BUSINESS AND
THE HUMAN RIGHTS ACT 1998

BUSINESS AND
THE HUMAN RIGHTS ACT 1998

Michael Smyth
Partner
Clifford Chance, Limited Liability Partnership

J O R D A N S
2000

Published by Jordan Publishing Ltd
21 St Thomas Street
Bristol BS1 6JS

British Library Cataloguing-in-Publication Data
A catalogue record for this book is available from the British Library.

ISBN 0 85308 565 X

Typeset by Mendip Communications Ltd, Frome, Somerset
Printed by MPG Books Ltd, Bodmin, Cornwall

'It is now plain that the incorporation of the European Convention on Human Rights into our domestic law will subject the entire legal system to a fundamental process of review and, where necessary, reform by the judiciary.'

(Lord Hope, *R v DPP, ex parte Kebeline* [1999] 3 WLR 972 at 988E)

FOREWORD

Readers who fear an overdose of commentaries on the effect of the introduction of the Human Rights Act 1998 into our law on 2 October 2000 should need no encouragement to add Michael Smyth's stimulating and instructive book to their essential reading list.

It is understandable that many authors, anxious to establish their pluralistic credentials, should have concentrated their efforts upon those rights which seek to protect and enhance liberty and quality of life. This book, however, throws light upon an important area of commercial activity, about which there has, hitherto, been less discussion and speculation. And yet commerce and industry are bound to feel, as Michael Smyth so well demonstrates, the impact of a momentous change in our law.

In the light of the substantial effect on an area of law, of which he has great experience, Michael Smyth has directed a thematic approach specifically to in-house lawyers and their commercial clients. But all who are concerned with *business* in its widest sense, employment lawyers, accountants, tax advisers, as well as their governmental and regulatory colleagues, will benefit from the learning in this book, particularly Chapters 6–9, which cover civil justice, privacy, the media and the protection of business assets.

Let no one think that, even absent horizontality, their business activities will remain unaffected by the Act and it will no longer be safe to advise clients without the assistance of this book. In his Reith Lecture, 'the Power and the State', in 1951, Lord Radcliffe said:

> 'The old glories of the liberal tradition, the passionate belief that political liberties are the essential condition of the greater liberties of thought, speech, and action, have shrunk to a meaningless constitutionalism which asserts that anything is all right if it is permitted, nothing is all right if it is forbidden, by an Act of Parliament.'

The European Convention and Strasbourg jurisprudence have begun to teach us to avoid the danger, which Lord Radcliffe feared, that the United Kingdom would lose its character but be 'left with its institutions: a result disastrous indeed'.

The Act will trigger a new determination to protect and enhance our liberties. This book will, I believe, provide an important guide as to how those objectives can be achieved in the world of business.

THE HON MR ALAN MOSES
Presiding Judge of the South Eastern Circuit

PREFACE

This book arose out of an article written for the *European Human Rights Law Review* in the spring of 1998.[1] Indications then were that the business community in the United Kingdom, although often well informed about legal developments affecting it, was unfamiliar with the European Convention on Human Rights. The media and utilities aside, industry particularly appeared slow to appreciate not just the commercial implications of the European Convention but the reasons why the Government's determination, in the Human Rights Act 1998, to give further effect to the rights guaranteed by the European Convention might actually be of some consequence for directors and managers.

More than 2 years on, and in the run-up to the wholesale implementation of the Act, it is not obviously apparent that much has changed. The sense persists that in boardrooms, as much as in taprooms, the Act is perceived as a statute intended to help those often relegated to society's margins, such as long-term prisoners, disability sufferers, asylum-seekers and transsexuals. The notion that the Act might impact on the interests of capital, for good or ill, has yet to secure a position in the corporate consciousness and if this book helps in any way to change that, it may have done some good.

There remains a coherent intellectual case to be made against the domestication of the European Convention through the medium of the Human Rights Act 1998. As a matter of electoral politics, however, that argument has been lost and this book largely passes over that debate. This volume is rather about the everyday outworkings of the legislation for a practically minded constituency facing, for example, regulatory inquiries, data protection complaints and tax disputes and (it is hoped) anxious to know what relevance the Act has in these areas.

In circumstances where the legislation is weeks away from coming into force, the systemic consequences of the Act will become apparent soon enough. Something is plainly astir when the best part of a year and a half is spent training the judges in European Convention law, when the additional burden on the legal aid budget which will be notionally attributable to the Act in its first 12 months of operation is predicted to be anything between £40m and £60m and when the number of High Court judges is substantially increased to accommodate the likely impact of the legislation. Plainly, the executive is preparing for an event of some moment.

Although it is hoped to contribute to the removal of that mixture of ignorance and misapprehension which currently characterises many reactions to this new law, this book is not meant to exaggerate the Act's relevance for business. The Act is likely to have its greatest impact in criminal cases, most of which (subject to those important exceptions examined in this book) will not involve the industrial and financial world. The fact that this book concentrates on those important, generally well-funded sectors should not cause the bigger picture to be missed.

---

1   M Smyth *The United Kingdom's Incorporation of the European Convention and its Implications for Business* [1998] EHRLR 273.

x *Business and the Human Rights Act 1998*

That bigger picture is one in which devolution features prominently. The view that the Act still has too low a profile can justifiably be criticised as London-centric to the extent that the European Convention has, at the time of writing, already been cited several hundred times in the courts of Scotland where devolved institutions are already obliged to behave in conformity with the Convention. Mindful of the fact that many businesses operate throughout the UK and are not confined to one of its constituent parts, a chapter of the book has been devoted to an examination of the implications of the Act in each of Scotland, Wales and Northern Ireland.

The book begins, however, with a short history of human rights so-called. It then seeks to explain why, despite the determination of the present Government to 'bring rights home', it remains important to know how the institutional machinery at Strasbourg for the supervision of the European Convention actually works.

In the section-by-section analysis of the Act which follows, particular concentration is paid to the position of those companies which are likely to be designated public authorities for the purposes of the Act on account of their public functions. For them, the Act is much more about risk than it is about opportunity and their potential exposure to claims gives the lie to those who (still) contend that the Act will be a capitalists' charter. Undeniably, however, the way in which the Act makes European Convention rights more directly accessible will present opportunities for swathes of the business community and, therefore, the greater part of this book examines those substantive rights which the European Convention aims to safeguard and which bear most obviously upon commerce.

What follows is not a comprehensive guide to the whole of Strasbourg law. That subject has generated a substantial publishing industry in its own right and this volume is not envisaged as any substitute for those excellent guides which are already available, not only to the European Convention but also to the Act. Its role, at best, is to complement such works of reference and it is targeted deliberately at non-specialists, specifically in-house lawyers and their internal (lay) clients.

Most books on the European Convention have adopted an Article-by-Article approach, examining each right in chronological order. A smaller number of works have adopted a thematic approach. This book attempts to do both (no doubt the worst option of all), to the extent that it tackles the key rights affecting the commercial sector (most obviously Arts 6, 8 and 10 and Art 1 of the First Protocol) in the order in which they appear in the text of the European Convention, whilst atempting to leave the narrative with sections outlining the possible domestic implications of the legislation in particular areas, even where this makes for a departure from the chronological treatment of the Articles. Thus, the consequences of the Act for environmental law is dealt with in Chapter 9, which examines the right to the protection of property in Art 1 of the First Protocol, even though the leading cases on the environment at Strasbourg have turned more on the provisions of Art 8, which guarantees the right to respect for homes and private lives. On balance, the view was taken that the environment was better looked at as part of a wider discussion on property than one on privacy.

Although the contents bear witness to the reality that it has been necessary to refer to most of the substantive European Convention rights, the fact is that this book is resolutely sector-oriented, which has meant that some issues fell on the wrong side of a conceivably arbitrary line and were omitted from any proper treatment. The impact of the legislation on employer–employee relations, specifically in terms of the right to freedom of association in Art 11 of the European Convention is therefore not dealt with on the basis that the book's focus is rather on the Act's consequences for corporate *trading* activity. For this reason, surveillance is discussed, because it is often carried out by commercial public authorities of one sort or another, even though it can also be a feature of staff monitoring.

The law is stated on the basis of materials available on 4 July 2000, less than 3 months before the Act comes fully into force and 50 years after the Council of Europe, under whose aegis the Strasbourg institutions operate, first met. There was a time when, on account of the limited early output of those institutions, the whole of the Strasbourg jurisprudence could be read in its entirety, from beginning to end. That is no longer possible (or, if it is, it is beyond this author). Most days, a decision, whether as to admissibility or merits, emerges from Strasbourg. So too, by the spring of this year, judgments bearing to some degree upon the European Convention and the Act were being handed down (it seemed) daily by the higher courts of the UK. Notwithstanding the clear steer of the House of Lords in the *Kebilene*[1] case that lawyers wait for their starters' orders on 2 October 2000, it is apparent that the Act has already undergone a process of *de facto* domestication and as much of this very recent material as possible (insofar as it is relevant) has been incorporated.

A considerable number of people at Clifford Chance need to be thanked for their assistance. They include (in addition to my very forbearing partners) Paul Ferguson (for his work on the media), Claire McDougall (for her text on general principles) and Karen Anderson (for her analysis of the Financial Services and Markets Act 2000). Maria Perdikis worked wonders in transforming a stone-age manuscript into an immaculate typescript, ably assisted by Sheila Reed. All the while Louize Green and James Baxter performed miracles in finding sources, however obscure, with Sonia Rabbetts supervising the footnoting. Khawar Qureshi of Serle Court did the early work on Art 6 as part of what had been envisaged as a joint venture before practice demands at the Bar got in the way. Particular thanks, therefore, must go to Nicola Greaney and Colin Thomann at 39 Essex Street for stepping boldly into a very large breach. Chapter 10 on the right to protection of property is very largely theirs.

Stephen Honey, commissioning editor at Jordans, showed infinite patience when deadline after deadline came and went in the face of assurances that there would be no more delays while Mollie Dickenson saw the project through to completion.

Mention should also be made of my friend, near neighbour and colleague, the late Peter Duffy QC, who excited an interest in this subject and whose masterful book *Human Rights: The 1998 Act and the European Convention* (written jointly with Stephen Grosz and Jack Beatson and published by Sweet & Maxwell) will doubtless frequently be cited in the months and years to come. It is a fitting legacy of a great scholar, a fine advocate and a very brave man. What price the Act, however, without Peter Duffy to argue its biggest cases?

Last of all, I owe a debt to my family who had as little idea as I did of what would be entailed. To Joyce and to William and Rachel for the lost weekends and for the

---

1   *R v Director of Public Prosecutions, ex parte Kebilene* [1999] 4 All ER 801.

constant mood swings this book is dedicated. Any mistakes in it are entirely my responsibility.

MICHAEL T SMYTH

200 Aldersgate Street, London EC1A 4JJ

12 July 2000

CONTENTS

APPENDICES

TABLE OF CASES

References are to paragraph numbers.

TABLE OF STATUTES

References are to paragraph numbers.

TABLE OF STATUTORY INSTRUMENTS AND CODES

References are to paragraph numbers.

TABLE OF INTERNATIONAL LEGISLATION

References are to paragraph numbers.

TABLE OF ABBREVIATIONS

the Act	Human Rights Act 1998
COB	Commission des Opérations de Bourse
CPR 1988	Civil Procedure Rules 1998
the European Convention or the Convention or ECHR	the Convention for the Protection of Human Rights and Fundamental Freedoms
FSA	Financial Services Authority
ICCPR	International Covenant on Civil and Political Rights
ICESCR	International Covenant on Economic, Social and Cultural Rights
ILO	International Labour Organisation
IMRO	Investment Management Regulatory Organisation
NIHRC	Northern Ireland Human Rights Commission
UN	United Nations
UNDR	United Nations Declaration of Human Rights

Chapter 1
INTRODUCTION

THE HISTORICAL BACKDROP

1.1 This book is about the Human Rights Act 1998,[1] the chief purpose of which is stated to be the giving of 'further effect to rights and freedoms guaranteed under the European Convention on Human Rights'.[2]

1.2 The Act is already proving to be expensive in inception[3] and profound in its consequences.[4] It will bear on many aspects of British life, such as policing,[5] housing, education, welfare, prisons and immigration.[6] A predictable list, it might be argued, for the operation of the criminal justice system (for example) will always be central to any discussion of human rights. The aim of this work, however, is to outline the implications of the Act for one constituency (the corporate

---

1   The Human Rights Act 1998 (referred to throughout as 'the Act') is reproduced in Appendix 1. The Home Secretary announced in a Parliamentary Written Answer on 18 May 1999 that the Act would come fully into force on 2 October 2000. Certain provisions came into force on 9 November 1998, the day the Act received Royal Assent. These provisions are identified in Chapter 3.

2   See the Long Title to the Act at **3.1**. The European Convention on Human Rights is reproduced in Appendix 2. Its formal title is the Convention for the Protection of Human Rights and Fundamental Freedoms. It is referred to throughout as 'the European Convention' or 'the Convention' or 'ECHR'.

3   Originally, £39m was earmarked for legally aided human rights cases brought between 1 April 2000 and 1 April 2001 (see the *Solicitors Journal*, 9 April 1999) although, by spring 2000, it was suggested that the likely cost was nearer £60m. A further £4.5m was allocated to cover judicial training (see the Lord Chancellor's Department's Press Release, 16 November 1998). For an indication of the way in which the training has been conducted, see P Tain 'Judges and Human Rights' in (1999) *Solicitors Journal* 1194.

4   For Professor Ewing 'it is unquestionably the most significant formal redistribution of political power in this country since 1911, and perhaps since 1688 ...' (see his article 'The Human Rights Act and Parliamentary Democracy' [1999] 62 MLR 79). For the Home Secretary, the Rt Hon Jack Straw MP, it is 'the most significant statement of human rights in domestic law since the 1689 Bill of Rights' (see his Foreword to *Blackstone's Guide to the Human Rights Act 1998* by J Wadham and H Mountfield (Blackstone Press, 1999). The Lord Chancellor, Lord Irvine of Lairg, has said that the legislative reforms of which the new law forms part are 'arguably the most radical programme of constitutional change since the Great Reform Bill of 1832' (see his Keynote Address to the Cambridge Centre for Public Law, reproduced in *Constitutional Reform in the United Kingdom: Practice and Principles* (Hart Publishing, 1998).

5   The Report of the Independent Commission on Policing in Northern Ireland entitled *A New Beginning: Policing in Northern Ireland* (September 1999) made explicit reference to the Act and recommended a new code of police ethics integrating the European Convention into police practice (para 4.8).

6   The Government's guidance to its own employees is illuminating: '[The Act] will have a significant impact on your work, whether you are involved in developing legislation, making decisions on behalf of a Minister or carrying out government policy, concerned with prosecutions or the enforcement of law or simply involved in the administration of a contract or working in personnel' (see *The Human Rights Act 1998 Guidance for Departments* at http://www.homeoffice.gov.uk/hract/guidance.htm).

sector) which does not come obviously to mind when considering human rights so-called.[1]

1.3   Companies are manifestly not 'human' and the notion that this piece of legislation may be deployed on behalf of corporations will strike many as odd and, indeed, objectionable. The intention in the pages which follow is not merely to explain the form which that deployment may take and the reasons for it, but also to describe how particular provisions of the statute equally pose difficulties for the business community because certain features of the Act place burdens upon commercial interests across a broad front. Such a threat – opportunity dynamic is an enduring theme of this work.

1.4   This is not a study of philosophy or of the political and social sciences and an analysis of the nature and development of human rights is beyond its scope. The already hackneyed term 'human rights'[2] is of modern derivation.[3] It is not found anywhere in King James's Authorised Version of the Bible, which was directed more at the prescription of individual behaviour than the regulation of the relationship between government and citizen, and it is that latter, traditionally top-down or vertical relationship upon which those who formulated the landmark human rights covenants of the mid-twentieth century chose primarily to concentrate their attention.

1.5   The Authorised Version of the Bible was first printed in 1611, almost 400 years after the signing of Magna Carta which, in addition to the other limitations it placed upon the sovereign's authority, provided in 1215 that:

> 'no Freeman shall be taken, or imprisoned, or be disseised of his Freehold, or Liberties, or Free Customs or be outlawed, or exiled, or any otherwise destroyed; nor will [the Crown] condemn him, but by lawful Judgment of his Peers, or by the Law of the Land.'[4]

---

1   A company has 'no body to be kicked or soul to be damned': Lord Denning in *British Steel Corporation v Granada* [1981] AC 1096.

2   'Few phrases are more often used or abused than "human rights". Its moral resonance makes it an attractive cause with which to be identified and the variety of its many supporters has led to some attenuation of meaning as widely differing protagonists have jostled for position under the same ethical roof' (see C Gearty 'European Court of Human Rights and the Protection of Civil Liberties: An Overview' in [1993] CLJ 89 at 93). In this context, see, for example, the comments of the Home Office Minister, Mr Mike O'Brien MP, speaking at the Capita Conference on Human Rights on 15 September 1999: 'I count myself a life-long supporter of human rights. Many of us came into politics precisely because we care about the human rights of ordinary people' at http://homeoffice.gov.uk/huract/capspee.htm.

3   As far as the courts of the UK are concerned, the earliest reference to 'human rights' found in *Lexis* is in the Privy Council case of *Bird and Others v O'Neal and Others* [1960] AC 907.

4   The original text of Magna Carta is reproduced by the United States National Archives and Records Administration at http://www.nara.gov. For a recent case in which Magna Carta was deployed in argument (and its relevance rejected by the judge), see *R v Bow County Court, ex parte Pelling* [1999] COD 277.

1.6   These were clear restrictions upon the exercise of monarchical power. Such words enshrined a due process standard[1] and explicitly recognised a right to the safeguarding of property not wholly dissimilar to that guaranteed by Art 1 of the First Protocol to the European Convention which is given direct effect by the Act.[2] The idea, therefore, that commerce should have a measure of *constitutional* protection has long pre-dated the capitalist era.

1.7   Nor was it just 'freehold' rights which were to be upheld by Magna Carta. King John was also to have regard for trade, to the extent that merchants were to:

> 'have their safe and sure Conduct to depart out of England, to come into England, to tarry in, and go through England … to buy and sell without any manner of evil Tolts [sic], by the old and rightful Customs, except in Time of War.'

1.8   Whatever the curbs placed upon the Crown, neither Magna Carta nor the Petition of Right of 1628 nor the Bill of Rights of 1689[3] (which prohibited the infliction of 'cruel and unusual punishments' in phraseology very similar to that used in the key human rights instruments of the last 50 years[4]) could sensibly be described as establishing a comprehensive framework of guarantees appropriate for a democratic society. By the end of the eighteenth century, however, an idea of rights came to be promoted to a contemporary audience in terms which now appear altogether more familiar.

INTERNATIONAL DEVELOPMENTS

1.9   Those who signed the Declaration of Independence of the 13 United States of America of 4 July 1776 famously held certain truths to be 'self-evident', namely:

> 'that all men are created equal, that they are endowed by the Creator with certain unalienable [sic] Rights, [and] that amongst these are Life, Liberty and the Pursuit of Happiness.'[5]

Included in the specific charges laid by the signatories at the door of the then King of Great Britain were the following:

– obstruction of 'the Laws for the Naturalisation of Foreigners';
– imposition of 'Taxes … without Consent'; and

---

1   Those who assembled at Runnymede would no doubt have been unnerved to know that their compact would be relied upon nigh-on eight centuries later as a defence against the perceived excesses of regulators in the City of London, a number of commentators having suggested that features of the Financial Services and Markets Bill were in breach of Magna Carta. See for example, the remarks of Anthony Speaight QC as reported in The Daily Telegraph on 26 and 27 March 1999. The Bill (now the Financial Services and Markets Act 2000) is the subject of a fuller treatment at **6.236** et seq.
2   See Appendix 2 below. Article 1 of the First Protocol is generally discussed in Chapter 9 below.
3   The text of The Bill of Rights is conveniently reproduced in *Towards a Constitutional Bill of Rights for the United Kingdom* by R Blackburn (Pinter, 1999), p 113.
4   See, for example, Art 5 of the Universal Declaration of Human Rights 1948 (later reproduced as Art 3 of the European Convention (see Appendix 2 below) and as part of Art 7 of the International Covenant on Civil and Political Rights 1976): 'No one shall be subjected to torture or to cruel, inhuman or degrading treatment or punishment'.
5   The text of the Declaration of Independence is reproduced in at http://www.nara.gov.

–   deprivation in many cases 'of the Benefits of Trial by Jury'.[1]

1.10   If the Declaration of Independence was, in appearance, a list of complaints about the past, the 1791 Constitution of the USA and, in particular, the amendments made to it on 15 December 1791 set out what was in effect a code of rights, secured for the future. Thus (and perhaps most obviously) the First Amendment says:

> 'Congress shall make no law respecting an establishment of religion, or prohibiting the free exercise thereof; or abridging the freedom of speech, or of the press, or of the right of the people peaceably to assemble, and to petition the Government for a redress of grievances.' [2]

This early formulation of a right to free expression remains a starting point when seeking to articulate the role of the media in a civil society.[3]

1.11   There were, in addition, other measures which helped philosophically to pave the way for the European Convention and which remain linchpins of the system in which US business operates. The Fourth Amendment to the US Constitution stipulates, for example, that:

> 'the right of the people to be secure in their persons, houses, papers, and effects, against unreasonable seizures, shall not be violated ...',

while the Fifth Amendment states that:

> 'in all criminal prosecutions, the accused shall enjoy the right to a speedy and public trial, by an impartial jury and to be informed of the nature and cause of the accusation; to be confronted with the witnesses against him; to have compulsory process for obtaining witnesses in his favour, and to have the assistance of counsel for his defence.'[4]

Nor was this promulgation of rights exclusively an American phenomenon, for equality before the law was also to be an important feature of the French *Déclaration des Droits de L'homme et du Citoyen* of 1789[5] and the *Code Napoléon* of 1804.

1.12   These various proclamations, on both sides of the Atlantic, were not made in an intellectual vacuum and were testimony to the influence of Locke, Rousseau, Paine and others. Their ideas, whilst still striking, share a characteristic which limits the extent to which they can be utilised by law-makers in our time: they were all developed before the factory age. The Spinning Jenny by then might already have been invented and the first joint-stock companies established, but it was the Industrial Revolution of the early- and mid-nineteenth century which arguably set in train the events ultimately giving rise to the much-vaunted concern

---

1   The text of the Declaration of Independence is reproduced at http://www.nara.gov.
2   The text of the US Constitution is reproduced at http://www.nara.gov. Its sublime ambition has not been realised comprehensively. 'The first ten amendments to the American Constitution did not save the American Negro from slavery for 82 years nor from discrimination for another 82 years': Lord Scarman, reported in Hansard HL, vol 519, col 911, 23 May 1990. The United States has in fact ratified fewer human rights treaties than many other countries.
3   See generally Chapter 8.
4   See fn 2 above.
5   An English translation of the French Declaration of the Rights of Man and of the Citizen is reproduced in Blackburn (see fn 3 on p3) at pp 443 et seq.

for human rights which every country, virtually without exception, now claims to have.[1]

THE MULTILATERAL COVENANTS OF THE TWENTIETH CENTURY

1.13 Global means of production and transportation made global conflict possible and, after war on an international scale began in 1914, it came widely to be recognised that multilateral agreements between countries might one day assist in the maintenance of peace. The League of Nations and the International Labour Organisation (ILO) were established in 1920 following the Versailles Conference. The League was intended primarily to regulate inter-State relations. The ILO's remit, by contrast, extended to the raising of living standards, the improvement of working conditions and the promotion of social and economic welfare; all matters affecting the domestic and industrial spheres. In terms of the subject-matter of this book, it is noteworthy that the aims of the ILO were (and are) much broader than those on which the European Convention came to be based 30 years later.[2] For all that, the bodies set up after Versailles were unable to prevent the totalitarian onslaught of the 1930s which led to the Second World War and, following fascism's defeat, there was, perhaps unsurprisingly, an emerging belief that improved structures were required to be developed.

1.14 Moves to found the United Nations (UN) were in place before the end of the Second World War and the United Nations Charter was signed in San Francisco on 26 June 1945, coming into force on 24 October that year. In its Preamble, the peoples of the UN determined:

> 'to reaffirm faith in fundamental human rights, in the dignity and worth of the human person, in the equal rights of men and women and ... to promote social progress and better standards of life in larger freedom.'[3]

One purpose of the UN was:

> 'to achieve international co-operation ... in promoting and encouraging respect for human rights and for fundamental freedoms for all without distinction as to race, sex, language or religion.'[4]

1.15 The UN proceeded to establish a Commission on Human Rights, chaired by Mrs Eleanor Roosevelt, which was charged with the drafting of an international human rights code. On 10 December 1948, that code was adopted by the UN

---

1 See generally the chapter by P Cumper in *Human Rights: Agenda for the 21st Century*, edited by A Hegarty and S Leonard (Cavendish Publishing, 1999), p 1. Evidence of the heightened importance (rhetorical or otherwise) attached by the British Government to this issue may be seen from the fact that there are now human rights units in both the Home Office and the Foreign and Commonwealth Office.

2 The ILO now functions as part of the United Nations (and much of its work is considered by trade unions to be of particular value).

3 The text of the United Nations Charter is reproduced in at http://www.un.org.

4 Article 1(3) of the United Nations Charter (see fn 3 above).

General Assembly as the Universal Declaration of Human Rights (UNDR),[1] a document encompassing not just civil and political rights (of the type later enshrined in the European Convention) but also a range of social, economic and cultural rights (which are notably absent from the European Convention),[2] such as the right to work, to rest, to an adequate standard of living and to education.[3] The UNDR, with its emphasis upon rights as inherent, inalienable and universal, was to become the mainspring for subsequent multi-lateral agreements on human rights, such as the American Convention on Human Rights (signed in 1969 by 12 Latin American states and which led 10 years later to the establishment of the American Court of Human Rights[4]) and the African Charter on Human and Peoples' Rights[5] (approved by the Organisation of African Unity in 1981).[6]

1.16   Whilst the UNDR could scarcely be described as a prominent feature of British jurisprudence,[7] it has been held up by the Foreign Secretary, Rt Hon Robin Cook MP, as constituting the 'rules of membership' of the international community applicable to every country.[8] It is not part of local law and it is unlikely that many of those who signed it intended it to be binding.[9] As its name suggests, they doubtless regarded it as declaratory only, or more like a manifesto, with largely moral authority.[10] However, the International Court of Justice has since stated that the UNDR constitutes a form of customary law and the arrival of the Act is likely to give the UNDR greater significance, particularly when considered together with the further UN instruments which came after it.[11]

1.17   On 16 December 1966, the UN General Assembly adopted an International Covenant on Civil and Political Rights (ICCPR)[12] and an International Covenant on Economic, Social and Cultural Rights (ICESCR).[13] These two documents were conceived as giving a practical focus to the UNDR and it may be anticipated that, notwithstanding their non-binding status and the fact that the Act does not incorporate them, efforts will be made increasingly by British lawyers to rely upon them, not least because the Strasbourg institutions have not felt constrained about referring to them, to the UNDR itself and to other UN human

1   The text of the UNDR is published in *Human Rights in International Law* (Council of Europe Press, 1998). Eight States abstained in the General Assembly vote on the adoption of the UNDR including the then Soviet Union and several other Eastern bloc countries along with South Africa and Saudi Arabia. No State opposed the motion.
2   See **2.9** et seq.
3   Respectively, Arts 23, 24, 25 and 26 of the UNDR.
4   The American Convention of Human Rights is reproduced in (1970) 9 ILM 673.
5   The African Charter on Human and Peoples' Rights is reproduced in (1982) 21 ILM 59.
6   There are also plans for an African Court of Human Rights. Regional human rights regimes in the Middle East and Asia appear, however, not to be in prospect.
7   A *Lexis* search on 10 May 2000 produced references in 49 cases heard in UK courts.
8   His speech can be found at http://www.fco.gov.uk.
9   The position of the UNDR is analysed by Professor Hannum in 'The Status of the Universal Declaration of Human Rights in National and International Law' (1998) 12 INTERRIGHTS Bulletin 3.
10   Roosevelt thought it 'might well become an international Magna Carta of all mankind'. The quotation appears in *The Power of Human Rights*, edited by T Risse, SC Ropp and K Sikkink (Cambridge University Press, 1999), p 1.
11   Such as, for example, the United Nations Standard Minimum Rules for the Administration of Juvenile Justice (the so-called 'Beijing Rules') referred to by Strasbourg in the James Bulger case (*T and V v United Kingdom* [2000] CLR 187).
12   The ICCPR is reproduced at http://www.pch.gc.ca.
13   The ICESCR is reproduced in at http://www.unhchr.ch.

rights instruments.[1] Courts in Belfast may be amongst the first in the UK to witness such a trend, for s 69(1) of the Northern Ireland Act 1998 provides that the Northern Ireland Human Rights Commission:[2]

> 'shall keep under review the adequacy and effectiveness in Northern Ireland of law and practice relating to the protection of human rights.'[3]

1.18   Section 69(11) of the Northern Ireland Act 1998 defines 'human rights' as 'including' the rights provided for in the European Convention. In other words, the term 'human rights' is not limited in this context to European Convention rights and hence the probability that other international standards will become an important part of the work of the Northern Ireland Human Rights Commission. Advocates will not be slow to make the point that such wider terms of reference should also inform the jurisprudence of England, Scotland and Wales.[4]

1.19   Quite apart from any impetus deriving from developments in Northern Ireland, in litigation involving the Act there is likely to be an increasing tendency to refer, for example, to cases from New Zealand[5] which (unlike the UK) ratified the ICCPR's First Optional Protocol on 26 May 1989, thereby permitting individuals who believed that their rights had been violated to petition the United Nations Human Rights Committee,[6] an important part of whose role is to ensure adherence by States to the provisions of the ICCPR. Over 90 States now accept the complaints procedure in the First Optional Protocol and it is noteworthy, in the context of the Government's promotion of the Act, that the UK is the only European Union State not to do so.[7]

1.20   It is therefore to be envisaged that, as part of the cultural shift to be brought about by the Act (so its proponents say),[8] greater emphasis will be placed

---

1   See, for example, *Muller v Switzerland* (1998) 13 EHRR 212 and *Groppera Radio AG v Switzerland* (1990) 12 EHRR 321, in which reference was made to Art 19 of the ICCPR in two cases on Art 10 of the European Convention (see Chapter 8 below).

2   As to which see Chapter 4.

3   See also the Written Answer of Mr George Howarth MP (Hansard HC, vol 14, cols 130–131, 2 November 1999), in which Mr Howarth said that the Rt Hon Marjorie Mowlam MP, then Secretary of State for Northern Ireland, had written to the Northern Ireland Human Rights Commission on 24 March 1999 inviting advice 'on the scope for defining, in Westminster legislation, *rights supplementary* to those in the European Convention ...' (emphasis added). The quotation is an extract from the Belfast Agreement of 1998, as to which see Chapter 4.

4   For an analysis of the relationship between the Human Rights Act 1998 and the devolution schemes in Scotland, Wales and Northern Ireland, see Chapter 4.

5   Or Hong Kong, whose Bill of Rights Ordinance (No 39 of 1991) expressly incorporates the ICCPR and is reproduced in at http://www.uni-wuerzburg.de.

6   For an account of the workings of the United Nations Human Rights Committee generally, see D McGoldrick *The Human Rights Committee* (Clarendon Press, 1991).

7   In July 1997 the Foreign Secretary, the Rt Hon Robin Cook MP, announced a review of the UK's position as regards the First Optional Protocol. His speech can be found at http://www.fco.gov.uk.

8   In his Preface to the White Paper *Rights Brought Home: The Human Rights Bill* (Cm 3782), the Prime Minister, the Rt Hon Tony Blair MP, said that the then Bill would 'enhance the awareness of human rights in our society. It stands alongside our decision to put the promotion of human rights at the forefront of our foreign policy'. The Lord Chancellor, Lord Irvine of Lairg, said on Radio 4 on 6 November 1997 that 'incorporation of the Convention is going to operate as a very substantial culture change. We want it to percolate into the workings of all the Courts, we want a human rights culture to develop throughout society'. The quotation appears in *A Human Rights Commission: The Options for Britain and Northern Ireland* by S Spencer and I Bynoe (Institute for Public Policy Research, 1998).

upon the global bench-marks set out in international texts such as these, specifically as regards issues such as workplace rights. It was more than 50 years ago that the ILO adopted conventions on freedom of association, the right to organise and free collective bargaining[1] and it would be surprising if lawyers representing employees did not attempt to use such conventions as templates. More to the point, if human rights are now (at least rhetorically) acknowledged world-wide, business will in the longer run need to plan its response to greater pressure for extended social and economic rights if, as has been said, the logic of the Act makes inexorable and 'unanswerable' the absorption of such broader international safeguards.[2]

1.21 There is, of course, a difference between human rights which are generally aspirational (such as those in the UNDR) and those which are legally secured (such as those in the European Convention). The difference is not obviously reconcilable and it is one currently confronting the UK as it participates in the drafting of a European Charter of Fundamental Rights[3] which, according to Germany, 'would have pride of place among Europe's treaties'.[4] At the Cologne Summit in June 1999 it was agreed that 'fundamental rights,' not only of the civil and political variety but also extending, for example, to bioethical, environmental, gender and data protection safeguards, should be consolidated in a charter. One of the British representatives in the drafting body of 62, who (significantly perhaps) describe themselves as 'a convention', is Lord Goldsmith, the distinguished barrister, and the exercise is led by Roman Herzog, a former president of Germany. It is anticipated that a document will be available at the Nice summit in December 2000, with the French promising to make the Charter a priority during their presidency of the EU.[5]

1.22 There has been press speculation[6] that the British Government is opposed to making the Charter legally binding, for fear that it will be seen to be a federalist stalking-horse. Certainly, the Prime Minister's stated position is that the initiative is about creating a text which is non-justiciable and which does not add to existing rights and obligations. It will in his view be declaratory only, setting out a small pledge card of rights and will not be incorporated into the EU Treaties. In particular, the Government has been at pains to stress[7] that the putative Charter should not replace or compete with the European Convention but rather

---

1   See ILO Conventions 87 and 98 of 1948 and 1949, respectively, which are reproduced at www.ilo.org. The incremental potential of ILO standards has been emphasised by Laura Cox QC, representative on the ILO Committee of Independent Experts, in 'The International Labour Organisation and Fundamental Rights at Work' [1999] EHRLR 451.

2   See Ewing (fn 4 on p 1) p 84. The potential for legal development along such lines was seen, for example, in a death penalty case heard by the Judicial Committee of the Privy Council, their Lordships (by 3:2) granting a stay of execution to the Trinidadian appellants pending the hearing of their application to the Inter-American Commission on Human Rights, whose authority derives from a treaty, the American Convention on Human Rights (see **1.15** above), which has not been incorporated in Trinidad: *Thomas and Hilaire v The Queen* [1999] 3 WLR 249.

3   See generally on this issue 'Human Rights in the EU: The Charter of Fundamental Rights' (House of Commons Research Paper 00/32, 20 March 2000) and the Report of the House of Lords' European Union Committe of 24 May 2000.

4   See *Europe's Path into the 21st Century* at http://www.bundesregierung.de.

5   See *The Times*, 5 May 2000.

6   See *The Independent* (8 February 2000) and *The Guardian* (5 April 2000).

7   In a letter by the Minister for Europe, Keith Vaz MP, to the *The Independent*, 11 February 2000.

complement it. The fear is that if the former is too expansionist in its reach, the latter will be undermined.

1.23   This response is unsurprising, but the Government is plainly very conscious of the fact that the Charter draftsmen propose to take account of social and economic rights, ie rights of the kind that, as shall be seen,[1] do not form part of the European Convention. If such rights eventually form part of the Charter, it can be guaranteed that pressure will begin to make them legally justiciable.

1.24   The point, in short, is that the Act is not the last word on human rights and the Charter is but the latest in a series of documents to which lawyers may in the future attempt to refer.

THE UK AND HUMAN RIGHTS IN THE MODERN ERA

1.25   The Act may appear at the outset to be merely a direct consequence of commitments made long ago by the UK in a multinational treaty (ie the European Convention), but on any long-range view of British legal and constitutional history it offers a marked if not revolutionary break with the past.[2]

1.26   It had for many years been a hornbook principle that British law did not enshrine rights, preferring instead to prescribe infringements of liberty, thereby identifying what might not be done (negative or residual rights) and not what might be done (positive rights). The most forthright exponent of this view was George Venn Dicey in his book *The Law of the Constitution*,[3] although the argument had much earlier been put by Blackstone in his *Commentaries on the Laws of England*.

1.27   Received wisdom, as passed on by Dicey's latter-day disciples, was that incorporation of multilateral obligations such as those set out in the European Convention was unnecessary as the guarantees provided in the European Convention were in large measure co-extensive with the common law. Supporters of the Act suggest that this strains the reality, which was that it was left to the judiciary and the legal profession 'unguided by legislation, to attempt to fill the gaps between Convention law and domestic law'.[4] Dicey, his critics say, would have us subjects, not citizens. According to the Lord Chancellor, Lord Irvine of Lairg, the Act 'represents Britain's recognition that freedom in the Diceyan sense is not coterminous with the protection of fundamental human rights'.[5] In other words, the Act might be said to have the aim of transforming liberties into rights. We are free because we have a right enshrined in law.

1.28   This difference in philosophical approach partly explains why the transformation of an international treaty (the UNDR) into a regional one (the European Convention) and thence into a piece of domestic legislation (the Act)

---

1   See **2.9** et seq. Article 1 of the First Protocol is arguably an exception (see Chapter 9 below).
2   See generally in this area the famous Blackstone Lecture of Dr FA Mann reproduced in [1978] LQR 512 entitled 'Britain's Bill of Rights'.
3   10th edn, 1985.
4   Lord Lester of Herne Hill QC in his article 'First Steps Towards a Constitutional Bill of Rights' [1997] EHRLR 124. That the gap should exist at all is said to be in large measure attributable to the fact that, alone amongst the larger democracies, the UK has had no codified constitution.
5   See his Keynote Address to the Cambridge Centre for Public Law (fn 4 on p 1).

should until comparatively recently have been vigorously resisted. As will become apparent, there were, however, other reasons for that resistance which bear directly upon the commercial focus of this book.

1.29   The movement to establish a continental rights regime on this side of the Atlantic was led by the Council of Europe, whose statute was signed in London on 5 May 1949 and part of whose function was stated to be 'the maintenance and further realisation of human rights and fundamental freedoms',[1] the enjoyment of which was to be accepted by Member States.[2] And yet, in July 1949, Foreign Office staff[3] were describing the possible establishment of a human rights court under the aegis of the Council of Europe as 'totally unacceptable', on the basis that British governments would become prey to actions brought by 'Communists, crooks and cranks of every type'.[4]

1.30   The prejudice of the diplomatic corps was wide of the mark in a number of respects, not least as regards the suggestion that the convention on human rights which had been mooted would become an agitational device for socialists, for a significant part of the British left, including the political masters at that time of those same civil servants, also had concerns about the Council of Europe's intentions, albeit from a very different political perspective. At a Cabinet meeting held on 1 August 1950, Sir Stafford Cripps, then Chancellor of the Exchequer, warned that 'a government committed to the policy of a planned economy' could not ratify the proposed convention.[5] Its terms 'would be acceptable only to those who believed in a free economy and a minimum amount of State intervention in economic affairs'.[6] From the start, therefore, the European Convention was seen as possibly over-protective of private industry.

1.31   Nor was it only the perceived fetter upon the ideological programme of Clement Attlee's Labour administration to which certain Ministers took objection. In a memorandum written some months later, the Lord Chancellor, Lord Jowitt, criticised the draft convention as being 'so vague and woolly that it may mean almost anything.'[7] The document for him reeked of 'compromise' and, above all else, was 'a monument of lack of precision'.[8]

---

1   See Art 1(b) of the Statute of the Council of Europe, reproduced at http://www.coe.fr.
2   See Art 3 of the Statute of the Council of Europe and fn 1 above. For a recent article critical of the Council of Europe's perceived equivocation on human rights issues, see *The Economist*, 27 November 1999, in which the Council is described as 'the least demanding Western club, and thus the one to which the countries escaping Soviet dominance could be admitted as a first reward for discarding communism'.
3   The paragraphs that follow rely extensively on G Marston's fascinating article 'The United Kingdom's Part in the Preparation of the European Convention of Human Rights, 1950' in (1993) 42 ICLQ 796.
4   See Marston (fn 3 above), p 806.
5   See Marston (fn 3 above), p 812.
6   The Lord Chancellor, Lord Jowitt, agreed with Cripps. He said that the proposed treaty was about 'some half-baked scheme to be administered by some unknown court' and complained that 'the standpoint [was that] of a laissez faire economy', whereas Jowitt believed that the early 1950s were 'an age of planned economy'. See Marston (fn 3 above), p 813.
7   He went on: 'Our unhappy legal experts – two distinguished Home Office officials – who would probably have expressed their complete inability to draft a Bill (for example) to prevent the docking and nicking of horses – have had to take their share in drawing up a code compared to which the Code Napoleon – or indeed the Ten Commandments – are comparatively insignificant.' See Marston (fn 3 above), p 818.
8   See Marston (fn 3 above), p 818.

1.32   Whether or not Cripps and Jowitt were won over is to be doubted but, at its meeting on 24 October 1950, the Cabinet, no doubt conscious of the overriding political imperative to be seen to be agreeing a European-wide programme of rights in the face of developing Cold War tension, unanimously resolved that the putative Convention be signed, a signing which took place in Rome on 4 November 1950.[1] At that moment, the private individual (including, for these purposes, the legal entity known as the company) was transformed, in the words of Hersch Lauterpacht, from 'an object of international compassion into a subject of international right'.[2]

1.33   The concerns of certain post-War politicians are not without relevance today. Cripps for one had explicitly recognised the possible impact of the Convention upon business life. He had worried, for example, that (what became) Art 8[3] of the Convention would limit the power of Inland Revenue inspectors to enter private premises,[4] while the Cabinet as a whole feared that its plans for the nationalisation of certain industries would be impeded. So it was that an article upholding a right to the protection of property[5] was omitted from the final text of the Convention. The right of parents to educate their children 'in conformity with their own religious and philosophical convictions'[6] (which might have threatened any plan to abolish independent schools) was also shelved.[7]

1.34   In signing the Convention, the post-War Labour Government had taken care not to permit British citizens and companies the right themselves directly to complain about Convention infringements to the then European Commission of Human Rights.[8] Nor was any legislation introduced to give effect domestically to the Convention's terms, so it remained no part of UK law in the years that followed. Efforts were made to persuade the Conservative governments of the 1950s to concede the right of individual petition, but these failed. Governments remained cautious, although caution soon gave way to hostility. In 1956, Greece brought a case against the UK about British-administered Cyprus, which led the then Foreign Secretary, the Rt Hon Selwyn Lloyd MP, to concede that he knew 'very little' about the European Convention and to express 'dismay and incredulity that the Convention could have got [his Government] into such a "fix"'. His Minister of State added: 'we never conceived of the Convention being used against us like this'.[9]

---

1   The UK deposited its instrument of ratification on 8 March 1951. It was the first country to do so.
2   International Law and Human Rights (1950).
3   See Appendix 2.
4   See Marston (fn 3 on p 10), p 812.
5   Now part of Art 1 of the First Protocol to the ECHR, see Appendix 2.
6   Now part of Art 2 of the First Protocol to the ECHR, see Appendix 2. The Independent Schools Information Service has for some time argued that removal of the *charitable* status of private schools would also be a breach of the Convention.
7   These limited concessions to socialist sensibilities did not last. Winston Churchill, when in opposition, had been an enthusiastic supporter of the Convention and, a year after the victory of the Conservative Party in the General Election of 1951 and his return as Prime Minister, both rights were included in the First Protocol to the Convention, which was ratified by the UK on 3 November 1952.
8   The right now set out in Art 34 of the ECHR, see Appendix 2. For a description of the functions of the European Commission of Human Rights, see **2.36** et seq.
9   All quotations from the article by AWB Simpson 'The Exile of Archbishop Makarios III' [1996] 4 EHRLR 391.

1.35   There the matter rested[1] until, following an exchange of notes between
Whitehall departments, the then Prime Minister, the Rt Hon Harold Wilson MP,
informed the House of Commons on 7 December 1965 that the right of individual
petition had been granted.[2] This single, executive action[3] was, over time, to
transform the European Convention's status in the UK. Whereas hitherto only
States, already parties to the Convention, could file petitions, it was now open to
any 'person, non-governmental organisation or group of individuals',[4] who
otherwise satisfied the requisite threshold criteria, to do so. Mindful of the extent
to which the Government had been exercised by this issue a generation earlier, it
is apparent that the thinking of (at least a part of) Labour's political establishment
had moved some distance. However, caution continued to be the overriding
sentiment and the European Convention still formed no part of domestic law. It
remained an international treaty, binding *on* the UK but not *in* the UK.[5]

1.36   It has since emerged that the parliamentary statement made at the end of
1965 was delayed, at the insistence of the Treasury, which was anxious to ensure
that the Burmah Oil Company did not petition the Strasbourg institutions.
Burmah Oil had been successful before the Judicial Committee of the House of
Lords in establishing a right to claim damages for the loss of its installations in
Burma in 1942.[6] Plant and machinery had been destroyed on the orders of the
local (British) military commander as part of a scorched-earth policy, the aim
being to prevent the seizure of such assets by the Japanese army.

1.37   The Government's response to Burmah Oil's legal victory was to pass the
War Damage Act 1965, which retrospectively abolished the duty to pay compensation for the lawful destruction of property in war-time. It was feared that Burmah
Oil would challenge this action on a European Convention basis, a possibility
which the Treasury was anxious to close off. Indications from Whitehall papers
released to public view some years ago are that the Prime Minister's announcement regarding the right of individual petition was timed to ensure that Burmah
Oil was outside the 6-month period for filing a petition under the Convention.[7]
Therefore, the episode is a luminous early example of an attempt by private
capital to exploit the European Convention and of the concern on the part of the
executive to which this gave rise.

---

1   'In 1966, the Convention was a sleeping beauty': see A Lester and D Pannick *Human Rights
     Law and Practice* (Butterworths, 1999) p 8.
2   The declaration under what was then Art 25 of the Convention was in fact made on 14
     January 1966. See the *Declaration recognising the competence of the European Commission of Human
     Rights to receive individual petitions and recognising as compulsory the jurisdiction of the European
     Court of Human Rights* (Cm 2894).
3   Albeit one initially made for only 5 years. In the event, the Declaration has been renewed
     ever since, the current recognition period starting in January 1996.
4   Article 34 of the European Convention, see fn 8 on p 11.
5   As succinctly expressed by Hans Christian Kruger, then Secretary to the European
     Commission of Human Rights, in his article '*Current Topic: The Practicalities of a Bill of Rights*'
     in [1997] EHRLR 353 at 354.
6   *Burmah Oil Co (Burma Trading) Ltd v Lord Advocate* [1965] AC 75.
7   See Lester and Pannick (fn 1 above), p 8.

THE PUSH FOR INCORPORATION

1.38   In 1968 the barrister Anthony Lester (now Lord Lester of Herne Hill QC), who made a signal contribution to the introduction of the Act, published a Fabian Society pamphlet[1] calling for a domestic Bill of rights. Thus, arguably, the debate was inaugurated that culminated in the passing of the Act 30 years later. There followed in the early 1970s the tabling of several private members' Bills in Parliament, each having broadly the same objective, but none of which succeeded. Meanwhile other senior lawyers proceeded to take up Lester's call, most notably the then Sir Leslie Scarman[2] and Professor Michael Zander.[3]

1.39   To the extent that there was any political support for incorporation (or at least some form of human rights entrenchment), it was largely articulated by committed individuals in the Conservative and Liberal parties. Incorporation was far from being a headline issue, indeed the atmosphere of the time has been described as characterised by 'persistent background rumbling'.[4] In 1975, the Rt Hon Sir Keith Joseph MP, a significant ideological influence upon Margaret Thatcher's thinking, was calling for a Bill of rights 'to subject Parliament to the rule of law'; otherwise, he suggested, an untrammelled executive might, for example, issue compulsory purchase orders without restraint.[5] In other words, he feared that Parliament could no longer be relied upon in all circumstances to protect property interests, a view which commentators on the right were unsurprisingly not inclined to advance in the years which followed the defeat of the Labour Government in the General Election of 1979. Just, however, as their political concerns in this regard subsided, events in the courts were to ensure that the debate on incorporation became increasingly polarised.

1.40   Judicial review of administrative action increased markedly under the Conservatives.[6] Not that it was Government-inspired – quite the reverse. Joshua Rozenberg has described how in the 1980s and early 1990s judicial review was to become a 'theatre of war',[7] – a view shared by a number of senior lawyers. Lord Mustill also relied on metaphor when famously observing that

---

1   *Democracy and Individual Rights*, Fabian Tract No 390 (1968).
2   See *English Law – The New Dimension* (Stevens, London, 1974).
3   See *A Bill of Rights?* 3rd edn (Oxford University Press, 1985).
4   Professor ATH Smith in his article 'The Human Rights Act: The Constitutional Context' reproduced in *The Human Rights Act and the Criminal Justice and Regulatory Process* (Hart Publishing, 1999).
5   An extract from his speech to the Conservative Political Centre Conference on 26 January 1975 is quoted in P Wallington and J McBride *Civil Liberties and a Bill of Rights* (Cobden Trust, 1976).
6   A trend by no means confined to the UK. See, for example, *The Economist*, 7 August 1999 at p 33. In 1981, four Queen's Bench Division judges handled judicial review cases. By 1999, there were 24, including 2 drawn from the Chancery Division, with more appointed in 2000 to meet an expected increase in work as a result of the Act. As to this, see Chapter 10 below.
7   See his book *Trial of Strength* (Richard Cowen Press, 1997). Sir Stephen Sedley has used a similar analogy. During this period, he said, 'the courts were waiting with refined instruments of torture for ministers and departments' (see his article 'The Sound of Silence: Constitutional Law without a Constitution' [1994] LQR 270 at 283). See also, this time in a private law context, Lord Browne-Wilkinson (dissenting) in *Kleinwort Benson v Lincoln City Council* [1998] 4 All ER 513: 'the theoretical position ... that judges do not make or change law ... is ... a fairy tale in which no one any longer believes. In truth, judges make and change law.'

'to avoid a vacuum in which the citizen would be left without protection against a misuse of executive powers, the courts have had no option but to occupy the dead ground [left by Parliament] in a manner, and in areas of public life, which could not have been foreseen 30 years ago.'[1]

1.41   Whether the Bench smelled blood or not, it is oddly coincidental that, during the tenure as Prime Minister of Mrs Thatcher's successor, the Rt Hon John Major MP, certain of the most eminent and intellectually able judges began to call for the incorporation of the European Convention into UK law, all this when more than a hundred significant changes to regulations and administrative practices affecting civic rights had already resulted from decisions of the European Convention institutions.[2]

1.42   Lord Bingham of Cornhill LCJ, now the senior Lord of Appeal in Ordinary, said in his Denning Lecture on 2 March 1993 that 'it would be naïve to suppose that incorporation of the Convention would usher in the new Jerusalem', but such a change 'would over time stifle the insidious and damaging belief that it is necessary to go abroad to obtain justice. It would restore this country to its former place as an international standard-bearer of liberty and justice'.[3] According to Lord Woolf, the domestication of the European Convention would also change legal perspective, for 'it [would] no longer in the public law field be focusing upon the rights of the individual'; rather it would be 'investigating whether infringement of those rights can be justified'.[4]

1.43   By 1993, the then leader of the Labour Party, the Rt Hon John Smith QC, MP, was also in favour of incorporation (even though his party had opposed private members' Bills on the subject in the 1980s) and a policy statement that year made incorporation only the first step towards a fully blown bill of rights. This may have been a tribute to the perceived role of the judiciary in curbing aspects of the Conservative Government's legislative zeal (which the official opposition had singularly failed to do) or an early acknowledgement that Labour, in seriously contending for power, would abandon the kind of radical programme that might be constrained by certain of the provisions of the European Convention (the same provisions that Cripps had once feared).[5] It may, however, have stemmed more from a pragmatic acceptance that this was an idea whose time, for whatever reason, had come. If nothing else, it served to differentiate Labour from the governing party, for the Conservatives were by 1995 expressing profound disenchantment with the European Convention institutions and were briefing the media about the possible removal of the right of individual petition in the wake of

---

1   *R v Home Secretary, ex parte Fire Brigades Union* [1995] AC 513 at 567.
2   According to Lord Hutchinson, as reported in *A Path to a Bill of Rights* by P Cumper [1991] NLJ 100.
3   See R Gordon QC and R Wilmot-Smith QC in *Human Rights in the United Kingdom* (Oxford University Press, 1996), p 11. The role of the senior judges (apart, that is, from Lord McCluskey) in enthusiastically supporting a measure (most obviously in the debates on the Human Rights Bill) which would inevitably add to their constitutional importance has gone largely without comment (although, see Ewing (fn 4 on p 1), p 85). In the period after enactment, however, there has been widespread criticism of the multi-purpose role of the Lord Chancellor as a Cabinet Minister, head of the justice system and presiding judge. As to that, see **6.204** and **10.2**.
4   '*Judicial Review – The Tensions between the Executive and the Judiciary*' (1998) 114 LQR 578 at 592.
5   See **1.30** et seq.

the European Court's ruling in a case arising out of the shooting of three IRA members in Gibraltar.[1]

1.44   So it was that in the period following John Smith's premature death and in the run-up to the General Election victory of the Labour Party on 1 May 1997, the notion of European Convention incorporation began to attract substantial left–liberal support in a loose consensus that had not existed previously and it was that consensus which enabled the Blair Government to introduce the Human Rights Bill in October 1997.

THE INTRODUCTION OF THE HUMAN RIGHTS BILL[2]

1.45   Many Labour Party representatives and supporters had traditionally regarded the judiciary as hostile to the working-class interest,[3] which was in their terms more likely to be advanced by political action than by intervention of the High Court. The prospect that the authority of the Bench would be greatly enhanced if it was given the job of enforcing the European Convention domestically was viewed by some socialists with suspicion. That notion of judges as the class enemy was, however, to recede from view following Tony Blair's election as Leader of the Labour Party, and in December 1996 the party released a Consultation Paper unambiguously inclining in favour of European Convention incorporation, thereby accepting and indeed promoting an extended role for the judges in the policing of the rights and freedoms set out in the European Convention.

1.46   In its Introduction, the Consultation Paper[4] acclaimed the virtues of incorporation in terms both prosaic and unideological. Repatriating rights would, it was said, 'cut costs, save time and give power back to British courts'.[5] In addition, the authors claimed, incorporation would be popular, as opinion poll evidence suggested that people wanted to protect individual liberty. What was more, many senior judges and a prominent Conservative agreed that incorporation was a good idea! Expressed in such terms, the document encapsulated a key characteristic of the Blair project – the emphasis upon administrative efficiency.

1.47   If the Consultation Paper disclosed any philosophical vision at all, it was in an idea of personal freedom which certain of the founders of the party of organised labour would not have viewed with favour. Incorporation would help to 'change the relationship between the State and citizen, and to redress the dilution of individual rights by an over-centralising government that [had] taken place

---

1   *McCann and Others v United Kingdom* (1996) 21 EHRR 97.
2   A useful survey of the historical developments giving rise to the Act is the House of Commons Research Paper (98/24) on the Human Rights Bill. Appendix III to that Paper lists the 24 (failed) attempts made since 1970 to introduce human rights legislation in Parliament.
3   For an academic perspective of the 'myth' of courtroom neutrality, see JAG Griffith *The Politics of the Judiciary* 5th edn, (Fontana Press, 1997). See also M Phillips *The Sunday Times*, 14 November 1999.
4   *Bringing Rights Home: Labour's plans to incorporate the European Convention on Human Rights into UK law* by the Rt Hon Jack Straw MP, (then) Shadow Home Secretary, and Paul Boateng MP, (then) Shadow Minister for the Lord Chancellor's Department (December 1996). The text is reproduced in [1997] EHRLR 71.
5   *Bringing Rights Home* (see fn 4 above), p 1.

over the past two decades'.[1] In addition, 'by increasing the stake which citizens [had] in society through a stronger constitutional framework of civil and political rights' the Government would encourage citizens 'to better fulfil their responsibilities ... an essential part of [a] strategy to re-establish a balanced relationship between rights and responsibilities'.[2]

1.48   The Consultation Paper was attacked by two academic lawyers, Professors Ewing and Gearty, who dismissed Mr Straw's appeal to 'the true believers', warning that incorporation would 'almost certainly endanger our civil liberties more than it would protect them' and 'would give the lawyers' profession a new lease of litigious life'.[3] It

> 'would guarantee supremacy to [the European Convention's] narrowly individualistic view of society and would then make it impossible or extremely difficult to undermine or overthrow this ideology through the ordinary democratic process. As such [incorporation] represents the triumph of liberalism over socialism and as such fixes that triumph irrevocably into the constitution.'[4]

Whether Mr Blair and his colleagues privately endorsed the Ewing/Gearty analysis (albeit from a diametrically opposed perspective) or not, within days of the Labour landslide of 1 May 1997 the new Government's legislative priorities became apparent, with European Convention incorporation high on the action list.[5]

1.49   At this stage, the form of European human rights entrenchment had still not been established. As the Lord Chancellor put it at the time:

> 'the ... question is how to graft incorporation into our existing court systems. Wherever possible we will build on existing court procedures. The whole point of incorporation is to weave it into the existing fabric of legislative, executive and judicial responsibilities. Incorporation can only work if the courts are comfortable with their new responsibilities'.[6]

In the period immediately before the introduction in Parliament of the Human Rights Bill, debate therefore focused less on the principle of incorporation and

---

1   *Bringing Rights Home* (see fn 4 on p 15), p 14.

2   Ibid, p 14.

3   See their article 'Rocky Foundations for Labour's New Rights' [1997] EHRLR 146, and also their (undated) pamphlet for the Society of Labour Lawyers entitled 'Democracy or a Bill of Rights'. See also Ewing (fn 4 on p 1).

4   The barrister Murray Hunt suggests, however, that the Act is 'more communitarian than libertarian in its basic orientation', introducing 'a distinctively social-democratic model of human rights protection'. See 'The Human Rights Act and Legal Culture: The Judiciary and the Legal Profession' 26 [1999] 1 JLS 86 at 89.

5   *The Observer*, 11 May 1997, regarded incorporation as 'a big shift in the balance of constitutional power between Parliament and the judiciary' and *The Guardian* thought Labour deserved 'a hosanna' for it. Its leading article (13 May 1997) proclaimed that this was 'a victory for the small man, not the well-heeled corporation or aloof administrator'. An altogether different tone was struck by the former Conservative Attorney-General, Sir Nicholas Lyell, QC, MP, who said: 'we have a highly sophisticated legal system in this country. Indeed, I must declare an interest. My friends in the profession are in the most honourable sense rubbing their hands to at the thought of widening their practices in European Convention work' (Hansard HC, vol 294, col 301, 16 May 1997).

6   He was delivering the keynote speech at a Conference entitled 'A Bill of Rights for the United Kingdom' on 4 July 1997 held at University College, London.

more on its mechanical form. The significance of that debate is such as to justify a summary here of the views of the various protagonists.

1.50 Sir Stephen Sedley, one of the country's most incisive judicial thinkers, explained why the form of implementation mattered:

'the problem is that by legislating to give effect to a supra-national instrument [ie the European Convention] which binds legislature, executive and judiciary alike, Parliament will make it impossible to keep away from the courts the question whether primary legislation breaches the Convention.'[1]

There could be no clearer demonstration of this, it was said, than if incorporation allowed judges to strike down statutes which infringed the European Convention.[2]

1.51 This is broadly the position that obtains in Canada, where the 1982 Canadian Charter of Rights and Freedoms (a document much influenced not only by the UNDR and the ICCPR but also by the European Convention itself) allows judges to grant remedies, including the striking-down of statutes, where such statutes breach the Charter, unless, that is, the statutes are themselves expressly stated to have force and effect *notwithstanding* the principles in the Charter.[3] If need be, therefore, Parliament in Ottawa still has a legislative override.

1.52 In New Zealand, on the other hand, under the local Bill of Rights Act 1990 (based on the 1982 Canadian Bill of Rights) judges can only *declare* statutes to be inconsistent with human rights standards and cannot impliedly repeal or revoke them.[4] At one time, it was this solely interpretative option which enjoyed the most support among those British judges and politicians in favour of Convention domestication.[5]

1.53 Not that the Canadian and New Zealand precedents were the only ones. The maximalist approach favoured by barrister Ben Emmerson[6] would have called for a provision analogous to that in EC law, whereby, in the event of an irreconcilable conflict between UK law and a provision of directly effective European Community law, local law could be declared invalid and Community law would prevail.

1.54 David Pannick QC[7] summarised these approaches before calling for the adoption of a fourth, previously advocated by Lord Lester, whereby existing legislation that was found to offend the European Convention was impliedly repealed. In this way, judges would strive to construe laws made after incorporation so as to be consistent with the Convention, but if that was not possible, no remedy would lie.

---

1 In a speech delivered to the Law and Justice Conference held at Lincoln's Inn on 1 August 1997, reproduced in revised and annotated form in [1997] EHRLR 458.
2 A view supported by *The Financial Times* in a leading article on 17 September 1997.
3 The Canadian model was also supported by John Wadham of Liberty. See his Comment in the *Law Society Gazette* on 9 July 1997 and his article in the *Solicitors Journal* on 16 May 1997.
4 See generally in this area *The Impact of the Human Rights Act: Lessons from Canada and New Zealand* (Constitution Unit, May 1998).
5 According to Lord Lester in his article 'First Steps towards a Constitutional Bill of Rights' (fn 4 on p 9 above), p 146.
6 Writing in *The Times*, 22 July 1997.
7 Writing in *The Times*, 12 August 1997.

1.55   To the lay reader, these arguments may appear to have been a pre-millennial exercise in dancing on pin-heads. However, the debate was important because, in re-shaping the British constitution, form (ie the mechanics of incorporation) was to be as important as substance (ie the fact of incorporation).

1.56   Before describing the 'distinctively British'[1] approach the Government in the event chose to adopt in the Act,[2] there follows a short review of the European Convention and its workings.

---

1   The phrase used by the Lord Chancellor in his University College address (see fn 6 on p 16 above).

2   See Chapter 3.

Chapter 2

THE STRASBOURG SYSTEM

THE SCOPE OF THE EUROPEAN CONVENTION

2.1   The European Convention was the first treaty to give explicit legal content to the key provisions of the UNDR. It was also the first multinational attempt to devise machinery for the supervision and enforcement of human rights. The Preamble stressed the signatories' 'common heritage of political traditions, ideals, freedom and the rule of law'.[1]

2.2   The Convention purports to guarantee the following 17 rights as being inherent (in that they are considered to derive from our humanity), inalienable and universal:

–   right to life[2] (Art 2);
–   prohibition of torture (Art 3);
–   prohibition of slavery and forced labour (Art 4);
–   right to liberty and security (Art 5);
–   right to a fair trial (Art 6);
–   no punishment without law (Art 7);[3]
–   right to respect for private and family life (Art 8);
–   freedom of thought, conscience and religion (Art 9);
–   freedom of expression (Art 10);
–   freedom of assembly and association (Art 11);
–   right to marry (Art 12);
–   right to an effective remedy (Art 13);[4] and
–   prohibition of discrimination (Art 14).

2.3   First Protocol:

–   protection of property (Art 1);
–   right to education (Art 2); and
–   right to free elections (Art 3).

2.4   Sixth Protocol:

–   abolition of the death penalty.

2.5   The European Convention's raison d'être was from the outset that it should operate primarily at the level of domestic law. Article 1[5] provides, in terms, that it is the Contracting States who are to secure the relevant rights, leaving it to the institutions at Strasbourg to discharge an essentially supervisory role. Therefore, it would not be correct to describe the Strasbourg judges as constituting a European supreme court. Their function is not akin, for example,

---

1   See Appendix 2.
2   These are the official headings to be found in the European Convention. They were only added on 1 November 1998, when Protocol 11 came into force (see Appendix 2). Article 1 (with Art 13) has been excluded from the provisions of the Act (see Appendix 2).
3   This is a prohibition on retroactive criminal legislation (see Appendix 2).
4   Excluded (with Art 1) from the provisions of the Act.
5   See Appendix 2.

to that of the Judicial Committee of the Privy Council and the primary obligation to police the European Convention is placed upon Member States.

2.6 The European Convention is a mixture of negative and positive obligations. Therefore, signatories must not enslave their citizens, but must at the same time (for example) guarantee their freedom of expression.[1] Although there is no express hierarchy of rights, some rights (ie Arts 2,[2] 3, 4(1) and 7) are absolute and may not be made the subject of derogations (ie suspensions), restrictions or other limitations on the basis that they are so fundamental. There is no question of balancing them against other competing considerations. As a matter of European Convention law, no Contracting State, therefore, can ever torture its citizens,[3] not even when the victims' involvement in terrorism or organised crime is suspected.

2.7 There is then a separate class of rights (ie Art 4(2) and (3), and Arts 5 and 6) which, although unqualified in their nature and not susceptible to any restriction by governments purportedly acting in the public interest, are potentially derogable. So it is that the right to a fair trial could conceivably be the subject of a specific derogation by the UK in war-time. Finally, there are provisions (ie Arts 8–12) which are both qualified and susceptible to restriction[4] and in respect of which the wider public interest may be taken into account by Contracting States.

2.8 In terms of the focus of this book, some of those qualifications are highly significant and their express elaboration in the European Convention distinguishes it from other covenants (such as the US Constitution), where such qualifications tend to be implied. Much of the difficulty, in terms of assessing the implications of the Act for commerce, derives from the fact that these qualified rights will from now on be the subject of judicial interpretation, which must perforce take account of jurisprudential concepts developed by the Strasbourg institutions such as proportionality, legality and democratic necessity.[5]

2.9 It has become trite to note that the European Convention is a product of its time, a meaningless statement in circumstances where it could hardly be anything else. The Treaty's detractors regularly point to the fact, for example, that the right to life is, while absolute, qualified. Capital punishment is expressly permitted by the European Convention in the execution of a sentence of a court following conviction for a violation for which execution is provided by law.[6] What is more, there will not be an Art 2 violation where death 'results from the use of force which is no more than absolutely necessary'. Given that the most ardent supporters of European Convention domestication in the UK have tended to include many civil libertarians, these exceptions may appear surprising. Abolitionism was, however, a minority pursuit in the years after the end of the Second World

---

1   Subject, in the case of free expression, to the permissible restrictions set out in the Convention (see Appendix 2).

2   Although Art 2(1) is limited by Art 2(2).

3   Two countries have been condemned by the European Court for precisely this offence: Turkey in the case of *Cyprus v Turkey* (1976) 4 EHRR 282 and France in the case of *Selmouni v France* (2000) 29 EHRR 403.

4 ·   See also **3.198**.

5   As to which, see Chapter 5 below.

6   Article 2 (see Appendix 2). The subject featured in the Parliamentary debates on the Human Rights Bill and led to a change in the law (see **3.22** et seq).

War when the critical priority was 'to reconstruct durable civilisation on the mainland of Europe'.[1]

2.10 The European Convention is, it must be stressed, about civil and political rights (the so-called 'first generation' rights) and in the Labour Party's own estimation it is not about the 'social and economic rights [the so-called "red rights"] which have surfaced in advanced industrial societies in the past two or three decades'.[2] It has been suggested that this is because so-called 'red' or 'second generation' rights are not susceptible to legal determination, but this explanation is rejected by some commentators, who point to the fact that provisions of the European Social Charter are, for example, subject to a collective complaints mechanism. The allegedly incomplete span of the European Convention (despite the fact that many of its Articles are in broad terms) therefore has continued to attract complaint, partly because not even all civil and political standards are protected, such as the right to seek information from public bodies (the so-called 'right to know').

2.11 Critics on the left assert that the European Convention's protection of workplace rights (Art 11 aside)[3] is also arguably meagre. They lament the fact that there is in it (predictably) no reference to the rights to shelter and water which form part (for example) of the 1996 Constitution of the Republic of South Africa. The newly fashionable 'green' or 'third generation' rights affecting the environment are also missing. Nor, notes Sir Stephen Sedley, does the Convention take any account of the right to be free from the fear engendered by so-called 'hate' speech. Speaking in 1994, he described the Convention as 'a full generation out of date', based as he believed that it was 'on the nineteenth-century paradigm of the individual whose enemy is the State'.[4]

2.12 Even where the European Convention purportedly reproduces standards found in the UNDR, it has been attacked for its narrow focus. The bar on discrimination is allegedly weaker in Art 14 of the European Convention than in Art 26 of the ICCPR, because Art 14 can only be invoked in combination with some other European Convention claim.[5] Article 26 of the ICCPR is, by contrast, a free-standing or autonomous non-discrimination standard. It also promotes equality (as does the Canadian Charter), again unlike Art 14 of the European Convention.

2.13 Conceivably, however, these limitations have helped to make the European Convention the most successful human rights instrument the world has seen so far. It is precisely because it operates at the level of the lowest common denominator and looks anxiously for an existing continental consensus on any

---

1 *Rights Brought Home: The Human Rights Bill* (see fn 8 on p 7), para 1.1.

2 *Bringing Rights Home* (see fn 4 on p 15) at p 3. It is a noteworthy example of the transformation wrought to the Labour Party by Mr Blair that such a statement should have attracted virtually no comment.

3 See KD Ewing 'The Human Rights Act and Labour Law' [1998] ILJ 275. He says (at p 279) that 'the contribution of Article 11 to date has been disappointing, failing to deliver any meaningful protection for trade union activities, while being used as an instrument for undermining trade union security'.

4 *The Times*, 10 October 1994. See also, for example, Ewing and Gearty (fn 3 on p 16), p 151. Lord Lester takes a rather different view in *First Steps* (see fn 4 on p 9), p 126, footnote 10. See also in this context T Campbell 'Human Rights: A Culture of Controversy' 26 [1999] 1 JLS 6.

5 See **5.44** et seq for a fuller description of Art 14.

given issue that its institutions have been able to flourish and disputes with Member States have largely been avoided.

COMPANIES AND THE EUROPEAN CONVENTION

2.14	The view has been expressed that, if men and women world-wide are to have meaningful freedoms, the European Convention and other multilateral covenants must be adapted to police global capitalism.[1] Bad enough, it is said, that to date big business has not been made fully accountable in key human rights treaties, but much worse that it is able to exploit such instruments on its own behalf. In examining the Government's proposal to bring in the Act, Professors Ewing and Gearty cited the applications to Strasbourg made in recent years by, amongst others, the Fayed brothers, Ernest Saunders and Air Canada.[2] The political reality, the writers said, was that

> 'outside the arena of the criminal law, these [were] the sort of "people", some real and wealthy, some wholly artificial and corporate, who would overwhelmingly have resort to the Convention if it were incorporated into British domestic law.'[3]

2.15	This view is far from being without adherents. For all the supposed universality of human rights in the modern era, it would appear that some constituencies are more entitled to rights and freedoms than others, with business occupying a position far from the top.

2.16	John Wadham, the Director of Liberty, the campaigning organisation, has in the past said that only individuals can have human rights and that a domestic bill of rights should be able to be invoked by them alone, for fear that companies would otherwise 'dominate' any new system.[4] Similarly, the leading barrister, Sir Sydney Kentridge QC, in urging 'public support' for the Act has warned that 'it must be understood as a protection against power and not as a Rogues' Charter'. He feared that it might be invoked by 'unappealing litigants' and cited the success in Canada of tobacco manufacturers in striking down prohibitions on tobacco advertising as an infringement of free speech. He also noted the unsuccessful attempt of drinks companies which sought to persuade the Constitutional Court in South Africa to strike down a law prohibiting Sunday trading in off-licences on the ground that it purported to infringe the religious freedom of would-be drinkers.[5]

2.17	More importantly perhaps, at least one highly influential judge at one time felt uneasy about the possibility of corporates exploiting the European

---

1	See A Byrnes' article 'The Implementation of Rights' (1998/99) 12 INTERRIGHTS Bulletin at p 10.
2	So, too, Abbas Gokal, serving 14 years for his involvement in the BCCI affair, is petitioning the European Court: see *The Times*, 16 November 1999.
3	See Ewing and Gearty, (fn 3 on p 16), p 149. Professor Ewing has, in a separate piece, described the notion of corporate human rights as an oxymoron: see his article 'The Human Rights Act and Labour Law' (fn 3 on p 21), p 291.
4	See his article 'Why Incorporation of the European Convention on Human Rights is Not Enough' in *Human Rights in the United Kingdom* (see fn 3 on p 14), p 34.
5	See his article 'The Incorporation of the European Convention on Human Rights' in *Constitutional Reform in the United Kingdom: Practice and Principles* (see fn 4 on p 1), p 70.

Convention's provisions. Sir Stephen Sedley has remarked that he once regarded the ability of companies to rely upon the European Convention as the 'acid test of the desirability of enacting a domestic Bill of rights.' His view now is that

> 'unless they are brought within a cascade effect of the Human Rights Act, corporations will be getting both the penny and the bun: a multi-national news corporation will rank as a potential victim of human rights abuse at the hands of the state, able to complain loudly of official violations of its right of free expression – yet people whose privacy it invades in the name of free expression will be said to have no constitutional redress against it.'[1]

2.18 Such views are extremely significant. They suggest that the ability of companies to utilise the provisions of the Act will not be straightforward. The risk is that a relativist approach to business rights will fail to acknowledge that freedom of contract is (for example) just as much part of the common European heritage alluded to in the European Convention's Preamble as the other rights and freedoms the Treaty's draftsmen no doubt had in mind.[2] Just as in Canada, so too in New Zealand companies have traditionally been able to enjoy 'human rights',[3] a point of some significance in circumstances where case-law from both countries is likely frequently to be cited in litigation brought under the Act.

2.19 The Act eschews any notion that companies should be beyond its reach, no doubt in part because otherwise the Act would not obviously have been reconcilable with Arts 6 and 14 of the Convention,[4] but firms who in the future seek to rely on the Act should brace themselves nevertheless, as some judges may be anxious to ensure that 'it is not those with the sharpest elbows and lawyers who get to drink at the well'.[5]

THE REMAINING IMPORTANCE OF THE STRASBOURG INSTITUTIONS

2.20 The fact that the rights supervised by the European Convention's institutions[6] from their base in Strasbourg have been (in the time-worn phrase used by the Government) brought home does not of itself signify that the

---

1   Delivering the 1998 Hamlyn Lecture, published under the title *Freedom, Law and Justice* (Sweet & Maxwell, 1999), p 31.
2   And not just contract. According to Blackstone, 'there is nothing which so generally strikes the imagination and engages the affections of mankind as the right of property': *Commentaries on the Laws of England* vol II, p 2.
3   See s 29 of the New Zealand Bills of Right Act and the Canadian case of *R v Big M Drug Mart Ltd* 18 DLR (4th) 321 (1985).
4   The European Court suggested in the case of *Casado Coca v Spain* (1994) 18 EHRR 1 that to differentiate on the basis of whether or not an applicant's aims were profit-making might be discriminatory within Art 14.
5   Sir Stephen Sedley, in his address to the Law and Justice Conference at Lincoln's Inn on 1 August 1997, revised, annotated and published in *Opinion: A Bill of Rights for Britain* [1997] EHRLR 458 at 464.
6   The three institutions originally established by the Council of Europe to administer the European Convention were the European Commission of Human Rights, the European Court of Human Rights and the Committee of Ministers. With effect from 1 November 1998, the European Commission was merged with the European Court by virtue of Protocol 11 to the Convention (see **2.45** below).

institutions have been an unqualified success. The European Convention's credibility inevitably derives in the main from the support its Member States give it and it has been argued that aspects of Strasbourg's recent history were not wholly satisfactory and made the UK's repatriation of rights both necessary and timely – a case perhaps of rights brought home just in time.

2.21   It is perhaps rather odd that, half a century after the making of the Treaty and 30 years after the effective beginning of a campaign for the Treaty's incorporation into local law, it should be argued that the Act enables the UK to jettison some of the less successful features of the Strasbourg regime. What is said is that the effort required to keep together the increased number of countries now represented in the Strasbourg Court[1] will stretch the necessarily elasticated notion of the margin of appreciation[2] too far and that the reasonable political desire to accommodate so far as possible new members from States with very disparate legal and philosophical origins (and, in some instances, no sustained history of Parliamentary democracy at all)[3] will contribute to a decline in the quality of Strasbourg jurisprudence, or at least to an increasing tendency towards conservative decision-making.

2.22   The worry of certain commentators that the European Court could include former Communist apparatchiks[4] would not be material if the Act had removed the need to go abroad for justice. In fact it does not, and, therefore, an analysis of the way in which the European Convention's machinery has worked so far remains important, not just because the Act requires British judges to take Strasbourg law into account[5] but also because individuals and companies will continue, notwithstanding the introduction of the Act, to petition the European Court for many years to come. Indeed, the Government's very public celebration of the Act as a jewel in its legislative programme may induce sufficient consciousness-raising amongst British lawyers to ensure that the cliché-ridden road to Strasbourg becomes congested as never before. Thus, far from the Act effectively dispensing with Strasbourg applications (one of the largest claims made for the legislation), the outcome may be quite the reverse.

2.23   Specifically, there are three chief reasons why commercial lawyers still need to know how Strasbourg works.

---

1   See **2.26** below.
2   The margin of appreciation is the measure of discretion which the Strasbourg institutions have traditionally accorded a State when determining whether that State has acted in conformity with the European Convention. It is more fully dealt with at **5.35** et seq.
3   Lord Browne-Wilkinson remarked during the Parliamentary debates on the Human Rights Bill: 'there are now a number of judges [at Strasbourg] from jurisdictions which in the past at least have not been famous for their defence of human rights' (Hansard HL, vol 584, col 1269, 19 January 1998), while Lord Lester of Herne Hill QC has complained that the European Court may be more lenient when dealing with cases from former Eastern bloc countries (see his article in *The Guardian*, 31 May 1994 and his earlier article 'Universality versus Subsidiarity: A Reply' [1998] EHRLR 73, where he quotes from his own earlier report to the Proceedings of the 8th International Colloquy on the European Convention on Human Rights in describing the margin of appreciation as being 'as slippery and elusive as an eel' (at p 75)).
4   See, for example, J Langland 'Why Activists and Communists Will Soon Run British Justice: A Shocking Account of How Power in the Courts has been Handed to Europe by New Labour' (*Mail on Sunday*, 13 February 2000).
5   Section 2 of the Act (see Appendix 1).

– As will be seen, despite lavish statements about rights (like football) coming home, not all the benefits of the European Convention have been made directly enforceable by the Act and these will necessarily have to be secured by complaint to the European Court in the traditional way. Critically missing from the Act is Art 13 of the European Convention, which provides that 'everyone whose rights and freedoms ... are violated shall have an effective remedy before a national authority ...'.[1] The ostensible justification for that omission is discussed elsewhere.[2]

– Firms dissatisfied with the decisions of British courts in future cases raising a European Convention point (whether because local judges are believed to have got the European Convention wrong or, right or wrong, have declined to grant any relief) may still as a last resort wish to seek a review of those decisions (and it is a review and not an appeal) in Strasbourg.[3] It is a tactic of last resort because it is mandatory, before the European Court's procedures may be invoked properly, for prospective petitioners first to exhaust those legal possibilities available to them domestically.[4] This is a general principle of international law and it is unchanged by the Act. Subject to this, however, companies unhappy with rulings on the European Convention given in UK courts remain able to go to Strasbourg afterwards. Indeed, traditionally, most complaints from those Member States that domesticated the European Convention some time previously have reached the European Court on this basis.

– Even if a corporate claimant succeeds in establishing before a UK court that (say) an existing statutory provision breaches the European Convention, it may still be deprived of the fruits of its success if the Government declines, in the face of the court's decision, to change the offending measure or declines to do so retrospectively. The scheme of the Act is one whereby Parliamentary sovereignty is preserved[5] and, even where a British judge has declared that a particular statute is incompatible with the Act, the Government is not obliged to amend the statute.[6] A refusal to grant retrospective relief will, for example, continue to be of especial significance for businesses in dispute with customs or revenue authorities[7] and the ultimate option for such businesses will remain that of a complaint to the Strasbourg Court, the decisions of which are final and unappealable.

---

1 See Appendix 2. Provisions of this sort appear in many human rights treaties. They require States to ensure that the obligations to which they have committed are carried through domestically by the setting-up of credible and accessible forms of redress. See, for example, Art 2(3)(a) of the ICCPR, which obliges the Member States to that Covenant 'to ensure that any person whose rights or freedoms ... are violated shall have an effective remedy, notwithstanding that the violation has been committed by persons acting in an official capacity'.
2 See **3.10** et seq.
3 As the European Court is a court of review only, it cannot overturn a criminal conviction or order the release of prisoners, such as the killers of toddler James Bulger, even when it finds that the European Convention has been violated. Unlike the European Court of Justice in Luxembourg, it does not carry out reviews on the basis of a reference from a national court. There is no such mechanism in the Act.
4 See **2.48** et seq.
5 See **3.2** et seq.
6 Section 10 of the Act, see **3.178** et seq.
7 See, for example, the case brought by several British building societies, discussed at **9.20** et seq: *National & Provincial Building Society v United Kingdom* (1997) 25 EHRR 127.

2.24   In short, the Strasbourg regime and its procedures continue to matter profoundly and any notion that the Act will put an end to European Court complaints is wide of the mark.

A SHORT HISTORY OF THE STRASBOURG INSTITUTIONS

2.25   In view of the very high profile they now enjoy, it may appear surprising that, for all the concerns expressed by certain members of the Attlee adminis-tration,[1] the European Convention's institutions were slow to make their mark. There were no elections to the European Commission until 1954 and no judicial appointments to the European Court until 1959, by which time eight Member States (only) had accepted its compulsory jurisdiction. Not until 1 July 1961 was the first judgment delivered on the merits of a petition and in the following quarter of a century the European Court gave little more than a hundred further merits-based decisions. Therefore, litigation arising out of the Act will not draw upon 50 years of unbroken Strasbourg jurisprudence. For years, the European Court sat for only one week each month and a description of it in the early 1980s as the most significant and authoritative human rights tribunal in the world might have appeared greatly exaggerated to many. Such reputation as it has largely derives from developments since then.

2.26   One of these developments has been a surge in the European Court's popularity, insofar as this is to be measured in terms of the increasing number of States which have signed the European Convention. Whereas the treaty was adopted in 1950 by only 15 countries,[2] it has now been ratified by 41 nations.[3] Only Ireland (the written constitution of which is by no means European-Convention-proof) has not domesticated it, although indications are that it may do so shortly.[4] Therefore, if the buoyancy of any organisation is to be assessed, at least in part, by reference to the number of people wishing to join it, the Strasbourg institutions must currently be judged to be very successful and many politicians no doubt wish that the process of European Union enlargement could be as painless.

2.27   The fact is that most citizens of the former Soviet Union are now (in principle) as amenable to human rights protection as those resident in Western Europe. Mindful of this book's focus, this is significant because multi-national corporations now know that there exists enforcement machinery, the ostensible purpose of which is to ensure that such protection under the European

---

1   See **1.29** et seq.
2   Austria, Belgium, Denmark, France, Germany, Greece, Iceland, Ireland, Italy, Luxembourg, The Netherlands, Norway, Sweden and the UK.
3   In addition to the original signatories, these are Albania, Andorra, Bulgaria, Croatia, Cyprus, the Czech Republic, Estonia, Finland, Georgia, Hungary, Latvia, Liechtenstein, Lithuania, Macedonia, Malta, Moldova, Poland, Portugal, Romania, Russia, San Marino, the Slovak Republic, Slovenia, Switzerland, Turkey and the Ukraine. The parties to the 1995 Dayton Agreement on Bosnia and Herzegovina committed to adhere to the terms of the European Convention and certain other international human rights treaties. The Agreement can be found at http://www.bosnianembassy.org/bih/dayton.
4   See *The Irish Times*, 27 October 1999, 29 February 2000 and 21 April 2000. It is a requirement of the Belfast Agreement (as to which see **4.18** et seq) that Ireland gives further consideration to Convention incorporation and latest indications are that the Dublin Government will attempt to do so by October 2000.

Convention as they enjoy in the UK also broadly extends (application of the margin of appreciation apart) to their interests in, for example, Russia.[1] Of course, practice may not coincide with theory on this score but, a generation ago, not even the theoretical option existed.

2.28   In this context, it is to be noted that a significant feature of the Strasbourg system is that the European Convention can be invoked by parties which are not nationals of the State believed to be in violation of the Treaty or by nationals of any State which is a party to the Convention.[2] Therefore, a US firm, for example, can proceed against the UK for a perceived Convention breach.

2.29   As it has become fashionable to ratify the European Convention, so its agencies have become noticeably busier. There were, as already noted,[3] barely a hundred substantive decisions made by the European Court in the period from 1961 to the end of 1987. By contrast, in the ensuing 5 years, around 200 such judgments were given.[4] In 1999, the last year for which statistics are available, 177 judgments were delivered against a year-on-year increase in the European Court's workload of 25%.[5]

2.30   Such exponential growth may usefully be compared to the increased use made of the European Convention in UK litigation. The first English (or Welsh) citation was in the case of *Zoernsch v Waldock* in 1964.[6] The European Convention was mentioned in reported cases a further four times in the 10 years after 1974 but, until relatively recently, sightings in British courtrooms have remained an exotic and rare occurrence.[7] The figures for the last 3 years, however, show (following a *Lexis* search) that the European Convention was referred to in 124 English (or Welsh) cases in 1997, 71 cases in 1998 and 170 cases in 1999.

2.31   Whatever the Government's timetable and notwithstanding the fact that the Act comes fully into force on 2 October 2000, it is apparent that the European Convention, through the Act, has already incrementally become a necessary part of the British lawyer's legal armoury.[8]

---

1   In fact, the Council of Europe has threatened to suspend Russia's membership of the Council unless its human rights record in Chechnya improves (see, for example, *The Times*, 5 April 2000).

2   See *Soering v United Kingdom* (1989) 11 EHRR 439.

3   See **2.25** above.

4   There is an analysis of these figures in DW Jackson *The United Kingdom Confronts the European Convention on Human Rights* (University Press of Florida, 1997) at pp 16 et seq.

5   It was reported in mid-1999 that 700 letters a day were being received by the Strasbourg Secretariat (Press Association, 24 June 1999). As at 16 June 1999, there were 4,457 provisional case files registered against the UK alone, with just seven lawyers processing them (*The Independent*, 28 June 1999). By mid-February 2000, there were apparently more than 47,000 provisional files and more than 12,600 registered applications (*The Times*, 15 February 2000) and the President of the European Court was talking about the need for yet further procedural changes.

6   [1964] 1 WLR 675. A *Lexis* search has found no other reference in the 1960s.

7   See M Hunt *Using Human Rights Law in English Courts* (Hart Publishing, 1997) which lists all references to the European Convention to the end of 1996.

8   On the other hand, research suggests that, although there were 316 European Convention citations in UK courts between 1976 and 1996, the Convention had a bearing upon the outcome in only 16 cases: see F Klug and K Starmer: 'Incorporation by the Back Door' [1996] PL 223.

2.32   In any event, local lawyers have been accumulating more direct European Convention experience by actually taking cases to Strasbourg – numbers of which have been successful.[1] This country's record before the European Court is not as discreditable as has been widely claimed[2] but, according to the Labour Party's Consultation Paper, it 'does little for the reputation of Parliament, government or the courts', affecting as it does 'the UK's international standing on human rights as well as weakening the position of individual UK citizens'.[3]

2.33   The cumulative impact of a series of adverse findings at Strasbourg was sufficient to enrage the Conservative Government of the day.[4] All the more remarkable then that British lawyers should have secured such victories abroad by using institutional machinery generally recognised to be inadequate.

THE OLD STRASBOURG PROCEDURES

2.34   Days before the Act received Royal Assent, the procedural regime at Strasbourg changed radically.[5] Before describing the new arrangements,[6] it may be helpful briefly to explain how the Convention machinery used to work, on the basis that Strasbourg decisions arising under the old regime will from now on frequently be cited in UK courts.[7]

2.35   At the outset the Convention had provided that:

1   Mr Peter Hain MP, a Foreign Office Minister, said in Parliament on 18 April 2000 that, in 1999, 429 applications involving the UK were registered before the European Court, of which 32 were declared admissible.
2   In answer to the charge see, for example, AW Bradley and KD Ewing *Constitutional Law* (Harlow Addison Wesley, Longman, 1997), p 471. France and Italy, for example, have committed more violations than the UK, even though the French conceded the right of individual petition only in 1981. More worrying, perhaps, is the fact that the violations by the UK have extended across a broad range of the European Convention's Articles, compared to Italy, for example, and that more than half have occurred since 1990. At one point in the 1980s, 60% of the cases taken to Strasbourg were about delays in the Italian legal system and the European Court's current President, Judge Wildhaber, has expressed public concern about this problem of 'repetitive violations', specifically as regards continuing delays in the Italian justice system (see his article 'Some Reflections on the First Year of Operations of the "New" European Court of Human Rights' in *The Clifford Chance Millennium Lectures* at p 217). Virtually identical complaints pose a resource burden in his view and reduce Strasbourg's credibility.
3   *Bringing Rights Home* (see fn 4 on p 15), p 5.
4   See Lord Irvine's comments in 'The Development of Human Rights in Britain' [1998] PL 221 at 232–233.
5   The (new) Rules of Procedure of the European Court of Human Rights are to be found in Section II of the Convention (see Appendix 2).
6   See **2.45** et seq.
7   Two of the best guides to the Strasbourg system generally are L Clements, N Mole and A Simmons *European Human Rights: Taking a Case under the Convention* (Sweet & Maxwell, 1999) and K Reid *A Practitioner's Guide to the European Convention on Human Rights* (Sweet & Maxwell, 1998). It is a mark of the very recent popularity of the European Convention that there was no practical text for British lawyers until 1994. The Research and Policy Planning Unit of the Law Society published a Research Study (No 28) entitled *Practising Human Rights* in 1998, which documented some British lawyers' experiences of Convention work. One half said that they took less than 5 hours to make a Convention application.

'to ensure the observance of the engagements undertaken by the High Contracting Parties there [should] be set up:

(a) a European Commission of Human Rights, hereinafter referred to as "the Commission"; [and]

(b) a European Court of Human Rights, hereinafter referred to as "the Court".'[1]

2.36 It was the job of the European Commission to investigate complaints that the European Convention had been breached[2] (almost always on the basis of paper applications, many of which were less formulaic and were certainly shorter than old-style British court pleadings) and, if possible, to assist in the securing of a so-called 'friendly settlement'.[3] Otherwise the European Commission would report whether, in its view, there had been a violation of the European Convention.[4] If, in the opinion of the European Commission, the facts disclosed a breach of a State's obligations, the European Commission's report was delivered to the third European Convention institution, the Committee of Ministers of the Council of Europe, which could then decide to remit the matter to the European Court.[5]

2.37 In discharging this role, the European Commission was once described as 'the obligatory pathway to the European Court'[6] and as the 'spinal cord of the Convention system'.[7] Its critical importance is not surprising in circumstances where, at one point, approximately 90% of applications to Strasbourg were declared inadmissible by the European Commission. Although the proportion is now closer to one in five, companies need to bear this in mind before confidently telling shareholders and the market generally that their complaints will go to a successful adjudication at Strasbourg, as the reality is that most cases do not get past first base.

2.38 On 21 January 1959, the compulsory powers of the European Court were first recognised, the Member States undertaking to abide by the decisions of the Strasbourg judges in any cases to which they were party.[8] In the past, judgments of the European Court would be transmitted to full-time politicians sitting in the Committee of Ministers who would supervise execution of the judgments,[9] even though the European Convention had then (and still has) no specific power to punish Member States in the event of their failure or refusal to comply with the decisions of the European Court.[10]

---

1   Article 19 of the European Convention before the implementation of Protocol 11. This earlier text can be found in *Human Rights in International Law* (Council of Europe Press, 1998). References to the Articles applicable before the Protocol 11 changes were introduced are prefaced here by the adjective 'Old', as in Old Art 20 and so on. These (Old) Articles, it must be emphasised, have been abrogated by Protocol 11, as to which see **2.45**.

2   Old Art 28(1)(a), see fn 1 above.

3   Old Art 28(1)(b), see fn 1 above.

4   Old Art 31(1), see fn 1 above.

5   Old Arts 35 and 32, see fn 1 above.

6   See DJ Harris, M O'Boyle and C Warbrick *Law of the European Convention on Human Rights* (Butterworths, 1995), p 571.

7   Ibid, p 574.

8   Old Art 53, see fn 1 above.

9   Old Art 28, see fn 1 above.

10 Albeit that 'the level of state compliance with judgments of the Court is generally recognised to be exemplary' (Harris, O'Boyle and Warbrick at fn 6 above), p 702.

2.39   To this day, the Committee of Ministers is able to make non-binding recommendations, certain of which have in the past been of significance for the corporate sector on issues such as copyright and data protection. That part of its remit has not proved to be contentious. This could not, nevertheless, be said for its historical power to determine whether there had been a violation of the European Convention in cases not referred to the European Court.[1] This jurisdiction has been criticised over the years for the way in which it permitted politicians to make legal determinations. However, it reflected the exigencies facing those who first drafted the Convention at a time when certain States were not prepared to accept the compulsory jurisdiction of the European Court. The European Convention has always been something of a fix, conceived of and agreed to by politicians and supervised by them – hence the old, hybrid role of the Committee of Ministers.

2.40   Compared to some of the labyrinthine aspects of old-style English civil procedure, the European Convention machinery was at least readily understood by most of those required to operate it. By the beginning of the 1990s, however, it was straining at the seams. Specifically:

'. . . it had become quite clear that on a purely mechanical level the existing structure needed a considerable overhaul if the achievements of the Convention's first 40 years were to be preserved. In addition to this considerable structural difficulty, which would only be aggravated by the arrival of new Contracting States, political attitudes had undergone a substantial change since 1950. The hesitations that had prompted the original compromises appeared largely to have been dissipated; there was now general agreement that the system of protection of human rights under the Convention should be fully judicial.'

2.41   This statement may safely be regarded as authoritative as it was made by the late Rolv Ryssdal, then President of the European Court.[2] It was, in effect, his own machinery about which he was complaining. Given the statistics, however, his concern was far from being misplaced.

2.42   The Council of Europe disclosed in 1994[3] that the number of applications registered with the European Commission increased from 404 in 1981 to 2,037 in 1993 and, during this period, a growing number of complaints were filed through lawyers – perhaps a further indication of the European Convention's heightened profile. Before 1988, there were never more than 25 cases referred to the European Court in any one year, whereas 52 were referred in 1993 alone. The upwards-only curve in completed adjudications from the bench was even more stark, as we have seen.[4] The Court delivered no judgments in the 1950s, 10 in the 1960s, 26 in the 1970s, 169 in the 1980s and 177 in 1999 alone.[5]

---

1   Old Art 32, see fn 1 on p 29.
2   He was delivering the third Doughty Street lecture on 2 November 1995, reproduced in an annotated, revised version in [1996] EHRLR 18. See also M Janis, R Kay and A Bradley *European Human Rights Law Text and Materials* (Oxford University Press, 1996) in which it is suggested (at p 88) that systemic problems arose because of the Convention's 'deepening' and 'widening'. 'Deepening' was the overload caused by an increase in the cases referred to Strasbourg, while 'widening' stemmed from the enlarged number of Member States.
3   In its Explanatory Report to Protocol 11 (H(94) 5E), p 19.
4   See **2.29**.
5   See Janis, Kay and Bradley (fn 2 above), p 113. This created a 'congestion of the system' which by now was 'running the risk of choking on its own success': Trechsel in (1987) 8 *Human Rights Journal* 11 at 13, reproduced in Janis, Kay and Bradley (fn 2 above), p 115.

2.43   The delay caused by this congestion has been a regrettable characteristic of the Strasbourg institutions in recent years; embarrassing too, because many cases reviewed at Strasbourg had as their subject-matter delays before the courts of Member States.[1] As we shall see, Art 6(1) of the Convention provides that 'everyone is entitled to a . . . hearing within a reasonable time.'[2] Given that, by the mid-1990s, it was generally taking 5–6 years (and not infrequently longer) for a complaint to go from first registration with the European Commission to final judgment by the European Court, the question arises as to whether the Strasbourg institutions themselves were effectively in violation of Art 6(1) of the European Convention. It is likely that, during this period, many prospective claimants, not least companies, declined to take up the option of a Strasbourg complaint.

2.44   No doubt conscious of this, in May 1993 the Committee of Ministers of the Council of Europe resolved that the European Convention be amended in order to improve efficiency and shorten the time taken for individual applications. The Eleventh Protocol to the European Convention was the result. On 11 May 1994, it opened for signature in Strasbourg and it came into force on 1 November 1998. The rolling-out of the procedural changes embodied in the Protocol was accompanied by conspicuous editorial praise for the Strasbourg institutions, some of it tending to the hyperbolic. The press reported that the 'most successful human rights machinery in the world [was] moving into a new age'[3] with a jurisdiction stretching 'from Vladivostock to the Atlantic'.[4] Whether, over time, the reality matches the rhetoric remains to be seen.

THE NEW PROCEDURES[5]

2.45   The most significant change effected by the Eleventh Protocol was that the European Commission and European Court metamorphosed into one, a development first mooted in 1982. There is now a single European Court which performs the functions previously carried out both by the Commission and the Court. The first hearing of the new European Court took place on 12 November 1998 and its first judgment was handed down on 21 January 1999. Its jurisdiction extends to 'all matters concerning the interpretation and application of the Convention'.[6] It now sits on a permanent basis[7] and consists (as before) of a number of judges equal to the number of High Contracting Parties (currently 41).[8] The judges are (still) elected[9] (albeit for 6 years[10] rather than the 9 years of old) and are subject to retirement at the age of 70.[11] The previous rule whereby no

---

1   See fn 2 on p 28, regarding delays in the Italian legal system.
2   See Appendix 2.
3   *The Guardian*, 3 November 1998.
4   *The Irish Times*, 2 November 1998.
5   See generally the chapter by the President, Judge Wildhaber, in *The Clifford Chance Millennium Lectures* (see fn 2 on p 28), p 215. He has been a member of the European Court since 1991 and has warned that a further major restructuring of Strasbourg procedures may be necessary.
6   Art 32(1), see Appendix 2.
7   Art 20, see Appendix 2.
8   Art 22, see Appendix 2.
9   Art 20, see Appendix 2.
10   Art 22, see Appendix 2.
11   Art 23(1), see Appendix 2.

two judges could share the same nationality is abolished. The current British judge is Sir Nicholas Bratza.[1]

2.46   When considering cases, the Court sits either in a Committee of three judges, in Chambers of seven judges or in a Grand Chamber of 17 judges.[2] It can also sit in plenary session. A committee of judges acting unanimously may declare an application inadmissible or strike it out.[3] Otherwise the decision is left to a Chamber of judges,[4] unless it in turn wishes to relinquish its jurisdiction in favour of the Grand Chamber of 17 judges in cases raising a serious question affecting European Convention interpretation or where there is a risk of reaching a decision potentially inconsistent with a previous judgment of the European Court.[5] Relinquishing jurisdiction in this manner, however, can be prevented by the objection of the claimant or respondent. The supervisory authority of the Committee of Ministers as regards the execution of judgments is retained,[6] but its highly contentious role in making legal determinations has gone.

2.47   Shorthand descriptions of the new procedures might suggest that the European Commission had merely been folded into the Court, but President Ryssdal was anxious to stress that the changes accomplished by the Eleventh Protocol amounted to much more than that. In his view, what had been created instead was 'an entirely new entity which will have to find its own way as regards its organisation and, in particular, its procedure, whilst preserving and building on the achievements of the established Convention case-law'.[7] As far as he was concerned, the Convention had come of age, as

> '... the Convention Community [had] shown itself to be sufficiently mature to rid itself of those features that were the result of a reluctance – understandable in 1950 – on the part of Contracting States to commit themselves fully to an international judicial system of human rights protection.'[8]

BRINGING A CASE TO STRASBOURG

Admissibility at Strasbourg

2.48   As stated already,[9] not every case has in the past or will in the future benefit from a substantive review by the European Court and for many years the great bulk of filings at Strasbourg were found to be inadmissible for one reason or

---

1   Another British judge, Sir John Laws, stood in for him to hear the case from Guernsey of
     McGonnell v United Kingdom [2000] 8 BHRC 56, Sir Nicholas having previously heard the case
     in his former capacity as a member of the European Commission (see (1999) *The Times*, 28
     September). Lord Reed then substituted for Sir Nicholas in the case arising out of the killing
     of James Bulger (*T and V v United Kingdom* [2000] CLR 187), in which Sir Nicholas had also
     had an earlier involvement (see (1999) *The Express*, 17 December).
2   Art 27(1), see Appendix 2.
3   Art 28, see Appendix 2.
4   Art 29, see Appendix 2.
5   Art 30, see Appendix 2.
6   Art 46, see Appendix 2. The Committee of Ministers were supervising the execution of 28
     judgments against the UK on 8 February 2000 (Hansard HL, vol 609, Written Answer 82).
7   See Ryssdal (fn 2 on p 30), p 29.
8   See Ryssdal (fn 2 on p 30), p 29.
9   See fn 1 on p 28.

another.[1] This is because it has from the outset been an indispensable and unsurprising feature of the Strasbourg regime for certain threshold criteria to be met by every applicant and these are set out in Arts 34 and 35 of the European Convention.[2]

2.49 Complaints may be made by 'any person, non-governmental organisation or group of individuals' provided, that is, they claim 'to be the victim of a violation by one of the High Contracting Parties of the rights set forth in the Convention or the protocols thereto'.[3] This formulation does not expressly give corporations standing to complain of a Convention breach, indeed the term used in the French text of the European Convention[4] is *personne physique*. For all that, the European Court has traditionally held that companies may (other procedural requirements aside) properly claim to be victims of Convention violations. Thus, by way of example, the publishers of *The Sunday Times* were able to petition the court in the so-called *Thalidomide* case[5] alongside the newspaper's editor and journalists. On the other hand, a trade union cannot, without more, file a complaint in its own name on behalf of its members.[6] It may do so only if it identifies these members 'directly affected' by the alleged European Convention breach and is shown to have due authority from these members to bring the case.[7]

2.50 Nor can a local council or other perceived emanation of the State bring a case under the European Convention[8]. This is potentially a very significant limitation in the context of the Act and, as we shall see, may place certain British companies in a double-bind, whereby they are liable to be proceeded against under the Act whilst, if they are public authorities, themselves being arguably unable to rely on the Act's terms.[9]

2.51 On a number of occasions shareholders have sought to bring complaints to Strasbourg in their own right, most obviously where the company of which they are members has gone into liquidation. The Court has permitted this with obvious reluctance, saying that

'the piercing of the "corporate veil" or the disregarding of a company's legal personality will be justified only in exceptional circumstances, in particular where it is clearly established that it is impossible for the company to apply to the Convention

---

1   See, for example, the statistics cited by Janis, Kay and Bradley (fn 2 on p 30), pp 35 et seq.
2   See Appendix 2.
3   Art 34, see Appendix 2. The 'victim' requirement as carried over into the Act is dealt with more fully at **3.129** et seq.
4   As to which see **5.6**.
5   *The Sunday Times v United Kingdom* (1979) 2 EHRR 245. See also **8.86** et seq below for an account of that case. In the case of *Autronic AG v Switzerland* (1990) 12 EHRR 48 and see **8.68** et seq below) the applicant company complained of a violation of its rights to free expression. The Court held (at para 47) that 'neither Autronic AG's legal status as a limited company nor the fact that its activities were commercial nor the intrinsic nature of freedom of expression each deprive Autronic AG of the protection of Article 10. The Article applies to "everyone", whether natural or legal persons. The Court has, moreover, already held on three occasions that it is applicable to profit-making corporate bodies'.
6   *Swedish Engine Drivers Union v Sweden* (1976) 1 EHRR 617.
7   *Zentralrat Deutscher Sinti und Rome and Rose v Germany* (1997) 23 EHRR 209.
8   *Ayuntamiento de M v Spain* (1991) 68 DR 209.
9   See **3.139**.

institutions through the organs set up under its articles of incorporation or – in the event of liquidation – through its liquidators.'[1]

2.52   In the *Agrotexim* case, the petitioner shareholders at least held the majority of the shares in the company and the European Court appears to have been influenced by the fact that the company's liquidation constituted a form of State control, making a complaint by the company wholly unlikely.

2.53   In the *Pine Valley* case,[2] the two claimant companies were adjudged at Strasbourg to be victims even though one had been struck off the Irish Companies Register and the other was in receivership. The European Court's rationale was apparently that these were the corporate vehicles through which the third applicant, a private individual, had sought to develop a site. The company struck off had, in any event, earlier initiated proceedings in Ireland.

2.54   On the other hand, policyholders in an insurance company were once held by the European Commission not to be victims, as they did not have any legal claim to direct ownership of the insurance company's assets.[3] Similarly, a disappointed shareholder in the parent company of Yarrow Shipbuilders could not complain when Yarrow was nationalised. Only the parent company had that right.[4]

2.55   A company registered outside a European Convention Member State (in, for example, an offshore tax haven with perhaps only a name-plate operation in the UK) can potentially make a Strasbourg complaint. The only requirement is that the applicant is susceptible to the jurisdiction of the High Contracting Party which is the subject of the Strasbourg proceedings at the time the supposed European Convention violation took place.

2.56   Companies have no standing to complain of breaches of certain European Convention rights, such as the right to education (Art 2 of the First Protocol),[5] the right not to endure inhuman or degrading treatment (Art 3)[6] and the right to freedom of conscience (Art 9)[7]. Perhaps oddly, freedom of religion, however, can be exercised by a legal, non-natural person.[8]

2.57   An application which is purely hypothetical will not be permitted,[9] nor will a complaint brought by way of *actio popularis*. In other words, the putative victim must be personally affected, or risk being personally affected, even if not

---

1   *Agrotexim Hellas SA and Others v Greece* (1996) 21 EHRR 250.
2   *Pine Valley Developments v Ireland* (1993) 16 EHRR 379 (but contrast *Mendes Godinho and Filhos v Portugal* Appl 11724/85, (1990) 64 DR 72).
3   *Wasa Liv Ömsesidigt* Appl 13013/87, (1988) 58 DR 163 at 183–185.
4   Appl 9266/81, (1983) 30 DR 155 at 184–185.
5   *Ingrid Jordebo Foundation of Christian Schools and Ingrid Jordebo v Sweden* (1987) 51 DR 125 at 128.
6   *Purcell v Ireland* Appl 1540/89, (1991) 70 DR 262 at 273.
7   *Verein Kontakt Information Therapie and Hagen v Austria* Appl 11921/86, (1988) 57 DR 81 at 88. As for the extent to which British companies enjoy a right to privacy, see **7.12** below.
8   *Church of Scientology v Sweden* Appl 8282/78, (1981) 21 DR 109 at 109–110.
9   See *Klass v Germany* (1978) A No 28. A wife seeking a judicial review of a decision not to permit her husband permanently to reside in the UK can be a victim even if she (unlike her husband) is not the principal victim of the alleged breach: *Abdulaziz, Cabales and Balkandali v United Kingdom* (1985) 7 EHRR 471.

necessarily prejudiced or the subject of some direct form of detriment.[1] It is all a question of degree and the claimant must show at least a reasonable likelihood of his or her being prey to a breach of the European Convention.[2] As already seen,[3] trades unions and indeed other interest groups are not generally victims, even when charged with safeguarding the interests of their members, although they can provide legal representation for members.

2.58   The European Court has power under Art 19[4] to ensure that the European Convention's provisions are adhered to and, therefore, it need not restrict itself to an investigation of the particular facts before it. It must be doubted, however, whether judges in the UK would generally be willing, Strasbourg-style, to pursue a case in the public interest after the claimant has withdrawn it on the basis 'that the interests served by the protection of human rights and fundamental freedoms granted by the European Convention extend beyond the individual interests of the person concerned'.[5]

2.59   Applications to Strasbourg are also subject to a time-bar. Cases must be brought not more than 6 months after 'a final decision' has been taken locally[6] (a provision generally applied strictly). Following the Act's introduction, British lawyers may be negligent if they do not first take European Convention points (where possible) before local courts and are as a consequence later unable to proceed at Strasbourg. If only on account of this need to run a Convention point from the outset, British legal practice has been changed by the Act.[7]

2.60   There is also provision for the European Court to declare inadmissible and reject any application which is incompatible with European Convention provisions or is 'manifestly ill-founded, or an abuse of the right of application'.[8]

Friendly settlements at Strasbourg

2.61   If a case is admissible, the European Court will examine it.[9] It will also (and this, the advent in England and Wales of the Civil Procedure Rules 1998

---

1   See the case of *Groppera Radio AG v Switzerland* (1990) 13 EHRR 321. Women capable of having children had standing as victims to seek a review at Strasbourg of the decision of the Irish Supreme Court to grant an injunction restraining the provision of information about abortion facilities outside Ireland: *Open Door Counselling and Dublin Well Woman Centre v Ireland* (1992) 15 EHRR 244. Compare the more restrictive decision in *Leigh and Guardian Newspapers Ltd and Observer Ltd v United Kingdom* Appl 10039/82, (1984) 38 DR 74, in which reporter David Leigh (who had been given papers by Harriet Harman which had been read in open court) was not allowed to proceed with his claim that his (and his paper's) rights of free expression had been infringed by the House of Lords' finding that Harman's actions were a contempt. According to the European Commission, the violation complained of was too remote and indirect.
2   *Hilton v UK* (1981) 3 EHRR 104.
3   See **2.49**.
4   See Appendix 2.
5   *Gericke v Federal Republic of Germany* Appl 2294/64, (1965) Yearbook VIII 314 at 320. See also *Heinz Kornmann v Federal Republic of Germany* Appl 8282/78, (1966) Yearbook IX 494 at 506–508, 'The claim to be a victim goes to the question of standing; being a victim goes to the merits': see FG Jacobs and RCA White *The European Convention on Human Rights* 2nd edn (Clarendon Press, 1996), p 352.
6   Article 35(1), see Appendix 2.
7   See **6.169** et seq as regards waiver of European Convention rights generally.
8   Articles 35(3) and 35(4), see Appendix 2.
9   Article 38(1)(a), see Appendix 2.

notwithstanding, is a differentiating characteristic of the Strasbourg system) 'place itself at the disposal of the parties concerned with a view to securing a friendly settlement of the matter on the basis of respect for human rights as defined in the Convention and the Protocols thereto'.[1]

2.62 The ability of the European Court to give non-binding indications to the parties and, in particular, to broker friendly settlements has been described as 'perhaps the centre-piece of the Convention'.[2] It perhaps has a particular attraction for companies who are unlikely at the outset to have filed complaints at Strasbourg in order to establish an important human rights principle for the benefit of the 800m people and innumerable business entities now potentially able to enjoy the benefits of the European Convention. Corporations (in the UK at least) generally owe fiduciary obligations only to their shareholders (ignoring legal obligations to employees and creditors) and the prospect therefore of an agreed, negotiated outcome to a Strasbourg complaint which saves time and legal expense is an attraction for the commercial sector.[3]

2.63 The Act gives further effect to the Convention rights (Arts 1 and 13 excepted).[4] It does not domesticate Strasbourg's procedural rules, however. So, for example, under the Act neither the Court of Session nor the High Court will be able to procure a friendly settlement, although the increased incidence of various forms of Court-driven mediation in our justice system arguably suggests a trend in a not dissimilar direction.

2.64 There are no evidential rules at Strasbourg and parties are not required to adhere to their respective national laws in that regard. There is, therefore, no formal allocation of the probative burden in favour of one party or another and hearsay material is not prohibited. In broad terms, however, it is for the applicant to show that there has been an interference with a European Convention right and for the State respondent to justify it.

2.65 The European Court cannot compel witnesses to appear or call for the disclosure of documents. Therefore, its forensic powers are limited. In common with civil law systems generally, its procedures are paper-based and, therefore, it is not a tribunal before which British advocates can generally practice their oratorical skills. Questions are rare and, prior to the introduction of the Eleventh Protocol, the procedure was for each side to have about 15 minutes to make their

---

1 Article 38(1)(b), see Appendix 2.
2 See Clements, Mole and Simmons (fn 7 on p 28), p 74.
3 And not just corporates. 'The government may be content to cut its losses in the context of a private arrangement which usually attracts little publicity even where it includes an undertaking to introduce new legislation or to change an administrative practice. It is really not surprising that experience has taught governments to adopt a less combative approach in cases where it can be reasonably predicted that continued resistance to an inevitable result may be financially, legally and politically costly': N Bratza QC and M O'Boyle in 'Opinion: The Legacy of the Commission to the New Court under the Eleventh Protocol' [1997] EHRLR 211 at 221.
4 See **3.10** et seq.

submissions with about 15 minutes to reply. The submissions will have been filed beforehand to permit translation.[1]

Damages at Strasbourg

2.66 The European Court can award compensation and costs.[2] It cannot, however, grant injunctions. Nor, as already stated,[3] can it punish Member States for failing to change the law. To the extent that it is notorious that a company cannot have hurt feelings and can only be injured in its pocket, such limitations on the European Court's powers may not matter to the corporate sector. On the other hand, when it comes to damages,[4] the meagre awards often made at Strasbourg for non-pecuniary loss may come as a disappointment to boards of directors.

2.67 It has become commonplace for the European Court to award no more than half of the sums claimed by applicants. For some time now there has been a broad tariff of between £10,000 and £15,000 in non-pecuniary cases. This is a remarkably low figure when it is considered that £10,000 was awarded in a case against the UK where the claimant, Mr Johnson, had been unlawfully detained as a mental patient for 4 years.[5]

2.68 Substantial awards are not, however, unknown. In the case of *Sporrong and Lönnroth v Sweden,*[6] the applicant, whose property had (wrongly) been the subject of planning blight for over 20 years was awarded approximately £100,000. In the *Pine Valley* case,[7] around £1.2m was awarded, purportedly on the basis that this was the development value of the land which was the subject of the complaint less its rental value, while in the *Stran Greek* case,[8] the European Court said that the applicants were entitled to approximately £24m (£9m of which was accrued interest).

2.69 To date, there have been no awards which have included an element of aggravated, exemplary or punitive damages (although they appear rarely to have been asked for). More often than not, the European Court has indicated that its declaration in favour of the claimant (if it makes one) is itself 'just satisfaction',[9] reflecting the reality that most Strasbourg applicants have traditionally sought

---

1   In 1999, the parents of murdered toddler James Bulger were allowed to file a written submission and make oral representations at Strasbourg about the inadequacy of 'victims' rights' before British courts. This was in response to the application brought by the boy's killers, Jon Venables and Robert Thompson. The European Court's hearing was in private (apparently to avoid damaging the killers' prospects of rehabilitation). The Court gave its decision in December 1999, finding an Art 6 violation (see *T and V v United Kingdom* [2000] 2 All ER 1024).
2   To be paid within three months: see *Preora de Azevedo v Portugal* Appl 11296/84.
3   See **2.38**.
4   See **3.155** et seq as regards the availability of damages under the Act.
5   *Johnson v United Kingdom* (24 October 1997). In the torture case against France (*Selmouni* (2000) 29 EHRR 403) the applicant was awarded FFr613,000, approximately one-quarter of the amount his lawyer had asked for.
6   (1984) 7 EHRR 256. For a fuller description of this case, see **9.119**. See also generally the very helpful treatment in Chapter 7 of Clements, Mole and Simmons fn 7 on p 28).
7   (1993) 16 EHRR 379. See also **2.53**.
8   See **9.17**.
9   See, for example, *Kamasinski v Austria* (1991) 13 EHRR 36.

vindication above all else. However, the motivation of most corporate petitioners will be rather different.

2.70   No consistent principle can be extracted from the approach of the Strasbourg institutions to the question of damages and such reasoning as can be eked out has been described as 'inconsistent and weak'.[1] The parsimonious approach of the Strasbourg judges, if followed locally, will dismay corporate claimants whilst delighting public authority respondents who also happen to be companies.

Costs at Strasbourg

2.71   Costs may be awarded, but only where those costs are reasonable as to amount and have been actually and necessarily incurred. In the case of *Young, James and Webster v United Kingdom*[2] the European Court said 'the high costs of litigation may themselves constitute a serious impediment to the effective protection of human rights', adding that 'it would be wrong for the European Court to give encouragement to such a situation in its decisions awarding costs'.

2.72   When Ernest Saunders successfully petitioned the European Court,[3] he sought costs and expenses of almost £550,000. The Court awarded him only £75,000 while, in the case of Alison Halford,[4] the European Court appears to have accepted the British Government's argument that her lawyers should have an expense rate roughly half that for which they were contending.

2.73   There is no reason in principle why a successful applicant should not claim those costs incurred in proceedings before domestic courts, although the European Court has in the past expressed concerns about the high level of legal fees in the UK when compared to those prevailing in other parts of Europe. Legal aid is available at Strasbourg, but only where it is clear that the applicant lacks means.

2.74   Having briefly explained the way in which the institutions of the European Convention work, it may be convenient to analyse the way in which the European Convention has been given further effect in local law.

---

1   See A Mowbray 'The European Court of Human Rights' Approach to Just Satisfaction' [1997] PL 647.
2   (1981) 4 EHRR 38.
3   *Saunders v United Kingdom* (1996) 23 EHRR 313 (and see **6.132** et seq).
4   *Halford v United Kingdom* (1997) 24 EHRR 523 (and see **7.35** et seq).

Chapter 3

THE PROVISIONS OF THE HUMAN RIGHTS ACT 1998

THE LONG TITLE

3.1   Bearing in mind its likely reach and long-term significance, the Act is impressively succinct. The Long Title states that it 'is to give *further effect* to rights and freedoms guaranteed under the European Convention on Human Rights . . .' (emphasis added).[1] This is arguably a down-beat introduction to legislation described by Lord Lester as a 'legal poem',[2] whose importance the Government has not obviously been keen to under-play.

Non-incorporation

3.2   Neither in the Long Title nor in the substantive parts of the statute is there any reference to the actual incorporation of the European Convention into municipal (ie local) law. Although the European Convention's guarantees are made 'more immediate and relevant',[3] by the Act, the Treaty is not entrenched by the Act. This is because, despite widespread claims to the contrary (and unlike the manner in which the Treaty of Rome was implemented locally through the European Communities Act 1972), the Act does not in strict terms incorporate the European Convention into domestic law. Therefore, the European Convention's rights have not become 'fundamental law' and, in theory, the Act can be amended or repealed in its entirety at some point in the future.

3.3   When the Human Rights Bill was debated in Committee in the House of Lords, the retired judge, Lord Simon of Glaisdale, complained that the use of the word 'further' in the sense of *further effect* really gave 'no indication to the courts of *how much further*' (emphasis added).[4] He proposed an amendment to give the European Convention rights forming part of the Act 'domestic' as opposed to 'further' effect. However, the Lord Chancellor, Lord Irvine of Lairg, was not persuaded by this, saying:

> 'I believe that the Long Title to the Bill is admirably clear to a layman and to lawyers. The reason the Long Title uses the word "further" is that our courts already apply the convention in many different circumstances ... If the common law is uncertain, unclear or incomplete, the courts will rule whenever possible in a manner which conforms with the Convention. That is English law today.'[5]

---

1   The Act is to be found at Appendix 1.
2   *The Independent*, 15 June 1999.
3   Home Secretary (Hansard HC, vol 306, col 771, 16 February 1998).
4   Hansard HL, vol 583, col 470, 18 November 1997.
5   Hansard HL, vol 583, col 478, 18 November 1997. There is a substantial literature as regards the extent to which the Convention was already part of British law in the period before the Act. See, for example, M Beloff and H Mountfield 'Unconventional Behaviour? Judicial Uses of the European Convention in England and Wales' [1996] EHRLR 467 and M Hunt *Using Human Rights Law in English Courts* (see fn 7 on p 27).

3.4   Attempts will doubtless be made by lawyers to confer upon remarks such as these, made by the head of the justice system, some added significance because of the earlier decision of the House of Lords in the case of *Pepper v Hart*,[1] where it was held to be permissible to refer to Parliamentary debates as an aid to the identification of the legislative intention behind a statutory provision. Litigation which raises issues affecting the Act are likely to be characterised by references to statements made during the passage of the Human Rights Bill. Not that every speech about the provisions of the Human Rights Bill may legitimately be relied upon, however, as the judges in *Pepper v Hart* were clear that reference should be limited to statements by a Government Minister or other promoter of the legislation in question and that, just as important, reference should only be made where the Bill under scrutiny was ambiguous or obscure or literally absurd.

3.5   Why did the Act not merely provide for the incorporation of the European Convention wholesale?[2] The Lord Chancellor conceded in debate that at least a kind of incorporation was involved:

> 'As the Long Title states the [Act] gives further effect to rights and freedoms guaranteed under the European Convention ... but in a particular way with a very distinctive scheme of incorporation. It achieves the purpose of the Long Title by requiring primary and secondary legislation to be read and given effect so far as possible in a way that is compatible with convention rights.
> ... The Convention rights will not, however, in themselves become part of our substantive domestic law.'[3]

3.6   Party political considerations conceivably played a role in ensuring that the Convention was not introduced into the UK in the same manner as the Treaty of Rome.[4] Had it been incorporated, in its strictest sense, the cry would doubtless have gone up that Westminster had been made subservient to the judges, both in Strasbourg and at home. As the Lord Chancellor observed, however, the rationale for the Act was:

> '. . . to make provision so as to respect the sovereignty of Parliament for the continuing force and effect of legislation held by the courts by way of a declaration of incompatibility[5] to be incompatible with the Convention rights. If those Convention rights were themselves to constitute provisions of domestic United Kingdom law there would be obvious scope for confusion when the courts were obliged to give effect to legislation that predated the coming into force of the [Act].'[6]

3.7   In other words, the European Convention rights are not made directly justiciable by the Act. As explained below, the scheme has been one whereby they are secured by putting in place a particular form of statutory interpretation of the European Convention rights and by requiring a designated class – public authorities – to behave in a way compatible with European Convention.

1   [1993] AC 593. The implications of *Pepper v Hart* in the context of the Act are arguably overstated, see **3.49**. All the key ministerial references are, however, helpfully collated by F Klug in 'The Human Rights Act 1998, Pepper v Hart and All That' [1999] PL 246.
2   The Convention does not itself in fact require its incorporation into the law of each Member State: see the case of *Swedish Engine Drivers Union v Sweden* (1976) 1 EHRR 617.
3   Hansard HL, vol 583, col 508, 18 November 1997.
4   To the extent that European Convention is a part of EC law, Parliament (and not just public authorities as provided for in the Act) requires to conform to it. For the relationship between the European Convention and EC law generally, see **5.55** et seq.
5   Section 10 of the Act. See **3.178**.
6   Hansard HL, vol 583, col 509, 18 November 1997.

3.8   Does any of this matter? Probably not,[1] provided it is understood that the aim of the Act is to give the relevant European Convention rights a defined, so-called 'higher order' status in UK law.

SECTION 1

3.9   The Introduction to the Act is set out in ss 1 and 2. Section 1(1) provides that 'the Convention rights' as referred to in the Act

> 'means the rights and fundamental freedoms set out in –
> (a)   Articles 2 to 12 and 14 of the Convention,
> (b)   Articles 1 to 3 of the First Protocol, and
> (c)   Articles 1 and 2 of the Sixth Protocol,
>
> as read with Articles 16 to 18 of the Convention.'

The missing rights

3.10   It will be apparent that Arts 1 and 13 of the European Convention are missing and, as a consequence, are not given 'further effect' by the Act. Article 1 imposes an 'obligation to respect human rights'[2] and is, it might be thought, thoroughly unobjectionable. Why, therefore, was it omitted from the Act's scope? The answer is because the obligation to which it refers is placed on 'the High Contracting Parties' (such as, for example, the UK) who are 'to secure to everyone within their jurisdiction the rights and freedoms defined in [the] Convention'.[3] As Lord Lester pointed out in the House of Lords' debates on the Human Rights Bill, this is an inter-State obligation inappropriate for inclusion in domestic legislation,[4] not least when the domestic legislation (ie the Act) purports to carry out that obligation by virtue of the duty it places upon public authorities to act in conformity with the Convention.[5] Article 1 is, nevertheless, important in terms of the positive obligation it places upon States to secure Convention rights and freedoms without interference. It is not devoid of content and is likely to be the subject of citation in local courts, particularly when used to buttress the argument that, for example, the UK should be proactive in establishing a coherent regime for the protection of privacy in conformity with Art 8 of the European Convention.[6]

3.11   The position in respect of Art 13, which is also outside the Act's scope, is, however, less straightforward. Described as 'the heart of the Convention',[7] it says that

> 'everyone whose rights and freedoms as set forth in [the] Convention are violated shall have an effective remedy before a national authority notwithstanding that the violation has been committed by persons acting in an official capacity.'[8]

---

1   Not at least to Government ministers, who frequently refer to the incorporation of the European Convention.
2   See Appendix 2.
3   See Appendix 2.
4   Hansard HL, vol 583, col 467, 18 November 1997.
5   By virtue of s 6 of the Act, see **3.73** et seq.
6   As to which, see Appendix 2.
7   Richard Gordon QC and Tim Ward writing in *The Guardian*, 19 May 1998.
8   See Appendix 2 below. Article 2 of the ICCPR is in similar form.

Is the Act already a lifeless corpse if it lacks the Convention's beating heart?

3.12   The Government's White Paper[1] did not mention the fact that Arts 1 and 13 were not to be 'brought home' and their omission was the subject of criticism and comment inside and outside Parliament. The Strasbourg Court itself has confirmed in the case of *Boyle and Rice v United Kingdom*[2] that Art 13 (unlike Art 14), may be invoked independently of other Convention provisions. That now makes it a free-standing right of some importance. It has been described as the 'link' between the European Convention and national legal systems[3] on the basis that by requiring Member States to establish effective local mechanisms it discourages recourse to Strasbourg save where all other options have been exhausted. The UK, like the other Member States, is accorded a margin of appreciation as regards the means by which it discharges its Art 13 obligations, provided the means are fit for the purpose in terms of safeguarding the various European Convention rights of substance and making them effective.[4] The mechanism required may vary depending upon the right engaged. The more important the right, the more effective the Art 13 remedy may need to be.[5]

3.13   The centrality of Art 13 is such that it has been incorporated by all the other Member States which have domesticated the European Convention[6] and the retired judge, Lord Ackner, himself a supporter of the legislation, said in Parliament that he feared that 'a failure to provide the means to enforce renders the [European Convention] rights valueless'.[7]

3.14   Opinions vary as to why the Government should have risked criticism for on the one hand ostensibly giving citizens the substantive European Convention rights while arguably taking them away with the other by omitting the European Convention guarantee of an effective remedy for the securing of those rights that is enshrined in Art 13. The omission was plainly not accidental, but was, it was suggested, meaningless on the basis that, as Lord Lester pointed out in Parliamentary debate, British courts will in the future have regard to Art 13 whether made part of the Act or not,[8] just as they have done in the past.

3.15   The Lord Chancellor was not persuaded that giving further effect to Art 13 by including it in the Act was 'either necessary or desirable'. He said:

> 'The [Act] gives effect to Article 1 by securing to people in the United Kingdom the rights and freedoms of the Convention. It gives effect to Article 13 by establishing a scheme under which Convention rights can be raised before our domestic courts. To that end, remedies are provided in section 8.[9] If the concern is to ensure that the [Act]

1   *Rights Brought Home: The Human Rights Bill* (Cm 3782).
2   (1998) 10 EHRR 425. As regards Art 14, see **5.44** et seq.
3   Lester and Pannick (see fn 1 on p 12) p 217.
4   *Askoy v Turkey* (1997) 27 EHRR 553.
5   *Klass v Germany* (1983) 2 EHRR 214.
6   See the article by the Constitution Unit *Rights Brought Home: a briefing on the Human Rights Bill with amendments* [1998] 1 EHRLR 9. Lord Lester said that the 'curious' Art 13 'gap' was 'one of only three imperfections in this otherwise brilliant Bill' in Hansard HL, vol 584, col 1264, 19 January 1998.
7   Hansard HL, vol 582, col 1285, 19 January 1998.
8   Hansard HL, vol 583, col 467, 18 November 1997. The Court of Appeal referred to it in, for example, Esther Rantzen's libel case against Mirror Group Newspapers (*Rantzen v Mirror Group Newspapers (1986) Ltd* [1994] QB 670). It was also referred to in *R v Khan* [1997] AC 558 and in *R v Secretary of State for the Home Department, ex parte Brind* [1991] 1 AC 696 .
9   Section 8 of the Act is dealt with at **3.155** et seq.

provides an exhaustive code of remedies for those whose Convention rights have been violated, we believe that [s] 8 already achieves that and that nothing further is needed .... The courts would be bound to ask themselves what was intended beyond the existing scheme of remedies set out in the [Act]. It might lead them to fashion remedies other than the section 8 remedies, which we regard as sufficient and clear.'[1]

3.16 On being further pressed by Lord Lester, in the House of Lords, the Lord Chancellor added:

'... the courts may have regard to Article 13. In particular, they may wish to do so when considering the very ample provisions of section 1 ... Knowing the remedial amplitude of the law of the United Kingdom, I cannot see any scope for the argument that English or Scots law is incapable within domestic adjectival law of providing effective remedies.'[2]

3.17 A further clue regarding the Cabinet's thinking was provided in the House of Commons by the Home Secretary, the Rt Hon Jack Straw MP, who admitted that he had some concern that Art 13, if included in the legislation, might lead the courts to award damages across a broader front than the Government had envisaged and that successful claims against Government-financed bodies would have implications for the public purse.[3]

3.18 The implications of Art 13's omission from the Act are for the present unclear.[4] It creates a dissonance of the very kind which the Act was supposed to remove and the Lord Chancellor's claim that the inclusion of Art 13 was unnecessary because of the 'remedial amplitude' of local law is on its face no more persuasive than the claim made years earlier by the Rt Hon John Major MP, when Prime Minister, that a bill of rights was unnecessary in this country because 'we have freedom'.[5] In the wake of unsuccessful attempts in both Houses of Parliament to amend the Human Rights Bill expressly to incorporate Art 13, the suspicion must remain that the chief reason for its omission was to insure against the possibility of a UK court reading into Art 13 implications that might expand the scope of judicial review.[6] Indeed, the judgment of the European Court in the so-called 'gays in the military' case (in which an Art 13 violation was established) suggests that Government knew precisely what it was doing when omitting Art 13

---

1 Hansard HL, vol 583, col 475, 18 November 1997.

2 Hansard HL, vol 583, col 477, 18 November 1997. To put the matter beyond doubt, he later added that: 'during the earlier course of the debate I did not say that Article 13 was incorporated. The debate is about the fact that it is not incorporated. In reply to the noble Lord, Lord Lester, I said that in my view the English courts, in the example which he offered, would be able to have regard to Article 13': Hansard HL, vol 583, col 479, 18 November 1997.

3 He said in Parliament: 'we are dealing with breaches of rights by public bodies, some of which are financed by Government – whose purse is, apparently, endless and seamless – whereas others do not have access to the full resources of Her Majesty's Government and the Bank of England printing works in my home town of Loughton in Essex. We had to think carefully about the scope of the remedies that we should provide': Hansard HC, vol 312, col 979, 20 May 1998.

4 The significance for judicial review is examined at **6.308** et seq.

5 Mr Major's remark has been alluded to by the Lord Chancellor on a number of occasions. See, for example, Lord Irvine's Keynote Address reproduced in *Constitutional Reform in the United Kingdom* (see fn 4 on p 1) and his speech at University College London on 4 July 1997 (see fn 6 on p 16).

6 See Dr G Marshall in 'Patriating Rights – with Reservations: The Human Rights Bill 1998' in *Constitutional Reform in the United Kingdom* (fn 4 on p 1) p 77.

from the legislation. In that case,[1] the Strasbourg judges stated that the level of scrutiny permitted local judges in domestic judicial review was *not* adequate to ensure that the applicants had an effective remedy as guaranteed by Art 13. Put simply (and notwithstanding the Government's acknowledgement that the courts here may have regard to it), the express inclusion of Art 13 in the Act might have made easier (and indeed required) more intensive judicial review of decision-making in this country.

3.19   Section 1(1)(b) gives further effect to Arts 1–3 of the European Convention's First Protocol. Included, therefore, are the rights to protection of property (Art 1 of the First Protocol),[2] to education (Art 2 of the First Protocol) and to free elections (Art 3 of the First Protocol).

3.20   The Fourth Protocol to the European Convention, however, is also missing from the Act. Although signed by the UK in 1963, that protocol has not yet been ratified. Arguably, it already has indirect effect through European Community law. Its First Article provides that 'no one shall be deprived of his liberty merely on the ground of inability to fulfil a contractual obligation'[3] (as to which business may respond with a mixture of relief and disappointment),[4] while the Second Article of the Fourth Protocol provides that everyone has 'freedom to choose his residence'.[5]

3.21   The White Paper[6] described the guarantees in the Fourth Protocol as 'important', reflecting as they did similar rights in the ICCPR and to which the Government wished to give formal recognition in local law. It warned, however, that ratification was not likely to happen before potential conflicts with domestic laws (regarding entry rights in particular) were resolved.[7]

Abolition of the death penalty

3.22   The Act explicitly gives further effect to the First and Second Articles of the European Convention's Sixth Protocol, concerning the abolition of the death penalty.[8] Following a spirited campaign by a Labour back-bencher, Kevin McNamara MP (against the wishes of the Government), these two Articles were made part of the Act by amendment and their effect is to abolish in the UK the death penalty for military offences. Although this development is of only esoteric interest to company directors and their advisors, Mr McNamara's successful

---

1   *Lustig-Prean v United Kingdom* (1999) 29 EHRR 548. See also **6.289** et seq.
2   Article 1 of the First Protocol is more fully dealt with in Chapter 9.
3   See Appendix 2. See also Written Answer 134 of Baroness Scotland of Asthal in the House of Lords on 9 November 1999.
4   This is not directed at debtors who have acted fraudulently or refused to disclose the whereabouts of assets (see *X v Germany* (1971) Appl 5025/71, (1971) 14 Yearbook 692). It is unlikely that it would bear upon a claimant's ability to obtain a freezing injunction, but see generally Chapter 6.
5   See Appendix 2.
6   At **4.10** and **4.11**.
7   Article 2(1) of the Fourth Protocol provides that freedom of movement may be restricted 'in accordance with law and justified by the public interest in a democratic society'. For an analysis of the concept of necessity in a democratic society, see **5.29** et seq.
8   See Appendix 2. The immediate post-War environment in which the European Convention was drafted is evident from the fact that Art 2 of the Sixth Protocol does not, in itself, prohibit the death penalty (see **2.9**). No human rights instrument drafted today is likely to be cast in such terms.

efforts are of wider interest to the extent that they may be considered emblematic of the way in which the Act may encourage a rights culture to develop by accretion. The Government had said in debate that it was concerned that maintenance or abolition of the death penalty was *par excellence* a matter of private conscience for determination in a Parliamentary free vote (and numbers of Conservative members supported that view). The inclusion of the Sixth Protocol in the Act led, however, to the Government's decision on 27 January 1999 to ratify the Sixth Protocol. Going further, the Home Secretary announced on 3 March 1999[1] that the UK would also ratify the Second Optional Protocol to the ICCPR, requiring States to abolish the death penalty. What is more, the Home Secretary has indicated that the Government now proposes to go further than the McNamara amendment by declining to make a declaration under the Protocol which would still permit the use of the death penalty in wartime.[2]

Articles 16–18

3.23   As already noted, all of the European Convention rights, as defined in the legislation, are to be 'read with Articles 16 to 18 of the Convention'.[3] These Articles permit a variety of limitations upon the operation of European Convention rights. Article 16, for example, legitimises restrictions on the political activity of aliens, notwithstanding the provisions of Art 10 (on freedom of expression), Art 11 (on freedom of assembly and association) and Art 12 (on the right to marry). There has only been one case brought to the Strasbourg Court under Art 16[4] (and that was in a non-business context) and it has been described as 'a dead letter to be abolished'.[5]

3.24   Article 17 forbids any abuse of the Convention's rights. No Member State, group or person can purportedly rely upon the European Convention to engage in any activity or perform any act 'aimed at the destruction of any of the rights and freedoms set out in the Convention'.[6]

3.25   Article 17 is directed both at governmental and individual abuses of rights and bears directly on that long-standing liberal dilemma: to what extent can restrictions properly be placed upon the freedoms of those who would otherwise seek to rely upon such freedoms (as provided, for example, in the European Convention) to diminish or remove the freedoms of others? The difficulties were illustrated at Strasbourg in the *Lawless* case,[7] where the European Court held that, even if the applicant Lawless had been involved in IRA activities, on account of

---

1   Home Secretary's Statement, 3 March 1999.
2   The UK is still not a party to the Seventh Protocol, which expressly provides for freedom from double jeopardy. Here too, however, it has said that it will become a signatory after ironing out some inconsistencies regarding domestic family law matters, Home Secretary's Statement, 3 March 1999. See also Written Answer 82, Hansard HL, vol 609, 8 February 2000.
3   Section 1(1) of the Act, see Appendix 1.
4   *Piermont v France* (1995) 20 EHRR 301.
5   P van Dijk and GJH van Hoof *Theory and Practice of the European Convention on Human Rights* (Kluwer Law International, 1998).
6   See Appendix 2.
7   *Lawless v Ireland* (1961) 1 EHRR 15.

Art 17 he was entitled in prison to invoke (in that case) Art 5 (the right to liberty and security) and Art 6 (the right to a fair trial).[1]

3.26   Article 17 of the Convention has been described as 'an instrument of last resort',[2] perhaps because, like Art 16, it concedes as permissible a measure of discrimination. However, its justification is clear, namely 'to protect the rights enshrined in the Convention by safeguarding the free functioning of democratic institutions'.[3]

3.27   Article 18 provides that 'the restrictions permitted under [the] Convention to the [relevant] rights and freedoms shall not be applied for any purpose other than those for which they have been prescribed'.[4] As such, the UK and the other Contracting States which are parties to the European Convention are barred from using the permissible restrictions in the European Convention for any purpose other than those intended.[5]

3.28   The effect of s 1(1) of the Act is that, when interpreting the European Convention, the UK courts are to have regard for the same limitations upon the operation of European Convention rights (ie as set out in Arts 16 to 18) as would the European Court.

Section 1 – additional provisions

3.29   Section 1(2) states that those Convention Articles forming part of the Act are to have effect 'subject to any designated derogation or reservation (as to which see ss 14 and 15)',[6] while s 1(3) provides that the European Convention Articles forming part of the Act are to be found in Sch 1. Section 1(4) permits the Secretary of State by order to 'make such amendments to the Act as he considers appropriate to reflect the effect, in relation to the United Kingdom, of a protocol'.[7] 'Protocol' is defined in s 1(5) to mean a protocol to the Convention:

'(a)   which the United Kingdom has ratified; or
(b)   which the United Kingdom has signed with a view to ratification.'[8]

3.30   Section 1(6) provides that no amendment made under s 1(4) of the Act (ie to reflect the effect of a protocol) can come into force before the relevant protocol is in force in relation to the UK.[9]

3.31   The effect of these essentially technical measures is to ensure that the Act is not preserved in legal aspic as at its accession date (9 November 1998). Its reach may develop and extend over time in conformity with any further protocol which

---

1   Article 17 has on occasions been in issue at Strasbourg in business cases, such as when the
     applicant is making a claim under Art 1 of the First Protocol (see P van Dijk and GJH van
     Hoof (fn 5 on p 45), p 753).
2   Harris, O'Boyle and Warbrick (fn 6 on p 29) p 511.
3   *Kommunistiche Partei Deutschland v Germany*, Appl 20/57, (1955–1957) 1 Yearbook 222 at 223.
4   See Appendix 2.
5   Here too, the Strasbourg institutions have generally been reluctant to treat Art 18 as decisive,
     although it was the subject of some discussion in the important property case of *Sporrong and
     Lönnroth v Sweden* (1982) 5 EHRR 35, see **9.119** et seq.
6   For a description of ss 14 and 15, see **3.195** et seq.
7   See Appendix 1. A protocol in this context is an amendment or a modification to an existing
     treaty. It is itself a treaty and as such requires to be negotiated and agreed in the usual way.
8   See Appendix 1.
9   See Appendix 1.

the UK may in the future enter into. However, the Act does not permit legal effect to be given locally to a protocol before the UK has an obligation internationally to give effect to the rights set out in that protocol. Thus, the European Convention rights to which the Act gives further effect must in every case *succeed* those secured by this country internationally and may not *precede* them. Section 1(5) does nevertheless mean that, for example, the Fourth Protocol to the European Convention,[1] which the UK has signed but not ratified and the Seventh Protocol[2] of the European Convention, which the UK has neither signed nor ratified, could be introduced at some future date (together, that is, with protocols that do not yet exist).

SECTION 2

3.32   The marginal heading to s 2 is 'Interpretation of Convention Rights'. Section 2(1)[3] provides that, when a court or tribunal in the UK considers a question which 'has arisen in connection with a Convention right', it *must take into account* judgments, decisions, declarations or opinions[4] of the respective Strasbourg institutions whenever made or given (ie whether before or after the coming into force of the Act and whether or not the UK was directly the subject of the particular Strasbourg determination[5]), provided they are, in the view of the court or tribunal, relevant.

3.33   The obligation to take into account is placed only on courts and tribunals in the UK, not public authorities, unlike the position in respect of s 3 which deals with the interpretation of domestic legislation. This suggests that, for example, an industry regulator could in theory disregard the accumulated weight of Strasbourg jurisprudence. Of course, the risk would be that, in doing so, he might end up acting in a way that was incompatible with the Convention and thereby be in breach of s 6(1).[6]

THE WEIGHT TO BE ATTACHED TO THE CONVENTION JURISPRUDENCE

3.34   Section 2 requires account to be taken of Strasbourg jurisprudence, as a result of which not merely the Convention but also its case-law has been

---

1   See **3.20** et seq.
2   The Lord Chancellor has indicated that the legislation necessary to remove obstacles to the ratification of the Seventh Protocol will be put in train when Parliamentary time allows: Written Answer 141, Hansard HL, 9 November 1999.
3   See Appendix 1.
4   The European Court cannot (by Art 47(2)) in fact give an opinion (as opposed to a judgment) on any question affecting the European Convention's rights and freedoms, so this is unlikely to be an issue in future British litigation. Similarly, it is difficult to see how a decision of the politicians sitting in the Committee of Ministers could tip the balance in a British court.
5   The Lord Chancellor, Lord Irvine, confirmed this during the Report stage debate in the House of Lords (see Hansard HL, vol 584, col 1271, 19 January 1998).
6   The Lord Chancellor's confirmation in debate that judges may have regard for Art 13 presumably makes that and Art 1 relevant in this context, even though they are not Convention rights as defined in the Act.

domesticated. This begs the question: how much account? As explained earlier, the European Commission no longer exists[1] but, by virtue of s 2(1) of the Act, its decisions and opinions will remain highly relevant for British lawyers. However, those determinations (and decisions of the Committee of Ministers which are made by politicians in any event) are likely to continue not to be accorded the same weight as decisions of the European Court, particularly as regards the European Commission's many decisions on matters affecting admissibility and not dealing with matters of substance. Determinations of the European Commission sitting on a plenary basis will be more substantial than determinations made by a chamber and the same goes for decisions of the European Court. Unanimous (or near unanimous) judgments of the European Court are more authoritative than those in respect of which the European Court judges have obviously been split, while greater significance arguably attaches to recent decisions than older ones on the basis that the European Convention is to be interpreted in light of contemporary attitudes.[2]

3.35   Section 2(2) and (3)[3] provides that the manner in which the 'wealth'[4] of Strasbourg jurisprudence (past and future) may properly be relied upon in proceedings under the Act is to be set out in new court (or tribunal) rules.[5]

3.36   In circumstances where Convention cases have been cited in UK courts for many years,[6] the provisions of s 2 might be regarded as unnecessary.

3.37   When the duty it places upon British courts and tribunals as regards European Convention jurisprudence is one of *consideration* but not of *adherence,* does s 2 add anything to existing practice? What impact does it have for existing rules of precedent? As to that, Lord Browne-Wilkinson, then the senior member of the Judicial Committee of the House of Lords, told his fellow peers that:

> '... the doctrine of *stare decisis,* the doctrine of precedent, whereby we manage to tie ourselves up in knots for ever bound by an earlier decision of an English court, does not find much favour north of the Border, finds no favour across the Channel and is an indigenous growth of dubious merit.'[7]

3.38   What appears clear is that *must take into account* does not mean *must follow* and the Government resisted an opposition amendment that it should do. This was, according to the Lord Chancellor, because British:

> '... courts must be free to develop human rights jurisprudence by taking into account European judgments and decisions but they must also be free to distinguish them and to move out in new directions in relation to the whole area of human rights law.'[8]

3.39   Making Strasbourg law binding would remove 'from the judges the flexibility and discretion that they require in developing human rights law'.[9] As one way of exercising that discretion, local judges may conceivably attach less

---

1   Pursuant to the Eleventh Protocol, effective from 1 November 1998, see **2.44** et seq.
2   See also **5.4** on construing the Convention.
3   See Appendix 1.
4   A word used by the Lord Chancellor: Hansard HL, vol 582, col 1230, 3 November 1997.
5   A draft of which appeared in spring 2000.
6   See **2.30**.
7   Hansard HL, vol 583, col 513, 18 November 1997. The role of precedent at Strasbourg is dealt with at **5.11** below.
8   Hansard HL, vol 583, col 835, 24 November 1997.
9   Hansard HL, vol 584, col 127, 19 January 1998.

significance to some of the earliest pronouncements of the European Court, which are not necessarily a reliable pointer to the meaning of the European Convention today. That is not to say, however, that *must take into account* is synonymous with *may take into account* and an amendment to that effect was withdrawn during the Parliamentary passage of the Human Rights Bill.

3.40   Whilst the wording *must take into account* imposes a mandatory obligation to examine relevant Strasbourg jurisprudence and, thus, undeniably extends the reach of the European Convention, it nevertheless remains open to British courts in effect to side-step this obligation. For all that, instances in the future of local judges in substance ignoring Convention authorities are likely to be rare. As a matter of international law, the UK is already bound (if only bound) by those decisions of the European Court in cases in which it is a party and the scheme of the Act as a whole plainly does not contemplate that Strasbourg jurisprudence be disregarded wholesale. This is most obviously illustrated by s 3 of the Act.

SECTION 3

3.41   Section 3(1)[1] provides that, 'so far as it is possible to do so' primary and subordinate legislation[2] must be read and given effect in a manner which is compatible with the European Convention rights which are domesticated by the Act. Although it does not say so in terms, this interpretative obligation almost certainly extends to the common law which, according to the Lord Chancellor,[3] will be adapted and developed by the Act, a view shared by two of the law Lords, Lord Cooke and Lord Steyn. The duty in s 3 is not expressly limited to courts or tribunals and is to be read as applying not only to public authorities but also to private bodies and to citizens at large – in other words, to anyone relying on legislation. The Lord Chancellor considers that it makes for a 'strong' form of incorporation.[4] In his view, if a statute is capable of two different constructions – one compatible with the European Convention and one not – the statute will henceforth be construed in the way that is compatible with the European Convention. Put another way, the judges in their decisions will at least be required to adopt the most generous and favourable construction of the European Convention so far adopted in the UK. However, the worry has been expressed that while local courts cannot now back away from existing generous exercises in construction already engaged in by UK judges, they may, in areas so far not the subject of judicial comment in the UK, adopt the least flexible interpretation of the European Convention.

3.42   Section 3 certainly requires UK courts to do more than they have traditionally done, which was (very broadly) to use the European Convention to resolve ambiguity in a statute, as an aid to the exercise of judicial discretion, or in

---

1   See Appendix 1. See also F Bennion *What interpretation is 'possible' under section 3(1) of the Human Rights Act 1998?* [2000] PL 77 (spring) and Hunt (see fn 7 on p 27) at 97–99.
2   The definition of primary and subordinate legislation is to be found in s 21(1) of the Act, see Appendix 1.
3   Hansard HL, vol 583, col 785, 24 November 1997.
4   Hansard HL, vol 582, col 1230, 3 November 1997.

determining the scope of the common law.[1] On the other hand, it requires them to do no more than they presently do when construing UK statutes compatibly with the UK's EC obligations.[2]

3.43   Under the Act, the courts (and indeed all of us) are now required to interpret legislation, whenever enacted, so that it accords with European Convention rights. This interpretative obligation will most obviously be relevant in three types of situation:

–   where the legislation under scrutiny is ambiguous;
–   where the legislation is not ambiguous, but can be construed so as to conform with European Convention rights by means of 'reading in' or 'reading down' (ie by the implication of additional words or the attenuation of existing words)[3]; and
–   where the legislation is clear in intent and that intent does not allow for any interpretation in accordance with Convention rights.

3.44   When the Human Rights Bill was introduced, the intention to extend the traditional British canons of legal interpretation was made clear in the White Paper.[4] As Lord Cooke pointed out in the House of Lords debates,[5] and as confirmed by his fellow member of the Judicial Committee, Lord Steyn, writing extra-judicially,[6] this marks a radical departure from previous practice, as s 3 requires local courts to search for possible meanings (in the hope that they are compatible with the European Convention) as opposed to the traditional search for the one true meaning,[7] even though this exercise in divination should stop

---

1   See, for example, the cases of *R v Secretary of State for the Home Department, ex parte Brind* [1991] AC 696 (HL) (the case on the so-called Sinn Féin broadcasting ban) and *R v Ministry of Defence, ex parte Smith* [1996] QB 517 (CA) (the so-called 'gays in the military' case). See also Hunt (see fn 7 on p 27) at Chapters 5 and 6 and M Beloff and H Mountfield.
2   See **5.55** et seq as regards the relationship between EC law and the European Convention.
3   The techniques used by the House of Lords in the case of *R v Secretary of State for the Home Department, ex parte Simms and O'Brien* [1999] 3 All ER 400 suggest that the process of 'reading in' has already begun. Lord Steyn observed that in that case there was 'at stake a fundamental or basic right, namely the right of a prisoner to seek through oral interviews to persuade a journalist to investigate the safety of the prisoner's conviction ... In these circumstances even in the absence of express words [in the Prison Act] there comes into play a presumption of general application operating as a constitutional principle as Sir Robert Cross explained ... This is called "the principle of legality ..." Applying this principle I would hold that [prison standing orders] leave untouched the fundamental and basic rights asserted by the prisoners'.
4   *Rights Brought Home: The Human Rights Bill* (Cm 3782).
5   He said: 'Traditionally, the search has been for the true meaning; now it will be for a possible meaning that would prevent the making of a declaration of incompatibility ... The shift of the criterion to a search for possible compatible meanings will confront the courts with delicate responsibilities ... In effect, the courts are being asked to solve ... problems [of interpretation] by applying a rebuttable presumption in favour of Convention rights': Hansard HL, vol 582, cols 1272 and 1273, 3 November 1997.
6   In his article 'Incorporation and Devolution – A Few Reflections on the Changing Scene' [1998] EHRLR at 155.
7   Hansard HL, vol 583, col 533, 18 November 1997.

short, in the words of the Home Secretary, of any attempt 'to contort the meaning of words to produce implausible or incredible meanings'.[1]

3.45   The Lord Chancellor said in Parliament that he expected that, in 99% of cases, British judges (presuming Parliament has legislated in conformity with the European Convention) would be able to interpret legislation so so as to avoid the need for a declaration of incompatibility.[2] Lord Lester has suggested that they 'will do so by construing existing and future legislation as intended to provide the necessary safeguards to ensure fairness, proportionality and legal certainty, as required by the Convention'.[3] If the judges read in and read down as asked of them, it is likely that the Lord Chancellor's prediction will be borne out in practice, with a declaration of incompatibility very much a 'last resort'.[4] A further inducement to find a meaning that is compatible with the European Convention is, of course, the likelihood that an incompatible construction will be the subject of an application to Strasbourg in the traditional way. This possibility was referred to in Parliament by Lord Cooke, reminding his peers in debate that the European Court 'retains all its power and can always have the last word'.[5] In this respect, local courts will, as already stated, be performing a similar role to that involved when confronted by legislation on which EU rights have a bearing. It may be helpful to describe briefly how they have discharged that role in the past.

3.46   In the *Litster* case,[6] the House of Lords was concerned with the transfer of a business in which employees had been dismissed just prior to the transfer. A previous ruling from the European Court of Justice had interpreted a provision in the Acquired Rights Directive to mean that employees in such a position were to be considered as still employed in the affected business at the time of transfer. The position in English law was governed by reg 5 of the Transfer of Undertakings (Protection of Employment) Regulations 1981, dealing with the transfer of employment contracts to new owners of businesses taken over where the relevant employees were 'employed [as such] immediately before the transfer'.

3.47   In the face of such clear wording, the House of Lords in *Litster* implied additional words into the text of the regulation so as to make it consistent with the EC Directive, thereby merely extending its reach to those employees employed 'immediately before the transfer or who would have been so employed if [they] had not been unfairly dismissed [by reason of the transfer]'.[7]

---

1   Hansard HC, vol 313, col 422, 3 June 1998. For an insight into the way in which the Law Lords may approach s 3 as regards the issue of reverse onus provisions, see the speech of Lord Hope in *R v Director of Public Prosecutions, ex parte Kebilene* [1999] 3 WLR 972 at 988. See also **6.300**.

2   Hansard HL, vol 585, col 840, 5 February 1998. Previously during the Committee stage debate in the House of Lords, the Lord Chancellor had stated that 'we want the courts to strive to find an interpretation of legislation that is consistent with Convention rights, so far as the words of the legislation allow, and only in the last resort to conclude that the legislation is simply incompatible with them': Hansard HL, vol 583, col 535, 18 November 1997.

3   Hansard HC, vol 582, col 1240, 3 November 1997. As to proportionality, see **5.21** et seq.

4   The words used by the Lord Chancellor: Hansard HL, vol 583, col 535, 18 November 1997.

5   Hansard HL, vol 582, col 1272, 3 November 1997.

6   *Litster v Forth Dry Dock and Forth Estuary Engineering* [1990] 1 AC 546 (HL).

7   Ibid, at p 558 (per Lord Templeman) and p 557 (per Lord Oliver).

3.48   Save in cases where the legislation under review is clearly incompatible with European Convention rights, courts in the UK are likely to adopt a similar approach when addressing European Convention rights.

3.49   In *Pepper v Hart*,[1] their Lordships had held, as already noted, that recourse could be had to Hansard where it would assist in revealing the intention of Parliament and the court was otherwise presented with the task of interpreting an ambiguous statutory provision. However, in circumstances where Parliament is to be presumed not to have legislated ambiguously with reference to European Convention rights, it is odd that it should be suggested that any perceived ambiguity should potentially be resolved by reference to Hansard. Surely, instead, the court should look in future at legislation which throws up a human rights point in the context of the relevant European Convention right, as required by s 3 of the Act? At best, Parliament's intention as reflected in Hansard would show either that Parliament was oblivious to the Convention, sought to legislate in conformity with it, or consciously legislated in contravention of it. In all such cases, the court would derive no practical benefit from recourse to Hansard insofar as the interpretative obligation in the Act is concerned. The importance of references to Parliamentary proceedings in the present context, therefore, may have been exaggerated, although the Government's coyness in debate in explaining the relationship between s 3 and traditional rules of construction may have owed something to a concern about the operation of *Pepper v Hart.*[2]

3.50   In searching for the legislative meaning which is compatible with European Convention rights, as opposed to the more traditional 'natural' meaning, a UK court may in the future conclude that a statutory provision cannot be interpreted compatibly with a European Convention guarantee and, indeed, that it is manifestly incompatible with it. In that event, the incompatible legislation cannot be struck down by the court and will remain valid, fully operational and capable of enforcement.[3] The status quo is preserved, subject only to the remedial procedure outlined in s 10 of the Act.[4] It is not for a court to strike down or quash laws violating the European Convention and it is for Parliament then to remedy the position.

3.51   The determination of the legislature to prevail over the judiciary in this context was underlined by the Home Secretary during the Second Reading debate on the Human Rights Bill in the House of Commons, when he stated:

> 'The sovereignty of Parliament must be paramount. By that, I mean that Parliament must be competent to make any law on any matter of its choosing … To allow the courts to set aside Acts of Parliament would confer on the judiciary a power that it does not possess, and which could draw it into serious conflict with Parliament … The courts and the senior judiciary do not want such a power, and we believe that the people do not wish the judiciary to have it.'[5]

---

1   *Pepper (Inspector of Taxes) v Hart* [1993] AC 593 (HL). See also **3.4**.
2   Michael Beloff QC has described *Pepper v Hart* as being of little assistance to him as an advocate. In his experience, 'the ratio is of the order of one hundred pieces of chaff to one grain of wheat' (see his chapter 'What Does it All Mean?' in Betten (ed) *The Human Rights Act 1998: What it Means* (Martinus Nijhoff Publishers, 1999).
3   Section 3(2)(b).
4   See **3.178** et seq.
5   Hansard HC, vol 306, col 772, 16 February 1998.

3.52   The accuracy of that statement is questionable in circumstances in which British courts already have the power to grant relief to disapply clear legislative provisions which are incompatible with EC rights,[1] but the political imperative of being seen to preserve Parliamentary sovereignty was at least clear.

3.53   It must be emphasised that the High Court can already strike down subordinate legislation and regularly does so, as the Home Secretary indicated during the debates on the Human Rights Bill.[2] The Act does not affect that. Where, however, subordinate legislation is incompatible with European Convention rights, it cannot be struck down by the courts where primary (or so-called 'mother') legislation would prevent the removal of the relevant incompatibility.[3] This appears obscure, but was explained during the Committee stage debates in the House of Commons by Geoffrey Hoon MP, then Parliamentary Secretary at the Lord Chancellor's Department, when he said:

> 'The nature of the primary legislation under which an order is made may be such that any subordinate legislation will necessarily be in conflict with Convention rights. If the courts were to have the power to strike down such subordinate legislation, it would, at least indirectly, amount to a challenge to the primary legislation itself. That would place the courts at odds with Parliament.'[4]

3.54   In other words, the secondary and primary legislation are so closely connected that removing the incompatibility in the secondary measure would challenge the status of the primary measure. Hence the phrase 'dependent secondary legislation'.

3.55   Section 3 shows the limits deliberately placed upon European Convention domestication. There is no question of the Strasbourg guarantees prevailing over existing (or indeed future) legislation and the suggestion, in effect, that the Act would allow for the implied repeal of laws violating the European Convention was not to be. On the other hand, s 3 does not merely govern the interpretative responsibilities of judges, but also governs the behaviour of anyone (including lawyers and their clients) who are construing legislation.

3.56   Professor Gearty has warned about the practical difficulties that may arise if the interpretative obligation in s 3(1) is used in such a way as to confer a form of retrospective effect. He uses the example of prisoners in jail who would not now be incarcerated if a particular statute had been interpreted in a way that is compatible with the European Convention as it will be in future. Can such prisoners sue for compensation and demand to be released? Or consider the position of a company prosecuted and fined for a criminal offence which would not now happen because the relevant law under which it was punished has been read down to conform with the European Convention. This is a very real issue which corporates will surely wish to pursue.

3.57   Section 3 only *expressly* requires statutes to be reconciled to Strasbourg law. Is this because 'the judges are free to develop the common law in their own independent judicial sphere'[5] as suggested by the Lord Chancellor? So long as the

---

1   See, for example, *R v Secretary of State for Transport, ex parte Factortame (No 2)* [1991] 1 AC 603.
2   Hansard HC, vol 314, col 1128, 24 June 1998.
3   Section 3(2)(c) of the Act.
4   Hansard HC, vol 313, col 433, 3 June 1998.
5   Hansard HL, vol 583, col 784, 24 November 1997.

courts, as public authorities in their own right,[1] do not breach the Convention, it would appear that they are to be allowed to get on with their traditional job of developing non-statutory law, which conceivably means that the judges, for example, can proceed in a more progressive direction, relying upon the European Convention, in extending the common law, than would be the case if they were construing a statute. This could pose interesting questions in future cases, for example, raising issues of personal privacy.[2]

SECTION 4

3.58   Section 4[3] explains what happens when the higher courts in the UK encounter a statute which is not compatible with the European Convention, 'reading in' and 'reading down' having proved impossible. It is one of the distinguishing features of the legislation, but it is predicted that it will rarely be encountered by business. Where primary legislation of this sort is found, or where secondary legislation is also adjudged incompatible but is incapable of being struck down because primary legislation prevents the removal of the incompatibility, higher courts[4] in the UK may make 'in these rare cases'[5] a declaration (which has prospective effect only and thereby preserves Parliamentary sovereignty) as to the incompatibility of the relevant provision.[6] That is all they can do and even that limited power does not need to be exercised. It is a pointed contrast to the position in, for example, the USA or Germany, where the supreme courts of those countries can declare statutes to be void. Ironically, therefore, if British judges are effectively to police the European Convention in the future, they will first need to find the law under scrutiny to be in conformity with the European Convention. Only then can they go further and determine whether or not there has been a violation of the European Convention and whether or not a remedy should be available for any violation that is found.

3.59   It may be because of the acknowledgement that a declaration of incompatibility will automatically render further judicial involvement nugatory that it is widely believed that such declarations will be exceptional. Quite apart from the interpretative obligation set out in s 3, which is plainly also intended to discourage declarations of incompatibility, the jurisdiction (in common with any

---

1   See **3.78** et seq.
2   See Chapter 7.
3   See Appendix 1.
4   The courts which are empowered to make declarations of incompatibility are identified in s 4(5) as the High Court, the Court of Appeal, the Judicial Committees of the Privy Council and the House of Lords, the Courts Martial Appeal Court and the Court of Session, but not criminal courts, for fear that trials might be upset 'by declarations of incompatibility that may go to the very foundations' of a prosecution: Lord Irvine (Hansard HL, vol 583, col 551, 18 November 1997). Employment tribunals are also excluded.
5   Lord Irvine: Hansard HL, vol 582, col 1231, 3 November 1997.
6   Section 4(1), (2), (3) and (4).

other form of declaratory relief), as already stated, will be purely discretionary.[1] Moreover, during the Committee stage debate in the House of Lords, the Lord Chancellor adverted to possibilities (such as the existence of a statutory appeal route) which judges might consider should be exhausted first and these too should preclude the making of a declaration of incompatibility.[2] In any event, there may have been a declaration made in a similar case which is under appeal, or the Government may have recognised the incompatibility and moved to introduce a legislative amendment to remove it.

3.60 These are but some of the factors which may persuade a court that a declaration of incompatibility is inappropriate in the case before it. That said, the Lord Chancellor also confirmed in Parliament that he expected courts 'generally to make declarations of incompatibility when they find an Act to be incompatible with the Convention'.[3]

3.61 The right to grant declarations of incompatibility will probably have no material impact upon businesses. If anything, it could prove something of an irritant. A s 4 declaration will not be accompanied by any other form of relief (save perhaps an award of costs in favour of the party which had raised the point)[4] and will not be binding on the parties to the proceedings in which it is made.[5] One commentator has suggested that it creates an (unsatisfactory) 'halfway house between legality and illegality'.[6] Sir William Wade has suggested that a stay of the relevant litigation be ordered while the Government considers the position, but this raises procedural complications.[7] Above all else, a declaration of incompatibility will have no effect on the validity, continuing operation and enforcement of the legislation declared to be incompatible with European Convention rights.[8]

3.62 The Lord Chancellor explained in debate that the narrow basis of the power was intended, once again, to preserve the doctrine of Parliamentary sovereignty, although he conceded that Westminster would have to heed such a judicial pronouncement.[9] The Home Secretary indicated that Westminster would want to do so 'pretty rapidly',[10] having been given a 'clear signal'.[11] To this extent, another Law Lord, Lord Hoffman, has suggested that 'the political pressure upon the Government and Parliament to bring the law into line will be hard to resist'.[12]

---

1   There has been some debate as to whether it is still appropriate to maintain judicial discretion in granting relief in the face of unlawfulness in the area of judicial review. *JUSTICE* in its report *Administrative Law – Some Necessary Reforms* concluded that there is a strong argument for removing judicial discretion where courts find grounds exist for relief.
2   Hansard HL, vol 583, col 546, 18 November 1997.
3   Hansard HL, vol 583, col 546, 18 November 1997.
4   Hansard HL, vol 583, col 546, 18 November 1997.
5   Section 4(6)(b), see Appendix 1.
6   See S Green *A Guide to The Human Rights Act* 1998 (1999) 24 EL Rev 1 at p 15.
7   *Rights Brought Home: The Human Rights Bill* (Cm 3782), para 2.10.
8   Section 4(6)(a), see Appendix 1.
9   He said on Second Reading: 'A declaration of incompatibility will not itself change the law. The statute will continue to apply despite its incompatibility. But the declaration is very likely to prompt the Government and Parliament to respond'. Hansard HL, vol 582, col 1231, 3 November 1997.
10   Hansard HC, vol 317, col 1306, 21 October 1998.
11   Hansard HC, vol 306, col 780, 16 February 1998.
12   See his article *Human Rights and the House of Lords* [1999] 62 MLR 159 at 160.

3.63   The few declarations of incompatibility that are made, therefore, will bring to the attention of the executive and the legislature the fact that a breach of European Convention rights has taken place, even though the ministerial indications during the debates on the Human Rights Bill were less forthright than the statement in the White Paper to the effect that a declaration of incompatibility would 'almost certainly prompt the Government and Parliament to change the law'. The decision then will rest with the executive as to whether to cure the offence (or 'systemic failure' in Lord Lester's words[1]) by using subordinate legislation, introduced pursuant to the 'fast track' mechanism provided for in s 10 of the Act.[2] Beyond that, s 4 will be of limited consequence and this inability (in terms of the Act) of senior British judges to grant relief requiring Government action sits uneasily with the reality that, for many years now, Parliament has been obliged to change the law following adverse judgments against the UK delivered by continental judges at Strasbourg, albeit that such changes have been made to comply with the obligation under international law to adhere to the terms of the European Convention as a treaty.[3]

3.64   Should the higher courts make a declaration of incompatibility and the Government (through Parliament) fail to amend the offending legislation, it will of course remain possible for an application to be made to the European Court.[4] This is also unsatisfactory in circumstances where, in reality, a form of violation of the European Convention will already have been found (as otherwise it is not apparent that a declaration of incompatibility could have been made), even though the relevant British court may not have considered whether, in the instant case, the applicant's European Convention rights had been breached. The applicant who elects to petition Strasbourg in this situation will face further delays which could lead to an argument that the Act is itself inadequate to secure for the applicant an effective remedy before a national authority as required by Art 13 of the European Convention.[5]

3.65   The deliberate limitation placed upon British judicial authority in this area may become less significant over time as, from 24 November 1998, the Government Minister charged with conducting the passage of a new Bill through Parliament has been required by s 19 of the Act to make a written statement as to the compatibility of the proposed legislation with European Convention rights.[6] No such statement needs to be made in respect of legislation which pre-dates the Act, but at least Government, judges, citizens and businesses alike know that, from now on, new laws are expressed to conform to the European Convention unless no such expression is made.

3.66   The disregarding of Convention rights is not a step likely to be taken by any Government, whatever its composition and it would be puzzling if the Government chose not to amend parts of a statute found by judges to be incompatible with the Convention, particularly where in the future the relevant

---

1   Hansard HL, vol 582, col 1240, 3 November 1997.
2   See **3.178** et seq.
3   A point raised by Robert MacLennan MP (see Hansard HC, vol 306, col 806, 16 February 1998).
4   See **2.38**.
5   See **3.11** et seq.
6   Section 19(1)(a) of the Act (see **3.202**).

statute will be given a clean bill of health at the outset in terms of a s 19 statement that it is in fact compliant with the European Convention.

3.67 The limitation placed upon the types of court able to make declarations of incompatibility is not surprising when considering the risk of a multitude of inconsistent decisions on similar facts emerging from lower courts. No doubt Ministers had in mind particularly the systemic implications of (for example) one magistrates' court decision declaring incompatible a provision of road traffic or theft legislation. However, that is not to say that magistrates cannot give an opinion as to whether a provision is in conformity with the European Convention, not least when it is central to the bench's s 3 obligations.[1] As such, there is no reason why a magistrates' court cannot now choose, in a matter raising a European Convention point, not to follow an existing decision of the House of Lords.

SECTION 5

3.68 Section 5 of the Act must be considered together with s 4. It provides that, where a court which is capable of making a declaration of incompatibility pursuant to s 4 is considering such a step, the Crown[2] is entitled, upon being given advance notice by the court,[3] to be joined as a party to the relevant proceedings.[4] The notice can be given at any stage in the proceedings,[5] but there is no express power for notice also to be given to any other party to intervene, a power available to the judges at Strasbourg.[6]

3.69 The rationale for this early warning system is to enable the Crown to be made aware formally of the course the court is considering and to enable it to make representations should it choose to do so. There is no obligation upon the Government to intervene through its lawyers, but it would be highly unusual indeed for there to be no representation of the Crown, given that declarations of incompatibility are envisaged by the Lord Chancellor as 'serious'.[7] Interventions under s 5 will often be unnecessary in any event, for the Crown will in many instances already be a party to cases with a European Convention dimension.

3.70 Attempts in Parliament to get the Crown to meet the costs of such interventions failed[8] and that issue remains one for judicial discretion.

3.71 One consequence of the Crown's becoming a party to criminal proceedings (outside Scotland) is that it will be able, with leave, to exercise a right of appeal to the House of Lords should a declaration of incompatibility be made.[9]

---

1 See **3.41** et seq.
2 In the shape of a Minister of the Crown or a person nominated by him, a member of the Scottish Executive, a Northern Ireland Minister or a Northern Ireland department: s 5(2) (see Appendix 1). In other words, the person with most knowledge of the legislation under scrutiny can appear. The Lord Chancellor observed that a Minister might nominate, for example, a utilities regulator or the Director General of Fair Trading to be joined as a party (Hansard HL, vol 583, col 555, 18 November 1997).
3 Section 5(1), see Appendix 1.
4 Section 5(2), see Appendix 1.
5 Section 5(3), see Appendix 1.
6 By virtue of Art 36 (see Appendix 2).
7 Hansard HL, vol 582, col 1231, 3 November 1997.
8 Hansard HL, vol 583, col 557–559, 18 November 1997.
9 Section 5(4), see Appendix 1.

This right so to appeal in criminal proceedings is not one generally available to the Crown.

SECTION 6

3.72   Sections 6–9 deal with the acts of public authorities and are the crux of the legislation in terms of its unfolding, practical effect upon commerce.

3.73   Section 6(1)[1] of the Act provides that it is 'unlawful for a public authority to act in a way which is incompatible with a Convention right'.[2] This is central – no body other than a public authority is *expressly* required to comply with the provisions of the Act and European Convention rights can be relied upon directly only in respect of the actions of public authorities.[3] The Act says nothing, however, about the position of bodies which are not public authorities but which act in a manner incompatible with a provision or provisions of the European Convention. As to those bodies, the likelihood is that local courts will employ the European Convention as a multipurpose tool in the development of the common law, aiming where possible to ensure parity of protection for citizens affected by the human rights infractions of non-public authorities.[4]

VERTICALISTS AND HORIZONTALISTS – THE GREAT DEBATE

3.74   Does the centrality of the role of public authorities in the Act mean that the statute has *vertical* consequences only, ie that it solely governs the behaviour of the State (in all its manifestations and emanations) in relation to its citizens and does not, by contrast, have a *horizontal* effect, ie it does not govern the behaviour of one citizen towards another? These geometric terms are borrowed from EC law and one senior judicial figure[5] has suggested that the very language of horizontality and verticality is unhelpful because the analogy with the Community legal order is inapt. Whether or not that be so, the terms are now so much part of the common currency when discussing the Act that their use is adopted here also.

---

1   See Appendix 1.
2   For a good general treatment of s 6 (albeit principally in the employment law context), see GS Morris *The Human Rights Act and the Public/Private Divide in Employment* [1998] ILJ 29 and A Sherlock *The Applicability of the United Kingdom's Human Rights Bill: Identifying 'Public' Functions* [1998] EPL 593.
3   See *Marshall v Southampton AHA* [1986] 2 QB 584, which confirms the analogous position in EC law.
4   An outcome which would, again, be analogous to the position in the European Community legal order. See *Marleasing SA v La Commercial Internationale de Alimentation SA* [1990] ECR I-4135.
5   Sir Richard Buxton in 'The Human Rights Act and Private Law' [2000] 116 LDR 48. The literature is substantial. See also M Hunt 'The Horizontal Effect of the Human Rights Act 1998' [1998] PL 423; G Phillipson 'The Human Rights Act, "Horizontal Effect" and the Common Law: A Bang or a Whimper?' [1999] 62 MLR 824; and Sir Sydney Kentridge in *Constitutional Reform* (see fn 4 on p 1) at p 70.

3.75   If the Act is (only) vertical in effect, it would at least conform to the classical human rights model that the draftsman of the Convention principally had in mind, ie the protection of the citizen from the excesses of the State. It is perhaps odd then that there is only limited support amongst judges and academic lawyers for the proposition that the Act will be strictly vertical in its impact.

3.76   Certainly, the Government has been at pains to stress that the Act is not intended to have direct horizontal effect, ie to regulate relationships between citizen and citizen and, at first sight, it would not appear possible to deploy the Act in litigation between two private companies, a view that the Lord Chancellor appeared to confirm when addressing the issue during the Parliamentary debates on the Human Rights Bill, when he said:

> 'What the Bill does not do is to make the Convention rights themselves directly a part of our domestic law in the same way that, for example, the civil wrongs of negligence, trespass or libel are part of our domestic law. Claims in those areas are all actionable in tort in cases between private individuals ... We have sought to protect the human rights of individuals against the abuse of power by the State, broadly defined, rather than to protect them against each other. That is the only practical difference between the full incorporation of the Convention rights into our domestic law and the actual effect of the Bill.'[1]

3.77   However, the position is not as clear as Lord Irvine suggested and the preponderant view appears to be that the Act will have a form of *indirect* horizontal effect in that, although European Convention rights will bear on litigation between purely private interests, they will, in terms of the way in which pre-existing law is applied, infuse local jurisprudence in an indirect way only. This prediction of *indirect* horizontalism is based very largely on an assumption as to the implications of s 6(3) of the Act.

3.78   Section 6(3) states that courts and tribunals are public authorities in their own right. This has a number of consequences. It means, most obviously, that courts and tribunals in the UK must, in carrying out their activities (and not just their judicial functions but their administrative ones too), behave in conformity with the European Convention. More than that, however, it means that courts and tribunals have been fixed with the chief responsibility for ensuring that, within the UK, the European Convention's rights and freedoms are upheld and this obligation would extend, it is said, to the judges' conduct of proceedings between private parties. So, for example, parts of the media have contended that the High Court will seek to discharge its s 6(3) obligation to police the European Convention by seeking to remedy the gap in our system attributable to the absence of a regime for the protection of privacy here by endeavouring to fashion a nascent privacy tort, relying upon Art 8 of the European Convention.

3.79   When as distinguished a commentator as Sir William Wade suggests that the legislation will have full-blooded horizontal effect the appropriate response is to pay careful attention. Certainly, the question of the Act's significance for private law disputes is arguably the key issue calling for early consideration by the UK's most senior judges. There is, in fact, a greater measure of agreement in this area than the volumes of academic discussion might at first indicate, as a result of which certain observations can be made specifically regarding the future role of the judges.

---

1   Hansard HL, vol 585, col 840, 5 February 1998.

3.80	First, if future litigation turns on the provisions of a statute, the compatibility of that statute with the European Convention will be a relevant matter for submission and this will be so in private law cases as much as in public law cases. Therefore, in cases between companies engaging a particular statutory term, local judges are obliged, in accordance with s 3(1) of the Act, to strive for a meaning that is compatible with the European Convention. In this way, the European Convention, through the Act, has horizontal effect. A further implication is that judges must be prepared to abandon traditional adherence to the doctrine of binding precedent where a failure to do so might make it otherwise impossible for them to act in a way that is compatible with the Convention.

3.81	Secondly, if British courts or tribunals innocently (or otherwise) miss a European Convention point (perhaps because it was not referred to them), they may be found to have acted in a way that is incompatible with the Convention, pursuant to s 6(1) and (6)[1] of the Act, on the basis that s 6(6) defines an act incompatible with the Convention as including a 'failure to act'.

3.82	Thirdly, the judges will use the European Convention, as given further effect by the Act, to develop the common law in the way they always have, and this will bear on directly private relationships, parties and disputes. The Lord Chancellor acknowledged this during the parliamentary debates on the Human Rights Bill:

'We ... believe that it is right as a matter of principle for the courts to have the duty of acting compatibly with the Convention not only in cases involving other public authorities but also in developing the common law in deciding cases between individuals. Why should they not? In preparing this Bill, we have taken the view that it is the other course, that of excluding Convention considerations altogether from cases between individuals, which would have to be justified. We do not think that that would be justifiable; nor indeed, do we think that it would be practicable.'[2]

3.83	Fourthly, on the other hand, litigants in private common-law actions will continue not to be able to rely on European Convention rights *simpliciter*. They will still need to identify an existing cause of action on to which they must hope to graft one of the European Convention guarantees.

3.84	Fifthly, ss 2 and 3 of the Act require not only that European Convention jurisprudence be taken into account, but also that legislation be given an effect consistent with the Convention. A clear duty is placed by Strasbourg upon Member States to take positive steps to protect European Convention rights,[3] such as the right to respect for a private life enshrined in Art 8,[4] a duty which may call for judicial intervention on European Convention grounds in disputes between private, non-State interests, quite outwith the obligations placed upon courts and tribunals as public authorities in s 6(3) of the Act. Although the European Court has eschewed the development of any 'general theory of positive obligations',[5] States (and in terms of the Act that means judges) may be required to do what is necessary to establish a mechanism for the effective protection of European Convention rights and to prevent Convention violations.

1	See, in relation to omissions generally, Mr O'Brien MP at Hansard HC, vol 314, col 1097, 24 June 1998.

2	Hansard HL, vol 583, col 783, 24 November 1997.

3	See also **5.17** et seq.

4	See Chapter 7.

5	*Platform Artze für das Leben v Austria* (1991) 13 EHRR 204.

3.85   Finally, the greater the horizontal effect of the Act, the less relevant the debate will be about whether a given respondent is a public authority or not.[1] If the Act was not meant to have a form of horizontal effect, s 6(3) is otiose.

Public authorities – a problem of definition

3.86   In its White Paper, the Government explained that, prior to the introduction of the Act:

> 'although the United Kingdom [had] an international obligation to comply with the Convention, there ... [was] ... no requirement in our domestic law on central and local government, or others exercising similar executive powers, to exercise these powers in a way which [was] compatible with the Convention.'[2]

3.87   Although it was this perceived deficit which the Act was apparently supposed to change, there is nothing in the extract cited from the White Paper which obviously suggests that an obligation to conform to the European Convention was to be placed upon parts of industry, unless it could be said that elements of the corporate sector exercise 'similar executive powers' to the Government. Even with regard to the largest of the privatised entities, this is implausible. Nevertheless, this is what s 6 seeks to do (as the White Paper proceeded to explain) and it is the reason why, for certain companies, the coming into force of the Act is an event of strategic significance. Whether or not in years to come such companies are classified as public authorities is no mere question of semantics. It may affect the way in which corporate public authorities are expected to act towards customers, suppliers and society at large. As will be seen, it may burden such corporates with additional overheads and leave them at a disadvantage *vis-à-vis* those of their competitors who, in terms of the Act, are not adjudged to be public authorities. In such circumstances, it is regrettable that the statutory definition of corporate public authorities remains obscure, despite the critical role that the Act requires such bodies to fulfil. The vertical/horizontal debate aside,[3] the issue as regards whether one firm is a public authority while another is not is the other most important matter calling for urgent judicial clarification – hence the lengthy discussion that follows.

3.88   The White Paper asserted that the legislative definition of a public authority would be in broad terms. The Lord Chancellor indicated that this was because the boundaries of the State have been changing and would continue to change in the future.[4] The following were identified in the White Paper as the core bodies that would be caught by the legislation in terms of being required to conform to European Convention standards: 'central government (including executive agencies); local government; the police; immigration officers; prisons; courts and tribunals ...'.[5] When discharging their public duties, such bodies are generally already susceptible to judicial review, in terms of local law, so this is no

---

1   As far as the definition of a public authority is concerned, see **3.86** et seq.
2   *Rights Brought Home: The Human Rights Bill* (Cm 3782), p 8.
3   See **3.74** et seq.
4   In his opening address to the Clifford Chance Conference on 28 November 1997 published in *The Impact of the Human Rights Bill on English Law* (Oxford University Press, 1998).
5   *Rights Brought Home* (see fn 2 above), p 8.

surprise, albeit that the Act now requires them to act compatibly with the European Convention in *everything* they do.[1]

3.89   The step-change contemplated by s 6, however, is the likely designation (albeit that this is a matter of judicial discretion) of the following as public authorities: 'to the extent that they are exercising public functions, companies responsible for areas of activity which were previously within the public sector, such as the privatised utilities'.[2] In other words, the Act bears upon the activities of corporates which would, but for the Act, largely have fallen outside the purview of UK administrative law.

3.90   Reference to the White Paper is of some limited assistance in circumstances where the Act is in its terms wholly imprecise. Section 6(3) states merely that 'public authority' includes a court or tribunal,[3] and: 'any person certain of whose functions are functions of a public nature, but does not include either House of Parliament or a person exercising functions in connection with proceedings in Parliament.'

3.91   This carve-out, whereby Parliament (including, for these purposes, select committees), the most public institution of all in our democracy, is made exempt from the legislation, is philosophically sustainable on the basis that, without it, Westminster's sovereignty would have been impaired by being made susceptible to judicial review.[4]

3.92   So Parliament is not a public authority. Who, however, are the entities 'certain of whose functions are functions of a public nature'? According to Lord Williams, speaking for the Government during the debates on the Human Rights Bill, the term 'any person' was 'well known as a term of art in our law. It [was] defined in the Interpretation Act 1978 ... as including any person or body of persons corporate or unincorporate', and was thereby 'clearly wide enough to cover the natural or legal person ...'.[5] 'Any person' can therefore be a company.

3.93   Some very limited elaboration is provided in s 6(5), which says that 'in relation to a particular act, a person is not a public authority ... if the nature of the act is private'.[6] As to this, Lord Coleraine, in Committee-stage debate in the House of Lords, thought it 'bizarre to read that a person may ape the chameleon and be a public authority at one moment in relation to an act the nature of which is not private, but be a public authority the next moment where the nature of the act is private'.[7]

3.94   However, Lord Williams, replying for the Government, was in no doubt about the legislation's remit:

---

1   In line with the European Court's decision in the case of *Swedish Engine Drivers' Union v Sweden* (1976) 1 EHRR 617 at para 37, holding that there was no difference between the public acts of a State body and its acts *qua* employer.
2   *Rights Brought Home: The Human Rights Bill* (Cm 3782), p 8.
3   See **3.78** et seq.
4   However, politicians punished for misdemeanours may continue to have a right of recourse to Strasbourg direct. See *Demicoli v Malta* (1992) 14 EHRR 47, where it was held by the European Court that disciplinary proceedings by the Parliament of Malta against a member fell within Art 6 of the European Convention.
5   Hansard HL, vol 583, col 803, 24 November 1997.
6   See Appendix 1.
7   Hansard HL, vol 583, col 757, 24 November 1997.

'When the [Act] is enacted, one will be dealing with two types of public authority – those which everyone would recognise as being plainly public authorities which are public authorities because, in part of their functions, they carry out what would be regarded as public functions. Examples vary, but I believe that the courts will have in mind changing social economic and cultural conditions when they come to consider particular decisions on particular aspects of a public authority.'[1]

3.95 It is far from apparent what 'changing social economic and cultural conditions' are in this context. The UK has blazed a trail for privatisation over the last generation. Has this (and the popular response to it) given rise to a change in underlying conditions which is 'social' or 'economic' or 'cultural'? Presumably not, as it is to be inferred from Lord Williams' comments that privatisation is incidental to the enduring reality that, in terms of human rights at least, what was once part of the public sector before becoming private is still functionally public. This echoes the sentiments of Hoffman LJ (as he then was) in the *Aga Khan* case, when he said that 'a body which exercises governmental powers is not any the less amenable to public law because it has contractual relations with its members.'[2]

3.96 The Government later suggested in the Parliamentary debates on the Human Rights Bill that an entity spending taxpayers' money or with Government appointees on its governing body was likely (although it was a matter for the courts) to be a public authority. This is better, but does London Transport spend taxpayers' money directly? There is no hypothecated payment made by the capital's citizens for the purposes of the operators of the Underground, so, in this respect at least, London Transport is *not* a public authority, even though it is state-supported. What then of a start-up company in Scotland, Wales or Northern Ireland that receives regional grant aid? Is it a public authority? Or what of a public–private partnership? Do the participants in a private finance initiative (PFI) project become public authorities?

3.97 Lord Williams' description, however general, was at least some advance upon the distinction drawn by the Lord Chancellor, when introducing the legislation, between 'obvious' public authorities 'such as government depart-ments and the police . . . and bodies which are public in certain respects but not in others'.[3]

3.98 One answer to the definitional problem would have been to draw up a list of public authorities, as the Government has (in effect) done (albeit in different contexts) in its Freedom of Information Bill and in the Defamation Act 1996 but, according to the Lord Chancellor, it was decided for policy reasons not to publish a list because 'it would be easy to regard it as exhaustive or to suggest that any non-listed body could be a public authority only if it was sufficiently analogous in its essential characteristics to a body that had qualified in the list'.[4] Some weeks later, he said in a conference speech that 'any attempt to define or limit the list of bodies which would be subject to the Act would risk leaving out bodies to whose activities Strasbourg would rule that the Convention should apply'.[5]

---

1   Hansard HL, vol 583, col 758, 24 November 1997.
2   *R v Disciplinary Committee of the Jockey Club, ex parte the Aga Khan* [1993] 2 All ER 853.
3   Hansard HL, vol 582, col 1232, 3 November 1997.
4   Hansard HL, vol 583, col 796, 24 November 1997.
5   In his keynote address, reproduced in *Constitutional Reform* (see fn 4 on p 1).

3.99   It remains unclear, however, why a de facto list should be deemed appropriate in identifying for the purposes of defamation law those bodies (such as the Broadcasting Standards Commission), reports of whose determinations may be protected by qualified privilege, whilst compiling a list of bodies (again such as the Broadcasting Standards Commission) whose actions are now likely to have to be compliant with the European Convention is deemed inappropriate for the purposes of the Act.[1] Nor, notwithstanding the comments of the Lord Chancellor, is it a solution to identify likely public authorities by reference to European Convention practice, as the decisions made at Strasbourg in this area are not necessarily consistent with existing UK law. For example, private schools traditionally have not been susceptible to judicial review locally on the basis that they are essentially regulated by contract.[2] However, the Strasbourg judges have held that such establishments are sufficiently 'public' for the UK to be held responsible for violations of rights which occur within them.[3]

3.100   Which parts of the UK's corporate sector therefore will be obliged in the future to act in conformity with the Convention? Which are the companies made public authorities by the statute on account of the fact that certain of their acts are by their nature public? Whatever the Government might say, an application of the 'elephant' test (difficult to describe, but you know it when you see it) when determining whether a firm is a public authority or not is an inadequate way to proceed. Nor, it is submitted, can serious business planning be embarked upon relying solely on analogy.

3.101   The Act contemplates a two-tier test for determining whether bodies are caught by the Act in any given instance. The first requirement is to ask whether the bodies discharge certain functions of a public nature. If they do, it is then necessary to ask if the particular act of which complaint is made is one of those public functions. For whatever reason (and the political importance attaching to transport policy is an obvious starting-point), one company whose activities a number of Government Ministers have cited in this context is Railtrack plc – an example *par excellence* of a corporation whose functions (or many of them) were previously carried out by the State. Even before the Human Rights Bill was introduced, the Lord Chancellor had identified it as an entity liable to be caught by the legislation.[4] Later he suggested that Railtrack's acts 'would be covered in respect of its management of the national rail network where it is responsible for safety, but not in its commercial property dealings'.[5]

---

1   See Sch 1 to the Defamation Act 1996. Note that the Broadcasting Standards Commission is not referred to expressly.

2   See, for example, *R v Fernhill Manor School, ex parte Brown* (1993) 5 Admin LR 159.

3   For example, see *Costello-Roberts v United Kingdom* (1993) 19 EHRR 112. Note too that there have been reports that certain private schools will go to Strasbourg in an attempt to retain caning (*The Daily Telegraph*, 1 September 1999). For an examination of the inconsistency between UK and Convention approaches in this area, see N Bamforth 'The Application of the Human Rights Act 1998 to Public Authorities and Private Bodies' [1999] CLJ 159.

4   In his speech at University College, London on 4 July 1997 (see fn 6 on p 16).

5   In his keynote address reproduced in *Constitutional Reform* (see fn 4 on p 1), p 4. Lord Williams said in the debate at the Committee stage in the House of Lords: 'Railtrack has statutory public powers and functions as the safety regulatory authority; but, equally, it may well carry out transactions, such as the disposal of, the acquisition of, or the development of property' (Hansard HL, vol 583, col 758, 24 November 1997).

3.102 This application of a *functions* or *responsibilities* test in determining whether a particular company is a public authority for the purposes of the Act is also not free from difficulty. Concerns, for example, regarding passenger safety are such that few would consider that Railtrack's functions in that regard were not public simply because the company is not owned by the Government. Yet at an early stage of the Parliamentary debates on the Human Rights Bill, Lord Borrie, a distinguished lawyer and former Director-General of the Office of Fair Trading, raised the possibility that (what became) s 6 may operate unfairly among businesses working in the same industrial sector. He reminded his fellow peers that 'BT and British Gas – in providing their services to the UK public, are competing with other companies and that competition is encouraged. It is odd if one company in the field is considered to be a "public authority" and one of its competitors is not'.[1] It will cost money for the privatised utilities to conform to the safeguards in the European Convention in terms of staff training, the provision of information to customers and the improvement of procedures. What is the justification for placing that burden on them and not on their competitors? Is a *functions* test in any event adequate to track the changing nature of the modern economy? Microsoft is (US litigation aside) arguably the biggest publisher and information-provider in the world. Does that make it more *public* than it was when it was a mere software development company?

3.103 What, for example, of the Post Office, whose statutory monopoly over certain forms of mail delivery is being reviewed by the Government? In continuing to provide a universal service (at least), the Post Office is almost certainly a public authority. Does that mean that the Post Office will be prey to human rights litigation when competitor (private) courier companies will not be? Or are the latter too caught as companies undertaking work with a public element (mail delivery) in it? Can a company after time cease to be a public authority? Is Transco (formerly the contracting arm of British Gas) less of a public authority than BG Group, having been demerged by order of OFGAS? Is BP Amoco, the oil producer, any longer in any respect a public authority when few people probably recall that British Petroleum was once State-owned?

3.104 As far as such issues are concerned, the Government has been clear that its plans are not about 'hobbling authorities because they are now private whereas they used to be public authorities',[2] but it remains to be seen whether this will be so in practice, not least when the Lord Chancellor has said that the definition of public authority is intended to be wide-ranging and to be matched by a 'correspondingly wide liability'.[3]

3.105 The Government admittedly faced a difficult task in framing this part of the legislation, as the distinction between public and private law has been an enduring source of debate in the UK (and indeed in civil law jurisdictions too)

---

1   Hansard HL, vol 582, col 1277, 3 November 1997. The point was later developed in the debates in the House of Commons by David Ruffley, the Conservative MP, who feared 'a potential breach of competition or company law in this regard' Hansard HC, vol 314, col 432, 17 June 1998.
2   Lord Williams in Hansard HL, vol 582, col 1310, 3 November 1997.
3   Speaking at the Clifford Chance Conference (see fn 3 on p 61), p 11.

since the development of the modern concept of judicial review in 1977.[1] The problem for both claimants and corporate respondents, however, is that determining whether a corporation is a public authority or not may go not just to procedure but to substance too. Subject to the Act having a degree of horizontal effect,[2] a company which is *not* designated a public authority may not face a European Convention claim at all. That makes the question of public authority designation in the Act conceivably of much greater consequence than, for example, the dilemma administrative lawyers faced for years as to whether in a given situation to proceed by way a private law action or to seek a public law judicial review, which at least went only to procedure.[3]

3.106   Lord Lester, speaking in debate in the House of Lords at the Committee stage, was confident that, in circumstances where the courts had grappled with this issue for a generation, as a result of which they had 'developed clear and coherent criteria of a general kind to decide which side of the line a particular body comes from', thought it was better to have 'a broad and inclusive definition rather than some kind of exhaustive list'. He too proceeded by way of analogy, regarding it as 'unthinkable' if a body which was private in form, such as a privatised prison service, but public in function, could escape liability under the Convention.[4] Why so? For example, why is Group 4's status as a private security firm contracting with the Government to be distinguished from Railtrack's supposedly private role as a property developer which, as Wadham and Mountfield point out, makes it 'a statutory undertaker for the purposes of planning legislation ... [with] certain permitted development rights not afforded to ordinary private bodies'?[5] The retired judge, Lord Donaldson, raised another example during the Second Reading of the Human Rights Bill in the House of Lords:

> '... is Safeways conducting a business of a public nature?[6] It may be said that it is not but I am not quite sure why. There must be a better way of defining what is meant by a "public authority". It is quite clear that it does not mean a public authority; indeed this is a pure term of art. Whatever the definition, it must be made clear that it is only a term of art.'[7]

3.107   So far, it appears that when determining whether a commercial organisation is a public authority, 'the point is not the label or description: it is the

---

1   See, for example, *O'Reilly v Mackman* [1983] AC 237; *Mercury Communications Ltd v Director General of Telecommunications* [1996] 1 All ER 575; and *Trustees of Dennis Rye Pension Fund v Sheffield City Council* [1998] 1 WLR 840.
2   See **3.74** et seq.
3   Even though, at times, the consequences could be disastrous if a case was (wrongly) brought in private law proceedings which were subsequently out of time for being made the subject of an application for judicial review.
4   Hansard HL, vol 583, col 792, 24 November 1997. The incarceration example was also used by the Lord Chancellor: 'A private security company would be exercising public functions in relation to the management of a contracted-out prison but would be acting privately when, for example, guarding commercial premises': at col 811.
5   Wadham and Mountfield (see fn 4 on p 1), p 37.
6   See Hansard HL, vol 582, col 1293, 3 November 1997. In later exchanges in the House of Commons, the Parliamentary Under-Secretary of State for the Home Department (Mr Mike O'Brien MP) said that Tesco would not be acting as a public authority in bringing a private shoplifting prosecution: see Hansard HC, vol 314, col 1057, 24 June 1998.
7   Hansard HL, vol 582, col 1293, 3 November 1997.

function'.[1] As to functionality, one possible definition offered by Lord Simon of Glidsdale in Parliament and taken from existing UK race relations legislation would have brought within the range of the Act 'any person concerned with the provision to the public or a section of the public (whether for payment or otherwise) of any goods, facilities or services'.[2] This *marketplace* formulation was rejected by the Lord Chancellor as far too broad, on the basis that it would catch (he noted with politically incorrect candour) 'window cleaners, jobbing joiners, the girl who keeps the window cleaners' accounts and the boy who delivers the flyers from the local restaurant'.[3]

3.108 Some further elaboration was forthcoming in the debates on the Human Rights Bill in the House of Commons. Sir Norman Fowler MP, for the Conservatives, wanted the definition of a public authority to be limited to:

'any person or body which:

(a)   is established and regulated by statute; or

(b)   has ministerial appointments on its governing body;

and ... such a person or body ... is only a public body when acting in the discharge of its statutory functions.'[4]

3.109 The Home Secretary rejected the proposal, citing the Panel on Takeovers and Mergers as an example of one body which would not be caught by the proposed amendment, even though the Panel 'plays a crucial role in the regulation of markets and competition policy and has been regarded by our domestic courts as susceptible to judicial review'.[5] Mr Straw was, however, alive to the danger of a perceived unfairness if, for example, a privatised telecommunications company was susceptible to the operation of the European Convention while its direct competitors fell outside the Treaty's reach. He said: 'I am absolutely clear that we must, to use the old cliché, provide a level playing field between BT and other, wholly private operators. They would have to be treated the same under the Act'. He continued:

'That is why we do not want to go down the road advocated [by the amendment] which, with commercial property developers, for example, would treat Railtrack more onerously than any other body – such as the wholly private developer McAlpine ... – simply because Railtrack happens to be a statutory body. I do not want to do that.'[6]

3.110 In *Pepper v Hart*[7] terms, it was perhaps these and other remarks made by the Home Secretary on 17 June 1998 which are likely to be cited most frequently in

---

1   Lord Williams (Hansard HL, vol 582, col 1310, 3 November 1997). The South African courts have looked at this broad issue in connection with the South African Bill of Rights, posing the following questions: is the relevant body operating in the public domain? To what extent (if any) are its private functions entwined with its public functions? Are the functions State-approved? See the case of *Barlow v University of Boputhatswana* (1995) (4) SA 1997 and the helpful article by A Henderson *The Human Rights Act and JR: A South African Perspective* [1999] JR 118.

2   Hansard HL, vol 583, col 789, 24 November 1997

3   Hansard HL, vol 583, col 797, 24 November 1997.

4   Hansard HC, vol 314, col 399, 17 June 1998.

5   Hansard HC, vol 314, col 407, 17 June 1998. See also the cases involving the Takeover Panel beginning with *R v Panel on Takeovers and Mergers, ex parte Datafin plc* [1987] QB 815.

6   The true position is perhaps more complex. See Professor Hepple's chapter 'The Impact on Labour Law' at the Clifford Chance Conference (see fn 4 on p 61) at p 80.

7   See **3.4** and **3.49**.

court in disputes as to whether or not a respondent is a public authority within s 6 of the Act. Mr Straw said that, in framing the legislation, the Government's 'most valuable asset' had been the judicial review cases and that the 'best' approach was to adhere to the concept of 'a public function'.[1] The Lord Chancellor had articulated the functionality test 6 months earlier but, unlike him, however, the Home Secretary went further in identifying three types of body the legislation had in mind. The first comprised 'organisations which might be termed "obvious" public authorities, all of whose functions [were] public. The clearest examples [were] Government Departments, local authorities and the police. There [was] no argument about that.'

3.111   'The second category [included] organisations with a mix of public and private functions.' In that regard, the Home Secretary referred, like his colleagues before him, to Railtrack, confirming that he did not want the legislation to catch 'the commercial activities of Railtrack or, for example, of the water companies – which were nothing whatever to do with the exercise of public functions'. He also reached for the prisons analogy:

> 'Private security firms contract to run prisons. What Group 4, for example, does as a plc contracting with other bodies is nothing whatever to do with the State, but, plainly, where it runs a prison, it may be acting in the shoes of the State ... those organisations, unlike the "obvious" public authorities, will not be liable in respect of their private acts. The third category is organisations with no public functions – accordingly, they fall outside the scope of [section] 6.'[2]

3.112   The Home Secretary was circumspect about the extent to which European Court decisions could be looked to for guidance in this area. He said:

> '... we could not directly replicate the definition of public authorities used by Strasbourg because ... the respondent to any application in the Strasbourg court is the United Kingdom, as the State. We have therefore tried to do the best we can in terms of replication by taking into account whether a body is sufficiently public to engage the responsibility of the State.'[3]

3.113   The problem with even that limited reliance on existing European Convention authorities is that, quite apart from the fact that the Act does not wholly reflect Strasbourg case-law to date,[4] the European Court's jurisprudence offers little assistance in determining what is a State concern for European Convention purposes.[5] Indeed, it might be said that the Strasbourg institutions have tended in the past to duck the very analysis that courts in the UK now face. The judges of the European Court in the main have circumvented the need directly to identify the criteria for determining whether, for example, nationalised industries are, for European Convention purposes, emanations of the State by

---

1   Hansard HC, vol 314, col 410, 17 June 1998.
2   Hansard HC, vol 314, col 409, 17 June 1998.
3   Hansard HC, vol 314, cols 406 and 432, 17 June 1998.
4   See Morris (fn 2 on p 58), p 305 et seq.
5   Although it has at least been clear that a Member State cannot divest itself of its European Convention obligations by contracting-out what would otherwise be a public service: *Costello-Roberts v United Kingdom* (1982) 4 EHRR 38.

instead focusing on the obligation placed upon Member States to take positive measures to guarantee adherence to European Convention rights.[1]

3.114 Perhaps the only relevance of the Strasbourg jurisprudence in this context is to suggest an answer to the question whether this is a body in respect of whose actions the UK would be notionally responsible before the Strasbourg Court. If so, it will almost certainly be a public authority in terms of the Act. Beyond that, it could be that judges will batten on to the thinking of the European Court of Justice in Luxembourg, which has said that a body is an emanation of the State if, whatever its legal form, it 'has been made responsible, pursuant to a measure adopted by the State, for providing a public service under the control of the State and which has for that purpose special powers beyond those which result from the normal rules applicable in relations between individuals'.[2] This is readily understandable, but also problematic, as the test was formulated against a background involving the failure of EU Governments to implement certain EC Directives.

3.115 Beyond that, reference will perforce be made to the existing British administrative law authorities and the leading text-books. De Smith, Woolf and Jowell[3] have succinctly distilled, from the mass of decisions in this area, the following questions (summarised by the writer) to be put when seeking to determine whether a non-statutory body performs public functions:

(1) but for that statutory body, would the Government have had to intervene to regulate the activity that is being scrutinised?
(2) does the Government underpin the work of this particular body by 'weaving' it into the 'fabric' of public regulation or by establishing it with the Government's authority?[4]
(3) does it exercise monopolistic powers?
(4) does it confer some form of collective benefit?
(5) has anyone aggrieved by it at the same time agreed to be bound by it?

3.116 Here too, however, it is apparent that the scheme of the Act cannot readily be made to fit. These questions (and the answers they suggest) would appear to mean that, for example, the telecommunications regulator is a s 6 public authority but its regulated company BT is not.

---

1   See, for example, *Hilton v United Kingdom* Appl 12015/86, (1988) 57 DR 108, where the issue regarding the BBC's status as a state entity was never decided. The position of the Post Office was equally not clarified in the case of *Malone v UK* (1985) 7 EHRR 14, nor was the role of British Rail made clear in *Young, James and Webster v UK* (1981) 4 EHRR 38.
2   *Foster v British Gas plc* [1990] 3 All ER 897. See also *Griffin v South West Water* [1995] IRLR 15, where it was held that a privatised water company was a State emanation. The Pharmaceutical Society of Great Britain is a public authority in EU terms. See *R v The Pharmaceutical Society, ex parte Association of Pharmaceutical Importers* (1989) ECR 1295.
3   *Judicial Review of Administrative Action* (Sweet & Maxwell, 1995), para 3–021. See also Lester and Pannick (fn 1 on p 12) on the different approaches adopted in Canada and Hong Kong (p 32) and J Coppel *The Human Rights Act* (John Wiley & Sons, 1999), p 21 on the relevant decisions in New Zealand. See also the key characteristics identified in the Core Guidance for Public Authorities produced by the Home Office's Human Rights Task Force: http://www.homeoffice.gov.uk/hract.
4   See *R v Disciplinary Committee of the Jockey Club, ex parte Aga Khan* [1993] 1 WLR 909 (see also **3.95**).

3.117   It can at least be said with some confidence that a body already susceptible to judicial review in the UK in relation to all or part of its activities will almost certainly be a public authority in relation to the same or a greater part of its activities by virtue of the Act.[1] This is not to say, however, that a body which has not traditionally been judicially reviewable will fall outside the provisions of the Act. On the contrary, as we have seen, the reverse may be the case. Sporting bodies are a good example. It has been trite in English law to point out that their relationship with members is a matter of private law (generally the law of contract), but it must be doubted whether this line can be held after the Act comes fully into force.[2]

3.118   Likewise, Lloyd's of London has so far been found not to be susceptible to judicial review in general terms, but in discharging its public functions (and this must cover its disciplinary procedures), it is likely to be a public authority under the Act. The same goes for the General Medical Council, the Law Society and the plethora of other bodies that have a disciplinary remit. Charities may be caught where they have prosecutorial powers as have, for example, the NSPCC and the RSPCA, or where they discharge functions which otherwise would be discharged by the State, such as the residential care offered by Barnardos or by private nursing homes.

3.119   It will be apparent from this treatment of the key definitional issue presented by the legislation (namely the designation of public authorities) that wholly private companies (but including public limited companies for this purpose) which have never been in the public sector (such as Group 4) may be public authorities under the terms of the Act as regards certain of their activities. So too, companies which were once State-owned but are now squarely within the private sector (such as BT). In either case, the pool of those potentially affected is very considerable indeed and, as such, the lie is surely given to the claim that the domestication of the European Convention has been an occasion of unalloyed joy in company boardrooms.

A public authority's defence

3.120   Section 6(1) enunciates a simple free-standing test. For a claim to be made against it under the Act, the relevant public authority must have acted in a way which is incompatible with the relevant European Convention rights.

3.121   Public authorities found to have acted in a way that is incompatible with the European Convention have one defence only – that of statutory obligation.[3] Consistent once again with a determination to maintain Parliamentary sovereignty and ensure that incompatible primary legislation remains fully effective, the Act provides that a public authority does not act unlawfully if, as a result of one

1   The Director of Gas Supply was proceeded against in a judicial review case about customer disconnection. See *R v Director of Gas Supply, ex parte Sherlock & Morris N Ireland* 29 November 1996 (unreported) (QB). See also *R v Northumbria Water, ex parte Able UK* (1996) COD 187.
2   See, for example, *R v Disciplinary Committee of the Jockey Club, ex parte Aga Khan* (fn 1 on p 63). The fact that the Football Association may take decisions involving hundreds of millions of pounds in a very public arena has hitherto not been sufficient to make it judicially reviewable in England and, indeed, the Home Secretary has said that it will not be a public authority under the Act. The Scottish Football Association has, however, been the subject of a judicial review: *St Johnston FC v Scottish Football Association* [1965] SLT 171.
3   Section 6(2), see Appendix 1.

or more provisions of a statute, the relevant authority could not have acted differently or if, in the case of one of more provisions of a statute which cannot be read or given effect in a way which is compatible with the relevant European Convention rights, the authority was acting so as to give effect to or enforce those provisions.[1] In other words, if Westminster has decreed by statute that privatised utilities must, for example, discharge their functions in a particular way, those utilities will not be at risk in terms of the Act.

3.122   As if to put beyond any doubt the residual and pre-eminent authority of the legislature, s 6(6) of the Act[2] provides that a public authority acts unlawfully when it *fails* to act but not where the failure in question is a failure to introduce or make legislation. That failure, however, could still be a European Convention violation where the right in question is one which the UK and other Member States have a positive obligation to secure, if need be by the introduction of legislation. Absent some imaginative common-law decision-making, the victim may be without a remedy in this situation save, that is, for a complaint to Strasbourg.

3.123   Here too then, the less-than-wholesale incorporation of the European Convention is apparent. The UK, like other Member States, has an obligation under the European Convention to take positive action to uphold its provisions, but the effect of s 6(6) is to exempt public authorities from liability where the failure to act compatibly with the European Convention is a failure by Westminster to legislate. EC law, by contrast, allows for damages to be awarded where the UK has failed to give effect to EC law.[3]

SECTION 7

The new tort

3.124   Section 6 of the Act establishes in UK law a new cause of action, the public law tort (to which public authorities are susceptible) of acting 'in a way which is incompatible with a Convention right'.[4] Section 7 of the Act, headed (in the margin) 'Proceedings', sets out the manner in which this cause of action is to be enforced by stating that:

> 'A person who claims that a public authority has acted (or proposes to act) in a way which is made unlawful by section 6(1) may—
> (a)   bring proceedings against the authority under [the] Act in the appropriate court or tribunal, or
> (b)   rely on the Convention right or rights concerned in any legal proceedings, but only if he is (or would be) a victim of the unlawful act.'[5]

3.125   On this basis, it is provided that public authorities can be challenged not just in respect of their *past* actions but where they are *about to act* in a way that is

---

1   Section 6(2), see Appendix 1.
2   See Appendix 1.
3   See *Francovich v Italy* [1991] ECR I–5357.
4   Section 6(1), see **3.73** and Appendix 1.
5   Section 7(1), see Appendix 1.

incompatible with the Convention. A claimant can sue under the Act alone, confirming in the process (as already stated) the creation of an entirely new and free-standing basis for court action. Alternatively, the claimant can rely upon the Act in any (other) kind of proceedings,[1] most obviously perhaps by alleging a new head of illegality in the context of an application for judicial review.[2] Equally, there is no reason why the Act could not be used to bolster a claim for, say, negligence against a council operating a children's home or for breach of confidence against the BBC or, further, in the context of an appeal on the basis that a new ground of appeal will be that the judge's order at first instance was in violation of a provision of the European Convention. So, too, the illegality of the actions of a public authority in European Convention terms may properly be relied upon even where the public authority is not a party to the relevant proceedings. In such ways, the Act will insinuate itself into British litigation across a broad front.

3.126   The ability to invoke the Act in legal proceedings is not limited to claimants. Defendants to actions brought by public authorities (whether civil or criminal) may seek to rely on their s 6 rights[3] by way of defence,[4] a possibility specifically acknowledged by the Home Secretary during the Parliamentary passage of the legislation.

3.127   Detailed provisions regarding the rules of court governing proceedings under the Act are to be found at s 7(9)–(13).[5] In March 2000, the Lord Chancellor's Department produced a Consultation Paper on the subject,[6] reflecting the Government's commitment during the Parliamentary debates on the Human Rights Bill to ensure that s 7 proceedings would use existing court procedures so far as possible.[7] The Consultation Paper sensibly proposes to insert in the Practice Direction to Part 16 of the Civil Procedure Rules 1998 (Statements of Case) the requirement that claimants issuing proceedings under s 7(1)(a) of the Act state that fact in their claim forms and identify the European Convention right ostensibly infringed.

3.128   Section 7(11)[8] arguably belongs more to s 8 of the Act, dealing with remedies.[9] It permits the Government to supplement the forms of relief or remedies available to a tribunal (or the grounds on which relief or remedies may be granted) to ensure that the relevant tribunal can provide an appropriate remedy in relation to behaviour of a public authority which is incompatible with a Convention right.

---

1   Section 7(1)(b), see Appendix 1.
2   A subject discussed more fully in relation to Art 6. See Chapter 6.
3   See **3.72** et seq.
4   Section 7(6) of the Act provides that 'legal proceedings' includes: '(a) proceedings brought *by or at the instigation of* [writer's emphasis] a public authority; and (b) an appeal against the decision of a court or tribunal'. See Appendix 1. In addition, s 7(2) of the Act (see Appendix 1) provides that proceedings against an authority include 'a counterclaim or similar proceeding', for example such as an appeal.
5   See Appendix 1.
6   See http://www.open.gov.uk.
7   See, for example, the Home Secretary, Mr Straw, at Hansard HC, vol 306, col 780, 16 February 1998.
8   See Appendix 1.
9   As to which, see **3.155** et seq.

Victims

3.129 Questions of horizontality aside, the Act contemplates only two forms of human rights litigant – victims and public authorities.

3.130 The ability to invoke s 7 is limited solely to those who are or would be victims, for the purposes of Art 34[1] of the European Convention, in proceedings brought before the European Court.[2] In this respect at least, Strasbourg law appears to be decisive and not merely persuasive.

3.131 This victim threshold has been widely criticised, not least because it represents a retreat from the position outlined in the Labour Party's pre-election Consultation Paper, which had eschewed Strasbourg's requirement that victimhood first be established before a European Convention complaint could be considered on its merits and instead had suggested that an applicant would need to have (only) a 'sufficient interest' in the ostensibly unlawful behaviour of the relevant public authority in order to bring a claim – in other words, the same requirement as to standing that is used in domestic judicial review cases.[3] As to that, the Act provides at s 7(3) that, where proceedings are brought on an application (outside Scotland) for judicial review, 'the applicant is to be taken to have a sufficient interest in relation to the unlawful act *only* if he is, or would be, a victim of that Act' (emphasis added).[4]

3.132 The Act's precision in narrowly identifying in s 7 those who may bring claims under the Act has been contrasted with the absence of any precise identification in s 6 of those who may be sued under the Act.[5] The Act throws up, as it were, a very broad range of targets, but not everyone will be permitted to take aim at them. The Government feared that a more relaxed approach to standing would lead to 'a raft of test cases increasing the work of the courts',[6] although it was strongly argued in Parliament that the result might in the event be precisely what Ministers had sought to rule out, namely 'a proliferation of litigation that might have been avoided, had the full range of issues pertinent to the consideration of a specific case ... been deployed by an interested party'.[7] Mr O'Brien, for the Government, said that the purpose of the 'victim' requirement in s 7 was

'... not to create opportunities to allow interest groups ... to venture into frolics of their own in the courts. The aim [was] to confer access to rights, not to licence interest groups to clog up the courts with test cases, which [would] delay victims' access to the

---

1   See **2.49** et seq and Appendix 2.
2   Section 7(7), see Appendix 1.
3   The term 'sufficient interest' was conceived 'as one which would sufficiently embrace all classes of those who might apply and yet permit sufficient flexibility in any particular case to determine whether or not "sufficient interest" was in fact shown': see *Inland Revenue Commissioners v National Federation of Self-Employed Small Business Ltd* [1982] AC 617.
4   See Appendix 1.
5   See, for example, the comments of Edward Leigh MP (Conservative) in the Committee-stage debate in the House of Commons on the Human Rights Bill (Hansard HC, vol 314, col 421, 17 June 1998).
6   Robert Maclennan MP, Hansard HC, vol 314, col 1068, 24 June 1998.
7   Mr Maclennan (see fn 4 above) at col 1069. John M Taylor MP (Conservative) disagreed. He said that he had about 35 constituents who wrote letters to him in green ink and who would 'burst through the door' once the Human Rights Bill had Royal Assent (Hansard HC, vol 314, col 1072, 24 June 1998). He worried too (at col 1073) about claims by 'those politically motivated law centres' and wanted 'the most restrictive interpretation possible of who can petition' (at col 1081).

courts. There [was] nothing undemocratic about conferring rights on victims, rather than interest groups that [were] non-victims. Interest groups [could] always support victims and that [was] enough.'[1]

3.133   That statement may reflect a reasonable apprehension about the opening of floodgates, but it is inadequate to assist lawyers and business clients in addressing a quite separate problem, namely the difficulty in reconciling the tension between what will henceforth be different tests for standing in UK public law litigation, ie between the traditional requirement in judicial review applications (of a sufficient interest)[2] and the requirement laid down in the Act (of victim status).[3]

3.134   The narrow claimant threshold in the legislation assists corporate public authorities on two grounds – first, on the basis that it reduces the number of potential claimants able to sue them; and, secondly, because the victim test in the Act is one with which commerce is already familiar, in the sense that a putative public-law victim is broadly analogous to a claimant alleging breach and loss in a private-law contract and tort action.

3.135   Civil libertarians have complained that the introduction of the victim requirement is particularly regrettable in circumstances where judges in judicial review cases over time have developed flexible rules on standing which have enabled relief to be sought by a variety of interest groups who, although not victims, are agents or representatives of victims.[4] Indeed, the European Court itself has permitted third-party interventions by a variety of interested bodies such as Amnesty International and Liberty[5] and has said that construing the European Convention as a 'living instrument'[6] applies as much to matters of procedure as

---

1   Hansard HC, vol 314, col 1086, 24 June 1998.
2   See RSC Ord 53.3(7) in CPR 1998, Sch 1.
3   Lord Lester put the point in context during the debates in the House of Lords: 'The Act is traditionally British in its main principles, respecting both the English constitutional doctrine of Parliamentary sovereignty and the need to provide effective British judicial remedies for breach of Convention rights. The [Act] is also British in empowering all our courts and tribunals to interpret and apply the Convention rather than to establish a special constitutional court. The [Act] is British too, in requiring our courts to take into account the European jurisprudence from Strasbourg but not to be ruled by it. Yet [s] 7 makes a curious and anomalous departure from this very British scheme. Instead of relying upon the well-developed public-law concepts – judicial review concepts – of legal standing for judicial review and other proceedings, the [Act] imports a test of legal standing derived from the concept of a victim to be used by the European Court of Human Rights in interpreting and applying Article 34 of the Convention ...': Hansard HL, vol 583, col 823, 24 November 1997.
4   Beneficiaries of this approach have included the Child Poverty Action Group (see *R v Secretary of State for Social Services, ex parte Child Poverty Action Group* [1990] 2 QB 540), the Equal Opportunities Commission (see *R v Secretary of State for Employment, ex parte Equal Opportunities Commission* [1995] AC 1), the Joint Council for the Welfare of Immigrants (see *R v Secretary of State for Social Security, ex parte Joint Council for the Welfare of Immigrants* [1997] 1 WLR 275) and, more significantly for business, Greenpeace (see *R v HM Inspectorate of Pollution, ex parte Greenpeace Ltd (No 2)* [1994] 4 All ER 329). By contrast, it is suggested that the provisions of s 7 may in fact extend the scope of judicial review in Scotland, where traditionally standing has been more narrowly interpreted than in England.
5   More relevantly for the commercial sector, there has been participation in cases by trade unions. See the cases of *Malone v United Kingdom* (1984) 7 EHRR 14 and *Young, James and Webster v United Kingdom* (1981) 4 EHRR 38, where the then Post Office Engineering Union and the Trades Union Congress (respectively) made submissions, and the case of *Lingens v Austria* (1986) 8 EHRR 407, in which the International Press Institute appeared.
6   As regards the introduction of the European Convention, see **5.4** et seq.

matters of substance and there is no reason why the victim criterion should not be considered flexibly in this context.[1]

3.136   The need for victimhood as expressed in Art 34 of the European Convention has, however, still not been dispositively reviewed by the European Court[2] and, as it stands, campaign groups may have to omit a challenge based upon an alleged violation of the European Convention from any forthcoming judicial review application in which they have standing to appear unless, that is, they can find a 'victim'. It was precisely that hunt for a representative victim, who might have no specialist knowledge (however profoundly affected by the matter complained of) or adequate resources which English judges had increasingly come to regard as synthetic and unnecessary and which the Government, in the Act, has seen fit to make necessary once more.

3.137   Lord Lester expressed the fear in Parliament that in the future there could be up to five different tests for legal standing in UK courts, depending on whether the relevant case involved:

(1)   'ordinary' common law;
(2)   common law embodying Convention rights;
(3)   European Community law;[3]
(4)   European Convention rights alone; and
(5)   any combination of the above.[4]

3.138   In response, the Lord Chancellor conceded that a narrower filter now applies to claims brought on European Convention grounds than to other forms of judicial review, although he has held out the prospect of making special arrangements 'for cases that raise issues of wider public interest'.[5] (At the time of writing, no such arrangements had been made.) The stricter European Convention test for standing should not, furthermore, affect the growing practice of the House of Lords (although it is so far only the House of Lords) of permitting non-governmental organisations to intervene and file amicus briefs (both orally and in writing), even where they cannot appear as parties[6] and it is unlikely that any of the higher courts will exclude evidence filed by public interest groups, particularly if it involves expert testimony or research which may assist the tribunal.

3.139   In one respect, in any event, the standing threshold is arguably more relaxed as, prior to the Act, it was not generally possible for proceedings to be brought by a claimant *at risk* of being affected by a future act of a public authority,

---

1   *Loizidou v Turkey* (1995) 20 EHRR 99. Far from narrowing the standing rules, some Commonwealth States appear to be moving in the opposite direction. See M Plimmer 'Standing in Someone Else's Shoes' [1998] NLJ 1026. Section 6 of Barbados' Administrative Justice Act 1980 already permits 'any other person' to apply for judicial review if justified on a public interest and circumstantial basis.

2   Much of the case-law derives only from European Commission decisions on the threshold question of admissibility.

3   See *Foster v British Gas plc* [1991] 1 QB 405.

4   Hansard HL, vol 583, col 828, 24 November 1997.

5   Hansard HL, vol 583, col 831, 24 November 1997.

6   Practice Direction and Standing Orders Applicable to Civil Appeals, House of Lords (January 1996), Direction 34.1. See *R v Khan (Sultan)* [1996] 3 All ER 289. See, also, the case involving the killers of James Bulger (*R v Secretary of State for the Home Department, ex parte T and V* [1998] AC 407) and the Pinochet case: *R v Bow Street Stipendiary Magistrate, ex parte Ugarte* [1999] 2

although such claims are admissible at Strasbourg[1] and, consistent with that, the Act permits applications by those who 'would be' victims. Pressure group lawyers will be particularly keen to ensure that those words are given a flexible meaning in the first appeals as regards issues of standing which are heard after the Act comes fully into force. Otherwise, it generally will be the case that claimants who fail to establish that they are victims will, in seeking to rely upon the European Convention, be thrown back on the principles developed before the introduction of the Act.[2]

Public authority victims

3.140   There is a further twist to the victim requirement. State bodies (including local authorities) traditionally have not been regarded by the European Court as victims for European Convention purposes, although, admittedly, the case-law is sparse.[3] In the early days of the European Convention this may have made sense philosophically. After all, the European Convention was intended to function as a bulwark against the abuse of executive power and it would have been perverse if States could also have used the European Convention to protect their own interests. This rationale is too simplistic, however, in an era when much State power across Europe (and particularly in the UK) has been hived off by privatisation, contracting out and the process of compulsory competitive tendering. Much of the British economy has shifted from the public to the private sector and it would be unfair and indeed odd to see privatised utilities (for example) only as putative offenders of the Act's provisions.

3.141   As matters currently stand, however, Railtrack, BT and local councils (for example) are potentially liable as public authorities in terms of the Act but, at least insofar as their public functions are concerned, arguably cannot themselves invoke the provisions of the Act. Would that therefore deprive Railtrack of any legal remedy (in the context of the Act) if the railway network were to be taken back into public ownership, as continues in some quarters to be mooted? As it happens, Railtrack issued proceedings in 2000 against the Rail Regulator in the wake of his indication that he was minded to fine Railtrack a very substantial sum if it failed to meet punctuality standards. Is Railtrack prevented from raising a point under the Act because of its public authority status in relation to those (public) parts of its functions which are precisely those in respect of which the Rail Regulator is minded to impose a financial penalty? Does this not patently engage Art 13? This too is an issue which senior British judges will need to resolve early. It may be anticipated that industry regulators may not wish to be seen to take such an unattractive and technical argument against one of their own regulated entities, but this may not always be the case.

3.142   There is no indication that the legislation was intended to place privatised utilities (and other former public sector entities) in a straight-jacket of

---

WLR 827. The Public Law Project filed an affidavit in a case about the removal of the exemption of those on a low income from paying Writ fees: *R v Lord Chancellor, ex parte Witham* [1998] 2 WLR 849.

1   See **2.49** et seq.

2   See s 11 of the Act at **3.188** et seq and Appendix 1.

3   See *Austria Municipalities v Austria* (1974) 17 Yearbook 338. See also **2.49** et seq and *Ayuntamiento de M v Spain* (1991) 68 DR 209. A more recent case is *Sectio De Commune D'Antilly v France* Appl 45129/98, 23 November 1999, where an application by a local

this sort and it is to be hoped that the judiciary will seek to ensure that corporate public authorities are not left in such a position. Conceivably, a way through is to look not at the capacity of the human rights complainant (provided the complainant is, of course, a victim) but solely at that of the respondent. The Rail Regulator (continuing the analogy) is unarguably acting as a public authority when threatening to fine Railtrack. He must act in a way that is compatible with the Convention and, if he does not, a claim should lie in favour of any body that he regulates, such as Railtrack, notwithstanding the fact that, for other purposes, Railtrack itself is a public authority under the Act.

Limitation

3.143   The first four sub-sections of s 7 describe those who may make claims under the Act. Section 7(5) prescribes the period during which such claims are to be brought. It provides that proceedings against a public authority for allegedly acting in a manner incompatible with a European Convention right must be brought before the end of:

'(a)   the period of one year beginning with the date on which the act complained of took place; or

(b)   such longer period as the court or tribunal considers equitable having regard to all the circumstances;

but that is subject to any rule imposing a stricter time-limit in relation to the procedure in question.'[1]

3.144   The Human Rights Bill, as originally published, contained no such time-bar, which was introduced by Government amendment during the Committee-stage debate in the House of Commons. The provision means that a *claimant* seeking to invoke the Act has a year from the date of the alleged European Convention breach in which to do so. Where the Act is relied upon in any other context (most obviously as a defence), the limitation period applicable to the relevant charge (in criminal proceedings) or cause of action (in civil proceedings) will govern the position, so that a defence may exist under the Act long after the first anniversary of the date on which a conceivable cause of action under the Act accrued.

3.145   Whether as claimants or defendants, however, litigants are circumscribed by the all-important proviso to s 7(5) cited above which means that, in very many cases, the applicable time-bar will be shorter than one year. The requirement in judicial review applications for cases to be brought promptly and in any event within 3 months of the date on which grounds for complaint first arose is obviously relevant here,[2] and it could be that commercial enterprises will barely be affected by the 1-year time-bar laid down in the Act to the extent that, to a large degree, the exposure of firms (which are not themselves public authorities)

---

authority was declared inadmissible because it was a form of 'public-law legal entity administering assets and rights in the general interest and did not fall within Article 34'. Compare, however, *NUT v St Mary's Church of England (Aided) Junior School* [1997] ICR 334.

1   Section 7(5), see Appendix 1.
2   See CPR 1988, Sch 1, RSC Ord 53.4(1). Mr O'Brien said during the debate in the House of Commons at the Committee stage that 'it would not be right' for applicants in judicial review cases to avoid the requirement of promptitude by relying upon the 12-month time-bar otherwise provided for in the Act (Hansard HC, vol 314, col 1095, 24 June 1998).

to the Act is likely to be confined to its deployment as an additional argument in judicial review proceedings in which they are claimants.[1]

3.146   Existing time-limits in for example, judicial review, libel and personal injury litigation can of course already be extended with the court's permission and it may be that judges in the UK will be generous in allowing points to be taken under the Act 'where a rigid 1-year cut off could lead to injustice'[2] and (perhaps) through fear that Arts 6 (with its right to court access) and 13 and/or 14 would otherwise be breached.[3] Here too a challenge to the Act on the basis that it is not itself compatible with the Convention may be anticipated and, for this reason, there must at least be a prospect that the requirement of promptitude in judicial review applications will be relaxed where a human rights point is raised.

3.147   Robert Maclennan MP, for the Liberal Democrats, had sought in the House of Commons to amend the time-bar provision by adding a power for British courts to have regard to all the circumstances when determining whether complaints were out of time,'including the time by which the complainant knew or ought reasonably to have known of the substance of the complaint and the time by which he was reasonably able to bring the proceedings'.[4]

3.148   He contrasted the position in New Zealand and Canada, which have statutes analogous to the Act,[5] but in respect of which the courts apply the (more generous) limitation period affecting civil proceedings generally. He worried that, with a narrow victim test[6] and with no human rights commissioner to help in the bringing of claims, it could be that good cases would go by default. Mr O'Brien, replying for the Government and no doubt with *Pepper v Hart*[7] very much in mind said:

> '... there is no off-the-shelf answer to the question of how long the limitation period for claims under [the Act] should be. What we have tried to do in our amendment is to strike a balance between the legitimate needs of the plaintiff and the legitimate needs of the defendant, which is what all limitation periods should do.'

3.149   He went on:

> 'Having a 3-month period ... would be unduly strict. Equally, we think that, in the majority of cases, it is reasonable to expect challenges solely on Convention grounds to be brought within 12 months. A longer limitation period would skew the balance too much against public authorities. We want to ensure that public authorities are made subject to the legislation, but we want to do that in a fair and balanced way, remembering that public authorities are often acting in the interests of the taxpayer and the citizen, so it is right that fairness should apply to them as well.'[8]

3.150   The Government thought it impossible to provide an exhaustive list of circumstances justifying an extension of time. The Maclennan amendment, it was

---

1   Although it has been argued that ss 6 and 7 of the Act together create 'a *sui generis*' European Convention right to judicial review subject only to the 1-year time-limit laid down in the Act (see D Nicol 'Limitation Periods under the Human Rights Act and Judicial Review' (1999) 115 LQR 216).
2   Mr O'Brien MP (Hansard HC, vol 314, col 1096, 24 June 1998).
3   See *Stubbings v United Kingdom* (1996) 23 EHRR 213.
4   As referred to by Mr Garnier MP at Hansard HC, vol 314, col 1093, 24 June 1998.
5   See **1.51** et seq.
6   See **3.129** et seq.
7   See **3.4** and **3.49**.
8   Hansard HC, vol 314, col 1095, 24 June 1998.

said, might have been reasonable in the context of personal injury claims, but the Act was different in contemplating proceedings that might potentially be issued across a broad front.[1] Nor, it was pointed out, was the Government's tough stance a ground-breaking one, as it was similar to that adopted in existing sex and race discrimination legislation,[2] where a comparable discretion has been exercised generously.

3.151 Whatever the Government's concerns about the striking of a balance between the interests of victims and those of public authorities, the 1-year limitation period laid down in the Act is likely to give rise to a degree of procedural confusion and complexity, in circumstances where attempts will no doubt be made to put cases on a European Convention basis in order to fall within the Act's more generous timetable, when previously they would have been characterised as fairness challenges[3] subject to the traditional judicial review requirement that they be litigated promptly and in any event within 3 months. Using the Act in this collateral way is, of course, artificial and some judges may wish to exercise a striking-out power in this context.

3.152 Opacity as regards the operation of the victim requirement is another issue calling for early judicial clarification. For now, the absence of any reference to the relevant considerations to be taken into account when the court is minded to extend the time-bar in the Act (unlike the position in s 33 of the Limitation Act 1980 in the case of personal injury actions) conceivably indicates that this is one provision at least which will be liberally construed, subject, that is, to the Government's emphasis that the intention behind the legislation is not to create a vast array of 'novel features that would allow litigants to pursue cases in courts in a way that the courts and Parliament had not intended'.[4]

Breach of the Act is no crime

3.153 Section 7(8) of the Act provides that nothing in it creates a criminal offence. That is not to say, for example, that a torturer found to be in breach of Art 3 of the European Convention will escape punishment. He will, on the contrary, be dealt with by existing criminal law in the normal way.

3.154 The fact that a breach of the Act is not made a crime may be of some reputational importance to public authorities who are found to violate the European Convention. It may also be of great commercial significance in circumstances where some standard-form loan agreements provide that banking covenants can be breached where the borrower is convicted of a criminal offence.

SECTION 8

3.155 Section 6 of the Act[5] identifies those who (broadly) may be sued under the Act while s 7[6] identifies those by whom the putative defendants identified in s 6

---

1   See Mr O'Brien (fn 2 on p 78) at col 1097.
2   See, for example, s 76(5) of the Sex Discrimination Act 1975 and s 68(6) of the Race Relations Act 1976.
3   For the implications of the Act for domestic judicial review, see **6.308**.
4   Mr O'Brien (see fn 2 on p 78) at col 1099.
5   See **3.72** et seq and Appendix 1.
6   See **3.124** et seq and Appendix 1.

may be sued. Section 8 sets out the remedies available to s 7 victims in dispute with
s 6 public authorities.

3.156   Section 8(1) provides in very wide terms that a court (which includes a
tribunal for these purposes)[1] may grant such relief or remedy, or make such order
as it considers just and appropriate in relation to an act or proposed act of a public
authority which the court finds is (or would be) unlawful[2] in the sense of being
incompatible with a European Convention right.[3] The use of the word 'may' in
this context makes clear that, although s 8 is cast in very broad terms, the power to
grant a remedy is discretionary. The court may, furthermore, only make an order
that is within its powers. This too is central. It means that, while the Act creates a
new cause of action, that cause of action gives rise to no new remedy or relief
where it succeeds.[4]

3.157   This theme is continued in s 8(2), which provides that damages under
the Act may be awarded 'only by a court which has power to award damages, or to
order the payment of compensation, in civil proceedings'.[5] 'Damages' for these
purposes mean 'damages for an unlawful act of a public authority'.[6] The scheme
of the Act, therefore, appears to preclude the award of damages for breach of a
European Convention right by a criminal court.[7] Thus, a company director who
successfully sets up an Art 6 defence[8] when prosecuted for, say, insider dealing
would need, after his acquittal, to take separate (civil) proceedings when seeking
compensation.

3.158   This prohibition on damages awards by criminal courts was the subject
of some criticism in Parliament[9] and, in terms of *Pepper v Hart*,[10] it may be
convenient to reproduce the Lord Chancellor's very clear views at some length,
for they appear to put the position beyond any doubt. He said:

> 'So as to make the intention plain, it is not the [Act's] aim that, for example, the
> Crown court should be able to make an award of damages where it finds, during the
> course of a trial, that a violation of a person's convention rights has occurred. We
> believe that it is appropriate for an individual, who considers that his rights have been
> infringed in such a case to pursue any matter of damages through the civil courts
> where this type of issue is normally dealt with; in other words, to pursue the matter in

---

1   Section 8(6), see Appendix 1.
2   Section 8(1), see Appendix 1.
3   Section 8(6), see Appendix 1.
4   The wording of s 8(1) is similar to that in the 1991 Hong Kong Bill of Rights Ordinance and
      the Canadian Charter of Fundamental Rights 1982.
5   See Appendix 1.
6   Section 8(6), see Appendix 1.
7   Section 8(2), see Appendix 1.
8   See Chapter 6.
9   Lord Mackay of Drumadoon feared that an individual who had successfully established a
      European Convention infringement before a criminal court would have to 'raise a second
      action at further expense to himself, to others and the court system itself' (Hansard HL, vol
      583, col 853, 24 November 1997). However, the Lord Chancellor was unmoved: 'A criminal
      court need not be able to award damages for a convention breach, even if it currently has the
      power to make a compensation order unless it also has the power to award damages in civil
      proceedings': Hansard HL, vol 583, col 854, 24 November 1997. This would at least appear to
      allow for the possibility of a claim for damages before the Court of Appeal (which can make
      awards), whilst depriving the criminal courts of the right to extend their existing powers of
      compensation.
10   See **3.4** and **3.49**.

the courts that are accustomed to determining whether it is necessary and appropriate to award damages and what the proper amount should be.'

3.159   He went on:

'We say that the Crown court, in cases of crime, should not award damages. The remedy that the defendant wants in a criminal court is not to be convicted. We see very considerable practical difficulties about giving a new power to award damages to a criminal court in Convention cases. It would seem to me to open up the need for representation in the Crown court to any person whom it might appear in the course of criminal proceedings might be at risk of damages. We believe that that would be potentially disruptive of a criminal trial . . .

We believe that it is appropriate that the civil courts, which traditionally make awards of damages, should, alone, be enabled to make awards of damages in these Convention cases.'[1]

The basis for damages awards

3.160   The likelihood is that damages claims will be a standard feature of claims under the Act.[2] Whether they are in fact awarded and whether, if awarded, they will amount to much is an entirely different matter. The Act sets out the principles to which courts are to have regard when determining whether damages should be awarded. Section 8(3) provides that:

'no award of damages is to be made unless, taking account of all the circumstances of the case including:

(a)   any other relief or remedy granted, or order made, in relation to the act in question (by that or any other court) and

(b)   the consequences of any decision (of that or any other court) in respect of that act,

the court is satisfied that the award is necessary to afford just satisfaction to the person in whose favour it is made.'[3]

3.161   Therefore, establishing a breach of a European Convention right is not enough. It is not axiomatic that a damages award will follow, indeed the most obvious construction of s 8(3) is that damages should be awarded only as a last resort. In effect, this is the obverse of the test to be applied by a judge asked to award an injunction. An injunction will generally not be granted where the claimant can adequately be compensated in damages. Section 8(3) makes it plain that damages will not be awarded where some other remedy will lie.

3.162   An award, therefore, will not be necessary where the victim can be compensated by a remedy other than the award of a monetary sum. This might be, for example, a declaration as to his rights or an order of *certiorari* to quash a decision of a public authority which was incompatible with the European Convention. Corporate claimants might conceivably be denied damages where, say, the defendant public authority is a local council and where the ultimate burden of meeting any award would be borne by the council tax-payer.

---

1   Hansard HL, vol 583, col 855, 24 November 1997.
2   As to whether such damages will be taxable in the hands of the successful litigant, see
      J Peacock 'Human Rights Abuse' in (1999) *The Tax Journal*, 3 May.
3   See Appendix 1. The court is empowered under s 8(5) (see Appendix 1) to order the making
      of a contribution, in accordance with existing legislation, where more than one public
      authority is found to be at fault.

Conversely, could a business successfully obtain damages under the Act in circumstances where a judge, exercising his discretion in an application (say) for judicial review declined for the sake of good administration to overturn the relevant public authority's decision, concluding that the corporate claimants could be compensated financially instead? The answer would appear to be yes.

3.163   It has been seen that, in order to establish a claimant's victim status, express regard is to be had to the provisions of the European Convention.[1] Explicit regard for Strasbourg jurisprudence will also be relevant in determining whether to award damages and, if damages are to be awarded, the amount of any award. Specifically, s 8(4) stipulates that henceforth UK courts must take into account the compensation principles applied by the European Court under Art 41 of the European Convention.[2] This is straightforward. The reality is, however, that the case-law of the European Court throws up little consistent thinking in this area. The 'principles' referred to in s 8(4) are not easy to find, if indeed they exist at all.

3.164   Article 41 provides that if the European Court finds:

'... that there has been a violation of the Convention or the protocols thereto, and if the internal law of the High Contracting Party concerned allows only a partial reparation to be made, the Court shall, if necessary, afford just satisfaction to the injured party.'

3.165   This text is problematic, not merely because the term 'just satisfaction' is a Strasbourg import hitherto not generally used in local law. Beyond that, the question arises as to whether an 'injured party' is the same as a 'victim'?[3] Certainly the Strasbourg cases suggest so,[4] but reference to 'partial reparation' is also troublesome in this context. Should damages only be awarded where a victim who succeeds on a European Convention point can otherwise not be compensated in full?

3.166   It is clear that the power to award damages has traditionally been regarded by the European Court as discretionary.[5] As already noted,[6] the Strasbourg judges will often conclude that a merits vindication of the applicant is award enough. Where, however, the Strasbourg judges do have regard for the compensatory principle then, as with the test for damages in an English tort claim, the claimant so far as possible is to 'be put in the position he would have been in had the requirements of [the Convention] not been disregarded'.[7] In such instances, there needs to be a nexus established between breach and loss.[8]

3.167   In the *Papamichalopoulos*[9] case, the European Court quoted with approval a 1928 decision of the then Permanent Court of International Justice when saying that:

---

1   See s 7(7) in Appendix 1 and see also **2.66** et seq as regards the level of Strasbourg awards.
2   Section 8(4) is reproduced in Appendix 1. Article 41 is reproduced in Appendix 2.
3   See the analysis of victim status at **3.128** et seq.
4   See, for example, *Airey v Ireland* (1979) 2 EHRR 305 and *Le Compte, Van Leuven and De Meyere v Belgium* (1983) 5 EHRR 183. Both cases are dealt with more fully in Chapter 6.
5   See *Guzzardi v Italy* (1981) 3 EHRR 333.
6   See **2.69**.
7   *Piersack v Belgium* (1982) 5 EHRR 169.
8   See, for example, *Saunders v United Kingdom* (1996) 23 EHRR 313 and *Darby v Sweden* (1991) 13 EHRR 774.
9   *Papamichalopoulos and Others v Greece* (1996) 21 EHRR 439.

'reparation must, as far as possible, wipe out all the consequences of the illegal act and re-establish the situation which would, in all probability, have existed if that act had not been committed. Restitution in kind, or, if this is not possible, payment of a sum corresponding to the value which a restitution in kind would bear; the award, if need be, of damages for loss sustained which would not be covered by restitution in kind or payment in place of it such are the principles which should serve to determine the amount of compensation due for an act contrary to international law.'[1]

3.168 Damages are often expressed as being awarded equitably, but no one at Strasbourg has explained when equity will intervene. The judges of the European Court plainly have had reservations in the past about some of the people appearing before them but without usually saying so.

3.169 Therefore, the claimant's behaviour may have a bearing upon the amount he receives.[2] Attempts to mitigate on the part of Contracting States may also be relevant. In the *Airey* case[3], for example, when determining the level of compensation to be awarded, the Court took into account the fact that the Irish Government had indicated before proceedings were initiated that it would pay a certain amount by way of compensation. Of course, it is likely that such a pre-action offer would be highly relevant in future domestic proceedings in light of the provisions of Part 36 of the Civil Procedure Rules 1998. Non-compensatory awards have also been made where the underlying facts remain in dispute[4] and where the Strasbourg judges reject the applicant's quantum calculation.[5]

3.170 Judges in the UK will not of course be bound by the previous decisions of the Strasbourg Court as regards damages or anything else.[6] The Government's aim, however, is to ensure that 'people should receive damages equivalent to what they would have obtained had they taken their case to Strasbourg'.[7] In circumstances where it is almost impossible in a Strasbourg complaint reliably to predict the damages (if any) to be awarded, it is clear that this is another area of uncertainty created by the legislation. It is perhaps understandable that a court exercising supervisory powers of the kind available to the Strasbourg judges should not necessarily consider the award of monetary compensation as its first function. Where, however, the *measure* of loss in a Strasbourg case tends (if it can be identified at all) often to be the same as in a UK case, there must be some prospect that judges here, if they consider that damages should be awarded (and often they will not), will not follow Strasbourg in setting a low tariff but instead will approach matters in the same way they would if hearing, for example, a claim for professional negligence. What approach will British courts adopt, however, when assessing the quantum of damages after liability is established for a breach of contract (as opposed to a tortious breach) attributable to a European Convention violation (in, for example, the employment context)?

---

1   Ibid at para 36.
2   A factor to which the Government drew attention during the debates on the Human Rights Bill (see Mr O'Brien MP at Hansard HC, vol 314, col 1114, 24 June 1998). In the *McCann* case, no award was made because the application was made on behalf of three IRA terrorists planning to bomb Gibraltar.
3   See fn 4 on p 82.
4   *Gaygusuz v Austria* (1997) 23 EHRR 362.
5   *Matos e Silva v Portugal* [1997] EHRLR 109.
6   Section 2(1) of the Act. See **3.32** et seq and Appendix 1.
7   The Lord Chancellor, speaking during the Second Reading debate in the House of Lords: Hansard HL, vol 582, col 1232, 3 November 1997.

3.171	Companies which are not also public authorities will welcome the scope for compensation in the Act, but they need to bear in mind that if, as the Lord Chancellor has suggested, awards are to follow those that would otherwise have been made in Strasbourg, they are likely to be low.[1] Indeed, it may be anticipated that, in most instances, any sum ordered to be paid by a public authority will be less than the claimant company's irrecoverable costs of the litigation. In strict monetary terms alone, the game of litigating a European Convention point may, for much of the business sector, simply not be worth it.

3.172	In practice it is difficult to say more than that, because of the Act, damages claims are likely to become a more popular feature of applications for judicial review.

Damages for maladministration

3.173	By permitting British courts to award compensation for a breach of the Act, s 8, whilst providing no new remedy, arguably extends the common law which, in the judicial review context, broadly provides that damages will only lie where, if the case had been brought in a private-law context, damages could have been awarded. Before the Act, generally there was no common law right to damages for maladministration save where a state of mind connoting misfeasance in public office (or rank bad faith) could be established.[2] The Act creates greater flexibility on this score than had hitherto existed.

3.174	On this particular point, case-law from the Commonwealth again is likely throw up popular citations, particularly *Nilabati Bahero v State of Orissa*[3] from the Supreme Court of India and *Simpson v Attorney-General* (otherwise known as *Baigent's* case)[4] from the New Zealand Court of Appeal. In the first case, it was held that a *constitutional* claim could give rise to strict liability and, what is more, an award of exemplary damages. The judges in the second case looked at damages in the context of the New Zealand Bill of Rights Act 1990.

3.175	The liability of the executive in human rights terms was an issue raised by Lord Lester in the debates on the Human Rights Bill, in which he reminded his peers that the European Convention might award compensation for a so-called government tort giving rise to direct loss, whereas existing law in this country generally did not permit it.[5] If that dissonance continues, this may be an area in which undomesticated Art 13[6] comes into play.

3.176	Finally, in this context, it should be noted that damages can of course be awarded where a Convention violation gives rise to an existing cause of action and the Act does nothing to change this.[7]

1	See **3.169**.
2	See, for example, *Three Rivers District Council v Bank of England* [2000] 3 All ER 1.
3	ACR 1993 SC 1960.
4	[1994] 3 NZLR 667. See also, in this context, *Osman v United Kingdom* [1999] 1 FLR 193, where the European Court held that the blanket immunity from suit enjoyed by the police here was excessive. That case is more fully discussed in Chapter 6.
5	See Hansard HL, vol 583, col 854, 24 November 1997. He cited the *Pine Valley* case (see **2.68**) as one in which the European Court awarded compensation for breach of the applicant's legitimate expectations in the planning context.
6	See **3.10** et seq and Appendix 2.
7	See s 11 at **3.188** et seq.

SECTION 9

3.177   Section 9 has the marginal title 'judicial acts'.[1] It provides in s 9(1) that any claim based upon an alleged breach of the Act by a court or tribunal (and it refers to no one else) may be pursued only by appeal, by application for judicial review or in a forum 'prescribed by rules'.[2] In other words (and consistent with the philosophy underpinning the Act as a whole), the Act does not introduce or indeed permit new techniques for challenging judicial decisions. Nor, where a court or tribunal has acted in good faith, may damages in respect of judicial conduct be awarded in proceedings under the Act. As the Home Secretary noted during the Parliamentary debates on the Human Rights Bill, this preserves the general and long-standing principle of judicial immunity.[3] The only exception is where a claimant (in proceedings under the Act) has been the victim of arrest or detention in contravention of Art 5(5) of the European Convention (the right to liberty and security),[4] in which case he has 'an enforceable right to compensation'.[5] White-collar crime lawyers will take due note.

SECTION 10

3.178   The Act preserves Parliamentary sovereignty and, as such, no judge can strike down primary legislation on the basis that it violates the European Convention. Pursuant to s 4 of the Act,[6] however, he may declare such legislation to be incompatible with the European Convention and, in that event, the Act provides in s 10 that Parliament may use a novel 'fast-track' procedure to move to amend the statute found to be incompatible with the European Convention.

3.179   The s 10 mechanism is only triggered where there has been a declaration of incompatibility made pursuant to s 4 of the Act and any appeal has been exhausted or abandoned, or where the Government concedes that the European Court has found in a UK case, decided after 2 October 2000, that a provision of national legislation is incompatible with an obligation of the UK arising from the European Convention (including, presumably, Arts 1 and 13, which are not given further effect by the Act).[7]

3.180   In circumstances where s 4 declarations are envisaged as being rare,[8] s 10 interventions may equally be unusual. It is only in the circumstances identified above that a Government Minister may, if he considers there are 'compelling reasons' for invoking s 10, 'by order make such amendments to the [Convention-incompatible] legislation as he considers necessary to remove the incompatibility'.[9] In other words, s 10 is not triggered by cases heard at Strasbourg before s 10 comes into force nor by decisions in Strasbourg cases not involving this country.

---

1   See Appendix 1.
2   See Appendix 1.
3   Hansard HC, vol 306, col 781, 16 February 1998.
4   Section 9(3), see Appendix 1.
5   Section 9(3), see Appendix 1.
6   See **3.58** et seq and Appendix 1.
7   Section 10(1)(b), see Appendix 1. As to Arts 1 and 13, see **1.10** et seq and Appendix 2.
8   See **3.58**.
9   Section 10(2), see Appendix 1.

3.181   It is not clear what makes for a 'compelling'[1] reason in this context but, bearing in mind that s 10 operates as an addition to the general power of the Westminster Parliament to amend or abrogate legislation at any time, it is presumably intended to operate where the Government's law-making timetable does not readily permit the early introduction in the normal way of a bill to amend legislation that constitutes a European Convention breach.[2]

3.182   Section 10 has attracted the attention of constitutional specialists on the basis that it permits the amendment of primary legislation by statutory instrument, a controversial technique patented in the sixteenth century by Henry VIII. The fact that s 10 does not oblige the Government to take action (for the power is discretionary) did not quell concern in Parliament, particularly about s 10(2) – a Henry VIII clause *par excellence.* The Government therefore inserted the require-ment for 'compelling reasons' to exist before the fast-track can be followed where previously the Human Rights Bill had permitted ministerial intervention to amend incompatible primary legislation where 'appropriate'. As the Home Secretary saw it, the need for 'compelling reasons' was 'a very high test'[3] and was proof of the Government's assurance that it would not use the s 10 mechanism routinely. He justified the rolling-out of such a special procedure as necessary to cure 'a degree of paralysis'[4] which was, he said, to no one's advantage.

3.183   Lord Lester did not believe it represented 'a sinister sapping of parliamentary powers'. Amending primary legislation that was incompatible with the Convention by new primary legislation was 'a slow and cumbersome way of complying with our international obligations'[5] and it is certainly true that the s 10 procedure allows for greater Parliamentary control than is permitted in relation to matters affecting the UK's EU obligations, which can be made law by statutory instrument without the need for affirmative resolutions at Westminster.

3.184   Section 10(3) provides for similar powers of ministerial intervention as regards provisions of *subordinate* legislation made under *primary* legislation found to be incompatible with the Convention.[6]

3.185   The details of the Parliamentary procedure to be followed under s 10 are set out in Sch 2 to the Act.[7] In summary, Sch 2 provides that a draft of the proposed order purporting to remove the original incompatibility (and which may provide for amendment or revocation)[8] must be laid before Parliament,[9] accompanied (helpfully) by information explaining (a) the incompatibility to be removed by the order, including (where appropriate) details of the relevant

---

1   It is 'a strong word' according to Mr O'Brien (Hansard HC, vol 317, col 1330, 21 October 1998).
2   The Home Secretary suggested it might be used where the question involved an interference with 'the liberty of the subject' (Hansard HC, vol 314, col 1137, 24 June 1998).
3   Hansard HC, vol 314, col 1138, 24 June 1998.
4   Hansard HC, vol 306, col 772, 16 February 1998.
5   Hansard HL, vol 582, col 1241, 3 November 1997.
6   See Appendix 1.
7   See Appendix 1.
8   Schedule 2, para 1(2), see Appendix 1.
9   Schedule 2, para 2, see Appendix 1.

judicial decision (whether in the UK or at Strasbourg) and (b) the reasons for using the s 10 mechanism.[1]

3.186   There then follows a 60-day period for the making of representations.[2] If representations are made, these are to be summarised and any changes made as a consequence of them detailed in a statement accompanying the draft to be laid before Parliament.[3] No order can be made after that until there has been an affirmative vote in both Houses of Parliament to take place at the end of a further period of 60 days.[4] There is then a different procedure for urgent cases which dispenses with the need for a draft first to be approved.[5] Even then, representations can still be made and must be noted and there must be a vote.[6]

3.187   These requirements are strict, but not so strict as to prevent interested groups from making their own representations about prospective remedial orders to the relevant Government ministers. The Home Secretary has stressed that the 'fast-track' procedure in s 10 'is not to take away anyone's rights; it is to confer rights'.[7] As such, even though remedial orders can have retrospective effect,[8] they may not create retrospective criminal liability.[9] A consideration for businesses, therefore, is what steps they should take in the event that a remedial order changes the statute that gave rise to the proceedings to which they were parties in which a declaration of incompatibility was made. It may be worth a speculative return to court to see if damages would be available, even though they were not possible when the declaration of incompatibility was made.

SECTION 11

3.188   The marginal title to s 11 reads 'Safeguard for *existing* human rights' (emphasis added).[10] This is a reminder that the scheme of the Act is not that it is intended comprehensively to modify human rights law in the UK, but to complement and enhance it. The phrase confirms that a citizen's reliance upon the European Convention rights does not restrict:

'(a)   any other right or freedom conferred on him by or under any law having effect in any part of the United Kingdom; or

(b)   his right to make any claim or bring any proceedings which he could make or bring apart from sections 7 to 9.'[11]

3.189   The Act does not take away or replace existing rights. It adds to them by offering easier and more effective access to them. There is now a 'floor of rights; and if there are different or superior rights or freedoms conferred by or under any law having effect in the United Kingdom, this is [an Act] which only gives and does

---

1   Schedule 2, para 3(2) and para 5, see Appendix 1.
2   Schedule 2, para 3(1)(b), see Appendix 1.
3   Schedule 2, para 3(2), see Appendix 1.
4   Schedule 2, para 2(a), see Appendix 1.
5   Schedule 2, para 4, see Appendix 1.
6   Schedule 2, para 4(2) and (4), see Appendix 1.
7   Hansard HC, vol 306, col 773, 16 February 1998.
8   By virtue of Sch 2, para 1(1)(b), see Appendix 1.
9   Schedule 2, para 1(4), see Appendix 1.
10   Section 11, see Appendix 1.
11   Section 11, see Appendix 1.

not take away'.[1] If future (and better) rights come along, citizens and companies can rely upon them by virtue of s 11(b) and if there are existing rights which are (by inference) broader in scope than those available under the European Convention, they can continue to be invoked. In much the same way, Art 53 of the European Convention itself provides that:

> '... nothing in [the] Convention shall be construed as limiting or derogating from any of the human rights and fundamental freedoms, which may be ensured under the laws of any High Contracting Party or under any other agreement to which it is a Party.'[2]

3.190   The 'floor' metaphor was extended by Lord Lester. The Act, for him, did not create a 'ceiling' of rights. It was neither a 'minimum' nor a 'maximum' and the key was to 'approach Convention rights *through* our common law and through the statute book, not *round* the common law or the statute book' (emphasis added).[3]

SECTION 12

3.191   Sections 12 and 13 of the Act were added during the Parliamentary passage of the Human Rights Bill in response to pressure from media and church interests. Section 12 makes important provisions regarding freedom of expression. It departs fundamentally from the Parliamentary draftsmen's carefully crafted scheme and is examined in more detail later,[4] when consideration is given to the implications of European Convention domestication for the media here.

SECTION 13

3.192   Section 13, the marginal title of which is 'Freedom of thought, conscience and religion', provides that, where a court or tribunal decision might bear upon the exercise by a religious body of the European Convention right to freedom of thought, conscience and religion, it must have particular regard to the importance of that right.[5]

3.193   Arguably, the Church secured a bigger coup than did the media in s 12 in that s 13 requires freedom of thought, conscience and religion to be considered (where relevant) during *all* stages of proceedings, whereas s 12 only operates when the court is considering whether to grant relief,[6] although it is not clear that this will make any difference in practice.

3.194   Perhaps the most salient feature of s 12 and s 13 is that the s 2 obligation to take European Convention law into account is replaced by an obligation to have *particular regard* for (respectively) the European Convention's guarantees of freedom of expression and freedom of conscience.

---

1   The Lord Chancellor: Hansard HL, vol 583, col 510, 18 November 1997.
2   See Appendix 2.
3   Hansard HL, vol 585, col 411, 29 January 1998.
4   See Chapter 8.
5   Lester and Pannick (see fn 1 on p 12) explain (at pp 50 and 52) why they consider that, like s 12, s 13 'serves no sensible purpose'.
6   Section 12(1), see Appendix 1.

SECTIONS 14–17

3.195 As explained earlier,[1] not all the rights and freedoms promulgated by the European Convention are absolute. Some are derogable, ie they may legitimately be suspended. Thus, Art 15 of the European Convention provides that:

> '... in time of war or other public emergency threatening the life of the nation any High Contracting Party may take measures derogating from its obligations under [the] Convention to the extent strictly required by the exigencies of the situation, provided that such measures are not inconsistent with its other obligations under international law.'[2]

3.196 Article 15(2) of the European Convention[3] provides that some rights are non-derogable, such as Art 2 (right to life – and even then there are exceptions),[4] Art 3 (prohibition of torture), Art 4 para 1 (the ban on slavery or servitude) and Art 7 (no punishment without law).[5] Otherwise, however, it is possible for a Member State to give notice of its determination no longer to be bound by a particular provision of the European Convention.

3.197 The Act contemplates just such a possibility for the scheme whereby the Act gives further effect to the European Convention's rights and freedoms is expressly made subject to any designated derogations or reservations entered by the UK.[6] A reservation for these purposes is an instrument submitted by (for example) the UK purporting to exclude or modify the legal effect of particular provisions of a treaty (such as the European Convention) prior to its ratification. Article 57 of the European Convention provides that: 'Any State may ... make a reservation in respect of any particular provision of the European Convention to the extent that any law then in force in its territory is not in conformity with the provision'.[7]

3.198 Derogations and reservations are not intended to be permanent. Indeed, derogations should be regarded as a last resort. In the past, the British Government has entered derogations in relation to Northern Ireland and its 1988 notification regarding prevention of terrorism legislation is to be found in Sch 3, Part I to the Act.[8] The UK has also entered a reservation in relation to Art 2 of the First Protocol, whereby Member States undertake to respect the rights of parents to ensure that their children's education conforms to the parents' own religious and philosophical convictions.[9] This has been accepted by the UK 'only so far as it is compatible with the provision of efficient instruction and training and the avoidance of unreasonable public expenditure'.[10]

3.199 Sections 14, 15, 16 and 17 of the Act are technical in appearance and are intended amongst other matters to put on a statutory basis the current derogation

---

1   See **2.26** et seq and Appendix 1.
2   See Appendix 2.
3   See Appendix 2.
4   See Appendix 2.
5   See Appendix 2.
6   Section 1(2), see **3.9** et seq.
7   See Appendix 2.
8   See Appendix 1.
9   See **1.33**.
10   Schedule 3, Part II, see Appendix 1.

and reservation, to circumscribe the period for which designated derogations are to have effect and to provide for a periodic review of designated reservations.[1] These provisions are a reminder that, by Government action, parts of the European Convention can be limited in their scope, but otherwise have little specific relevance for business. That does not mean that in wider political terms they are unimportant, and Liberty has condemned the 5-year period for which specific derogations are to have effect[2] as being too long. It has also criticised the Government's approach to reservations generally.

SECTION 18

3.200   Section 18, which came into force the day the Act received Royal Assent (9 November 1998), deals in some detail with the appointment of British judges to the Strasbourg Court. In short, it provides that any senior UK judge[3] can become a judge of the European Court without being required to relinquish his office in the UK.[4] For so long as he is a judge at Strasbourg, however, he will not be required to perform his domestic judicial duties.[5]

3.201   In the past, British appointees at Strasbourg had to give up their positions on the bench in the UK with no guarantee that they would be re-appointed at the end of their term abroad. It is hoped that the Act's removal of this requirement will encourage the best local judicial talent to become available for appointment to the Strasbourg panel.[6] As already noted,[7] the current British judge at Strasbourg is Sir Nicholas Bratza, who previously had been the British member of the European Commission.

SECTION 19

3.202   Section 19 provides that a Government Minister who is in charge of a Bill (whether in the House of Commons or the House of Lords) must, before the Second Reading of the relevant bill:[8]

    '(a)   make a statement to the effect that in his view the provisions of the Bill are compatible with the Convention rights ("a statement of compatibility"); or

---

1   A defined term – see s 15(1) of the Act in Appendix 1.
2   By virtue of s 16(1)(a) and (b), see Appendix 1.
3   Which means a High Court or Circuit judge or above in England and Wales, a judge of the Court of Session or Sheriff in Scotland or a High Court or County Court judge (or above) in Northern Ireland: s 18(1), see Appendix 1. This excludes by implication a member of the Judicial Committee of the House of Lords.
4   Section 18(2), see Appendix 1.
5   Section 18(3), see Appendix 1.
6   The Lord Chancellor specifically alluded to the disincentive which had operated in the past: Hansard HL, vol 583, col 1160, 27 November 1997 and at vol 585, col 413, 29 January 1998.
7   See **2.45**.
8   It is included alongside the Explanatory and Financial Memorandum accompanying the relevant Bill.

(b) make a statement to the effect that, although he is unable to make a statement of compatibility, the Government nevertheless wishes the [relevant] House to proceed with the Bill.'[1]

3.203   Even though Ministers were already under an obligation to take account of European Convention obligations,[2] this is likely to be one of the most enduring provisions of the legislation. It came into force on 24 November 1998.[3] Although Parliamentary sovereignty is preserved by dint of the fact that legislation can continue to be introduced in the absence of a statement of compatibility, it is now necessary for the executive to have European Convention rights and freedoms in mind when bringing forward a legislative measure.[4] A similar provision exists in New Zealand (the certification there being provided by the Attorney-General), where the courts have held that it confers no rights on individuals.[5] Therefore, if some new measure affecting business cannot be made the subject of a statement of compatibility because it is incompatible with the Convention, there will not be a basis for a legal challenge.[6]

3.204   Section 19 illuminates the step change represented by the Act.[7] According to one commentator, this will become the Government's very own internal audit procedure.[8] In the meantime, Lord Hoffman has said that he would take a statement of compatibility 'extremely seriously and would be very reluctant to decide that such a measure [in respect of which a statement under s 19(1)(a) had been made] was not in fact compatible'.[9] The Lord Chancellor explained that s 19 was 'in itself a very large gesture, as well as being a point of substance, in favour of the development of a culture of awareness of what the Convention requires in relation to domestic legislation'.[10] Inevitably, ministers will be anxious to be seen to be making positive statements about the draft laws for which they are

---

1   Section 19(2), see Appendix 1.
2   See the *Ministerial Code: A Code of Conduct and Guidance on Procedure for Ministers* (Cabinet Office, 1997).
3   Human Rights Act 1998 (Commencement) Order 1998, SI 1998/2882.
4   The Government, however, does not need to make a s 19 statement in relation to a private member's Bill or a private Bill. See, for example, the arguments surrounding the City of London (Ward Elections) Bill (Press Association, 24 January 2000).
5   See the case of *Mangawaro Enterprises Ltd v Attorney-General* [1994] 2 NZLR 451. See also s 3 of the Canadian Bill of Rights 1960.
6   See G Marshall's comments in 'Patriating Rights – with Reservations' in *Constitutional Reform* (fn 4 on p 1), p 78, where he doubts whether any great significance can be attached to s 19 statements and cites the disparate nature of the annual Budget legislation to show the difficulties Ministers will have 'ahead of time and in advance of litigation' in saying that nothing in a particular Bill could be held to be an infringement of some Article of the European Convention. As if to make Dr Marshall's point, the first Bill to be subject to the s 19 procedure was the Access to Justice Bill, a measure of very considerable complexity. See also [1999] BTR 330 as regards Finance Acts and s 19 of the Act.
7   The obligation on civil servants in advising Ministers is set out in some detail in *The Human Rights Act 1998 Guidance for Departments*, see fn 6 on p 1, at paras 32–37. The terms of the s 19 statement are set out in Annex A to the Guidance as follows: 'In my view the provisions of the … Bill are compatible with the Convention rights'.
8   Blackburn (see fn 2 on p 2), p XXIV. Conceivably, the Parliamentary Joint Committee on Human Rights that has been established will be, in effect, the auditors. It was reported in Parliament on 18 April 2000 that the Committee will start its work before 2 October 2000.
9   In his view, it was important that the executive should not approach compatibility statements as a mere formality, because they would 'carry great weight with the courts'.
10   Hansard HL, vol 583, col 1163, 27 November 1997.

responsible,[1] although at the outset the Government stopped short of accepting a Liberal Democrat amendment which would have required the s 19 statement of compatibility to include reasons for the relevant Bill's supposed compatibility with the Convention.[2]

3.205   Since the Act was passed, the Government has relaxed its position regarding s 19, the Home Secretary having said that a Minister introducing secondary legislation 'should always volunteer' his view regarding the measure's compatibility with the Convention. Likewise, in his opinion, the Minister should now give a view where secondary legislation amending primary legislation is incompatible. What is more, a Minister introducing a Bill should be prepared to explain his thinking on the compatibility of particular provisions of the Bill with Convention rights and be ready to give a general outline of the arguments reflected in the s 19 statement.

3.206   Where a statement of compatibility henceforth cannot be made (something 'rare and exceptional' according to Mr O'Brien MP[3]), the Lord Chancellor has envisaged that Parliamentary scrutiny of the measure will be 'intense'[4] – not just in Parliament, but outside it too.[5] It could be that, in order to forestall difficulties later on, the implications of s 19 will encourage the Government to introduce a form of pre-legislative scrutiny, as otherwise in the event that a judge subsequently makes a declaration of incompatibility 'it is hard to see how a Minister could withhold remedial action'.[6]

3.207   There is already some evidence of this happening. On 28 April 1999, for example, the First Report of the Joint Committee of both Houses of Parliament on the then draft Financial Services and Markets Bill was published.[7] The Joint Committee heard evidence from, amongst others, legal practitioners in the City of London and suggested that the Government obtain advice as to whether aspects of the draft legislation gave rise to Convention difficulties. The Government responded by way of a Treasury memorandum to the effect that the draft statute complied with the Convention, but it is noteworthy that it also undertook to ensure (and indeed did ensure) that certain draft provisions were amended and that additional European Convention safeguards were put in place. At the time of

---

1   See the Home Secretary's comments during the debate in Second Reading in the House of Commons: Hansard HC, vol 306, col 781, 16 February 1998. See also the Lord Chancellor's comments in the same vein: Hansard HL, vol 582, col 1233, 3 November 1997.

2   See The Lord Chancellor's answer to Baroness Williams: Hansard HL, vol 583, col 1163, 27 November 1997.

3   Hansard HC, vol 317, col 1352, 21 October 1998. He cited new anti-terrorist legislation as a possibility. In the devolved institutions created in Edinburgh, Cardiff and Belfast it is not possible to state that the legislation introduced by those institutions is not compatible with the European Convention, as all such devolved laws must be European Convention-compatible. That is not to say that they will in fact be Convention-proof. See Chapter 4.

4   Hansard HL, vol 582, col 1233, 3 November 1997. See also S Tierney 'Human Rights Bill: Incorporating the European Convention on Human Rights into UK Law' [1998] EPL 299 at 302.

5   Liberty has wanted the Government to go further and have a so-called Human Rights Impact Assessment for all legislation to ensure conformity not only with the European Convention but also other international human rights instruments. In 1999, *JUSTICE* began a 1-year pilot project considering the process for carrying out a human rights audit of legislation.

6   Lord Chancellor: Hansard HL, vol 582, col 1229, 3 November 1997.

7   For a fuller analysis of what is now the Financial Services and Markets Act 2000, see **6.230** et seq.

writing, attention was also turning to the Local Government Bill, in respect of which the Rt Hon John Prescott MP, the Deputy Prime Minister, was unable to give a s 19 statement[1] in the House of Commons.

3.208   Business needs to be in a position to respond effectively to what may become a popular way of making new law, as amongst the measures introduced by way of the draft Bill procedure are some of great importance to commerce, such as the Freedom of Information Bill, the Food Standards Agency Bill and the Limited Liability Partnerships Bill. In the future, it may well make more sense for firms to seek to challenge up-coming legislation on the ground that it might breach the European Convention before it reaches the statute book than to litigate over the legislation after it has come into force.

SECTIONS 20–22

3.209   The remainder of the Act sets out supplemental provisions. Section 21 is the interpretation provision.[2] Section 22(2)[3] lists those parts of the statute (with one exception, none of them is of significance for business) which came into effect when the Act received Royal Assent (on 9 November 1998). Section 22(3)[4] in the meantime provides that the other provisions of the Act come into force on such day 'as the Secretary of the State may by order appoint' and that 'different days may be appointed for different purposes'.[5]

3.210   Following the (largely) trouble-free Parliamentary passage of the Human Rights Bill, a number of commentators called for the legislation's key features to be brought into force as soon as possible. Some senior judges on the other hand urged patience, principally because of the need to roll out programmes for judicial training.[6] At one point, the press speculated that the bulk of the Act would not come into force until 2001, but the matter was put beyond doubt on 18 May 1999 when the Home Secretary announced that the remaining provisions of the Act would come into force on 2 October 2000.[7] In the run-up to that date, there is a transitional provision of some importance and it is regrettable that it appears at no stage to have been discussed during the Parliamentary debates on the legislation.

3.211   Where a company (or indeed any natural person) is being proceeded against by a public authority, it appears to be able to rely on its European Convention rights whenever the relevant act of the public authority which is

---

1   See Hansard, HC, vol 348, col 496, 13 April 2000.
2   During the Parliamentary debates it was confirmed that the phrase 'primary legislation' covered statutes made before the Scottish and Irish Acts of Union of 1707 and 1801, respectively. Lord Hardie: Hansard HC, vol 585, col 416, 29 January 1998.
3   See Appendix 1.
4   See Appendix 1.
5   The rest of the Act comes into force on 2 October 2000. The Home Secretary signed the Commencement Order to that effect on 12 July 2000.
6   See, for example, Lord Bingham of Cornhill, then Lord Chief Justice, speaking on 9 January 1999: 'If I had to put money on a date, rather as if it were a general election, I should choose 1 October 2000'. See his keynote speech to the University of Cambridge Centre for Public Law reproduced in *The Human Rights Act and the Criminal Justice and Regulatory Process* (Hart Publishing, 1999).
7   See Home Office Press Release of 18 May 1999.

alleged to be incompatible with the European Convention took place.[1] This gives
the Act a form of retrospective effect and it means that public authorities cannot
assume that successful efforts on their part to comply with the Convention by 2
October 2000 will render them invulnerable in respect of their Convention-
incompatible acts before that date. As a result, it has been possible, since 9
November 1998, for the Act to be used by respondents in litigation (under
s 7(1)(b) of the Act),[2] initiated by a public authority or where the lawfulness of the
public authority's conduct in European Convention terms is in issue. However,
the Act cannot be used to initiate claims (under s 7(1)(a) of the Act)[3] against
public authorities for acts committed before the relevant part of the Act came into
force.[4] The scope of s 22(4), admittedly, is not entirely free from doubt in that a
defence raised under s 7(1)(b) is based on the unlawful act of a public authority as
defined in s 6(1) of the Act,[5] a section which only comes into force on 2 October
2000.[6]

The position of the offshore dependencies

3.212   Section 22(6) provides that the Act extends to Northern Ireland and
the statute's important place in the Government's programme of devolution
there and indeed elsewhere in the UK is looked at later.[7] Although the Act applies
to every part of the UK (with its three distinct legal jurisdictions: England and
Wales, Scotland and Northern Ireland), it does not apply to the Isle of Man or the
Channel Islands, which have important offshore financial centres, even though
the UK is under the European Convention responsible for them and obliged to
ensure that they comply with the European Convention.[8]

3.213   This is no mere exotic constitutional detail. Landmark cases from the
Isle of Man and the Channel Islands have in the past proceeded to Strasbourg and
led to findings of violations by the UK.

3.214   Certain features of the justice system in Guernsey, for example, were
thrown into sharp relief by the recent case of *McGonnell v United Kingdom*[9] in which
both the European Commission (Sir Nicholas Bratza QC concurring) and the
European Court (with Sir John Laws concurring) found that it was a breach of
Art 6 of the European Convention for Guernsey's Bailiff to have exercised both
legislative and executive functions in a local planning matter.[10] Towards the end
of 1997, during the Report stage of the debates on the Human Rights Bill, Lord
Henley had speculated in the House of Lords:

'... whether it would be possible for the court of appeal in Guernsey to say that
legislation relating to, for example, the outlawing of offshore trusts, something which

---

1   Section 22(4) of the Act, which is already in force. (See Appendix 1.)
2   See Appendix 1.
3   See Appendix 1.
4   See also s 7(1)(b) at **3.124** et seq and Appendix 1.
5   See Appendix 1.
6   See *Current Law Week*, vol 7, issue 6/99 and the case of *R v DPP, ex parte Kebilene* [1999] 3 WLR
     972.
7   See Chapter 4.
8   See Lord Williams' Written Answer of 12 January 1998.
9   (2000) 8 BHRC 56.
10   The case is more fully dealt with at **6.98**.

we have been promised by this Government, could be in breach of their human rights?'[1]

3.215   Lord Williams, replying for the Government, indicated that the Isle of Man and the Channel Islands did not (then) wish European Convention rights and freedoms to be incorporated into their own laws.[2] He said that the Isle of Man was planning to introduce a law of its own,[3] although the relevant authorities in the Channel Islands did not propose to follow suit, even if they had not ruled it out for the future.[4]

3.216   On 3 June 1998, during the debate at the Committee stage in the House of Commons, the matter was again raised, this time by Mr Austin Mitchell MP. His sympathies were clear:

'Rights should be protected in these small democracies and dependencies, which are intimate and closed – they are, in many respects, living loopholes from the twentieth century. There is no real party democracy that could make the legislature account-able, no open government and no base for dissent. The islands have their own tax regimes, which must cost our Exchequer billions of pounds in lost revenues. They do not have clear, powerful, effective financial regulations – they have become little offshore entrepots for the manipulation of money.

The islands have all the intimacies and pressures of any small community – they are like Salem without the witches ... The islands have been humorously described – by me – as one-party States run by the freemasons.'[5]

3.217   Such general, if colourful, references obscure the reality that the corporate and fiscal regimes that operate in these islands are not identical. Guernsey is not the same as Jersey, and Sark[6] is different from both. The newspaper proprietors, David and Frederick Barclay, filed a complaint at Strasbourg about Sark's feudal land-holding system and, specifically, the oper-ation of primogeniture, which they said prevented their settling the neighbouring island of Brecqhou (not recognised by the brothers as part of Sark) on their children.[7] In the event, on 24 November 1999, the relevant public authority on Sark, the Court of Chief Pleas, abandoned the principle of primogeniture, to all appearances an example of legislative change emanating from a Strasbourg complaint[8] (albeit one that had not been heard) without the need to give direct effect domestically to European Convention rights.

---

1   Hansard HL, vol 584, cols 1306 and 1307, 19 January 1998.

2   Hansard HL, vol 584, cols 1307 and 1308, 19 January 1998.

3   In one respect at least, the Isle of Man is further away from any domestication of the Convention in that the right to individual petition was removed from local people in 1976. The European Court had held in *Tyrer v United Kingdom* (1979) 2 EHRR 1 that judicial birching on the island violated Art 3 of the European Convention. In response, the British Government was induced by local interests to remove the islanders' Art 34 right.

4   Hansard HL, vol 584, col 1308, 19 January 1998.

5   Hansard HC, vol 313, col 465, 3 June 1998.

6   'I was told ... that a man in Sark still has the right to beat his wife provided that the stick is thinner than his thumb and he does not draw blood. I do not want to provoke a rush of public school Conservatives wanting to settle in the island as a result of that revelation, but it is a sign of the feudal nature of the regime in Sark and the abuses of rights that it produces': Austin Mitchell MP, Hansard HC, vol 313, col 467, 3 June 1979.

7   For an article critical of the Barclays' use of the Strasbourg institutions in this context, see *The Daily Telegraph*, 18 November 1999.

8   The Barclays have been reported as saying that the new law is inadequate (*The Times*, 10 December 1999).

3.218   By the middle of 1998, the Home Secretary was able to express confidence that law-makers on the islands wanted 'to bring rights home to the islands, just as [the Government was] ... doing in the United Kingdom'.[1] One may speculate as to the pressures exercising island administrators around this time. By September 1999, Jersey had begun work on draft legislation obviously based (subject to some limited local adaptation) upon the Act. A draft Bill was passed on 8 February 2000.[2] In the meantime, the Guernsey Parliament has been considering a form of incorporation along the lines of the Act. The expectation in both islands is that any legislation will come into force in 2002 at the earliest.

3.219   This has practical implications for business lawyers. The Act should enable financial institutions, for example, to rely on certain Art 6 safeguards in the event that disciplinary proceedings are instituted against them in the City of London. However, for the present, Jersey or Guernsey trust company subsidiaries of those same institutions will not be able to rely directly on such safeguards when proceeded against by regulators there (perhaps on charge which is virtually identical). The same goes for trust companies based on the Isle of Man. All the while, although branches of the relevant institutions based in Charlotte Square in Edinburgh are able to rely upon the Act, they may witness its application by Scottish judges in quite a different way from its application in England – an issue to which attention is now turned. In this way, the Act makes forum considerations of considerable practical significance.

---

1   Hansard HC, vol 313, col 471, 3 June 1999.
2   See http://mornet/library_new/Legislation/Draft_HumanRights_Law/ draft_human_rights-law.htm. The States Assembly, the Jersey Parliament, is (unsurprisingly) not to be a public authority under the legislation 'save that it will be unlawful for the Assembly to make subordinate legislation which is incompatible with a European Convention right or to acquire land by compulsory purchase pursuant to powers contained in any enactment which is incompatible with a Convention right'.

Chapter 4

HUMAN RIGHTS AND THE UK'S DEVOLVED INSTITUTIONS

4.1   In his Preface to the Government's White Paper on the Human Rights Bill,[1] the Prime Minister said that his administration was 'pledged to modernise British politics'. It was 'committed to a comprehensive programme of constitutional reform' with increased individual rights, decentralised power, open government and a reformed Parliament. One element of this programme was the move to give direct effect in local law to the European Convention. Another involved a determination to establish devolved administrations in Edinburgh and Cardiff with the aim of 'giving the people of Scotland and Wales more control over their own affairs within the United Kingdom'.[2]

4.2   This was not the first occasion on which a nexus had been suggested between devolution and human rights domestication. In 1977, the Conservative, Leon Brittan MP (then a Shadow spokesman), had suggested that the European Convention be incorporated in Scotland and Wales. This was at a time when the then Labour administration had introduced Scottish and Welsh devolution proposals.[3] That attempt at devolution failed and it is only recently, with the establishment of a Scottish Parliament and Assemblies in Wales and Northern Ireland, that the connection between devolution and human rights has again been made. It is an issue which has a considerable bearing upon the subject of this book, even though it is one which has been neglected by a number of the commentaries on the Act published so far. Its relevance derives from the fact that few British corporates are based solely in one of the four constituent parts of the UK and the differentiated approach to the Act which is likely to be taken in each makes a coordinated and pre-planned approach by businesses and their advisors to the legislation all the more difficult.

SCOTLAND

4.3   The Government's approach to devolution has been asymmetrical – deliberately so. This coincidentally parallels the distinct attitudes historically adopted towards the European Convention by judges in particular parts of the UK. Prior to the Act, the European Convention had only rarely been cited in Scottish courts, not least on account of local judicial hostility to it, to the extent that it could not, for a long period, be used (even) as an aid to construction, unlike

---

1   *Rights Brought Home: The Human Rights Bill* (Cm 3782) at p 1.
2   *Rights Brought Home* (see fn 1 above) at p 1. The Government has expressed confidence that none of these developments will encourage separatism. It is interesting to note in that context that a key reason for the introduction of the Canadian Charter of Rights and Freedoms was the perceived need for the whole of Canada to cohere around a set of common values in the face of secessionist pressure in Quebec. See R Penner's article 'The Canadian Experience with the Charter' [1996] PL 104.
3   Ironically, he was opposed by John Smith MP, then a junior Government Minister.

the position reached in England.[1] Only with the decision in the case of *T Petitioner*[2] did Scottish law come to enunciate an approach broadly similar to that prevailing in England.[3]

4.4   Against this background, it might have been assumed that the learning-curve to be plotted before the European Convention could be utilised creatively locally would be, if anything, steeper for Scottish lawyers and their business clients than for their counterparts south of the border. In the event, it has been the Scots who have been first to give a form of direct effect to the European Convention rights at the domestic level, albeit that they have done so not by invoking the Act, the relevant parts of which were not at the applicable time in force, but by invoking the Scotland Act, which created Scottish devolution.[4]

4.5   The Act, as has been seen, explicitly preserves Westminster's sovereignty. As a result, the position in Scotland with regard to statutes of the UK Parliament is the same as in England and Wales, ie the House of Commons and House of Lords together remain able to legislate in a way that is incompatible with the Convention. To the extent that the Act applies throughout the whole of the UK, Scottish courts are now required by ss 2 and 3 of the Act to take account of the European Convention and Strasbourg jurisprudence in just the same way as courts in other parts of the UK.

4.6   Whilst Westminster remains supreme, the subordinate position of the Scottish Parliament (at least as regards European Convention compliance) was flagged at the outset. The White Paper on the Human Rights Bill made the position clear: 'The Scottish Parliament will have no power to legislate in a way which is incompatible with the Convention'.

4.7   Similarly:

'... the Scottish Executive will have no power to make subordinate legislation or to take executive action which is incompatible with the Convention. It will accordingly be possible to challenge such legislation and actions in the Scottish courts on the ground that the Scottish Parliament or Executive has incorrectly applied its powers. If

---

1   See, for example, the comments of Lord Ross in *Kaur v Lord Advocate* [1981] SLT 322 and *Moore v Secretary of State for Scotland* [1985] SLT 38. See also JL Murdoch 'The European Convention on Human Rights in Scots Law' [1991] PL 40. The only judge to speak in opposition to the Human Rights Bill in the House of Lords was the distinguished Scottish peer, Lord McCluskey, as regards whom see **6.212**.
2   [1997] SLT 724 (Lord Hope).
3   Traditionally, few Scottish cases have proceeded to Strasbourg, although it is not clear that this was attributable solely to hostility to the European Convention on the part of Scottish judges. Scottish lawyers as a whole appeared less inclined to use the European Convention on behalf of clients, particularly when compared to lawyers in Northern Ireland. Admittedly the events there of the last 30 years have prompted the generation of a number of landmark Northern Ireland decisions in Strasbourg. See, for example, *Tinnelly and Sons Ltd and McElduff v United Kingdom* (1999) 27 EHRR 249, *Ireland v United Kingdom* (1978) 2 EHRR 25 (where the UK was taken to the European Court by another Member State (Ireland)) and *McCann v United Kingdom* (1996) 21 EHRR 97. Not all the cases have been a consequence, direct or indirect, of the terrorist campaign. See, for example, *Dudgeon v United Kingdom* (1981) 4 EHRR 149.
4   An excellent general treatment of the position in Scotland is A O'Neill *Judicial Review in Scotland* (Butterworths, 1999).

the challenge is successful then the legislation or action would be held to be unlawful.'[1]

4.8   The position, in short, is that the Act's provisions can be used to police the Edinburgh parliament and that parliament has no power to modify or abrogate the Act.

4.9   The relationship between the devolved administration in Edinburgh and the European Convention is set out in s 29 of the Scotland Act 1998. An act of the Scottish parliament is not law so far as any provision of that act is outside the parliament's legislative competence.[2] Section 29(2) provides that a 'provision' is outside that competence if, amongst other matters, 'it is incompatible with any of the Convention rights or with Community law'.[3] Indeed a measure 'incompatible with any international obligations' (and not just European Convention ones) may be stopped by the Secretary of State for Scotland.[4] Section 57(2) of the Scotland Act 1998 then provides that members of the Scottish Executive (who are the Ministers of the Scottish parliament and who include the Lord Advocate, Scotland's most senior law officer) cannot make Scottish laws or do any other act which is incompatible with Convention rights.

4.10   An interesting question arises as to what would happen if an act of the Scottish parliament were in substantially identical terms to an act of the Westminster Parliament. The latter, whether or not the subject of a compatibility statement under s 19(1)(a) and whether or not it results in a s 4 declaration of incompatibility, can potentially only be trumped by a judgment of the Strasbourg Court. The former is simply not a competent action of the Scottish parliament. The scenario is perhaps unlikely and indeed naïve in political terms, but it shows the potential for differential effect across the UK.

4.11   This is readily understood. The law of unforeseen consequences, however, has overtaken the Government as a consequence of the fact that the Scotland Act came into force long before the bulk of the provisions of the Act. The requirement in the Scotland Act that officers of the devolved institutions and the institutions themselves conform to the European Convention has meant, as is later explained,[5] that litigants before Scottish courts are able to assert their European Convention rights, albeit through the Scotland Act rather than the Act itself.

4.12   If a question arises as to whether the 'purported or proposed' exercise of a function by members of the Scottish Executive or the failure to act by a member of the Scottish Executive is incompatible with a European Convention right, it falls

---

1   *Rights Brought Home* (see fn 1 on p 97) at p 11.
2   Section 29(1) of the Scotland Act 1998.
3   Section 29(2)(d) of the Scotland Act 1998.
4   Section 35(1)(a) of the Scotland Act 1998. This is analogous to s 26(1) of the Northern Ireland Act 1998 (see **1.18**).
5   See **4.23** et seq.

to be disposed of as a so-called devolution issue and the Judicial Committee of the Privy Council is the final court of appeal for the determination of such issues.[1]

4.13   In any proceedings to be brought under the Scotland Act 1998 for breach of provisions of the European Convention, the necessity to establish victim status is the same as that set out in the Act.[2] Similarly, no damages can be awarded in a devolution case for an act incompatible with the European Convention if those damages could not be awarded under the Act.[3] While there is a time-bar of 1 year (subject to extension by exercise of discretion) upon the bringing of claims under the Act,[4] there is no time-bar in the Scotland Act upon the bringing of proceedings for breach of the European Convention. Lawyers will no doubt attempt to exploit this creatively, with human rights cases in Scotland acquiring a devolution gloss in order (it is hoped) to bring them within the Scotland Act when otherwise they would be out of time if brought under the Act.

WALES

4.14   England and Wales form one jurisdiction. In legislating for Welsh devolution, the Blair administration again determined that Westminster's overall sovereignty should be preserved and that adherence to the European Convention be made explicit. Thus, it was stated at the outset that:

> '... the Welsh Assembly [would] not have power to make subordinate legislation or take executive action which is incompatible with the Convention. It will be possible to challenge such legislation and action in the courts, and for them to be quashed, on the ground that the Assembly has exceeded its powers.'[5]

4.15   So, in the same manner as in Scotland, the Cardiff administration may not make, confirm or approve any subordinate legislation or do any other act incompatible with any European Convention right.[6] So, too, the requirements as to standing and for claiming damages are the same as provided in the Act.[7] As in Scotland, there is no limitation period for claims made under the Government of Wales Act 1998, according to which the final court of appeal is (once again) the Judicial Committee of the Privy Council.[8]

---

1   For example, the Privy Council is expected later in 2000 to hear an appeal in the important case of *Brown (Margaret) v Stott* [2000] SLT 379, in which the defendant established that a provision of the Road Traffic Act (not incidentally a devolved matter), making it an offence not to tell the police who was driving the defendant's vehicle, infringed the right to silence and against self-incrimination. The case has been described as 'momentous' and of potential UK-wide application (see *The Independent*, 9 February 2000).
2   Section 100(1) of the Scotland Act 1998.
3   Section 100(3) of the Scotland Act 1998.
4   Section 7(5) of the Act, see **3.143** et seq.
5   *Rights Brought Home* (see fn 1 on p 97) at p 11.
6   Section 107(1) of the Government of Wales Act 1998.
7   Section 107(2) and (4) of the Government of Wales Act 1998.
8   Whether or not it is a reflection of the fact that the Welsh Assembly has considerably less authority than the Scottish Parliament, it is noteworthy that Welsh devolution (and, in particular, its operation in the human rights context) has spawned little legal writing, quite unlike the position in Scotland.

4.16   Welsh lawyers were given a fillip when it was announced that applications for judicial review on devolution matters might be heard in Cardiff and that the Privy Council would be able to sit (for the first time) in Wales.[1]

NORTHERN IRELAND

4.17   The Northern Ireland Act 1998 provides for devolution in Northern Ireland. In terms of adherence to the European Convention, the regime is, for all material purposes, broadly the same as that established for Scotland and Wales. The White Paper in 1997 provided that:

> 'Acts of the Westminster Parliament will be treated in the same way in Northern Ireland as in the rest of the United Kingdom. But Orders in Council and other related legislation will be treated as subordinate legislation. In other words, they will be struck down by the courts if they are incompatible with the Convention.'[2]

4.18   Unlike other parts of the UK, Northern Ireland has by statute its own Human Rights Commission, which has already been established.[3] As already noted,[4] the Northern Ireland Human Rights Commission (NIHRC) has the power to consider human rights standards other than the European Convention and it would be surprising if campaign groups did not have it in mind to induce the NIHRC to advance proposals across a broad front in the hope that enhanced human rights guarantees will in due course be extended to the rest of the UK. The NIHRC is, for example, to help formulate 'rights not to be discriminated against and to equality of opportunity in both the public and private sectors'.[5]

4.19   In future, Bills of the Northern Ireland Assembly will require, following their introduction, to be sent to the NIHRC for advice as to their compatibility with Convention rights.[6]

4.20   A Bill of rights is to be introduced in Northern Ireland which will (notably) promulgate rights '*supplementary* to those in the [European Convention], to reflect the particular circumstances of Northern Ireland, drawing

---

1   *Practice Direction (Devolution Issues: Wales)* [1999] 3 All ER 466 per Lord Bingham of Cornhill LCJ.
2   *Rights Brought Home* (see fn 1 on p 97) at p 11.
3   It is defined as a non-departmental public body funded by grant aid of £750,000 per annum for its first 3 years (Written Answer by Mr George Howarth MP on 19 January 2000). By April 2000, the NIHRC had already intervened in seven court cases in terms of submitting *amicus* briefs (see *The Irish Times*, 3 April 2000).
4   See **1.18**.
5   Belfast Agreement (Cm 3883), para 4 of the section headed 'Rights, Safeguards and Equality of Opportunity'. See also the article by the NIHRC's First Commissioner, Brice Dickson 'New Human Rights Protection in Northern Ireland' [1999] 24 *EC Rev Human Rights Survey* 13.
6   Northern Ireland Act 1998, s 69(4)(a).

as appropriate on international instruments and experience' (emphasis added).[1]

4.21 As in Scotland and Wales, there are limitations on the matters to be devolved to the Northern Ireland Assembly. Reserved matters of relevance to business include:

–   data protection;[2]
–   consumer safety;[3]
–   regulation of anti-competitive practices;[4] and
–   stamps and postal regulations.[5]

THE INTERACTION TO DATE OF HUMAN RIGHTS AND DEVOLUTION

4.22 To the extent that the Act is an entrenched feature of the law of every constituent part of the UK,[6] it has a status not dissimilar to the Acts of Union (a fact upon which nationalist opinion may not wish to dwell), although its subordination to the sovereignty of Westminster arguably makes it less significant than the European Communities Act 1972.[7] The Government's own Guidance to (White-hall) Departments acknowledges[8] that human rights claims may be brought both under the Act and under the applicable devolution statute or under either of them and this has not been lost on practitioners in Scotland.

4.23 The European Convention had reputedly been cited in 374 devolved matters north of the border in the period to 2 March 2000, although it was reportedly decisive in only 10 of these, where in most instances the complaint was of unreasonable delay in court cases.[9] A startling example of the transformation of legal practice in Scotland is the *Starrs* case,[10] in which it was held that it would be a process breach in terms of Art 6 of the European Convention if a temporary sheriff (ie a part-time judge) were to hear a criminal case, because his appointment (like that of other temporary sheriffs) was in the gift of the Lord Advocate who, in his other capacity as chief prosecutor, is a party to all criminal proceedings north of

---

1   Belfast Agreement (fn 5 on p 101), para 4 of the section headed 'Rights, Safeguards and Equality of Opportunity'. A Parliamentary Human Rights Committee has been established at Westminster and a human rights commission is likely to be established in Scotland (see *Scotland on Sunday*, 23 April 2000). See also Lord Woolf's preface to Spencer's book (see fn 6 on p 7), where he said as regards the idea that there be a human rights commission for the whole of the UK: 'The most important benefit of a commission is that it will assist in creating a culture in which human rights are routinely observed, without the need for continued intervention in the courts'. Commissions have existed in France, Canada, New Zealand and Australia for some time and more recently were established in India, South Africa, Latvia, Sri Lanka and Uganda, to name but a few.
2   Northern Ireland Act 1998, Sch 3, para 40.
3   Northern Ireland Act 1998, Sch 3, para 37.
4   Northern Ireland Act 1998, Sch 3, para 26.
5   Northern Ireland Act 1998, Sch 3, para 7.
6   See, for example, s 129(2) of the Scotland Act 1998 and s 153(2) of the Government of Wales Act 1998.
7   See s 2(1) of the European Communities Act 1972.
8   See fn 6 on p 1, para 110.
9   Press Association, 2 March 2000.
10 A number of other significant Scottish cases are dealt with later, chiefly in Chapter 6.

the border. He also happens to be a member of the Scottish Executive and, thus, by virtue of s 53 of the Scotland Act 1998, susceptible to the provisions of the Act, including the need to conform to the European Convention. Claims will doubtless follow by those imprisoned by any of the 129 such sheriffs since 20 May 1999, when the Scotland Act 1998 came into force.[1] Politicians in the Edinburgh parliament have been quick to respond to a perceived lack of preparedness for such cases on the part of the Scottish Executive.[2] Indeed, it is suggested that the very first law passed by the Scottish parliament (amending existing mental health legislation) may violate the European Convention.[3]

4.24 The Government's devolution programme raises a wider question regarding the possible renaissance within the UK of forum-shopping – the notion that by electing in favour of one jurisdiction as opposed to another some tactical advantage may be secured.

4.25 Most domestic lawyers have tended to study forum-shopping in the international context, but henceforth they will need to have a more detailed knowledge of the differences characterising the three jurisdictions within the UK. The establishment of the NIHRC suggests that practitioners will also have to have more than a passing knowledge of multilateral covenants other than the European Convention.

---

1   It is all the more surprising that this debacle should have come about when the issue had apparently been a talking point in Scottish legal circles in recent years. See A Bonnington 'Scotland pays the price of justice on the cheap', in *The Times*, 13 November 1999.

2   See *The Daily Mail*, 15 February 2000.

3   See A Bonnington *The Times*, 15 February 2000 about the Mental Health (Public Safety and Appeals) (Scotland) Act 1999.

Chapter 5

KEY EUROPEAN CONVENTION CONCEPTS

5.1 The coming into force of the Act means that it is unlawful for a public authority (which includes a court) 'to act in a way which is incompatible with a Convention right'.[1] Furthermore (and as already noted[2]), an interpretative duty is imposed on British judges to 'read and give effect to primary legislation in a way which is compatible with the Convention rights' (insofar as it is possible to do so)[3] and to 'take into account' Strasbourg case-law when 'determining a question which has arisen in connection with a Convention right'.[4]

5.2 These obligations will not only have a considerable bearing upon traditional canons of interpretation that have been ingrained in the British judicial psyche but will also change the way in which public authorities go about their activities. In this chapter, the aim is to explain those core principles underpinning the Strasbourg jurisprudence which have emerged from decisions of the European Commission or the European Court and to which local judges (in particular) will need to have regard.

5.3 The explanation is in general terms only, as reference will be made to specific concepts when describing those particular European Convention rights of most significance for business. Beyond that, the aim is to highlight the considerations to be borne in mind when approaching any possible Convention-based issue.

CONSTRUING THE EUROPEAN CONVENTION

5.4 The primary role of interpreting the European Convention lies with the Strasbourg institutions. It is for them 'to elucidate, safeguard and develop the rules instituted by the Convention, thereby contributing to the observance by the [Contracting] States of [their] engagements'.[5]

5.5 The European Convention is a multi-lateral treaty (albeit a rather special one) to be construed in accordance with international law as set out in the Vienna Convention on the Law of Treaties 1969,[6] Art 31(1) of which requires that a treaty 'shall be interpreted in good faith in accordance with the ordinary meaning to be given to [its] ... terms in their context and in the light of its object and purposes'. The 'ordinary meaning' is not necessarily that used in the relevant Contracting State. As will be seen below (most importantly in connection with the right to a fair trial in Art 6[7]), the European Court, like the European Court of Justice in Luxembourg, has sought where necessary to identify an autonomous approach to

---

1   Section 6(1) of the Act. See **3.73** et seq and Appendix 1.
2   See **3.41** et seq.
3   Section 3(1) of the Act. See Appendix 1.
4   Section 2(1) of the Act. See **3.32** and Appendix 1.
5   *Ireland v United Kingdom* (1978) 2 EHRR 25.
6   Cm 7964. See also *Golder v United Kingdom* (1975) 1 EHRR 524.
7   See Chapter 6.

questions of construction – autonomous, that is, of constructions adopted locally. Contextual assistance (albeit limited) may be derived from the European Convention's Preamble and from the *travaux préparatoires*,[1] the preliminary work on the text which gave rise to the Treaty. The latter were, for example, reviewed in an important case from the UK on the compensation payable under Art 1 of the First Protocol for the expropriation of property.[2] Following the domestication of the European Convention, it is unclear to what degree local courts will choose (or need) to refer to the broad statements of principle to be found in the Preamble as regards, for example, the achievement of greater unity among Contracting States.

5.6   Unsurprisingly, the English and French language versions of the European Convention have equal status and are assumed to have the same meaning.[3] If differences do emerge between them, the task is to seek to reconcile the two, having regard to the European Convention's 'object and purpose'[4] and construing the Treaty as a whole.

5.7   When addressing the substantive rights forming part of the Convention, it will be for British judges 'to seek the interpretation that is most appropriate in order to realise the aim and achieve the object of the treaty, and not that which would restrict to the greatest possible degree the obligations undertaken by the parties'.[5] This adherence to a purposive (or so-called teleological) approach as opposed to a legalistic or technical one was shown by the case of *Pepper v Hart*[6] not to be unknown in local law[7] – indeed, EC law requires it – but it has in the past generally only been invoked where there is ambiguity. As a result of the Act, that limitation has now gone.

5.8   The Strasbourg institutions address questions of construction mindful of the importance of securing the objects of the European Convention, although they have also emphasised the importance of adhering to a text-based approach.[8]

5.9   This is not an entirely ground-breaking approach for commercial lawyers in the UK to assimilate. The European Court of Justice conceives part of its role as being 'to apply a body of unwritten legal principles which are common to the national legal and political systems of the [EU] Member States'. In other words, an aspect of the Court's role is to 'contribute to forming that philosophical, political and legal substratum common to the Member States from which emerges through the case-law an unwritten Community law, one of the essential aims of which is precisely to ensure ... respect for the fundamental rights of the individual'.[9]

---

1   Although, arguably, the use of such historical reference points is inconsistent with the need to look at the Convention in contemporary terms. See **5.12** et seq.
2   *James and Others v United Kingdom* (1986) 8 EHRR 123.
3   Article 33(3) of the Vienna Convention (see fn 6 on p 105).
4   Article 33(4) of the Vienna Convention (see fn 6 on p 105) and *James and Others v United Kingdom* (fn 2 above).
5   *Wemhoff v Germany* (1968) 1 EHRR 55 at para 8. This is, in fact, a departure from the general presumption of international law that treaty obligations should be construed narrowly as they are a derogation of sovereignty.
6   [1993] AC 593. See also **3.4** and **3.49**.
7   See Lord Diplock's comments in *Carter v Bradbeer* [1975] 1 WLR 1204 at 1206–1207.
8   There is a very helpful treatment of this area in JG Merrill's *The Development of International Law by the European Court of Human Rights* Manchester University Press, 1993, Chapter 4.
9   *Internationale Handelsgesellschaft GmbH v Einfuhr-und Vorratstelle für Getreide und Futter* [1972] CMLR 255 at 271.

British businesses have been litigating before Community courts on just this basis for almost 30 years.

5.10   The European Court considers that the European Convention is unlike other international treaties because it 'comprises more than mere reciprocal engagements between Contracting States'. Rather 'it creates, over and above a network of mutual, bilateral undertakings, objective obligations which, in the words of the Preamble, benefit from a "collective enforcement" '. This is because:

> '... the [European] Convention allows Contracting States to require the observance of those obligations without having to justify an interest deriving, for example, from the fact that a measure they complain of has prejudiced one of their own nationals.'[1]

THE ROLE OF PRECEDENT

5.11   One cultural and professional adjustment which local private lawyers are required to make as a result of the Act is to use as a professional tool a corpus of law (ie the Strasbourg jurisprudence) developed without any formal adherence to *stare decisis*. The European Court, however, has stressed that it 'usually follows and applies its own precedents, such a course being in the interest of legal certainty and the orderly development of the Convention'.[2] However, the judges do not make any distinctions between the *ratio* of any given case and its *obiter dicta*.

THE EUROPEAN CONVENTION AS A 'LIVING INSTRUMENT'

5.12   It is the broad framework in which the European Convention was necessarily drafted that facilitates its operation as a 'living instrument'.[3] Thus, in a case about birching policy in the Isle of Man (in which the phrase was first used) the Strasbourg judges considered that they could not 'but be influenced by the developments and commonly accepted standards in the penal policy of the Member States of the Council of Europe in this field'.[4] The term is generally understood to mean that the European Convention is to be interpreted in the light of the moral and social attitudes prevailing at the time any institutional decision is taken at Strasbourg and not when the Treaty was drafted. This undercuts the argument of those who would criticise the European Convention for its overt, post-War feel, and is wholly different from the traditional practice of British courts (in effect entrenched by *Pepper v Hart*[5]) of seeking to divine what the legislature had in mind when the statute under scrutiny was introduced.

5.13   In this way, the scope of and meaning attaching to the safeguards enshrined in the European Convention may evolve over time and one reason why previous Strasbourg decisions may, in effect, be disregarded is because of the need

---

1   *Ireland v United Kingdom* (1978) 2 EHRR 25.
2   *Cossey v United Kingdom* (1968) 1 EHRR 35.
3   *Tyrer v United Kingdom* (1978) 2 EHRR 1 at para 31.
4   Ibid at para 15.
5   See fn 6 on p 106.

to adapt the European Convention to changing conditions on the ground. As already noted, Strasbourg cases on similar facts will be persuasive but, unless involving the UK, will not be binding on British judges[1] and UK courts will be under a duty to test and reassess previous determinations of the European Court[2] in order to benchmark them against relevant societal changes. This living-instrument approach has been seen at work in the determinations of the Strasbourg institutions on questions of sexual orientation. In *Dudgeon v United Kingdom,*[3] it was held that the criminalisation of certain homosexual acts between consenting adults in Northern Ireland amounted to a breach of Art 8's guarantee of respect for private and family life.[4] The willingness of the judges in that case to recognise changing attitudes was reflected in their belief that:

> 'Although members of the public who regard homosexual acts as immoral may be shocked, offended or disturbed by the commission by others of private homosexual acts, this cannot on its own warrant the application of penal sanctions when consenting adults alone are involved.'[5]

5.14   Not only is the European Convention *not* to be preserved in a form of legal aspic, but it is also not to be construed literally. So it was that in the *Golder*[6] case the European Court determined that the fair trial guarantee in Art 6(1)[7] of the European Convention imported a right to legal representation, even though no such safeguard is to be found in the text of Art 6. Such inventiveness may make for a difficult process of adjustment on the part of some private lawyers in the UK following the domestication of the European Convention. It also does little to help practitioners predict the outcome of European Convention cases that come before the British courts. As van Dijk and van Hoof observe: 'the principle of evaluative interpretation begs the question where treaty interpretation ends and where treaty amendment begins'.[8] Unless care is shown, judicial interpretation of the European Convention should become judicial legislation, both in Strasbourg and London. It is reasonably clear from the jurisprudence that the European Court acknowledges the distinction, hence the decision in *Johnston v Ireland,*[9] where it was held that the Art 12 right to marry does *not* import a right to divorce, even though, at that time, divorce was permitted throughout most of Europe.

5.15   Some means of identifying what amounts to a contemporary continental standard should be a necessary element of the Strasbourg approach but, with countries as disparate as those now forming the Member States of the Council of Europe, eking out such a standard is necessarily problematic. The search for a consensus, or at least a consensus among a 'great majority of Contracting States',[10] is perfectly legitimate and probably inevitable, but its operation in practice has proved to be difficult.

---

1   Section 2 of the Act, see **3.22** et seq and Appendix 1.
2   And the other Strasbourg institutions: see s 2 of the Act (ibid).
3   (1981) 4 EHRR 149.
4   See Chapter 7 and Appendix 1.
5   A similar attitude has been evident in cases concerning illegitimacy (see, for example, *Marckx v Belgium* (1979) 2 EHRR 330 and corporal punishment in schools.
6   *Golder v United Kingdom* (1975) 1 EHRR 524. The case is discussed more fully at **6.75**.
7   See Appendix 2.
8   See fn 6 on p 45, at p 79.
9   (1986) 9 EHRR 203.
10   See *Marckx* (fn 6 above).

5.16 Some commonality in thinking may readily characterise State approaches to, for example, issues of national security, but as regards the status of, for example, transsexuals, there remain significant disparities in approach, so that the European Court has been obliged to say 'that the need for legal measures affecting transsexuals should be kept under review having regard in particular, to scientific and societal developments', as transsexuality touches 'on areas where there is little common ground amongst the Member States of the Council of Europe and, generally speaking, the law appears to be in a transitional stage, as a result of which the relevant respondent State must be afforded a wide margin of appreciation'.[1] In other words, where no consensus can (yet) be found, States will, depending upon the substantive European Convention right that is engaged, have a substantial area of discretion. This important subject is addressed below.[2]

POSITIVE AND NEGATIVE OBLIGATIONS

5.17 In one of its earliest pronouncements, the European Commission stated that:

> 'The obligations undertaken by the High Contracting Parties in the [European] Convention are essentially of an objective character, being designed rather to protect the fundamental rights of individual human beings from infringement by any of the High Contracting Parties than to create subjective and reciprocal rights for the High Contracting Parties themselves.'[3]

5.18 The European Convention does not lay down best-practice standards but minimum guarantees only. It is not intended to be the blueprint *par excellence* for human rights attainment – that is the job of national governments – and the fact that one country adheres to a higher standard than another does not without more mean that the latter is guilty of a European Convention violation.

5.19 The Treaty is predicated on the basis that States discharge *negative* obligations by refraining from unlawful interference with human rights whilst also taking *positive* steps to secure human rights.[4] Positive obligations may be the subject of express inclusion in the text of the European Convention[5] (although this is unusual) or otherwise have been enunciated (particularly recently) by the Strasbourg judges, most obviously in connection with Art 8's guarantee of respect for private life.[6] The need for positive steps to be taken by public authorities will be an important feature of the litigation arising out of the Act, for claimants will maintain that it may require the Government (if need be through the courts) to secure the requisite European Convention guarantees by intervening in matters affecting relations between private interests, thereby arguably giving the Act a form of so-called horizontal effect.[7]

---

1 *X, Y and Z v United Kingdom* (1997) 24 EHRR 143. See also *Rees v United Kingdom* (1987) 9 EHRR 56, *B v France* (1993) 16 EHRR 493, *Cossey v United Kingdom* (1993) 13 EHRR 622 and *Sheffield and Horsham v United Kingdom* (1999) 27 EHRR 163.
2 See **5.35** et seq.
3 *Austria v Italy* Appl 788/60 (1961) 4 Yearbook 116 at 138.
4 See Art 1 of the Convention at **3.10** et seq and Appendix 2.
5 Such as the obligation to organise free elections (in Art 3 of the First Protocol (see Appendix 2).
6 See Chapter 7.
7 See **3.74** et seq.

5.20   A positive obligation may require a State to take infrastructural, procedural or managerial steps to facilitate the attainment of a particular European Convention right where otherwise there might be a risk of individuals (including companies) infringing the human rights of others. In theory, such an obligation can be identified in relation to any European Convention safeguard. In fact, the Strasbourg institutions have identified positive obligations on a wholly piecemeal, case-by-case basis to date, with the nature of the right in issue and the seriousness of the alleged violation tending to be the most material considerations for the European Court in seeking to determine whether a (new) positive objection should be promulgated. Even then, however, it will generally be left to national governments to determine how their positive obligations come to be discharged.

PROPORTIONALITY

5.21   The idea of proportionality tends to attract overworked metaphors, but it was encapsulated in the era long before European Convention domestication by Lord Diplock, when saying that 'you must not use a steam hammer to crack a nut'.[1] Put another way, it is about the achievement of a reasonable relationship between ends and means. In circumstances where certain of the European Convention rights may be in competition,[2] the Strasbourg judges traditionally have been anxious to ensure that Contracting States strike a balance between 'the demands of the general interest of the community, and the requirements of the protection of the individual's fundamental rights'.[3] Central to the idea of a 'fair balance'[4] is the doctrine of proportionality. The concept is commonly described as having an all-pervasive influence upon the European Convention, even though it is nowhere referred to in the text.

5.22   British judges as a rule were reluctant to embrace the doctrine of proportionality, fearing that its application locally could be an 'abuse of their supervisory jurisdiction'[5] but, in fact, they have been determining questions involving proportionality for some time where EC law matters are in issue and the likelihood must be that that experience will be looked to when European Convention points call for determination.

5.23   In defining proportionality, the European Court of Justice in Luxembourg has said that a measure:

> '... should not exceed the limits of what is appropriate and necessary in order to obtain the objectives legitimately pursued by the legislation in question; when there is a choice between several appropriate measures, recourse must be had to the least onerous and the disadvantages caused must not be disproportionate to the aims pursued.'[6]

---

1   In *R v Goldstein* [1983] 1 WLR 151 at 155.
2   Most obviously, between Art 8's guarantee of respect for private and family life and the right to free expression in Art 10 (as to which see Chapters 7 and 8 respectively).
3   *Soering v United Kingdom* (1989) 11 EHRR 439 at 468.
4   Ibid.
5   *R v Secretary of State for the Home Department, ex parte Brind* [1991] 1 AC 696.
6   Case C-331/88 *Fedesa* [1990] ECR I-4023 at para 13.

On this basis, the obligation upon a public authority to be proportionate involves an analysis of the means to be engaged to secure a particular end and of the extent to which (if at all) those means are excessive in all the circumstances.

5.24   It has already been noted that, while some of the safeguards in the European Convention are absolute in nature,[1] others (generally including those of most relevance to business)[2] are not and it is primarily to such qualified rights that the doctrine of proportionality attaches. The qualified rights adhere to the same broad structure, whereby, in respect of each guarantee, the substantive protection is first identified before the forms of permissible State interference with that protection are made explicit. In other words, national authorities may legitimately apply limitations to qualified European Convention rights so far as permitted by the Treaty's express terms and those terms require that such limitations be 'in accordance with'[3] or 'prescribed by law'[4] and 'necessary in a democratic society'[5] – requirements to which attention is now turned.

The need for legality

5.25   The requirement for limitations upon European Convention rights to be *in accordance with* or *prescribed by* law (and the phrases are treated as synonymous) is an obvious constraint upon arbitrary action by the State. The need for an identifiable legal prescription is to ensure that, *as a minimum*, any interference by the State should have something more than a simple cosmetic basis in domestic law and that citizens ought to be able to identify in advance the legal basis for governmental activities. It is part of the rule of law whereby people are entitled to know where they stand so that they can regulate their conduct.[6]

5.26   While the democratic imperative behind such phraseology is clear, it is by no means certain what is meant by *law* in this context. Proceeding on the basis of a narrow construction, the European Court tends to look at 'the quality of the law, requiring it to be compatible with the rule of law'.[7] Therefore, there must be a legal regime which is readily ascertainable. It need not be statute-based and a common-law standard may suffice, provided it is decipherable and predictive. So too, the rules of a professional association such as the Law Society could be 'law' in European Convention terms.[8] On the other hand, 'a bare resolution in the breast of the legislator, without manifesting itself by some external sign, can never properly be law for it is requisite that this resolution be notified to the people who are to obey it'.[9] The legality requirement is therefore about ensuring that, where States want to curb rights for purported public interest reasons, they go about it in a transparent, coordinated way and, from now on, it is unlikely to be enough for

---

1   See, for example, Art 3 prohibiting torture or inhuman or degrading treatment and see also **2.6** et seq.
2   See, for example, Arts 8, 9 and 10 of the Convention.
3   Article 8, see Appendix 2.
4   Article 9, see Appendix 2.
5   Article 10, see Appendix 2.
6   See *Sunday Times v United Kingdom* (1979) 2 EHRR 245 at para 49.
7   *Malone v United Kingdom* (1985) 7 EHRR 14.
8   See, for example, *Barthold v Germany* (1985) 7 EHRR 383.
9   See H Mountfield *Fundamental Human Rights Principles: Defining the limits to Rights. The Concept of a Lawful Interference with Fundamental Rights.* UCL/JUSTICE Seminar notes, 5 October 1999, at p 3.

public authorities in the UK to seek to limit human rights on the basis of, for example, guidelines which have not been made public.

5.27   Whilst the Strasbourg judges have for a long time recognised that it is highly desirable that citizens are able to identify in advance the rules to which they are subject, they equally acknowledge that it may be appropriate in some circumstances to confer a discretion as regards the application of the law, as 'many laws are inevitably couched in terms which, to a greater or lesser extent, are vague and whose interpretation and application are questions of practice'.[1] What is essential in such circumstances is for the discretion not to be so wide or inchoate as to preclude an individual or corporate citizen from being able to determine quite how his or its conduct should be regulated.[2]

The need for a legitimate aim

5.28   National law can, of course, be a model of precision to which public authorities can point as unambiguously identifying limitations on rights, and which citizens (individual and corporate) would need to concede leave them in no doubt as to their position. However, that is not necessarily sufficient in European Convention terms, as any State-sanctioned interference with the rights espoused in Arts 8–11 must also be in pursuit of a *legitimate aim*. In seeking to identify the aim of any interference, the explanation put forward by a Contracting State will not necessarily be considered by the Strasbourg institutions to be in fact the real basis for the interference. Generally, however, the European Convention jurisprudence suggests that national governments are able to satisfy this requirement.

The democratic requirement

5.29   The European Convention resonates with democratic values to the extent that 'any interpretation of the rights and freedoms guaranteed [has] to be consistent with the general spirit of the Convention, an instrument designed to maintain and promote the ideals and value of a democratic society'.[3] The phrase 'necessary in a democratic society' has been described as requiring States to show that any interference with qualified European Convention rights 'corresponds to a pressing social need, and is proportionate to the legitimate aim pursued'.[4] It is for national authorities to make the initial assessment in each case as to the existence of a pressing social need.[5] *Necessary* means that the interference must be *needed* and the Strasbourg judges have emphasised that the word does not have the flexibility of such phrases as 'useful', 'reasonable' or 'desirable'.[6] It means also that the requirement for a *pressing social need* justifying the interference in question is unlikely to be met unless the interference is capable of meeting the relevant need and bears least onerously on the citizen, consistent with achieving

---

1   See *Sunday Times v United Kingdom* (1979) 2 EHRR 245 at para 47.
2   This is illustrated by certain telephone tapping cases considered later in relation to Art 8, see Appendix 2.
3   *Soering* (see fn 3 on p 110) at para 87.
4   *Silver v United Kingdom* (1983) 5 EHRR 344.
5   *Dudgeon v United Kingdom* (see fn 3 on p 108).
6   *Handyside v United Kingdom* (1976) 1 EHRR 737.

the purpose of the interference. In other words, the democratic imperative and the obligation of proportionality are to be considered together.

5.30   The Strasbourg judges have said that:

'... a restriction on a Convention right cannot be regarded as "necessary in a democratic society", two hallmarks of which are tolerance and broadmindedness, unless, amongst other things, it is proportionate to the legitimate aims pursued.'[1]

In cases involving the Act, it will be for public authorities convincingly to establish necessity in this context.

5.31   Democratic necessity does not mean bare utilitarianism, however. On the contrary, in the case of *Young, James and Webster v United Kingdom*, the European Court said that:

'Although individual interests must on occasion subordinate to those of a group, democracy does not simply mean that the views of a majority must always prevail: a balance must be achieved which ensures the fair and proper treatment of minorities and avoids any abuse of dominant position.'[2]

5.32   How is the doctrine of proportionality to be applied to the obligation upon States to ensure that certain limitations upon European Convention rights are borne of a democratic necessity? Coppel[3] succinctly picks out five tests to be applied:

–   a 'balancing' test, which essentially involves a weighing up of the relative impact (most obviously on the applicant) of the restriction imposed, and consideration whether this is justified by the reasonableness and importance of the end to be derived;[4]
–   a 'relevant and sufficient reasoning' test, which dictates that an interference will not be proportionate if it is not supportable in compelling terms;
–   a 'test of careful design', by which is meant that the interference should not be so wide as to have, for example, blanket application but should instead be tailored to the issue to be addressed;
–   an 'essence of the right' test, which holds that a restriction will infringe the proportionality test if it strikes at the heart of the right itself; and
–   an 'evidential' test, which requires that adequate factual justification will need to be adduced before an interference will be held to be proportionate.

5.33   The interaction between the requirement to identify a pressing social need (before State inference with a qualified European Convention right can be justified) and the doctrine of proportionality was addressed by the European Court in the *Dudgeon* case,[5] about the law then affecting homosexuals in Northern Ireland. There the European Court said:

'It cannot be maintained in these circumstances that there is a "pressing social need" to make such [ie homosexual] acts criminal offences, there being no sufficient

1   See *Dudgeon v United Kingdom* (see fn 3 on p108).
2   (1981) 4 EHRR 38.
3   J Coppel *The Human Rights Act 1998*, at pp 161–164.
4   See, in this context, *Thompson Newspapers Co Ltd v Attorney-General of Canada* [1998] 5 BHRC 567.
5   See fn 3 on p 108.

justification provided by the risk of harm to vulnerable sections of society requiring protection or by the effects on the public. On the issue of proportionality, the Court considers that such justifications as there are for retaining the law in force unamended are outweighed by the detrimental effects which the very existence of the legislative provisions in question have on the life of the person of homosexual orientation like the applicant ... Accordingly, the reasons given by the [British] government, although relevant, are not sufficient to justify the maintenance in force of the impugned legislation in so far as it has the general effect of criminalising private homosexual relations between adult males capable of valid consent.'[1]

THE EFFECTIVENESS PRINCIPLE

5.34   The Strasbourg institutions have constantly stressed the importance of rendering European Convention rights 'practical and effective' rather than 'theoretical and illusory'.[2] In determining whether rights have been infringed or (alternatively) adequately secured, the European Court will look beyond form to concentrate on the substance of the applicant's position. This emphasis on *effet utile* overlaps with the European Court's evolutive approach to construction and its interpretation of positive obligations, both already referred to.[3] The omission of Art 1 and, more particularly, Art 13 from the Act,[4] leaves uncertain the status of the effectiveness principle in local law.

THE MARGIN OF APPRECIATION[5]

5.35   Central to the jurisprudence developed by the Strasbourg institutions as regards their relationship with national authorities is the principle that there is a *margin of appreciation* by virtue of which Contracting States are granted a sphere of influence and a legitimate discretion in determining how they should implement and safeguard Convention rights. It is borne of a recognition that Member States have democratically elected administrations which should be permitted some latitude as regards the way in which they safeguard the rights in the Treaty, a latitude that reflects the history, culture and political philosophy of the various Member States. Like the idea of proportionality, the notion pervades Strasbourg law and extends beyond the key, qualified rights to be found in Arts 8–11. This principle of marginal appreciation is arguably a feature of the EC law notion of subsidiarity, the idea that the social, political and cultural traditions of a particular Member State are to be respected even if the area of competence of a supranational institution (such as, in the EC context, the European Commission

---

1   This statement is significant in its historical context in that in the 1950s the European Commission on a number of occasions dismissed applications by homosexuals as 'manifestly ill-founded'. See, for example, *X v Germany* Appl 5025/71, (1971) 14 Yearbook 692.
2   See, for example, *Airey v Ireland* (1979) 2 EHRR 305 and **6.79** et seq.
3   At **5.4** et seq and **5.17** et seq.
4   See **3.10** et seq.
5   See generally on this subject the Editorial in [1996] EHRLR p 229 at 230–232 and N Lavender *The Problem of the Margin of Appreciation* [1997] EHRLR 380. As to whether the margin of appreciation has any role after the Act, see **6.300**.

in Brussels) is thereby restricted.[1] Van Dijk and van Hoof suggest that it is a kind of 'counterweight' to the Strasbourg judges' interpretative activism[2] and that it is, in principle, relevant in all situations where proportionality is called for, with competing interests having to be weighed in the balance.[3]

5.36   The existence of a margin of appreciation in European Convention terms, is a recognition that, in relation to human rights:

> '... it is not possible to find in the domestic law of the various Contracting States a uniform European conception of morals. The view taken by their respective laws of the requirements of morality varies from time to time and from place to place, especially in an era which is characterised by a rapid and far-reaching evolution of opinions on the subject. By reason of their direct and continuous contact with the vital forces of their countries, State authorities are in principle in a better position than the international judge to give an opinion on the exact content of the requirements [of morals] or the "necessity" of a "restriction" or "penalty" intended to meet them.'[4]

5.37   The importance of the idea of a margin of appreciation therefore lies in its deference to local customs and practices, and the fact that it represents a form of philosophical devolution of authority from Strasbourg. It has been described as 'a lubricant at the interface between individual rights and public interest'[5] and as a means of preserving 'the marvellous richness and inexhaustible variety' of Europe.[6] Optimists would say that it complements continent-wide supervision of human rights because the deference accorded natural governments is residual – they are only given the room for manoeuvre which the Strasbourg institutions say they should have. Certainly, it is consistent with the notion of the European Convention's text as a living and evolutive instrument. If the European Convention is to be truly reflective of the changing values of European society, then who better to dictate or at least define those values than the Contracting States of the Council of Europe? What is more, it is suggested that the doctrine makes for transparent and consistent judicial reasoning at Strasbourg[7] and that 'Through the margin of appreciation the [European] Court sends the message that it will not disregard national particularities'.[8]

5.38   That is one view. The margin of appreciation has also been described as a 'hackneyed phrase',[9] and as 'a spreading disease'.[10] The counter-argument is that the scope of the margin of appreciation is hopelessly difficult to define in the abstract because it is, by definition, in a constant state of flux, changing in accordance with particular national circumstances. It does not lend itself to the

---

1   The Brussels comparison is apt, as John Major's administration (which faced such difficulties over EU matters) was at one time reported as wanting to see a wider application of the doctrine when London's relationship with Strasbourg cooled. See, for example, *The Irish Times*, 7 May 1996.
2   See fn 6 on p 45, at p 95.
3   Ibid, at p 85.
4   See *Handyside v United Kingdom* (1976) 1 EHRR 737.
5   DJ Harris, M O'Boyle and C Warbrick *Law of the European Convention on Human Rights* (Butterworths, 1995), pp 15–16.
6   Judge Matscher in 'Methods of Interpretation of the Convention' in Macdonald, Matscher and Pitzhold *The European System for the Protection of Human Rights* (Martinus Nijhoff, 1993).
7   Van Dijk and van Hoof (see fn 6 on p45) at pp 93–95.
8   Ibid, at p 93.
9   Judge de Meyer in *Z v Finland* [1997] EHRLR 439.
10   Van Dijk and van Hoof (fn 6 on p 45).

articulation of a coherent set of principles and, indeed, it is conceivably used to avoid the need to articulate them. Lord Lester, for example, has lamented the fact that 'the concept of the margin of appreciation has become as slippery and elusive as an eel'.[1]

5.39 The margin of appreciation does not preclude Strasbourg review. On the contrary, the European Court has stressed that the margin of appreciation goes 'hand in hand with European supervision ... which obliges it to pay the utmost attention to the principles characterising a "democratic society" '.[2] Therefore, the claim by a Contracting State that a particular matter falls within the margin of appreciation is not treated as conclusive in European Convention terms. The greater the interference with human rights that is in issue, the better the justification for the interference will need to be. National governments may make the initial determination, but that will not deprive the Strasbourg judges of their broad, supervisory powers.

5.40 The margin is, by definition, not therefore a uniform one and 'not only the nature of the aim of the restriction but also the nature of the activities involved will affect the scope of the margin of appreciation'.[3] Thus, in the *Dudgeon* case, which concerned 'a most intimate aspect of private life', the European Court held that 'there must exist particularly serious reasons before interference on the part of the public authorities can be legitimate for the purposes of paragraph 2 of Article 8'.[4] So too:

> 'In spheres such as housing, which plays a central role in the welfare and economic policies of modern societies, the [European] Court will respect the legislative's judgment as to what is in the general interest unless that judgment is manifestly without reasonable foundation.'[5]

5.41 In broad terms, it may be stated that the margin operates across a spectrum and will be widest (ie most deferential to States) where, for example, a public emergency or national security issue is involved (as the UK argued for many years with considerable success in relation to cases emanating from Northern Ireland) or where matters of profound personal belief affecting religion or morality (often highly disputatious) are in issue. The deference accorded a Member State will also be wide where the matter in issue is a conflict or tension between two or more European Convention rights and where the conflict may arise as a function of the historic and cultural values in a particular Member State. As will be seen in connection with the analysis of certain substantive European Convention rights that follows, the margin of appreciation is often invoked when the qualified rights in Arts 8–11 and Art 1 of the First Protocol[6] are in issue,[7] but its role is more limited when determining technical, procedural issues arising in connection with Art 6 and no limit on its application to particular rights has ever been put.

---

1   In his article *Universality versus Subsidiary: A Reply* [1998] ERLR 73 at p 75. See also **2.21**.
2   *Dudgeon v United Kingdom* (see fn 3 on p 108) at paras 48–49.
3   Ibid.
4   Ibid.
5   *Immobiliare Saffi v Italy* [1999] 7 BHRC 256.
6   See Chapter 9 and Appendix 2.
7   Especially in relation to revenue and planning matters, as to which see Chapter 9.

5.42   The Strasbourg jurisprudence suggests that the boundaries of the marginal appreciation doctrine will vary depending on whether a consensus can be identified among Member States, on the basis that, where 'the Contracting States reveal a fairly substantial measure of common ground' in a particular area, 'more extensive European supervision corresponds to a less discretionary power of appreciation'.[1] Put another way, if a continent-wide standard is adjudged to exist, there is logically less scope for the residual operation of the margin of appreciation. The fact that many people in Northern Ireland had a different opinion regarding homosexual practices from many citizens in the rest of Europe did not therefore justify the continuing criminalisation of such practices in the Province in circumstances where it was for the European Court to make the final determination.

5.43   The margin of appreciation is an international doctrine and, as such, should have no strict place in local law following the domestication of the European Convention.[2] While the doctrine was introduced as a reflection of the practical difficulty in a multilateral setting of reconciling all disparate local, political and cultural traditions, it can have no domestic role to play within a State, not least when the doctrine of proportionality is flexible and broad enough to allow for deference to public authorities in areas of policy sensitivity. Whether, in fact, it does insinuate itself into British courts through the Act is one of the most interesting jurisprudential questions thrown up by the legislation. Certainly, it is the case that it is the margin of appreciation which, all other issues aside, has been decisive in very many Strasbourg complaints and, as Coppel reminds us,[3] whether it be termed a margin of appreciation or not, the notion that public authorities have a residual area of permissible discretion is a basic feature of our common law and that residual area of legitimate movement will continue to be accepted by judges here for the foreseeable future.[4]

DISCRIMINATION

5.44   Critics on the left have long complained that the European Convention does not promulgate a right to equality or even a wholesale guarantee against discrimination.[5] Art 14 provides as follows:

'*Prohibition of Discrimination*

The enjoyment of the rights and freedoms, set forth in this Convention[6] shall be secured without discrimination on any ground such as sex, race, colour, language, religion, political or other opinion, national or social origin, association with a national minority, property, birth or other status.'[7]

---

1   *The Sunday Times v United Kingdom* (1979) 2 EHRR 245 at para 59.
2   See, for example, Lord Woolf in *Attorney-General of Hong Kong v Lee Kwong-Kut* [1993] AC 951 at 966–967.
3   See fn 3 on p 113, at p 165.
4   For an analysis of the implications of the Act for domestic judicial review generally, see **6.308** et seq.
5   See **2.12**.
6   Including all the various protocols.
7   See Appendix 2.

5.45   The complaints attaching to Art 14 have been such that, since the 1960s, consideration has been given to the incorporation of an explicit right to equality in the text of the European Convention. A draft text, which would be introduced in what would become the treaty's Twelfth Protocol, is currently under discussion. It includes the covenant that 'No-one shall be discriminated against by any public authority' on any ground *such as* those already identified in Art 14.[1]

5.46   Wadham and Mountfield[2] describe Art 14 as 'a guarantee of equality before the law of the Convention' rather than a condemnation of discrimination *per se*. It has, as already noted,[3] a parasitical relationship with the other substantive rights in the European Convention in that it cannot be invoked on a free-standing basis – hence its description as 'an accessory right'[4] importing 'an autonomous though complementary guarantee'.[5] Although Art 14 must be invoked in combination with some other right, it is not necessary for an arguable violation of that other right to be established, provided the facts in issue 'fall within the ambit' of another European Convention right (and it must be a European Convention right)[6] – a requirement which tends readily to be met,[7] even where the essence of the complaint is the discrimination element.[8] Where a violation of an Article other than Art 14 is established, the European Court will generally not consider the question of discrimination unless it is perceived to be a fundamental feature of the case.[9]

5.47   The categories of unjustified, unequal treatment expressly set out in Art 14 are, by virtue of the phrase *such as*, plainly intended to be relied upon by way of example and are not definitive. Despite that, many complaints of discrimination at Strasbourg fail as a result of a lack of evidence, the complainant being unable to establish a relevant benchmark or analogy. The treatment of married couples may not therefore be compared with the treatment of unmarried couples[10] or pupil barristers be compared to apprentices in other professions.[11] What needs to be established is more than a difference in treatment. Also material will be the existence of any purportedly legitimate aim for the differentiation and a consideration of the effect of the measure about which complaint is made. The existence of a 'reasonable relationship of proportionality between the means employed and the aim sought be realised'[12] will be significant too. Companies which are public authorities will need to consider what justification they can offer for a measure which is otherwise discriminatory. Could any alternative be found?

1   See, generally, G Moon *The Draft Discrimination Protocol to the European Convention on Human Rights: A Progress Report* [2000] EHRLR 49.
2   See fn 4 on p 1.
3   See **2.12**.
4   Van Dijk and van Hoof (see fn 6 on p 45) at p 711.
5   Ibid at p 716.
6   See *Marckx v Belgium* (1979) 2 EHRR 330 at para 50.
7   See, for example, *Schmidt and Dahlström v Sweden* (1979–1980) 1 EHRR 632.
8   See *Rasmussen v Denmark* (1984) 7 EHRR 371 at para 29.
9   See, for example, *Airey v Ireland* (1979) 2 EHRR 305 at para 30. A good recent example of the European Court's determination to deal expressly with the discrimination aspect even though another Article violation had been established is *Chassagnou v France* (2000) 29 EHRR 615, as to which see Chapter 9.
10   See *Lindsay v United Kingdom* (1986) 49 DR 181.
11   See *Van der Mussele v Belgium* (1985) 6 EHRR 163.
12   See *Case Relating To Certain Aspects Of The Laws On The Use Of Languages In Education In Belgium* (1968) 1 EHRR 252.

5.48   Discrimination is constituted not merely by treating similar cases differently. It can also arise where the different is treated as being the same. In the recent case of *Thlimmenos v Greece*,[1] the European Court said that 'The right not to be discriminated against in the enjoyment of rights guaranteed under the Convention is also violated when States without an objective and reasonable justification fail to treat differently persons whose situations are significantly different'.

5.49   Even in matters of discrimination, a margin of appreciation exists, although its scope may vary depending upon the kind of discrimination in issue, with complaints based on sex and nationality requiring very serious justification if a violation is not to be shown.[2]

5.50   Arts 6 and 14 were considered together in the so-called *Belgian Linguistics (No 2)* case,[3] which confirmed that, where a Contracting State goes beyond what the European Convention may otherwise require in terms of safeguarding a right, Art 14 may still have a bearing upon that added-value right. Thus:

> 'Article 6 of the Convention does not compel States to constitute a system of appeal courts. A State which does set up such courts consequently goes beyond its obligations under Article 6. However, it would violate that Article, read in conjunction with Article 14, were it to debar certain persons from these remedies without legitimate reason while making them available to others in respect of the same type of actions.'[4]

5.51   *Indirect* discrimination (ie discrimination deriving from a practice applied without differentiation, but bearing disproportionately on one group) is probably caught by Art 14, although there is no direct authority on the point. A tax case from the UK suggests on the other hand that *positive* discrimination may not be a European Convention violation on the basis that the aim of addressing some perceived form of historical inequality is ostensibly a legitimate one. Thus, taxing women more favourably than men in an equivalent position in the hope of encouraging the former to stay in work was not a breach of Art 14.[5] Differential tax treatment on the ground of administrative convenience is not, however, permissible.[6]

5.52   The grossest forms of discrimination (generally on grounds of sex or race) may conceivably engage Art 3 as being degrading treatment.[7] Regional differences within Contracting States may not, however, necessarily be discriminatory where the difference is a matter of geography and not characteristics personal to the complainant. Introducing the poll tax in Scotland before England and Wales, therefore, was not an Art 14 violation.[8] This is unsatisfactory. It is unlikely that the Strasbourg judges would ever adopt a position whereby laws would be required to operate identically within a country, but what about the tuition fee debate in Scotland or the refusal of the Labour Party to admit to

---

1   Appl 34369/97, 6 April 2000.
2   See, for example, *Lithgow and United Kingdom* (1986) 8 EHRR 329 and *James v United Kingdom* (1986) 8 EHRR 123.
3   See fn 12 on p 18.
4   Ibid.
5   *Lindsay v United Kingdom* (see fn 10 on p 118).
6   *Darby v Sweden* (1990) 13 EHRR 744 at para 33.
7   See, for example, *East African Asians v United Kingdom* (1973) 78 DR 5 and *Abdulaziz, Cabales and Balkandali v United Kingdom* (1985) 7 EHRR 471.
8   Appl 13473/87, 11 July 1988.

membership residents in Northern Ireland?[1] Are these not issues affecting a national minority as understood in Art 14?

5.53   Not every difference is discriminatory in European Convention terms, indeed to forbid every difference in treatment might produce 'absurd results',[2] the European Court has said, seeking to quell fears deriving from a concern about the wider scope of the French text and its reference to *sans distinction aucune*.

5.54   Article 14 is wider in scope than the existing domestic law and may make a difference in relation to discrimination complaints based on sexual orientation, age, property or religion not yet statutorily covered in the UK (save, so far as religion is concerned, in Northern Ireland). Insofar, however, as the provision does not embody a right to work, it may be much less significant in the employment context. A treatment of the European Convention's approach to discrimination has been included here because Art 14 needs to be looked at closely in addressing the limitations to the substantive rights in Arts 8–11 (which will have significance for the commercial sector) to ensure that those limitations are not applied in a discriminatory way.

THE RELATIONSHIP BETWEEN EC LAW AND THE EUROPEAN CONVENTION

5.55   The relationship between Brussels and Strasbourg jurisprudence is not straightforward. Certainly, it has yet to be delineated coherently. In circumstances where in 1993 it was estimated that nearly 70% of commercial law in the future was likely to derive from the EU,[3] the uncertainties in this area are all the more regrettable.

5.56   The Treaty of Rome, which established the European Economic Community and is, like the European Convention, a framework treaty to be construed dynamically, made no reference to the European Convention (nor indeed to human right concepts of any sort) and although all the Member States of the EU are signatories to the European Convention, the EU itself is not. As such, therefore, the Strasbourg judges cannot review (in a supervisory sense) the decisions of the European Court of Justice in Luxembourg[4] as the European Convention binds EU Member States, but not Community institutions.

5.57   Some of the early case-law emanating from the ECJ exhibited a reluctance to accept the notion that the European Convention had any part to play in EC law.[5] Over the last 30 years, however, the ECJ has come to acknowledge that a discrete and autonomous slew of fundamental human rights must be given effect to as part of the general principles of EC law[6] and, further, that 'respect for

---

1   It is, of course, arguable that a political party is not a public authority.
2   See the *Belgian Linguistic* case (fn 12 on p 118).
3   See the *Review of the Implementation and Enforcement of EC Law in the United Kingdom* (DTI, 1993).
4   See *CFDT v European Communities* (1978) DR 13 231.
5   See, for example, *Stork v High Authority* [1959] ECR 17 and *Ruhr v High Authority* [1960] ECR 47.
6   For a recent case confirming the principle, see *Emesa Sugar (Free Zone) NV v Aruba (C17/98) (No 2)* (2000) *The Times*, 29 February.

human rights is a condition of the lawfulness of Community acts'.[1] Specifically, the Luxembourg Court has said that a Community measure which infringes a fundamental human right will be struck down by the European Court of Justice.[2] The Court has also confirmed that fundamental human rights are capable of limiting the legislative competence of the Community institutions themselves and that respect for fundamental rights forms an integral part of the general principles of law protected by the Court,[3] deriving as such rights do from the 'international treaties for the protection of human rights on which Member States have collaborated or of which they are signatories'.[4]

5.58   Explicit institutional acknowledgement of the extent to which the European Convention now bears directly on EC norms can be found in Art F(2) of the Treaty on European Union (as amended by the Amsterdam Treaty of 10 October 1997) which states that: 'The Union is founded on the principles of liberty, democracy, respect for human rights and fundamental freedoms'. It continues: 'the Union shall respect fundamental human rights as guaranteed by the [European Convention] and as they result from the constitutional traditions common to the Member States, as general principles of Community law'. The effect of this provision is to transform the European Convention from being a 'source of inspiration' into an *incorporated* part of EC law's general principles.[5]

5.59   Notwithstanding the fact that the European Convention now enjoys 'special significance' within the Community legal order (and is indeed a condition of Community membership), it remains kept within bounds and the ECJ has stressed that 'it is not bound, insofar as it does not have systematically to take into account, as regards fundamental rights under Community law, the interpretation of the Convention given by the Strasbourg authorities'.[6] Nor, furthermore, has the ECJ any power to examine the compatibility with the European Convention of national legislation falling outside the scope of EC law.[7]

5.60   It is on this basis that the ECJ's fundamental rights doctrine remains distinct from that enshrined in the European Convention. To a degree, this is understandable, for although the EU exists to discharge a greater variety of objectives, its foremost driver is economic considerations, whereas the Strasbourg system is concerned only with human rights protection. Each has different imperatives and this is doubtless the principal reason why EU accession to the European Convention is unlikely for the foreseeable future, as it would entail the EU joining a different multilateral system with its own enforcement machinery, the institutional implications of which would conceivably require amendment of the Treaty of European Union.[8] It follows that the ECJ will not have regard for

---

1   Paragraph 34 of Opinion 2/94 on Accession by the Community to the ECHR [1996] ECR I-1759.
2   *Stauder v City of Ulm* [1969] ECR 419.
3   *Internationale Handelsgesellschaft v Est* Case 11/70, [1970] ECR 1125.
4   *Nold v Commission* Case 4/73 [1974] ECR 491 at 507, para 13. In *Rutili v Minister for the Interior* [1975] ECR 1219 at para 13 the ECJ decided that it was in fact the European Convention which was the source of the Community law principle that human rights ought to be respected.
5   See *Elliniki Radiophonia Tileorassi AE v Dimotiki Etairia Pliroforissis* [1991] ECR I–2925 at para 41.
6   *Orkem v Commission* [1989] ECR 3283 at para 140. See also **6.130**.
7   *Demirel v Stadt Schwabish Gmund* [1987] ECR 3719 at para 28.
8   See Opinion 2/94 (fn 1 above).

European Convention jurisprudence save insofar as it bears upon European Community issues. Where it does, the ECJ's interpretation and application of the European Convention will, within the ECJ's own jurisdiction, prevail.

5.61   As will be seen, this uneasy relationship has given rise to a number of examples of inconsistencies between decisions emanating from Luxembourg and from Strasbourg, where very different conclusions on similar facts have been reached in cases involving, for example, Art 10[1] and Art 8.[2]

5.62   This is not satisfactory and, in relation at least to fair trial procedures, the Advocate-General of the European Court of Justice has said that it is 'far from unimportant to avoid conspicuous discrepancies'.[3] If a local court is forced, because of inconsistency between the two, to choose between the European Convention and EC law, it must defer to the latter because it is obliged to do so by virtue of the European Communities Act 1972, and that reality is entirely unaltered by the Act's domestication of the European Convention. To that extent, companies who challenge the legality of dawn raids will still have to overcome the decision in, for example, the *Hoechst*[4] case, notwithstanding the later, more helpful, decision of the European Court in *Niemietz*.[5]

5.63   In tactical terms, this could mean that in certain circumstances Community law may offer more for the business litigant than the European Convention. It may also mean that the best way to exploit European Convention rights is *through* Community law because of the latter's ability to prevail over inconsistent domestic law and because the European Convention's guarantees, now part of EC law, can by the EC route be made to trump domestic law too. In this way (only) are the European Convention's guarantees fully incorporated in the UK.[6]

5.64   Some of the advantages to be derived from putting a case on a Community as opposed to a European Convention basis will be procedural (involving the different rules as to standing for example),[7] but others will concern the substance of rights protection – the High Court being able to disapply statutes inconsistent with directly effective EC law (but not other forms of law), whereas a Convention-incompatible statute cannot be disapplied, only made the subject of a declaration of incompatibility under s 4 of the Act.[8] A European Convention right may therefore be better protected if it can be subsumed within an EC law argument and policed outside the reach of the Act, an ironical outcome perhaps

---

1   Cf *SPUC v Grogan* [1991] ECR I-4685, where the European Court of Justice held that a prohibition against dissemination of information in Ireland about the availability of abortion services was not a breach of EU law and where it did not address the suggestion of a breach of Art 10 of the Convention and *Open Door Counselling and Dublin Well Woman v Ireland* (1993) 15 EHRR 244, where the European Court held that such a prohibition would breach Art 10.

2   See *Hoechst AG v Commission* [1989] ECR 2859 and *Niemietz v Germany* (1993) 16 EHRR 297 for inconsistencies as regards Art 8 and *Orkem v Commission* (fn 6 on p 121) and *Funke v France* (1992) 16 EHRR 297 for inconsistencies regarding Art 6. See also Chapters 7 and 6 respectively.

3   *Al Jubail Fertiliser Co and Saudi Arabian Fertiliser Co v Council* [1991] ECR I-3187.

4   See fn 2 above.

5   See fn 2 above.

6   See *Johnston v Chief Constable of the RUC* [1986] ECR 1651 as an example of the use of EC law in this way.

7   See **3.129** et seq.

8   See **3.58** and Appendix 1.

but one emanating directly from the fact that Parliament is not made a public authority in the Act and is not as such required in theory to adhere to the European Convention.

5.65 Although the conflict between EC law and European Convention law (specifically, in terms of this book's focus, as regards rights protection in the context of competition inquiries) remains unresolved,[1] it must be emphasised that the European Court of Justice has taken account of the European Convention since 1975[2] (although the Strasbourg jurisprudence was first adverted to in 1996 only).[3] Many of the key principles discussed in this chapter, such as proportionality, non-discrimination and the need for legal certainty, are common to both courts. As such, it has been said that 'the principles, though not the text of the (European) Convention, now inform the law of the European Union'[4] and if the Strasbourg approach may accurately be described as teleological, so too is the Luxembourg one.

5.66 The single key message for the business lawyer and his client is not perhaps of the tensions existing between both systems but of the fact that the Act leaves unaffected the ability to challenge primary Westminster legislation[5] and if need be, to seek its dis-application, for failing to meet the standards for EC human rights protection. This could conceivably be of real, tactical significance in commercial litigation. In short, Strasbourg jurisprudence is moving centre stage, not just in London, but (albeit at a slower velocity) in Brussels and Luxembourg too.

---

1   See generally in this area the chapter by D Spielmann 'Human Rights Case Law in the Strasbourg and Luxembourg Court: Conflicts, Inconsistencies, and Complementarities' in P Alston (ed) *The EU and Human Rights* (Oxford University Press, 1999).

2   *Rutili v Minister for the Interior* (see fn 4 on p 121) at para 32.

3   In the case *P v S and Cornwall County Council* [1996] ECR I-2143 at 2164. There were three other references between 1996 and 1998.

4   Sedley J (as he then was) in *R v Home Secretary, ex parte McQuillan* [1995] 4 All ER 400 at 422.

5   See, for example, *Elliniki Radiophonia Tileorassi AE v Dimotiki Etairia Pliroforissis* (see fn 5 on p 121).

Chapter 6

LITIGATION AND REGULATION AFTER THE ACT

6.1 The citizen's fundamental constitutional right to a fair hearing has been such an indispensable feature of our legal system for so long that it might be regarded as trite to say so. Indeed Lord Bingham, when Lord Chief Justice, said that it called for no citation of authority.[1] The notion is also central to the jurisprudence of the European Court, even though the European Convention does not, in terms, define a fair hearing.

6.2 Across the Continent the right to a fair hearing is an aspect of the rule of law, a feature of the common heritage that in part encouraged the Contracting States to draft the Treaty in the first place. It is also held to be a prominent feature of a democratic society[2] and is to be given a flexible interpretation – indeed, there can be no justification for construing it narrowly.[3] The key at all times is fairness – more than justice, a word not mentioned in Art 6, the part of the European Convention that articulates the fair trial guarantee. More than any other, it is this safeguard which will generate (and be a feature of) domestic litigation arising from the Act. There is already some sign of this happening on an incremental basis, with 181 reported references to Art 6 in UK courts in the period from the day on which the Act obtained royal assent (9 November 1998) to 24 May 2000,[4] less than 5 months before the Act's wholesale introduction. Numbers of those references were in civil cases, a pattern likely to be repeated in the future, although it is in the criminal sphere that the impact of the Act will probably be greatest, reflecting the relevance in the criminal context not only of Art 6 but also of Arts 5[5] and 7[6] of the European Convention.[7]

6.3 Article 6 provides:

'Right to a fair trial

1.   In the determination of his civil rights and obligations or of any criminal charge against him, everyone is entitled to a fair and public hearing within a reasonable time by an independent and impartial tribunal established by law. Judgment shall be pronounced publicly but the press and public may be excluded from all or part of the trial in the interest of morals, public order or national security in a democratic society, where the interests of juveniles or the protection of the private life of the parties so require, or to the extent strictly necessary in the opinion of the Court in special circumstances where publicity would prejudice the interests of justice.

2.   Everyone charged with a criminal offence shall be presumed innocent until proved guilty according to law.

3.   Everyone charged with a criminal offence has the following minimum rights:

---

1   In *R v Director of Public Prosecutions, ex parte Kebilene and Others* [1999] 3 WLR 972.
2   *De Cubber v Belgium* (1991) 13 EHRR 422.
3   *Delcourt v Belgium* (1970) 1 EHRR 355 and *Moreira de Azevedo v Portugal* (1990) 13 EHRR 721.
4   According to a *Lexis* search carried out on 24 May 2000.
5   See Appendix 2.
6   See **6.265** and Appendix 2.
7   More than half the judgments of the Strasbourg judges have concerned criminal trials.

(a) to be informed promptly, in a language he understands and in detail, of the nature and cause of the accusation against him;

(b) to have adequate time and facilities for the preparation of his defence;

(c) to defend himself in person or through legal assistance of his own choosing or, if he has not sufficient means to pay for legal assistance, to be given it free when the interests of justice so require;

(d) to examine or have examined witnesses against him and to obtain the attendance and examination of witnesses on his behalf under the same conditions as witnesses against him;

(e) to have the free assistance of an interpreter if he cannot understand or speak the language used in Court.'

6.4   The thrust of these provisions is not new. There was a process right in Magna Carta[1] and it has been a requirement of our common law for hundreds of years that natural justice be adhered to.[2] The Fifth and Fourteenth Amendments to the US Constitution cover much the same ground, whilst Art 10 of the UNDR states that: 'Everyone is entitled in full equality to a fair and public hearing by an independent and impartial tribunal in the determination of his rights and obligations and of any criminal charge against him'.[3] By contrast, the ICCPR follows more obviously the extended definition in the European Convention rather than the UNDR and adds further rights that are in substance reproduced in the Seventh Protocol to the European Convention, which is not given further effect in the Act[4] but which the Government has said it hopes to ratify as soon as possible. For the present, the Seventh Protocol is not part of domestic law.

6.5   In these circumstances, it is perhaps unsurprising that the Judicial Committee of the House of Lords should have suggested in the case of *Khan*[5] that the requirements of a fair trial are the same in London as in Strasbourg. To use the words of Lord Nicholls in that case, they 'march hand in hand'. Whilst the European Court's Art 6 jurisprudence will be unfamiliar to many, the concepts underpinning it are therefore likely to be familiar and this common approach may explain why, notwithstanding the habitual condemnation in recent years of the UK's record before the European Court, Art 6 violations involving this country have been relatively rare[6] although, as will be seen, this country has nevertheless stood condemned for a number of process breaches in significant areas. The bulk of European Convention case-law rather derives from violations by civil law countries such as Italy, and European Convention complaints regarding delays before Italian tribunals at one time constituted a very significant proportion of the workload of the Strasbourg institutions.

6.6   When British lawyers henceforth come to consider the European Court's judgments on Art 6, it will be relevant to bear in mind that such determinations, by definition, were all retrospective and that as a consequence the Strasbourg judges

---

1   See **1.5** et seq.

2   See, for example, *Dr Bentley's Case* (1723) 1 Stra 557.

3   This is to be read in conjunction with the presumption of innocence set out in the first paragraph of Art 11 of the UNDR.

4   See **3.1** et seq.

5   *R v Khan* [1996] 3 WLR 162. In that case, their Lordships were content to refer to the European Convention and accept its relevance.

6   Indeed arguably the *Bulger* decision in December 1999 was the first occasion on which UK trial procedure was found to be in violation: *T and V v United Kingdom* [2000] CLR 189.

had on each occasion the opportunity to review the integrity of the antecedent proceedings as a whole. In terms of their obligations under the Act, local judges have no such luxury. They now need to make their decisions on the hoof as regards the operation of Art 6's process guarantees in the very cases they are determining. For example, in civil litigation Art 6 will now be measured against the delegated legislation that is the Civil Procedure Rules 1998 (CPR 1998) which were introduced in the wake of the Civil Procedure Act 1997 but the contents of which were not prescribed by that statute. From now on, the Civil Procedure Rules will, so far as possible, need to be interpreted in conformity with the European Convention.

THE SCOPE OF ARTICLE 6

6.7   The structure of Art 6 is such that the essential minimum requirements of all legal proceedings, *both civil and criminal*, are first identified (in Art 6(1)). The remainder of the Article (ie Art 6(2) and (3)) then sets out explicitly the irreducible requirements of fair criminal proceedings. The commercial sector in the UK traditionally has had more involvement in civil than criminal trials. That is not to say, however, that the business community does not need to have regard for the additional guarantees enshrined in Art 6(2) and (3), as there is no reason in principle why British advocates should not seek to measure the extent to which non-criminal matters are susceptible to a fair disposal by reference to the particular ingredients of Art 6(2) and (3).

6.8   A feature of the European Court's decisions in recent years has been the extended reach of Art 6. It applies not only to set-piece trials in a court, but also to certain (but not all) forms of administrative decision-making. Therefore, a key challenge for UK corporations facing regulatory proceedings threatening commercial licences and indeed livelihoods will be to see whether the alleged offences can in Strasbourg terms be characterised as criminal charges, thereby making them susceptible to determination not only on the basis of the requirements of Art 6(1), but also on the basis of the extended guarantees provided for in Art 6(2) and (3).[1] As will be seen, the reasoning of the Strasbourg institutions, in this area as in others, has been neither clear nor certain. The draftsmen of the Treaty conceived of Art 6 with the classical courtroom in mind and not the plethora of statutory and non-statutory agencies which police modern commercial life and whose actions can have very significant consequences. Indeed, so significant that they can appear to have more power than judges.

6.9   Article 6 is not a complete fair trial code and the civil or (more particularly) criminal process may frequently make relevant other provisions of the European Convention. Thus, directors may need also to have regard for Art 5(1)(b),[2] which expressly upholds a State's right to deprive a citizen of his liberty 'for non-compliance with the lawful order of a court or in order to secure the fulfilment of any obligation prescribed by law'. The power to jail for contempt of court (for example) is thereby upheld. Article 2 of the Seventh Protocol (which

---

1   The suggestion that market offences in the City of London should be regarded as criminal in nature has been a prominent feature of the concerns expressed about aspects of the Financial Services and Markets Act 2000, as to which see **6.233** et seq.

2   See Appendix 2.

is not yet part of UK law)[1] explicitly upholds the right to appeal (subject to exceptions identified in Art 2(2)) to 'everyone convicted of a criminal offence', a right not expressly provided for in Art 6. Article 7, on retrospective punishment, may bulk large in disciplinary proceedings in the City of London,[2] while Art 13[3] also bears upon rights and obligations to the extent that it upholds the right to an effective remedy, although this need not (but can be) provided by a court.

6.10   To the extent that the ingredients of Art 13 are less explicit than those of Art 6, a case that establishes a violation of Art 6 at Strasbourg is not one which need in addition involve a consideration of Art 13, indeed its requirements tend to be 'absorbed' [4] by Art 6. Beyond that, in the (it is to be hoped) unlikely event that the inquisitorial techniques of, for example, the police or industry regulators are excessive in the extreme, it is conceivable of course that Art 3 of the European Convention,[5] barring 'inhuman or degrading treatment' could be invoked.[6] The fact that libel is primarily a criminal matter across much of Europe obviously engages Art 10,[7] while the continuing criminalisation of certain sexual offences has implications for Art 8.[8] In these latter two instances, the imposition of a conviction may therefore breach European Convention rights entirely outside Art 6. In this light, it will be seen that Art 6, whilst absolutely critical, does not incorporate the whole of the European Convention's process safeguards.

STRASBOURG'S LIMITED FORENSIC ROLE

6.11   It is a feature of European Convention practice and jurisprudence that the Strasbourg institutions have been careful not to seek to second-guess the findings of fact made by a national court in any given case. In so doing, they have adhered to the *quatrième instance* doctrine, ie they do not function as a fourth instance court. A complaint to Strasbourg is not an appeal. The judges of the European Court are concerned more with systemic unfairness at a national level and generally will not enter into a merits examination of individual cases, even where a miscarriage of justice is alleged. The convicted men in the so-called 'Birmingham Six' case therefore lost their application to Strasbourg when arguing that new evidence emerging after their original trial should have been heard by a jury and not by the Court of Appeal. A difficulty they faced is that juries are not commonplace in European Convention countries. The European Convention does not, in any event, guarantee a retrial. The men's petition was rejected.[9]

---

1   See **6.4** and Appendix 2.
2   See **6.265**.
3   See **3.10** et seq and Appendix 2.
4   *Sporrong and Lönnroth v Sweden* (1982) 5 EHRR 35.
5   See Appendix 2.
6   In the case of *Smith and Grady v United Kingdom* (2000) 29 EHRR 493 (the so-called 'gays in the military' case), the applicants claimed at Strasbourg that their treatment by military investigators breached Art 3. The argument failed on the facts, although the European Convention was in other respects held by the European Court to have been violated (see also **6.290** et seq).
7   See Chapter 8.
8   See, for example, *Dudgeon v United Kingdom* (1981) 4 EHRR 149 and **5.40**.
9   *Callaghan v United Kingdom* Appl 14739/89, (1989) 60 DR 296.

6.12   Just as issues affecting the admissibility and relevance of evidence will rarely be considered at Strasbourg, sentencing matters will tend only to be the subject of a review by the European Court where a question of discrimination is raised. Criticism of judicial behaviour in national courts is rare and it is really only when there is some form of gross unfairness that the Strasbourg judges reach their own view based on the substance of the underlying case.

6.13   The intention in the pages that follow is to analyse the constituent parts of Art 6. Its implications for disciplinary proceedings in the City of London and for domestic judicial review are then looked at separately and in some detail.

CRIMINAL CHARGES AS UNDERSTOOD AT STRASBOURG

6.14   Article 6 is engaged when a crime comes to be determined. This immediately gives rise to a difficulty, as the European Convention's definition of a crime is not necessarily the same (although it often will be) as the definition of a crime in the UK. Nor is it solely a matter of definitional differences. The approach to criminal investigations and prosecutions in continental countries (where the process is often judge- or magistrate-led) is distinct from the UK's (Scotland aside) and in utilising European Convention jurisprudence this always needs to be kept in mind.

6.15   As regards this question at least, the Strasbourg court laid down a helpful three-part test in the case of *Engel*,[1] holding that the relevant factors in determining whether or not an offence was criminal in nature were:

–   the local definition of the offence;
–   the nature of the offence; and
–   the severity of the punishment for the offence.

Each of these is now examined in turn.

The local definition of the offence

6.16   The importance of categorising a particular matter as *criminal* in European Convention terms is that it then becomes susceptible to the whole panoply of Art 6 protection. In approaching this question of categorisation, the classification of the offence which is locally adopted is plainly relevant. If it is designated locally as *criminal*, that designation will be conclusive for European Convention purposes. Where the particular offence is, however, designated by a national State as other than criminal, that local designation is not conclusive. It remains relevant but, according to the European Court, it is only 'a starting point'.[2] This is because the word *criminal* is accorded at Strasbourg an autonomous meaning. Were it not so, Member States could in effect limit their Art 6 obligations merely by classifying particular matters as civil in nature thereby, it has been said, subordinating European Convention guarantees to the 'sovereign will' of a particular State, which could in turn lead to results 'incompatible with the purpose and object of the Convention', such as the widening of differences between one Contracting State's laws and those of another. This is far from being

---

1   *Engel and Others v The Netherlands* (1976) 1 EHRR 647.
2   Ibid. See also *Benham v United Kingdom* (1996) 22 EHRR 293.

an issue of narrow theoretical concern, as the legislative history of the Financial Services and Markets Act 2000 shows all too clearly.[1]

6.17   If an offence is not defined as a crime in the UK, it will also be relevant to look at its categorisation in other countries, an exercise which again illustrates the need for British lawyers in the future to approach legal analysis of European Convention problems on a comparative basis.

The nature of the offence

6.18   In analysing the nature of the putative offence, it is pertinent to consider to whom it applies. If the offence is general in effect it is probably criminal in nature,[2] but if those potentially subject to it are limited in number, it may not be criminal but rather, for example, be disciplinary in nature.

The severity of the punishment for the offence

6.19   The third *Engel* stipulation in considering whether a particular offence is criminal in essence is to look at the scale of the penalty attaching to a conviction. If imprisonment is a possibility[3] and/or a fine may be imposed whose effect is 'appreciably detrimental', the matter is likely to be considered to be criminal. Several cases heard at Strasbourg may be illustrative in this regard.

6.20   In *Engel* itself, the Strasbourg judges had to consider offences under Dutch military law arising out of the publication of a periodical ostensibly tending to undermine discipline and the reckless driving of an army vehicle. Such offences could potentially lead to a period of imprisonment of several months and the European Court had no difficulty in concluding that, therefore, they were criminal in nature. In contrast, it was found in another case that placing a soldier in solitary confinement for less than a week for disobeying orders was a disciplinary or non-criminal matter as the 'nature, duration or manner of execution of the imprisonment' was not, in the view of the European Commission, 'appreciably detrimental'.[4] In the case of *Campbell and Fell v United Kingdom*,[5] the European Court had to look at matters affecting prison discipline in the context of violent behaviour by inmates including assault. The consequences for the prisoners involved was loss of remission of sentence of up to 18 months' duration. Considering the matter as a whole, the Strasbourg judges concluded that these were criminal offences.

6.21   Regulatory and disciplinary matters may attract the full measure of Art 6's protection where the seriousness of the offence in question and the severity of the sanction warrants it. The case of *Oztürk*[6] was about careless driving. This was classified as a regulatory and non-criminal matter in Germany, although it was

1   See **6.233**.
2   See *Oztürk v Federal Republic of Germany* (1984) 6 EHRR 409 and *Lauko v Slovakia* [1998] HRCD 838.
3   Such as for tax evasion: see *Bendenoun v France* (1994) 18 EHRR 54.
4   *Eggs v Switzerland* Appl 7341/76, (1976) 6 DR 170. See also *Pelle v France* Appl 11691/85, (1986) 50 DR 263.
5   (1984) 7 EHRR 165.
6   See fn 2 above.

categorised as criminal across most of the Continent. The European Court concluded that this was a criminal offence because of its general application and the perception that the fine imposed had punitive and deterrent characteristics. The fact that the actual fine for the relevant offence was relatively meagre was not decisive.

6.22   Fiscal cases present particular difficulties in this context. In *AGOSI v United Kingdom,*[1] a seizure of krugerrands by HM Customs & Excise was held not to be a criminal matter, nor was the action of HM Customs & Excise in impounding an Air Canada jet when drugs were found on board.[2] Likewise, revenue inquiries have in the past not been considered criminal matters,[3] save where the penalties have been very substantial and were essentially punitive rather than restitutionary.[4] Proceedings for non-payment of council tax have been held to be criminal in nature because imprisonment was a possible sanction[5] and (significantly in terms of this book's focus) the same has been the case where a fine has been imposed for breach of competition rules.[6]

6.23   Other offences *not* traditionally falling within the Strasbourg definition of criminal matters include cases where a licence to trade has been revoked for failure to comply with its conditions[7] and cases where disciplinary charges have been laid against members of 'liberal' professions, such as doctors,[8] although these matters may instead be regarded as involving civil rights and obligations and as such amenable to a degree of Art 6 protection.

6.24   If such distinctions between criminal and non-criminal matters appear arbitrary and unsatisfactory, it is because the jurisprudence of which they form part is opaque. It might not unreasonably be presumed that, when advising a business accused of, for example, regulatory offences, a substantial clue as to whether a matter is likely in European Convention terms to be designated criminal is to consider what is at stake for the client if the offences are proved. What, short of imprisonment, could be a more severe sanction than the threatened withdrawal of a licence to trade or a licence to practice, particularly where the offences involve allegations of unethical behaviour? As matters currently stand, however, there is every prospect that such cases would not be judged by the European Court to be criminal matters, even where they involve an individual's dismissal and his or her loss of earnings.

6.25   The aim of the commercial lawyer in arguing that the offence with which his client is charged is criminal in nature is not, of course, to criminalise his client;

---

1   *Allgemeine Gold-Und Silberscheideanstalt v United Kingdom* (1987) 9 EHRR 1. See also **9.35** et seq.
2   *Air Canada v United Kingdom* (1995) 20 EHRR 150. See also **9.36**.
3   See, for example, *Abas v The Netherlands* Appl 27943/95.
4   See, for example, *Bendenoun v France* (see fn 3 on p 130).
5   *Benham v United Kindom* (see fn 2 on p 129).
6   *Société Stenuit v France* (1992) 14 EHRR 509.
7   *Tre Traktörer Aktiebolag v Sweden* (1989) 13 EHRR 309. See also **9.16**.
8   *Albert and Le Compte v Belgium* (1983) 5 EHRR 533. News reports have suggested that the Government is proposing to ban doctors who have been struck off from returning to the medical register for at least 5 years and perhaps life. (See, for example, *The Guardian*, 18 March 2000.) The General Medical Council apparently wants a 3-year ban and states that it has been advised that 'universal or selective' life bans would violate the European Convention. (See *The Times*, 18 March 2000.)

rather it is to ensure that his client is able to rely upon the whole of Art 6's guarantees. The extent to which disciplinary and regulatory disputes will, in proceedings under the Act, be adjudged to be criminal is likely to be very considerable practical significance for business and it is considered more fully in the context of the reforms introduced by the Government to the regulation of market behaviour in the City of London.[1]

WHEN IS ARTICLE 6 ENGAGED IN CRIMINAL MATTERS?

6.26   It will often be important to determine when Art 6 first becomes engaged in the criminal context. This may, for example, be of very real significance to firms facing interrogation by competition or customs officials. There will be little doubt that a charge has been laid when official notification is given to an individual by a competent authority of an allegation that he has committed a criminal offence.[2] There may, however, be situations in which this does not occur, or where there is a delay before a charge is formally laid. In such instances, the European Convention approach is to examine the facts to determine whether the relevant individual has *effectively* been made the subject of a charge. If, on examination, he has been (even if the charge has not formally been put to him), then from that point onwards the Art 6 safeguards (including the individual's right to a hearing within a reasonable time)[3] will apply.

6.27   The term *charge*, like the word *criminal*, is to be given an autonomous meaning. In this regard also, the definition in domestic law is not conclusive. It is its interpretation in the Strasbourg context which counts. This is because:

> 'The prominent place held in a democratic society by the right to a fair trial favours a "substantive" rather than a "formal" conception of the "charge" referred to in Article 6; it impels the European Court to look behind the appearances and examine the realities of the procedure in question in order to determine whether there has been a charge within Article 6.'[4]

6.28   This is a further example of the need to construe European Convention rights in such a way as to ensure that they are made effective. In assessing whether in any given situation a criminal charge is in issue, the Strasbourg approach therefore is to look at the realities of the procedure involved rather than the label given to that procedure by the relevant national authority.[5] As a result, it may be that, even though no charge has formally been put, there has been some course of conduct or act by the relevant authority which implies the commission of a criminal offence and 'substantially affects the situation of the suspect'.[6]

6.29   Once Art 6 has been engaged, it will continue to be engaged for the entirety of the criminal process leading to conviction and sentence (if need be)

---

1   See **6.233** et seq.
2   *Corigliano v Italy* (1983) 5 EHRR 334. The reference to an official notification by a competent authority is significant in circumstances where it does not appear that there is any protected right in the European Convention to bring a private prosecution: see *Helmers v Sweden* (1991) 15 EHRR 285.
3   See **6.184** et seq.
4   *Adolf v Austria* (1982) 4 EHRR 313.
5   See *Deweer v Belgium* (1980) 2 EHRR 439.
6   See *Corigliano* v *Italy* (fn 2 above).

and indeed to any appeals against conviction and sentence, even where such appeals take place some considerable time later.[1]

DETERMINING CIVIL RIGHTS AND OBLIGATIONS

6.30   For Art 6 to be engaged in a civil context, there has to be a *determination*. It is not clear what this means. There is no reference, for example, to the word *dispute* in the English text of the European Convention, although the French language version refers to a *contestation*. Some elaboration was provided in the case of *H v Belgium*,[2] where the European Court stated that:

> 'Article 6(1) extends only to *contestations* (disputes) over (civil) "rights and obligations" which can be said, at least on arguable grounds, to be recognised under domestic law; it does not in itself guarantee any particular content for (civil) "rights and obligations" in the substantive law of the Contracting States.'

6.31   In identifying, therefore, whether a European Convention dispute exists, it is necessary to look at the underlying reality, for: 'Conformity with the spirit of the Convention requires that the word [ie *contestation*] . . . should not be construed too technically and should be given a substantive rather than a formal meaning'.[3] The following points may be distilled from the Strasbourg jurisprudence to date in assessing whether the determination of a civil right and obligation is in issue.

–   There must be a dispute which is genuine (an ingredient which is presumed), serious,[4] arguable (as opposed to merely hypothetical)[5] and which has a basis in local law. The applicant's tenuous connection with the matter in issue therefore will not be enough to engage Art 6(1).[6] So it was held in the case of *Agrotexim*[7] that shareholders could not pursue a complaint which more properly belonged to the company of which they were members,[8] while there has been a series of recent decisions in environmental cases in which it has been held that Art 6(1) did not apply because the impact upon the applicant protestors was too remote.[9]
–   The matter must be justiciable, in the sense that it involves an issue capable of judicial evaluation, rather than an issue which is more susceptible to a process of assessment. This is of practical significance for British business lawyers, for it may be argued that impositions (however severe) placed upon their clients are merely the result of a technical process of assessment falling outside the protective ambit of Art 6(1). In the case of *Van Marle v Netherlands*,[10] for example, the European Court split 11:7 in finding that Art 6(1) was not

---

1   See the cases of *Eckle v Germany* (1983) 5 EHRR 1 and *Callaghan v United Kingdom* (see fn 9 on p 128) – the application made by the Birmingham Six.
2   (1988) 10 EHRR 339.
3   *Tre Traktörer Aktiesbolag v Sweden* (1989) 13 EHRR 309. See also fn 7 on p 131.
4   *Benthem v The Netherlands* (1986) 8 EHRR 1.
5   But a claim for a declaration will suffice: *Helmers v Sweden* (1993) 15 EHRR 285. See also fn 2 on p 132.
6   *Agrotexim v Greece* (1996) 21 EHRR 250. See also **2.51** et seq.
7   Ibid.
8   Compare the more recent case of *Pafitis and Others v Greece* (1999) 27 EHRR 566.
9   See, for example, *Balmer-Schafroth v Switzerland* (1998) 25 EHRR 598 and *Zander v Sweden* (1994) 18 EHRR 175.
10   (1986) 8 EHRR 483.

engaged in circumstances where the applicants had complained that their fitness to be accredited as accountants had been improperly assessed by their professional body. The Strasbourg judges considered that this was not a matter on which it could properly adjudicate as the accreditation process was more akin to an examination than the exercise of a judicial function.

– While the dispute may not of itself concern the actual existence of a right, it may relate to the scope of the right and the manner in which it can be exercised.[1]

– The issue may concern a question of fact or law.[2] Even though it may involve an application for a declaration, it is still likely to be a *contestation* if it leads to a result which demonstrably impacts in a 'directly decisive' manner upon the rights and obligations which are the subject-matter of the dispute.

6.32 The most salient message for commerce in this is that not all prejudicial decisions affecting it may be susceptible to Art 6(1) protection. That is not to say that British business is without a remedy wherever decisions are made detrimental to its interests. It will have available to it the legal armoury it had before the European Convention was given direct effect locally. What it will not have, however, is the super-added protection of the European Convention's fair trial covenant and this will be so in a number of different contexts.

CIVIL RIGHTS AND OBLIGATIONS

6.33 The need for a determination is in respect of *civil rights and obligations* (*droits et obligations de caractère civil* in the French text). At the outset, the Strasbourg institutions broadly interpreted civil rights and obligations as excluding what would be regarded in this country as public-law matters, even though nothing in the Treaty's *travaux préparatoires*[3] suggested that civil rights and obligations were to be regarded as co-terminous with private rights and obligations. Here too, the jurisprudence is very far from being coherent, with the European Court and European Commission regularly split within and between each other, as they deliberately eschew the formulation of a generic description of civil rights and obligations. This at least allows ample room for manoeuvre on the part of the judges here when discharging their obligations under s 2 of the Act.[4]

6.34 What can be said is that the civil rights and obligations referred to in Art 6(1) are not bound to be the same (although they may well be) as the substantive rights guaranteed by the European Convention. The latter comprise the specific guarantees to be found in the Treaty. The former are rights and obligations recognised by the national laws of the respective Contracting States. Where a European Convention right does not exist as a national right (such as, in the case of the UK, a generic right to privacy), a claim for a European Convention violation may lie (in the case of privacy, under Art 8). A claim that due process had been breached in violation of Art 6 on account of the absence locally of a protected European Convention right (such as the right to privacy) would not, however, lie.

---

1   *Le Compte, Van Leuven and de Meyere v Belgium* (1982) 4 EHRR 1.
2   *Albert and Le Compte v Belgium* (see fn 8 on p 131).
3   See **5.5**.
4   See **3.32** et seq and Appendix 1.

6.35   The rights and obligations must be *civil* (a word missing from the UNDR's fair trial guarantee). The problem is that not all the rights that a UK lawyer would regard as civil are civil in European Convention terms and some (such as certain matters affecting tax)[1] fall outside the reach of Art 6 altogether. Once again, the existence of a uniform European standard may be relevant in helping to establish that a given matter engages Art 6(1).[2] The autonomous definition of *criminal* confirmed by the European Court in the *Engel* case applies also in the civil context and the domestic definition of *civil* will not therefore be conclusive.[3] The key is to focus upon the 'character of the right'[4] in issue. This requires further elaboration.

6.36   As might be expected, matters in issue in civil cases between private parties will tend to constitute civil rights as understood by Art 6(1). In this respect, the European Court has moved away from its original approach when holding that Art 6(1) did not include public law claims. More and more, the Strasbourg judges are inclined to concede that matters in issue between private interests and national authorities (such as property disputes) will involve civil rights within the scope of Art 6(1). In other words, a civil matter as now understood by the European Court may not merely involve what would be regarded as private law issues but may also cover administrative law issues. Thus, in the *Ringeisen*[5] case, the decision of an Austrian land tribunal engaged Art 6(1) because its finding (in effect although not expressly) not to allow the applicant to have a parcel of land was determinative of his rights and obligations, although the determination was ostensibly an administrative one not made by a court. The critical factor was that the decision was dispositive because it prevented the applicant from completing a contract to buy the land which he had already entered into. To that extent, the ruling was 'directly decisive' of the applicant's 'relations in civil law'.[6] In other words, if public law proceedings are dispositive of civil rights and obligations, Art 6(1) is invoked.

6.37   In this area, as in others, the Strasbourg institutions have declined to adopt an analytical approach and, in coming to the jurisprudence generated by them, it is necessary by default to proceed by way of analogy. So far as business is concerned, the authorities suggest, for example, that disputes about land,[7] tort,[8] commerce,[9] the withdrawal of a licence[10] or directly applicable EC rights[11] will be civil matters for the purposes of Art 6(1). So, too, in disciplinary cases a more

---

1   See also **6.40** and **9.93** et seq.
2   See, for example, *Feldbrugge v The Netherlands* (1986) 8 EHRR 425 and *Dreumeland v Germany* (1986) 8 EHRR 448.
3   See *Stran Greek Refineries and Stratis Andreadis v Greece* (1994) 19 EHRR 293 and **9.17**.
4   *Konig v Germany* (1978) 2 EHRR 170.
5   *Ringeisen v Austria* (1971) 1 EHRR 455.
6   Thus, too, the regime in Sweden for revoking the licences of taxi drivers was decisive of a civil right and obligation: *Pudas v Sweden* (1998) 10 EHRR 380. Even a first-time applicant for a licence may have a civil right: *Benthem v The Netherlands* (1986) 8 EHRR 1.
7   See, for example, *Pretto v Italy* (1983) 6 EHRR 182; *Sporrong and Lönnroth v Sweden* (1983) 5 EHRR 35.
8   See, for example, *Axen v Germany* (1984) 6 EHRR 195.
9   See, for example, *Edificaciones March Gallegosa v Spain* [1998] HRCD 287.
10   See, for example, *Tre Traktörer Atkiebolag v Sweden* (1989) 13 EHRR 309. This case is dealt with more fully in Chapter 9. See also *Kingsley v United Kingdom* Appl 35605/97, where an Art 6 complaint about the revocation of a gaming licence was declared admissible.
11   *Van de Hurk v The Netherlands* (1994) 18 EHRR 481.

settled position appears to be emerging that complaints laid against individuals which could determine whether they are still able to practice in certain professions are civil matters within Art 6(1).[1]

6.38   On the other hand, there will be bona fide disputes of great importance to those involved which, as has been seen, are not generally deemed to be within Art 6(1). For example, disputes involving the recruitment and career progression of civil servants are generally not conceded at Strasbourg to involve the determination of civil rights[2] – the rationale historically being that such cases solely raise public-law considerations as opposed to private rights. On the other hand, it would appear that Art 6(1) will be engaged where an issue arises as to, for example, the salary or pension rights of civil servants.[3] The relevant authorities in this area derive in the main from continental jurisdictions and cannot readily be reconciled with the legal position in this country, which traditionally has been that civil servants may not normally seek a judicial review of decisions to dismiss them, but should instead proceed by private law action.[4] This relationship between public sector employment and Art 6, following the introduction of the Act, risks giving rise to confusion in this country. The Strasbourg jurisprudence on the subject is confused and the confirmation of some clear principles by local judges in early course would be welcome.[5]

6.39   Of more direct concern to business is the fact that it still appears as though Art 6(1) cannot be invoked by those subject to a tax assessment, as this ostensibly involves a pure public-law matter,[6] unless, that is, the taxpayer has issued proceedings seeking restitution of an overpayment, there being 'quantifiable sums of money' involved.[7] Conceivably, therefore, UK firms in receipt of a multi-million pound revenue demand cannot claim, without more, that the process right in Art 6(1) is available to them. Equally important for the commercial sector here (but in a very different context), the European Court has held that company investigations carried out in this country by inspectors appointed by the Department of Trade and Industry do not engage Art 6(1) as they are not determinative of legal rights but are investigative in substance.[8]

6.40   Whether the process of change is wholly coherent or not and notwithstanding the exceptions noted above, the Strasbourg institutions appear to have

---

1   See *Konig v Germany* (1978) 2 EHRR 170; *Wickramsinghe v United Kingdom* (1998) EHRLR 338 and *X v United Kingdom* (1998) EHRR 480. See, however, Appl 11869/85, suggesting that professional disciplinary proceedings will not engage Art 6 if they could not lead to suspension.
2   See, for example, *Neigel v France* Appl 18725/91, 14 March 1997 (unreported), *Huber v France* (1998) 26 EHRR 457 and, more recently, *Argento v Italy* (1999) 28 EHRR 719. However, *Pellegrin v France* Appl 28541/95 (8 December 1999) suggests some relaxation in approach.
3   Rights derived from the contract of employment of a National Health Service employee are civil rights: *Darnell v United Kingdom* (1994) 18 EHRR 205.
4   See, for example, *McLaren v Home Office* [1990] 1 ICR 82.
5   There is a helpful treatment of the subject in Supperstone, Goudie and Coppel *Local Authorities and the Human Rights Act 1998* (Butterworths, 1999) at p 45. See also the recent French cases including *Le Calvez v France* Appl 2554/94, 29 July 1998, *Couez v France* Appl 24271/94, 24 August 1998 and *Maillard v France* Appl 26586/95, 9 June 1998.
6   *Schouten and Meldrum v The Netherlands* (1995) 19 EHRR 432.
7   *National & Provincial Building Society, The Leeds Permanent Building Society and the Yorkshire Building Society v United Kingdom* (1997) 25 EHRR 127. This case is more fully dealt with in Chapter 9.
8   *Fayed v United Kingdom* (1994) 18 EHRR 393. This subject is more fully dealt with at **6.48** et seq.

relaxed their earlier, more dogmatic approach and appear to have moved to a broad position whereby increasing numbers of situations now involve civil rights and obligations within Art 6(1) that would be considered justiciable public law matters in the UK. A hint as to the European Court's posture in the future was provided in the case of *Editions Periscope v France*,[1] where the judges suggested that public law rights of a *pecuniary* nature are probably (but not always[2]) *civil* in the sense understood by Art 6(1).

6.41   It is not clear that this distinction between matters of a pecuniary and non-pecuniary nature is helpful, but at least it marks a further break from the rigidity of the past. That is not to say, however, that local judges taking account of the Strasbourg jurisprudence will be keen to widen the scope of Art 6(1). On the contrary, indications are that local courts may be slow to widen the categories of civil rights and obligations. In, for example, the case of *R v Secretary of State for Health, ex parte C*,[3] the Court of Appeal said that the maintenance of the Consultancy Service Index, which lists those who may not be suitable to work with children, did not engage Art 6 as it was not determinative of any civil right. On the other hand, it has recently been held that a compulsory scheme of arrangement may engage Art 6. [4]

WHEN DOES ARTICLE 6(1) BECOME RELEVANT IN CIVIL MATTERS?

6.42   Article 6(1) will be engaged when court proceedings are instituted[5] and it will continue to apply until the proceedings have ended. Thus, it covers more than the dispositive hearing itself.[6] Strangely perhaps, the right to an appeal in civil cases is not made expressly in the European Convention. Such a right in the criminal context is to be found in the Seventh Protocol,[7] but whether there is an inalienable right of appeal in a non-criminal case remains unclear. However, by now it is well established in the Strasbourg jurisprudence that where there is laid down in national law a right to a civil appeal the requirements of Art 6(1) attach to that appeal. If a case from Spain[8] is any guide, making the appeal subject to a requirement of leave is probably not a European Convention violation.

6.43   Article 6(1) also applies to matters affecting the enforcement of judgments so that, for example, Greece was held liable by the European Court for taking more than 5 years to comply with a tribunal decision.[9] It is relevant too where there is a preliminary issue on liability[10] and where damages are being set.[11]

---

1   (1992) 14 EHRR 597.
2   *Schouten and Meldrum v The Netherlands* (1995) 19 EHRR 432.
3   [2000] 1 FLR 627. It does not appear that the Court was referred to Art 8, which would perhaps have been a more fruitful basis for complaint.
4   See *Re Hawk Insurance Co Limited* (24 January 2000, unreported).
5   *Guincho v Portugal* (1994) 17 EHRR 223.
6   In the criminal context, police investigations may fall within it: see *Imbroscia v Switzerland* (1994) 17 EHRR 441.
7   See **6.9** and Appendix 2.
8   *Brualla Gomez de la Torre v Spain* [1998] HRCD 191.
9   See *Hornsby v Greece* (1997) 24 EHRR 250.
10   See *Obermeier v Austria* (1990) 13 EHRR 290.
11   *Silva Pontes v Portugal* (1994) 18 EHRR 156. Less satisfactory are those decisions suggesting that Art 6 does not apply to applications for interim relief (see *Austerlund v Sweden* (1998) 56

THE CONTENT OF CIVIL RIGHTS AND OBLIGATIONS

6.44   Article 6 is in essence about procedural safeguards. The European Court has repeatedly stated that this particular provision of the European Convention does not of itself 'guarantee any particular content of rights and obligations in the substantive law of Contracting States'.[1] This means that a claim for (in substance) a privacy violation that is henceforth made in a British court (the strict cause of action very likely being an existing common-law tort, such as breach of confidence) will probably engage the substantive right in Art 8 of the European Convention,[2] but not the fair trial right in Art 6.

6.45   Article 6 is, in other words, about the regulation of the *processing* of legal entitlements. The *content* of those entitlements (or indeed their absence) is, generally, a separate matter. As such, where, for example, the system for statutory leasehold enfranchisement in the UK had the effect of depriving certain Strasbourg applicants of their property rights (for which they had no legal remedy in the UK), the absence of that remedy did not of itself mean that there had been a breach of Art 6.[3] The applicants having no right to a remedy domestically, no determination could ever take place which could be measured against the standards of Art 6.

6.46   British applicants were also disappointed in a case at Strasbourg concerning complaints by owners of property near enough to Heathrow Airport to be affected by noise from over-flying aircraft.[4] The difficulty they faced was that liability for trespass and nuisance had been excluded by statute and the European Court held that any question as to the possible application of Art 6 could not arise.

LIMITATIONS UPON RIGHTS

6.47   Perhaps conscious of the unfairness that may result from an overly strict adherence to this approach, the European Court of late has been examining more critically the basis for limitations upon rights. In determining whether Art 6(1) is applicable, it now appears necessary to ask whether a substantive legal right is being barred or whether the limitation relates instead to the remedy for a breach of that right. The latter engages Art 6(1), the former does not.

6.48   The *Fayed* case[5] arose out of the contested take-over of House of Fraser, owners of Harrods, which led to an investigation of Mohamed Fayed and his two brothers. The investigation was carried out by inspectors appointed by the Secretary of State for Trade and Industry. Their subsequent report was distinctly

---

DR 229) or to applications for leave to petition the House of Lords (see *Porter v United Kingdom* (1987) 54 DR 207). In the latter case, it was held that the dismissal of an application for leave to appeal to the House of Lords was not dispositive in terms of Art 6(1).

1   See *H v Belgium* (1987) 10 EHRR 339.
2   See Chapter 7.
3   *James v United Kingdom* (1986) 8 EHRR 123. This case, concerning the estate of the Duke of Westminster, is discussed more fully at **9.50** et seq.
4   *Powell and Rayner v United Kingdom* (1990) 12 EHRR 355. In the event, the applicants also failed to establish violations under Art 8 and Art 1 of the First Protocol, see also **9.189** et seq.
5   *Fayed v United Kindom* (1994) 18 EHRR 393.

unfavourable towards the Fayeds, who proceeded to Strasbourg on the following two principal grounds.

–   They asserted that the inspectors' report was flawed. Specifically, it was argued that when the inspectors had taken evidence for the purposes of their report, they should have complied with the safeguards in Art 6(1) because they were engaged in a process which ultimately impacted upon the Fayeds' reputational rights.
–   The Fayeds could not sue the inspectors for defamation in circumstances where it was agreed on both sides that the inspectors had a (good) defence of qualified privilege. This meant, according to the Fayeds, that they had been denied the opportunity to have their civil rights determined in a manner consistent with Art 6(1)'s guarantees.

6.49   The judges at Strasbourg held that the inspectors' report was investigative in nature and was not dispositive of the Fayeds' civil rights. As such, Art 6(1) was not applicable. There had been no determination of the Fayeds' rights, at a national level, even though they had been severely criticised and the report thereby bore upon their right to a good reputation. Even if, however, Art 6(1) had been engaged (which the judges believed it had not been), the existence of the defence of qualified privilege to a potential claim for defamation was legitimate, operating in this instance to enable investigations of large companies in the public interest to be undertaken 'with courage and frankness'. It was within the UK's margin of appreciation.[1]

6.50   The judges recognised that they needed coherently to distinguish between substantive and procedural limitations on rights. As to the latter, they said:

> '... whether a person has an actionable domestic claim may depend not only on the substantive content, properly speaking, of the relevant civil right as defined under national law but also on the existence of procedural bars preventing or limiting the possibilities of bringing potential claims to court. In the latter kind of case Article 6(1) may have a degree of applicability. Certainly the Convention enforcement bodies may not create by way of interpretation of Article 6(1) a substantive civil right which has no legal basis in the State concerned. However, it would not be consistent with the rule of law in a democratic society or with the basic principle underlined in Article 6(1) – namely that civil claims must be capable of being submitted to a judge for adjudication – if, for example, a State could, without restraint or control by the Convention enforcement bodies, remove from the jurisdiction of the courts a whole range of civil claims or confer immunities from civil liability on large groups or categories of persons.'

6.51   In circumstances where much of the Strasbourg jurisprudence is not the product of any obvious analytical approach, this attempt to articulate the difference between substantive and procedural rights is helpful, even if its application in the *Fayed* case remains unpersuasive. In the end, the Fayeds were left without a remedy and, unless their case is understood in terms of the operation of the margin of appreciation to be accorded the UK in relation to public company investigations, the outcome appears to be unjust. The odds are, however, that it will be followed by judges here and, as a consequence, directors

---

1   As to which, see **5.35** et seq.

who are the subject of criticism in statutory inquiries are unlikely (at least at the moment of criticism) to be able to rely upon Art 6(1) in their defence.

THE IMPACT OF THE ACT UPON THE LAW OF NEGLIGENCE

6.52   The fact that Art 6(1) does not prescribe the content of particular legal rights in the UK does not mean that it will have no impact upon substantive aspects of local law such as, for example, traditional common-law immunities from suit. It had, for example, for many years been hornbook law in this country that local authorities, even where negligent, could not successfully be sued.[1] Permitting litigation in this context would, it was argued, divert public resources and cause institutions such as the police and fire service to perform their duties defensively. Such immunities were created and developed on straightforward policy grounds. However understandable (and indeed justifiable), they have the effect of leaving without a remedy those deleteriously affected by the actions of public services. What is more, as a result of their (necessarily) absolute nature, such immunities make irrelevant any idea of proportionality.[2] Is this a process breach in Strasbourg terms?

6.53   In the *Osman* case,[3] it was the immunity from suit of the Metropolitan Police that was in issue. The Osman family (mother and son) argued that officers had been negligent in failing (despite repeated warnings) to prevent a teacher, who had formed an obsessive attachment to their son, from murdering the boy's father. Their High Court claim was struck out.[4] All 17 judges of the European Court (including the British representative, Sir Nicholas Bratza) found, however, that denying the Osmans a trial was a violation of Art 6.[5] The premise on which the police's immunity from suit was based was legitimate and States were to be afforded a margin of appreciation in this area, but the existence of a *blanket* immunity in this instance was disproportionate. After all, the police were being made exempt from a law that applied to ordinary members of the public and the so-called exclusionary rule deprived a domestic court of the opportunity to weigh competing public interest considerations. The decision of the English judges to strike out the action restricted the Osmans' right of access to a court[6] to pursue a claim in negligence. That claim might not have succeeded, but the police should at least have been obliged to give an account of their actions before a legal tribunal.

---

1   See, for example, *X v Bedfordshire County Council* [1995] 2 AC 633 on social services, since considered by the European Court as *X and Another v United Kingdom* (together with *TP and KM v United Kingdom* [2000] 2 LGLR 181), *Hill v Chief Constable of West Yorkshire* [1999] AC 53 on the police and *Stovin v Wise* [1996] 3 All ER 801 on highway improvements.

2   See **5.21** et seq.

3   *Osman v United Kingdom* (1999) 1 EHRR 193.

4   *Osman v Ferguson* [1993] 4 All ER 344. The Court of Appeal had acknowledged that a duty of care might arise between the police and someone in Mrs Osman's position, but public policy dictated that there should be immunity from liability. Leave to appeal to the House of Lords was refused.

5   The applicants also complained (unsuccessfully) under Arts 2 and 8.

6   For a description of right of access see **6.74** et seq.

6.54   The Osman decision has been criticised, most obviously by Lord Browne-Wilkinson in the case of *Barrett v London Borough of Enfield*.[1] He found it 'extremely difficult to understand', confusing as he saw it a matter of procedure 'with what is in truth a matter of substantive domestic law'. He also feared for the uncertainty to which it would give rise. One of his fellow Law Lords, Lord Hoffman, went further when writing in an extra-judicial capacity. For him the case, 'dealing with the substantive civil law right to financial compensation for not receiving the benefit of a social service, is as far as one can imagine from basic human rights'.[2] However, Lord Woolf has suggested that 'there may well be a more positive consequence of the *Osman* decision' to the extent that it draws 'attention to the fact that in this area of the law there is a danger that statements made in judgments will be applied more widely and more rigidly than was in fact intended'.[3]

6.55   In *Jarvis v Hampshire County Council*,[4] the Court of Appeal emphasised that nothing in *Osman* should prevent a court from not striking out a claim which is in all other respects justified. This was supported some months later by a different Court of Appeal in *DS v Gloucestershire County Council*,[5] where the bench distinguished claims raising resource-allocation points (which were simply not justiciable) and claims raising questions of reasonableness, where some detailed merits review might be appropriate. These read like elegant, if anguished, attempts to give *Osman* a soft landing locally.

6.56   Most British lawyers (and, at a guess, most companies), who recognise the systematic importance of certainty in any legal system, will nevertheless be minded to agree with Lords Browne-Wilkinson and Hoffman. On the other hand, they now need to adjust to the reality of practice after *Osman*, a decision with great potential influence upon tort law in the UK. *Osman* may, conceivably, result in fewer successful striking-out applications where negligence claims are brought against public authorities and a decline in reliance solely or principally upon public policy or floodgates-type arguments as justification for the existence of blanket immunities. In increasing numbers of cases, a merits examination will now be required. In the *Barratt* case, Lord Browne-Wilkinson specifically alluded to the fact that if the appeal in that instance was not allowed, it was 'at least probable' that the case would go to Strasbourg. It is conceivable that, over time, comprehensive exclusions will have to give way to case-by-case analyses, and municipal indemnity insurance will doubtless become more expensive as a result, even though the Strasbourg judges were anxious in *Osman* to ensure that no 'impossible or disproportionate burden' was placed upon authorities.

6.57   Where there is a de facto immunity from suit, such as in *Fayed*, which is perceived to be a proportionate and legitimate restriction, it is likely to be

---

1   [1999] 3 All ER 193.
2   (1999) 62 MLR 159. He thought it 'inconceivable' that a domestic court could have come to the same conclusion as the Strasbourg judges.
3   See *Kent v Griffiths and Others* [2000] 3 All ER 474, holding that the ambulance service is under a duty of care to arrive on time.
4   [2000] 2 FCR 310.
5   The appeal was heard at the same time as that in *RL v Tower Hamlets LBC and Havering LBC* [2000] 1 FLR 825. See also *Palmer v Tees Health Authority* [2000] 2 LRLR 69.

upheld.[1] As a consequence, it may be anticipated that many judges will strive to be seen to be engaging in an impeccable *Osman*-style analysis before reaching the same result they would have reached pre-*Osman*, albeit by a different route. They will, however, have had to preside over some (at least limited) form of merits review so that, if nothing else, it is likely that negligence cases in this country will increase in number (because fewer will be struck out and more begun) and will become longer in duration and exponentially more expensive – all this despite the fact that the Court of Appeal in the *DS* case[2] stressed the power in Part 24 of CPR 1998 whereby defendants (and not just claimants) can apply for summary judgment.

6.58   Will the operational techniques of the police need to be changed as a result of the Convention?[3] It has already been reported that the family of murdered black musician Michael Menson have petitioned Strasbourg, arguing that Art 6 imports a right to the proper investigation of a crime.[4] Does *Osman*, however, mean that going beyond the legal position of the emergency services, the scope of qualified privilege in libel (which has potentially been greatly extended as a result of the *Reynolds* case[5]) is now vulnerable to attack on Art 6 grounds, notwithstanding its survival unscathed in *Fayed*? With the immunity of barristers from suit having just gone (at least in part on Art 6 grounds),[6] what of the policy-driven determination of the House of Lords that auditors should owe no duty to potential investors in companies whose books they audit?[7] Or what if a court deprives itself of jurisdiction over all or part of a case? More generally, to what extent will human rights concepts infuse the common law of negligence going forward? For example, it has been suggested that a long-term consequence of *Osman* is to shift the focus in immunity-type cases from duty to breach considerations.[8] Does the decision make more likely challenges to the historical constraints in local law on seeking damages for purely economic loss? Must every allegation as to the existence of a duty of care, however tangential, now result in a

---

1   *Osman* was, for example, followed by *Waite and Kennedy v Germany* [1999] 6 BHRC 499, where the European Court held that diplomatic immunity (enjoyed by the European Space Agency) had a legitimate objective and was proportionate. It was 'an essential means of ensuring the proper functioning of organisations ... free from unilateral interference by individual governments'. See also *Holland v Lampen-Wolfe* [2000] 1 WLR 1573, in which the sovereign immunity of the United States was held to trump the appellant's Art 6 rights.
2   See **6.56**.
3   See Lord Wilberforce in *Anns v Merton LBC* [1978] AC 728 and see generally A Sprince and J Cooke 'Article 6 and immunity in tort: let the facts speak for themselves' (1999) *Professional Negligence*, vol 15, no 4 and the article by P de Prez 'Proportionality, symmetry and competing public policy arguments: the police force and civil immunity' (1999) *Professional Negligence*, vol 15, no 4. Nothing in *Osman* suggests that Art 6 can be relied upon in arguing that the State is obliged to prosecute merely because of the existence of sufficient evidence.
4   The parents of the murdered black teenager Stephen Lawrence are also suing the Metropolitan Police for investigative failures (*Law Society Gazette*, 23 March 2000.)
5   *Reynolds v Times Newspapers Limited* [1999] 4 All ER 609. For a fuller treatment of this case, see **8.115** et seq.
6   *Hall v Simons* (unreported) 20 July 2000 (HL), and see Sir Richard Buxton in [2000] 116 LQR at p 62.
7   See *Caparo Industries plc v Dickman* [1990] 2 AC 605. Lord Browne-Wilkinson raised this point in *Barrett* (see fn 1 on p 141).
8   See *Barrett, Negligence and Discretionary Powers in Public Law* by P Craig and D Fairgrieve [1999] PL 626.

merits review? In any event, if European Convention considerations now come to inform the domestic law of negligence, why not contract law too?

6.59   At this stage, it is difficult to predict the reaction of the local judiciary to these wider considerations. However, such is the apparent hostility to *Osman* that, although the European Court's decision appears destined to affect the future disposal of negligence claims against certain public services, it would be surprising if UK courts were anxious to extend it to private-law negligence claims of the type with which companies are more familiar.

IMMUNITY CERTIFICATES

6.60   The use of public-interest immunity certificates was reviewed in *Tinnelly*,[1] a case from Northern Ireland in which the applicant alleged it had been denied a public works contract on religious grounds in the face of the Secretary of State's certification that the true reason was national security considerations. The European Court held that such certification could not be conclusive and the fact that it was treated as such in a subsequent judicial review application in Belfast was a process breach under Art 6. According to the European Court:

> '... the right guaranteed to an applicant under Article 6(1) of the Convention to submit a dispute to a Court or to a tribunal in order to have a determination on questions of both fact and law cannot be displaced by the *ipse dixit* of the executive.'

6.61   In other contexts, it had been possible to balance the need for procedural fairness with the need to safeguard national security and the Strasbourg judges in *Tinnelly* were not persuaded that the same could not be done on this occasion, where no opportunity had been given to scrutinise the substantive basis for the certificate. Security considerations, of course, were important, but the action taken was disproportionate.[2]

6.62   Both *Tinnelly* and *Osman* are examples of the Strasbourg juridical technique *par excellence* in that the applicable European Convention guarantee was first identified (the right to a fair trial) before consideration was given to the legitimacy or otherwise of any interference with that right. Understood in this light, the decisions are less surprising than they might at first appear. It was the blanket, all-encompassing nature of the immunities which the judges evidently found most objectionable and of which local courts henceforth need to have regard, not just in civil litigation but, as appears below, in criminal matters also.

6.63   In the case of *Davis and Rowe v United Kingdom*,[3] the European Court had to consider whether the prosecution's failure in a British case to disclose material evidence (not just to the defence but also to the judge) on the ground of public interest immunity[4] was a violation of Art 6. The Court of Appeal had looked at the withheld material (again, not provided to the defence) and ruled against disclosure. When European Convention complaints were made, the Strasbourg

---

1   *Tinnelly and Sons Ltd and Others v United Kingdom* (1999) 27 EHRR 249.
2   In the case of *Johnson v Chief Constable of Royal Ulster Constabulary* [1986] ECR 1651, the same reasoning was applied, albeit by the European Court of Justice in Luxembourg.
3   *Rowe (Raphael) and Davis (Michael) v United Kingdom* (2000) TLR, 1 March.
4   The argument was that the immunity was necessary to protect police informants.

judges confirmed their traditional reticence as to the determination of evidential matters. They acknowledged the competing considerations that might be involved in such cases, but concluded that a procedure whereby the prosecution determined whether it was in the public's interest to embargo certain evidence without any opportunity for independent scrutiny by the trial judge could not comply with Art 6 and that, furthermore, the process breach at first instance had not been cured by the Court of Appeal.

6.64   In two accompanying complaints[1] the Strasbourg judges found by the narrowest of margins (9:8) that there was no violation where the non-disclosure of evidence was the subject of an application to the trial judge on notice to the defence. The defence had at least been heard, even if it had not seen the relevant material (as regards which orders for non-disclosure were in fact made).

6.65   This issue of undisclosed material also arose in the context of the debates about the Financial Services and Markets Act 2000[2] and the judgment in *Rowe and Davis* will inevitably increase pressure for a change to prosecutorial practice in white-collar cases (and, indeed, generally).

THE IMPACT OF THE ACT UPON ADMINISTRATIVE DECISIONS

6.66   Article 6, as already explained,[3] does not apply to all public-law matters. On the contrary, the likelihood is that an issue, however disputatious, will be regarded by the Strasbourg Court as *not* engaging Art 6 in the following circumstances:

–   where the determination is not adjudicative or judicial (ie the *Fayed* scenario);
–   where the issues involved are highly technical (eg as regards matters of planning or finance);[4] or
–   where the decision is made by a body which does not conform to the Art 6 notion of a tribunal, provided an appeal lies from that non-compliant tribunal to a judicial body with 'full jurisdiction'.[5]

6.67   In circumstances where administrative decisions bear significantly upon many parts of British commercial life (and can affect livelihoods), this is particularly problematic, as many administrators in this country are far from being compliant with the Convention. Fortunately for them, the Strasbourg institutions have long held that Art 6(1) does not require every *initial* decision determining civil rights and obligations to be made by a tribunal satisfying Art 6(1)'s requirements.[6] The key, as already noted, is the ability, in the wake of any such unfavourable decision, for the person or company aggrieved to have available

1   *Jasper v United Kingdom* Appl 27052/95 and *Fitt v United Kingdom* Appl 29777/96.
2   See **6.233**.
3   See **6.36**.
4   See, for example, *Zumbotel v Austria* (1994) 17 EHRR 116, where property valuation evidence was called in a compensation claim and where the European Court said that it might legitimately be expedient for national courts to restrict their review of such decisions.
5   As to which, see **6.69**.
6   *Kaplan v United Kingdom* (1980) 4 EHRR 64.

to them a process whereby objectionable administrative decisions can be challenged in a forum that provides the relevant Art 6 guarantees. This might mean a merits-based appeal, going to issues of both fact and law, or a process of judicial review limited to a scrutiny of the legality of the relevant decisions. Once again, no clear reasoning has emerged from Strasbourg, although certain broad themes have.

6.68   In the case of *Albert and Le Compte*,[1] doctors disciplined by their professional society had a domestic right of appeal to a further professional tribunal, followed thereafter by an appeal to the Belgian Court of Cassation. The judges at Strasbourg concluded that the disciplinary proceedings involved were a determination of the civil rights and obligations of the doctors (namely their right to continue to practise) and that, as a consequence, Art 6 was relevant. This meant that the medical tribunals had to conform to Art 6 or, if they did not, the Belgian Court had to have 'full jurisdiction'. On the facts, the European Court held that Art 6 was violated because the professional panels had sat in private (a feature inconsistent with Art 6's fair hearing guarantee) and because the subsequent review by the Court of Cassation could only consider points of law. Therefore, a tribunal bound by findings of fact on material issues will not have 'full jurisdiction' in the sense meant by Art 6.[2] Whereas 'demands of flexibility and efficiency' might justify the use of administrative panels at the outset, at some point, cases of this sort needed to come before an Art 6(1) compliant tribunal with authority, if need be, to assess whether the penalty meted out was disproportionate.[3]

6.69   The case of *W v United Kingdom*[4] involved a father's challenge to the decision of a local authority to restrict access to his children, who were in care. In the UK the only legal basis for any challenge was by bringing an application for judicial review or by the institution of wardship proceedings, both of which were held by the European Court to be inadequate, on the basis that neither allowed for a review of the merits of the underlying decision regarding access arrangements made by the relevant local authority. Here too, then, there was an Art 6 violation. By contrast, in the case of *Oerlemans v The Netherlands*[5] there was no Art 6 violation in a land-use dispute because the Dutch court was able to carry out a full review on matters of fact and law, even though it lacked the power to nullify the original administrative decision of which the applicant complained. It could, however, award damages or grant an injunction against the execution of the decision.

6.70   In the case of *Bryan v United Kingdom*,[6] the judges at Strasbourg were required to review the process by which planning disputes are dealt with in the UK. They found that the planning inspector's decision, to which Mr Bryan objected, was susceptible to appeal to the High Court on a point of law. Mr Bryan argued, however, that this was inadequate in circumstances where the High Court

---

1   (1995) 21 EHRR 342.
2   See also *Terra Woringen v The Netherlands* (1996) 24 EHRR 456.
3   *Diennet v France* (1996) 21 EHRR 554.
4   (1998) 10 EHRR 29. The judges also suggested that Art 6 does not require every decision
      determining a civil right to be heard by a court provided that the court can determine
      substantial disputes.
5   (1991) 15 EHRR 561.
6   See (1995) 21 EHRR 342. The case is also generally considered in connection with Art 1 of
      the First Protocol, see Chapter 9.

was neither capable of reviewing the inspector's finding of fact (even though the facts were not in dispute) nor of substituting its own decision for that of the inspector.

6.71   In a judgment that will have been greeted with relief by British administrators in a variety of sectors, the European Court concluded that the process of appeal to the High Court in *Bryan* did comply with Art 6. It was influenced by the following factors.

–   The case concerned a specialised planning-law matter. Restricting an appeal to points of law only was not unusual or indeed unacceptable where it was more practical for an administrative body with specific expertise (such as the planning inspector) to eke out the relevant facts. The planning inspector, rather than the High Court, was also better qualified to take policy considerations into account.
–   Even though the planning inspector was not fully independent of the executive,[1] the procedure was quasi-judicial in nature with an emphasis upon openness, impartiality and fairness.
–   The High Court had been able to deal with the grounds of appeal and there had been no absence or denial of jurisdiction. Any findings of fact disputed by the applicant had not been the subject of the appeal,[2] although if they had been, the High Court's limited powers would probably have prevented it from considering them.

6.72   The position therefore is that, where an administrative decision is being taken by a public authority in the UK, under the Act it must conform to the safeguards in Art 6 if the decision is determinative of civil rights and obligations (and, as already seen, in some significant instances it may not be). Where those safeguards are not met, there must at least be made available a process whereby the decision can be challenged before a tribunal of 'full jurisdiction' that itself meets the requisite Art 6 standards.

6.73   The reality in the UK is that much administrative decision-making, insofar as it affects commerce, violates Art 6. There is, therefore, little doubt that the outcome of much of the litigation in this area will, as a consequence, turn upon the extent to which such defects as characterise the process at the outset are cured by the intervention of a court of 'full jurisdiction'. That in turn raises an issue as to whether the most normal legal mechanism for challenging administrative decisions in this country, namely an application for judicial review, *itself* passes muster in terms of Art 6. This will depend on the subject-matter of the dispute in question. In the cases of *W* and *Tinnelly* domestic judicial review was found wanting. In the case of an area of specialist activity, such as planning, it was held in *Bryan* to be Convention-compliant. This is an issue of very practical moment for business clients and their lawyers, and later in this chapter the consequences of the Act for domestic judicial review are considered further.[3]

---

1   As regards Art 6(1)'s requirement for an independent and impartial tribunal, see **6.194** et seq.
2   See the case of *ISKCON v United Kingdom* (1994) 76A DR 90, which concerned a planning violation and an appeal on a point of law, where it was found that the applicant had been able to advance all his arguments and where the European Commission found no violation of Art 6.
3   See **6.289** et seq.

THE RIGHT OF ACCESS TO A COURT

6.74   This is a central and inherent right (even though it is not spelt out in Art 6(1)) for if there is no access, there can, by definition, be no fair hearing or indeed any hearing at all. In the landmark case of *Golder*[1] the European Court held that for the Home Secretary to inform a prisoner that any letter he wrote to a solicitor would be intercepted, in circumstances where the prisoner was seeking advice as regards the bringing of a defamation action against a prison officer, amounted to a denial of access to a court. This was so even though the prisoner never actually attempted to write a letter seeking advice and was later released before the limitation period for any defamation action would have expired. The deciding factor for the Strasbourg judges was that, at the moment when Mr Golder in fact contemplated seeking legal advice, he was told he would be prevented from doing so.

6.75   Robertson and Merrills[2] describe *Golder* as one of the European Court's most important cases, on the basis that it shows how the reach of the European Convention can be increased by imaginative interpretative techniques. That may be so, but, for British practitioners professionally inured to the role of precedent and legal certainty, cases such as *Golder* throw the interpretative challenge to which the Act gives rise into sharp relief. In fact, the European Court in *Golder* was anxious to explain that its decision was:

> '... not an extensive interpretation forcing new obligations on the Contracting States: it [was] based on the very terms of the first sentence of Art 6 ... [r]ead in its context and having regard to the object and purpose of the Convention, a law-making treaty ... and to general principles of law.'

6.76   Access to a court can, of course, be barred in a myriad number of ways and in the pages that follow an attempt is made to identify those aspects of local procedure affecting access rights which may pose difficulties for UK courts in terms of Art 6. As regards, first, the jurisprudence of the Strasbourg institutions, it is to be noted that access to a court was found, for example, to have been denied, in violation of Art 6, in the following instances:

- where a tribunal determined an issue relating to compensation without consideration of any submissions by any of the parties;[3]
- where there was a denial of *locus standi* to a father wishing to challenge the placing of his child for adoption;[4] and
- where a party was not given adequate notice of an administrative decision to enable it adequately to be considered and (if need be) challenged.[5]

6.77   The European Court has, in addition, held that *statutory* restrictions upon the right of access breached Art 6 where, for example:

---

1   *Golder v United Kingdom* (1975) 1 EHRR 524.
2   AH Robertson and JG Merrills *Human Rights in Europe* (Manchester University Press, 1993) at p 86.
3   *Georgiades v Greece* (1997) 24 EHRR 606.
4   *Keegan v Ireland* (1994) 18 EHRR 342.
5   *De la Pradelle v France* Appl 12694/87, 16 December 1992. A group of landowners was unable to appeal in time against a decree restricting land use. Publication of the decree in the *Official Gazette* was held not to be adequate or reasonable notice.

–   there was a requirement that a professional's fees could only be recovered through legal proceedings if they were brought by his professional body, which had total control over the proceedings.[1] (This raises issues about subrogation, particularly in the insurance context; for example, the question recently arose as to whether the proceedings of the Motor Insurers Bureau, which determines compensation under the Untraced Drivers' Agreement, conformed to Art 6);[2] and

–   legislation which prevented religious institutions from bringing legal proceedings against the State in respect of its actions over their property.[3]

Access must be effective

6.78   In the *Golder* case, access to the legal process was deliberately impeded. In the case of *Airey*,[4] the argument was that access was *effectively* impeded in circumstances where Mrs Airey was unable to retain a lawyer to act for her in an action for judicial separation in Ireland (there being at that time no ability to divorce in that jurisdiction) for which no legal aid existed.

6.79   The European Commission in *Airey* had been unanimous in finding an Art 6 violation. However, the Strasbourg judges split. The majority was not persuaded by the Irish Government's argument that Mrs Airey could avail herself of the court process by acting in person or by paying for a lawyer. This was perceived to be unrealistic, not least against a background which showed that, in hundreds of earlier cases of judicial separation, the applicants had been legally represented. The European Court emphasised that: 'The Convention is intended to guarantee not rights that are theoretical or illusory but rights that are practical and effective'. It went on: 'this is particularly so of the right of access to the courts in view of the prominent place held in a democratic society by the right to a fair trial'. Not just that, but the inevitable emotional involvement of Mrs Airey in the instant case, which entailed complicated procedures, difficult questions of law and highly personal issues, buttressed her entitlement to objective legal representation.

IS THERE A RIGHT TO CIVIL LEGAL AID?

6.80   The submissions made in *Airey* are of continuing relevance at a time when the legal aid system has been curtailed in the UK – an issue which is likely to form the basis of an early challenge under the Act.[5] *Airey* is not, however, authority for the proposition that the European Convention enshrines an entitlement to legal aid in civil cases,[6] and the European Commission subsequently held in

---

1   *Philis v Greece* (1991) 13 EHRR 74.

2   *Evans v Secretary of State for the Environment, Transport and the Regions and Another* (unreported) 17 March 2000.

3   *Holy Monasteries v Greece* (1994) 20 EHRR 1.

4   *Airey v Ireland* (1979) 2 EHRR 305. See also *McTear v United Kingdom* Appl 40291/98, 7 September 1999, where the fact that lawyers were acting without a fee meant that the access right had not been violated.

5   It has been reported that Leading Counsel has advised that features of the Access to Justice Act 1999 (which, amongst other matters, has the effect of ending legal aid for personal injury claims) are in violation of Art 6. See *The Lawyer*, 19 July 1999.

6   For the position in relation to criminal cases, see **6.250**.

another case that restricting civil legal aid by reference to the means of applicants and the likelihood of their succeeding was permissible, even though this might, in effect, be a denial of court access.[1] The European Commission has also accepted that the refusal of civil legal aid for an appeal by the Moors Murderer, Ian Brady, was legitimate to the extent that he had no obvious prospect of success and the costs involved in comparison to the benefit to be gained were disproportionate.[2]

6.81   The absence of any legal aid for defamation actions in the UK has previously been the subject of complaint at Strasbourg.[3] The challenges have failed so far, but there is no reason to believe that, as a consequence of the Act, the argument will not now be made locally. After all, defamation actions often involve highly technical points of law, while the performance of witnesses under cross-examination can have a very material bearing upon the outcome of cases. In such a context, experienced advocacy can have a significant bearing upon jury perception. If Mrs Airey needed help, why not John McVicar, who lost a libel action against Linford Christie and who is reported to have petitioned Strasbourg on this and other points concerning domestic libel law?[4]

6.82   *Airey* suggests that there may be circumstances in which Art 6 is violated when legal aid is not made available and when an individual will be so handicapped by the absence of legal representation that the very rights and obligations which are in issue in the underlying proceedings cannot be dealt with adequately, as a result of which the individual's ability to vindicate his or her position is undermined. This was demonstrated in *Faulkner*,[5] a case from the Channel Islands, in which the European Commission unanimously found an Art 6 violation in circumstances where the applicant was unable to pay for a lawyer to act for him in a claim for, amongst other matters, false imprisonment. In the wake of this decision, a friendly settlement was concluded, whereby Guernsey undertook to establish a system of civil legal aid.

6.83   Corporates in the UK will obviously look closely at any challenges in this area which, if successful, may lead to an increase in litigation against business. In particular, companies sued by litigants in person may be caught up in Art 6 challenges where the litigation is inherently complex (as it was perceived to be in *Airey*). Landlord and tenant disputes come to mind in this regard, as do minority shareholder petitions pursuant to s 459 of the Companies Act 1985.[6]

6.84   Access issues have a further indirect affect upon businesses. Damages awards at Strasbourg are often not substantial.[7] The Act makes clear that damages are to be awarded in accordance with Strasbourg principles.[8] If human rights points brought locally generate meagre awards, it could be that few cases concerning the Act will be taken on the basis of a conditional or no-win, no-fee

---

1   See, for example, *X v United Kingdom* (1981) DR 95.
2   *Stewart-Brady v United Kingdom* (1997) 24 EHRR CD 38.
3   See the European Commission cases of *Winer v United Kingdom* (1986) DR 154 and *Munro v United Kingdom* Appl 10594/83.
4   See also **8.146** et seq.
5   See *Faulkner v United Kingdom* Appl 30308/96, 30 November 1999.
6   But see also *R v Secretary of State for the Environment, Transport and the Regions ex parte Challenger* (unreported) 15 June 2000: claim that Article 6 would be breached if objectors at planning enquiry could not pay for counsel was dismissed.
7   See **2.66** et seq.
8   Section 8. See **3.160** et seq and Appendix 1.

arrangement. As such, putative litigants may have no alternative but to make an *Airey*-type challenge.

THE IMPACT OF THE ACT UPON VEXATIOUS LITIGANTS

6.85   Any notion that giving direct effect to Art 6 will extend the freedom to litigate of the vexatious is likely to prove to be wide of the mark. This issue was looked at by the European Commission some years ago and it accepted that it was a legitimate aim for the UK to require such persons to seek judicial permission before embarking upon further court action.[1] On this basis, it would appear difficult to mount a challenge based on the European Convention to the provisions of s 42 of the Supreme Court Act 1981.

LITIGANTS IN PERSON

6.86   Numbers of Contracting States do not permit litigants in person to appear in their highest courts and to that extent the practice in the UK is more liberal, thereby reducing the likelihood of Art 6 infractions.[2]

PERMISSION REQUIREMENTS

6.87   A number of legal systems (and not just that of the UK) demand that the permission of a court be obtained before particular forms of proceedings may be instituted. In one case from the UK the exclusion in the Mental Health Act 1959 of claims by mental patients against those responsible for their care *save on substantial grounds* was held not to be an Art 6 violation.[3] The European Court considered that the essence of the patients' right to litigate had not been impaired, whilst a proportionate safeguard against the possible harassment of staff had been put in place.[4]

6.88   However, what about the need established by the CPR 1998 to seek permission to appeal at the end of virtually all first instance hearings?[5] The obligation to seek permission before proceeding to the House of Lords has been upheld at Strasbourg,[6] but the systemic implications of requiring parties *at first instance* to obtain leave before proceeding further are more serious. Is the new system risk-free in the context of Art 6?

---

1   *H v United Kingdom* Appl 11559/85, (1985) 45 DR 281.
2   See the article by Sir Robert Walker *Opinion: The Impact of European Standards on the Right to a Fair Trial in Civil Proceedings in United Kingdom Domestic Law* [1999] EHRLR 4.
3   *Ashingdane v United Kingdom* (1985) 7 EHRR 528, where a mental patient had sought access to court for the purposes of *habeas corpus* proceedings. Compare, however, *Aerts v Belgium* (2000) 29 EHRR 50. Restrictions on the ability of bankrupts to sue have also been upheld as Convention-compliant: see *M v United Kingdom* (1987) 52 DR 269.
4   By analogy, it would appear difficult to object on European Convention grounds to the requirement in CPR 1998, rr 6.17–6.31 that permission be obtained before certain forms of proceedings are served out of the jurisdiction. See also **6.99** et seq.
5   CPR 1998, r 52.3.
6   *Porter v United Kingdom* (1987) 54 DR 207.

ACCESS AND COURT FEES

6.89   Court fees have risen steeply in recent years, ostensibly on account of the fact that it is the Government's aim to make the justice system self-financing. The CPR 1998 aim to treat litigation as a last resort and this has at the same time contributed to a substantial decline in the number of claims brought.[1] Reports suggest that filing fees will increase exponentially to cover the shortfall that is accruing. Is this consistent with the access principle if the net effect is that people cannot, *Airey*-style, obtain effective access in complicated matters? Are claims to be allowed where payment of court fees is offered by instalments? The argument that the courts should pay their own way may be a legitimate aim in European Convention terms, but is the range of fees proportionate? How will local judges discharge the duty placed upon them by CPR 1998, r 1.1 to have regard for the financial position of the parties in seeking to ensure that equality of arms is achieved?[2]

6.90   At this stage, it may not be possible to say more than that the Court Service would do well to look again at its regime for the payment of scale fees in the context of Art 6. Beyond that, the question arises as to whether a claim should, on European Convention grounds, be reinstated where it has been struck out for non-payment of fees and where the party in default subsequently offers to make the requisite payment.

PERMISSIBLE LIMITATIONS UPON ACCESS

6.91   Clearly, if there were no boundaries placed upon access to the justice system, there would exist a real danger that the courts could be derailed by a torrent of unmeritorious claims, which could itself cause unfairness to others. The European Court accepted in the *Golder* case that limitations could be imposed in this area because the access right 'by its very nature' called for regulation by the State – regulation which might vary in time and place according to the needs and resources of the community and of individuals.[3] In such circumstances, Robertson and Merrills[4] suggest that Art 6(1) is more about 'a guarantee of ultimate judicial control than ... a right of instant access'. Therefore, limitations are possible, provided the 'very essence' of the underlying right is not impaired (as it was in *Airey*[5]), the restrictions pursue a legitimate aim, are not uncertain in scope and content, and are not disproportionate. In other words, in future in approaching the question of access restrictions, domestic courts should adhere to the same

---

1   In 1999 79,068 High Court actions were begun, compared with 152,412 the year before.
2   Compare the decision in *R v Lord Chancellor, ex parte Witham* [1998] 2 WLR 849, where it was held that withdrawing the exemption from the requirement to pay court fees for those on income support was invalid, and *R v Lord Chancellor, ex parte Lightfoot* [1999] 4 All ER 583, where the requirement to pay £250 to present a bankruptcy petition was not invalid. It was held that a constitutional right was involved in the first case but not in the second. For an explanation of the concept of equality of arms, see **6.159** et seq.
3   See **6.75** et seq.
4   See fn 2 on p 147 at p 87.
5   See also *Canea Catholic Church v Greece* (1999) 27 EHRR 521, where it was held that a determination after more than a century that the Catholic Church in Greece had no legal personality and, therefore, could not bring proceedings imposed a real and permanent restriction and impaired the very essence of the Art 6 right.

broad analytical approach used in considering alleged violations of Arts 8–11 of the European Convention.[1]

6.92   If, as predicted, the UK were to witness a US-style tort explosion, a clash between access rights in group actions and the need to manage court lists efficiently would appear all but guaranteed. Local courts already have considerable experience as regards the logistical handling of multi-claimant actions, but the giving of direct effect to the European Convention requires the difficult considerations involved to be approached within a new conceptual framework. One Strasbourg decision that is highly material in this context is that of *Lithgow v United Kingdom*,[2] where the statutory scheme established by the British Government to handle claims following shipbuilding nationalisation, which provided for a collective form of arbitration, was adjudged a legitimate device for the avoidance of a multiplicity of claims, and where the applicant shareholders were still able to participate in the compensation regime provided for in the legislation.[3]

LIMITATION PERIODS

6.93   Time-bars *prima facie* prevent court access, but they are permissible in European Convention terms where they are proportionate, promote legal certainty and avoid the difficulties and conceivable injustice arising out of litigation many years after the material events have taken place, when witness recollection has often gone and relevant documentation may no longer exist. In the case of *Stubbings*,[4] claims for assault had been brought by adults alleging sexual abuse during childhood. The applicants had petitioned Strasbourg in the wake of the House of Lords' judgment in the case of *Stubbings v Webb*[5] that civil proceedings for assault were subject to a 6-year limitation period which could not be extended, unlike the position in respect of personal injury claims, where the applicable 3-year time-bar can be extended at the court's discretion.[6]

6.94   The applicants had stressed the long-term nature of the damage caused by sexual abuse and the risk that their legitimate claims might be statute-barred before they even realised that they had a cause of action. Nevertheless, they lost their case at Strasbourg under Art 6 and Art 14.[7] The European Court reiterated its view that limitation periods must be legitimate in aim and proportionate in effect. There were, however, countervailing considerations. In this area, as in so many others, a margin of appreciation existed, there being no uniform standard across Europe. It was significant, said the Strasbourg judges, that limitation periods in personal injury cases are a common feature of the domestic legal systems of the Contracting States. What is more:

---

1   See Chapter 5.
2   (1986) 8 EHRR 329. See also Chapter 9.
3   See also **6.113** et seq as regards Art 6 and arbitrations.
4   *Stubbings v United Kingdom* (1997) 23 EHRR 213. The case of *R v Secretary of State for Trade and Industry, ex parte Greenpeace Limited* [2000] 2 CMLR 94, suggests that limitation periods will not readily be regarded as incompatible with the Convention.
5   [1993] AC 498.
6   Sections 11–14 of the Limitation Act 1980.
7   The prohibition on discrimination: see **5.44** et seq and Appendix 2.

'They serve important purposes, namely to ensure legal certainty and finality, to protect potential defendants from stale claims which might be difficult to counter and to prevent the injustice which might arise if courts were required to decide upon events which took place in the distant past on the basis of evidence which might have become unreliable and incomplete because of the passage of time.'

6.95 The European Court noted, in addition, that there was no limitation period in the UK for criminal proceedings and, taken as a whole, they concluded that the applicants' access rights had not been violated, although they conceded that victims of child sexual abuse were a special case and that the issue might need to be revisited in the future.

6.96 The judicial observation reproduced above is, of course, entirely in keeping with the common law's traditional promotion of finality in litigation, but it will nevertheless be of comfort to insurers and their corporate assureds fearful of long-tail liabilities.

6.97 What, however, of the time-bars in the CPR 1998 that are not the subject of statutory provision in the Limitation Act 1980? It may be anticipated, for example, that the requirement of promptitude in bringing judicial review applications will be tested on European Convention grounds. There will be pressure upon judges, in cases raising European Convention points, to relax the requirement that applications for leave be made promptly and in any event within 3 months of the act complained of. The argument will be made that this is to be construed by reference to the 2-year period for the bringing of claims laid down in s 7(5) of the Act.[1] Quite apart from the fact that the Act stipulates that the 1-year limitation is expressly subject to any rule imposing a stricter time-limit as regards the procedure in question (for example the stiffer requirement in applications for judicial review), such an argument looks unlikely to prevail in circumstances where there is a saving provision enabling applications for judicial review to be made after the 3-month long-stop and where, more importantly, there is a good policy reason for requiring public-law claimants to proceed promptly, namely that good administration would be impeded if claims could be made long after the material event.

QUALIFYING PERIODS

6.98 Some countries require a certain period of time to elapse before a claim can accrue. This too may be permissible in European Convention terms. Thus, the (then) 2-year qualifying period in the UK before most claims for unfair dismissal and redundancy payments could be brought was held not to violate Art 6.[2]

JURISDICTIONAL REQUIREMENTS

6.99 Some claimants will argue that the cases they have instituted in the UK should not be stayed on jurisdictional or forum grounds if the effect would be to deprive them of their European Convention rights.[3] It will be said that, in the wake

---

1   See **3.138** et seq and Appendix 2.
2   *Stedman v United Kingdom* [1997] 23 EHRLR 545. See also *Dobbie v United Kingdom* Appl 28477/95.
3   See *Lubbe and Others v Cape plc* (2000) 1 WLR 1545.

of the *Osman* decision at Strasbourg, judges here are no longer permitted to screen out claims at an interlocutory level on conflicts grounds. Against such submissions, the argument will be put that the imposition of a stay on proceedings in this country does not dispositively determine rights and objections.

6.100   In any event, stays are only imposed after judicial determination, following the filing of evidence and the making of oral submissions. In such circumstances, it is more than likely that the philosophical basis in comity for rules regarding conflicts of laws will not give rise to a European Convention difficulty.

PROCEDURAL TIME-LIMITS

6.101   These will generally be permissible, provided they are proportionate in the circumstances. A refusal to give further time to a litigant has been adjudged at Strasbourg to be reasonable, even where the order was a final one which could not be waived and when new evidence had emerged after the allotted time had expired.[1] Conversely, a 3-day time-limit for setting aside a judgment has been held to be overly strict.[2]

SECURITY FOR COSTS[3]

6.102   Requiring a party to litigation to secure the costs of his opponent may have the effect of stifling the litigation, thereby denying access to court. In the *Tolstoy* case[4] the Court of Appeal[5] took into account Tolstoy's prospects of success in his appeal from a High Court trial for libel which he had lost. It ordered Tolstoy to provide £124,900 to secure the costs of the appeal. This was not, in the view of the European Court, a violation of Art 6. Tolstoy had had the benefit of a 40-day hearing at first instance. He was unlikely to win on appeal in which event his opponent would conceivably be left with substantial costs which were irrecoverable. The Strasbourg judges found the principle of security for costs to be legitimate before turning to consider whether its operation in the *Tolstoy* case was proportionate.[6] They concluded that it was.

6.103   That is not to say that orders for security for costs are, in all respects, Convention-compliant. If Tolstoy's prospects on appeal had been better, or he had not appeared able to provide security, the result might have been different, as indeed it was in the case of *Aït-Mahoub v France*,[7] in which the European Court held that a requirement for an applicant with no income to lodge FFr80,000 before he could pursue his claim against two police officers violated his access right. This case can perhaps be distinguished from *Tolstoy* on the basis that Tolstoy had had

---

1   *X v Sweden* (1992) 31 DR 223. See too the reluctance in one recent case to stay English proceedings pending an application to Strasbourg: *Locabail (UK) Ltd and Another v Waldorf Investment Corporation and Others (No 4)* (2000) *The Times*, 13 June.
2   *Perez de Rada Cavanilles v Spain* (2000) 29 EHRR 109.
3   CPR 1998, Part 25. See also fn 3 on p 152.
4   *Tolstoy Miloslavsky v United Kingdom* (1995) 20 EHRR 442. See also *Les Travaux du Midi v France* (1991) 70 DR 47.
5   In a hearing which itself took 6 days of oral argument.
6   The need for proportionality in applications for security for costs was confirmed in a recent duty tribunal case: see *Anchor Foods Limited* Lon/94/7403.
7   [1998] HRCD 976.

his day(s) in court and had a poor case to take to appeal. In *Aït-Mahoub* the security was sought at first instance.

6.104   In this area at least, the Act is likely to change domestic civil procedure and judges will need to have regard for *Aït-Mahoub* before exercising their discretion in favour of an award of security for costs in cases where there has not already been a first instance decision, as there was in *Tolstoy*.

6.105   A likely clue as to the approach to be adopted by domestic courts in the wake of the Act has been provided in the case of *Hadkinson*,[1] where the Court of Appeal held that Art 6(1) was not violated by an order for the costs of an appeal to be secured. That was, however, an appeal from a summary judgment, placing it on all fours with neither *Aït-Mahoub* nor *Tolstoy*.

STRIKING-OUT POWERS AFTER THE ACT

6.106   The power to strike out claims, which traditionally has been available to British courts and is now the subject of increasingly interventionist judicial behaviour under the CPR 1998 is a *prima facie* denial of access to court. From now on, the power will need to be exercised with the *Osman* decision in mind. Its use will not in many instances, however, be an Art 6 process breach, not least because the exercise of the power is one way to secure the due process rights of the party which successfully obtains a striking-out decision. This is, nevertheless, subject to the proviso that the interference of the court be proportionate, and it is noteworthy that, for example, in the case of *Annodeus Entertainment Limited v Gibson*[2] an appeal against a striking-out order was successful in circumstances where the claimant could have been sanctioned in costs and/or by denial of some of its claim for interest.

6.107   More likely than not, local judges will cite with approval the words of Lord Woolf in the recent case of *Kent v Griffiths*,[3] in which it is plain that a marker was being laid down for the future. He said:

> '... it would be wrong for the *Osman* decision to be taken as a signal that, even when the legal position is clear and an investigation of the facts would provide no assistance, the courts should be reluctant to dismiss cases which have no real prospect of success. Courts are now encouraged, where an issue or issues can be identified which will resolve or help to resolve litigation, to take that issue or those issues at an early stage of the proceedings so as to achieve expedition and save expense. There is no question of any contravention of Article 6 of the ECHR in doing so. Defendants as well as claimants are entitled to a fair trial and it is an important part of the case-management function to bring proceedings to an end as expeditiously as possible. Although a strike-out may appear to be a summary remedy, it is in fact indistinguishable from deciding a case on a preliminary point of law.'

6.108   In much the same context, the Court of Appeal has also been quick to say that the summary judgment jurisdiction in local law is not incompatible with Art 6.[4]

---

1   *Federal Bank of Middle East Ltd v Hadkinson and Others* (1999) TLR, 7 December.
2   (Unreported) 2 February 2000.
3   (Unreported) 3 February 2000. Lord Woolf's observations were quoted by Lord Justice Tuckey in *Outram v Academy Plastics* 19 April 2000, when striking out a case.
4   See *Monsanto plc v Tilly and Others* (1999) *The Times*, 30 November.

6.109   So too in *Canada Trust Company v Stolzenberg and Others*,[1] Rattee J held that the making of an *unless* order was not an Art 6 violation on the basis that the defendant was not deprived of a fair hearing in circumstances where he had excluded himself from the court by his failure to comply with court orders. A similarly robust approach was adopted in the *Hadkinson* case,[2] regarding a related issue, namely the extent to which Art 6 may be engaged where proceedings are stayed pending the purging by a litigant of his contempt.[3] In that action, Arden J stressed that the fair trial guarantee was not unqualified. She emphasised that there was 'a paramount importance' in ensuring compliance with court orders and directed that certain costs be paid by the applicant before a stay was lifted. If *Hadkinson* is any guide, it could be that the role of Art 6 in attacking peremptory orders of the court in substantial cross-border commercial litigation may be limited.

ARTICLE 6 AND COSTS AWARDS

6.110   The so-called 'English rule', whereby costs have historically tended to follow the event (notwithstanding the greater judicial discretion permitted by the CPR 1998),[4] has previously been considered by the Strasbourg institutions not to be an Art 6 infringement.[5] Although there is no European Convention right to litigate at no cost to the litigant, the decision in *Airey*[6] shows that, if legal costs are so high as in effect to prohibit access to a court, Art 6 may be engaged.

6.111   Wasted costs orders made against lawyers as a mark of judicial displeasure have been held to fall outside Art 6 on the basis that they are not determinative of civil rights and obligations nor of a criminal charge.[7] This seems unpersuasive. Such orders are made in the context of subsisting proceedings. If the procedure for the assessment of court costs is justiciable within Art 6,[8] then so too, surely, should be the sanctioning of lawyers on account generally of their conduct in litigation.

6.112   Peremptory orders for costs made in summary assessments may have the effect of denying claimants, who cannot pay the sums ordered, a hearing. Here too, then, Art 6 may be engaged. What if the claimant offers to pay by instalments?

RETROSPECTION AND ARTICLE 6

6.113   Companies are on occasions denied their right to a hearing by the introduction of retrospective legislation. That was what happened to Burmah Oil

---

1   (Unreported) 13 October 1998.
2   See fn 1 on p 155.
3   See also *Daisystar Limited v Woolwich plc* 16 March 2000, unreported, in which the Court of Appeal looked at Art 6(1) in the context of a complaint that 'unless orders' made in that case were disproportionate and that refusal of an adjournment had denied the appellant a fair trial. The Court of Appeal held that it was the appellant's fault and that fairness was to be judged in terms of history of the litigation as a whole.
4   Parts 43–47 of CPR 1998.
5   Appl 15434/89, 64 DR 232.
6   See **6.79** et seq.
7   See **6.30** et seq and **6.14** et seq.
8   See *Robins v United Kingdom* (1997) 26 EHRR 527.

after the Second World War[1] and it happened to three British building societies much more recently.[2] Introducing statutes with retrospective effect is not *per se* a process breach, although it will be looked at very closely on the basis that 'respect for the rule of law and the notion of fair trial require that the reasons adduced to justify such measures be treated with the greatest possible degree of circumspection'.[3]

ARBITRATION AND MEDIATION

6.114   In most arbitrations the parties will have agreed to waive recourse to a court except for limited and stated purposes. This is permissible in European Convention terms, where it is based upon consent given freely.[4]

6.115   However, what if a local court, pursuant to r 26.4 of the CPR 1998, orders a form of alternative dispute resolution (such as mediation) in the absence of consent? To the extent that the mediation is by definition non-binding, this is unlikely to be a European Convention violation, a fair hearing being at worst postponed and not denied, but what if the claimant could show that he would be unable to proceed to trial on costs grounds if the mediation were to fail? What about the requirements in many consumer contracts that the consumer go to arbitration? There is scarcely equality of bargaining power in such cases. What about the requirement of arbitration that generally characterises non-negotiable tender offers? Is Art 6 engaged in such situations?

THE ENTITLEMENT TO A HEARING THAT IS FAIR

6.116   Article 6(1) explicitly guarantees the right to a hearing that is fair without identifying the constituent elements of fairness. Conceptions of fairness may change over time, something the Strasbourg judges acknowledged some years ago when saying that the fair trial concept had 'undergone a considerable evolution in the [European] Court's case-law, notably in respect of the importance attached to appearances and to the increased sensitivity of the public to the fair administration of justice'.[5]

6.117   The ingredients of fairness, therefore, are neither definitive nor conclusive and, even when uncovered, will often overlap. A greater latitude in approach is traditionally conceded by the Strasbourg institutions to national courts in civil[6] as opposed to criminal cases, as regards which the European Court often talks about fairness in terms of the rights of the defence. However, the question to be asked in every case (and whether it is civil or criminal in derivation)

---

1   See **1.35**.
2   *National and Provincial Building Society and Others v United Kingdom* (1998) 25 EHRR 127.
3   In the *National and Provincial* case. That case is dealt with more fully in Chapter 9. See also *Pressos Compania SA and Others v Belgium* (1996) 21 EHRR 301 and *Stran Greek Refineries v Greece* (1995) 19 EHRR 293, where the European Court was more hostile to retrospective legislation and **9.17** et seq.
4   *Deweer v Belgium* (1980) 2 EHRR 439. As regards waiver of Art 6 rights generally, see **6.170** et seq.
5   *Dombo Beheer BV v The Netherlands* (1993) 18 EHRR 213.
6   Ibid.

is this: were the proceedings conducted in such a manner that demonstrably impacts upon their fairness as seen by the applicant?[1]

6.118   In endeavouring to answer this question, the Strasbourg judges will not concentrate (unduly) upon technical lapses but instead will review the fairness of the relevant proceedings in their entirety, seeking (a) to identify the source of the unfairness and (b) to determine whether it created a significant impediment to the fair disposal of the proceedings.[2]

6.119   The most fundamental ingredients of fairness affect evidence, the trial process and judgment, and these are examined below.

Evidential fairness

6.120   The domestic rules of evidence, in relation both to criminal and civil procedure, are well developed and of long standing. In European Convention terms, such rules are largely a matter for the UK, and the European Court has laid down no strict safeguards in this area provided that hearings, considered in the round, remain fair.[3] In the UK, evidence obtained by theft, trespass or unlawful interception may, for example, be admissible, subject to the court assessing the weight to be attached to that evidence by virtue of the circumstances of its production.[4] In criminal cases, a judge here may exclude such evidence if its 'prejudicial impact outweighs its probative value',[5] but a major issue under the Act is very likely to be the extent to which the limited disclosure obligations of the Police and Criminal Evidence Act 1984 are consistent with Art 6, for denying the defence access to certain materials is not obviously reconcilable with the European Convention imperative to secure a fair trial.[6]

6.121   In *Schenk v Switzerland*,[7] the judges at Strasbourg concluded that evidence obtained by illegal telephone tapping, which was used to convict the appellant of incitement to murder, did not need to be excluded. The admissibility of such evidence was a matter to be regulated by national law. On the particular facts of that case, there was other evidence to convict the appellant, who had in any event been able to challenge questions of evidential admissibility before the relevant national court. By implication, however, if illegally obtained material is the only or principal evidence against an accused, the European Court might take a different view. Indications are that counsel for the defence will press British

---

1   See, for example, *Miailhe v France (No 2)* (1997) 23 EHRR 491.
2   *Nielson v Denmark* (1988) 11 EHRR 175. See also *Barbera Messeguè and Jabardo v Spain* (1988) 11 EHRR 360 and *Stanford v United Kingdom* Appl 16757/90. In the latter case the defendant to criminal proceedings had not been able to hear the witness properly. The trial was not unfair, said the European Commission, because the defendant had been represented by experienced counsel with whom he had been able to communicate.
3   There are many cases in point. See, for example, *Nielsen v Denmark* (see fn 2 above), *Mailhe v France* (fn 1 above), *Barbera, Messeguè and Jabardo v Spain* (see fn 2 above) and *Stanford v United Kingdom* (see fn 2 above).
4   *R v Khan Sultan* [1997] AC 558. A complaint to Strasbourg in that case was declared admissible on 20 April 1999 (Appl 35394/97) and judgment was delivered on 12 May 2000 (2000) *The Times*, 23 May.
5   Section 78 of the Police and Criminal Evidence Act 1984.
6   See *Kremar and Others v Czech Republic* Appl 35376/97, 3 March 2000: there was an Art 6(1) violation where the complainant was not shown documents relied upon by the national court.
7   (1991) 13 EHRR 242.

judges to adopt a position analogous to that in New Zealand, whereby evidence obtained in violation of the local bill of rights is *prima facie* inadmissible.[1]

DISCLOSURE AND EVIDENTIAL FAIRNESS

6.122   Disclosure in the context of civil proceedings has been the subject of a number of determinations at Strasbourg. Where documents are withheld and not made available, a violation of Art 6(1) may be found.[2] For example, the case of *McGinley and Egan v United Kingdom*[3] arose out of the campaign for compensation brought by veterans of nuclear tests in the Pacific. They alleged that documentation had been suppressed which could have assisted them in establishing that they had been subjected to deleterious levels of radiation when serving in the armed forces. The applicants' claim was rejected, but the European Court stated that:

> '... if there were a case that the respondent State had, without good cause, prevented the applicants from gaining access to, or falsely denied the existence of, documents in its possession which would have assisted them in establishing before the Pensions Appeals Tribunal that they had been exposed to dangerous levels of radiation, this would have been to deny them a fair hearing in violation of Art 6(1).'

6.123   It is a moot point as to whether in the future a claim could be made that the requirement to disclose, for example, medical information or to submit to a medical examination was a breach of a party's right to respect for private life as safeguarded by Art 8 of the European Convention.[4] This could become an issue in personal injury cases, which would make litigation more difficult in future for insurance lawyers in cases where they suspect malingering. What, indeed, of any filming that they make of the alleged malingerer?[5] This too may raise questions under Art 8,[6] in addition to Art 6.

6.124   An interesting insight into the interaction between the CPR 1998 and the European Convention in the run-up to the wholesale coming into force of the Act was provided in the case of *General Mediterranean Holdings SA v Patel*,[7] where Toulson J held that legal professional privilege (together, it should be noted, with the guarantees in Art 8) outweighed Art 6 considerations of evidential fairness

---

1   See *R v Goodwin* [1993] 2 NZLR 390 and *R v Te Kira* [1993] 3 NZLR 257.
2   See the case of *Feldbrugge v The Netherlands* (1986) 8 EHRR 425. There was an Art 6(1)
     violation where there was a failure to disclose expert evidence in connection with
     proceedings before a welfare benefits tribunal. See also *McMichael v United Kingdom* (1995) 20
     EHRR 205.
3   (1998) 27 EHRR 1. See also **9.203**.
4   See Chapter 7. In *MS v Sweden* [1997] 3 BHRC 248, it was held that, on the ground of privacy,
     disclosure should be strictly controlled in medical cases.
5   See, for example, *Ford v GKR* [2000] 1 All ER 302.
6   See also the case of *Chappell v United Kingdom* (1990) 12 EHRR 1, more fully dealt with at
     7.27. Although a search order (the old *Anton Piller* order) was held in that case not to violate
     the European Convention it, together with the injunction to make a freezing order (the old
     Mareva injunction), raises questions under not just Art 6 but also Arts 8 and 1 of the First
     Protocol, the right to property.
7   [1999] 3 All ER 673. See too, in this context, the deference paid by Neuberger J to privacy
     rights in refusing to order disclosure to be given by a third party not involved in proceedings:
     Anselm v Anselm (unreported) 29 June 1999. See also *R v Middlesex Guildhall Crown Court and
     Another, ex parte Tamosius and Partners (A Firm)* [2000] 1 WLR 453.

when the disclosure of an exchange of correspondence between lawyers and their clients was sought in a wasted costs application. Privilege, according to the judge, was a matter of substantive law and not evidence. More than that, it was a matter of constitutional importance in the administration of justice that engaged fundamental rights. Rule 48.7(3) of the CPR 1998, which required disclosure of the documents, was held to be *ultra vires.*

6.125 What about the end of the 'train of enquiry'[1] test for disclosure? Is the new (and less onerous)[2] requirement of a reasonable search adequate to guarantee a fair hearing? More likely than not it is, because the tribunal retains a residual discretion exercised, Strasbourg-style, on a case-by-case basis, and because a more rigorous approach to disclosure (which is not in any event accorded the same significance in civil law countries) could be a denial of the process rights of the parties from whom disclosure is sought. However, can a reconciliation be achieved by local judges between attempts, on the one hand, to push forward 'open justice' arguments, now buttressed by the free expression covenant in Art 10 of the European Convention[3] and, on the other, the limited information right in Art 8 and the fair trial guarantees in Art 6? Will the European Convention make it easier for companies to inspect court files, even when they are not parties to litigation?[4]

Expert testimony and fairness

6.126 The CPR 1998 ,[5] as already noted, encourage judicial interventionism and, understandably, the question whether expert testimony is necessary in any proceedings is being scrutinised more closely than it was in the past. It may be predicted that litigants will now argue that, where expert evidence is necessary for a fair trial to take place,[6] British judges must permit its introduction and, where parties are unable to meet the costs of such an expert, it will no doubt also be contended that legal aid should be provided for that purpose.[7] The key determinant in the event of such a dispute will necessarily be the issue of proportionality.[8] Otherwise, it may be anticipated that an Art 6 argument may be raised where the judge limits expert testimony to a single, joint witness in the absence of the consent of the parties.[9] Is a single, joint expert more likely to meet the requirements of Art 6(1) in some types of claim but not in others?[10] What are

---

1   See *The Peruvian Guano Company* [1983] QB 55.
2   See Part 31 of the CPR 1998.
3   See Chapter 8.
4   See *Smithkline Beecham Biologicals SA v Connaught Laboratoires Inc* [1998] 4 All ER 498; *GIO Personal Investment Services Limited v Liverpool and London Steamship Protection and Indemnity Association Limited (FAI General Insurance Co Limited Intervening)* [1999] 1 WLR 984 and *Barings plc and Others v Coopers Lybrand and Others* (unreported) 5 May 2000.
5   See CPR 1998, Part 35.
6   See *Stevens v Gullis* [2000] 1 All ER 527.
7   See the cases of *H v France* (1990) 12 EHRR 74, *Mantovanelli v France* (1997) 24 EHRR 37 and *Martins Moreira v Portugal* (1991) 13 EHRR 517. The French tradition of a single, court-appointed expert has been a frequent subject of Strasbourg complaints.
8   See *Vernon v United Kingdom* Appl 38753/97, 14 September 1999 on the disclosure of expert evidence.
9   See *Daniels v Walker* (unreported) 3 May 2000 and Chapter 10.
10 See, for example, *S (A Minor) v Birmingham Health Authority* (1999) *The Times,* 23 November, where a single, joint expert on liability was deemed not appropriate in a medical negligence case.

the Art 6 implications of a judge's refusal to adjourn a trial date, notwithstanding the inability of an expert to attend?[1]

COMPANY DIRECTORS AND THE PRIVILEGE AGAINST SELF-INCRIMINATION

6.127   The privilege against self-incrimination, like the right to remain silent, is 'at the heart of the notion of fair procedure under Art 6'.[2] In criminal cases it arises expressly out of Art 6(2), but it has equally formed part of the broader fair trial guarantee in Art 6(1).[3] The principle is that a person cannot be compelled to provide evidence in response to questions which is subsequently used against him. The rule is a long-standing feature of the common law,[4] but it has been restricted in its application by various statutory provisions which require answers to be given to questions on pain of punishment by fine and/or imprisonment. Statutes containing such provisions and which enable the evidence so provided to be used in criminal proceedings against the provider include:

- s 43(1) of the Insurance Companies Act 1982;
- s 436 of the Companies Act 1985;
- ss 236 and 237 of the Insolvency Act 1987;
- ss 94, 105, 177 and 178 of the Financial Services Act 1986;
- s 2 of the Criminal Justice Act 1987;
- ss 41 and 42 of the Banking Act 1987; and
- ss 82 and 83 of the Companies Act 1989.

6.128   The principle of freedom from self-incrimination (strictly it was the right to silence) was first articulated by the European Court (overruling the European Commission) in the case of *Funke v France*.[5] M Funke had been under criminal investigation (for possible exchange control offences) by the French customs authorities who had demanded he produce bank statements and legal papers after a search of premises had failed to locate them. He refused and was fined. No other prosecution was initiated against him, but the Strasbourg judges nevertheless decided (M Funke having died in the meantime) that France had infringed his right to silence by prosecuting him for failing to produce potentially incriminating evidence. It is significant that no distinction was drawn by the European Court between compelled testimony and the compelled provision of documents and it was the failure to produce the documents which had led to the violation, not their subsequent use (potentially).

---

1   See, for example, *Matthews v Tarmac Bricks and Tiles* [1999] CPLR 463.
2   *Murray v United Kingdom* (1996) 22 EHRR 29 at para 45. See too *Brown v Procurator Fiscal of Dunfermline* [2000] UKHRR 239, where it was held that the Art 6 right to silence and not to incriminate oneself implicitly applied to a suspect under questioning and would certainly apply to the use of any answers at trial.
3   As a result of the centrality of privilege in terms of Art 6(1), it was considered appropriate to deal with it here, after discussing evidentiary issues.
4   See the case of *In Re O* [1999] 2 WLR 475, but see also the case of *AT&T Istel Limited v Tully* [1993] AC 45, where the House of Lords held that, in the context of civil proceedings, so long as safeguards can be put in place (such as restricted disclosure), there was no reason why evidence should not be produced which had the potential otherwise to incriminate.
5   (1993) 16 EHRR 297.

6.129   The decision in *Funke* came some years after that reached by the European Court of Justice in the case of *Orkem*[1] where the Luxembourg Court determined in the context of a competition inquiry that:

> 'As far as Article 6 of the European Convention is concerned, although it may be relied upon by an undertaking subject to an investigation relating to competition law, it must be observed that neither the wording of that Article nor the decisions of the European Court of Human Rights indicates that it upholds the right not to give evidence against oneself.'

6.130   The Court ruled in *Orkem* that the EC Commission could not force a business to answer questions which might constitute an admission of a competition infraction, but deprived this statement of much of its content by confirming that undertakings were compelled to hand over materials even if they 'may be used to establish ... the existence of anti-competitive conduct'. The conclusion apparently to be drawn from *Orkem* is not 'that there are certain matters about which questions may not be asked but only that there are certain types of questions which may not be asked'.[2]

6.131   *Funke* and *Orkem* are not obviously consistent, but the importance attaching to competition inquiries in the European Community legal order is such that it must be doubtful whether the Court would in a future case abandon *Orkem*, not least when the Court in addition can point to its decision in *SA Musique Diffusion Française et al v EC Commission*[3] to the effect that the Brussels Commission is itself not a tribunal for Art 6 purposes.[4]

6.132   *Funke* was followed shortly afterwards by the landmark case of *Saunders*.[5] Ernest Saunders was one-time Chief Executive of Guinness Plc and was charged (together with others) with false accounting and conspiracy arising out of an illegal share support scheme operated during Guinness' contested bid (which ultimately succeeded) for Distillers Company Plc. Before and after he was charged, Saunders had been interviewed by inspectors appointed by the Department of Trade and Industry to investigate the circumstances of the bid. His answers when interviewed *after* he was charged were not put before the jury at his trial, but those given *before* he was charged were. In the face of Saunders' objections, part of the transcript of his interview was read out to the jury over 3 days.

6.133   The Court of Appeal saw no basis for disturbing the verdict below, but both the European Commission and the European Court held that there had been a process breach under Art 6 and that the undoubted public interest in

---

1   *Orkem v Commission* [1989] ECR 3283. As regards this vexed question of conflict between European Community and European Convention law, see also **5.55**.
2   According to the Advocate-General in the case of *Otto v Postbank* [1993] ECR J-5683.
3   [1983] ECR 1825.
4   On the other hand, the European Commission's unanimous view in *Société Stenuit v France* (1992) 14 EHRR 509 was that a fine imposed upon a French company on competition grounds was 'criminal' in nature, not least because the fine could be imposed in relation to a proportion of a company's annual turnover (broadly, the provision now imported into the Competition Act 1998, see **6.282** et seq. As to the relationship between EC law and European Convention law, see **5.55** et seq.
5   (1996) 23 EHRR 312, a case in which the pressure group Liberty submitted an *amicus* brief at Strasbourg, as they also did in the case of *Halford* (see Chapter 7).

prosecuting serious fraud could not justify such a violation of the applicant's rights. The Strasbourg judges considered that:

> '... the right to silence and the right not to incriminate oneself [were] generally recognised international standards ... [t]heir rationale lies, *inter alia*, in the protection of the accused against improper compulsion by the authorities, thereby contributing to the avoidance of miscarriages of justice and to the fulfilment of the aims of Article 6.'[1]

6.134   Had Saunders not answered the questions put to him, he would, under s 436 of the Companies Act 1985, have risked being (in effect) in contempt and punished as such. It was irrelevant, said the European Court, that the evidence Saunders had provided might not, in fact, be incriminating (if, for example, it included exculpatory remarks), as a skilful prosecutor could deploy potentially neutral evidence in a way which could damage a defendant. According to the Strasbourg judges:

> 'The right not to incriminate oneself, in particular, presupposes that the prosecution in a criminal case must prove their case without resort to evidence obtained through methods of coercion or oppression in defiance of the will of the accused.'

6.135   The European Court emphasised in *Saunders* that 'its sole concern' was with the use later made of the statements at Saunders' trial – what has been called a 'subsequent use' immunity by Professor Davies[2] – rather than a condemnation of compelled evidence generally. The protection conferred by the European Court in the *Saunders* case was against the subsequent use of testimony (and not merely incriminating testimony), not the use of compulsion under s 432 of the Companies Act 1985 to obtain the testimony. That, according to the Strasbourg judges, was permissible.[3]

6.136   In early 1997, the Court of Appeal was faced in a criminal case with a concession made by the prosecution that convictions for insider trading had been based upon compelled evidence which violated Art 6.[4] In what Professor Davies

---

1   A more recent European Court pronouncement on the right to silence in criminal cases is in *Condron v United Kingdom* 2 May 2000, where two convicted drug dealers were each awarded £15,000 after an Art 6 breach was unanimously found by the Strasbourg judges, who considered that the jury had been misdirected about the couple's refusal to answer police questions. Silence was not 'an absolute right', but the jury should have been directed that 'if it was satisfied that the applicants' silence ... could not sensibly be attributed to their having no answer, or none that would stand up to cross-examination, it should not draw an adverse inference'. It is not clear, in light of *Condron*, whether the Court of Appeal in the UK will any longer be able to say that a conviction at first instance was *safe*, whether or not it was *fair*.

2   See his chapter 'Self-incrimination, Fair Trials and the Prevention of Corporate and Financial Wrong-doing' in *The Impact of the Human Rights Bill on English Law* (Clarendon Press, Oxford, 1998) at p 33.

3   In August 1999, the European Court said in a preliminary ruling that three of Saunders' co-defendants, Gerald Ronson, Jack Lyons and Anthony Parnes, had admissible arguments that they had been denied a fair trial on the basis, in part, that there had been an 'impermissible degree of co-operation' between the Department of Trade and Industry inspectors and other agencies as regards the transcripts of evidence (given to the inspectors). The applicants are raising additional arguments as regards the length of the trial and the use of undisclosed evidence. A full hearing is anticipated in late 2000. See, for example, *The Guardian*, 4 August 1999.

4   *R v Staines; R v Morrisey* (1997) 2 Cr App Rep 426. See also *R v Faryab* [1999] BPIR 569 – compelled testimony given pursuant to s 433 of the Insolvency Act 1986 could not be used in the accused's later criminal prosecution (for handling stolen goods).

has described as a 'flat refusal to come to grips' with the *Saunders* decision, the Court of Appeal conceded that there was indeed a conflict with the views of the European Court, but refused to interfere with the convictions on the ground that to do so:

> '... would amount to the repeal, or a substantial repeal, of an English statutory provision [ie s 78 of the Police and Criminal Evidence Act 1984] which remains in force in deference to [the *Saunders* decision] which does not have direct effect and which, as a matter of law, is irrelevant.'[1]

Plainly this approach is, as a consequence of the Act, no longer sustainable.

6.137   The Government has indicated that it will legislate to bridge the *Saunders* gap. In the meantime, it is now prosecutorial practice, following a Guidance Note from the Attorney-General on 3 February 1998, for such forms of compelled evidence no longer 'normally' to be used in criminal trials.[2] Nevertheless, this may remain a problematic area as the courts will be unable to disapply the Police and Criminal Evidence Act 1984, and where, as a result, it is conceivable that a declaration of incompatibility will be made.

6.138   A recent domestic case in which the techniques of the inspectors of the Department of Trade and Industry were successfully challenged (partly on European Convention grounds and prior to the coming into force of the Act) involved Kevin Maxwell.[3] The background was that the relevant inspectors had been asked to investigate certain affairs of Mirror Group Newspapers. They declined to interview Maxwell while criminal proceedings were pending against him. After his acquittal, however, they sought to interview him on 131 topics. He declined to assist on the basis that, among other matters, the voluminous materials sent to him constituted an unlawful demand by the inspectors for him 'to perform forced or compulsory labour' (under Art 4(2) of the European Convention)[4] under threat of penalty. In proceedings brought against Maxwell by the inspectors for failing to co-operate, the then Vice-Chancellor, Sir Richard Scott, found that the inspectors could not place demands upon witnesses that were unreasonable as to time or expense.

6.139   Ernest Saunders' success at Strasbourg has tended to obscure the fact that the European Court's earlier finding in *Fayed*,[5] that the Department of Trade and Industry's inspectors' role was adjudicative only (thereby putting their actions outside Art 6), was followed in *Saunders*, thus pointing up again the distinction drawn by the European Court between the process of investigation, often regarded as administrative in nature and not bearing upon Art 6 (whatever the panoply of powers available to the investigator), and the trial process.[6] The

---

1   See also in this context the case of *Re Atlantic Computers – Secretary of State for Trade and Industry v McCormick* (unreported) 29 April 1997, where Rimer J said that it was tenable that Saunders had 'no directly analogous application to civil disqualification proceedings' and *Secretary of State for Trade and Industry v Hinchcliffe* (1998) *The Times*, 2 February 1998. See also *Nottingham City Council v Amin* (1999) *The Times*, 2 December.

2   See also the analysis of the Financial Services and Markets Act 2000 (see **6.233**) and, in a different context, *Nottingham City Council v Amin* [2000] 2 All ER 946, where Lord Bingham reviewed the Strasbourg jurisprudence on *agents provocateurs* when considering s 48 of the Police and Criminal Evidence Act 1984.

3   *Re an Inquiry into Mirror Group Newspapers plc* [1999] 2 All ER 641.

4   See Appendix 2.

5   See **6.48**.

6   See, as regards Art 6 and administrative decisions, **6.66** et seq.

distinction is, of course, of enormous assistance to agencies such as the Department of Trade and Industry. There must be a real doubt, however, whether this distinction could credibly be maintained in an investigation by the Department of Trade and Industry, for example, into possible insider dealing where the nexus between the investigation and potential prosecution is direct and clear and where the Art 6 safeguards should conceivably encompass the legal process in its entirety.

6.140   As has been seen, the privilege against self-incrimination applies not only to the power to compel the giving of oral testimony, but also to the production of documents.[1] This is not merely a matter of common law. It is also the European Court's position as outlined in *Funke*.[2] The *Funke* decision, however, does create practical difficulties. Many regulators in the UK require those engaged in regulated activities to maintain logs and other data to ensure that effective monitoring can take place and regulators will no doubt argue that a distinction can be drawn between the exercise of a compulsory power to provide testimony and a compulsory power to hand over documents which already exist.

6.141   Perhaps mindful of this, the Strasbourg judges stressed in *Saunders* that the right not to incriminate oneself was not absolute. In a further respect, it was:

> '. . . primarily concerned . . . with respecting the will of an accused person to remain silent. As commonly understood in the legal system of the Contracting Parties to the Convention and elsewhere, it does not extend to the use in criminal proceedings of material which may be obtained from the accused through the use of compulsory powers but which has an existence independent of the will of the suspect such as documents acquired pursuant to a warrant, breath, blood and urine samples and bodily tissue for the purpose of DNA testing.'

6.142   There is something odd about this attempt on the part of the European Court to maintain a distinction between documents seized by the authorities (which may fall outside the ambit of the privilege against self-incrimination because of their so-called *independent* existence) and documents otherwise obtained under compulsion (but, following the decision in *Funke*, within the privilege). Documents in the first category may, as the Strasbourg judges expressly contemplated in *Saunders,* often be seized under warrant, which is self-evidently a form of compulsion. It is therefore by no means clear what status local judges will confer upon *Funke*.

6.143   The use of compulsory testimony in disciplinary proceedings is also likely to be problematic in terms of Art 6(1). In the *Nawaz* case,[3] which involved the Institute of Chartered Accountants of England and Wales, Sir Stephen Sedley held that answers given under compulsion to a professional body might expose an individual to loss of livelihood. This was in the nature of a penalty as a consequence of which the privilege against self-incrimination was engaged. On the facts, however, Sir Stephen found that Mr Nawaz had waived[4] his privilege when he agreed to become a member of the Institute. The Court of Appeal[5] accepted this analysis, noting that when individuals participate in the activities of

---

1   See *AT&T Istel Limited v Tully* [1992] 3 All ER 523 (see also fn 4 on p 161) and *Rank Film Distributors v Video Information Centre* [1981] 2 All ER 76.

2   See **6.128**.

3   *R v Institute of Chartered Accountants of England and Wales ex parte Taher Nawaz* [1997] PNLR 433.

4   As to the waiver of European Convention rights generally, see **6.170** et seq.

5   (Unreported) 25 April 1997.

an organisation in a way that expressly renders them subject to that organisation's rules (including a rule providing for compulsory questioning), they waive any privilege which might otherwise have been capable of being asserted.[1] It is not apparent then that Art 6 will necessarily have much bearing upon the use of compelled evidence in professional disciplinary proceedings.[2]

6.144   The House of Lords has recently exhibited a determination to keep *Saunders* narrowly confined in a case involving Hertfordshire County Council,[3] in which their Lordships looked at the European Convention in connection with s 33(1)(a) of the Environmental Protection Act 1990, which gave effect in the UK to an EC Council Directive. A failure without reasonable excuse to answer a request for information under s 71(2) of the Environmental Protection Act is a criminal offence and the appeal arose out of the Council's refusal to confirm that any response to its request would not be used in a subsequent prosecution. In his speech, Lord Hoffman was clear that Art 6(1) was only engaged if the information provided was used at trial. Administering the request was an extra-judicial matter which did not engage Art 6(1). It was not an adjudication, either in form or substance. The privilege against self-incrimination did not arise (not least because 'the right not to give evidence against oneself is basically a right of an individual, not a legal entity or company') and the questions, seeking to elicit purely factual information without inviting admissions of wrongdoing, had to be answered. Signs are, therefore, that local judges will work hard to maintain *Saunders* and *Funke* within bounds.

DISQUALIFICATION ORDERS AND ARTICLE 6[4]

6.145   The issue of subsequent use testimony arose in the case of *Official Receiver v Stern and Another,*[5] where the Court of Appeal held that the use of statements provided under the compulsory powers in s 235 of the Insolvency Act 1986 would not breach Art 6(1) or, indeed, EC law. Disqualification proceedings were not criminal proceedings, although serious in nature and potentially involving stigma. Insolvency law had a range of coercive powers giving rise to a range of conceivable prejudice. Section 235 was not directed exclusively at incriminating material, and exclusively self-incriminating material had not in fact emerged in this instance. Fairness was to be reviewed in the round. It had not been affected in the instant case and was best left to the trial judge.

6.146   *Stern* suggests that the domestic threshold for determining a *criminal charge* in terms of Art 6(1) remains high and that disqualification proceedings under the Company Directors Disqualification Act 1986 will for the foreseeable future be treated as civil in nature, as a result of which the allegations regarding the respondent director need not be pleaded with the degree of particularity expected in a criminal case,[6] where the burden of proof will therefore be the civil

---

1   Judgment dated 25 April 1997.
2   Its use in disciplinary proceedings instituted by financial services regulators in the City of London may, however, be different, as to which see **6.233** et seq.
3   *R v Herefordshire County Council, ex parte Green Environmental Industries Ltd and Another* [2000] 1 All ER 773.
4   See generally in relation to this subject (2000) *The Company Lawyer* vol 21, no 3, p 90.
5   [2000] ILR 10.
6   See, for example, *Re Continental Assurance Co of London plc* [1997] 1 BCLC 48.

one[1] and where compelled testimony will not necessarily be excluded,[2] even though obtained under compulsion and used in subsequent proceedings bearing directly upon livelihoods.

6.147   The then Vice-Chancellor, Sir Richard Scott, had relied at first instance in *Stern* upon the decision of the European Court in *DC, HS and AD v United Kingdom*[3] in finding that the disqualification proceedings involved the determination of civil rights and obligations but not a criminal charge. Company director disqualification, the Strasbourg judges had said, was a regulatory matter in the UK, leading not to a fine or imprisonment but rather to a prohibition on acting as a company director without leave. In particular, the European Court noted in that case 'the importance in modern economic life of public confidence in limited companies, and it [accepted] that regulatory mechanisms to ensure respect for directors' duties [were] one way of maintaining the necessary confidence'.

6.148   Compulsion does of course impact upon fairness. Quite outwith any invocation of the privilege against self-incrimination, attention in local courts may now shift to the argument that evidence obtained by compulsion offends against the right to a fair trial generally. In the civil context, oral evidence sought by compulsory powers may already be adjudged to be oppressive when directed at a third party or someone against whom allegations of fraud or dishonesty are made.[4]

THE IMPACT OF THE ACT UPON COMPANY INVESTIGATIONS GENERALLY

6.149   The European Convention's implications for company investigations would appear to be as follows.

(1) The compulsory powers deriving from the statutes identified earlier[5] remain available to domestic authorities so long as they are part of a (genuinely) investigative process and are, to that extent, outside the provisions of Art 6. The decision in *Stern* is significant local confirmation of this.

(2) Where an investigation is closely bound up with the likely prosecution of specific offences (such as insider dealing) there may be scope for arguing that the process, considered as a whole, engages Art 6, but the House of Lords' decision in the *Hertfordshire County Council* case,[6] in which the questions were administered by the very authority which had power to prosecute, suggests that this argument will encounter a good deal of judicial scepticism in the UK.

(3) In later criminal trials, compelled testimony cannot be used directly or collaterally because, as found by the Strasbourg judges in *Saunders*, it might otherwise be deployed:

---

1   See *Living Images Limited* [1996] 1 BCLC 348.
2   See *R v Secretary of State, ex parte McCormick* [1998] BCC 379.
3   Appl 39031/97, 14 September 1999. See also *EDC v United Kingdom* [1998] BCC 370.
4   See *Cloverbay Limited v Bank of Credit and Commerce International SA* [1991] 1 All ER 894, where the court refused to grant orders for oral examination pursuant to s 236 of the Insolvency Act 1986. See also *England v Purves* (1998) *The Times*, 29 January, sub nom *Re JN Taylor Finance Pty Ltd* [1999] BCLC 256 and *Re Atlantic Computers* (1997) *The Times*, 25 April.
5   See **6.127**.
6   See **6.144**.

'... to contradict or cast doubt upon other statements of the accused or evidence given by him during the trial or to undermine his credibility. Where the credibility of an accused must be assessed by a jury, the use of such testimony may be especially harmful.'[1]

For this reason, the use of coercive powers is likely to continue to be directed more at putative witnesses in criminal proceedings than putative defendants.

(4) Where compelled testimony leads to other testimony which is unlikely otherwise to have been revealed, the fact that such additional material has an existence independent of the compelled testimony is likely to mean that the additional material is not embargoed against subsequent use. There is, as yet, no clear European Convention authority on the point, but a Canadian case under s 7 of the Canadian Charter of Rights (which is broadly analogous to Art 6) confirms this approach.[2]

THE PRESUMPTION OF INNOCENCE

6.150   Closely linked to the right to silence and the privilege against self-incrimination is the presumption of innocence. Consequently, although the presumption is the subject of express protection in Art 6(2), it is for convenience dealt with now.

6.151   The presumption of innocence is central to the fair trial guarantee and, therefore, a broad interpretation of it is appropriate. It will:

'... be violated if, without the accused's having previously been proved guilty according to law and, notably, without his having had the opportunity of exercising his rights of defence, a judicial decision concerning him reflects an opinion that he is guilty. This is so even in the absence of any formal finding; it suffices that there is some reasoning suggesting that the Court regards the accused as guilty.'[3]

6.152   British lawyers will no doubt look to invoke the Art 6(2) guarantee in any 'reverse-onus' case, in circumstances where the Strasbourg judges have said that presumptions against the interests of the accused must be confined 'within reasonable limits which take account of the importance of what is at stake and maintain the rights of the defence'.[4] In other words, reverse-onus provisions are not barred in European Convention terms, but are susceptible to a form of fair balance adjudication.

6.153   The importance of the presumption to the Strasbourg institutions is part of a wider safeguard which is intended to ensure that the individual facing a public authority (most obviously in criminal proceedings) should not be unfairly disadvantaged. The theory is that, so far as possible, the State (with the vast array of resources at its disposal) should not be able to use its position to exert undue pressure upon the individual. On the contrary, the individual should be afforded

---

1   At para 71.
2   *Thompson Newspapers Limited v Director of Investigations and Research* (1990) 47 DLR (4th) 161 at pp 252–253 per La Forrest J.
3   *Minelli v Switzerland* (1983) 5 EHRR 554 at para 37.
4   It has been suggested that the Proceeds of Crime Act 1995 may be vulnerable in terms of Art 6(2) as requiring the defendant to demonstrate the innocent origin of his assets.

additional protection to guarantee that the serious issues that will often be at stake, whether they be deprivation of liberty, employment or reputation, are capable of being properly understood and addressed by him. In this context, the presumption is, as already noted, closely connected with the privilege against self-incrimination.[1] The latter can protect the individual against the subsequent use of compelled evidence. The former requires the prosecution to prove its case.[2]

6.154   The presumption, like the right to silence, has been stated to lie at the heart of the European Convention's conception of a fair procedure,[3] just as in the common law it cannot ostensibly be challenged.[4] That is not to say, however, that it is unlimited in extent. There is no Strasbourg authority for the proposition that the criminal burden of proof is beyond a reasonable doubt. However, where there is an evidential doubt, it 'should benefit the accused'.[5] Where an individual refuses to answer questions in circumstances where he has been warned that adverse inferences may be drawn against him and which 'clearly call for an explanation from him' and where other evidence of wrong-doing is 'formidable', a trier of fact is entitled to draw adverse inferences from the failure to answer, so long as reasons are given for doing so.

6.155   *Murray* was a case from Northern Ireland involving a terrorist offence and where the judge sat without a jury.[6] Murray had been found in a house where a man was being held captive by the IRA. He failed to explain why he was there. His conviction was not an Art 6 violation according to the Strasbourg judges (by 14:5). Provided evidence was not obtained under compulsion, the fact that a local statute permitted the drawing of inferences did not move the probative burden from the prosecution to the defence. The Strasbourg judges considered that an experienced judge would recognise this and it is conceivable that, in a jury trial, the result might be different.

6.156   Strict liability offences do not offend against the presumption,[7] provided that the burden of establishing the *actus reus* is upon the prosecution. Companies vulnerable to, for example, environmental charges of a strict liability nature, therefore, are likely to receive little assistance from Art 6.

6.157   The presumption has been raised in a variety of different contexts.[8] In the landmark free expression case of *Lingens*[9] (which arose out of a prosecution for *criminal* libel), it was held that the requirement in Austrian defamation law for the defendant to prove certain elements of his case was not, without more, a breach. Similarly, the French rule of law whereby a company director is deemed to be responsible for a company's debts has also been found not to be a violation.[10] So

---

1   See **6.127** et seq.
2   See *Funke* (**6.128** et seq) and also *Barbera, Messeguè and Jabardo v Spain* (1998) 11 EHRR 360.
3   *Murray v United Kingdom* (1996) 22 EHRR 29.
4   See Lord Bingham in *Kebilene* [1999] 3 WLR 175 at 188.
5   *Barbera, Messeguè and Jabardo v Spain* (see fn 2 above).
6   In what was then popularly known as a Diplock court.
7   See *Bates v United Kingdom* [1996] EHRLR 312 and *Salabiaku v France* (1988) 13 EHRR 379. *X v United Kingdom* (1972) 42 CD 135 suggests that statutory presumptions are also not a violation.
8   For example, in the case of *Albert and Le Compte v Belgium*, it was considered to encompass disciplinary actions against members of the medical profession. See also **6.23**.
9   See **8.15** et seq.
10   *G v France* (1988) 57 DR 100.

too, complaints to Strasbourg about the extent to which the Dangerous Dogs Act 1991 in the UK might undermine the presumption (in circumstances where dogs are assumed to be of a defined, dangerous breed unless otherwise shown to be the case) failed because the UK courts retained, in the view of the European Commission, an area of discretion, albeit constrained.[1]

6.158   Despite the limited reach of the presumption suggested by these cases, the Strasbourg institutions have stated repeatedly that great care must be taken to avoid any perceived determination of guilt on the part of court officials in comments preceding any judicial finding.[2] The aim at all times should be to be 'guilt neutral'. The Swiss Minister of Justice managed to avoid a finding of an Art 6 violation when saying of a suspected terrorist held in detention that she had committed 'common-law offences'. However, the Minister added that she did not know whether the alleged terrorist would be convicted. The European Commission suggested that this was an assertion of suspicion and not a determination of guilt – an unsatisfactory conclusion by any standard.[3]

6.159   Connected with this, the Strasbourg institutions have recognised that adverse publicity which is directed intentionally at the accused may violate the presumption, particularly where the trial is to take place before a jury.[4] This bears directly upon issues affecting the hearing itself which are examined below.

THE TRIAL PROCESS

6.160   The European Convention upholds a general principle of equality of arms (*égalité des armes* in the French text),[5] an aspect of the fair trial guarantee but not co-extensive with it. It is a requirement of open justice and applies in both the civil and criminal law spheres and not just in relation to Art 6.[6]

6.161   The idea is that in litigation there should be a level playing field, that parties to legal proceedings[7] should engage in similar conditions in order to ensure that a fair balance is maintained between them. In its classical formulation, it is about ensuring that litigants have reasonable opportunities to present their cases in an environment that does not place one at a substantial disadvantage *vis-à-vis* the other.[8] Thus, for example, in a case about the compulsory expropriation of shares, both parties had, as part of this Art 6(1) guarantee, the right to 'have knowledge of and to comment on the observations filed or evidence adduced by the other party'.[9]

---

1   See *Bates v United Kingdom* Appl 26280/95, *Foster v United Kingdom* Appl 28846/95 and *Brock v United Kingdom* Appl 26279/95.
2   See, for example, *Allenet de Ribemont v France* (1995) 20 EHRR 557. In that case, a police officer had said at a press conference before the appellant's trial that the appellant was the 'instigator of a murder'. This violated the presumption.
3   *Krause v Switzerland* (1978) 13 DR 73.
4   *X v Austria* (1963) 11 CD 31. In such cases, the key is for the judge to give careful directions to the jury to disregard the publicity.
5   The phrase was first used in the case of *Neumeister v Austria* (1960) 1 EHRR 91.
6   It may, therefore, encompass proceedings engaging Art 5(4).
7   Including Strasbourg proceedings: see *Lawless v Ireland* (1961) 1 EHRR 15 .
8   *Dombo Beheer BV v The Netherlands* (1994) 18 EHRR 213, where the prohibition on the applicant's calling a witness while the other side could was held to violate Art 6.
9   *Ruiz-Mateos v Spain* (1993) 16 EHRR 505. See also *Borgers v Belgium* (1993) 15 EHRR 92.

6.162   A feature of the principle of equality of arms is that the dispute resolution process should be adversarial.[1] *Adversarial* in this context does not mean combative as such. It refers instead to the ability of parties to present their respective cases, whether civil or criminal[2] and to see and test their opponents' evidence and all other evidence placed before the tribunal or relied upon by it.

6.163   Local judges, in exercise of their trial management powers in civil litigation, are becoming more vigorous in limiting cross-examination and their control of evidence generally. In the future, they will need to be Convention-proof in so doing, which may not be straightforward when, on the one hand, they are charged with disposing of cases expeditiously and cheaply in accordance with the overriding objective of CPR 1998[3] whilst, on the other hand, the European Convention demands that a tribunal 'conduct a proper examination of the submissions, arguments and evidence adduced by the parties, *without prejudice to its assessments of* [sic] *whether they are relevant to its decision'* (emphasis added).[4] If it is for the parties at the outset to determine relevance (as this statement suggests), a clash between the CPR 1998 and Art 6 would appear inevitable.

6.164   The need for equality of aims may arise in a great variety of different contexts, affecting, for example, the role of experts[5] or being infringed where legislation is passed to stymie an existing claim.[6] If there is no equality of arms, the overriding safeguard of fairness may be infringed, even if no actual unfairness takes place. In a criminal trial, if a prosecutor is afforded greater facilities or access to the court, the impression may be created that there is a reasonable doubt as to the existence of equality of arms. This will suffice to render the proceedings unfair.[7]

6.165   By definition, equality of arms is more difficult to achieve in a criminal case and, therefore, the need for vigilance is all the greater in that context. A prosecutor must, as such, disclose all relevant material which would enable the defendant to prepare his defence, including material which could undermine prosecution evidence[8] and could also assist in mitigating the consequences of any determination of guilt.

6.166   Examples of the innovative application of the principle of equality of arms include the defamation case of *De Haes*,[9] in which a refusal to admit expert evidence was held to be a process breach under Art 6, which was also violated in the case of *Mantovanelli v France*,[10] where the national court asked its own expert

---

1   See the cases of *McMichael v United Kingdom* (1995) 20 EHRR 205 and *Ruiz-Mateos v Spain* (fn 9 on p 170).
2   See *Lobo Machado v Portugal* (1997) 23 EHRR 79 and *Vermeulen v Belgium* Appl 19075/91 and *Niderost-Huber v Switzerland* (1998) 25 EHRR 709.
3   CPR 1998, r 1.1.
4   *Kraska v Switzerland* (1993) 18 EHRR 188, para 30.
5   *Bönisch v Austria* (1987) 9 EHRR 191.
6   See *Stran Greek Refineries and Stratis Andreadis v Greece* (1994) 19 EHRR 293. See also **9.17**.
7   See *Borgers v Belgium* (1991) 15 EHRR 92, a criminal case in which the procurator appeared and made submissions before the Court of Cassation and then retired with the Court while it deliberated. This was standard practice in Belgium at the time. The procurator did not participate in the vote, but the impression created was one of inequality.
8   See the cases of *Jespers v Belgium* (1981) 27 DR 61 and *Edwards v United Kingdom* (1992) 15 EHRR 417. See also *Rowe and Davis v United Kingdom* (fn 3 on p 143).
9   *De Haes and Gijsels v Belgium* (1997) 25 EHRR 1.
10   (1996) 24 EHRR 370.

certain questions, the answers to which were likely in reality to be dispositive of the matter and to which the applicant had no ability, realistically, to contribute.

PRESENCE AT TRIAL

6.167   The defendant in a criminal case has the right to be present at his trial,[1] unless there is a real threat to witnesses or the defendant otherwise behaves in a disruptive manner.[2] Furthermore, the right to a fair trial pre-supposes that the trial be by way of oral hearing.[3]

6.168   In civil litigation, there is no European Convention right for an individual necessarily to be present at all stages of proceedings (albeit that there is generally no bar on this), except in those situations where his behaviour or character may be in issue, in which case there is probably a right to be present at all times.[4] The principle is more easily stated than applied in practice. What of interlocutory hearings without notice? Does an application for a freezing order against a company on the basis that its managing director is liable to dissipate corporate assets involve just his or the company's behaviour or character? Must the party seeking the freezing order at a hearing without notice raise this?[5]

6.169   On occasions, a litigant can waive his right to be present at trial and this is dealt with below in the context of a more general analysis of the extent to which European Convention rights can generally be waived.

WAIVER OF EUROPEAN CONVENTION RIGHTS

6.170   Notwithstanding the centrality of Art 6, it is possible for certain of its safeguards to be waived and derogated from when 'strictly required by the exigencies of the situation'.[6] Notwithstanding the European Convention's express qualification of a number of its substantive rights, this may seem remarkable. In fact, the extent to which waivers will be permitted is limited.

6.171   In express terms, the European Convention neither permits nor prohibits a waiver of its safeguards or the giving of consent to what might otherwise give rise to a European Convention violation. Different approaches have been adopted by the Strasbourg institutions in relation to different parts of the European Convention. Thus, giving oneself up to the police voluntarily has not been considered automatically to give rise to a waiver of the citizen's Art 5 right to liberty,[7] just as it is difficult to see how one could consent to forced or

---

1   Although this may not extend to his presence at an application for leave to appeal, where counsel can make the necessary submissions on his behalf: see *Monnell and Morris v United Kingdom* (1987) 10 EHRR 205. Even then, where the actual appeal considers questions of fact, there is surely an argument that the presence of the affected individual is necessary.
2   See *Ekbatani v Sweden* (1988) 13 EHRR 504 and *X v Denmark* (1981) 23 DR 50.
3   See *Fredin v Sweden (No 2)* (1994) Series A, No 283-A.
4   See *X v Sweden* [1959] 2 Yearbook 354 and *Muyldemans v Belgium* (1991) 50 EHRR 204.
5   See s 12 of the Act as regards without notice applications affecting the media (see **3.184** and **8.212** et seq).
6   See *Ireland v United Kingdom* (1978) 2 EHRR 25.
7   See *De Wilde, Ooms and Versyp v Belgium (No 1) (Vagrancy Cases)* (1971) 1 EHRR 373.

compulsory labour as understood in Art 4(2) of the European Convention.[1] On the other hand, the European Commission has stated that an employee may lawfully contract to limit his right to freedom of expression and that enforcement of that limitation will not violate Art 10(1).[2]

6.172 Within the specific confines of Art 6(1), limited forms of waiver may be upheld. In the case of *Albert and Le Compte*,[3] the European Court confirmed that a litigant could waive, of his own free will, the right to have a hearing in public,[4] provided, that is, that the waiver was clear and unambiguous. In that case, no waiver was in fact established, which meant that Art 6 had been violated, but the Strasbourg judges' principled support for the operation of waivers in this area may be helpful to businesses faced, for example, with disciplinary proceedings which they are anxious to keep from the public gaze.[5] If an individual or institution which is the subject of disciplinary proceedings perceives that a request for a public hearing will be turned down because hearings have been held in private *as a matter of course*, it is conceivable that there will *not* be a tacit waiver where the individual or institution seeks no public hearing, on the basis that the very essence of the Art 6(1) safeguard has not been made effective.[6]

6.173 In the *Håkansson* case,[7] a majority of the Strasbourg judges suggested that there was no process breach under Art 6 where there was a right to a public hearing but the applicant failed to apply for one. In a minority judgment, however, Mr Justice Walsh (from Ireland) objected to the notion of a tacit waiver in such circumstances. In his view:

> 'The public hearing requirement of Article 6(1) [was] enshrined in the Convention because the Contracting States thought it important, not because a party may think it important. The administration of justice in public is a matter of paramount importance in every democracy and is one of the cornerstones put in place in the Convention to guarantee the impartial administration of justice and the defence of the rights guaranteed by the Convention. The fact that the public may not manifest any particular interest in a given case is not a consideration. Equally, a lack of interest in having a hearing in public on the part of one or both parties to a suit does not alter the matter. Only where both parties agree to a hearing other than in public can the mandatory provisions of Article 6(1) be waived.'

6.174 Proceeding by analogy, it would appear that where, in the future, a regulator consents to a request that disciplinary proceedings be held in private, no European Convention breach will arise unless this would be to 'run counter to any important public interest',[8] such as (most obviously) the demand of the media to be present on account of the high-profile status of the relevant matter. This will

---

1   See Appendix 2. See also the case of *Van der Musselle v Belgium* (1982) 6 EHRR 163.
2   See *Vereniging Rechtswinkels Utrecht v The Netherlands* Appl 11308/84, (1986) 46 DR 200.
3   (1983) 5 EHRR 533.
4   As regards the Art 6(1) right to a public hearing, see **6.178** et seq.
5   See also *H v Belgium* (1988) 10 EHRR 339 and *Håkansson and Sturesson v Sweden* (1991) 13 EHRR 1. In the latter case, it was noted that proceedings were routinely conducted by the Swedish courts in private, absent a request by any party that a hearing be in public or where a public hearing was considered necessary by the courts. The applicant had not requested a public hearing and this was deemed in the circumstances to be an effective waiver of his right to a public hearing.
6   See *H v Belgium* (fn 5 above).
7   See fn 5 above.
8   *Håkansson* (see fn 5 above).

surely be a feature of commercial life from now on, with the press demanding access to regulatory tribunals held in private by consent of all parties.

6.175   It is possible for an individual to waive the right *to be present* at an oral hearing so long as the waiver is unequivocal and has been provided freely.[1] In a criminal case, if an individual waives the right to be present, legal representation must still be allowed.[2]

6.176   A trial may take place in the absence of a party so long as genuine steps have been taken a reasonable time beforehand to bring the proceedings to his personal attention.[3] If a trial *in absentia* does take place, an accused who has not absconded or waived his right to be present at the hearing (and any such waiver must, as already stated, be based on clear evidence) may well be able to argue that Art 6(1) has been violated.

6.177   The importance attaching to the impartiality of a tribunal is such that this requirement can probably not be waived.[4]

THE RIGHT TO A PUBLIC HEARING

6.178   As already noted (in context of waiver),[5] the right to a public hearing is a central feature of Art 6 (and also of local law).[6] It is intended to prevent the administration of justice in secret and to enable the public and the media to scrutinise the judicial process, which the European Court has described as being vital to the promotion of understanding and the maintenance of confidence in the legal system.[7] Lord Woolf has warned that the growing practice whereby judges read documents in their rooms 'away from the public gaze, should not be allowed adversely to affect the ability of the public to know what was happening in the course of the proceedings'[8] and he has acknowledged that the Act may cause a 'tension' in this area. Thus, the circumstances justifying the absence of a public hearing determining guilt or civil rights and obligations need to be compelling, even though Art 6(1) expressly permits the press and public to be excluded:

> '... from all or part of the trial in the interests of morals, public order or national security in a democratic society, where the interests of the parties so require, or to the extent strictly necessary in the opinion of the court in special circumstances where publicity would prejudice the interests of justice.'

6.179   These carve-outs appear on their face to allow for the exercise of a very broad discretion. It is interesting too that the press (presumably including

---

1   *Postrimol v France* (1994) 18 EHRR 130.
2   See *Pelladoah v The Netherlands* (1994) 19 EHRR 81.
3   See *Stamoulakatos v Greece* (1994) 17 EHRR 479 and *Colozza and Rubinat v Italy* (1985) 7 EHRR 516. In the civil context, judgments in default are not *per se* a violation of Art 6(1), provided a warning has been given.
4   See *Pfeifer and Plankl v Austria* (1992) 14 EHRR 692 and see **6.194** et seq.
5   See **6.170** et seq.
6   See *Storer v British Gas plc* [2000] 2 All ER 440.
7   See *Pretto v Italy* (1983) 6 EHRR 182 and *Diennet v France* (1995) 21 EHRR 554. In the latter case, the European Court held that disciplinary proceedings before a French medical association should be heard in public. See also *Mahon and Kent v Rahm* (unreported) 8 June 2000.
8   *Barings plc (in liquidation) v Coopers and Lybrand and Others* (2000) *The Independent*, 10 May.

broadcasters) and the public are differentiated.[1] In practice, the exceptions have been construed narrowly. Thus, according to a unanimous European Commission, it was an Art 6 violation where county court debt proceedings dealt with in the UK by way of arbitration were not the subject of the public hearing that the applicant had asked for.[2] The fact that the county court judge considered it a 'run of the mill' case was not the point, nor did the availability of an appeal to the Court of Appeal cure the defect. Exclusion of the public was only permissible 'to the extent strictly necessary in the opinion of the court in special circumstances where publicity would prejudice the interests of justice'. The British Government conceded that there had been a violation.

6.180   Among the compelling situations justifying a hearing other than in public will be cases involving public order issues or the disruptive behaviour of a party to the proceedings.[3] Hearings can also exclude the public where the subject-matter is particularly sensitive, such as divorce proceedings or where the testimony of child witnesses is being given.[4]

6.181   Also of relevance in this context are the indications to date of the Strasbourg institutions to the effect that:

– an appeal hearing on points of law only is not necessarily in breach of Art 6 if it is not in public, provided the hearing below was a public one;[5]
– it is not necessary that public notification be given of a hearing, provided the public is not excluded from attending;[6]
– private hearings before High Court masters are probably not a violation of Art 6(1); and
– only exceptionally is a public hearing not also an oral hearing.[7]

6.182   Predictions are that this long-standing Strasbourg safeguard will, in terms of the Act, have less impact in the High Court than in the regulatory sphere.[8]

PREJUDICIAL PRESS COVERAGE

6.183   Whilst Art 6(1) explicitly permits the removal of the press from court hearings, the Strasbourg institutions have tended to adopt a media-friendly position in their approach to wider coverage of legal proceedings. In the case of *X*

---

1   See **6.183** below as regards reporting restrictions generally and the televising of trials.
2   See *Scarth (Norman) v United Kingdom* Appl 33745/96.
3   See *Campbell and Fell v United Kingdom* (1984) 7 EHRR 165. That case arose out of prison disciplinary proceedings held *in camera*. The European Court held that this was justified in the circumstances.
4   See *X v United Kingdom* [1977] 2 Digest 452 and *X v United Kingdom* [1980] 2 Digest 456, where witness testimony was given on film for safety reasons. See also *T and V v United Kingdom* [2000] CLR 187 in this context.
5   *Helmers v Sweden* (1993) 15 EHRR 285 and *Ekbatani v Sweden* (1991) 13 EHRR 504.
6   *X v United Kingdom* [1979] 2 Digest 444. See also the case of *Atkinson, Crook and The Independent v United Kingdom* (1990) 67 DR 244, where the European Commission rejected the applicants' complaint that sentencing had taken place in private.
7   *Fischer v Austria* (1995) 20 EHRR 349 and *Allan Jacobsson v Sweden* (1990) 12 EHRR 56.
8   As far as the implications of the Act for the financial services industry are concerned, see **6.233** et seq.

v United Kingdom,[1] the European Commission found that any pre-trial publicity which had had a prejudicial effect on the jury could be cured, if need be, on appeal. This is not obviously reconcilable with the traditional judicial approach in this country to the reporting of contemporaneous legal proceedings. Relying on the decision in *X*, British publishers will no doubt argue from now on that the fact that jurors have taken an oath and are generally told to ignore press coverage disposes of any Art 6 problem. This issue is dealt with more fully in Chapter 8 below, dealing with Art 10's right to freedom of expression, but there must be grave doubts as to whether local judges will permit the importance of Art 10 materially to alter the long-standing emphasis on preserving the integrity of the trial process at all costs, even if this means that the privilege of journalists to write freely about hearings is limited effectively to fair and accurate reporting of the relevant day's proceedings in court.

THE RIGHT TO A TRIAL WITHIN A REASONABLE TIME

6.184　　Neither the UNDR (which preceded the European Convention) nor the ICCPR (which followed it) has any express provision requiring the dispensation of justice within a reasonable time. Article 6(1), however, does make the right explicit and no other single issue has been the subject of more frequent complaint to Strasbourg. The right applies to all forms of litigation and local judges will not be slow to rely on this part of the Treaty when declining applications for adjournments, specifically as regards trial dates.[2]

6.185　　The notion that justice delayed is justice denied is, of course, a well-established feature of English law. In European Convention terms, the obligation is to ensure that hearings in both civil and criminal cases should take place without excessive procedural delay, as otherwise confidence in the justice system is undermined and the rights and obligations which the European Convention is supposed to guarantee may be rendered nugatory. Contracting States should therefore order their legal systems in such a way as to ensure that this is achieved[3] and listing congestion is not therefore excusable if it was foreseeable and nothing was done about it.[4]

6.186　　What constitutes a reasonable time (the French phrase in the European Convention is *dans un délai raissonable*) first depends in any given case upon identification (which may be subjective) of the start and end date of the legal process. In civil litigation, time begins to run from the point at which proceedings are commenced[5] and when determining whether a civil case has been heard within a reasonable time, the following factors have been held to be relevant as a matter of European Convention jurisprudence.

1　　*X v United Kingdom* Appl 3860/68. By Strasbourg standards, this is now an old case not necessarily to be regarded as symptomatic of the European Court's current view. As regards reliance on Strasbourg decisions generally, see **5.11** et seq.

2　　See *H v France* (1990) 12 EHRR 74 and *Stogmuller v Austria* (1969) 1 EHRR 155.

3　　See *Pammel v Germany* (1998) 26 EHRR 100 at para 68.

4　　See *Zimmerman and Steiner v Switzerland* (1984) 6 EHRR 17 and *Guincho v Portugal* (1994) 7 EHRR 223.

5　　See *Ausiello v Italy* (1996) 24 EHRR 568.

–   The behaviour of the applicant – has he been responsible for the delay by using delaying tactics or being obstructive?[1] Parties are expected to proceed expeditiously with claims and to avail themselves of any procedural assistance. Ultimately it is for Contracting States to ensure that court procedures are such as not to result in unreasonable delay.[2]

–   The complexity, in factual and/or legal terms, of the issues at stake – do they, indeed, have consequences which extend beyond the parties to the instant litigation?[3]

–   Whether the issue is time-critical, ie whether delay would render the proceedings pointless or otherwise undermine the applicant's position.[4] Where a civil claim was brought by an HIV patient who allegedly contracted the disease after a negligent blood transfusion, the Strasbourg judges said that expedition was appropriate in circumstances where the applicant's life expectancy was limited. Two years was too long.[5] Urgency may also be appropriate in employment cases[6] and those involving land.[7]

–   Whether the State has been responsible for the delay[8] – if so, was it avoidable? The European Court has, for example, held that the listing congestion in national courts attributable to the restoration of democracy in both Portugal and Spain was not totally unforeseeable and the efforts made by the respective Contracting Parties were inadequate to deal with it.[9] So too, in a case from Ireland, the European Commission criticised the fact that it took a year for the Supreme Court to give judgment and 14 months for the trial judge to approve a transcript.[10]

6.187   An interesting question aries where the delay is not caused by a Member State but by the EU, specifically where competition investigations often last for a number of years. Chances are that, considerations of complexity, high politics and a desire not to reach a decision inconsistent with the position of the European Court of Justice in this area will make a successful Art 6(1) challenge on this score difficult.

DELAY IN CRIMINAL CASES

6.188   In criminal cases there tends to be even greater emphasis at Strasbourg upon the need for the expeditious dispensation of justice. This is on the basis that

---

1   See, for example, *Proszak v Poland* [1998] HRCD 162, where the applicant had declined a medical examination or *Ciricosta and Viola v Italy* Appl 19753/92, where the applicants had sought 17 adjournments over the years and not objected to six others sought by the other party. The case lasted 15 years in all. It was held that there was no process breach as the primary responsibility for the delay lay with the applicants.

2   See *Bucholz v Germany* (1981) 3 EHRR 597.

3   See *Kalte Klitsche de le Grange v Italy* (1994) 19 EHRR 368.

4   See *X v France* (1992) 14 EHRR 483.

5   The applicant indeed died and his case was taken to Strasbourg by his parents.

6   See, for example, *Bucholz v Germany* (1981) 3 EHRR 597.

7   See, for example, *Hentrich v France* (1994) 18 EHRR 440.

8   The case of *Süssman v Germany* (1996) 25 EHRR 64 suggests that cases heard before constitutional courts may need to be looked at differently in this context because of their political implications.

9   See *Guincho* (fn 4 on p 176) and *Union Alimentaria Sanders v Spain* (1990) 12 EHRR 24.

10 See *Reilly v Ireland* Appl 21624/93.

the defendant can generally do little (even if he tries) to lengthen proceedings and it is incumbent upon national courts in such circumstances not to delay matters, especially when the defendant is in custody.[1]

EXAMPLES OF UNREASONABLE DELAY

6.189   In this area, as in so many others, British lawyers looking for a European Convention answer need to proceed by way of analogy. Although it may be stated in general terms that the Strasbourg institutions are becoming less tolerant of delay, their approach is largely to have regard for the particular facts of the cases before them and, save for the broad issues identified above, to eschew the making of principled statements.

6.190   Delays have been held to be unreasonable where:

–   it took 6½ years for a civil dispute to be determined which was 'not particularly complex',[2] but a straightforward case that took a year longer did not give rise to an Art 6 violation because it was the applicants who had prolonged matters;[3]
–   a debt action took 5 years;[4]
–   company director disqualification proceedings that began in August 1991 were not disposed of until January 1996;[5]
–   costs proceedings in the UK took more than 4 years to complete;[6]
–   unfair dismissal proceedings in the UK (allowing for appeals) lasted almost 7 years;[7]
–   a pensions appeal took 2 years 8 months;[8] and
–   child care proceedings in the UK took more than 2½ years to be determined.[9]

6.191   It is doubtful whether the requirement of Art 6(1) of (reasonably) swift justice will lead to the inauguration of great changes following the wholesale introduction of the Act, not least given continuing active case management on the part of the local judiciary. Courts in the UK are likely to be slow to accept that a violation has been established on the ground of delay alone in circumstances where they will doubtless be aware of the systemic implications of so doing. As regards criminal matters there have, for example, been reports[10] of the efforts made to get as many fraud cases as possible to trial before October 2000 in order to see off delay applications (conceivably, it is suggested, by Mr Asil Nadir among others).

---

1   See *Foti v Italy* (1982) 5 EHRR 313, *Eckle v Germany* (1983) 5 EHRR 1 and *Abdoella v The Netherlands* (1995) 20 EHRR 585.
2   *Neves e Silva* Series A No 153-A, 27 April 1989.
3   See *Neubeck v Germany* App1 9132/80.
4   *Zimmerman and Steiner v Switzerland* (1983) 6 EHRR 17.
5   *EDC v United Kingdom* [1998] BCC 370. Consider in this context the Art 6 implications of long-running enquiries by the Serious Fraud Office or the DTI.
6   *Robins v United Kingdom* (1998) 26 EHRR 527.
7   *Darnell v United Kingdom* (1994) 18 EHRR 205.
8   *Styranowski v Poland* [1998] HRCD 1001.
9   *H v United Kingdom* (1988) 10 EHRR 95.
10   *The Guardian*, 20 March 2000.

6.192   What if a trial is held up by ancillary disciplinary proceedings or vice-versa? In some criminal cases the appropriate sanction for delay could, of course, be a reduction in sentence, but what of a civil case?

6.193   These issues will no doubt be thoroughly canvassed in the near future. However, it is important to emphasise that, although the UK has been found in violation of Art 6(1) on delay grounds, its record in this area is creditable when compared to that of Italy, for example.

THE RIGHT TO AN INDEPENDENT AND IMPARTIAL TRIBUNAL ESTABLISHED BY LAW

6.194   The characteristics of a tribunal as contemplated in this part of the European Convention were set out in the case of *Belilos v Switzerland*,[1] where the European Court stated that:

> '... a tribunal is characterised in the substantive sense of the term by its judicial function, that is to say determining matters within its competence on the basis of rules of law and after proceedings conducted in a prescribed manner.'

More than that, however, a tribunal

> 'must also satisfy a series of further requirements – independence, in particular of the executive; impartiality; duration of its members' terms of office; guarantees afforded by its procedure – several of which appear in the text of Art 6(1) itself.'

6.195   It is the judicial nature of the function performed by the body in question which characterises it as a tribunal in European Convention terms. The definition extends beyond courts and tribunals as generally recognised to include 'jurisdictional organs of professional associations'.[2] A tribunal that meets the standards of Art 6(1) should have the power to make a binding decision, but its composition need not be judicial and, subject to satisfying requirements of independence, civil servants and lay people can be members of administrative and disciplinary tribunals.[3] Likewise, although Art 6(1) does not import an automatic right to trial by jury, where there is a jury, the jurors must be independent and impartial.

6.196   The High Court judge, Sir Stephen Richards, when writing extra-judicially, has observed that UK courts generally have been concerned less with issues of independence than with those of impartiality.[4] Whether that remains so is another matter. From what appears below, it seems that, as a consequence of the Act, the issue of the relevant tribunal's very integrity may become an increasing feature of domestic litigation, even in the commercial context.

INDEPENDENCE

6.197   Independence means independence from the executive. In this regard, the European Court has identified the following factors as important:

---

1   (1988) 10 EHRR 466.
2   *De Cubber v Belgium* (1991) 13 EHRR 422.
3   See *Campbell and Fell v United Kingdom* (1984) 7 EHRR 165 at paras 33 and 81.
4   See his article *The Impact of Art 6 of the ECHR on Judicial Review* [1999] JR 106.

- the manner of appointment of tribunal members, their term of office and basis for removal;
- the existence of any guarantees against outside influence; and
- the appearance of independence to an objective viewer.

6.198   Judged by these criteria, planning inspectors in the UK have been found not to be independent.[1] Despite the obligation on them to be impartial, such inspectors held their appointments from the Secretary of State and could have them revoked by him at any time. Furthermore, the minister could short-circuit planning appeals by taking the matter from the requisite planning inspector and himself determining the appeal. The fact that the power was seldom used was not, in the view of the Strasbourg judges, material.

6.199   Appointment by the executive is not of itself objectionable (for how otherwise would judges be appointed) and in exceptional circumstances (such as misconduct) the removal of judges or tribunal members will not infringe Art 6(1). Membership of the executive, whilst also discharging a judicial function, is another matter altogether and has provoked several significant recent decisions both at Strasbourg and in the UK. There was, for example, a European Convention breach when the Rt Hon Michael Howard MP, as Home Secretary, set the sentencing tariff for the killers of James Bulger. This was the exercise of an Art 6 function which should not have been carried out by the minister to the extent that he was not independent of the executive.[2]

6.200   The strategic (if not perhaps the party political) implications of that determination at Strasbourg pale beside the ramifications of the more recent decision in the Scottish case of *Starrs*,[3] where the Scottish High Court held that Art 6 would be violated for lack of independence if a hearing took place before a temporary sheriff who held office at the pleasure of a member of a Scottish Executive, the Lord Advocate.[4] No surprise that, on 12 April 2000, it was announced that the position of Assistant Recorder was, in effect, to be abolished, a further example of a radical change to the structure of the judicial system here undeniably attributable to European Convention considerations and one coming about, what is more, before the wholesale coming into force of the Act.

6.201   The European Court held in the case of *McGonnell* (which came from Guernsey)[5] that the position of Bailiff in Guernsey was incompatible with the European Convention's requirement of judicial independence in circumstances where the Bailiff was a senior member of the local judiciary, legislature and executive. There was no question of actual bias on the Bailiff's part. Instead the question to be determined was whether he had the necessary appearance of

1   *Bryan v United Kingdom* (see **6.71** and Chapter 9). However, the Strasbourg judges found on different grounds that there had been no Art 6 violation.
2   *T and V v United Kingdom* [2000] CLR 187. See also fn 8 on p 6.
3   *Starrs v Ruxton* [2000] JC 208. See also *Clancy v Robin Dempsey Caird* [2000] SLT 546, where a challenge to a temporary judge (ie not a Sheriff) failed, but that was a civil case in which it was found that the claimant had waived his right to object to the temporary judge by not taking the point earlier. As regards waiver in relation to the European Convention generally, see **6.170** et seq.
4   See Chapter 4 above for the interplay between the Act and the Scotland Act 1998. The implications of *Starrs* are even greater in England, where 90% of criminal cases are heard by lay magistrates.
5   *McGonnell v United Kingdom* [2000] 8 BHRC 56.

independence. In Mr McGonnell's case a doubt had been created and, 'however slight its justification', it was sufficient to constitute an Art 6 violation. *McGonnell* in this way echoed the earlier decision in *Procola*,[1] in which the European Court found an Art 6 violation where four members of Luxembourg's *Conseil d'Etat* discharged advisory and judicial roles in the same case.

6.202   Independence will also not be achieved if the relevant decision-making body is too closely linked to the executive. The court-martial regime in the UK, for example, was found at Strasbourg not to be independent in the case of *Findlay v United Kingdom*[2] on account of the fact that the officer who convened the court-martial was responsible for appointing the panel to hear the case (who were all his subordinates), where he acted as prosecutor and where he ratified the decision of the court-martial in his capacity as so-called confirming officer. The Armed Forces Act 1996 has since remedied these deficiencies.

6.203   A systemically important determination as regards judicial indepen-dence in the labour law context is that of *Smith*.[3] In that case, the appellant had been seeking leave to appeal from a decision of an employment tribunal. In granting permission, Mr Justice Morrison said in the Employment Appeal Tribunal as follows:

> 'The question at issue was whether the employment tribunal was an "independent and impartial" tribunal in relation to a determination of claims brought by complainants against the Secretary of State and Industry . . . It was something of an anomaly that the employment tribunal should have such close links with an executive arm of the Government. They were paid for, largely appointed and administered by the Employment Tribunal Service, a Department of Trade and Industry agency. There was a real and troubling question as to whether they might properly and lawfully adjudicate on claims made against the Secretary of State, having regard to Art 6 of the Convention.'[4]

6.204   The issue which has most readily engaged the attention of the media in this context is the position of the Lord Chancellor in the wake of *McGonnell*.[5] In Parliament, Lord Irvine has expressed confidence that his position (as head of the justice system, member of the cabinet, Speaker of the House of Lords and presiding judge) was 'unaffected'[6] by the case, although he counselled his fellow Lords of Appeal in Ordinary 'to abstain from concluded views of a judicial character on issues which might later disqualify them from adjudicating should those issues come before them'. Nevertheless, Lord Irvine may need to consider whether he should sit any longer in a judicial capacity in the House of Lords in a case involving legislation he first tabled in Parliament. Arguably then, the Lord Chancellor should not adjudicate in any case testing the ambit of the Act, which

---

1   *Procola v Luxembourg* (1996) 22 EHRR 193.
2   (1997) 23 EHRR 221. See also *Van de Hurk v The Netherlands* (1994) 18 EHRR 481, *Hood v United Kindom* (2000) 29 EHRR 65 and *Jordan v United Kingdom* Appl 30280/96, 17 March 2000. The last of these was, in fact, a case about Art 5(3) and (5), but it established that the powers and position of a commanding officer meant that he could not be considered independent. See also J Mackenzie *A fair and public trial* [2000] NLJ 516.
3   *Smith v Secretary of State for Trade and Industry* [2000] ICR 69.
4   The employment tribunal set-up in Scotland is slightly different.
5   See, for example, H Young in *The Guardian*, 20 April 2000.
6   Hansard HL, vol 610, col 655, 2 March 2000. Since *McGonnell*, a Government-funded report by Professor Diane Woodhouse has suggested that the position of Lord Chancellor be abolished. See, for example, *The Guardian*, 21 March 2000.

he introduced as a bill in the House of Lords. Indeed, it may be safer for him not to appear in any appeal involving a scrutiny of statutes passed in this Parliament.[1]

6.205   In a short period, the Strasbourg requirement that a tribunal be independent has led to the transformation of the court-martial system in the UK, the coming to an end (in effect) of the system of temporary judges, the articulation of doubt as to whether the employment tribunal system can continue as presently constituted and the expression of concerns as regards the multi-faceted role of one of the great offices of the British State, that of Lord Chancellor. This is heady stuff and very likely there is more to come. In the future, a European Convention issue may, for example, arise as regards the role of clerks in magistrates' courts who, in some forms of proceedings, put questions to alleged defaulters before advising justices.[2]

6.206   These are, in the main, systemic matters affecting the structure of courts here and they may, as a consequence, bear little on businesses involved in particular cases. On the other hand, commerce may be much more readily affected by the allied European Convention requirement for Art 6(1) tribunals to be impartial, to which attention is now turned.

Impartiality

6.207   A court or tribunal must, both subjectively and objectively, be free of prejudice or bias.[3] The test developed by the European Court in the case of *Piersack* was as follows:

> 'A distinction can be drawn between a subjective approach, that is endeavouring to ascertain the personal conviction of a given judge in a given case, and the objective approach, that is determining whether he offered guarantees sufficient to exclude any legitimate doubt in this respect.'

6.208   In that case the European Court adopted with approval the common-law due process standard that justice not only be done but be seen to be done. The compliment was repaid by the Court of Appeal in the recent case of *Locabail,*[4] where the European Convention right to a fair hearing was described as 'fundamental' on the basis that:

> 'All legal arbiters are bound to apply the law as they understand it to the facts of individual cases as they find them. They must do so without fear or favour, affection or ill-will, that is without partiality or prejudice. Justice is portrayed as blind not because she ignores the facts and circumstances of individual cases but because she shuts her eyes to all considerations extraneous to the particular case.'

6.209   The bench in *Locabail* referred to the key Strasbourg cases, including *Piersack,* but otherwise based its decision on existing English (and some

---

1   In 1999 the Lord Chancellor withdrew from a case concerning police liability for the suicide of a man held in custody. See *The Guardian,* 4 March 1999. Lord Steyn, writing extra-judicially, has warned of the likelihood of a successful complaint to Strasbourg in certain situations if the position remains unchanged.

2   See *R v Corby Justices, ex parte Mort* (1998) *The Times,* 13 March. A complaint is pending at Strasbourg on this very point.

3   *Piersack v Belgium* (1983) 5 EHRR 169.

4   A number of appeals raising impartiality issues were heard together. The lead case was *Locabail (United Kindom) Ltd v Bayfield Properties Ltd* [2000] BHRC 583. See also the decision of the House of Lords in *R v Bow Street Stipendiary Magistrate, ex parte Pinochet Ugarte* (1999) 2 WLR 272.

Commonwealth) authorities. Although there is a sense that the judges were anxious to close off a plethora of European-Convention-based challenges on partiality grounds, the fact that they allowed one appeal will do nothing to discourage activity in this area. The relevant appeal, in the case of *Timmins v Gormley*, was upheld on the basis that a personal injury claim had been heard at first instance by a recorder who had in certain articles expressed 'pronounced pro-claimant anti-insurer views'. In general terms, their Lordships expressed the view that: 'Anyone writing in an area in which he sits judicially has to exercise considerable care not to express himself in terms which indicate that it may not be possible for him to try a case with an open mind'.

6.210   It would appear on this basis that in appropriate cases which raise questions involving a balance of interests in society, non-negligent lawyers will need to reflect carefully upon the extra-judicial activities of the tribunal. From now on, the persuasive precedents in the Strasbourg jurisprudence will be another depository on which to draw. By training (and perhaps even cultural disposition), it will be difficult for practitioners (less so their business clients) to make this adjustment, but make it they must.

6.211   What then are the Art 6 implications of the many pronouncements made by senior judges in recent years about, for example, privacy rights?[1] Should they recuse themselves in the early cases raising Art 8 points? What about the role of Lord Woolf as Master of the Rolls in presiding over cases turning upon the operation of the CPR 1998, of which he is (in effect) the architect?[2] Most salient of all perhaps, can anything be done if a case under the Act is heard by a local judge known to have been strongly in favour of or (less likely) strongly against European Convention domestication?

6.212   Lord McCluskey, the senior Scottish judge, and two colleagues were obliged in early 2000 to stand down from a part-heard appeal in a drugs case[3] (in which they had already sat for 10 days) on account of the defence argument that Lord McCluskey had a pronounced hostility to the European Convention. In particular, complaint was made of an article he wrote for *Scotland on Sunday* referring to the 'devastating' local effects of the European Convention, which was in his view a 'Trojan Horse'. Judges were entitled, in the words of Lord Rodger, 'to criticise developments in the law, whether in the form of legislation or judicial decisions'. On the other hand:

> '... what judges could not do with impunity was to publish either criticism or praise of such a nature or in such language as to give rise to a legitimate apprehension that, when called upon in the course of their judicial duties to apply that particular branch of the law, they would be able to do so impartially.'

6.213   The principle does not merely cover courts of law. In *Demicoli*[4], for example, it was held by the European Court that the House of Representatives in Malta was not an impartial tribunal to hear charges of breach of parliamentary

---

1   See **8.188** et seq.
2   To the extent that the CPR 1998 were substantially based upon his report *Access to Justice* (1995). It is interesting to note that, in May 2000, it was announced that Lord Woolf would become Lord Chief Justice, thereby making unlikely his need in the future to preside in appeals based on the CPR 1998.
3   *Hoekstra v HM Advocate* (2000) TLR, 14 April.
4   *Demicoli v Malta* (1992) 14 EHRR 47.

privilege laid against a member who had published a satirical leaflet. This was so in circumstances where some of those satirised played an active role in the proceedings.

6.214   Impartiality is taken as a given, unless the contrary be shown.[1] The concept is so central that the right decision, taken by a judge giving an appearance of bias, should not stand.[2] So too an appellate judge should not hear appeals from his own first instance decisions.[3]

6.215   All of this appears clear but consider, in a very different context, the fact that applications for judicial review in England and Wales are on occasions heard by the same judge at the substantive hearing who initially gave permission for the application to proceed. This might be welcomed by the applicant where permission was given without difficulty, but not where the applicant has obtained permission by the narrowest of margins. What in any event of the position of the respondent? The same issue arises where judges who hear applications for interim injunctions without notice then preside at trial.[4] The Court of Appeal's reasoning in *Locabail* suggests that judges will be reluctant to hold that this gives rise to a European Convention difficulty unless, that is, the relevant judge has already expressed views on the credibility of witnesses or otherwise exhibited behaviour suggesting that he can no longer approach the case with an open mind.[5]

6.216   Is impartiality achieved merely by imposing a straightforward bar upon participation in disciplinary tribunals by those who have personal knowledge of a case? Not necessarily, according to the Privy Council in the case of *Stefan*,[6] in which the General Medical Council's insistence on such a bar was held not to be of itself enough to ensure impartiality. Any deficiencies in procedure were, however, cured by the existence of an appeal from the General Medical Council to the Privy Council, which was Art 6-compliant.

6.217   There will, of course, be cases of importance to companies where the tribunal comprises not just a judge but a jury too. The impartiality of jurors also engages Art 6(1) and was the subject of an application in Scotland in the wake of the *Starrs* case.[7] In *Crummock (Scotland) Limited v Her Majesty's Advocate*,[8] the appellant argued in the context of a health and safety prosecution that an Edinburgh jury would be likely to include some of the people affected by the water allegedly contaminated by the appellant's activities. Lord Weir questioned this assumption and said that any concern about a juror's impartiality could be dealt with in the directions that the trial judge could be expected to give the jury.

6.218   Similar views were expressed some few weeks later by Sir Nicholas Bratza in a dissenting judgment at Strasbourg in the case of *Sander v United Kingdom*,[9] but

---

1   *Le Compte, Van Leuven and de Meyere v Belgium* (1981) 4 EHRR 1.
2   *Piersack v Belgium* (1982) 5 EHRR 169.
3   *De Hann v The Netherlands* (1998) 26 EHRR 417.
4   See *Woolwich v Daisystar (No 2)* (unreported) 16 March 2000 and *Khreino v Khreino* [2000] 1 FCR 75.
5   See also in this context *Seer Technologies v Abbas* (unreported) 2 February 2000, where it was considered 'completely unacceptable' to seek to recuse a judge, who was Jewish, from hearing a case in which the defendant was an Arab.
6   *Stefan v General Medical Council* [1999] 1 WLR 1299.
7   See **6.170**.
8   (2000) *The Times*, 9 May.
9   9 May 2000.

it is noteworthy that, in that matter, a majority in the European Court found that unacceptable conduct on the part of one juror (such as the making of racist jokes) was enough to violate Art 6(1), notwithstanding the fact that a clear warning had been given by the trial judge to the jury as to how they should behave. On the facts, the Strasbourg judges considered by 4:3 that the jury should have been discharged. It can be anticipated that the senior judiciary here will be very reluctant to follow the European Court in this respect for fear of encouraging wholesale attacks on jury conduct and this may be one area in which Strasbourg jurisprudence is taken account of, but not followed.

6.219   The judges in the *Locabail* appeals plainly wanted to discourage legal adventurism in this area. However, the introduction of the Act has encouraged the genie to escape from the bottle and it will not readily be put back. For example, it has been reported that a decision of Lord Millett is now the subject of a complaint to Strasbourg arising out of a case in which he, a leading Mason, refused leave to appeal from a first instance decision given by an alleged Mason in which the solicitor of the applicant's opponent was also (it is said) a Mason.[1]

6.220   There is a long tradition in the USA of seeking to recuse judges on grounds of partiality and indications are that it will become more commonplace here. One result may be that the recent tendency of the senior judges to become more accessible in terms of their extra-judicial writing and contributions at conferences will be curtailed. Not just that, but it may be predicted that lawyers will now collate materials about the antecedents of those appearing on tribunals. This will apply not only to the judiciary but also to those sitting on disciplinary panels in, for example, the City of London.

TRIBUNAL ESTABLISHED BY LAW

6.221   Article 6(1) provides that a court or tribunal must not only be independent and impartial, but also be *established by law*. This means that, for example, the relevant body should not exist at the *discretion* of the executive as this might militate against its independence.[2] In other words, the aim is to ensure that such control as is exercised over a court or tribunal is exercised by the legislature (in Parliament) and not by the executive.

ARTICLE 6 AND APPEAL PROCEEDINGS

6.222   Where, as has been seen, a determination is made by, say, a disciplinary tribunal of a professional association which does not comply fully with Art 6 standards, the existence of an appellate body with 'full jurisdiction' to determine issues of law and fact may well cure any process breach.[3]

6.223   In contrast, a court in the strict sense (in other words, one which is 'integrated within the standard judicial machinery of the [relevant] country') must comply fully with Art 6, both at first instance and on appeal.[4] Here too,

---

1   *The Independent*, 6 April 2000.
2   See *Zand v Austria* (1980) 15 DR 7 at 80.
3   *Le Compte, van Leuven and de Meyere* (see fn 1 on p 184) at para 15.
4   *De Cubber* (see fn 2 on p 125) at para 32.

however, a *prima facie* violation at first instance may conceivably be rectified on appeal,[1] in which case there will be no European Convention breach on the basis that the Strasburg jurisprudence requires the instant proceedings to be looked at as a whole.[2]

PUBLIC PRONOUNCEMENT OF JUDGMENT

6.224   This right is not subject to any of the restrictions in Art 6(1) which enable the press and public alike to be barred from certain forms of proceedings. They can be kept away from a hearing but may not be barred from receiving judgment. The rationale is to prevent the dispensation of justice in secret and to encourage scrutiny and debate.[3] Not that it is necessary for judgment to be rendered in open court orally, a requirement that would cause difficulties in many civil law countries where this often does not happen and where decisions are instead made available through the court registry, a practice which is, in any event, becoming more popular in this juridiction, albeit that an appointment for the delivery of a judgment is still fixed, even if the text of the decision is not read out in full. What matters is the *availability* of the judgment. The fact that it is handed down in writing to the litigants and is also otherwise available should be sufficient. This raises interesting questions, however, as to the current inspection regime in the High Court, which journalists have suggested is more restricted than in the past.

6.225   The Strasbourg judges have said relatively little about the form of judgments, save that they must be reasoned with sufficient clarity to ensure that a right of appeal can be exercised on an informed basis, although it is not necessary for every argument to be dealt with in detail[4] and an appellate court can adopt the reasoning of the first instance court.[5]

6.226   It had historically been a feature of many disciplinary tribunals in this country that they did not give full or indeed any reasons for their decisions and this may need to change on account of the Act. As regards the Strasbourg authorities[6] (and, specifically, the domestication of Art 6(1)) Lord Clyde said in the case of *Stefan* that the Act had 'created a possibility of a "re-appraisal of the whole position" concerning the giving of reasons'. As a minimum, regulators[7] wanting to avoid Art 6 difficulties (specifically in the disciplinary context) will likely need to articulate their decisions in the way suggested by His Lordship:

---

1   *Edwards v United Kingdom* (1992) 15 EHRR 417.
2   See also *R v Secretary of State for the Home Department, ex parte Garner and Others* [1999] 11 Admin LR 595.
3   For a recent decision which suggests that the existing common-law position is the same in substance as that in the European Convention, see *Trustor AB v Smallbone and Others* [2000] 1 All ER 811.
4   *Van de Hurk v The Netherlands* (1994) 18 EHRR 481 and *Heinrich v France* (1994) 18 EHRR 140. See also the 11-point analysis by Lord Bingham regarding the local law on the giving of reasons in *R v Ministry of Defence, ex parte Murray* [1998] COD 134.
5   *Garcia Ruiz v Spain* Appl 30544/96, 21 January 1999.
6   *Stefan v General Medical Council* [1999] 1 WLR 1293. See also *R v General Medical Council, ex parte Toth* (unreported) 23 June 2000 and *Hiro Balani v Spain* (1995) 19 EHRR 566.
7   Section 10 of the Tribunals and Inquiries Act 1992 already requires designated tribunals to give reasoned decisions.

'They need not be elaborate nor lengthy. But they should be such as to tell the parties in broad terms why the decision was reached. In many cases a very few sentences should suffice to give such explanation as was appropriate to the particular situation.'

ARTICLE 6(3)

6.227 Article 6(3) provides five key *minimum* guarantees in criminal trials. Because they are explicitly stated to be minima, they can be augmented, just as the fact that they are present may not be enough to secure a fair trial. They are 'not an aim in themselves, and they must accordingly be interpreted in the light of the function which they have in the overall context of the proceedings'.[1] Just as importantly, there is no reason why these elements should not be constituent features in civil cases of the broader Art 6(1) guarantee of a fair trial,[2] on the basis that the relationship between Art 6(1) and (3) has been described as 'that of the general to the particular'.[3]

6.228 The additional safeguards are as follows.

(1) There must be prompt and intelligible notification of the nature of the charge laid against any individual. The evidence in support of the charge does not need to be disclosed when an individual is charged, provided the accused is given some information as to the factual basis for the charge.[4]

(2) Adequate time and facilities must be given to the accused for the preparation of his defence. This may entail a positive obligation to take the necessary steps to achieve equality as between the defence and the prosecution.[5] The absence of such steps may make for unfairness in the proceedings.[6] The amount of time which is adequate will plainly vary from case to case. In general terms, however, the more complex the issues involved, the more time that will be required.[7]

(3) The accused is entitled to legal representation of his choosing.[8] He may represent himself if he prefers. Such legal representation as is provided, however, should (so far as possible) meet with the approval of the defendant.[9] Where this is not possible (as is likely in legal aid cases), alternative representation will be permissible so long as there is no prejudice to the accused and the lawyer appointed is able to provide *effective* assistance. That lawyer should as a rule, therefore, be someone in whom the defendant has confidence[10] and there may be an Art 6(3) breach where representation is not effective because it was inadequate.[11] Free legal aid should be available

---

1   *Can v Austria* (1986) 8 EHRR 14.
2   *Albert and Le Compte v Belgium* (1983) 5 EHRR 533.
3   *Jespers v Belgium* (1981) 27 DR 61.
4   *Brozicek v Italy* (1990) 12 EHRR 371.
5   See *Jespers v Belgium* (see fn 3).
6   *X v Belgium* (1970) 13 Yearbook 690.
7   *Albert and Le Compte* (see fn 2 above).
8   A right confirmed by Neuberger J in the case of *Maltez v Lewis* (1999) *The Times*, 4 May as being a fundamental right integral to a free society.
9   *Goddi v Italy* (1994) 6 EHRR 457.
10   *Croissant v Germany* (1992) 16 EHRR 135.
11   *Artico v Italy* (1980) 3 EHRR 1, where the European Court said 'Article 6(3)(c) speaks of "assistance" and not "nomination".' See also *Daud v Portugal* [1998] 4 BHRC 522.

where the means of the accused is limited, the issues are complex and there is a risk of sentence or a fine.[1]

(4) The defendant has the right to cross-examine prosecution witnesses and the assistance of free interpretation facilities.[2] Restrictions can be placed upon the scope of the right to cross-examine[3] and hearsay evidence can be relied upon against the defence provided there are sufficient countervailing factors.[4] Anonymity can be conferred if it will protect a witness from harassment or intimidation.[5] This is because witnesses too are entitled to a fair trial guarantee. However, any evidence obtained anonymously should not be the sole basis for conviction.[6] More generally though, Art 6(3)(d) encompasses the notion that all evidence should be produced in the presence of the criminal accused.

6.229   Perhaps strangely, nowhere is the right of a criminal accused to communicate privately with his lawyer made explicit in the European Convention. The European Court has, however, made it clear that it 'is part of the basic requirements of a fair trial in a democratic society'.[7]

ARTICLE 6 AND THE CIVIL PROCEDURE RULES: AN OVERVIEW

6.230   It is not difficult to imagine Art 6 points being taken in a multitude of ways in civil proceedings. In addition to the instances already identified, these might include complaints about:

– the requirement to pay for transcripts, which arguably prejudices *effective* access;
– the absence of sound-recording facilities in Masters' appointments, conceivably disadvantaging litigants in person who cannot take notes whilst otherwise participating in the proceedings;

---

1   See the cases of *Benham v United Kindom* (1996) 22 EHRR 23 and *Perks and Others v United Kingdom* (1999) *The Times*, 12 October, both cases concerning non-payment of poll tax in which the absence of free legal representation was considered (in Strasbourg and London respectively) to be a violation of Art 6(3)(c).

2   Interpreters should be paid for by the court: see *Luedicke Belkacem and KOC v Germany* (1978) 2 EHRR 149. But see also *Zideault v France* (1986) 48 DR 232. It is to be noted that the existing Practice Direction on costs in criminal proceedings (93 Cr App R 89 Part IV) gives a court discretion to order the defence to meet such costs. The right to an interpreter in Art 6(3) has already been considered by the High Court before the wholesale coming into force of the Act: see *R v West London Youth Court, ex parte N* [2000] 1 All ER 823. The argument that a Welsh (and English) speaker had the right, bolstered by Arts 10 and 6, to require that the proceedings of the Employment Appeal Tribunal in London be conducted in Welsh was rejected in *Williams v Cowell* [2000] 1 WLR 187.

3   The trauma suffered by rape victims cross-examined by their alleged assailants has long been the subject of concern and is now the basis for an Art 6 complaint to Strasbourg by an applicant interrogated for 6 days. The law is being changed to prevent such abuses.

4   *Kostovski v The Netherlands* (1989) 12 EHRR 434. See also *Blastland v United Kingdom* Appl 12045/86, (1987) 52 DR 273.

5   See the decision of the Court of Appeal in the case of *R v Lord Saville of Newdigate and Others, ex parte B* (1999) *The Times*, 29 July, where the decision of the Bloody Sunday Inquiry to refuse witness anonymity to former paratroopers was quashed as being unfair.

6   *Doorsen v The Netherlands* (1996) 22 EHRR 330.

7   *S v Switzerland* (1992) 14 EHRR 670 at para 48.

- the refusal to adjourn trial dates, the argument being that the party refused the adjournment will be ill-prepared and, thereby, denied a hearing that is fair;
- ceilings on awards in unfair dismissal cases, which may make such cases financially unattractive for lawyers to take them on; and
- the refusal of some judges to allow litigants in person to be supported by McKenzie friends,[1] thereby allegedly denying them effective representation.
- the operation of the law and practice regarding forfeiture and the enforcement of recognisances[2];
- the narrow appeals regime in CPR 1998 Part 52 introduced on 2 May 2000.

6.231   Although this list could readily be extended, it will be surprising if whole swathes of the CPR 1998 are struck down as a consequence of the Act. To date, domestic civil procedure has emerged largely unscathed at Strasbourg and it would be odd indeed if the CPR 1998, predicated as they are on the need for lawyers, clients and indeed judges to behave proportionately, were to be found wanting. The scope for legal creativity, however, is clear and change in relation to the approach to security for costs applications and in other areas will be needed. Undeniably the increased case management powers conferred by the CPR 1998[3] are not in all respects reconcilable with the process rights safeguarded by the European Convention. There is, therefore, tension in terms of Art 6, between the systemic efficiencies achieved by sanctions-driven techniques[4] and the denial of justice to which this may understandably give rise to individual cases and this is likely to give rise to a number of courtroom challenges in the coming period. Specifically, issues may arise in this context as regards:

- judicial exclusion of evidence;[5]
- the application of penalties (most obviously in costs) for failure to adhere to pre-action protocols;[6]
- the imposition of very short interlocutory time-limits for compliance with orders.[7]

6.232   Having deconstructed Art 6, attention now turns to its application in practice for a very important part of the British commercial sector.

ARTICLE 6 AND FINANCIAL SERVICES

6.233   The Labour Party assumed power in 1997 determined to reform the UK's financial services industry extensively. As has been seen,[8] it also had a manifesto commitment to domesticate the European Convention. Few in the Government or outside it could have predicted in advance that the latter would

---

1   See *R v Bow County Court, ex parte Pelling* [1999] 2 All ER 582, where it was held that the judge's refusal to allow the claimant to act as a McKenzie friend was not inconsistent with Art 6(1), which permitted the public to be excluded in designated circumstances.
2   See *R v Stipendiary Magistrate for Leicestershire, ex parte Kaur* [2000] COD 109.
3   See Part 3, 26–29 and 32.
4   See, for example, CPR 1998, Part 3.4(3).
5   See, for example, *Grobbelaar v Sun Newspapers* (1999) *The Times*, 12 August.
6   See CPR 1998, Parts 44–47.
7   See *Peres de Rada Cavanilles v Spain* [2000] 29 EHRR 109.
8   See **1.45** et seq.

bear so profoundly upon the former. In what has been described as an unusual and scenic route taken from the Treasury to Buckingham Palace,[1] the Financial Services and Markets Act 2000 was subjected to an unprecedented level of intensive pre-legislative and legislative scrutiny, much of it on human rights grounds. What follows is a description of that process and of the way in which Art 6 may henceforth be relied upon in the City of London. The history of the legislation is dealt with first.

6.234   Until 1988, there was no comprehensive regime for the regulation of the UK's financial services markets. The sector was largely self-regulated, albeit that the system of self-regulation was augmented by piecemeal statutory inter-vention with an ultimate sanction in the form of prosecution where the criminal law was breached. With, however, the increasing globalisation of markets that was encouraged by the abolition of exchange controls and 'Big Bang' structural reforms on the one hand, and the dramatic increase in private investment in equity markets and pension plans triggered by the Conservative Government's privatisation programme on the other, new forms of control offering greater protection for investors were clearly required. This was the aim of the Financial Services Act 1986, which came into force in 1988. Under that Act, the Securities and Investments Board was given overall control of self-regulatory bodies in the investment sector.

6.235   In the event, several spectacular collapses that undermined public confidence (most obviously affecting two banks, BCCI and Barings) occurred in the 10 years after the Financial Services Act 1986 was introduced. This encouraged a perception that the self-regulatory nature of the then existing regime would never be sufficiently robust to prevent such scandals, particularly in terms of its ability to police and, if need be, punish those in senior management who presided over systemic failures of control. There was also a widely held belief that the criminal law had not been capable of dealing effectively with the more serious offences (particularly insider dealing and market manipulation). Of over 100 cases of suspected insider dealing referred to the authorities by the recognised investment exchanges (as defined) between 1993 and 1998, there were just five successful prosecutions and eight acquittals.[2] Indeed it was reported late in April 2000 that, since the Labour Government came to power, not one insider dealing case had by then been pursued by the Crown Prosecution Service.[3]

The Financial Services and Markets Act 2000

6.236   In July 1998, the Government published for consultation a first draft of its Financial Services and Markets Bill. This was an unusual form of Parliamentary procedure to adopt but, as it transpired, the widespread discussion which it facilitated was beneficial in terms of the change to Government thinking to which it contributed.

---

1   The phrase as used by Howard (now Sir Howard) Davies, head of the Financial Services Authority (FSA) in his speech to the Chancery Bar Association and Combar at Lincoln's Inn on 3 March 1999: see http://www.fsa.gov.uk/pubs/speeches/sp23.html.
2   Statistics quoted by Mr David Kidney MP on 16 March 1999 in the examination of Howard Davies by the Joint Parliamentary Committee on Financial Services and Markets; see also Howard Davies' speech to the Chancery Bar Association (see 1 above).
3   Complinet, 20 April 2000.

6.237 The Financial Services and Markets Act 2000 aims to provide a fully statutory scheme under which a single regulator (and undoubted public authority in human rights terms), the Financial Services Authority (FSA), replaces a range of existing City regulators. Therefore, the statute brings together nine bodies responsible for banking supervision, investment business, insurance companies, building societies, the recognition and supervision of investment exchanges and clearing houses, and the regulation of Lloyds of London. From summer 2001, the Financial Services Authority will, in addition, supervise all mortgage lenders.

6.238 The Financial Services and Markets Act 2000 gives the FSA very broad powers of investigation, intervention, sanction, suit and prosecution across a wide spectrum. Although most of its authority derives from the various powers available to one or more of the nine regulatory bodies which the FSA supersedes, no single regulator under the old system had available to it the full armoury now in the hands of the FSA, including the power to introduce a *civil* fines regime to deal with those guilty of market abuse.[1]

6.239 One effect of the end of self-regulation is that the new financial services regulator (and the Government) can no longer rely on market participants to take their medicine without protest, for the good of their club. Those subject to the stringent new statutory powers in the Financial Services and Markets Act 2000 are more likely to question whether they have been treated fairly and in accordance with their human rights. From the outset, therefore, the Government's proposals have raised concern about the extent of the powers to be conferred on the FSA, a private company limited by guarantee. In particular, the Government's statement, when introducing the draft Bill, that its provisions were compatible with the European Convention, was to come under close scrutiny.

6.240 In the period of open consultation on the draft Bill, certain of the larger law firms and trade associations expressed concern about what they perceived to be the potential inconsistencies between aspects of the draft Bill and provisions of Strasbourg jurisprudence. In particular, they contended that local courts would likely construe the new offences to form part of the disciplinary and market abuse regimes in the legislation as *criminal charges* for the purposes of Art 6. If this was correct, the argument ran, the proposals as then drafted would not, to begin with, adequately safeguard the presumption of innocence in Art 6(2).[2]

6.241 The law firms proceeded to retain Lord Lester to advise and he concluded,[3] based on the draft Financial Services and Markets Bill and upon draft Guidance and Codes published under the draft Bill, that the provisions as they then stood were likely to contravene not only Art 6 of the European Convention but also Art 7(1) and Art 4 of the Seventh Protocol (albeit that the latter remains to be ratified by the UK). [4]

---

1   See Part VIII of the Financial Services and Markets Act 2000.
2   See **6.150**.
3   In a joint opinion with Javan Herberg to be found at Annex C to the First Report of the Joint Committee on Financial Services and Markets, HL Paper 50–1. The opinion also appears as an appendix to *The Human Rights Act and the Criminal Justice and Regulatory Process* (Hart Publishing, 1999), which, in addition, reproduces the second opinion given by Lord Lester, this time jointly with Monica Carrs-Frisk (also reproduced in the First Report of the Joint Committee).
4   See fn 2 on p 45 and Appendix 2.

6.242   In November and December 1998, the Treasury Select Committee conducted a short inquiry into financial services regulation, during which the Chief Secretary to the Treasury announced a series of measures designed to ensure that the enforcement procedures of the putative regulator were fair and transparent.[1] By February 1999, the Treasury Select Committee was stating in a report[2] that it expected 'the Government to respond in detail to the concerns [raised] about natural justice and the European Convention on Human Rights'. It went on:

> 'Given the substantial powers given to the [Financial Services Authority], and the complaints from independent financial advisers about the current disciplinary process run by the [Personal Investment Authority], it is easy to perceive the disciplinary process as one in which the [Financial Services Authority] holds all the cards. For that reason, the initial process, not just the Appeals Tribunal, must be – and be seen to be – fair, accessible, inexpensive and transparent.'[3]

6.243   Shortly afterwards, a joint committee of both Houses of Parliament was appointed to consider the draft Financial Services and Markets Bill and report by 30 April 1999. The Joint Committee heard extensive evidence from all sectors of the financial services industry and on behalf of consumers. Its first report (delivered on 27 April 1999),[4] again expressed anxiety, amongst a raft of recommendations regarding the draft Financial Services and Markets Bill, about possible European Convention infractions in the proposed legislation.

6.244   In the wake of that report, both Houses of Parliament instructed the Joint Committee to make a further report by 27 May 1999, specifically on the European Convention implications of particular features of the proposals. The Economic Secretary to the Treasury, Patricia Hewitt MP and her legal advisers, Sir Sydney Kentridge QC and James Eadie, gave oral evidence and, in a memorandum published on 14 May 1999, the Treasury (finally) recognised the possibility that certain of the fining powers to be given to the Financial Services Authority might be classified as criminal for European Convention purposes. The Joint Committee commended the Government's response, but recommended that further thought be given to the possibility that the disciplinary proceedings mooted in the draft Financial Services and Markets Bill might also in certain circumstances be held to be criminal in nature, given the conflicting legal arguments advanced in written evidence to the Joint Committee by (respectively) the Treasury, Lord Lester and two law lords, Lords Hobhouse and Steyn.[5]

6.245   Following the Joint Committee's second report, the Financial Services and Markets Bill was further revised. No longer in draft form, it was presented to the House of Commons (accompanied by a s 19 statement of compatibility made by the Chancellor of the Exchequer)[6] on 17 June 1999 before being examined and

---

1   See HM Treasury News Release, 22 December 1998, http://www.hmt.gov.uk/press/1998/p217_98.html

2   Treasury Select Committee, Third Report, Financial Services Regulation, 4 February 1999, HC 73–1, http://www.parliament.the-stationery-office.co.uk/pa/cm199899/cmselect/cmtreasury/73/73.

3   At para 81. The form of the disciplinary process in the Financial Services and Markets Act 2000 is dealt with at **6.248** et seq.

4   HL Paper 50–1; HC Paper 328-I, 1998–1999.

5   See Appendices 1, 2 and 3 to the Second Report of the Joint Committee, published on 27 May 1999 (HL Paper 66, HC Paper 465, 1998–1999).

6   As regards s 19 statements generally, see **3.195** et seq.

amended at length in Standing Committee. It moved to the House of Lords in February 2000, went back to the House of Commons on 5 June 2000 and received Royal Assent on 14 June 2000, albeit amidst protests for it to be delayed for further consideration. It is likely to come into force during 2001.

6.246   The form of pre-legislative scrutiny to which the Financial Services and Markets Act 2000 was subjected was highly unusual and the process by which it eventually became law illustrates the extent to which the Act will not only change legal proceedings, legal culture and the activities of public authorities generally, but will also change statute-making procedures.

6.247   What follows is an explanation of the substantive implications of the Financial Services and Markets Act 2000 in European Convention terms.

Statutory immunity

6.248   The Financial Services and Markets Act 2000 confers upon the FSA statutory immunity from suit for damages.[1] Initially, the proposed immunity extended to anything done or omitted in the discharge or purported discharge of the Authority's functions (but not where the act or omission was shown to have been in bad faith). However, it was suggested in evidence before the Joint Committee[2] that such a blanket immunity might not be compatible with Art 6's access right, particularly in the light of the European Court's decisions in *Tinnelly*[3] and *Osman*.[4] As a result, the Government amended the Financial Services and Markets Bill to provide that the exemption from liability for damages would not apply to prevent an award of damages made in respect of an act or omission on the ground that the act or omission was unlawful as a result of s 6(1) of the Act.[5] In so doing, the Financial Services and Markets Act 2000 explicitly notes the connection between the Authority's discharge of its activities and its obligations *qua* public authority under the European Convention.

Enforcement

6.249   The essence of the regulatory regime in the Financial Services and Markets Act 2000 is prohibitive – no person may carry on a regulated activity in the UK unless authorised to do so (or exempted from doing so) by the FSA.[6] The Authority is empowered to grant and to withdraw authorisation and, in respect of authorised persons, to prohibit or restrict their activities, the solicitation of business and the disposal of or dealing with assets. It can require the transfer of assets to a trustee, the disposal of investments and the maintenance in the UK of assets of specified value. In cases of urgency, many of these powers can be exercised peremptorily and the person affected will not have the opportunity to make representations. The power to compel the giving of answers by witnesses (including suspects) is confirmed.[7]

---

1   Schedule 1, para. 19. See also s 102.
2   See the First Report of the Joint Committee (fn 3 on p 191) at para 141.
3   *Tinnelly and Sons Ltd and Others and McElduff and Others v the United Kingdom* (see **6.60** et seq).
4   *Osman v the United Kingdom* (see **6.53** et seq).
5   Schedule 1, para 19. See also s 102.
6   Section 19.
7   Sections 171, 182 and 177.

6.250   The legislation establishes a framework for the exercise of disciplinary powers over authorised persons (firms or individuals carrying on regulated activities) and approved persons (individuals employed in particular capacities by authorised persons). Specifically, the FSA is given the power to fine, to publish a statement of misconduct and/or to order restitution or disgorgement of profits. To this list was added, during the parliamentary debates, persons who contravene rules in respect of listed securities.[1] Quite separately, under Part VIII of the Financial Services and Markets Act 2000, the Authority may impose unlimited civil fines on persons (whether regulated or not) who commit market abuse.

6.251   Before taking disciplinary or other regulatory action (except in cases of urgency), the Financial Services and Markets Act 2000 requires the FSA to publish a 'warning notice' describing its proposed fine or statement. The notice is required to contain the Authority's reasons, but not to set out the evidence on which its conclusions are based. The recipient of such a notice is then given at least 28 days to make representations. If the FSA decides (within a reasonable time) to proceed with sanctions, a decision notice has to be issued setting out the date on which the decision will take effect, the FSA's reasons, and an explanation of the right to appeal.

6.252   Under the draft Financial Services and Markets Bill, parties were to have the right to appeal against the imposition of sanctions by reference to a single, independent appeal tribunal[2] managed as part of the Court Service. This body would be able to consider new evidence or hear new arguments (except as specified by the Lord Chancellor). In addition, it would be able to confirm, vary or set aside the decision, remit the matter to the FSA, impose, revoke or vary fines, make recommendations as to the Authority's regulatory provisions or procedures or make any other decision which the Authority itself could have made. The appeal tribunal would be part of the High Court[3] (in Scotland, the Court of Session) and would hear appeals on points of law alone.

6.253   These measures, as initially proposed in the draft Bill, raised a number of serious concerns in relation to Art 6. The measures were not to go forward unamended and are considered below.

The right to a court

6.254   The FSA originally proposed that an enforcement committee be established to consider cases where the exercise of the Authority's powers to impose disciplinary sanctions, restitution orders or civil fines for market abuse was being considered. Such a committee would consider staff recommendations as to whether a warning notice should be issued. Where such recommendations were accepted, the committee's chairman would issue the warning notice, consider any responses received to it and decide whether any further enquiries were

---

1   Part VI of the Bill (relating to Official Listing) first appeared in the Bill as presented to the House of Commons in June 1999.

2   In the Act, this right is now termed a right of 'reference'. The tribunal is to be known as the Financial Services and Markets Tribunal: see s 132 of the Financial Services and Markets Act 2000.

3   The Act now provides that appeals will be to the Court of Appeal or Court of Session: see s 137.

needed, if necessary hearing oral representations and deciding whether a decision notice should be issued. In addition, the Authority at one time considered that the committee chairman should be involved in the development of regulatory policy (particularly enforcement policy) by the FSA.

6.255   The intention was evidently to create an administrative (or at most a quasi-judicial) decision-making process. By establishing an enforcement committee it was not intended to duplicate the role of the appeal tribunal. As an administrative body combining the roles of investigator and prosecutor, which was, furthermore, to retain the proceeds of fines as well as costs orders made in its favour, the FSA was never likely to be able itself to fulfil the requirements of Art 6(1), however elaborate its internal procedures. Thus, the model initially relied upon the 'full jurisdiction' of the appeal tribunal[1] to deliver compliance with Art 6, at least in respect of the right to an independent and impartial tribunal and the right to a fair hearing generally.

6.256   Provided the appeal took the form of a full *de novo* hearing, so that the burden of proof remained on the FSA, and the firm or individual concerned was not prejudiced by the FSA's initial decision, Art 6(1) safeguards would very possibly have been met. Clause 68(3)(c) of the draft Bill suggested, however, that the appeal tribunal's power to receive fresh evidence or hear fresh arguments not raised at the time of the FSA's initial decision might be restricted in specified circumstances and Lord Lester considered that, in so far as a defendant could thereby be prevented from raising arguments he reasonably did not make to the Authority, this might breach Art 6.[2] In the event, in a News Release on 22 December 1999, the Treasury announced that it proposed to remove from the Financial Services and Markets Bill the power to make rules as to when relevant evidence might not be admissible before the appeal tribunal.

The definition of a criminal charge

6.257   This most important issue – as to whether the disciplinary system in the Financial Services and Markets Act 2000 is likely to be classified in European Convention terms as criminal in nature – remains unclear. The Government considers (and no-one would seriously challenge it) that the protection of the public justifies the imposition of a requirement to become part of a regulated group on those who choose to undertake financial services business (whether as authorised persons or as approved persons).

6.258   As the disciplinary regime in the Financial Services and Markets Act 2000 is limited in scope to a defined (if substantial) number of persons who are part of a regulated community, the Government has argued throughout that the conduct covered by the regime is comparable to that covered by the regulation of a profession. The Joint Committee did not entirely accept this analogy,[3] noting that, although there is to be substantial practitioner input into the work of the FSA, it is a body of a very different character from (for example) the Law Society or the General Medical Council. In rejecting this, Sir Sydney Kentridge QC had

---

1   See **6.66** et seq.
2   In his Joint Opinion with Javan Herberg, see fn 3 on p 191.
3   In its Second Report (see fn 5 on p 192) at para 14.

relied on the case of *Wickramsinghe v United Kingdom*,[1] but that was a case dealing with the striking-off powers of a professional body (in that instance the General Medical Council), as indeed were the other cases referred to in the Treasury's memorandum and by counsel for the Treasury.[2]

6.259   The Government also argued that, although disciplinary action for breach of market rules may have a deterrent effect, the regime is intended primarily to be protective rather than punitive. This contention may be difficult to sustain, however, in relation to the power to discipline (for misconduct) approved persons who are not directly carrying on a regulated activity (although they are approved to carry on related functions) and still less tenable in respect of directors of listed companies who contravene listing rules.

6.260   During the debates on the Financial Services and Markets Bill, the Government never conceded that the nature and unlimited size of the penalties which can be imposed under the Financial Services and Markets Act 2000 should of themselves lead to the conclusion that proceedings under the Act are criminal in nature. It has throughout emphasised that such fines are recoverable as civil debts and that there is no provision for imprisonment in default of payment.[3] However, in his second opinion,[4] Lord Lester made the point that the fact that an offence is not punishable by imprisonment and does not give rise to a criminal record is not decisive in European Convention terms.[5]

6.261   He also referred to the decision of the French courts in the *Oury* case[6] as supporting the proposition that, where significant financial sanctions are imposed by a disciplinary tribunal (of, for example, the Paris Stock Exchange) as a punishment, the offence is properly to be regarded as criminal for the purposes of Art 6 and, therefore, susceptible to the full protection of the procedural safeguards in that Article. On the other hand, Sir Sydney Kentridge contended that *Oury* dealt with conduct more akin to market abuse than to disciplinary action, while Lord Steyn concluded that, where disciplinary matters closely overlapped with serious abuse, the question remained open.[7]

---

1   [1998] EHRLR 338. Although it should be noted that in *APB Ltd v United Kingdom* Appl 30552/96, 15 January 1998, the European Commission concluded that disciplinary proceedings brought by IMRO were civil in nature.

2   Reproduced in the Minutes of Evidence before the Joint Committee on 19 May 1999; see the Second Report (fn 5 on p 192).

3   See s 390(9). The Government relied in this regard on the case of *Irving-Brown v United Kingdom* Appl 38644/97, 24 November 1998, where the European Court treated a £10,000 fine imposed upon a solicitor as a civil matter, because the Solicitors Complaints Tribunal had no power of imprisonment and the charge related to the disciplining of a member of a specified group and not a member of the general public. See also *Air Canada v United Kingdom* [1995] 20 EHRR 150 and see **9.36**.

4   At para 15, see Annex D to the First Report of the Joint Committee (see fn 3 on p 191).

5   See, for example, *Lauko v Slovakia* [1988] HRCD 838 and *Ozturk v Germany* [1984] 6 EHRR 409.

6   *Oury c/- Agent Judiciaire du Trésor,* Cour de Cassation, 1 December 1998. See also *Commission des Opérations de Bourse c/- Oury,* Cour de Cassation, 5 February 1999 and *Haddad c/- Agent Judiciaire du Trésor,* Cour de Cassation, 9 April 1996. In March 2000, the Commission des Opérations de Bourse (COB) suspended all pending administrative sanction cases following the decision of the Court of Appeal of Paris in *Société Fiducière v COB* that the COB's procedures violated the right to a fair trial under Art 6. New legislation is to be passed to enable the COB to fulfil its regulatory duties in compliance with the decision.

7   See Appendix 3, Second Report of the Joint Committee (see fn 5 on p 192).

6.262   It remains possible, therefore, that in the early human rights cases that now ensue, the courts may conclude that, as the sanctions imposed in City disciplinary proceedings are punitive in nature and unlimited in size, *all* of the FSA's disciplinary proceedings should be classified as criminal, the dispositive factor being not so much the seriousness or ambit of the offence but the nature and size of the penalties imposed on conviction.[1]

6.263   If all of the FSA's disciplinary proceedings are to be classified as criminal, then the additional Art 6 considerations discussed below in respect of market abuse offence will be equally applicable to disciplinary proceedings. In particular, the FSA would not be entitled to rely on answers obtained under compulsion from witnesses.

6.264   So too the withdrawal of authorisation or approved status – as opposed to a decision not to confer it – could conceivably be classified as criminal for European Convention purposes because of the potentially very serious impact on the persons concerned.[2]

6.265   For the present, all that may be said reliably is that some City disciplinary offences will very likely be designated by local judges to be civil matters in Art 6 terms, while some serious charges are equally likely to be classified as criminal, either because the alleged misconduct is essentially criminal in nature or because sanctions are threatened primarily for punitive rather than compensatory reasons.

CITY OFFENCES AND ARTICLE 7

6.266   Article 7 of the European Convention provides as follows:

'No punishment without law

1.   No-one shall be held guilty of any criminal offences on account of any act or omission which did not constitute a criminal offence under national or international law at the time when it was committed. Nor shall a heavier penalty be imposed than the one that was applicable at the time the criminal offence was committed.
2.   This article shall not prejudice the trial and punishment of any person for any act or omission which, at the time when it was committed, was criminal according to the general principles of law recognised by civilised nations.'

6.267   Article 7 contains the Treaty's only reference to general principles of law.[3] It has also generated very few complaints at Strasbourg. It constitutes not merely a ban on the retrospective application of the criminal law but:

'... also embodies, more generally, the principle that only the law can define a crime and prescribe a penalty (*nullum crimen, nulle poene sine lege*) and the principle that the criminal law must not be extensively construed to the accused's detriment, for

---

1   See, for example, *Ozturk v Germany* (fn 5 on p 196 and **6.19**).
2   In its Consultation Paper 17, the Financial Services Authority expressly recognises the potentially damaging effects of the withdrawal of authorisation (at para 210) .
3   It has been suggested that it was at the outset considered inevitable that the European Convention would proceed on the basis of such principles and that there was no need for the proposition to be stated in broad terms. This begs the question, however, as to why the reference should appear in Art 7(2).

instance by analogy; it follows from this that an offence must be clearly defined in law.'[1]

In other words, Art 7 enshrines the notion of legal certainty, in common with other European Convention provisions. It applies both to the common law and to statutes.

6.268   Here too, an autonomous approach[2] is to be adopted. In looking to see whether any measure engages Art 7, it is necessary to look at substance more than form. Relevant factors include 'the nature and purpose of the measure in question and its characteristics under national law – the procedures involved in the making and implementation of the measure – and its severity'.[3] In particular, does the activity under scrutiny potentially attract a fine or imprisonment?[4] Art 7 in one respect adheres to the classical European Convention formula affecting qualified safeguards whereby the substantive right is first articulated before the permissible restrictions upon the operation of that right are set out. [5] In this instance, however (and unlike Art 10 in particular), the restrictions are narrowly confined and Art 7, because of its importance, is non-derogable even in wartime or during an emergency. Nevertheless, it does not go so far as to prohibit retrospection generally – that is prohibited only as regards crimes[6] – nor does it prohibit double jeopardy. The Seventh Protocol, not yet part of local law, needs to be relied upon for that prohibition.

6.269   Judges can continue to clarify and interpret the existing law without violating Art 7; indeed not doing so might mean that the law did not reflect changing circumstances generally, which is considered at Strasbourg to be a desirable aim.[7] However, what courts cannot do is fit existing offences to facts which did not previously attract criminal liability,[8] create new offences, or define offences in a wholly imprecise way. Criminal law is very much the preserve of Parliament in the UK and it would be surprising if such occurrences were to be encountered in commercial practice.

6.270   This diversionary explanation of Art 7 has been necessary because Art 7 is highly relevant in the financial services context. If the disciplinary offences in the Financial Services and Markets Act 2000 are eventually classified as criminal in nature, they will need to comply with the principle of legal certainty enshrined in Art 7 insofar, that is, as the definition of *criminal offence* in Art 7 is regarded as synonymous with the term *criminal charge* in Art 6. [9]

6.271   The FSA's Consultation Paper 13, published in September 1998, set out the FSA's proposed Principles for Business. These were drafted in very broad terms, although they were designed to impose binding 'obligations'. While the Authority has proposed to elaborate on the Principles in binding rules, evidential

---

1   *Kokkinakis v Greece* (1994) 17 EHRR 397 at para 52. See also *Dharmarajeu Sabapethee v The State* [1999] 1 WLR 1836.
2   As regards the need for an autonomous approach in addressing Arts 6 and 8, see **6.16**.
3   *Welsh v United Kingdom* (1995) **20 EHRR 247.**
4   See *Harman v United Kingdom* Appl 10038/82, (1984) 38 DR 53 (1984).
5   See in this regard, Arts 8 and 10, dealt with more fully in Chapters 7 and 8 respectively.
6   An attempt was made in the case of *National and Provincial Building Society v United Kingdom* (1997) 25 EHRR 127 to rely on Art 7 outside the criminal sphere, but this failed.
7   See *CR v United Kingdom* and *SW v United Kingdom* (1996) 21 EHRR 363.
8   See *X Limited and Y v United Kingdom* (1982) 28 DR 77.
9   See van Dijk and van Hoof (see fn 6 at p 45) p 479.

provisions and guidance, it has nevertheless indicated that there may be instances when disciplinary action will be taken in respect of conduct which is not identified in any such rule, evidential provision or guidance.

6.272   The comments of Sir Henry Brooke in a case involving a criminal conviction for breach of a local by-law requiring licensees to maintain good order on licensed premises,[1] could well be applied in this context:

> 'The Council would do well, in my judgment, to tighten up the language of [the relevant by-law] if it wishes to be able to use it to prohibit activities like these on licensed premises after the Human Rights Act 1998 comes into force. The extension of the very vague concept of the maintenance of good order to the control of the activities of prostitutes may have passed muster in the days when English common law offences did not receive critical scrutiny from national judicial guardians of a rights-based jurisprudence, but those days will soon be over. English judges will then be applying a Human Rights Convention which has the effect of prescribing that a criminal offence must be clearly defined in law. I do not accept ... that it is impossible to define the kind of conduct [the Council desired] to prohibit with greater precision.'

6.273   Lord Lester advised[2] that the FSA's Principles were so widely and vaguely drafted that the conviction of a person for a disciplinary offence on the basis of an alleged breach of a Principle alone would amount to an Art 7 breach. In his view, it would not be reasonable to expect a firm to foresee that acts and omissions falling outside the FSA's detailed rules, evidential provisions and guidance might render it liable to disciplinary action for breach of a Principle. Although knowledge of technical provisions may be assumed of those who work in a technical field, this is surely right.[3]

The market abuse regime

6.274   Part VIII of the Financial Services and Markets Act 2000, entitled *Civil Fines for Market Abuse,* gives the FSA the power to impose unlimited fines on persons engaging in market abuse or inducing others to do so by taking or refraining from any action. Market abuse is defined as behaviour of a particular kind occurring in relation to investments (prescribed by the Treasury), including investments whose subject-matter is a prescribed investment, on markets (prescribed by the Treasury) which are likely to affect the confidence of informed market participants that the market is a true and fair one.

6.275   Although the regime was characterised as *civil* in the draft Financial Services and Markets Bill, this characterisation is, as has been seen, not conclusive in European Convention terms.[4] In reviewing the nature of the proposed offences at the time of the draft Bill, Lord Lester noted[5] that the fines proposed were of a

---

1   *Westminster City Council v Blenheim Leisure (Restaurants) Limited and Others* (1999) *The Times,* 24 February. See also *R v Thames Magistrates' Court, ex parte Acadamy International plc* (1999) *The Times,* 23 June, and *Hashman and Harrup v United Kingdom* Appl 255/94 25 November 1999.

2   See para 7 of the Joint Note of Advice of Lord Lester of Herne Hill QC and Monica Carss-Frisk, Annex D to the First Report of the Joint Committee (see fn 3 on p 191).

3   See Appl 8141/78, (1979) 16 DR 141 about a butcher convicted in a food standards case.

4   See *Engel v The Netherlands* (1976) 1 EHRR 647 and **6.15** et seq.

5   At para 29 of his Joint Opinion with Javan Herberg, Annex C to the First Report of the Joint Committee (see fn 3 on p 191).

generally binding character, unlike the disciplinary systems of the then existing self-regulating organisations which took effect by virtue of the contractual relationship between the self-regulating organisations and their members.[1] In addition, the new regime extends beyond the regulated community to any person guilty of the requisite behaviour and Lord Lester drew attention to the similarities between the market abuse offences that were then envisaged and the existing criminal offences of insider trading and market manipulation, in terms of the nature, severity and purpose (ie deterrence) of the penalties involved.

6.276　　Initially, the Government and the FSA strongly defended the proposals outlined in the draft Bill, arguing that, although the monetary penalties were substantial, no term of imprisonment was prescribed, that the purpose of the fining power was to protect organised markets and compensate those markets (and people involved in them) for the costs of abuse and of policing them, that the scope of the regime was limited to those who chose to take advantage of organised investment markets and that the criminal courts would not be involved.[2] Nonetheless, under pressure from the Treasury Select Committee and the Joint Committee, the Government has since accepted that there is a 'real possibility' that the provisions for fines for market abuse in the Financial Services and Markets Act 2000 will be classified as *criminal* for European Convention purposes.

6.277　　The Government now acknowledges that its market abuse regime is not solely concerned with regulating the entry to a regulated community and the conduct and standards applicable to it, but also applies to anyone who participates in the financial markets (a much wider group, defined by economic activity, rather than by privileged access to a regulated occupation). Therefore, it has agreed that the market abuse regime in the Financial Services and Markets Act 2000 shall apply only to market participants.[3] Just as important, the Government has conceded the relevance of the significant similarities, in terms of scope, content and purpose, between the market abuse regime and existing criminal offences of insider dealing and market manipulation.

6.278　　If a market abuse offence is a *criminal* charge in European Convention terms, the provisions of Arts 6(2) and (3) additionally become applicable and this too was a feature of the debates regarding the Financial Services and Markets Bill. Following presentations made to it, the Government made concessions as regards the following.

(1) The presumption of innocence: in its original Consultation Paper 10 on Market Abuse, the FSA suggested[4] that it would only be required to prove a breach on the civil law basis of a balance of probabilities. Before the Joint Committee, the FSA accepted,[5] however, that the appropriate standard of proof was a 'sliding scale', which in serious cases is very close to the criminal level of proof.

1　　See *APB Ltd and Others v IMRO United Kingdom* Appl 30552/96, 15 January 1998, in which judicial review was considered adequately to comply with Art 6(1). See also fn 1 on p 196.

2　　Howard Davies, speech to the Chancery Bar Association, 3 March 1999 (see fn 1 on p 190).

3　　See para 1 of the Minutes of Evidence of 19 May 1999 in the Joint Committee's Second Report. See fn 5 on p 192.

4　　At para 7, Part 1, see http://www.fsa.gov.uk.

5　　Through Philip Thorpe, in response to question 58. See the Evidence taken by the Joint Committee on 16 March 1999 (see fn 3 on p 191).

(2) The privilege against self-incrimination: the Act now ensures that protection against the use of compelled evidence is put in place where there are proceedings which may lead to the imposition of a fine for market abuse.[1] In its Explanatory Notes to the Financial Services and Markets Bill the Government accepted that this was necessary to take the *Saunders*[2] judgment into account.

(3) The right to legal assistance: certain former Morgan Grenfell executives, when defending disciplinary proceedings brought by IMRO, complained that the legal costs involved were so prohibitive that they were constrained to abandon their defences.[3] The Government now accepts that subsidised legal assistance will have to be made available in market abuse cases to those who do not have sufficient means[4] even though City institutions will ultimately pay for this on the basis that the Lord Chancellor will obtain the subsidy from the FSA, which is in turn funded by the industry.

(4) Article 7 and market abuse: the Government also took steps to deal with the other primary area of concern regarding the market abuse regime, namely whether, given their high level of generality, the relevant market abuse offences as set out in the Financial Services and Markets Bill were sufficiently clearly defined in law to enable an individual to foresee the legal consequences of his actions. The FSA's Consultation Document on its proposed Code on Market Abuse had itself thrown up a number of questions as to whether particular conduct not only *would be* but *should be* treated as falling within the statute's market abuse offences.[5] Lord Hobhouse noted that:

'... so long as the draft ... remains in its present form, there will be a serious risk that it will fail in its objective and, far from providing a scheme which will catch the unscrupulous, will provide them with a means of escape which a properly drafted provision would foreclose.'[6]

6.279   Lord Steyn considered that, while the proposed system continued to be underpinned by a vaguely worded Code, there was a 'substantial risk that in respect of market abuse the system will be held not to comply with the Convention principle of certainty'.[7] If the Code were to have the force of law instead of merely 'evidential' status, Lord Lester conceded that an objection based upon Art 7(1) would probably fail. However, he considered that it would be a breach of Art 7 for a person to be convicted of a market abuse offence where his conduct did not fall within conduct indicated by the FSA's own Code to constitute an offence – let alone where the conduct was actually permitted by the Code. At all events, the Financial Services and Markets Act 2000 now provides[8] that the Authority may not sanction an individual if,

---

1   Section 174(2).
2   See **6.32** et seq.
3   One of them, Glyn Owen, has petitioned Strasbourg on the basis (*inter alia*) that his right to a fair hearing was denied by virtue of the costs incurred by IMRO and the inequality of arms created by IMRO's rules whereby an individual was at risk of being ordered to pay all IMRO's costs if found guilty but was unlikely to recover his own costs if acquitted. Mr Owen subsequently established the pressure group Justice in Financial Services.
4   Section 134.
5   See para 63 of the Joint Opinion of Lord Lester and Javan Herberg (see fn 3 on p 191).
6   See Appendix 1 to the Second Report of the Joint Committee (see fn 5 on p 192).
7   See Appendix 3 to the Second Report of the Joint Committee (see fn 5 on p 192).
8   Section 123(2).

having considered representations, it is satisfied that the person had taken all reasonable steps to avoid market abuse, or reasonably believed that his behaviour did not amount to market abuse.

(5) Double jeopardy: Lord Lester raised in his opinion the possibility that the Financial Services and Markets Bill infringed Art 4 of the (as yet unratified) Seventh Protocol to the European Convention,[1] which provides that:

> '... no-one shall be liable to be tried or punished again in criminal proceedings under the jurisdiction of the same State for an offence for which he has already been finally acquitted or convicted in accordance with the law and penal procedure of that State.'

The issue arose because the FSA indicated in its Consultation Paper 17 that, as a matter of 'general policy', it would not seek to impose a civil fine on a person who was, or had been, the subject of criminal proceedings involving substantially the same allegations of fact.[2] In response to consultation, the Authority has now confirmed a policy not to do so.

6.280   Before offering some concluding observations upon the relationship between the Financial Services and Markets Act 2000 and the Human Rights Act 1998, some other issues of significance to City practitioners are dealt with.

CITY OMBUDSMEN

6.281   The role of certain financial services ombudsmen is problematic in European Convention terms. Some, such as the Pensions Ombudsman, investigate very substantial matters involving large sums before themselves reaching determinations. Does this make for an independent and impartial tribunal?[3] In the case of the Pensions Ombudsman, an appeal from his decision is to the High Court on a point of law only. Is this an exercise of 'full jurisdiction' or not?[4] In the past, a decision was reached in one case involving an alleged breach of trust by trustees where the trustees were not shown a material document or allowed to comment upon it.[5] Here, too, the implementation of the Act will doubtless lead to changed decision-making practices.

THE IMPLICATIONS OF THE ACT FOR COMPETITION LAW

6.282   Given the range of interests engaged by it, it is not surprising that the Financial Services and Markets Act 2000 should have provoked high-profile debate, not least on European Convention grounds. What is surprising, however, is that the Competition Act 1998, which came fully into force on 1 March 2000 (having, ironically, received Royal Assent on the same day as the Act, 9 November

---

1   See Appendix 2.
2   See para 126, Financial Services Authority Consultation Paper 17, *Enforcing the New Regime*.
3   See **6.190** et seq.
4   See **6.66** et seq.
5   See *Seifert v Pensions Ombudsman* [1997] 4 All ER 947.

1998), should not have generated much comment as regards its human rights implications, no doubt to the unspoken chagrin of financial service regulators.

6.283   The Competition Act 1998 contains new powers of company investigation and establishes a range of possible penalties for infringements, all done with the aim of bringing competition law in the UK into line with that prevailing in the EU. The following features of the new legislation raise obvious European Convention considerations.

(1) The power to enter premises, which may, for these purposes, include private homes.[1] Entry can be without warrant where the premises are occupied by those reasonably suspected of competition law infringements. Nor need entry be restricted to premises occupied by businesses believed to be engaging in prohibited activity, for the powers can be used against third parties who *may* have useful information. In determining whether such entry constitutes an Art 8 violation, will a British judge follow the Strasbourg case of *Niemietz* or the Luxembourg case of *Hoechst*?[2]

(2) The power to require explanations from 'any person' on pain of criminal sanctions.[3] What if subsequent use is made of those explanations? Is this consistent with the decision in *Saunders*?[4] Is Art 6 engaged (unlike in *Saunders*) because the link between the investigation and the suspected offence is clear?

(3) The power to impose a fine of up to 10% of the UK turnover of the undertaking in question for up to 3 years.[5] Such a fine would clearly not be compensatory but punitive, as to which the European Commission has already held that a fine (of as much as 5% of annual turnover) imposed under French national competition laws was criminal in nature in terms of Art 6.[6] The traditional approach of the European Court of Justice has been to say that competition procedures are administrative in nature and do not engage Art 6,[7] but in *Orkem*,[8] Art 6 was held to be relevant where a business was facing a competition investigation and the Advocate-General has said that certain competition law fines 'have a criminal law character'.[9]

(4) The provision of an appeal to a tribunal which can make any decision the regulator could have made. Is this a tribunal of 'full jurisdiction' in terms of Art 6?

6.284   Considered as a whole, the Competition Act 1998 contemplates something much more serious than an administrative investigation and it would not be surprising if one of the first business cases to test the Act derived from concerns not about the financial services regime in the City of London (which now looks rather different from its appearance in 1998) but about the activities of competition authorities in the UK.

---

1   Sections 27–28 of the Competition Act 1998.
2   See **7.19** et seq.
3   Section 26 of the Competition Act 1998.
4   See **6.132** et seq.
5   Sections 36–38 of the Competition Act 1998.
6   See *Société Stenuit v France* (1992) 14 EHRR 509. See also fn 4 on p 162.
7   See, for example, *Heintz van Landewyck and Others v Commission* [1980] ECR 3125.
8   See **6.130**.
9   See *Hercules Chemicals NV v Commission* [1991] ECR II–1711.

FINES AND PROPORTIONALITY

6.285　　　Fining powers have already been discussed in this book in a variety of contexts. In recent years a variety of domestic regulators have imposed monetary penalties upon regulated firms which appeared all too like exemplary measures *pour encourager les autres.* For example, in 1998, Central Independent Television plc was fined £2m by the Independent Television Commission for breaching programming guidelines. IMRO has in the past handed down a fine of £2m and the London Metal Exchange one of £6.5m. In early 2000, Railtrack was reportedly challenging the Rail Regulator's threat to charge it £4m for every percentage point by which it failed to meet punctuality targets.[1]

6.286　　　Faced by such a prospect, companies should in the future consider arguing:

– 　that the penalty is such as to make the matter a criminal one, thereby engaging the whole of Art 6 and requiring that adequate procedural safeguards exist before such a significant punishment is imposed;
– 　that the penalty is disproportionate, not least in terms of historical awards and awards in other applicable industries; and
– 　that it is uncertain – Railtrack is apparently contending that the Rail Regulator's determination to fine it if performance targets are not *in the future* met leaves it unable in advance to determine its maximum exposure and that this fails to meet the requirement of legal certainty.

6.287　　　These arguments, singly or together, may not be sufficient to prevent the use of 'naming and shaming' powers, but their deployment will at least require regulators to justify their actions in European Convention terms.

ARTICLE 6 AND COMMERCE: AN OVERVIEW

6.288　　　A number of the issues which have characterised the debate about the European Convention's relationship to the Financial Services and Markets Act 2000 are central to this book – hence the detailed discussion of the new law. Those issues, however, have application far beyond the City of London to the business sector generally. The success of interest groups in mitigating the severity of certain features of the Financial Services and Markets Act 2000 points up the importance to commerce as a whole of the following considerations.

(1)　The value of being able to establish that a particular offence is criminal in nature in order, potentially, to secure the full measure of protection under Art 6. The disadvantage is of course that if the offence is proved, the corporate defendant may reputationally be considered to be a criminal with the concomitant prejudice to livelihood that that implies. This is particularly pertinent in light of the fact that disciplinary and professional hearings are increasingly likely to be held in public with the media reporting not just the sentence but also the antecedent evidence and any mitigation material.
(2)　The need for regulators to establish barriers between discrete functions (in particular separating compliance, investigation and enforcement).

1　　Raising the interesting question as to whether Railtrack, as a hybrid public authority, can in fact invoke the European Convention on its own behalf: see **3.135** et seq.

(3) The requirement upon regulators to ensure that any prosecutorial policy is perceived to be consistent, proportionate and non-discriminatory. Can 'naming and shaming' really be done in a way that is compatible with the European Convention?

(4) The importance of action taken by commerce at the pre-legislative stage. Some (if not all) of the perceived unfairness of the Financial Services and Markets Act 2000 has undoubtedly been removed by a coordinated and effective campaign[1] inside and outside Parliament, a luminous example to other industrial sectors.

(5) The fact that there is no area of business activity which does not conceivably engage Art 6's guarantees at some point. Whether the post-War draftsmen of the Treaty had investment bankers in mind in this regard is not the point. The financial services community is but one sector liable to encounter the European Convention in a number of different ways and, having established its relevance, City institutions stand poised to invoke the Act across a broad front.

IMPLICATIONS OF THE ACT FOR PUBLIC LAW PROCEEDINGS

6.289   Much of the litigation generated by the Act will, in mechanical terms, be by way of applications for judicial review. As has been seen,[2] the Act places a statutory obligation upon public authorities to act in conformity with the European Convention. Many of those public authorities (such as local councils and statutory regulators) are already judicially reviewable and the aim in this section, therefore, is to concentrate not upon the procedural implications of the Act for domestic judicial review but upon the substantive effect which it may have. That the Act will have a considerable effect was illustrated by the announcement in a Practice Direction in March 2000 that the number of judges sitting in the Crown Office List (in which applications for judicial review are heard)[3] was, in preparation for the Act, to be increased for the period from May to the end of July 2000 in hope that a backlog of cases might be cleared.

6.290   A judicial review case raising a domesticated European Convention point from now on will not necessarily be susceptible to determination in the same way as a judicial review case which does not raise a European Convention point. This is so even though, as described earlier, the European Convention has long been a feature of public law in the UK, relevant as an interpretative device in resolving statutory uncertainty or ambiguity, for example.[4] Indeed, in a wider sense, human rights considerations (if not solely European Convention safeguards) have for years now infused the common law in so far as they bear on the question of whether a public body has behaved irrationally or not. As a result, the coming into force of the Act does not mean that local judges are engaging in

---

1   Approximately 1,450 amendments had been tabled by mid March 2000: see *The Financial Times*, 17 March 2000.

2   Section 6 of the Act. See **3.73** et seq and Appendix 1.

3   The Crown Office, in the wake of the report of Sir Jeffery Bowman, is to be renamed the Administrative Court.

4   See, for example, *R v Radio Authority, ex parte Bull* [1997] 3 WLR 1094 and see generally **3.42** et seq.

human rights adjudication for the first time. What may change is the *intensity* of that adjudication. In the case of *Bugdaycay*[1] Lord Bridge emphasised that a British court was:

> '... entitled to subject an administrative discretion to more vigorous examination, to ensure that it is in no way flawed, according to the gravity of the issue which the decision determines. The most fundamental of all human rights is the individual's right to life and when an administrative decision under challenge is said to be one which may put the applicant's life at risk, the basis of the decision must surely call for the most *anxious scrutiny*.' (author's emphasis)

6.291   This 'anxious scrutiny' test was developed some years later by Lord Bingham in the Court of Appeal, when he adopted with approval the following formulation by David Pannick QC in the *Smith* case:

> '[T]he court may not interfere with the exercise of an administrative discretion on substantive grounds save where the court is satisfied that the decision is unreasonable in the sense that it is beyond the range of responses open to a reasonable decision-maker. But in judging whether the decision-maker has exceeded this margin of appreciation the human rights context is important. The more substantial the interference with human rights, the more the court will require by way of justification before it is satisfied that the decision is reasonable in the sense outlined above.'[2]

6.292   In *Smith,* several former members of the armed forces failed to establish before UK courts that the Government acted unlawfully in having a policy which prohibited homosexuals from remaining in the services. The applicants proceeded to Strasbourg where, in the autumn of 1999, the European Court found that the UK was in breach of its European Convention obligations, not only as regards Art 8 but also Art 13[3] – the latter violation arising from the fact that domestic judicial review was adjudged not to afford the applicants an adequate remedy in the local context. The result is that, whether or not public-law litigation in the UK henceforth conforms to the *procedural* safeguards in Art 6 of the European Convention, wholly separate questions arise as to whether the rigour and scope of the *substantive* adjudication in an application for judicial review satisfies Art 13. In circumstances where commercial judicial review has enjoyed an exponential growth in recent years, the practical outworkings of the Strasbourg judges' decision in the *Smith* case has as much significance for the corporate sector as any other constituency.

6.293   Generations of British public lawyers were weaned on the case of *Associated Provincial Picture Houses v Wednesbury Corporation.*[4] *Wednesbury* established that an irrational decision was a decision which no decision-maker, seized of all the relevant facts, could properly have reached. Therefore, an irrational decision is not a determination which could readily have gone one way or the other and about which there could have been a sensible debate. Put like this, it is apparent that irrationality (otherwise known as *Wednesbury*-unreasonableness) is a very high hurdle for any claimant to jump and it is no surprise that it has acquired a

---

1   *R v Secretary of State for the Home Department, ex parte Bugdaycay* [1987] AC 514 at 531.
2   *R v Ministry of Defence and Others, ex parte Smith and Others* [1996] QB 517.
3   See also **3.10** et seq and Appendix 2. Not surprisingly, most Art 13 petitions have traditionally come from those Contracting States, including the UK, which hitherto have not domesticated the European Convention.
4   [1948] 1 KB 223.

'throw-away status'.[1] Boardrooms, however, traditionally have been obliged to become acquainted with the notion on the basis that unless, for example, an industry regulator has followed an unfair procedure (and the more sophisticated the regulator the more unlikely that will be) or exceeded its statutory powers (again a rare occurrence), there is no good prospect of overturning the decision of the regulator, however unfair, unless it is also shown to have been unreasonable in *Wednesbury* terms. It is against this background that companies have traditionally been only too aware that reversing regulatory decisions in court is notoriously difficult.

6.294   *Wednesbury* left British judges in the position, as Lord Bridge put it in *Brind*,[2] of needing to make a *secondary* judgment about the *primary* judgment of the original decision-maker. The Act changes this relationship. As Simon Brown LJ, one of the judges in the Court of Appeal, said in the case of *Smith*:

> '... if the European Convention ... were part of our law and we were accordingly entitled to ask whether the policy (ie on homosexuals in the armed forces) answers a pressing social need and whether the restriction on human rights can be shown to be proportionate ... then clearly the primary judgment (subject only to a limited margin of appreciation) should be for us and not for others; the constitutional balance would shift.'

6.295   This is potentially very significant and on any view it should lighten the mood of directors by now inured to receiving legal advice to the effect that an adverse public law decision cannot be successfully challenged in court unless shown to be 'so outrageous in its defiance of logic or of accepted moral standards that no sensible person who had applied his mind to the question to be decided could have arrived at it'.[3] The Act must, on account of the stop-charge to which Simon Brown LJ referred, offer the prospect of relief for the corporate sector in this context.

6.296   The *Wednesbury* doctrine may survive in litigation that does not engage the European Convention but, if local judges are fulfilling the interpretative obligation placed upon them by the Act, it would seem unlikely that claims against public authorities raising European Convention points can any longer be decided on a *Wednesbury* basis *simpliciter*, because that would, as one leading commentator has suggested,[4] surely not take account of the Strasbourg jurisprudence or indeed of the wider purpose of the legislation, which is to submit public authorities in judicial review litigation to a new formulation of the existing test of illegality. Before the Act, a public body could, in broad terms, behave disproportionately but lawfully. The Act changes that.

6.297   In the White Paper which accompanied the Human Rights Bill, the Government stressed that local courts would:

> '... be required to balance the protection of individuals' fundamental rights against the demands of the general interest of the community, particularly in relation to Arts 8–11 where a State may restrict the protected right to the extent that this is necessary in a democratic society.'[5]

---

1   Sir Stephen Sedley (see fn 1 on p 23) at p 21.
2   At 541.
3   Lord Diplock in *Council of Civil Service Unions v Minister for the Civil Service* [1985] AC 374.
4   M Hunt in [1999] EHRLR 15.
5   *Rights Brought Home* (see fn 2 on p 42), para 2.5

6.298 The Act on this basis requires British judges to adopt 'a more overtly principled'[1] approach to judicial review and to abandon the declaration by the House of Lords in the *Brind*[2] case (about the operation of the broadcasting ban of certain groups in Northern Ireland). Therefore, had the Act been in force when *Brind* was heard, it would surely not have been possible in the first place to legislate for the broadcasting restrictions in issue without complying with Art 10 of the European Convention. Put another way, the impact of the Act is now such that it will no longer, in the words of Sir Stephen Richards (speaking extra-judicially), be enough in a case with a human rights point to do as advocates did in the past, by 'taking a deep breath, submitting that recourse to the Convention was precluded by *ex parte Brind* and praying that it would not be necessary to go deeper into the merits than was required under *Wednesbury* principles'.[3]

6.299 As already stated, a decision which was irrational before the Act will, by definition, also have been disproportionate in terms of the Act. A disproportionate decision will not, however, in every instance have been an irrational one. Public authorities will therefore henceforth lose cases (on proportionality grounds) which they would previously have won (on irrationality grounds). Equally (and less satisfactorily) a case taken against a hybrid public authority (such as BT) on a European Convention point may be won (again, say, on pro-portionality grounds) when in the absence of a horizontal application of the Act[4] case against a private interest (such as another telecommunications company) may *substantially on the same facts* be lost.

6.300 Fears have been expressed that, over time, judges in the UK may seek to give a form of local application to the doctrine of margin of appreciation[5] – which, as an international law concept, should have no strict application domestically – and that it will metamorphose into *Wednesbury* by any other name. Despite the fact that both ideas have different antecedents and have had different functions, references to the operation of a margin of appreciation have become more common in local courts. In such a context, it is likely that the judiciary will turn with some enthusiasm to the observations of Lord Hope in *R v Director of Public Prosecutions, ex parte Kebilene*.[6] He considered that, when reviewing interferences with rights, on occasions it would be appropriate to defer 'on democratic grounds' to public authorities acting with a 'discretionary area of judgment' – the ambit of which might differ depending upon the issue in question. It would, for example, be broad (ie more deferential) in matters of social and economic policy and narrow (ie less deferential) in relation to constitutional questions or those which judges were well qualified to answer.

6.301 Companies supervised by statutory regulators are by definition operat-ing within limits imposed on policy grounds – the financial services sector is an

---

1   Lord Irvine in *The Development of Human Rights in Britain under an Incorporated Convention on Human Rights* [1998] PL 221.
2   *R v Home Secretary, ex parte Brind* [1991] 1 AC 696.
3   Addressing a Human Rights Act and Community Law training course organised by JUSTICE and Monckton Chambers. The address is reproduced in the JUSTICE Bulletin for spring 1999.
4   See **3.74** et seq.
5   See **5.35**.
6   [1999] 3 WLR 972.

obvious example – so these comments are a cautionary reminder that, from the perspective of the applicant, commercial judicial review will continue to be difficult, with judges reluctant to intervene in determinations involving highly technical, industry-specific considerations.

6.302   In the *Smith* case, the Strasbourg judges found that the irrationality threshold in local law was:

> '... placed so high that it effectively excluded any consideration by the domestic courts of the question of [sic] whether the interference with the applicants' rights answered a pressing social need or was proportionate to the national security and public order aims pursued, principles which lie at the heart of the [European] Court's analysis of complaints under Art 8 of the Convention.'[1]

6.303   The case therefore is to be contrasted with the earlier Strasbourg decisions *Soering*[2] and *Vilvarajah*,[3] in which domestic English judicial review emerged unscathed, but conceivably only because 'anxious scrutiny' was brought to bear in both cases.[4]

6.304   In recognition, perhaps, of the changed approach to judicial reasoning in public-law matters which the Act requires, Sir John Laws sought in a recent High Court decision to summarise the difference between the classical, domestic and continental approaches to supervision by the bench of administrative discretion. He said:

> 'The difference between *Wednesbury* and European review is that in the former case the legal limits lie further back. I think there are two factors. First the limits of domestic review are not, as the law presently stands, constrained by the doctrine of proportionality. Secondly, at least as regards a requirement such as that of objective justification in an equal treatment case, the European rule requires that the decision-maker provide a fully-reasoned case. It is not enough merely to set out the problem, and assert that within his jurisdiction the Minister chose this or that solution, constrained only by the requirement that his decision must have been one which a reasonable Minister could make. Rather the Court will test the solution arrived at and pass it only if substantial factual considerations are put forward in its justification, considerations which are relevant, reasonable and proportionate to the aim and view. But as I understand the jurisprudence the Court is not concerned to agree or disagree with the decision: that would be to travel beyond the boundaries of proper judicial authority, and usurp the primary decision-maker's function. Thus *Wednesbury* and European review are different models – one looser, one tighter – of the same judicial concept, which is the imposition of compulsory standards on decision-makers so as to secure the repudiation of arbitrary powers.'[5]

---

1   On the facts, the Strasbourg judges held that the applicants' Art 8 rights were breached on account of the way in which military investigations were carried out into their sexual orientation and by their subsequent discharge from the armed forces.

2   *Soering v United Kingdom* (1992) 14 EHRR 248, an extradition case.

3   *Vilvarajah v United Kingdom* (1989) 11 EHRR 439, an asylum case. In *Chahal v United Kingdom* (1996) 23 EHRR 413, the form of judicial review in this country was found to be inadequate in the context of Art 5(4).

4   The Court of Appeal in *Smith* had, arguably, given the Strasbourg judges something of a steer. Lord Bingham had said that there might well be room for argument that the interference with the applicants' Art 8 rights had been disproportionate and Simon Brown LJ thought that the balance of argument was with the applicants. His own view was that the days of the traditional policy towards homosexuals in the military was numbered.

5   *R v Ministry of Agriculture, Fisheries and Food, ex parte First City Trading* [1997] 1 CMLR 250.

6.305   The fact is that, under the Act, respondent public authorities (which may include companies) still stand every chance of being successful in litigation where they establish that:

–   they are pursuing an aim which justifies the restriction placed upon a European Convention right;
–   there is some rational nexus between the method of implementation of the aim and the aim itself; and
–   the method of implementation of the aim is just enough to meet the aim and there is, as such, no question of the authority's having 'gone over the top'.

6.306   For their part, British judges now have to:

–   identify whether a particular European Convention right is engaged;
–   identify any interference with that right;
–   establish whether the interference with a qualified European Convention right was prescribed by law;
–   (if it was) establish whether the prescription was legitimate; and
–   (if it was legitimate) establish whether it was proportionate.

6.307   There is no reason why respondent public authorities should not emerge from such an analytical process relatively unscathed, as there will continue to be a permissible area of discretion, however described, in which public authorities may operate lawfully. The size of this discretionary zone will vary from case to case. Companies can, for example, expect judges to police with some care the fair hearing rights of the business sector in terms of Art 6, but conceivably to be much more deferential towards public authorities interfering with the property rights of businesses in terms of Art 1 of the First Protocol.[1]

THE IMPACT OF THE ACT UPON JUDICIAL REVIEW PROCEDURE

6.308   In a case engaging the Act it will be for the claimant to establish a European Convention infringement and then for the respondent public authority, where a violation is found, to establish that there has been a proportionate response to it. It will be for the court to consider the extent to which it need involve itself in social, economic and political matters – so-called legislative facts – as opposed to its traditional preoccupation with purely 'adjudicative facts'. Lord Justice Henry, in the *Smith* case,[2] suggested, for example, that this might involve the submission of *Brandeis* briefs.

6.309   In an increasing number of claims, their obligation to take account of Strasbourg jurisprudence will oblige judges in the UK to engage in this wider form of analysis, for the requirements of proportionality will simply not be met in many instances unless socio-economic and other considerations are brought into account. The practical effect may well be that judicial review hearings might become longer and public law litigation more expensive with, the need for equality of arms notwithstanding,[3] an advantage conceivably lying with

---

1   See Chapter 9.
2   See fn 2 on p 206
3   See **6.160** et seq.

well-funded corporates and well-resourced lawyers. Not just that, but the traditional reluctance to order disclosure or cross-examination in such cases will need to be looked at afresh.

6.310　　Applications for judicial review in England and Wales are subject to a requirement for permission to be obtained at the outset, deliberately interposed to weed out weak claims. However, can an application for leave be dealt with any longer on the basis of a 'quick perusal'[1] on the part of the judge, when claimants will, in many instances, be filing evidence as regards the societal impact of an alleged European Convention breach? Even where the claimant's evidence does not go into such areas, the respondent in resisting the application may seek to justify a *prima facie* European Convention violation by adducing material dealing with complex policy considerations. It will be interesting to see whether central Government sets a lead in this area by not opposing the giving of permission in many instances.

THE ACT AND PUBLIC LAW: AN OVERVIEW

6.311　　Put at its lowest, the substantive effect of the Act on domestic judicial review is likely to be that the doctrine of proportionality will become relevant in many cases, as it already is in EC matters. The judges will need to engage in a new analytical approach based upon rights and justifiable interference with rights. However, if the sceptics are right in warning that the future of public law in this country can be characterised as a case of 'goodbye *Wednesbury*, hello margin of appreciation' it may be anticipated that a slew of complaints to Strasbourg based on undomesticated Art 13 of the European Convention will follow – an odd consequence of the legislation were it to happen.

1　　*R v IRC, ex parte National Federation of Self-employed and Small Businesses Limited* [1982] AC 617.

Chapter 7

PRIVATE LIVES AND BUSINESS AFTER THE ACT[1]

7.1   Just as it has been suggested that the notion of human rights for companies is a contradiction in terms,[2] so it has been argued that a business cannot, at least in some circumstances, have a private life.[3] As yet, the argument has not found favour at Strasbourg, but the issue is likely to feature prominently in future UK litigation regarding Art 8 of the European Convention, which bears the heading 'Right to Respect for Private and Family Life' (a heading added pursuant to the Eleventh Protocol).[4]

7.2   The main body of Art 8 provides that:

'1.   Everyone has the right to respect for his private and family life, his home and his correspondence.

2.   There shall be no interference by a public authority with the exercise of this right except such as is in accordance with the law and is necessary in a democratic society, in the interests of national security, public safety or the economic well-being of the country, for the prevention of disorder or crime, for the protection of health or morals, or for the protection of the rights and freedoms of others.'

THE SCOPE OF THE RIGHT

7.3   Some leading commentators contend that Art 8 could have a greater influence in reshaping British law than any other part of the European Convention,[5] though that view is not shared universally.[6] In structure, Art 8 is typical of those provisions of the Treaty which are not absolute and free from derogation. Like Arts 9, 10, 11 and 12, it promulgates a right (in its first part) and then in its second part itemises the permissible limitations upon the exercise of the right. Articles 10 and 11 do at least purport to guarantee the *substance* of particular rights (respectively, freedom of expression and association), whereas Art 8 oddly calls only for *respect* for private life, a notion belonging, it has been said, 'to the world of manners rather than the law'.[7] It is, on the other hand, a guarantee of respect in general and not just of respect by the State.

---

1   This chapter concentrates principally upon the implications of Art 8 for firms outside the media sector. The issue of press intrusion specifically and the implications that Art 8 may have for the media generally are dealt with in Chapter 8.

2   See **2.14** et seq.

3   See *R v Broadcasting Standards Commission, ex parte BBC* [2000] EMLR 587, discussed at **8.235** et seq.

4   See **2.44** et seq.

5   See, for example, Lester and Pannick, fn 1 on p 12.

6   Writing in early 1997, E Barendt suggested that, in the event of European Convention incorporation, privacy (not necessarily the same thing as the right to a private life (see **7.8** et seq)) would remain more a matter of social than legal significance. See his chapter 'Privacy as a Constitutional Right and Value' in *Privacy and Loyalty* edited by P Birks (Clarendon Press, 1997).

7   JES Fawcett *The Application of the European Convention on Human Rights* 2nd Edn (Oxford University Press, 1987), p 211.

7.4   The European Court has confirmed what might be regarded as self-evident in stating that 'the notion of "respect" is not clear-cut: having regard to the diversity of the practices followed and the situations obtaining in the Contracting States, the notion's requirements will vary considerably from case to case'.[1] Accordingly, 'this is an area in which the Contracting Parties enjoy a wide margin of appreciation[2] in determining the steps to be taken to ensure compliance with the Convention with due regard to the needs and resources of the community and of individuals'.[3] Therefore, the extent and scope of the protection deriving from Art 8 will vary among States. A number have privacy statutes, but few have given privacy the elevated status of a constitutional right. State discretion is not, however, unlimited in this area and it is to be approached restrictively.[4]

7.5   The inclusion in the European Convention of a guarantee respecting private lives arguably confirms its status as a civil and political right, but it may owe more to social, economic and cultural considerations. Is it, indeed 'no more than a luxury for the better-off in developed countries'?[5] Philosophical deliberations on this score would not generally have troubled British lawyers in the past, but the introduction of the Act conceivably makes them of some importance, for the less private lives are shown to be justiciable, the more they can perhaps be interfered with.

7.6   Article 8 was not the first multilateral attempt to create a standard affecting this sphere of human activity. Article 12 of the UNDR had earlier provided that:

> 'No-one shall be subjected to arbitrary interference with his privacy, family, home or correspondence, nor to attacks upon his honour and reputation. Everyone has the right to the protection of the law against such interference or attacks.'[6]

7.7   The UNDR text is plainly broader in scope than Article 8 and advocates in UK courts will doubtless attempt to rely upon the former for that reason. Its negative phraseology is redolent of an immediate post-War determination never again to witness the arbitrary infractions of the 1930s and 1940s, as exemplified by Nazi policies on marriage and the indoctrination of children. Interestingly, it also connects in one sentence and as overlapping safeguards two concepts (privacy and defamation) which the European Convention splits across two provisions (Arts 8 and 10)[7] and the tension between those two concepts underpins the whole of the debate about perceived media excesses in contemporary Britain. Article 12 of the UNDR entrenches defamation law by promulgating the civil right of the citizen to defend himself against reputational attack. The relevant text in the ICCPR is in very similar terms and is, again, wider than that in the European Convention. It states that:

---

1   *Abdulaziz, Cabales and Balkandali v United Kingdom* (1985) 7 EHRR 471, para 67.
2   As to which, see **5.35** et seq.
3   *Abdulaziz* (see fn 1 above), para 67.
4   *Silver v United Kingdom* (1983) 5 EHRR 347.
5   J Michael: *Privacy and Human Rights* (Dartmouth, 1994), p 1.
6   The first draft of Art 8 straightforwardly incorporated Art 12 of the UNDR, but this version was subsequently abandoned.
7   Reputational rights are entrenched in the European Convention as a restriction on free expression in Art 10. See Chapter 8.

'(1) No-one shall be subjected to arbitrary or unlawful interference with his privacy, family, home or correspondence, nor to unlawful attacks on his honour and reputation.

(2) Everyone has the right to the protection of the law against such interference or attacks.'[1]

7.8   Does it matter that the UNDR and the ICCPR refer to *privacy* while the European Convention refers to *private life*? The preponderant view appears to be that the difference is immaterial,[2] not least because the French texts of both the UNDR and European Convention use the same expression, *vie privée*. This is helpful, but it is unlikely to put an end to the suggestion that the right to privacy denotes a safeguarding of interests wider than those forming part of a private life.

7.9   The need to look again at this issue was highlighted in 1970 when the Consultative Assembly of the Council of Europe (under whose aegis the Strasbourg institutions operate) called for 'an agreed interpretation of the right to privacy [sic] provided for in Article 8 of the Convention . . . by the conclusion of a Protocol or otherwise, so as to make it clear that this right is effectively protected against interference not only by public authorities but also by private persons or the mass media'.[3] Ignoring in this context the fact that the word *privacy* is not used in Art 8, it is plain from this that the Consultative Assembly recognised the need to come up with a reformulated guarantee. Thirty years on, however, Art 8 remains unamended.

7.10   At least the members of the Consultative Assembly were in good company as, quite separately, the relationship between the press and private lives was over a number of years to be looked at extensively in the UK, with equally (if not more) inconclusive results, the Younger Report concluding in 1972 that privacy could not be satisfactorily defined[4] and Sir David Calcutt's Committee agreeing in 1990.[5] No assistance is to be found in the US Constitution which does not mention the word 'privacy' or 'private lives' as such, even though the first eight of its amendments bear upon aspects of the so-called right to be let alone, which is generally understood to cover broadly the same terrain. Whether however, that idea is greater or lesser in extent than anything connoted by Art 8 is not clear. Interestingly enough, it was this description, reminiscent of Garbo, that the European Commission sought to develop in 1974 in saying that the right to a private life was 'the right to live, as far as one wishes, protected from publicity, allied to which is the right to a certain degree to establish and develop relationships with other human beings, especially in the emotional field, for the development and fulfilment of one's own personality'.[6]

---

1   Article 17 of the ICCPR.
2   See, for example, Robertson and Merrills *Human Rights in Europe* 3rd edn (Manchester University Press, 1993).
3   Recommendation 582 of 1970, conveniently reproduced in Robertson and Merrills (see fn 2 above), p 131.
4   Report of the Committee on Privacy (Cm 5012) 1972, paras 57–61.
5   Report of the Committee on Privacy and Related Matters (Cm 1102) 1990, paras 3.1–3.8 See also R Bagshaw in 'Obstacles on the Path to Privacy Torts' in *Privacy and Loyalty* (see fn 6 on p 213 above), p 135, where he says that 'the problem is not that privacy is without value, but that the chaotic mix of values which coalesce under the "privacy umbrella" makes the concept useless for analytical or practical work'.
6   Appl 6825/74, (1976) 5 DR 86. See also *Van Oostrreijck v Belgium* (1979) B36, Com Rep, paras 30–41.

7.11   This broadly articulates the basis on which the Strasbourg institutions
have approached a number of cases on Art 8, although it does not extend to cover,
for example, protection from surveillance or from breach of confidence, both
indubitably Art 8 concerns. Perhaps all that can safely be said is that, over the years,
Art 8 has become 'a general charter of individual autonomy' covering activities as
diverse as the way in which the citizen dresses or conducts his sex life.[1]

7.12   Many of the leading Strasbourg authorities on Art 8 are of no direct
relevance to the corporate sector. There have been Art 8 cases about, for example,
marital separation in Ireland,[2] homosexual rights in Northern Ireland[3] and
deportation from the UK.[4] Such cases contain helpful statements of general
principle outlining the boundaries of the Article, but are on their facts far
removed from boardroom concerns. Business was, however, very much in the
thoughts of those who drafted Art 8. What appears now to be a remarkable
legitimisation of public authority interference with private lives in the interests of
'the economic well-being of the country' was apparently[5] inserted at the request of
those putative Contracting States who maintained exchange controls, which
could only be policed by exercise of the power to open mail. Such a power was of
course a feature of centre-left administrations of the time and it again shows the
extent to which a right, conceivably of benefit to the corporate sector, was made
subject to limitation at the request of socialist planners.

THE ANALYTICAL PROCESS

7.13   The European Court has tended to be imprecise in its analysis of Art
8(1), although this has at least allowed the Strasbourg case-law to develop by
accretion in a way that has taken account of social and technical developments.

7.14   In seeking to identify the conceivable relevance of Art 8 in a business
context, certain questions require to be posed. Equally, they need to be posed in
relation to questions arising under Art 10 or indeed under Arts 9 and 11. In short,
when approaching any of the key, qualified rights in the European Convention it
is necessary to ask:

–   is the interest that has, or is about to be, interfered with, within the reach of
      (in this case) Art 8(1)?
–   if it is, has a public authority, far from respecting the interest, interfered with
      it?[6]
–   if a public authority has interfered with it, did it do so:

---

1   M Janis, R Kay and A Bradley in *European Human Rights Law* (Clarendon Press, Oxford, 1995)
      at p 230. Reid believes that Art 8 is wider than a right to privacy. To her, 'the concept stands
      for the sphere of immediate personal autonomy'. See K Reid *Human Rights Act 1998: A
      Practitioner's Guide* (Sweet & Maxwell, 1998), p 323.
2   *Airey v Ireland* [1979] 2 EHRR 305. *Airey* is also an important case in the context of Art 6 (see
      6.69 et seq).
3   *Dudgeon v United Kingdom* (1981) 4 EHRR 149.
4   *Abdulaziz, Cabales and Balkandali v United Kingdom* (1985) 7 EHRR 471.
5   See Robertson and Merrills (fn 2 on p 215), p 128.
6   A temporary impediment inhibiting the effective exercise of the right may suffice. See *Golder
      v United Kingdom* (1975) EHRR 524 at para 26 and **6.75** et seq.

(a) in accordance with the law (and here the European Convention model clashes four-square with Dicey's idea of residual rights)?

(b) for one or more of the legitimate reasons set out (in this case) in Art 8(2)? and

(c) necessarily in a democratic society?[1]

7.15   In the *Marckx* case,[2] the European Court crucially held that it may not be sufficient for States merely to refrain from interference in private lives – States must also respect those lives and this may involve them in positive action, perhaps involving the taking of steps to protect privacy and to regulate with some precision those narrow purposes provided for in Art 8(2) whereby private lives may lawfully be interfered with. Specifically, the Strasbourg judges said that 'the object of [Art 8] is "essentially" that of protecting the individual against arbitrary interference by the public authorities'. Nevertheless, it does not merely compel the State to abstain from such interference. In addition to this primarily negative undertaking, there may be positive obligations inherent in an effective 'respect for family life'.

7.16   In circumstances where the application of Art 8 appears on its face to be limited to a prohibition of interference 'by a public authority', it is perhaps not surprising that the European Court should have been anxious to adopt such a construction. Therefore, Art 8 guarantees not only a substantive right but also the provision of procedural safeguards to protect that right.[3] These may be important to the extent that certain forms of regulatory behaviour directed at corporates (such as the investigations conducted by Department of Trade and Industry inspectors which do not engage the fair hearing requirements of Art 6)[4] may nevertheless engage Art 8 (as regards, for example, the circumstances in which such inspectors can call for documentation). In a different business context, Art 8 was, for example, referred to by Rattee J in holding that Jonathan Aitken's trustee in bankruptcy should not be able to sell Aitken's personal papers[5] and, on 20 June 2000, the European Court held that interference with a bankrupt's letters after the expiry of an order redirecting his mail to his trustee in bankruptcy was an Art 8 breach which was not necessary in a democratic society.[6]

7.17   However, there are limits to the scope and content of positive obligations. Article 8 only calls for *respect* after all and in:'determining whether or not a positive obligation exists, regard must be had to the fair balance that has to be struck between the general interest of the community and the interests of individuals'.[7] In trying to divine the implications in all of this for boards of directors, it is necessary to proceed substantially by use of analogy.

---

1   The nature of the qualified rights is more fully explained at **2.7** et seq, while the approach to European Convention interpretation is explained at **5.4** et seq.

2   *Marckx v Belgium* (1979) 2 EHRR 330.

3   See *McMichael v United Kingdom* (1995) 20 EHRR 205.

4   See **6.48** et seq and **6.149** et seq. See also *Harrison and Another v Bloom Camillin (a firm)* 14 April 2000, unreported, about the privacy of a prospective witness.

5   *Re Aitken* [2000] 3 All ER 80.

6   *Foxley v United Kingdom* Appl 33274/96, (2000) *The Times*, 4 July.

7   *Rees v United Kingdom* (1987) 9 EHRR 56 at para 37.

THE ACT'S IMPLICATIONS FOR SEARCH POWERS

7.18   To what extent may firms now be able to invoke the right to, for example, private correspondence that forms part of Art 8 to prevent the search of their premises by (say) the police, Her Majesty's Customs and Excise, or officials from Brussels? Art 8 was drafted with the Gestapo's knock in the middle of the night very much in mind. Indeed, Sir Gerald Fitzmaurice, then the UK's judge at Strasbourg, expressed concern in a 1979 case about illegitimacy that Art 8's original purpose was being stretched too far. For him, Art 8 was about 'domicilliary protection'.

7.19   In his view, its purpose was to prevent:

'... the whole gamut of fascist and communist inquisitorial practices such as had scarcely been known, at least in Western Europe, since the eras of religious intolerance and oppression, until (ideology replacing religion) they became prevalent again in many countries between the two world wars and subsequently.'

He added that it: 'was for the avoidance of these horrors, tyrannies and vexations that "private and family life ... home and correspondence" were to be respected – not for the regulation of the civil status of babies'.[1]

7.20   The reach of Art 8 in the business context was highlighted in the case of *Niemietz v Germany*,[2] which arose out of a search (conducted in the absence of any independent observer) of a lawyer's office as part of an on-going criminal investigation into 'insulting behaviour', the aim of the search being to seek to identify the writer of ostensibly insulting correspondence. Niemietz complained not only that respect for his home and correspondence had been impaired but (imaginatively) that the business goodwill and reputation of his firm, a tangible economic interest under Art 1 of the First Protocol,[3] had been damaged. The European Commission held unanimously that his Art 8 right had indeed been breached, as the interference was not necessary in a democratic society when unaccompanied by any safeguards which would protect against an abuse of power.

7.21   In its judgment the European Court confirmed the relevance of Art 8 for the corporate sector. There was, in its view:

'... no reason of principle why this understanding [ie the right to establish and develop relationships with other human beings] of the notion of "private life" should be taken to exclude activities of a professional or business nature since it is ... in the course of their working lives that the majority of people have a significant, if not the greatest, opportunity of developing relationships with the outside world.'

Any other decision would conceivably have discriminated against home workers by leading 'to an inequality of treatment, in that ... [Art 8's] protection would remain unavailable to a person whose professional and non-professional activities were so intermingled that there was no means of distinguishing them'. The Strasbourg judges emphasised that Contracting States were still able to 'interfere' to the extent permitted by Art 8(2), and interferences could conceivably be more far-reaching in the business sector than might otherwise be the case. Generally,

---

1   Delivering a dissenting opinion in the *Marckx* case (see fn 2 on p 217).
2   (1992) 16 EHRR 97.
3   As to which, see **9.13** et seq.

however, extending the concept of 'home' to include certain forms of professional or commercial activities was 'consonant with the essential object and purpose of Art 8, namely to protect the individual against arbitrary interference by the public authorities'. In principle, therefore, the 'home' can be the office (the word in the French text is *domicile*, which has a broader connotation in that language than *home* in any event) – a notion not unknown in modern professional life.

7.22 The European Court also acknowledged in its decision the extent to which work may be an essential element in the life of a liberal profession. Niemietz was a lawyer and the disproportionate risk of prejudice to third-party interests (ie those of his clients) was one the judges plainly had in mind. Whether the same level of protection would be extended to, for example, manufacturers or retailers is not clear.

7.23 The decision in *Niemietz* shows the European Court reaching for a broader understanding of private lives than that connoted by the Anglo-American notion of seclusion.[1] Distinguishing between the various parts of modern life was, the Strasbourg judges appeared to say, unnecessary and indeed fraught with difficulty in circumstances where an individual's work may 'form part and parcel of his life to such a degree that it becomes impossible to know in what capacity he is acting at a given moment in time'.

7.24 *Niemietz* was a case partly about the seizure of papers. It was followed in short order by the decision in *Miaihle*,[2] in which French customs authorities were found to have behaved disproportionately in indiscriminately seizing around 15,000 documents from the applicant's head office. It would appear wholly inconsistent with the evolutive tendencies of Strasbourg jurisprudence for these cases not now to extend to seizures of computer disks and other electronically-generated materials.

7.25 It is regrettable that, as far as the law regarding searches of companies is concerned, the European Court of Justice in Luxembourg and the European Court in Strasbourg have not been consistent in their thinking. In 1980, the European Court of Justice looked at Art 8 in the context of a search carried out by officials from Brussels without a warrant and in the absence of any legal representatives of the company (National Panasonic) whose premises were being searched.[3] When the company sought to rely on its Art 8 guarantee, the European Court of Justice, whilst at least acknowledging the safeguards in Art 8(1), also noted the permissible limitations in Art 8(2) and concluded that the use of the search power in such circumstances contributed 'to the maintenance of the system of competition intended by the Treaty [of Rome] which undertakings are absolutely bound to comply with'. The wider issue as to the interaction between European Community and European Convention rights was not addressed.[4]

---

1   According to Harris, O'Boyle and Warbrick (chapter 9 at pp 305 and 306).
2   (1993) 16 EHRR 332.
3   *National Panasonic v Commission* [1980] ECR 2057. See also *AKZO Chemie BV (The Netherlands)* and *AKZO Chemie UK Ltd v Commission* [1986] ECR 2585 and *Dow Benelux v Commission* [1989] ECR 3137. See also *Hoechst* case (see **7.2.6**).
4   See, generally, as regards conflicts between EC and European Convention law, **5.55** et seq.

7.26   In the case of *Hoechst AG v Commission*[1] the European Court of Justice had, before *Niemietz* (and indeed before there was any Strasbourg decision in this area), held that dawn raids by EU competition officials did not breach Art 8(1) on the basis that Art 8(1) was concerned with 'the development of man's personal freedom and may not therefore be extended to business premises'. Hoechst had argued that no search could be carried out without a court order which identified the scope of the inspection to take place. The European Court of Justice was unpersuaded. It was true that homes should be inviolate – a fundamental right forming, it confirmed, part of the EC's legal order – but the same was 'not true in regard to undertakings, because there are not inconsiderable differences between the legal systems of the [EC] Member States in regard to the nature and degree of protection afforded in business premises against intervention by ... public authorities'. In any event, Art 8(1), in the view of the European Court of Justice, was 'concerned with the development of man's personal freedom and may not therefore be extended to business premises'.

7.27   One suggested explanation for this divergence of opinion is that 'the Convention's aim is to protect the individual as a human being, while the Community's aim is to further economic and social integration',[2] but what will be the response of a British judge asked to determine whether a dawn raid, pursuant to the Competition Act 1998,[3] violates Art 8? Would he uphold the lawfulness of such action as being 'necessary in a democratic society ... for the prevention of disorder or crime'? Only, presumably, where the action was not disproportionate, as it was found to be in *Niemietz*, where the Strasbourg judges concluded that the German authorities had quite simply gone over the top. The suspected offence in that case had been a minor one and the warrant unjustifiably wide. Legal professional privilege had been breached and there was a risk that news of the search would have damaged the lawyer's business. In future litigation, it may conceivably be possible to reconcile *Hoechst* and *Niemietz*. *Niemietz* did not suggest that all raids on business premises were a violation of the European Convention. On the contrary, the Strasbourg judges said, as already noted, that the entitlement to interfere 'might well be more far-reaching where professional or business activities or premises were involved than would otherwise be the case' and, more likely than not, searches of commercial premises will be legitimate provided they are not disproportionate and are 'in accordance with the law'. Thus, the action of French customs officials in searching the applicant's home in *Funke* was held to be in breach of Art 8 because the rules regulating the behaviour of such officials were too 'lax and full of loopholes'. Beyond that, in many instances there will need to have been some form of independent judicial input into the process of carrying out a search (most obviously by the prior involvement of a magistrate in authorising a warrant).

7.28   Perhaps surprisingly, the *Anton Piller* or search order, which has been a high-profile feature of UK litigation for a generation, has withstood challenge at

---

1   *Hoechst AC v Commission* [1989] 3 ECR 2859. Nor was the decision in *Hoechst* unique. In the
      Funke case (see **6.138** et seq), the Strasbourg Court had held that Art 6 encompassed the right
      to remain silent and not to incriminate oneself, but in *Orkem* (see **6.130** et seq), the
      Luxembourg Court concluded that Art 6 did not, as regards the provisions of competition
      law, include a right against self-incrimination.
2   AG Toth *The European Union and Human Rights: The Way Forward* [1997] CMLR 491 at 499.
3   See **6.282** et seq.

Strasbourg. In the case of *Chappell*,[1] the European Court considered that, although features of the execution of such an order at a video club (where certain cassettes had been recorded in breach of copyright) were 'more oppressive' than they should have been, the order was made subject to safeguards ostensibly preventing arbitrary interference and abuse and the jurisdiction to make the order derived from a substantial body of precedent. However, the fact that the applicant's business premises and home were in the same building may have influenced the judges. *Chappell* will, however, now require to be considered afresh in the context of local courts' powers to order search and seizure under Part 25 of the CPR 1998. Indications are that judges here are already conscious of the need themselves to act proportionately in this context.[2]

HOSPITALS AS HOMES

7.29 *Niemietz*[3] showed that an office could be a 'home' for Art 8 purposes. A hospital can also be a home. In a case heard in 1999 (prior, therefore, to the wholesale coming into force of the Act) that has obvious commercial ramifications, not just for health trusts but also for private nursing home operators who provide residential care for patients under health authority contracts, the Court of Appeal found North-East Devon Health Authority to be in breach of its Art 8 obligations when it sought to close a cottage hospital in which the claimant lived.[4] The implications of the case will not have been lost on those campaigning against hospital closures and waiting lists[5] and it could be that Art 8 will become, with Article 2,[6] a popular basis for submissions in resource allocation litigation attacking the health service.

THE ACT'S IMPLICATIONS FOR SURVEILLANCE

7.30 In the German case of *Klass*,[7] it was accepted that secret surveillance by telephone tap was an undoubted interference under Art 8(1). The European Court, however, was satisfied that the interference was justified under Art 8(2) in circumstances where the relevant German legislation contained sufficient safeguards regarding the right to an independent review and where there was 'effective and continuous control' of the whole process. The French law on telephone tapping was, however, found to be insufficiently precise in the case of

---

1   *Chappell v United Kingdom* (1990) 12 EHRR 1. (No reference to *Chappell*, decided 6 months earlier, was made by the Court in *Hoechst* (see **7.26** et seq)).
2   See, for example, *Adams Phones v Goldschmidt* (1999) TLR, 17 August.
3   See **7.20** et seq.
4   *R v NE Devon Health Authority, ex parte Coughlan* (1999) Lloyd's Rep Med 306.
5   See *Passannante v Italy* (1998) 26 EHRR CD 153, in which the European Commission held that an excessive delay in providing medical treatment which deleteriously impacted upon the patient's health could engage Art 8.
6   See Appendix 2.
7   *Klass and Others v Federal Republic of Germany* (1978) 2 EHRR 214. In two recent cases, *Kopp v Switzerland* (1999) 27 EHRR 91 and *Valenzuela Contreras v Spain* (1999) 28 EHRR 483, the European Court found that the applicable legal regimes as regards interception in (respectively) Switzerland and Spain were not sufficiently foreseeable to be in accordance with the law and therefore gave rise to Art 8 violations.

Huvig.[1] So too the relevant Swiss law in the recent case of *Amman*,[2] where the European Court concluded that it was not just the tapping of the call but the keeping of a record confirming the fact that the applicant was a businessman and had made a telephone call to the then Soviet Embassy in Berne which engaged Art 8.

7.31   There were, for example, no limitations found in that case upon the duration of the tapping nor were the categories of those potentially susceptible to telephone tapping defined anywhere.

7.32   In the case of *Malone*,[3] telephone 'metering' (short of actual interception) by the British authorities was also found to be a violation of Art 8 because there was no single and comprehensive set of regulations governing the activity. The existence of a melange of common law and statutory prohibitions did not make the interference one that was in accordance with the law as required by the European Convention. Sir Robert Megarry, before whom the case had come in England,[4] had in fact looked at the Treaty and concluded that the then existing law in the UK could not be reconciled with the *Klass* case, but the unincorporated status of the European Convention prevented his making a declaration regarding the infringement of Mr Malone's privacy. The case therefore proceeded to Strasbourg, where the judges unanimously found that the UK had failed to show that the then applicable law in this country was laid out 'with reasonable precision in accessible legal rules that sufficiently indicated the scope and manner of exercise of the discretion conferred upon the relevant authorities'.

7.33   *Malone* is an important decision. Not only was it one of the first determinations at Strasbourg which led directly to the introduction of national legislation designed to cure a violation identified by the European Court,[5] but in it the British Government conceded that there was no difference in meaning between the words 'in accordance with the law' in Art 8(2) and 'prescribed by law' in Arts 9(2) and 10(2) of the European Convention. Indeed, in the case of all three provisions, the French text uses the identical term, *prévue par la loi.*

7.34   Company directors in the UK may dispute that the Strasbourg jurisprudence on surveillance is of relevance to them. Technological change suggests that that sentiment is no longer realistic. It has, for example, been reported that BP Amoco installed secret microphones at certain of its petrol stations to record customers' conversations, apparently to assist police in robbery investigations but without any warning being given to customers.[6] Does this engage the Convention? Even if such activity is unusual, the monitoring of staff telephones most certainly is not and a significant pronouncement of the Strasbourg judges bearing directly upon that practice is now considered in some detail.

---

1   *Huvig v France* (1990) 12 EHRR 528. See also the similar French case of *Kruslin v France* (1990) 12 EHRR 547.
2   *Amman v Switzerland*, Appl 27798/95, 16 February 2000. *Amman* raises obvious considerations regarding data protection, a subject dealt with at **7.51** et seq.
3   *Malone v United Kingdom* (1984) 7 EHRR 14.
4   *Malone v Metropolitan Police Commissioner* [1979] Ch 344.
5   The Interception of Communications Act 1985, which was considered to provide adequate Art 8 safeguards in the case of *Christie v United Kingdom* Appl 21482/93, (1993) 78A DR 119.
6   *The Herald*, 11 February 1999.

7.35   Alison Halford was a senior Merseyside police officer who filed a European Convention complaint,[1] alleging that her home and office telephones had been tapped as part of a campaign to discredit her. The British Government conceded that her *office* calls had been monitored, but argued that her employers were entitled to do this. The European Commission and Court, in separate determinations, comprehensively rejected this contention in the absence of any UK law justifying the interception of internal calls. Miss Halford had a reasonable expectation of privacy when making calls on her office line, not least where she had not been warned of the likelihood of surveillance. The interception was not prescribed by domestic law because the Interception of Communications Act 1985, introduced in the wake of the *Malone*[2] decision, did not cover the tapping or monitoring of *internal* telephone calls. As a consequence, Miss Halford's rights under Art 8 (and, indeed, under Art 13) had been violated.[3]

7.36   Miss Halford worked for a 'pure' public authority (the police) and it might be said that her victory only has implications for the UK public sector. There were additional case-specific matters which also suggest caution in its application, in particular the fact that the relevant telephone line in her office was a dedicated one installed for her personal use. What is more, she had been assured that she could use it in pursuing a sexual discrimination claim that she had brought. If she had been warned that her calls were liable to be monitored, it is not clear that her case would have succeeded.

7.37   The Strasbourg institutions authorities have clearly become worried about the activities of governmental agencies in this area. The *Lambert* case[4] came after the *Halford* decision and, in a powerful concurring opinion, Judge Pettiti there warned that:

> '... intercepting telephone conversations is one of the most serious temptations for State authorities and one of the most harmful for democracies ... In several Member States the supervision systems set up to control the monitors have proved inadequate and defective. Will it be necessary in the future, in order to protect privacy, to require people to get into "bubbles" in imitation of the practices of some embassies, in order to preclude any indiscretions? That would be to give in to Big Brother.'

7.38   In contemplating this neo-Orwellian nightmare, Judge Pettiti did not appear to have in mind the need for *private* sector employers also to look at the lawfulness of their procedures for staff monitoring. In the wake of *Halford*, however, the British Government appears to have recognised that the status quo cannot continue and that the current domestic mixture of inchoate, inadequate or non-existent guidelines[5] for the protection of staff privacy requires to be considered afresh and not just in the public sector context.

---

1   *Halford v United Kingdom* (1997) 24 EHRR 523.
2   See **7.32** et seq.
3   The European Court found that there was insufficient evidence to show that Miss Halford's line at home had been intercepted. The Home Secretary has since said that Miss Halford's treatment at the hands of the local police authority was 'outrageous' (*The Press Association*, 16 February 2000).
4   *Lambert v France* [1998] HRCD 806.
5   In 1972, the Younger Committee (see fn 4 on p 215) felt able to say (at para 95) that all that was needed was 'good relations between employer and employee'.

7.39   Evidence of this growing recognition that employees at work are to be protected by a form of telephonic *cordon sanitaire* came in 1999 in the form of a Home Office Consultation Paper.[1] It conceded at the outset that 'by its nature, interception of communications is a highly intensive activity, affecting the privacy of the individual'. This statement appears to recognise that the need to engage in surveillance for law enforcement purposes bears directly upon Art 8's guarantee. In its Consultation Paper the Government also acknowledged that Art 13 of the European Convention required the citizen to have available to him an effective remedy to challenge any interference with his Art 8 rights. This is, of course, the same Art 13 which the Government chose to exclude from the Act (whilst acknowledging that national courts may have regard for it).[2] The interaction of Arts 8 and 13 will likely be the focus of litigation from now on as creative British advocates seek to extend existing common-law causes of action to flesh out a domestic law of privacy (pursuant to Art 8), thereby securing the Art 13 remedy which the European Convention says is the citizen's due.

7.40   The Home Office additionally accepted in its Consultation Paper that legislation would be necessary to give effect to the Strasbourg judges' decision in *Halford*, specifically to outlaw interception on *non-public* networks. Such a statement is not inconsistent with the notion that the Act has vertical effect only.[3] With one eye upon the business community, however (and no doubt born of an acknowledgement that the Act will have some (albeit conceivably indirect) horizontal effect), the Consultation Paper added:

> '... there are perfectly respectable reasons for allowing employers to record telephone conversations in the work place; for example in order to provide evidence of commercial transactions or to counter fraud. But the practice needs to be regulated by law, in a way which ensures that the rights of employees are respected in circumstances where they have a reasonable expectation of privacy.'

7.41   Against this background, the Government proposed in the document the creation of a single interception regime covering all telecommunication networks (*including exclusively private ones*) and all forms of communications, including private courier delivery, e-mail and fax. It stated that it would be legitimate for commerce and industry to interfere with communications, but only where reasonable steps had been taken to bring to the attention of employees the kind of interference that might take place. The entire edifice would be underpinned by a code of practice.[4]

7.42   The Consultation Paper was followed by Guidance from OFTEL in August 1999 directed specifically at business[5] and which, interestingly enough, proceeded on the assumption that the reach of the European Convention would extend in this area to companies which were not public authorities. The Strasbourg implications were again made explicit. The Guidance reminded companies that, if they did not ensure that employees were able to make personal

---

1   *Interception of Communications in the United Kingdom* (Consultation paper) June 1999 (Cm 4368) at p 1.
2   See **3.10** et seq.
3   See **3.74** et seq.
4   There have been similar developments elsewhere. In April 2000, the Federal Government in Australia announced plans to extend privacy legislation to the private sector in its Privacy Amendment (Private Sector) Bill 2000: see http://www.privacy.gov.au/news.
5   See www.oftel.gov.uk.

calls that would not be recorded, Art 8 could become relevant. Although the press release that accompanied the Guidance did not say so explicitly, the inference was that this was a guarantee to be extended to all employees and not just those working for public authorities. If calls were permissibly to be recorded, staff needed to be made aware of that possibility, as one lesson to be derived from *Halford* (noted by the Guidance) was that there was a *reasonable expectation* of privacy for personal calls made at work.

7.43 In fact, the burden upon employers may not be as onerous as may at first appear, as OFTEL has suggested that the installation of payphones (which would not be monitored) may be one way of meeting employers' responsibilities. Beyond that, a clear explanation of a company's monitoring policies may be construed as *implied* consent to a *de facto* interference with privacy.

7.44 An earlier Home Office Circular,[1] addressed to Government departments and chief police officers, contained a suggested form of warning notice to employees which could usefully have an extended application throughout many parts of the private sector:

> 'You work with an organisation which deals with sensitive matters. Your job requires you to maintain high professional and ethical standards. In order to ensure that these sensitivities and high standards are maintained by all employees, telephone conversations may be recorded or monitored. Recorded material may be used in accordance with company guidelines.'

7.45 Privacy proponents have suggested that Whitehall is being less than straightforward in this area, in circumstances where (in particular) London and Washington have together agitated against the increasing use of encryption techniques (which are, after all, intended to safeguard privacy) which might make it more difficult for intelligence agents to eavesdrop on international telephone calls and e-mail messages.[2]

7.46 This inconsistency was highlighted in responses to the then draft Electronic Communications Bill (which has since been enacted).[3] Leading Counsel reportedly advised JUSTICE and the Foundation for Information Policy Research[4] that the Bill might conceivably raise concerns, not only under Art 8 but also Art 6, to the extent that the police were at one point to be allowed to access encrypted data (an obvious Art 8 interference) and to require users, on pain of imprisonment, to supply electronic encryption keys. This requirement might not only have infringed the presumption of innocence, but also the privilege against self-incrimination vigorously upheld by the Strasbourg Court in the *Saunders* case.[5]

---

1   HOC 15/1999, dated 23 March 1999.
2   See generally in this area *Under Surveillance: Covert Policing and Human Rights Standards* (JUSTICE Report, 1998); and S Fay 'Tough on Crime, Tough on Civil Liberties: Some Negative Aspects of Britain's Wholesale Adoption of CCTV Surveillance During the 1990s' (1998) 12 *International Review of Law Computers and Technology* at p 315.
3   (Cm 4417) published by the Department of Trade and Industry in July 1999 and intended to make the UK 'the best place in the world to do electronic business'. The Government gave a s 19 compatibility statement regarding the draft Bill. The Electronic Communications Act 2000 received Royal Assent on 25 May 2000.
4   See www.fipr.org/ecomm99/ecommand.htm.
5   See **6.132** et seq.

7.47   The Electronic Communications Act 2000 is directed at the work of law enforcement agencies, but it also engages issues involving personal autonomy generally and it has been introduced in the face of complaints by Internet service providers[1] about police surveillance of the Web (and private e-mail systems) without obtaining Home Office approval.[2] The Government appeared to heed the objections of campaigners to a degree when provisions permitting law enforcement agencies to access electronic communications were removed from the text of the then Electronic Communications Bill, only for certain of them to reappear in the separate Regulation of Investigatory Powers Act 2000, which received Royal Assent on 28 July 2000,[3] and which for the first time confers a statutory power to intercept and unscramble mobile telephones, pagers, e-mail and switchboards.

7.48   It is in one sense surprising that the Government should have got into difficulties in this area, for it has been anxious to stress that a prime concern from the outset has been to ensure that the powers envisaged are, in Strasbourg terms, properly prescribed by law.[4] For all that, it is profoundly questionable as to whether the Regulation of Investigatory Powers Act 2000 is European Convention-proof. The UK is conceivably the only country in the world to threaten to imprison those who fail to hand over electronic encryption keys, a move which may drive e-commerce offshore.[5] Safeguards in the Regulation of Investigatory Powers Act 2000 affecting the surveillance regime so far apply only to residential property, thereby appearing to reduce the scope of the European Court's decision in *Niemietz*.[6] Nor is it apparent, as JUSTICE has noted, that the covert surveillance for tax-gathering purposes which is sanctioned in the Act is in conformity with Art 8(2).[7]

7.49   The prediction that Art 8 concerns will lead to a change in the regime affecting the monitoring of staff calls throughout British industry does of course presuppose that the European Convention will be given a form of horizontal effect. If some element of horizontality does emerge (as appears likely) the implications for, for example, financial institutions in the City of London will be considerable. Banks (save perhaps for the Bank of England) are almost certainly not public authorities, hybrid or otherwise, in terms of the Act.[8] They routinely monitor calls, having done so for many years (and their employees generally know

1   The Internet is, unsurprisingly, outside the Interception of Communications Act 1985.
2   *The Sunday Times*, 7 February 1999.
3   *The Financial Times*, 11 February 2000.
4   The Home Secretary said: 'The Human Rights Act and rapid change in technology are the twin drivers of the new Bill ... What is new is that for the first time the use of these techniques will be properly regulated by law, and externally supervised' (Home Office Press Release, 11 February 2000).
5   To the Irish Republic, for example, where draft legislation states that law enforcement agencies will not have the right to compel the handing-over of encryption keys. See *The Irish Times*, 24 March 2000 and 7 April 2000.
6   See **7.20** et seq.
7   The Bill gives the authorities the right to monitor information on Internet traffic 'for the purpose of assessing or collecting any tax ... or charge payable to a government department'. See the article by M Colvin in *The Times*, 29 February 2000.
8   No doubt at some point it will be suggested that clearing banks discharge certain public functions bringing them within s 6 of the Act, but (by analogy with the Safeway analogy rejected by the Government during the debates on the Human Rights Bill (see **3.106** et seq)), it is surely unlikely that a judge would accede to this.

this), often at the direction of financial regulators. Assuming some horizontal application of the Act, this should continue to be permissible, provided, of course, that the interference fits within a coherent legal framework[1] and has been brought to the attention of staff in the form of notices which are not exorbitant in reach. Otherwise regulated institutions may find that Art 8 and the Strasbourg case-law deriving from it will become popular citations in claims for wrongful or unlawful dismissal brought by former members of staff terminated on account of matters caught on camera or on tape. One way or the other, workplace rights of privacy (conceivably encompassing calligraphy and isometric tests, security checks,[2] interception of mail, the provision of emergency contact details and compulsory medical examinations)[3] have been placed centre-stage by the Act. The insurance industry, which carries out a variety of inquiries when assessing risk, is only one industry likely to be directly affected by all of this.

7.50   The fact is that there continues in the UK to be no over-arching regulatory regime in the area of surveillance generally and nothing which satisfactorily takes account of rapid technological change. There is the *Halford* gap, deriving from the fact that the Interception of Communications Act 1985 does not extend to internal telephone systems.[4] There is also the fact that the statute does not appear to apply to mobile telephones,[5] to certain kinds of international telephone call, to the Internet or to infra-red cameras. Hence the need for Government action, but whether the new regime in the UK will preclude claims brought under the Act must be doubted.

DATA PROTECTION

7.51   Sir Brian Neill, the distinguished judge (now retired), has made the point that those in authority have sought to collect information since the time of Herod's census and before.[6] Of course, that does not make it permissible, not least when the processing and storage of information is circumscribed by data protection laws.

7.52   The interaction between the EC law requirement of data protection and the European Convention's requirement of privacy is not straightforward. On their face, they should not be in competition. Equally, they are not co-terminous. The 1978 Lindop Report on data protection stated that:

'... the function of a data protection law should be different from that of a law on privacy: rather than establishing a right, it should provide a framework for finding a

---

1   And complies, for example, with the data protection legislation (see **7.51** et seq).
2   The European Commission suggested in *Hilton v United Kingdom* Appl 12015/86 that security checks were not, without more, in violation of Art 8.
3   See *Chase née Julien v France* Appl 14461/88 holding that the maintenance of medical records engages Art 8.
4   Article 5 of the EU Telecommunications Data Protection Directive (No 97/66) closes the gap to a degree by requiring that interception or monitoring of communications on networks, whether public or private, can take place only when legally authorised.
5   See *R v Effik* [1995] 1 AC 309.
6   See his article *Privacy: A Challenge for the Next Century* in *Protecting Privacy* edited by BS Markesinis (Clarendon Press, Oxford, 1999), p 13.

balance between the interests of the individual, the data user and the community at large.'[1]

7.53   The Data Protection Act 1998 (which came into force on 1 March 2000) was introduced to implement the EU Data Protection Directive.[2] British businesses were already tolerably familiar with the previous regime (set out in the Data Protection Act 1984), which was never envisaged as a civil liberties measure but rather as a mechanism for facilitating Community trade in information, but the human rights overlay given by the Act to the new data protection statute undoubtedly adds an element of complication. The Deputy Data Protection Registrar,[3] who has, with his colleagues, the job of enforcing the legislation, plainly hopes that the Data Protection Act 1998 creates (or at least confirms) a privacy right, deriving in his view from Brussels and not from Strasbourg. He has said:

> 'If the 1998 [Data Protection] Act satisfies the Directive, then it serves to protect the right of individuals to privacy, at least in respect to [sic] the processing of personal data. If the 1998 [Data Protection] Act fails to protect personal privacy in accordance with the Directive, then the United Kingdom is in breach of its community obligations.'[4]

7.54   The different approaches in Europe and the USA (where there is no comprehensive data protection law) may possibly cause Art 8 to be engaged in the future.[5] Would a US company with operations in the UK be able to raise a European Convention point (under Art 1 of the First Protocol if not Art 8) if prevented from repatriating personnel records across the Atlantic? If it did so in a manner *permitted* by the Data Protection Act 1998, has there still been an interference the terms of Art 8?

THE IMPORTANCE OF POSITIVE OBLIGATIONS

7.55   As already noted,[6] when considering the likely future reach of Art 8, it must be borne in mind that the UK's relationship to the domesticated European Convention cannot merely be a passive one. The European Convention places positive obligations upon Member States too. In the words of the Strasbourg judges:

> 'although the object of Article 8 is essentially that of protecting the individual against arbitrary interference by the public authorities, it does not merely compel the State to abstain from such interference: there may, in addition to this primarily negative undertaking, be positive obligations inherent in an effective respect for private or family life. These obligations may involve the adoption of measures designed to secure respect for private life even in the sphere of the relations between individuals

---

1   Quoted in J Angel 'New Rights to Privacy' *Communications Law*, vol 3, No 5 (1998), p 169.
2   Specifically Directive 95/45/EC on the protection of individuals with regard to the processing of personal data and the free movement of such data.
3   Who became the Deputy Data Protection Commissioner on 1 March 2000.
4   FGB Aldhouse in 'Data Protection, Privacy and the Media' *Communications Law*, vol 4, no 1 (1999) p 8 at 11. In fact, the Data Protection Act 1998 nowhere mentions privacy.
5   A European Commission representative in Brussels has been quoted as saying 'Americans don't mind junk mail, and we do' *The Financial Times*, 9 June 1999.
6   See **5.17** et seq.

themselves. There are different ways of ensuring respect for private life and the nature of the State's obligation will depend upon the particular aspect of private life that is in issue. It follows that the choice of means calculated to secure compliance with this positive obligation in principle falls within the Contracting States' margin of appreciation.'[1]

7.56 This is clear, if unspecific, and it remains difficult to assess what impact Art 8's domestication will have on British corporate life. Insurers have apparently suggested that curbs on the ability to spy on fraudsters will drive up premiums.[2] This may be so, but costs in that industry may be more significantly altered over time by changes to the common-law tort of negligence in the wake of the *Osman* decision.[3] It has meanwhile been suggested that private detectives will be limited in what they can do.[4] Their interferences in private lives will be self-evident, but any suggestion that they will be hampered will depend to a large degree upon the approach of local judges to horizontality in this area. However loose-textured the principles applied at Strasbourg and however regrettable it is that the ambit of private lives (and the respect they are due) has not been more helpfully delineated by the Strasbourg judges, it is apparent that this is one part of the European Convention where the thinking of the Strasbourg institutions has evolved over time in keeping with changes in continental society at large, specifically as regards the rights of homosexuals, prisoners and transsexuals. There is no reason, therefore, why British judges should not be able to shape it as appropriate to accommodate contemporary conditions.

7.57 It is reported that a nursery in Croydon allows mothers to watch their children at play over the Internet.[5] A London hospital places CCTV cameras in women's toilets, apparently for security reasons. British call centres reputedly record conversations in the hope of confirming that their staff are 'cheerful' enough. Futurists predict that one day secretaries will monitor the movements of managers by use of implanted computer chips. Serious or not, these are but some of the activities thrown up by modern life which may engage Art 8 of the Convention. Indications are, however, that it will be the first Art 8 case to challenge the behaviour of tabloid reporters and not claims about (for example) staff surveillance, which will excite most attention in the period to come. This is addressed later,[6] after an explanation is first given in Chapter 8 of the implications of the Act for the media.

---

1   See *X and Y v The Netherlands* (1985) 8 EHRR 235, where the Dutch State was found to have failed to fulfil its positive obligations when a mentally disabled child was raped in a residential home and when civil law remedies in damages or for an injunction against a repetition of the offence were judged to be inadequate. It has been suggested in this context that Art 8 might be invoked to give victims the right to challenge decisions not to prosecute suspected child abusers: see A Gillespie 'Child Abuse Prosecutions and the Human Rights Act 1998' (2000) NLJ 620.
2   See *The Times*, 4 January 2000.
3   See **6.54** et seq.
4   There is a line of French cases constraining the right of creditors to trace trade debtors. This has been held not to be a breach of Art 8, but only where the inquiry is to protect a legal right or to enforce a judgment. See, for example, *SA Locumiviers v Hospices Civils de Lyon*, Cass Civ 1, 19 March 1991, D 1991 568–571 referred to by E Steiner in her chapter on France in *European Civil Liberties and the European Convention on Human Rights A Comparative Study* edited by CA Gearty (Martinus Nijhoff, 1997), p 286.
5   *The Observer*, 29 August 1999.
6   See **8.170** et seq.

Chapter 8

THE MEDIA AFTER THE ACT

8.1   As has been seen,[1] the campaign for European Convention incorporation had such a long and fitful history that the Blair administration could be forgiven some measure of satisfaction in observing that the Parliamentary passage of the Human Rights Bill was generally a tranquil affair. It is widely acknowledged that the debates at Westminster were of a high quality and that the Government's handling of the legislation was largely trouble-free. This is with one exception.

8.2   No constituency had followed the introduction of the Human Rights Bill with greater assiduity than press and broadcasting interests. Setting aside any suggestion that the newspaper industry (in particular) was motivated solely by an altruistic concern for the quality of our democracy, it was undeniably entitled on the ground of self-interest to have strong views about the shaping of the new law, for arguably no other part of the commercial sector will encounter, in such acute form, the risk/opportunity dynamic to which the Act gives rise. To use a metaphor from libel law, the statute contains both bane and antidote for the press.

8.3   The rewards and dangers which the legislation presents for this industry derive primarily from the tension between Art 8 (the right to respect for private and family life)[2] and Art 10 (the right to freedom of expression)[3] and it will be the job of in-house lawyers, journalists and judges alike to tease out a reconciliation of those provisions in the years following the wholesale introduction of the Act. As Lord Bingham once put it, where does free expression end and a right to privacy begin?[4]

FREEDOM OF EXPRESSION

8.4   Article 10 provides:

> '*Freedom of expression*
>
> 1.   Everyone has the right to freedom of expression. This right shall include freedom to hold opinions and to receive and impart information and ideas without interference by public authority and regardless of frontiers. This Article shall not prevent States from requiring the licensing of broadcasting, television or cinema enterprises.
> 2.   The exercise of these freedoms, since it carries with it duties and responsibilities, may be subject to such formalities, conditions, restrictions or penalties as are prescribed by law and are necessary in a democratic society, in the interests of national security, territorial integrity or public safety, for the prevention of disorder or crime, for the protection of health or morals, for the protection of

---

1   See **1.29** et seq.
2   For a general description of Art 8, see Chapter 7. See also **8.170** et seq for its possible operation in the media context.
3   There is also a tension (most notably as regards the operation of the law of contempt) between Art 6 (the right to a fair trial) and Art 10. For Art 6 generally, see Chapter 6.
4   Talking to Joshua Rozenberg on 4 October 1996, quoted in *Trial of Strength* (see fn 7 on p 13) p 119.

the reputation or rights of others, for preventing the disclosure of information received in confidence, or for maintaining the authority and impartiality of the judiciary.'[1]

8.5   This articulation of a freedom of expression right is far from being unique. It was not even the first such multi-national attempt, as Art 19 of the UNDR had earlier provided that: 'Everyone has the right to freedom of opinion and expression', a guarantee which 'includes freedom to hold opinions without interference and to seek, receive and impart information and ideas through any media and regardless of frontiers'. It is noteworthy that the UNDR includes a positive right to *seek* information and that it includes none of the provisos to be found in the second part of Art 10 of the European Convention, which conspicuously places considerable limits upon the operation of the freedom of expression right.

8.6   In this respect too then, the European Convention is shown to be less than revolutionary, and framing the contemporary debate about the Act's implications for the media in terms solely of a competition between Arts 8 and 10 is simplistic. Article 10, like other provisions of the European Convention, contains *within itself* elements that pull in different directions, enshrining a right whilst at the same time identifying permissible limitations upon the exercise of that right.

8.7   Freedom of expression has been described as: 'probably the most universally recognised human right',[2] with guarantees to be found in, for example, the ICCPR,[3] the Hong Kong Bill of Rights,[4] the American Convention of Human Rights,[5] the African Charter of Human Rights,[6] the New Zealand Bill of Rights Act 1990,[7] the Canadian Charter of Rights and Freedoms[8] and the South African Constitution.[9]

8.8   Pre-dating most of these by nearly two centuries is the First Amendment to the US Constitution, which extends the ambit of protection for publishers in America by providing that: 'Congress shall make no law . . . abridging the freedom of speech, *or of the Press* . . .' (emphasis added).[10] Are these two (ie freedom of speech and of the press) co-terminous, as the media would have us believe? The First   Amendment   is   certainly   the   only   provision   of   the   US

---

1   The provisions of Art 9 of the European Convention are beyond the scope of this book. However, it should be noted that its guarantee of freedom of thought, conscience and religion is a form of freedom of expression standard, albeit that its orientation is towards religious and philosophical views, whereas Art 10 tends more towards the civil and political. In the past, petitions have been filed at Strasbourg invoking both Articles. When in doubt, however, the Strasbourg institutions have tended to confer upon Art 10 more of a catch-all status.

2   In Janis, Kay and Bradley *European Human Rights Law* (Clarendon Press, Oxford, 1995), p 15, it is noted a 1978 survey of 142 States showed that 124 guaranteed freedom of expression while only 66 prohibited torture or cruel, inhuman or degrading treatment.

3   At Art 19. This was, for example, referred to by the European Court in the case of *Jersild v Denmark* (1994) 19 EHRR 1.

4   At Art 16.

5   At Art 13.

6   At Art 9.

7   At s 13.

8   At s 2.

9   At s 16.

10   A number of European Court cases on Art 10 contain references to First Amendment authorities.

Constitution which aims to safeguard a particular industry. This now appears remarkable in circumstances where there is a widely held view that the concentration of press ownership in a small number of hands is inconsistent with the achievement and maintenance of a plural democracy, the media having 'the colossal power not only of communication but of selection, comment and presentation.'[1] Indeed, for some time the danger has been recognised in UK law to the extent that s 59(3) of the Fair Trading Act 1973 requires the Monopolies and Mergers Commission (now the Competition Commission), when faced with newspaper acquisitions, to consider 'the need for accurate presentation of news and free expression of opinion'. Why, then, should the media have been deemed worthy of such protection by America's Founding Fathers and why should that emphasis have been carried over into all the great human rights ordinances of this century? On what basis did Hoffman LJ (as he then was) say in 1994 that 'there is no question of balancing freedom of speech against other interests. It is a trump card which always wins'?[2]

8.9 The point is of real significance because it can be predicted that an attempt will be made in early course to test the limits of Art 8 in a British context, specifically to see if the right to respect for private lives guaranteed in that Art can be used, as it were, as a bridge to what some envisage as a promised land, whose citizens are free from the perceived depredations of the media. This vision of the future is unlikely to come to pass because, as will be seen, Art 10 only gives way to Art 8 when the democratic imperative demands it. Nevertheless, there will be a heavy burden on those judges who hear the first media-related cases engaging the domesticated European Convention to determine the occasions when privacy should yield to free expression and vice-versa.

8.10 It has been suggested that: 'Freedom of expression has provoked some of the most concentrated and emphatic case-law from the Convention organs'. This is said to be because it involves 'the cleaner cases (fewer terrorists or other undesirables) and raises neat issues of principle for practitioner, politician, academic and civil right activists alike'.[3] Compared to the opacity that characterises other areas of Strasbourg jurisprudence, this may be so, but it would be wrong, nevertheless, to assume that the European Court has always spoken with one voice on this score. In the past, it has generally approached Art 10 issues more restrictively than the European Commission, albeit with some judges consistently putting a higher value than others on the exercise of freedom of expression across a broad front. Arguably, it is less a question of views changing over time – to be expected when, after all, the European Convention is to be looked upon as a living instrument[4] – than of enduringly different emphases on the part of different members of the bench. The fact is that, in a number of the key cases which it is appropriate now to consider, the Strasbourg institutions have each been split down the middle, while in others the European Court has reached a different conclusion from the European Commission. As one commentator put it, it may be

---

1   Sir Stephen Sedley in his chapter 'The First Amendment: a Case for Import Controls?' in I
     Loveland (ed) *Importing the First Amendment* (Hart Publishing, 1998), p 25.
2   In *R v Central Independent Television plc* [1994] Fam 192 at 203.
3   K Reid (see fn 7 on p 28), p 232.
4   See **5.12** et seq.

better therefore to refer to *trends* in this area, rather than 'unchangeable, unquestioned, positions set in stone'.[1]

8.11   In 1993, the Council of Europe, meeting in Vienna, stated that 'guaranteed freedom of expression and *notably* of the media ... must remain, in our view, decisive criteria for assessing any application for membership' (emphasis added). Where then does free expression rank? Is it 'the primary right', without which no effective rule of law is possible, as Lord Steyn has suggested?[2] Does it sit at the highest point of an apex of civil and political guarantees, higher even than the right to life? Whether or not it does, will any of this matter to those who are destitute, as another senior judge has suggested?[3]

ITS PLACE IN A DEMOCRATIC CONTEXT

8.12   The Strasbourg institutions have at least been clear that freedom of expression is no mere procedural right.[4] On the contrary, it:

> '... constitutes one of the essential foundations of ... [a democratic] society, one of the basic conditions for its progress and for the development of every man. Subject to paragraph 2 of Art 10, it is applicable not only to "information" or "ideas" that are favourably received or regarded as inoffensive but also to those that offend, shock or disturb the State or any sector of the population. Such are the demands of that pluralism, tolerance and broadmindedness without which there is no democratic society.'[5]

8.13   This is key – it is not just that free expression is important in itself but the fact that there is a vital nexus between the ability to exercise this right and the health of a functioning democracy. While the Soviet Constitution (for example) upheld free expression, it could not sensibly be maintained that the USSR guaranteed democratic standards. Therefore, it is not merely a question of individual liberty; there is a societal dynamic too.

8.14   As the European Commission once stated, 'freedom of expression is based on the need of a democratic society to promote the individual self-fulfilment of members ... and the striking of a balance between stability and change. The aim is to have a pluralistic open and tolerant society'.[6] Put in this way,

---

1   C McCrudden 'The Impact on Freedom of Speech' in *The Impact of the Human Rights Bill for English Law* edited by BS Markesinis (Clarendon Press, Oxford, 1999), pp 88–89. Clements, Mole and Simmons (see fn 7 on p 28) suggest that 'the European court swims with the tide of liberal opinion but no more' (p 192).

2   In *R v Secretary of State for the Home Department, ex parte Simms and O'Brien* (1999) 3 All ER 400. See also the article by Sir Sydney Kentridge QC 'Freedom of Expression – Is it the Primary Right?' [1996] 45 ICLQ 253.

3   Sir Stephen Sedley (see fn 1 on p 23), pp 46 and 54. He has also posed the question: 'Why then is it free speech, of all the rights which are regularly threatened, which is always at the head of the queue for judicial protection?' See his article 'The First Amendment: A Case for Import Controls' in *Importing the First Amendment* edited by I Loveland (Hart Publishing, 1998), p 25.

4   'It is both an end in the sense that open communication is a condition of self-realisation and a means because it enables claims to be articulated and thereby permits other rights to be protected': JG Merrills *The development of international law by the European Court of Human Rights* 2nd edn (Manchester University Press, 1993), p 134.

5   *Handyside v UK* (1976) 1 EHRR 737 at para 49.

6   See *Lingens v Austria* (1986) 8 EHRR 407.

an entrenched right to express oneself is a right that also triggers a freedom to associate (Art 11),[1] a freedom generally to hold ideas (Art 9)[2] and a right to participate in elections (Art 3 of the First Protocol).[3] Although it is about 'expression' in a broad sense (so that, for example, the way in which a person dresses may engage Art 10),[4] it is perhaps not surprising that the Strasbourg institutions should over the years have accorded a higher priority to the protection of speech rights, particularly to speech in a political context.

POLITICAL SPEECH

8.15   In the *Lingens* case,[5] the European Court was (perhaps significantly) unanimous in finding that there had been a violation of Art 10. The editor of a magazine in Vienna was the subject of a private prosecution for criminal defamation. He was convicted and fined after publishing two stories critical of the then Austrian Chancellor, Bruno Kreisky, who was variously described as opportunistic, immoral and a Nazi sympathiser. In England, Herr Lingens would have had the makings of a good defence based on fair comment, arguing that his pieces were based upon facts which were true, were of public interest and about which he was entitled in good faith to express a view. In Austria, however, he had by evidence to establish that the underlying statements were true.

8.16   The Strasbourg judges found that value judgments were not susceptible of truth and that there had been a disproportionate interference with Herr Lingens' Art 10 rights which was not necessary in a democratic society. On the contrary, criticism of this sort was an important function of the media, for 'freedom of political debate [was] at the very core of the concept of a democratic society which prevails throughout the Convention'. The European Court went on:

> 'Freedom of the press ... affords the public one of the best means of discovering and forming an opinion of the ideas and attitudes of political leaders ... The limits of acceptable criticism are accordingly wider as regards a politician as such than as regards a private individual. Unlike the latter, the former inevitably and knowingly lays himself open to close scrutiny of his every word and deed by both journalists and the public at large, and he must subsequently display a greater degree of tolerance.'

8.17   The approach to political reporting adopted in *Lingens* has been followed in a number of later cases (again from Austria). In *Oberschlick*,[6] for example, the Strasbourg judges approached the matter broadly in line with English defamation principles, finding that the underlying facts were true and

---

1   And, in that regard, a freedom not to express oneself. See the case of *Young, James and Webster v United Kingdom* (1981) 4 EHRR 38, on the operation of the trade union closed shop. For the text of Art 11, see Appendix 2.
2   See Appendix 2.
3   See Appendix 2.
4   See *Stevens v United Kingdom* (1986) 46 DR 245.
5   See fn 6 on p 234.
6   *Oberschlick v Austria* (1995) 19 EHRR 389.

that out of them the journalist concerned had extrapolated a value judgment, the truth of which he could not reasonably be required to establish.[1]

8.18   In other words, not just the rich are different. As a matter of European Convention law, so too are politicians. In *Lingens*, the European Court in effect declared that those reluctant to submit to a degree of editorial rough and tumble should not embark on a career in public life. That is not to say, however, that politicians are entirely unprotected in Strasbourg terms, as para (2) of Art 10 enables the reputation of all individuals to be protected. In yet another Austrian case, that of *Worm v Austria*,[2] it was stated that the pivotal role of the free press in a functioning democracy is to be protected, and that this protection extends to politicians, even when they are not acting in their private capacity, albeit that the Strasbourg judges have indicated that, in that event, the requirements of such protection have to be weighed in relation to the interest in open discussion of political issues. Therefore, where matters of genuine public interest are concerned, journalists will be afforded some flexibility in their treatment of politicians, even where their writing is provocative, prone to exaggeration or downright insulting, provided it is grounded in fact.[3] It will be interesting in this context to see if the British media, supported by Strasbourg jurisprudence, are given the benefit of the doubt by libel juries when ostensibly exposing as hypocrites politicians who campaign for so-called family values whilst adhering to rather different standards in their private lives.

8.19   There may be gradations of speech protection within the political arena. For example, the case of *Castells v Spain*[4] suggests that the ability freely to criticise is greatest when Government Ministers are the subject of attack and not merely elected politicians. Señor Castells was an opposition member of the Senate (and a lawyer), who alleged in a magazine article that the Spanish Government had been complicit in illegal counter-terrorist action in the Basque region. The Government succeeded in removing his parliamentary immunity from suit and he was convicted of 'insult' without being permitted to plead truth. The European Court held that the action taken against him was not necessary in a democratic society.

---

1   The same approach was also adhered to in the case of *Schwabe v Austria* Appl 13704/88. Yet another Austrian case, that of *Worm v Austria* (1998) 25 EHRR 454, again re-emphasised the pivotal role of the free press in a functioning democracy. Note too that the absolute privilege attaching to statements in Parliament has been upheld at Strasbourg: see *O'Faolain v Ireland* [1996] EHRLR 326.

2   (1998) 25 EHRR 454.

3   *Oberschlick v Austria (No 2)* (1997) 25 EHRR 357. In that case, Oberschlick had described Jorg Haider as an idiot (*trottel*). His conviction for this was disproportionate (the European Court said) and a breach of Art 10, not least because it appeared as if Haider had set out to provoke a robust reaction by suggesting that all military combatants in the Second World War, on whatever side, had fought for peace and freedom. See, however, that *Janowski v Poland* (2000) 29 EHRR 705 below. In yet another Austrian-derived case, the European Court recently found no Art 10 violation where an injunction was awarded *against* a politician and in favour of newspaper publishers accused by the politician of 'Nazi-journalism'. The Strasbourg judges were apparently influenced by the particular stigma attaching to a smear evoking Nazi connections: *Wabl v Austria* Appl 24773/94, 21 March 2000.

4   (1992) 14 EHRR 445. The *Castells* case would be unlikely here, where the applicant would have been able to rely on justification or the argument that no claim lay in circumstances where the claimant was a governmental body. In terms of the importance the European Court attaches to the free expression rights of political parties and their members, see also *Incal v Turkey* (2000) 29 EHRR 449.

Of course, States could protect themselves against claims that were 'devoid of foundation or formulated in bad faith'. Beyond that, however, the 'limits of permissible criticism [were] wider with regard to the Government than in relation to a private citizen, or even a politician'. It was especially important that the speech rights of an elected representative were preserved because 'he represents his electorate, draws attention to their preoccupations and defends their interests. Accordingly, interferences with the freedom of expression of an opposition MP call for the closest scrutiny on the part of the [European] Court'.

8.20   Likewise, the freedom to comment is exponentially wider in the run-up to an election. Phyllis Bowman, the anti-abortion campaigner, therefore succeeded (by 14:6) in establishing that a feature of local electoral law,[1] which capped expenses (at £5) on the part of those who were not themselves standing for election, could be in breach of Art 10. Whilst it was legitimate for States to conduct polls on the basis that candidates were, so far as possible, to be placed upon an equal footing, the Strasbourg judges considered that:

> '... free elections and freedom of expression, *particularly freedom of political debate*, together form the bedrock of any democratic system. The two rights are inter-related and operate to reinforce each other: as the Court has observed in the past, freedom of expression is one of the "conditions" necessary to "ensure the free expression of the opinion of the people in the choice of the legislature". For this reason it is particularly important in the period preceding an election that opinions and information of all kinds are permitted to circulate freely.'[2] (Emphasis added.)

8.21   Of course, political speech, like any other form of speech, can be abused, most clearly where it is at odds with democratic values (hate speech being the obvious example), in which case restrictions may be permitted by Art 10(2) to prevent 'disorder'.[3] Save for that, however, the European Court has been consistent in giving political speech a position at the head of a hierarchy of freedom of expression rights, even though the European Convention itself makes no explicit reference to any such hierarchy.

8.22   A similar approach has been adopted elsewhere, with judges in a number of countries coming increasingly to confer a different (and higher) status upon political discourse and whose decisions are already being used to bolster the Art 10 submissions of advocates in British courts.

8.23   There have been significant developments, for example, not only in India,[4] but also in Australia, where the High Court looked at the issue in the case of *Theophanous v The Herald and Weekly Times Limited and Another*.[5] Theophanous was an MP and Chair of the Standing Committee of the House of Representatives on Migration Regulations who had been attacked in a letter to a newspaper on a number of grounds (including an alleged pro-Greek bias). He sued for libel. The court was not unanimous in its decision, but Mason CJ spoke for the majority in finding that it was:

---

1   Specifically, s 75 of the Representation of the People Act 1983.
2   *Bowman v United Kingdom* (1998) 26 EHRR 1.
3   See *T v Belgium* (1983) 34 DR 158 and *De Becker v Belgium* (1962) 1 EHRR 43.
4   See *Rajagopal v State of Tamil Nadu* (1994) 6 SCC 632.
5   [1994] 124 ALR 1. See also the case of *Stephens v West Australian Newspapers Ltd* heard jointly with *Theophanous and Lange v Australian Broadcasting Corporation* (1997) 189 CLR 520. The Australian Constitution does not in fact have any guarantee of freedom of expression.

'... incontrovertible that an implication of freedom of communication, the purpose of which is to ensure the efficacy of representative democracy, must extend to protect political discussion from exposure to onerous criminal and civil liability if the implication is to be effective in achieving this purpose.'

8.24   He was supported in strikingly pungent terms by Deane J, who might conceivably have had a British audience in mind when stating that the:

'... use of defamation proceedings in relation to political communication and discussion has expanded to the stage where there is a widespread public perception that such proceedings represent a valued source of tax-free profit for the holder of high public office who is defamed, and an effective way to "stop" political criticism, especially at election times.'

8.25   *Theophanous* is emblematic of a developing international corpus of law entrenching the idea that political comment and opinion should be, so far as possible, unrestrained. The philosophical underpinning for this may differ from country to country. In the USA the approach has traditionally derived from the belief that 'the ultimate good ... is better reached in free trade in ideas – that the best test of truth is the power of the thought to get itself accepted in the competition of the market'.[1] Furthermore, in the celebrated case of *New York Times v Sullivan*,[2] Brennan J had emphasised that 'debate on public issues should be uninhibited, robust and wide open' even where it included 'vehement, caustic and sometimes unpleasantly sharp attacks on government and public officials'. It is perhaps not surprising, therefore, that the *Lingens* line of authorities at Strasbourg should be described as 'pure Sullivan'[3] even though the impetus behind such cases may have owed more to communitarianism than competitive markets, ie the need to promote tolerance if the ravages of the past were to be avoided in the future.

8.26   British media companies know all this, as the local decisions (dealt with later)[4] bear witness, and developments in this discrete area of political comment, deriving from the European Convention, may be less marked than in others. So-called commercial speech, for example, may more obviously be affected by the Act.

COMMERCIAL SPEECH IN THE ADVERTISING CONTEXT

8.27   The European Convention jurisprudence fails to confer upon commercial speech the same measure of protection that it confers upon political speech. This is broadly the position also adopted in the USA.[5] At one level, this is conceptually objectionable – does not all 'political' speech become 'commercial' when printed or broadcast for profit? Whatever happened to the free marketplace

1   Oliver Wendell Holmes in *Abrams v United States* (1919) 250 US 616.
2   (1964) 376 US 254. The Supreme Court of Canada in *Hill v Church of Scientology of Toronto* (1956) 126 DLR 129 declined, however, to make the *Sullivan* principle part of local law.
3   See I Loveland 'The Defamation Act 1996 and Political Libels' [1996] PL 113 at 123.
4   See **8.111** et seq.
5   See *Central Hudson Gas and Electricity Corporation v Public Service Commission of New York* (1980) 447 US 557. As Geoffrey Marshall has said of the position in the USA, 'where commerce enters the communications field ... the suppression of falsity appears to become necessary and content censorship respectable' in 'Press Freedom and Free Speech Theory' [1992] PL 40 at 53.

of ideas? It is said against this that there is not the same nexus between the need for commercial speech in a functioning democracy that there is for political speech (whatever might be said about the triumph of consumerism over ideology in the new millennium).

8.28   The reduced status conferred by European Convention law on trade speech was first explained in a case involving the Church of Scientology, which involved the claim that a so-called E-meter could measure the removal of sin from those upon whom it was used.[1] The European Commission noted the existence of laws against misleading advertising in a number of Member States and confirmed that it found in those countries a lower level of protection for commercial speech. What was more, the burden on a government of establishing that a particular interference with freedom of expression was necessary in a democratic society was less strict in the case of commercial speech. In short, the European Commission considered that 'the level of protection *must* be less than that afforded to the expression of "political" ideas, in the broadest sense, with which the values underpinning the concept of freedom of expression in the Convention are broadly concerned' (emphasis added).

8.29   A number of the most important Strasbourg decisions in this area have involved the professions – medical,[2] legal[3] and veterinary.[4] In the *Barthold* case a vet in Hamburg had given an interview to a newspaper in which he criticised the lack of 24-hour veterinary care in the city. His local professional association objected to the story, arguing that it was tantamount to an advertisement for Barthold's practice (which did offer round-the-clock cover). Such behaviour, it was said, was in breach of his code of ethics. Herr Barthold was sued for 'unfair competition' and an injunction restraining the repetition of certain statements was granted against him. On his complaint to Strasbourg, both the European Commission and the European Court found that the German court's injunction was not necessary in a democratic society. The fact that Barthold's name and practice details had been published did not constitute advertising and the interview with him was an exercise in freedom of expression. Attempts to police an ethics code in this way indeed risked 'discouraging the members of the liberal professions from contributing to public debate on topics affecting the life of the community if even there [was] the slightest likelihood of their utterances being treated as entailing, to some degree, an advertising effect [sic]'. Any other decision was 'liable to hamper the press in the performance of its task of *purveyor of information and public watchdog*' (emphasis added).

8.30   It is doubtful whether a case on these facts would now be litigated in the UK, the professions here having to varying degrees largely abandoned their traditional prohibition on promotional activity and where, as a medium, advertising generally is regarded with much less suspicion than in parts of continental Europe. The case does, however, highlight the importance attached by the European Court to the role of the press as scrutineer and information-

---

1   *X and Church of Scientology v Sweden* (1983) 5 EHRR 465.
2   See, for example, *Colman v United Kingdom* (1993) 18 EHRR 119, a case which was struck out following a friendly settlement between the parties (28 June 1993) and where the European Commission concluded, without examining the merits, that 'the Convention organs should not substitute their own evaluation for that of the competent medical authorities'.
3   See *Casado Coca v Spain* (1994) 18 EHRR 1 and **8.31** et seq.
4   *Barthold v Federal Republic of Germany* (1985) 7 EHRR 383.

provider. The judges in *Barthold* considered that any statement may, depending upon its content, contain a pure public interest element whilst also being an example of commercial speech. Where this was its content, the Strasbourg judges held that the statement was to have the wider protection of public interest speech. In this context, what about the likely attempts of 'big tobacco' to proceed against any government which bans cigarette advertising as an impermissible restriction upon free expression – is this commercial speech?[1]

8.31   In the case of *Casado Coca*,[2] the local bar took action against Señor Coca, ostensibly for infringing its prohibition on advertising. He was found to be in breach and proceeded to file an application at Strasbourg. The Spanish government there argued that the notices placed by the applicant in local newspapers:

> '… did not in any way constitute information of a commercial nature but [were] simply advertising … [which] did not come within the ambit of freedom of expression; an advertisement did not serve the public interest but merely the private interest of the individuals concerned.'

This is a remarkably broad proposition (which, on its face, would appear to extend to posters advocating, for example, safe sex techniques to prevent the spread of HIV) and it is perhaps unsurprising that the *Coca* case split the Commission.

8.32   When the case proceeded to the European Court it found that 'Article 10 guarantees freedom of expression to "everyone". No distinction is made in it according to whether the type of aim pursued is profit making or not and a difference of treatment in this sphere might fall foul of Article 14'.[3] It continued 'in its *Barthold* judgment the Court left open the question … [whether] … commercial advertising as such came within the scope of the guarantees under Article 10, but its later case-law provides guidance on this matter. Article 10 does not apply solely to certain types of information or ideas or forms of expression'.

8.33   The European Court described advertising as a 'means of discovering the characteristics of goods and services'. It might 'sometimes be restricted, especially to prevent unfair competition and untruthful or misleading advertising'. Indeed, 'in some contexts, the publication of even objective, truthful advertisements might be restricted in order to ensure respect for the rights of others or owing to the special circumstances of particular business activities and professions'. The Strasbourg judges warned that such restrictions would be closely scrutinised by the European Court, but Contracting States would be accorded a broad margin of appreciation in this area and, in this case, the actions of the Spanish Bar were found not to be disproportionate or unreasonable.[4]

---

1   See the Canadian case of *RJR MacDonald Inc* [1995] 3 SCR 199, in which the Canadian Supreme Court struck down a ban on tobacco advertising. See also the litigation involving tobacco companies in the UK: *R v Secretary of State for Health, ex parte Imperial Tobacco Ltd* [2000] 1 All ER 572.

2   See fn 4 on p 239. It concerned a lawyer in Barcelona. In addition to placing advertisements for his practice in several newspapers he also solicited a number of companies.

3   The prohibition on discrimination. See **5.44**.

4   Compare the very different approach of the US Supreme Court, which has said that 'commercial speech serves to inform the public of the availability, nature and prices of products and services, and this performs an indispensable role in the allocation of resources in a free enterprise system': *44 Liquormart, Inc v Rhode Island* (1996) 116 SCt 1495.

8.34   In an age of global branding, such a conservative adjudication is troubling and arguably leaves British advertisers and their clients, used to a more robust marketplace, at a disadvantage, at least so far as their operations in continental Europe are concerned. The difference in emphasis between the UK and Germany, for example, was underscored most obviously in the *Markt Intern* case[1] (even though, ironically, it was a British corporation which was seeking in that case to restrain publication). Markt Intern was a publishing company which sought to defend small retailers against big business. It produced a series of articles critical of a British mail-order firm, as regards which it advised its readers to be 'cautious' in their dealings. In Germany, an injunction was granted the firm to prevent the repetition of such statements and the Federal Constitutional Court held that freedom of expression could not prevail in circumstances where the disputed articles were intended to promote certain economic interests (in this case, retailers of beauty products) to the detriment of others. At Strasbourg, the judges at least recognised the reality of commercial life when saying that:

> 'In a market economy an undertaking which seeks to set up a business inevitably exposes itself to close scrutiny of its practices by its competitors. Its commercial strategy and the manner in which it honours its commitments may give rise to criticism on the part of consumers and the specialised press must be able to disclose facts which could be of interest to its readers and thereby contribute to the openness of business activity.'

8.35   Therefore, the valuable role of the consumer press was acknowledged, but that was all, as the case was in fact lost by the applicants. The European Court found that the national court had been acting within its margin of appreciation and that it was not part of Strasbourg's remit to re-examine the findings of local judges who had, on the basis of grounds found by them to be reasonable, considered the imposition of an injunction to be necessary, even though it restrained statements which were true. So it is that, as a Contracting State's area of permissible discretion is expanded in relation to commercial advertising, the level of Strasbourg jurisdiction contracts.

8.36   It is, as already noted, a regrettable characteristic of much European Convention jurisprudence that the Strasbourg institutions have been divided in a number of their most important cases. In *Markt Intern*, the European Court split down the middle with nine judges on each side, the President's casting vote ensuring that the decision went in favour of the Member State. Seven of the dissenting judges thought that commercial and political speech should attract equivalent measures of protection. In a joint opinion, they argued that 'the fact that a person defends a given interest, whether it is an economic interest or any other interest, does not ... deprive him of the benefit of freedom of expression'. Furthermore, in order: 'to ensure the openness of business activities, it must be possible to disseminate freely information and ideas concerning the products and services proposed to consumers. Consumers, who are exposed to highly effective distribution techniques and to advertising which is frequently less than objective, deserve, for their part too, to be protected, as indeed the retailers'.

8.37   Judge Martens, supported by Judge McDonald, said 'the socio-economic press is just as important as the political and cultural press for the progress of our modern societies and for the development of every man'.

---

1   *Markt Intern Verlag GmbH and Klaus Bermann v Federal Republic of Germany* (1989) 12 EHRR 161.

8.38   It will be apparent that, just as the operation of Austria's law of criminal libel in the political context has been a repeated subject of condemnation at Strasbourg, so too Germany's traditional suspicion of trade speech has come to be closely scrutinised, albeit with less clear results. The case of *Jacobowski v Germany*[1] was about the editor-in-chief of a news agency who was dismissed on a variety of different grounds (including, allegedly, incompetence) and was subsequently attacked in a press release issued by his former employers. He sent a file of unfavourable material about them to a number of journalists (all of them agency clients) with a covering letter that suggested that he might be setting up on his own account. Proceedings were issued against him under German unfair competition legislation and an injunction granted to prevent his sending out any further mailshots on the basis that these were giving him a commercial advantage that was unfair.

8.39   The German Government defended its national court's actions at Strasbourg by relying upon the operation of a margin of appreciation in this context and arguing that the control of unfair competition was a legitimate aim. However, the European Commission held unanimously that the national court's order was disproportionate in circumstances where Herr Jacobowski had been responding to a reputational attack. As such, the injunction awarded against him constituted an Art 10 infringement.

8.40   The European Court disagreed, accepting that the German court was exercising a margin of appreciation which was 'essential in commercial matters, in particular in an area as complex and fluctuating as that of unfair competition'. As the German court had correctly considered and balanced Herr Jacobowski's rights and had concluded that his principal motive was a competitive one, the German court had not stepped outside the range of permissible discretion available to it. After all, Herr Jacobowski could proceed other than by the dispatch of further mailshots. Here too, the European Court was not of one voice and, in a joint dissenting opinion, three of the judges reminded their colleagues that freedom of expression should be 'the guiding principle of the case', noting that the mailshots in question comprised clippings in the public domain and adding that the European Convention should be construed narrowly when exceptions to Art 10 were being contended for. The dissentients continued: 'To accept in this case a preponderance of the competitive element amounts to reducing the principle of freedom of expression to the level of an exception and to elevating the [German] Unfair Competition Act to the status of a rule. We cannot agree that this constitutes the proper way of exercising a European supervision'.

8.41   While deference paid by the European Court to the decisions of national courts in these German cases means that British companies may be constrained in their advertising activities in Germany, their marketing activities here are unlikely to be affected so long as the applicable legal and regulatory regime is complied with. This begs the question as to whether the wholesale introduction of the Act will lead to a relaxation in advertising controls in the UK. First indications are that it will do so.

8.42   In May 2000, the Independent Television Commission initiated a review into its own advertising regime, specifically directed at the 29 current prohibitions

---

1   (1995) 19 EHRR 64.

on different forms of broadcast advertising.[1] Announcing the review, the Independent Television Commission conceded that a driver for the review was the Act, which aims in its words 'to ensure that any restrictions on freedom of speech imposed by the [Independent Television Commission's] Advertising Code are proportionate and clearly related to potential viewer detriment'. Like other content regulators, the Independent Television Commission acknowledged that it needed 'to be confident that any absolute prohibition on categories of advertising [would] command public support and [be] consistent with the Convention'.

8.43 It would appear, therefore, that a further, very practical consequence of the Act will be a loosening of the restrictions on television advertising in the UK, with the present ban on (in particular) many forms of medical-related advertising due to disappear.

COMMERCIAL SPEECH OUTSIDE THE ADVERTISING CONTEXT

8.44 Commercial speech is not the same as speech about commerce and the latter may be accorded a higher degree of protection than the former on the basis that 'there is no warrant ... for distinguishing between political discussion and discussion of other matters of public concern'.[2] This is a developing Strasbourg theme[3] and is of obvious significance for the media in the UK. It suggests that higher-level protection may be conferred upon trade speech (and, indeed, other forms of non-political speech), but only where that speech touches upon public interest concerns, which most advertising does not.

8.45 In this context, British companies caught up in the current debate about food and public health should pay close regard to the recent case of *Hertel v Switzerland*,[4] where the European Court also took an opportunity to look critically at the operation of the margin of appreciation. It decided that the making of an injunction against Herr Hertel, to restrain him from repeating claims he had made about the danger posed by food which had been microwaved, was disproportionate. This was a form of censorship affecting Herr Hertel's right to 'participate in a debate affecting the general interest, for example, the public health [sic]'. Where something more was at stake than a narrow commercial advantage, the area of discretion available to a national court was to be reduced, whether or not the views in issue were those of a minority and even though they might be 'devoid of merit'. If nothing else, the *Hertel* case suggests that the consumer press stands poised, subject to the future development of local libel law, to secure a higher measure of protection than might previously have been acknowledged in the UK.

---

1   Reviewing the Commission's Code of Advertising Standards and Practice, First Consultation Paper, 8 May 2000.
2   So the European Court held in the case of *Thorqier Thorgeirson v Iceland* (1992) 14 EHRR 843, arising out of the conviction of a journalist for stories he had written about police brutality. An Art 10 violation was found. See also in this context *Bladet Tromsø and Stensaas v Norway* (2000) 29 EHRR 125 at **8.131** et seq.
3   See the views of seven of the dissentient judges in the *Markt Intern* case (**8.34** et seq).
4   (1999) 28 EHRR 534.

8.46   The role of the European Convention in relation to an unusual form of commercial speech was recently touched upon in the UK in a case[1] which arose out of an adjudication by the Advertising Standards Authority to the effect that an editorial paid for by a supermarket group was racist and offensive, and might incite violence. The High Court dismissed an application for judicial review brought by the retailer, but the judge (Sir Alan Moses) acknowledged that the Advertising Standards Authority's undoubted interference with an advertisement containing a political opinion would have to be revisited after the Act came fully into force.

8.47   Where the public interest is engaged, consumer reporting in European Convention terms is moving to a higher level of protection – close to that afforded political reporting. There is, in addition, a further respect in which Strasbourg law treats business and politics on a broadly comparable basis and that is as regards the ability to speak robustly of high-profile practitioners in both fields. The European Court's protection of those writing about politicians has already been referred to.[2] In the *Fayed* case,[3] it was, as already seen, the way in which businessmen were written about which was relevant (amongst other matters). The Fayed brothers argued at Strasbourg that the operation of the English law of qualified privilege as a defence to a claim for defamation meant that, in effect, they were left without a remedy when serious allegations were made against them by inspectors appointed by the Department of Trade and Industry looking into the brothers' acquisition of House of Fraser. This was in substance an Art 6 complaint, the Fayeds contending that they had been denied access to a court. The Strasbourg judges disagreed, however, confirming in the process the importance of the inspectors being able to report freely in this area. Specifically, the European Court said that 'the limits of acceptable criticism are wider with regard to businessmen actively involved in the affairs of large public companies than with regard to private individuals'.

8.48   This conclusion parallels the developments in the USA which gave rise to an extended public figure defence following *Sullivan*[4] (which had said that public figures needed to show 'actual malice' if they were to be able to recover damages for statements about their political activities). *Fayed* arguably justifies robust criticism of tycoons and those who 'thrust themselves to the forefront of particular public controversies'.[5]

8.49   In summary, it would appear that the advertising regime in the UK will be hedged about by fewer restrictions as a result of the Act (good for business), but that business journalists may, as a consequence of the Act, be encouraged to become more robust in their reporting. That may be good or bad for business. It is certainly good for the media.

---

1   *R v Advertising Standards Authority, ex parte Charles Robertson (Developments) Ltd* [2000] EMLR 463.
2   See **8.15** et seq.
3   *Fayed v United Kingdom* (1997) 18 EHRR 393. See **6.48** et seq.
4   See fn 2 on p 238.
5   *Gertz v Welch* 418 US 323.

ARTISTIC EXPRESSION

8.50   Article 10 is not merely a free speech standard. It is a guarantee of freedom of *expression*. In *Wingrove v United Kingdom*[1] the European Court had to consider whether British law on blasphemy (a crime at common law and which had been used to prevent the distribution of a film entitled *Visions of Ecstasy*) infringed the film-maker's Art 10 rights. The British Board of Film Classification had determined that the film, based upon the life and writings of St Teresa (a sixteenth-century Carmelite nun), was not only pornographic but also offensive to Christians, bound as it was 'to give rise to outrage at the unacceptable treatment of a sacred subject'. Therefore, it refused to give the film any classification.

8.51   The judges at Strasbourg held that simply because domestic law gave a public body a discretion – in this case whether or not to grant a classification – did not in itself mean that the offence was not 'prescribed by law' within the meaning of Art 10(2). As long as the *scope* of the discretion and the manner in which it was exercised were indicated clearly then, having regard to the legitimate aim in question (the operation of a film classification system), adequate protection existed to protect the individual from an arbitrary determination. A decision thus taken would be 'prescribed by law'. Against this background, the European Court dismissed the complaint, holding that the British Government (acting through the British Board of Film Classification) had not exceeded its margin of appreciation. In addition, the Strasbourg judges found that the film's blasphemous content 'could outrage and insult ... believing Christians and constitute a criminal offence'.

8.52   *Wingrove* was the latest in a line of Strasbourg cases confirming that national authorities have very considerable freedom of action when imposing restrictions on forms of artistic expression, with Member States and the courts of such States believed to be best placed to judge what their own citizens would find acceptable or offensive on account of the relevant States' 'direct and continuous contact with the vital forces of their countries'.[2] It appears clear that so-called 'fighting words' (most obviously pornography) lack the redeeming social value which would make them susceptible to the kind of added protection afforded to so-called 'speech-plus' (such as political comment).

8.53   This is apparent from the case of *Muller and Others v Switzerland*,[3] which arose out of the seizure and confiscation by Swiss officials of a number of paintings, some of them depicting bestiality. The European Court regarded the actions taken by the national authorities as not unreasonable, on the basis that morality was not to be defined or applied uniformly across Europe. In a dissenting opinion, however, Judge Spielmann emphasised that views in these matters tended to change – he noted that a conviction against Baudelaire for obscenity was not overturned until 80 years after the writer's death. He wanted States 'to take

---

1   (1996) 24 EHRR 1. See also, in this context, the European Commission's decision in *Gay News Ltd v United Kingdom* (1983) 5 EHRR 123, declining to find a breach after the successful prosecution in the UK of the editor of *Gay News* for blasphemy, the High Court having held that local blasphemy law was consistent with Art 10's notion of free speech in a pluralist society. The law may, however, now be ripe for a challenge on Art 7 grounds on account of its opacity. See **6.266** and Appendix 2.

2   *Handyside v United Kingdom* (1976) 1 EHRR 737.

3   (1991) 13 EHRR 212.

greater account of the relativity of values in the field of the expression of ideas'. As to the argument that Member States knew best, he said:

> '... it remains unacceptable in a Europe composed of States that the State in question should leave such an assessment to a canton or municipal authority. If this were to be the case, it would clearly be impossible for an international court to find any violation of Art 10 as the second paragraph of that article would always apply.'[1]

8.54   In comments reminiscent of *Muller* 6 years earlier, the judges found in the case of *Otto Preminger Institute v Austria*[2] that blasphemy had to be judged with one eye on the geographical area in which offence had apparently been given. In that case, advertisements in an Innsbruck cinema for a forthcoming attraction led to court orders for the seizure and forfeiture of a film. The Strasbourg Court regarded the fact that this had happened in the Roman Catholic heartland of the Tyrol as relevant. The Austrian authorities had 'acted to ensure religious peace in that region and to prevent some people being the object of attacks on their religious beliefs in an unwarranted and offensive manner'. That did not, however, deter the majority of the judges from themselves describing the film as 'scurrilous' and (oddly) 'ludicrous'.

8.55   It is not clear, therefore, that domestication of Art 10 will ineluctably lead to a more relaxed approach towards matters of taste and decency.[3] The media regulators (including the British Board of Film Classification for these purposes) will need *qua* public authorities to uphold the European Convention's guarantees, but when adjudicating upon what is obscene it is not anticipated that they will feel obliged (particularly in the absence of any enthusiasm from the politicians) to engage in a wholesale liberalisation of existing practices. They will, however, need to ensure that those practices are coherent and accessible (in other words, that they are prescribed by law) and this may be more difficult. Not only is there no codified obscenity statute in this country, but prosecutorial discretion is exercised differently in different areas. Consistent standards as regards what is permissible will now require to be applied.

8.56   One area where there may conceivably be a changed approach as a consequence of the Act is that of telephone sex lines. The relevant regulator, the Independent Committee for the Supervision of Telephone Information Services, may have to adjust its existing guidelines for fear of being met by the argument that its restrictions are not proportionate and do not meet a pressing social need.

THE ACT'S IMPACT UPON BROADCASTING LICENCES

8.57   It is often (wrongly) assumed that the limitations in the European Convention upon the exercise of the right to free expression derive solely from

---

1   Perhaps he had the *Handyside* case (see fn 2 on p 245) in mind. There the European Court had found more than 10 years earlier that the British Government had not breached Art 10 when seizing and confiscating as obscene an English-language version of the Danish work, the *Little Red School Book*. In the view of the Strasbourg judges, the British State was entitled to its own view as to whether the book would be detrimental to teenagers.

2   (1995) 19 EHRR 34.

3   See, for example, *R v Secretary of State for Culture, Media and Sport, ex parte Danish Satellite Television* [1999] 3 CMLR 919 where Laws J (as he then was) dismissed *inter alia* an Art 10 challenge to the proscription of a pornography channel.

the exceptions identified in Art 10(2). In fact, however, Art 10(1) itself (albeit indirectly) contemplates government interference with free expression by providing that nothing in Art 10 prevents Member States 'from requiring the licensing of broadcasting, television or cinema enterprises'. This carve-out was apparently justified at the time on account of the limited range of the spectrum, but it sits uneasily in the middle of a free expression right.

8.58 Broadcasting regulation in the UK is supposed to be carried out on a 'light-touch' basis, but to those the subject of regulation it can seem intensive. Every month franchises are bid for and awarded, whether they are to run radio stations or provide television services. The sums involved can be substantial and, in the past, some disappointed bidders have had resort to litigation.[1] As will be seen, the approach to date of the Strasbourg institutions to the State-sponsored licensing of broadcasting makes unrealistic any expectation that the wholesale introduction of the Act will lead to greater freedom of the airwaves.

8.59 The suggestion that the use of the plural *enterprises* in Art 10(1) meant that Member States were obliged to award broadcasting licences to more than one company (ie to allow for competition) was given short shrift at Strasbourg as long ago as 1967, in the case of *X v Sweden*,[2] a result which, given the development of State broadcasting monopolies in Europe after 1945, was less surprising than it might be considered now.[3] In that instance, the European Commission regarded the existence of a Swedish broadcasting monopoly as within Sweden's margin of appreciation, and much the same was said of the British system in 1971.[4] 'Enterprises' at that time was not necessarily to be qualified by the word 'private' and it took approximately 25 years for this to change.[5]

8.60 The treatment of broadcasting in Art 10(1) gives rise to a separate question as to whether or not it merely permits the granting of licences or goes further by permitting the prescription of terms to be placed upon licensees. If the latter, does the European Convention allow for the prescription of terms which would not generally be considered acceptable if applied to the print media? In other words, is there any continuing intellectual basis for treating broadcasting differently in an information age when media companies publish on-line, on paper and on television? Spectrum capacity issues notwithstanding, the justification for any enduring distinction appears unclear. It is noteworthy in this context that it was apparently a fear that Art 10(1)'s licensing proviso gave Contracting States too much latitude that led the proponents of the ICCPR to remove a similar provision from the draft of what became Art 19.[6]

8.61 A more flexible (perhaps realistic) approach became apparent in the case of *Groppera Radio AG and Others v Switzerland*,[7] which involved a radio station based in Italy that broadcast into Switzerland by way of cable re-transmission.

---

1   See, for example, *R v Independent Television Commission, ex parte TSW Broadcasting Ltd* [1996] EMLR 291 and *R v Independent Television Commission, ex parte Virgin Television Ltd* [1996] EMLR 318.
2   Appl No 3071/67, (1968) 26 CD 71. See also *Sacchi v Italy* Appl 6452/74, (1976) 5 DR 43.
3   See generally in this area R Crauford Smith *Broadcasting Law and Fundamental Rights* (Clarendon Press, 1997).
4   *X v United Kingdom* Appl No 4750/71.
5   In the case of *Informationsverein Lentia and Others v Austria* (1993) 17 EHRR 93. (See **8.65**.)
6   See Crauford Smith (fn 3 above), p 137.
7   (1990) 12 EHRR 321.

Groppera claimed that changes to Swiss regulations on radio station licensing had reduced the number of listeners able to pick up its programmes, thus cutting revenue and jeopardising its future. In the context of broadcasting regulation, the European Court construed the Convention thus:

> '... the purpose of the third sentence of Article 10(1) of the Convention is to make it clear that States are permitted to control by a licensing system the way in which broadcasting is organised in their territories, particularly in its technical aspects. It does not, however, provide that licensing measures shall not otherwise be subject to the requirements of Article 10(2), for that would lead to a result contrary to the object and purpose of Article 10 taken as a whole.'

8.62   In other words, regulation by licence was permissible to maintain an orderly development of the sector, but only so far as any license restrictions could be justified as a legitimate interference within the meaning of Art 10(2). Does that mean that a challenge could be mounted against those provisions of the Broadcasting Act 1990 which prevent particular political and religious organisations from holding broadcasting licences in the UK,[1] a prohibition that also raises questions in relation to Arts 9, 11 and 14 and Art 1 of the First Protocol?

8.63   As already noted, there have in recent years been a number of applications for judicial review in respect of the awards of the two bodies which currently grant broadcasting licences on behalf of the British State – the Independent Television Commission and the Radio Authority. So far as the author is aware, those challenges have all failed. Will the Act improve the odds which are currently stacked so obviously against disappointed bidders? The European Convention jurisprudence suggests not.

8.64   The criteria for selecting bidders for a broadcasting licence came up for review by the European Commission in the case of *Verein Alternatives*,[2] where it was held that the undoubted application of 'sensitive political criteria' in the decision-making process did not vitiate that process where the criteria were directed at the importance of achieving a regional balance as regards the maintenance of linguistic and cultural diversity within Switzerland. On this basis, the adoption of a similar approach by, say, the Independent Television Commission in considering a Welsh television licence would be likely to be legally invulnerable.[3]

8.65   The *Lentia* case is further authority for the proposition that State licensing bodies may have regard for 'the nature and objectives of a proposed station, its potential audience at national, regional or local level, the rights and needs of a specific audience and the obligations deriving from international instruments'. In this regard, 'quality and balance' may also be relevant. This view served to buttress earlier (non-enforceable) declarations of the Committee of Ministers[4] which, in its Declaration on Freedom of Expression and Information adopted on 29 April 1982, had stated that Member States 'should adopt policies

---

1   See Schedule 2, Part II, paras 1–6 of the Broadcasting Act 1990.
2   *Verein Alternatives Lokalradio Bern v Switzerland* Appl 10746/84, (1986) 49 DR 126.
3   It was, on the other hand, at one time reported that there was to be a challenge to the refusal of the Radio Authority to award a broadcasting licence to an evangelical station on the basis that the Broadcasting Act allows only the BBC to broadcast religious material nationally: see *The Sunday Telegraph*, 16 May 1999.
4   As to which, see **2.38** et seq.

designed to foster as much as possible a variety of media and a plurality of information sources'. In short, public authority licensors can have regard for considerations beyond the merely technical, particularly 'in an area as complex and fluctuating as that of radio or television broadcasting',[1] provided only that those considerations are proportionate and necessary.

8.66   It is, of course, conceivable that, where a future licence application in the UK is refused, a challenge based on the European Convention could lie where the effect of the licence denial could be to bar in a discriminatory way a particular group (such as a political party) from air-time. The European Court noted in *Groppera*[2] that 'it had frequently stressed the fundamental role of freedom of expression in a democratic society, in particular where, through the press, it serves to impart information and ideas of general interest which the public is moreover entitled to receive'. It went on: 'Such an undertaking cannot be successfully accomplished unless it is grounded in the principle of pluralism, of which the State is the ultimate guarantor'.

8.67   In *Groppera*, the Swiss Government had asked the court to consider the content of the station's output, arguing that a mix of light music and commercials could not constitute 'information' or 'ideas' for the purposes of Art 10. The European Court disagreed, ruling that 'both broadcasting programmes over the air and cable re-transmission of such programmes are covered by the right enshrined in the first two sentences of Art 10(1), without there being any need to make distinctions according to the content of the programmes'. In other words, the Strasbourg judges reiterated that, *so far as Art 10(1) is concerned*, it was the right to broadcast and not the content of the broadcasts which was key – a view which perhaps owes much to the recollection of the way in which Hitler had closed down independent parts of the media. Arguably, however, this approach is inconsistent. Encouraging pluralism is, after all, encouraging (however indirectly) a form of content control. The EU, in approving the Strasbourg Court's judgment in *Groppera*, met this point head-on by stating that 'pluralism is an exception to the principle of freedom of expression, designed to protect the rights of others'.[3]

8.68   The Strasbourg Court may in *Groppera* have been satisfied that the Swiss government was seeking only to prevent unauthorised cross-border use of Swiss frequencies, but to the Italian applicants it appeared like censorship, a point taken up by Judge Pettiti in a dissenting opinion. The Swiss authorities in fact had taken action against a Swiss-incorporated company which was re-transmitting Groppera's programmes from within Switzerland and it was only then that Groppera, based and incorporated in Italy, took legal proceedings. A majority of the European Court held that the Swiss Government's interference with transmission was not a form of censorship, but a measure taken against a broadcaster which the Swiss reasonably considered to be in reality a Swiss station which just happened to operate from the other side of the border in order to circumvent the statutory telecommunications regime that obtained in Switzerland.

8.69   In an age of global media operations and satellite television, this willingness of the European Court to border-hop is interesting, not least in the context of the perennial British phenomenon whereby pornography is trans-

---

1   *Lentia* (see fn 5 on p 247).
2   See **8.61**.
3   Green Paper on Pluralism and Media Concentration, EC Commission 1992.

mitted here from abroad by companies with no place of business in the UK. The case of *Autronic AG v Switzerland*[1] suggests that only exceptionally will Member States be permitted to restrict the reception of foreign transmissions, the European Court holding in that case that 'any restriction imposed upon the means [of transmission and reception] necessarily interferes with the right to receive and impart information'. The freedom of expression guarantee in any event applies 'regardless of frontiers' and, without more, this obliges the UK and the other European Convention Contracting States to admit cross-border information. The converse does not apply, however, and the UK is not obliged to ensure that local information is disseminated offshore.[2]

8.70   For all its progressive-sounding references to the importance of broadcasting pluralism, the European Court ultimately found in *Groppera* that the Swiss authorities were acting within their margin of appreciation, as it was acceptable for national authorities to regulate broadcasting where the applicable local regulations were framed and operated so as to regulate the industry on the basis of technology rather than content. The Strasbourg judges acknowledged the technological changes there had been in recent years but remained clear 'that States are permitted to control by a licensing system the way in which broadcasting is organised in their territories'.

8.71   The European Convention does not operate to support the right of every citizen to participation in the spectrum. As to that, there is no reason to believe that the Strasbourg institutions would today depart from the view expressed 30 years ago that there is no 'general and unfettered right for any private citizen or organisation to have access to broadcasting time on radio and television in order to forward its opinion'.[3]

8.72   The European Court had a further opportunity to consider media licensing generally in *Lentia*,[4] when five radio and television broadcasters, anxious to establish their own networks, petitioned Strasbourg in connection with the Austrian State's monopoly on broadcasting. Unlike in *Groppera*, there was no cross-border element and, bearing in mind the allowance made judicially for the margin of appreciation in this context, this may explain the European Court's more relaxed approach to licence restriction than in *Groppera*. The Strasbourg judges again stressed that the regulation of broadcasting was acceptable, but that the necessity and scope of any restriction had to be established convincingly, which it was not in *Lentia*. The judges held that:

---

1   (1990) 12 EHRR 485.
2   *Bertrand Russell Peace Foundation Ltd v United Kingdom* (1979) 14 DR 117.
3   *X v United Kingdom* Appl 4515/70. Therefore, the European Convention was not engaged when advertisements for Radio Caroline were banned as the station itself was a pirate one. So, too, the regulations of which complaint was made in *Groppera* may have been 'necessary in order to prevent evasion of the law'. Both cases confirm that licensing may be necessary and proportionate to prevent illegal activity. See also *Özkan v Turkey* Appl 23886/94 where the European Commission said that Art 10(1) was not engaged where a television programme had been interrupted on content grounds, on the basis that there were sufficient alternative sources for accessing the intercepted information. A similar conclusion (on very different facts) was reached in *De Geillustreerde Pers NV v The Netherlands* (1978) ECC 164, a case about television listings and one of the few copyright disputes to reach Strasbourg (but see also **8.245** et seq). Article 10(1) did not apply in circumstances where Dutch citizens could find out the broadcasting schedules by other means.
4   (1993) 17 EHRR 93.

'... [of] all the means of ensuring that [democratic] values are respected, a public monopoly is the one which imposes the greatest restrictions on the freedom of expression, namely the total impossibility of broadcasting otherwise than through a national station, and in some cases, to a very limited extent through a local cable station. The far-reaching character of such restrictions means that they can only be justified where they correspond to a pressing need.'

8.73   *Lentia* brought to a close the post-War statist approach of the Strasbourg institutions to broadcasting monopolies.[1] Its import is that each Member State should encourage a broad, diverse broadcasting sector, a requirement with which certain of the former Soviet States will doubtless be unfamiliar. Indeed, the European Court envisaged in the case that 'one-sided programmes must be possible wherever a sufficient number of frequencies [is] available'. Governments, of course, have content and technical concerns which are legitimate, but the European Commission believed in *Lentia* that these were dealt with by the imposition of licence conditions and a robust competition policy.

8.74   The government in Vienna found itself before the European Court again in *Radio ABC v Austria*,[2] where the judges restated their position as set out in *Lentia* and *Groppera*, noting that, 'as a result of technical progress made over the last decades, justification for [monopoly] restrictions like the one in issue could no longer be found in considerations relating to the number of frequencies and channels available'. The monopoly of the Austrian broadcaster ABC was disproportionate to the aim pursued and was not necessary in a democratic society, even though the Austrian government suggested that its regulations encouraged 'well-balanced, objective and pluralistic programmes'. It was, therefore, in violation of Art 10.[3]

8.75   The upshot of the European Convention cases on media licensing is that whereas public broadcasting monopolies are not illegitimate, they have, in Crawford Smith's words, only 'provisional legitimacy: acceptable only while States can establish that they are strictly necessary in a democratic society'.[4] The licensing right in Art 10(1), therefore, is no longer necessarily co-terminous with a State broadcasting right. That might have been acceptable in post-War Europe when no dynamic private television sector existed, but it is no longer acceptable.

8.76   What are the implications of all of this for the BBC? Independent television in the UK has long complained about the existence and operation of the licence fee by which the BBC is funded. It is not clear, however, that the BBC's current status raises any difficulty under Art 10(1) or (2).

8.77   Indeed, the position of the BBC (and, indeed, Channel 4) is arguably better than it has been for a long time because of the importance of maintaining plurality in an era of media concentration.

---

1   Compare, however, the approach of the European Court of Justice to what was, in substance, the same point in the ERT case (see fn 8 on p 121).
2   Where a private radio station challenged restrictions on the number of licences available to such stations.
3   Although the applicants were not awarded any damages. The European Court was not satisfied that, if the applicants had been able to apply for licences, they would in fact have been awarded them. This was consistent with the view of the European Commission in the case of *Verein Alternatives Lokalradio Bern v Switzerland* (see fn 2 on p 248), to the effect that no company has an Art 10 right to a broadcasting licence.
4   Crauford Smith (see fn 3 on p 247), p 209.

8.78   As to which, what about private monopoly interests? Could the European Convention be invoked against any of the well-known examples? Concerns about the abuse of private power in the broadcasting sector have been for some time a feature of cases before the French and Italian courts, although there has been little explicit reference to this issue in Strasbourg and it is likely that a more potent threat to any perceived over-concentration of media ownership will for the foreseeable future be found less in the European Convention and more in the anti-trust provisions of the Treaty of Rome.

8.79   Finally, what about the balance between the receipt and imparting of broadcast information? In the case of pirate broadcasting, it is arguable that the right to receive is greater than the right to impart. Have citizens the right to demand particular information or merely a lesser right to receive such information as is readily available? In circumstances where most viewers in the UK are no longer able to see many popular sporting events other than on a subscription-only or pay-per-view basis, this is a matter of some practical significance on which Strasbourg as yet offers no ready answer. The extent to which the European Convention confers a right to freedom of information at all is considered separately below.[1]

THE LIMITATIONS UPON FREE EXPRESSION

8.80   For all the claims made for the First Amendment, freedom of expression is not an absolute right in the USA. So too in the European Convention, for Art 10(2) sets out a series of permissible brakes upon the exercise of the right. As a result the British State explicitly remains able (and has always been able) not withstanding the Act, to maintain formalities, conditions, restrictions or penalties that serve to limit freedom of expression provided only that they are prescribed by law and are necessary in a democratic society:

–   in the interests of national security, territorial integrity or public safety (through, for example, laws on official secrecy);

–   to prevent disorder or crime (through, for example, laws against incitement or so-called 'hate speech');[2]

–   to protect health or morals (through, for example, laws against obscenity);

–   to protect reputations (through, for example, laws on defamation) or the rights of others (a restriction which does not appear in Arts 8, 9 or 11);[3]

–   to prevent the disclosure of information received in confidence (through, for example, the tort of breach of confidence); and

–   to maintain the authority and impartiality of the judiciary (through, for example, laws on contempt).

8.81   These curbs are specific to the operation of the free expression right in Art 10. There are, in addition, those restrictions to be found in Arts 15, 16 and 17 of the European Convention which, depending upon the circumstances, may reduce the ability of citizens (or merely some citizens) to rely upon any of the

---

1   See **8.159** et seq.

2   Albeit that there is no discrete hate speech law in the UK of the kind found elsewhere.

3   In 1993, the European Commission said 'the freedom conferred by Art 10 ... is not of an absolute, unfettered nature. It does not authorise the publication of defamatory material': *S and M v United Kingdom* (1994) 18 EHRR CD 172.

Convention's safeguards, including that of freedom of expression.[1] Article 10 is not referred to in Art 15(2), so it is not even non-derogable. Added to this list of restraints is the ability of courts to bar reporting of court proceedings.

8.82   These carve-outs, whether found in Art 10(2) or not, appear on their face to be very extensive and give an impression that freedom of expression is anything but untrammelled in its scope. In fact, however, the Strasbourg judges have been consistent in stating that the restrictions in Art 10(2) are to be construed narrowly,[2] and a Member State relying upon them must show that they are necessary, which means showing more than that the limitations are reasonable. Even if the restrictions do not need to be indispensable, there has to be a 'pressing social need' for them.[3] It is not a question of balancing the considerations in Art 10(1) against those in Art 10(2). British courts are now faced 'not with a choice between two conflicting principles but with a principle of freedom of expression that is subject to a number of exceptions'.[4] That sentiment appears media-friendly, but there are duties and responsibilities (uniquely for the European Convention) which go with the exercise of this particular freedom and, what is more, it comes with a margin of appreciation, which may be wider or narrower depending upon the restriction in Art 10(2) which is being relied upon,[5] being wider as regards, for example, issues of national security[6] or affecting the protection of morality.[7]

8.83   Against this background, why is it that editors in the UK appear to profess abiding faith in the progressive potential of Art 10? The question is particularly apt in circumstances where for years British judges have had regard to the European Convention in the media context, so a moot question going forward is (all-important privacy issues aside) whether the introduction of the Act will make any difference.

8.84   For a generation, judicial fealty was paid to the notion that European Convention law was in substance the same as English law. As Lord Goff once explained:

> 'The only difference is that, whereas Art 10 of the Convention, in accordance with its avowed purpose, proceeds to state a fundamental right and then qualify it, we in this country (where everybody is free to do anything, subject only to the provisions of the law) proceed rather on the assumption of freedom of speech, and turn to our law to discover the established exceptions to it.'[8]

8.85   In so saying, he echoed Lord Scarman who had, much earlier, confirmed the 'presumption, albeit refutable, that our municipal law will be consistent with our international obligations'.[9] Those international obligations were, however,

---

1   See **2.6** et seq and **3.23** et seq.
2   See *The Sunday Times v United Kingdom* (1979) 2 EHRR 245 at 281.
3   See *Handyside v UK* (see fn 2 on p 245).
4   *The Sunday Times v United Kingdom* (see fn 2 above).
5   See *The Sunday Times v United Kingdom* (1991) 14 EHRR 229 at 276.
6   See, for example, *Leander v Sweden* (1987) 9 EHRR 433.
7   See, for example, *Handyside* (fn 2 on p 245) and *Scherer v Switzerland* (1994) 18 EHRR 276.
8   *Attorney-General v Guardian Newspapers (No 2)* [1990] 1 AC 109 at 283.
9   *Attorney-General v BBC* [1981] AC 303 at 354. See also *John v Mirror Group Newspapers* [1996] 2 All ER 35 at 47, 51 and 58 and *R v Central Independent Television plc* [1994] 3 WLR 20 at 30–31. Lord Denning at one stage hinted that English common law was broader than Art 10 to the extent that it bore upon the actions of everyone and not just public authorities: see *Associated Newspapers v Wade* [1979] 1 WLR 697 at 709.

viewed rather differently by the European Court in a series of key decisions which may have popularised the view that the media did better in Strasbourg than in London and which are now examined.

STRASBOURG'S IMPACT UPON THE LAW OF CONTEMPT

8.86   In September 1972, *The Sunday Times*, then under the editorship of Harold Evans, had run an article entitled 'Our Thalidomide Children: A Cause For National Shame'. This was at a time when some court cases against the manufacturers of the fertility drug thalidomide had been compromised, but when hundreds of claims against the company were still pending. While attempts were being made to secure an across-the-board settlement, a story in the paper had trailed the fact that, in a future article, the origins of the matters giving rise to the litigation would be explained. In the event, the Attorney-General (2 months later) obtained an injunction[1] preventing the publication of any further article, arguing that it would constitute a contempt of court by virtue of its conceivable effect upon the negotiations that were taking place. There would be a serious risk that the course of justice might be interfered with.

8.87   The injunction was overturned by the Court of Appeal[2] (led by Lord Denning) on the basis that the balance of convenience test to be applied in local law when considering whether or not to invoke the exceptional jurisdiction of the court to grant an injunction lay in favour of publication. However, the injunction was later restored by the House of Lords.[3] Lord Reid recognised that 'responsible "mass media" will do their best to be fair, but there will also be ill-informed, slapdash or prejudicial attempts to influence the public', while Lord Cross warned about the possibility of a 'gradual slide towards trial by newspaper or by television'.

8.88   In the wake of its defeat, the newspaper publisher filed a complaint at Strasbourg, alleging a breach not only of Art 10 but also of Art 14[4] (because contempt proceedings had not been initiated against other newspaper publishers who had run similar stories) and Art 18.[5] By the time the European Commission delivered its report, the bulk of the thalidomide litigation had been settled and the ostensibly offending article was published, three-and-a-half years later than first anticipated. The European Commission found an Art 10 breach (but only on an 8:5 split) and referred the matter to the European Court, which divided 11:9 in favour of finding a European Convention breach.

8.89   None of the Strasbourg judges disputed that there had been an Art 10(1) interference. What was for determination was whether the interference by injunction was *necessary in a democratic society*, the dissenting judges believing that it was. The majority, on the other hand, considered that the thalidomide story was of great public concern, that the article had been written in a balanced way and that publication would not have threatened the authority of the judiciary in the

---

1   *Attorney-General v Times Newspapers Limited* [1972] 3 All ER 1136.
2   *Attorney-General v Times Newspapers Limited* [1973] 1 All ER 815.
3   *Attorney-General v Times Newspapers Limited* [1973] 3 All ER 54.
4   See **5.44** et seq.
5   See **3.23** et seq.

manner contemplated by the last limb of Art 10(2).[1] Necessity in this context meant more than what was merely 'desirable' or 'reasonable'[2] and the British Government had failed to show that there was any *pressing social need* for the injunction.

8.90   The Strasbourg judges additionally considered whether the restraint on which the UK had purported to rely was *prescribed by law*. They found that the relevant prescription would only be met if two criteria were satisfied:

> 'First, the law must be adequately accessible: the citizen must be able to have an indication that is adequate in the circumstances of the legal rules applicable to a given case. Secondly, a norm cannot be regarded as a "law" unless it is formulated with sufficient precision to enable the citizen to regulate his conduct: he must be able – if need be with appropriate advice – to foresee, to a degree that is reasonable in the circumstances, the consequences which a given action may entail.'[3]

The judges continued: ' "Sufficient" if not absolute precision is the key, for the need to avoid excessive rigidity and to keep pace with changing circumstances means that many laws are inevitably couched in terms which, to a greater or lesser extent, are vague and whose interpretation and application are questions of practice.'[4]

8.91   In the event, the European Court in the *Sunday Times* case found that the English common law of contempt was not sufficiently clear, even if its use by the Attorney-General could readily have been foreseen.

8.92   In domestic terms, the decision led (albeit 3 years later) to the introduction of the Contempt of Court Act 1981, the most salient feature of which in the free expression context is s 2(2), which stipulates that the test for a finding of strict liability contempt is the creation of 'a substantial risk that the course of justice in the proceedings in question will be seriously impeded or prejudiced'.

8.93   Following the introduction of the Act, how is the necessity for interfering with freedom of expression (whether or not to restrain a contempt of court) to be determined? The *Sunday Times* case suggests that the questions to be answered are as follows.

– Is the interference with free expression pursuant to a legitimate aim, ie one corresponding to a pressing social need?

---

1   This part of Art 10(2) was apparently included on the insistence of the British delegation when the European Convention was first drafted.

2   The European Convention doctrine of necessity also bulked large in the so-called 'gays in the military' case decided recently: see *Lustig-Prean v United Kingdom* (2000) 29 EHRR 548 and *Smith v United Kingdom* (2000) 29 EHRR 493.

3   *The Sunday Times v United Kingdom* (1991) 14 EHRR 229 at 271.

4   The *Sunday Times* case (ibid, at p 257). It was by this standard that the provisions of the Swiss law on obscenity, which were much later scrutinised in the *Muller* case (see **8.51** et seq) were sufficiently precise, as was the competition regime in Germany reviewed in *Markt Intern* (see **8.34** et seq). The Sunday Times' publisher returned to Strasbourg in 1983 arguing that, in the case of *Attorney-General v English* [1982] 2 All ER 903, the House of Lords had failed to adhere to the European Court's (majority) Strasbourg judgment in *The Sunday Times v United Kingdom* case and that editors had been left to operate in an area of continuing uncertainty as to the ambit of English contempt law. The European Commission found the application to be hypothetical and, therefore, inadmissible.

–   If so, is the interference proportionate to the legitimate aim pursued, ie is there a reasonable relationship between ends and means? (The injunction imposed in the *Sunday Times* case had purportedly been to safeguard the integrity of civil proceedings, but they had been dormant for a considerable time.)

–   If so, are the reasons given for the interference relevant and sufficient?

8.94   In determining necessity, British judges may in the future be apt to cite Lord Griffiths[1] when saying that:

> '*Necessary* is a word in common usage in everyday speech with which everyone is familiar. Like all words, it will take colour from its context ... I doubt if it is possible to go further than to say that "necessary" has a meaning that lies somewhere between "indispensable" on the one hand, and "useful" or "expected" on the other and to leave it to the judge to decide in any case toward which end of the scale of meaning he will place it on the facts of any particular case. The nearest paraphrase I can suggest is really necessary.' (emphasis added.)

8.95   The *Sunday Times* decision was the European Court's first finding of an Art 10 violation.[2] It changed the scope and form of the English law of contempt, 20 years before the wholesale implementation of the Act. The Strasbourg institutions have not said that the existence of a contempt jurisdiction is *per se* a breach of Art 10, as plainly the last limb of Art 10(2) permits it and, for example, in the case of *Worm v Austria*,[3] the European Court (overruling the European Commission) found that the conviction of an Austrian journalist for writing a story capable of prejudicing a criminal case was not a breach of Art 10.[4]

8.96   In circumstances where the European Convention has therefore already left its mark, it is not clear that the Act will herald further changes to the local law of contempt. Of course, should it come to be accepted judicially that s 2(2) of the Contempt of Court Act 1981 is to be 'read down'[5] as meaning that there must be a substantial risk that the course of justice will *necessarily* be impeded, it can be seen that the implications could be considerable and that a move towards the US approach to trial reporting might be initiated. As explained later, however, it is more likely that the local judiciary will continue to confer a higher priority upon the need to safeguard the (Art 6) rights of litigants and, specifically, those of the criminal accused.

8.97   A separate, but related question going forward, however, is whether contempt proceedings against journalists will be *criminal charges* for the purposes of Art 6.[6] It seems likely that they would, not least in view of the seriousness generally attaching to such matters.

---

1   In the case of *In re: Inquiry under the Company Securities (Insider Dealing) Act 1985* [1988] AC 660 at 704.
2   Next followed the decisions in *Barthold* (see **8.29** et seq) and *Lingens* (see **8.15** et seq).
3   (1997) 25 EHRR 454. See also fn 2 on p 236.
4   An inter-departmental working group is now examining how the requirements of the European Convention affect contempt proceedings (Press Release, Lord Chancellor's Department, 9 February 2000).
5   See **3.41** et seq.
6   See **6.14** et seq. In *Demicoli v Malta* (1992) 14 EHRR 47, the Maltese law of contempt was adjudged to be criminal in nature.

THE ACT'S IMPACT UPON PRIOR RESTRAINT

8.98   The publisher of *The Sunday Times* was back before the European Court in 1993 as part of the notorious *Spycatcher* litigation.[1] Injunctions to prevent the publication of articles in *The Observer* and *The Guardian* (but not *The Sunday Times*) had been obtained from the High Court in July 1986. After receiving legal advice that the injunctions did not extend to them, the publishers of *The Sunday Times* ran their own story, as a consequence of which the Editor, Andrew Neil, and his proprietors were found to be in contempt. They complained to Strasbourg that this was a breach of their rights under Art 7 of the European Convention (which outlaws retrospective punishment),[2] on the basis that, when they published their story, they were not guilty of an offence. The European Commission disagreed. Local contempt law was, in its view, by now tolerably clear-cut. What was more, 'the fact that the established legal principles involved were applied to novel circumstances (did) not render the offence retroactive in any way'. That disposed of the complaint brought on behalf of *The Sunday Times*.

8.99   At the same time, applications to Strasbourg had been filed on behalf of the publishers of *The Observer* and *The Guardian* which were substantially to turn upon Art 10(2)'s acknowledgement that restrictions may properly be placed upon freedom of expression on the basis of national security considerations. The European Court's reasoning on that score is sufficiently fact-specific as first to require an explanation of the background to the case and its chronology.

8.100   Peter Wright, retired and living in Australia, had written a book entitled *Spycatcher* about his years as an intelligence agent in MI5. As noted earlier, injunctions preventing the publication of disclosures from the book were served upon the publishers of *The Guardian* and *The Observer* in 1986 and substantially confirmed (albeit in a modified form) by the Court of Appeal.[3] However, this did not stop more disclosures, in different newspapers, the next spring, after the British Government's case against Wright had been lost in Australia and contempt applications in relation to those stories had failed.

8.101   By now, the book was on sale in the USA and, inevitably, copies were entering the UK, a phenomenon the Government did nothing to stop. In July 1987 the judicial restraints placed upon the publishers of *The Guardian* and *The Observer* (and, indeed, *The Sunday Times*) were removed, but they were restored by the Court of Appeal, albeit that the restraint was by now against publication of all or part of the book. The case proceeded to the House of Lords, which divided 3:2[4] in favour of a ban on publication until trial. At that trial (a year later), the Government lost in its attempt to secure a permanent ban, a defeat confirmed (5:0) in the House of Lords,[5] albeit that *The Sunday Times* was found to have misused confidential information in publishing extracts from the book.

---

1   See *The Observer and The Guardian v United Kingdom* (1992) 14 EHRR 153; *The Sunday Times v United Kingdom (No 2)* (1991) 14 EHRR 229.
2   See **6.265**.
3   *Attorney-General v Guardian Newspapers Ltd and Others* [1987] 3 All ER 316. *The Observer* had reported the year before that Wright was hoping to publish in Australia in order to block any Government attempts legally to gag him in this country.
4   See fn 1 above.
5   *Attorney-General v Guardian Newspapers Ltd and Others [No 2]* [1998] 3 All ER 545.

8.102   When the *Spycatcher* saga came to be reviewed by the European Court, the judges split. The majority (14:10) found that the injunctions awarded against the publishers of *The Guardian* and *The Observer* had at the outset pursued a legitimate aim, namely the preservation of national security and the authority of the judiciary. Up until the moment when *Spycatcher* came to be published overseas, the injunctions were necessary and were not a violation of Art 10. That determination went too far, however, for some judges, who thought that the injunctions violated the European Convention from the start, not least because some of Wright's charges had been published before by Chapman Pincher (in his book *Their Trade is Treachery*) and others.[1]

8.103   Once the book came to be published in the USA, it was the unanimous view of the European Court that the continuation of the injunctions 'prevented newspapers from exercising their right and duty to purvey information, already available, on a matter of legitimate public concern'.[2] If nothing else, therefore, one lesson to be derived from *Spycatcher* is that the media should highlight any apparent inconsistencies in attempts made to ban publication. The British Government had done nothing to prevent Wright's book being sold in the USA. As such, why, it was argued, seek to punish newspapers in the UK?

8.104   Gags of the type seen in *Spycatcher* were not of themselves a European Convention violation, said the Strasbourg judges, but they needed to be approached with extreme care. In the words of the European Court:

> '... the dangers inherent in prior restraint are such that they call for the most careful scrutiny on the part of the Court. This is especially so as far as the press is concerned, for news is a perishable commodity and to delay its publication, even for a short period, may well deprive it of all its value and interest.'[3]

8.105   The reaction of the British media to the finding of the majority of the Strasbourg judges in *Spycatcher* was understandable if overstated. The decision was far from being revolutionary, indeed the order made against the publishers of *The Sunday Times* to give an account of the profits attributable to their breach of confidence was held to be proportionate. Furthermore, the majority had not agreed with Judge de Meyer, who considered that:

> '... under no circumstances ... can prior restraint, even in the form of judicial injunctions either temporary or permanent, be accepted, except in what the Convention describes as a time of war or other public emergency threatening the life of the nation and even then only to the extent strictly required by the exigencies of the situation.'[4]

---

1   Two judges (Pettiti and Farinha) thought that the injunctions had been sought for fear of the disclosure of irregularities in MI5 and not to protect a confidence. The involvement of the press should have been incidental, in their view, to the battle between Her Majesty's Government and Peter Wright. See *The Observer* (fn 1 on p 257), p 201.

2   See *The Observer* (fn 1 on p 257), p 196. The British Government was ordered to compensate the publishers for their costs and expenses of the litigation. This, the Council of Ministers later held, was just satisfaction.

3   See *The Observer* (fn 1 on p 257), p 191. The effect of delay on freedom of speech has also long been regarded as significant. 'Under a system of prior restraints, speech never reaches the marketplace of ideas and, even if it does, it may well be obsolete stock': R Singh *The Future of Human Rights in the United Kingdom: Essays on Law and Practice* (Hart Publishing, 1997), p 76.

4   He was joined by Judges Pettiti, Russo, Foighel and Bigi: see *The Observer* (fn 1 on p 257), p 207.

8.106   Arguably, the most telling judicial observations in the whole *Spycatcher* affair were not those of any members of the European Court, but instead belonged to Lord Bridge, one of two dissenting judges in the House of Lords hearing to consider the interim ban on publication. He said:

> 'Having no written constitution, we have no equivalent in our law to the First Amendment to the constitution of the United States of America. Some think that that puts freedom of speech on too lofty a pedestal. Perhaps they are right. We have not adopted as part of our law the European Convention ... to which this country is signatory. Many think that we should. I have hitherto not been of that persuasion, in the large part because I have had confidence in the capacity of the common law to safeguard the fundamental freedoms essential to a free society. My confidence is seriously undermined by your Lordships' decision. Freedom of speech is always the first casualty under a totalitarian regime. Such a regime cannot afford to allow the free circulation of information and ideas among its citizens. Censorship is the indispensable tool to regulate what the public may and what they may not know. The present attempt to insulate the public in this country from information which is freely available elsewhere is a significant step down that very dangerous road. The maintenance of the ban, as more and more copies of the book *Spycatcher* enter this country and circulate here, will seem more and more ridiculous. If the Government are determined to fight to maintain the ban to the end, they will face inevitable condemnation and humiliation by the European Court. Long before that they will have been condemned at the bar of public opinion in the free world.'[1]

8.107   These statements were made in the last years before the Internet became publicly available. Satellite television in the UK had yet to be fully introduced let alone cable. Lord Bridge was plainly conscious of the difficulties in restraining publications internationally – how much more so now?

8.108   Rapid technological change also has a bearing upon the likely development of Art 8 in the context of prior restraints. A future claim for so-called 'breach of privacy' may in substance be nothing more than a claim to prevent the publication and repetition of gossip.[2] In medieval times, gossip may have been a matter solely of village concern. Now, however, it can be downloaded worldwide, as the activities of Matt *The Judge* Drudge in the USA bear witness. As one commentator has noted: 'The Internet constitutes Emerson's quintessential "free marketplace of ideas" ... [i]t provides an authentic rough-and-tumble environment of critical scepticism with the freedom to express the unenforceable, the unpalatable and the unconventional'.[3]

8.109   It is unclear whether the extended *Spycatcher* litigation was so much the product of a different political era that its like will not be witnessed again. In February 1999, the Home Secretary, Mr Straw (one of the architects of the Act), obtained an interim injunction against the publishers of *The Sunday Telegraph* to restrain the publication, several days before its official release date, of extracts from the Report of the Inquiry into the death of Stephen Lawrence. The after-hours restraint obtained from Mr Justice Rix took the form of a blanket ban, of the very type which risks being found to be disproportionate in terms of Art 10.[4]

---

1   *Attorney-General v Guardian Newspapers Ltd and Others* [1987] 3 All ER 316 at 346–347.
2   See **8.170** et seq.
3   R Wacks 'Privacy in Cyberspace' in *Privacy and Loyalty* (see fn 6 on p 213), p 106.
4   See, for example, *The Daily Telegraph* 23 February 1999 and see also **8.224**.

8.110   It would be dangerous to regard the European Court's decision in *Spycatcher* as now being the sole template for the development of the local law of prior restraint. The case was unusual as to its facts and the Strasbourg judges were split in any event. The starting point in now determining whether an application can ever again be made in the UK, on any ground, to prevent publication is s 12 of the Act and this is dealt with separately below.

THE ACT'S IMPACT UPON POLITICAL SPEECH

8.111   In the case of *Derbyshire County Council v Times Newspapers Limited*,[1] Lord Keith famously held that the House of Lords had no need to rely upon the European Convention on the basis that the principles it enshrined were not materially different from English common law (echoing Balcombe LJ, who said earlier in the same action in the Court of Appeal that Art 10 did not 'establish any novel proposition under English law'). In the process, Lord Keith and his colleagues found that Derbyshire County Council, as far as its governmental and administrative functions were concerned, should not be permitted to sue the publisher of *The Sunday Times* for libel.[2] The Court of Appeal had earlier reached the same result, not, however, by eschewing the relevance of the European Convention but, on the contrary, by relying expressly upon it to find that there was 'no pressing social need that a public authority should have the right to sue in damages for protection of its reputation'. In so doing, the Court of Appeal engaged in precisely the form of analytical exercise called for by Art 10 which will now become commonplace.[3]

8.112   *Derbyshire* confirms that the importance of a free exchange of views on certain political subjects had been acknowledged, well before the introduction of the Act, in British courts and the case was soon applied to prevent British Coal Corporation, described as 'an arm of Government' from suing for libel.[4] As a consequence *Derbyshire* reduces very considerably the scope of any public sector organisation to sue for libel in its own right and it may be anticipated that the argument will now be put that no public authority (as understood by s 6 of the Act),[5] should be able to enforce a reputational right.[6]

---

1   [1993] AC 534.
2   See also *Goldsmith and Another v Bhoyrul and Others* [1997] 4 All ER 268, establishing that a
      political party (in that case the Referendum Party) could not maintain an action for libel.
3   It was the Court of Appeal also which, in the case of *Rantzen v MGN* [1994] QB 670 looked at
      the discretion to award damages available to juries in English libel cases in terms of
      democratic necessity and pressing social need. Similarly, Laws J (as he then was) in a different
      context found that, when dealing with freedom of expression, the Advertising Standards
      Authority was only to be restrained on 'pressing grounds' (see *R v Advertising Standards
      Authority, ex parte Vernons Organisation* [1992] 1 WLR 1289 at 129A–B).
4   *British Coal Corporation v National Union of Mineworkers (Yorkshire Area)* (unreported) 28 June
      1996. In Zimbabwe, the Post and Telecommunications Corporation has been barred from
      bringing a libel action: see *Posts and Telecommunications Corp v Modus Publications (Private) Ltd*
      Civil (1998) (3) SA 1114.
5   See **3.139** et seq.
6   In *Derbyshire* considerable reliance was placed upon the South African case of *The Spoorbond v
      South African Railways* (1946) AD 999, in which the State-owned railway company was held not
      to be able to sue for libel.

8.113   The Court of Appeal in *Derbyshire* in effect domesticated the European Convention some years before this was institutionally achieved through the medium of the Act. If the Act had been in existence then, it is likely that the result would have been the same. In some matters affecting political speech, however, it is conceivable that the Act will have a considerable impact.

8.114   Some years ago, the British section of Amnesty International had sought a judicial review of the decision of the Radio Authority to ban certain of Amnesty's advertisements as 'political'. The first instance court was at pains to suggest that the European Convention was (at that time) not relevant, even though it proceeded to carry out a balancing exercise.[1] McCullough J did not believe that a ban upon political material was a significant interference with freedom of speech, not least because the rights of listeners in relation to unsolicited political opinions needed to be borne in mind, while Kennedy LJ worried about wealthy interests distorting the democratic process. Amnesty were no more successful in front of the Court of Appeal.[2] It is difficult to believe that, as a consequence of the Act, the traditional, very widespread limitations upon so-called political advertising will be able to stand any longer on the basis that it is not obvious at which pressing social need it could be suggested such limitations are directed.[3]

8.115   Strasbourg's higher-order protection of political debate was considered by the House of Lords in the case of *Reynolds v Times Newspapers Limited and Others*,[4] where the panel comprised two Englishmen (Lord Nicholls and Lord Hobhouse), a Scot (Lord Hope), a South African (Lord Steyn) and a New Zealander (Lord Cooke). Their Lordships sat in June 1999, four-and-a-half years after *The Sunday Times* wrote a story critical of the then Irish Prime Minister, Albert Reynolds. Reynolds sued for libel on the basis of the piece in *The Sunday Times*' British edition, which differed in a number of material respects from the story run the same day in the newspaper's Irish edition. The charge in substance was that Reynolds had deliberately and dishonestly misled the Dublin Parliament and his cabinet colleagues.

8.116   At trial, Reynolds was awarded nothing by the jury, the judge substituting an award of one penny. In approaching the question of costs, the trial judge held that the publisher could not assert a common-law privilege for political speech, ie 'information, opinion and arguments concerning government and political matters that affect the United Kingdom'. This was critical, as in

---

1   *R v Radio Authority, ex parte Bull* [1995] 3 WLR 572.
2   *R v Radio Authority, ex parte Bull* [1997] 2 All ER 561. Recent press reports suggest that the radio ban on political advertising may be lifted shortly, by implication because of fears about a claim under the Act.
3   A related question in this context is the extent to which groups such as Greenpeace and Amnesty International can rely upon their Art 10 rights in the hope of being given charitable status.
4   [1999] 4 All ER 609. The same judges who sat in the House of Lords to hear the *Reynolds* case also sat in the Privy Council very shortly afterwards to hear the case of *Lange v Atkinson and Australian Consolidated Press NZ Ltd* (Privy Council) [2000] 1 NZLR 257, which had regard to the decision in *Reynolds*. In *Lange*, Lord Nicholls said that 'one feature of all the judgments, New Zealand, Australian and English [cited in *Reynolds*], stands out with conspicuous clarity: the recognition that striking a balance between freedom of expression and protection of reputation calls for a value judgment which depends upon local political and social conditions. The conditions include matters such as the responsibility and vulnerability of the press'.

defamation cases the media has a good defence if it can show that its story was protected by a privilege which has not been lost by the presence of malice (ie they are shown not to have cared whether they told the truth or not). The Court of Appeal agreed as regards the privilege argument, also finding that the trial judge had misdirected the jury, and ordering a re-trial but not, however, before offering the view that it was desirable to have 'vigorous public discussion of issues including governance of public bodies, institutions *and companies* which give rise to a public interest in disclosure'[1] (emphasis added). Before the re-trial took place, the publisher was permitted to appeal on the question of privilege, arguing that it should extend (as a matter of English common law) to political information.

8.117   The House of Lords was plainly conscious of the need to contextualise its decision internationally. Its citations included cases from the USA, New Zealand, Canada, Australia, India and Strasbourg. As Lord Nicholls, who in October 1999 gave the leading speech, put it in his very first sentence, the appeal concerned 'the interaction between two fundamental rights: freedom of expression and protection of reputation'. He might equally have said that it was about the tension between Art 10(1) and (2). He rejected the newspaper's contention that, issues of malice aside, the publication of political information should be privileged, regardless of the status and source of the information and the circumstances of its publication. Otherwise, judges would be doing the jobs of editors and would be left in 'an undesirable and invidious role' as censor.[2]

8.118   Lord Nicholls obviously recognised an obligation to have regard for the Act, even though its implementation was then a year away. He posed the test to be applied in reconciling both parts of Art 10 thus: 'to be justified, any curtailment of freedom of expression must be convincingly established by compelling counter-vailing considerations, and the means employed must be proportionate to the end sought to be achieved'.[3]

8.119   Lord Nicholls found (as had certain of his colleagues in the past) that Strasbourg jurisprudence was on all fours with English law and he cited *Lingens*[4] as an example, particularly for the distinction drawn there between facts and value judgments. He also referred to the *Fressoz* case,[5] where the European Court had upheld the right of journalists to publish information on subjects of general interest, provided that they were acting in good faith on an 'accurate factual basis' and supplied precise information in an ethically justifiable way.

8.120   Considering these authorities and others from further afield, his Lordship concluded that political information should not be ring-fenced and afforded a higher degree of protection through the operation of qualified

1   *Reynolds v Times Newspapers Limited and Others* [1998] 3 All ER 981 at 1004 (CA).
2   *Reynolds* (see fn 4 on p 261) at 621.
3   *Reynolds* (HL) (see fn 4 on p 261) at 622.
4   See **8.15** et seq.
5   *Fressoz and Roire v France* [2000] 5 BHRC 654. This was, in fact, the first judgment of the newly constituted European Court. It dealt with the relationship between free expression and commercial confidences, *Le Canard Enchaîné* having printed leaked details from the tax statements of Peugeot's managing director. The fining of the magazine for breach of confidence, mindful of the importance of the material in its particular context, was held to be disproportionate in circumstances where the journalists concerned were adjudged to have the right to divulge information regarding public interest matters, provided they were ethical, accurate and acted in good faith.

privilege. To do so would not only provide inadequate protection for reputation, but would lead to the erection of a distinction between political discussion and discussion of other matters of serious public concern which would be 'unsound in principle'. He recognised, nevertheless, the key role of the press as public watchdog, observing that 'the freedom to disseminate and receive information on political matters is essential to the proper functioning of the system of parliamentary democracy cherished in this country'.[1]

8.121   Lord Steyn's speech also looked at the interaction between local (specifically English) law and the European Convention. The two were in harmony, he believed, because English law recognised the importance of liberty and enshrined a constitutional right to freedom of expression, thereby emphasising 'its higher normative force'.[2] In his view, the Act would reinforce this constitutional dimension. He approached matters on the basis that the Act would very soon be fully in force and supported Lord Nicholls in rejecting the notion of a 'generic' qualified privilege for political speech, but he did so by inclining, he said, towards the Strasbourg approach that eschewed categorisation in favour of individual evaluation based upon the facts of each case. He quoted with approval the European Court's decision in the case of *Castells*[3] where the Strasbourg judges had said:

> '... the pre-eminent role of the press in a State governed by the rule of law must not be forgotten. Although it must not overstep various bounds set, *inter alia*, for the prevention of disorder and the reputation of others, it is nevertheless incumbent on it to impart information and ideas on political questions and on other matters of public interest.
>
> Freedom of the press affords the public one of the best means of discovering and forming an opinion of the ideas and attitudes of their political leaders. In particular, it gives politicians the opportunity to reflect and comment on the preoccupations of public opinion; it thus enables everyone to participate in the free political debate which is at the very core of the concept of a democratic society.'

8.122   It is noteworthy that, in declining to identify a generic form of qualified privilege for political speech, Lord Steyn relied heavily on international jurisprudence, including that emanating from Strasbourg. So too did Lord Cooke, who found 'no trace' in the European Convention authorities of a generic privilege in the political context.[4]

8.123   The fact that none of the Lords of Appeal in Ordinary in *Reynolds* were prepared to acknowledge the existence of a discrete head of qualified privilege as political information *simpliciter* does not mean that the right enshrined in Art 10 will not copper-fasten freedom of expression in the UK, particularly so far as the exchange of political views is concerned. On the contrary, Lord Hope was in no doubt that what he referred to as the *incorporation* of the European Convention by the Act had strengthened the arguments in favour of the principles set out in Art 10.[5]

---

1   *Reynolds* (HL) (see fn 4 on p 261) at 621.
2   *Reynolds*, ibid, at 628.
3   *Castells v Spain* (1992) 14 EHRR 445 at 476.
4   *Reynolds* (HL) (see fn 4 on p 261) at 643. He was fortified in that view by the terms of s 12 of the Act (see **8.213** et seq).
5   Ibid, at 654.

8.124   English law, in the wake of *Reynolds*, affords political speech a status that stops short of the test outlined in *Sullivan*[1] (although the lawyers for *The Sunday Times'* publisher were understandably quick to emphasise that it was not their intention to import a *Sullivan* standard), but which leaves behind any residual notion that politicians are entitled to the same reputational protection as private citizens and which is broadly indistinguishable from the Strasbourg jurisprudence. As far as political speech is concerned, therefore, it is not apparent that the introduction of the Act makes much difference.

THE ACT'S IMPACT UPON NEWS REPORTING GENERALLY

8.125   Of much more potential significance is the effect that the domestication of the free of expression standard may have upon public interest stories *outside* the political context, an issue of practical moment not just for media companies, but also for putative corporate claimants.

8.126   As already noted,[2] the Strasbourg institutions have for some time sought to restrain interference with media activity which has a clear public interest dimension. In the *Thorgeirson* case,[3] for example, a reporter had been convicted of defaming unidentified policemen in Reykjavik. The European Court was clear that the requirement placed upon the journalist to establish the truth of allegations of police brutality made by his sources was 'an unreasonable, if not impossible task'.[4] A conviction in such a case would have had a potentially chilling effect upon open discussion in the future of matters of public interest. Application locally of the principle underpinning this case might conceivably deter the Police Federation from funding, as it has done, a stream of libel cases in recent years.

8.127   *Thorgeirson* presages later Strasbourg authority upholding in a broad sense the right of the media to report the unpalatable views of others. Thus, in the case of *Jersild v Denmark*,[5] it was held that a reporter found guilty of aiding and abetting the dissemination of racist remarks because he published the prejudiced views of a number of youths had had his Art 10 rights infringed. The European Court was obviously live to the dangers of convictions in such circumstances:

> 'News reporting based on interviews, whether edited or not, constitutes one of the most important means whereby the press is able to play its vital role of "public watchdog". The punishment of a journalist for assisting in the dissemination of statements made by another person in an interview would seriously hamper the contribution of the press to discussion of matters of public interest and should not be envisaged unless there are particularly strong reasons for doing so.'[6]

8.128   Public interest arguments on behalf of the media will, on the other hand, be looked at critically when the judiciary is attacked. In *Prager and*

---

1   See fn 2 on p 238 above. There is a helpful review of *Sullivan* by I Loveland 'Privacy and Political Speech' in *Privacy and Loyalty* (see fn 6 on p 213).

2   See **8.44** et seq.

3   *Thorgeir Thorgeirson v Iceland* (1992) 14 EHRR 843.

4   Ibid, at 866.

5   (1994) 19 EHRR 1. *Jersild* is to be compared to a number of applications made at Strasbourg challenging convictions for racist or other forms of so-called 'hate speech'. These have, it is believed, all failed on the basis that the underlying convictions were consistent with the European Convention's purposes.

6   Ibid, at 28.

Oberschlick,[1] the Strasbourg judges concluded that the Austrian State had not violated a journalist's Art 10 rights when proceeding against him for publishing a story critical of judges. This was on the basis that:

> 'Regard must ... be had to the special role of the judiciary in society. As the guarantor of justice, a fundamental value in a law-governed State, it must enjoy public confidence if it is to be successful in carrying out its duties. It may therefore prove necessary to protect such confidence against destructive attacks that are essentially unfounded, especially in view of the fact that the judges who have been criticised are subject to a duty of discretion that precludes them from replying.'[2]

8.129　So, too, in *Barfod v Denmark*,[3] where the imputation that two lay judges had a conflict of interest was held to be an imputation against the judges personally which was not part of a wider political discussion.

8.130　These cases are of limited relevance when transplanted into a UK context, being very much a product of the criminal law affecting press reporting that is a characteristic of many continental European countries. If any helpful prediction is to be made as regards the Act's implications for British journalism, attention rather needs to focus upon the European Convention's attitude towards the civil law of defamation, particularly in so far as the parties to libel proceedings are not public authorities.

8.131　The European Commission held in the *Bladet Tromsø*[4] case that 'freedom of the press would be extremely limited if it were considered to apply only to information which could be proved to be true. The working conditions of journalists would be extremely limited if they were limited to publishing such information'.[5] This is a very bold statement and it is perhaps not surprising that the European Court, in the same case, was more guarded in its comments. *Bladet Tromsø* is, for all that, an extremely important decision in the domestic context. On the basis that the more recent a European Court judgment, the more deference it should conceivably be accorded,[6] the case is likely to be a popular citation in British libel cases for the foreseeable future, bringing together, as it does, various of the abiding themes that characterise the Strasbourg jurisprudence on Art 10.

8.132　The background to the case was that a Norwegian newspaper had lost a libel action arising out of a story it had run which suggested that the claimant fishermen had been trawling in breach of seal-hunting regulations. The relevant article included an interview with a reporter turned seal-hunting inspector, who had been based on a fishing boat as part of a monitoring exercise. He had made allegations of cruelty which were vigorously denied by the claimants, all of whom were easily identifiable and who were subsequently awarded damages. When the

---

1　(1996) 21 EHRR 1.

2　Ibid, at 20. However, see the strong dissenting opinion of Judge Pettiti, a long-time staunch proponent of freedom of expression, who said that 'journalistic investigation of the functioning of the system of justice is indispensable in ensuring the verification of the protection of rights of individuals in a democratic society ... Judges, whose status carries with it immunity and who in most Member States are shielded from civil litigation, must in return accept exposure to unrestricted criticism where it is made in good faith' (at 22). He went on to consider the situation in the USA, where league tables grading judicial performance are published and criticism is full-blooded.

3　(1989) 13 EHRR 493. But see also *De Haes and Gijsels v Belgium* (1997) 25 EHRR 1 and **8.137**.

4　*Bladet Tromsø and Stenaas v Norway* (2000) 29 EHRR 125.

5　Ibid, at 155.

6　See, as regards the interpretation of the European Convention generally, **5.12** et seq.

newspaper and its editor complained to Strasbourg, the European Court found (by 13:4) that there had been an Art 10 violation. It could not 'find that the crew members' undoubted interest in protecting their reputation was sufficient to outweigh the vital public interest in ensuring an informed public debate over the matter of local and national as well as international interest'.[1] The 'most careful scrutiny' was called for when sanctions were imposed which might have the effect of discouraging 'the participation of the press in debates over matters of legitimate public concern'.

8.133   This was so even though the publishers of *Bladet Tromsø*[2] had, in breach of the Norwegian Code of Press Ethics, carried out no investigation to verify the relevant allegations independently, which would on the facts not have been impossible for them to do. As to that, the view of the European Court was that 'the press should usually be entitled, when contributing to public debate on matters of legitimate concern, to rely on the contents of official reports [in this case of the inspector] without having to undertake independent research', as otherwise 'the vital public watchdog role of the press [might] be undermined'. The Strasbourg judges were satisfied, that the newspaper had acted in good faith and, on the basis that there was no reasonable relationship of proportionality between the restrictions placed upon the newspaper publisher's free expression rights and the fishermen's legitimate reputational right, the Art 10 violation was made out.

8.134   Tromsø is the capital of the Norwegian seal-hunting industry and no doubt the article in question carried enormous resonance locally. The public interest in the story was obvious, but was that enough to justify the conclusion reached by the European Court? The judges at Strasbourg were exercising a supervisory jurisdiction and had no means effectively of testing the finding of the national court that the relevant allegations were untrue. If a good-faith publication on a matter of public interest is the key to an engagement of Art 10's freedom of expression standard, the Strasbourg judges may have begun to render the British media more or less libel-proof.

8.135   Perhaps it was this realisation that led to the strong dissenting opinion of Judges Palm, Fuhrmann and Baka. They reminded their colleagues that the European Convention imposed 'duties and responsibilities upon the media'.[3] The press, to use the European Court's own words in a case decided just 18 months earlier,[4] 'must not overstep certain bounds'. The *Bladet Tromsø* case was the first occasion on which an indisputable public interest publication had clashed with the reputational rights of *private* individuals *par excellence* and it was clear to the dissentients that the bounds legitimately circumscribing the conduct of the media had indeed been over-stepped.

8.136   In the view of the dissentients, the majority judgment in *Bladet Tromsø* sent 'the wrong signal to the press in Europe'.[5] They went on:

> 'Few stories can be so important in a democratic society or deserving of protection under Article 10 of the Convention, that the basic ethics of journalism – which require *inter alia* journalists to check their facts before going to press with a story in

1   *Bladet Tromsø* (see fn 4 on p 265) at 172.
2   Ibid, at 171.
3   *Bladet Tromsø* (see fn 1 above) at 175.
4   The case was *De Haes and Gijsels v Belgium* (1998) 25 EHRR 1.
5   *Bladet Tromsø* (see fn 1 above) at 182.

circumstances such as the present – can be sacrificed for the commercial gratification of an immediate scoop. We are not persuaded that the Court's approach in this case which has exonerated the applicant newspaper from this elementary requirement will actually advance the cause of press freedom since it undermines respect for the ethical principles which the media voluntarily adhere to. Article 10 may protect the right for [sic] the press to exaggerate and provoke but not to trample over the reputation of private individuals.'[1]

8.137 This ringing denunciation is likely to be read out in many subsequent cases in the UK and may find favour with local judges. Advocates for media companies will point to the fact that no State interest was engaged in the *Bladet Tromsø* case and that, whatever the horizontal application of the Act,[2] the view of the majority of the European Court should infuse the approach of British judges to libel cases on public interest stories. They will also make the point that *Bladet Tromsø* is not entirely novel in its approach, following as it did the decision in *Thorgeirson*[3] and in *De Haes*.[4] Although those two cases did not involve private law libels, all three decisions suggest a growing determination at Strasbourg to entrench the validity of robust democratic debate. These decisions are to be compared with the operation of local libel law after *Reynolds*, which, it should be remembered, principally involved the scope of common-law qualified privilege. In the case of *GKR Karate (UK) Ltd v Yorkshire Post Newspapers Ltd and Others*,[5] Popplewell J said that, as regards the operation of qualified privilege at common law 'a privileged occasion exists if the public is entitled to know the particular information. That is, if it was the journalists' social or moral duty to communicate it'. This is a statement capable of very considerable practical application, quite outwith the arrival of the Act.

8.138 What may be a crucial factor in future domestic libel cases is the extent to which any applicable code has been complied with. As shall be seen, this issue arose in the Parliamentary debates about the implications for the media of the Human Rights Bill and it may be anticipated that some judges will be keen to rely upon an infraction of a journalist's conduct handbook to see off a broad public interest defence based upon the majority decision in *Bladet Tromsø*. Generally, however, *Bladet Tromsø* appears likely to be used successfully to buttress claims to qualified privilege in contexts far removed from the political world. News reporting may be transformed as a result.[6]

THE ACT'S IMPACT UPON JOURNALISTS' SOURCES

8.139 Some years ago, the House of Lords ruled unanimously[7] that William Goodwin, a reporter for *The Engineer*, should be obliged to disclose his notes for a

---

1   *Bladet Tromsø* (see fn 4 on p 265) at 182.
2   See **3.74** et seq.
3   *Thorqier Thorgeirson v Iceland* (see **8.126** et seq).
4   *De Haes and Gijsels v Belgium* [1997] 25 EHRR 1, where a conviction arising out of criticism of judges in Antwerp was held to be an Art 10 violation. Key factors in the media's favour in that case were the thoroughness of the research done, the important subject-matter (suspected child abuse) and the wider public right to information. See also in this context *Fressoz* (see **8.119**) and *Hertel* (see **8.45**).
5   [2000] EMLR 410.
6   The liberal trend was recently confirmed in another Norwegian case, *Bergens Tidende v Norway* Appl 26132/95, 2 May 2000.
7   *X Ltd v Morgan-Grampian (Publishers) Ltd and Others* [1991] 1 AC 1.

story about Tetra Limited, a software house, even though this would have the effect of disclosing his source. Goodwin applied to Strasbourg,[1] where the European Commission found (11:7) that there had been a violation of Art 10. It said that the circumstances of the case were not exceptional and Tetra had already obtained an injunction barring publication of any information deriving from the source. A disclosure order could in the circumstances conceivably have a chilling effect on the readiness of potential informants to talk to journalists.

8.140   The European Court also split. The majority found that there had been a breach of Art 10(2) on the basis that the additional imposition of the disclosure order, on top of the injunction, was not necessary in a democratic society. The public interest in preserving the anonymity of the source outweighed the need to identify a disloyal member of staff. This was because: 'Protection of journalistic sources is one of the basic conditions for press freedom, as is reflected in the laws and the professional codes of conduct in a number of Contracting States'.[2] Any disclosure order would need to be justified by 'an overriding requirement in the public's interest' on account of the importance attached to 'the protection of journalistic sources for press freedom in a democratic society and the potentially chilling effect an order of source disclosure has on the exercise of that freedom'.[3] Notwithstanding this ringing declaration, a minority of seven judges thought that this was a case where the margin of appreciation should have operated in the national court's favour, on the basis that it was best placed to evaluate the significance of the competing factors that were in issue.

8.141   The local law on journalists' sources had, before the wholesale coming into force of the Act, already moved towards the position adopted by the European Court in *Goodwin*. In *John v Express Newspapers*[4] the Court of Appeal sought to mitigate the harshness (as perceived by the media) of the judgment in *Camelot Group plc v Centaur Communications Limited*,[5] where, notwithstanding *Goodwin*, it was ordered that leaked documents be delivered up, even though they would enable a source to be identified. In the *John* case an order to disclose the identity of the supplier of a copy of a draft opinion of Counsel was quashed, Lord Woolf finding that: '... before the courts require journalists to break what a journalist regards as a most important professional obligation to protect a source, the minimum requirement is that other avenues be explored'.[6] Although his Lordship did not refer to the Act anywhere in his judgment, this statement is a classical example of proportionality reasoning in action. Lord Woolf found that no inquiry had been carried out in a set of barristers' chambers as to how a copy of a draft opinion could have ended up in the hands of a newspaper journalist. What was more, the merits of source disclosure as clearly being in the public interest had not been established. Even though there had been further (limited) reproduction of the contents of the draft opinion on the Internet, this was 'still a one-off

1   *Goodwin v United Kingdom* (1996) 22 EHRR 123.
2   Ibid, at 143.
3   Ibid, at 143.
4   *John and Others v Express Newspapers plc and Others* [2000] 3 All ER 257.
5   [1999] QB 124. Compare the case of *BBC v United Kingdom* (1996) 21 EHRR 93, arising out of the murder of PC Keith Blakelock. The *Camelot* case has been described as a 'defiant gesture'. See L Clements 'The Human Rights Act – A New Equity or a New Opiate: Reinvesting Justice or Repackaging State Control' (1999) 26 1 JLS 72 at p 77.
6   *John and Others* (see fn 4) at 265.

infringement of professional legal confidentiality which [did] not justify making an inroad on the other privilege, the privilege of the journalist'.[1]

8.142   The *John* case would appear to have settled the domestic law on journalists' sources for the present, the position adopted chiming harmoniously with the majority view in *Goodwin* even though the influence of Strasbourg was not expressly acknowledged.

THE ACT'S IMPACT UPON DEFAMATION CLAIMS

8.143   The British media have complained for a long time about a number of features of the domestic law of defamation. The limited scope of the reporters' qualified privilege was one such feature and the level of damages awards was another. This latter issue has been considered by the Strasbourg judges, although not in a case involving a media defendant.

8.144   Lord Aldington's libel action against Nicolai Tolstoy arose out of the smear that Lord Aldington was the perpetrator of a major war crime. He was awarded damages of £1.5m (three times the then previous record-breaking award) along with a permanent injunction restraining any further publication of the pamphlet in which the allegation had been made. On Tolstoy's complaint to Strasbourg, the European Court found[2] (agreeing with the view of the European Commission) that the damages awarded were disproportionate, even though the gravity of the underlying allegation was recognised.[3] A libel jury, in the view of the Strasbourg judges, was not free to make any award it saw fit, as, under the European Convention, an award of damages for defamation must bear a reasonable relationship of proportionality to the injury to reputation suffered.

8.145   It is not clear what bearing this has upon the Court of Appeal's approval of an increase in awards in certain personal injury cases.[4] Will this, by analogy, lead to an increase in libel awards and be challenged by the media on Art 10 grounds?

8.146   On a separate issue the European Court disagreed with the European Commission in finding that the award of a permanent injunction was a logical consequence of the libel, whereas the European Commission had thought its scope too broad in this instance. The Strasbourg judges also found that the order that, as a condition of appealing, Tolstoy be required to provide security for costs in the sum of £124,900 was not a breach of his right to a fair hearing under Art 6.[5] That order pursued the legitimate aim of protecting Lord Aldington in the Court of Appeal in the event of Tolstoy's appeal failing, which appeared likely.

8.147   The *Tolstoy* case is a reminder that the European Convention does not import a right to defame. It also shows how libel potentially engages not only Arts 8 and 10 of the European Convention, but also Art 6, even though it is only in Art 10 that a reputational right is expressly alluded to. In process terms, citizens have a

---

1   *John* (see fn 4 on p 268) at 266.
2   *Tolstoy Miloslavsky v United Kingdom* (1995) 20 EHRR 442.
3   See also the Hong Kong case of *Cheung Ng Sheong Steven v Eastweek Publisher Ltd* [1995] HKC 601, where an award of HK$2.4m was held to violate the local Bill of Rights.
4   See *Heil v Rankin and Another* [2000] 2 WLR 1173.
5   See, more generally, **6.102** et seq.

general if not an absolute right to be able to come to court to pursue libel actions and any restrictions on that right must be necessary and proportionate.[1]

8.148   The most glaring feature of what the media claims to be the one-sided nature of domestic defamation law is the placing of the probative burden upon the defendant to make good his plea of justification.[2] In other words, it is for the journalist to back up his own story. In the *Reynolds*[3] case, Lord Steyn agreed with Tony Weir that libel was the 'oddest' of the local torts because the claimant 'can get damages (swingeing damages!) for a statement made to others without showing that the statement was untrue, without showing that the statement did him the slightest harm, and without showing that the defendant was in any way wrong to make it (much less that the defendant owed him any duty of any kind'.[4] This, together with the absence of legal aid for libel proceedings in the UK and the risk borne by printers and distributors as co-publishers of libels raises obvious difficulties in terms of Arts 6 and 10 and is now reportedly the subject of a complaint to Strasbourg by John McVicar, following his unsuccessful defence of a libel action brought by runner Linford Christie.[5]

8.149   In fact, the legal aid argument has been tested at Strasbourg before[6] with no violation found, the institutions there tending to accept the inevitability of rationing and looking less at the nature of the prohibition and more at the circumstances of each case. McVicar may be different to the extent that he was a defendant (and someone apparently also facing a claim for an indemnity from a distributor to boot), whereas in the earlier British complaints, the applicants had either initiated defamation actions or wanted to.

8.150   In these particular respects, the Act may, in terms of the future shape of local libel law, be a mixed blessing so far as the media are concerned. Strasbourg, as has been seen, appears to be moving towards a broad public interest defence (and not just in the political context) which parallels the progressive elaboration of common-law privilege that was witnessed in the *Reynolds* case. On the other hand, it may be anticipated that claimants may suggest that any attempt to develop a comprehensive reporters' privilege in the UK should be challenged as inconsistent with the European Court's hostility to blanket immunities from suit

---

1   The short limitation period for defamation (1 year) plainly has implications under Art 6. The media will argue that it should not be considered a violation in circumstances where there is a clear societal advantage in avoiding the litigation of stale claims about reputational issues which are, it will be said, generally ephemeral in nature in any event. The time-bar can, in any event, be lifted in an appropriate case: see the Defamation Act 1996.

2   The Act will also doubtless encourage the media to challenge the common-law presumption of damage and of a good reputation.

3   See **8.115** et seq.

4   See T Weir *A Casebook on Tort* 8th edn (Sweet & Maxwell, 1996), p 525.

5   In *Dalban v Romania* [2000] 8 BHRC 91, the European Court considered that it was 'unacceptable for a journalist to be deterred from expressing critical value-judgments unless he or she could prove their truth', echoing the majority view in *Bladet Tromsø*, so McVicar's argument plainly has some prospect of succeding.

6   See *Winer v United Kingdom* Appl 19871/84, (1986) 48 DR 154 and *Munro v United Kingdom* Appl 10594/83, (1987) 52 DR 158, where defamation proceedings were adjudged to be inherently high-risk in nature and a right to reputation not as vital as the right to family life at issue in the *Airey* case (see **6.78** et seq). The complaint of the so-called McLibel 2, forced to defend a libel action without legal aid, was also unsuccessful at Strasbourg: see *Steel and Morris v United Kingdom* Appl 21325/93.

as seen in *Osman.*[1] It could be that advances made by claimants on Art 6 grounds in the years to come (in the form of a more flexible judicial approach to the operation of the limitation period for libel, for example, or as regards the availability of legal aid) will mean that the Act leads to more and not fewer libel actions in the UK. They could, however, be actions in which the media stand a better prospect of succeeding then they do currently at least where the judges are minded to follow the majority in *Bladet Tromsø.*

THE ACT'S IMPACT UPON A RIGHT TO REPLY

8.151   The obligation under the Act to have regard for European Convention law extends to decisions of the Committee of Ministers taken under Art 46 of the Convention.[2] The European Convention on Transborder Television may be relevant in this context. It was made at Strasbourg on 5 May 1989 and entered into force on 1 May 1993.[3] It lays down certain minimum broadcasting standards and pays specific regard to Art 10. 'The free flow of information and ideas and the independence of broadcasting' is affirmed and broadcasting's role in the 'free formation of opinions in conditions safeguarding pluralism and equality of opportunity among all democratic groups and political parties' is emphasised. All entirely unsurprising, except perhaps that Art 8 of the Transborder Television Convention obliges broadcasters to 'ensure that every natural or legal person, regardless of nationality or place of residence, shall have the opportunity to exercise a right of reply or to seek other comparable legal or administrative remedies' as regards their programmes.

8.152   Nothing in the Transborder Television Convention suggests that Art 10 imports a right to reply. In the author's view, it does not. Indeed, it refers to 'a right of reply *or* other comparable ... remedies' (emphasis added).

8.153   As already seen,[4] radical feature of the judgment in the *Bladet Tromsø* was the fact that an Art 10 violation was found even though the newspaper had breached the Norwegian press ethics code by failing to give the subject of its attacks an opportunity to reply simultaneously. Even if the Act is not a catalyst towards the creation of a legally-enforceable right to reply, there must be a good prospect that the local media will need to revise its guidelines in this area in the absence of any power on the part of the existing media regulators in the UK to enforce such a right.

8.154   In those contracting States where a right to reply exists, it has been held not to infringe the Art 10 rights of the person required to publish the reply.[5]

---

1   See **6.54** et seq.
2   Section 2(1)(d). See **3.34**.
3   ETS No 132. There is an EC Directive covering much the same ground (Council Directive 89/552/EEC OJ 1989 298) and a UN Convention on the International Right of Correction (435 UNTS p 191).
4   See **8.131** et seq.
5   Appl 13010/87, 62 DR 247.

THE ACT'S IMPACT UPON REPORTING RESTRICTIONS

8.155   The free speech–fair trial dilemma is a long-standing one. UK law has traditionally prevented some forms of reporting in order to preserve the integrity of certain kinds of court proceedings. The statutory provisions, particularly those affecting the identification of children,[1] are complex and some are controversial.[2] The fact that reporters here have been traditionally barred from some hearings chimes to a large degree with the express terms of Art 6(1), whereby:

> '... the press and public may be excluded from all or part of [a] trial in the interests of morals, public order or national security in a democratic society, where the interests of juveniles or the protection of the private life of the parties so require, or to the extent strictly necessary in the opinion of the court in special circumstances where publicity would prejudice the interests of justice.'[3]

8.156   Such prohibitions on access would of course appear on their face to be Art 10 violations, particularly when the European Court has stated that 'whilst courts are the forum for the settlement of disputes, this does not mean that there can be no prior discussion of disputes elsewhere, be it in specialised journals, in the general press or amongst the public at large'.[4]

8.157   This appears on its face to adopt a more liberal approach towards media coverage of trials than the local law of contempt would necessarily permit. In reality, however, the Strasbourg institutions have tended to attach great significance to the need to secure the proper administration of justice, particularly during trials.[5] The publisher of *The Daily Mail* therefore failed to obtain a finding that the fines for contempt of court meted out to it and its journalist Jeremy Warner for their reports of the jury deliberations in the Blue Arrow trial were a European Convention breach.[6] Writing a research project about jury behaviour might conceivably have been different, but this was not that situation. A system for accrediting journalists at trials may also be legitimate.[7] More recently, the European Court found in the James Bulger case that it would be right to restrict press access to trials where otherwise child witnesses might be intimidated and a fair trial prejudiced.[8]

8.158   So, too, the broadcasting bans on Sinn Féin in the UK[9] and in Ireland[10] were adjudged at Strasbourg to be proportionate. The battle against terrorism was

1   See, in particular, s 49 of the Children and Young Persons Act 1933. See also *McKerry v Teesdale and Wear Valley Justices* (2000) *The Times*, 29 February.
2   One of the best surveys in this area is McNae's *Essential Law for Journalists* edited by T Welsh and W Greenwood (Butterworths, 1999). Newspaper organisations were at one time reported to be going to Strasbourg over planned changes in the Youth Justice and Criminal Evidence Bill which, it was said, would have prevented coverage of the Dunblane massacre. The Government later conceded an amendment permitting identification in the interests of justice. See *The Times*, 11 May 1999 and s 44 of the Youth Justice and Criminal Evidence Act 1999, which was, at the time of writing, not yet in force.
3   See **6.177** et seq.
4   *The Sunday Times v United Kingdom* (1979) 2 EHRR 249 at 280.
5   The fact that the European Court found no violation where hearings were closed to the press by consent of the parties would appear very strange to a US First Amendment lawyer: see *Le Compte, Van Leuven and De Meyere* (1981) 4 EHRR 1 at para 43.
6   *Associated Newspapers Ltd, Stewart Stevens and Clive Wolman v United Kingdom* Appl 24770/94.
7   *Loersch et la Nouvelle Association du Courtier v Switzerland* Appl 23869/94, (1995) 80-B DR 162.
8   *T and V v United Kingdom* [2000] CLR 187.
9   *Brind v United Kingdom* Appl 18714/91, (1994) 77 DR 42.
10   *Purcell v Ireland* Appl 15404/89, (1991) 70 DR 262.

in both cases recognised to be important, as was the capacity of the broadcast media to influence opinion. These were adjudged not to be bans on news coverage *per se* but rather restrictions on interviews. Likewise, it was proportionate to postpone a dramatic reconstruction of the appeal case of the so-called Birmingham Six until the Court of Appeal delivered its judgment some weeks later.[1] A proposed Channel 4 reconstruction of a spy trial was also legitimately banned because of the risk of prejudice if it was seen by jurors.[2] Reliant on these authorities, the media in the UK will still need to proceed with caution when reporting on jury trials. In particular, they must proceed 'with all discretion and circumspection necessary if the presumption of innocence is to be respected'.[3] Outside the jury arena, however, applications by the media for access to hearings are likely now to stand a better chance of success. As this book went to press, for example, the order that the Inquiry into the activities of Dr Harold Shipman be held in private was quashed by the Divisional Court.[4]

THE ACT'S IMPACT UPON FREEDOM OF INFORMATION

8.159   The Strasbourg judges regard the right to receive and impart information as an integral aspect of the right to freedom of expression – readers and publishers, listeners and broadcasters, all have separate Art 10 guarantees. That is not to say, however, that the Act secures for UK businesses the right to freedom of information. Article 10 does not uphold 'the right to know'. It omits any express reference to the right to seek information of the kind that appears in Art 19 of the ICCPR, and the European Court put the point beyond doubt in the case of *Leander*[5] when finding that 'the right to receive information basically prohibits a government from restricting a person from receiving information *that others wish or may be willing to impart to him*' (emphasis added). It went on: 'Article 10 does not ... confer on the individual a right of access to a register containing information on his personal position, nor does it embody any obligation on the government to impart such information to the individual'. Where, for example, a company is willing to disgorge information, *Leander* suggests that the law cannot intervene to prevent it.

8.160   Where a citizen has a right to receive information, there is no obligation in European Convention terms upon governments to provide it. In the case of *Gaskin v United Kingdom*,[6] the European Court concluded that Art 10 did not give rise to an affirmative right of access to government information, although Art 8 gave Mr Gaskin a right to certain information about his childhood in care.

---

1   Appl 14132/88, 61 D & R 285.
2   *Hodgson Woolf Productions, NUJ and Channel 4 v United Kingdom* (1987) 10 EHRR 503.
3   *Allenet de Ribemont v France* (1995) 20 EHRR 557. The BBC, for example, ran an Art 10 argument before the High Court in Edinburgh in seeking permission to televise the trial of the Lockerbie bombing suspects, but was unsuccessful. The judge at first instance accepted, however, that the European Convention was relevant: see *The Independent*, 8 March 2000. On appeal, it was held that the absence of a jury was an insufficient reason to depart from the normal rule prohibiting live transmission and it was for the broadcasters to establish that the administration of justice would not be impeded: see *The Times*, 13 June 2000.
4   *R v Secretary of State for Health ex parte Wagstaff; R v Secretary of State for Health ex parte Associated Newspapers Ltd* (unreported) 20 July 2000.
5   *Leander v Sweden* (1987) 9 EHRR 433.
6   (1989) 12 EHRR 36.

8.161 Freedom of information is something of a misnomer. What its proponents in substance seek is greater disclosure of public (and specifically governmental) information. As long ago as 1981, the Committee of Ministers of the Council of Europe issued a Recommendation calling on Member States to ensure 'the right to obtain, on request, information held by ... public authorities *other than legislative bodies* and judicial authorities'[1] (emphasis added). This was confirmed a year later, the Committee of Ministers resolving to pursue 'an open information policy in the public sector, including access to information, in order to enhance the individual's understanding of, and his ability to discuss freely, political, social, economic and cultural matters'. Local judges will need to have regard for these decisions if they are to meet their interpretative obligations in the Act.[2]

8.162 In the case of *Guerra v Italy*,[3] the European Court (overruling the European Commission) held that Art 8 required the Italian authorities to provide the applicants, as a positive obligation, with information about emissions from a nearby plant. So, too, in the case of *McGinley*[4] the European Court (whilst finding no violation) held that:

'... where a government engages in hazardous activities, such as those in issue ... [w]hich might have hidden adverse consequences on the health of those involved in such activities, respect for private and family life under Art 8 requires that an effective and accessible procedure be established which enables persons to seek all relevant and appropriate information.'

8.163 In *McGinley* the Strasbourg judges envisaged that Art 8[5] and not Art 10 would be invoked to bolster a (limited) information right and it is surprising that few attempts have been made at Strasbourg to utilise Art 10 for this purpose. Article 10 at least mentions a right to receive information, whereas Art 8, which is relied upon to eke some form of rudimentary access right, says nothing about a right to information.

8.164 A post-War fear of holding executive policy-making up to scrutiny may once have been understandable, but when so much of government has in the modern era been contracted out to other agencies, there are increasing calls for a change in attitude towards the disclosure of official information. The Freedom of Information Bill tabled by the Blair administration[6] has, as far as commerce is concerned, good and bad features, with the (helpful) prospect of perhaps finding out why tenders have been lost balanced by the (less happy) prospect that aspects of corporate activity will for the first time be susceptible to review by competitors.

8.165 This is a substantial subject that is beyond the scope of this book. Suffice it to say that some early attempt to use the Act to test the ambit of both Arts 8 and

---

1   Recommendation No R(81) 19.
2   See **3.32** et seq.
3   (1998) 26 EHRR 278. This case is dealt with more fully at **9.197**.
4   *McGinley and Eyan v United Kingdom* (1998) 27 EHRR 1. Compare *LCB v United Kingdom* (1998) 27 EHRR 212. Both cases arose out of British nuclear tests in the Pacific in the late 1950s.
5   See Chapter 7.
6   The Bill is reproduced at www.publications.parliament.uk.

10 in this area cannot be ruled out. The problem may be in finding a victim[1] and, as in *Guerra*, it may be in the environmental context that one emerges.[2]

THE ACT'S IMPACT UPON EMPLOYMENT[3]

8.166   It is possible for the citizen to agree to limit his right to freedom of expression and the European Commission has held that the enforcement of such a limitation in, say, an employment contract will not constitute an Art 10(2) infringement.[4] Gagging clauses in the service contracts of civil servants are, therefore, far from disappearing.[5]

8.167   The leading (recent) case at Strasbourg is that of *Ahmed and Others v United Kingdom*,[6] in which the applicants, who were local government officers, failed to show that restrictions placed upon their political activities were a violation of Arts 10 and 11 and Art 3 of the First Protocol.[7] These are, on the whole, matters of significance for civil service employment only and it is not envisaged that any horizontal application of the Act will be such as to lead to a slew of cases establishing the freedom of expression rights of private sector employees to speak out in breach of confidentiality covenants that have been freely entered into, not least on account of the specific limitation in Art 10(2) permitting laws intended to prevent the disclosure of information received in confidence.

8.168   On the other hand, it could be that Art 10 will be used to buttress the so-called whistleblowing provisions of the Public Interest Disclosure Act 1998[8] and employers must face the possibility that staff who speak out publicly on a subject that is not a protected disclosure within the specific classes set out in that statute may still have a measure of Art 10 protection, relying, for example, on the *Hertel* case.[9]

8.169   A separate question arises in this context as to the power of trade and professional bodies to restrain speech. It has been reported that the Football Association has reviewed its regulations for fear that its power to fine players and managers for their outbursts may give rise to Art 10 difficulties.[10] The story makes for good copy, but there is nothing in the European Convention which guarantees the right, for example, to be profane.

---

1   See s 7 of the Act. See also **3.128** et seq.
2   For the impact of the Act upon environmental law, see **9.178** et seq.
3   The labour law implications of the Act are beyond the scope of this book.
4   See *Vereniging Rechtswinkels Utrecht v The Netherlands* Appl No 11308/84, (1986) 46 DR 200. See also **6.170** above as regards waiver of Convention rights generally.
5   See *Rommelfanger v Germany* Appl No 12242/86, (1989) 62 DR 151, where it was held that the German State had not failed to protect the Art 10 rights of a doctor sacked by a Catholic clinic after speaking out in favour of abortion.
6   (2000) 29 EHRR 1.
7   See Appendix 2.
8   See L Vickers 'Whistleblowing in the Public Sector and ECHR' [1997] PL 594.
9   See **8.45**.
10   See *The Mirror*, 2 November 1999.

THE MEDIA AND PRIVACY UNDER THE ACT

8.170　　The broad scope of the free expression guarantee enshrined in Art 10 has been explained, as have the limitations which may legitimately be placed upon the exercise of that guarantee. What has not been considered so far is the tension between Arts 8 and 10, even though it was this tension (and specifically the risk that Art 8 would be conflated into a general law of privacy) which appeared to condition much of the British-based media's approach to the Act, as appears below.

8.171　　The Parliamentary debates on the Human Rights Bill would appear, on a review of Hansard, to have been high-calibre affairs. That is, perhaps, less surprising than the fact that they were so restrained in the main. A massive step-change in the development of the constitution of the UK was marked by limited fuss. Such bother as there was derived from the protests of two influential interests: the church and the media. The Lords spiritual led a campaign against the possibility that they would denominationally be designated public authorities. It was said that the spectre of priests being required to officiate at gay weddings loomed, with Christian evangelism assailed by political correctness. In the event (and in the face of the wrath of certain liberal commentators who railed against what they saw as a relativist approach to civil rights on the part of the churches), the fears of the prelates appear to have been assuaged by the Government's late amendment of the legislation, which became s 13 of the Act,[1] requiring courts and tribunals to have 'particular regard' to the importance of the right to freedom of thought, conscience and religion when determining any question regarding the exercise by a religious organisation of that right.

8.172　　The other constituency proactively (if also defensively) to engage with the Government was the media. In particular, it was the suggestion that for the first time the Act would inaugurate a privacy law in the UK that led to a number of vigorous exchanges and gave rise to an important ministerial concession when the draft legislation was part way through its Parliamentary passage.

8.173　　The media's ostensible concern was that a privacy law would stifle freedom of speech. It saw the European Convention as enshrining a right to privacy, *ergo* the Act, in giving further effect to the European Convention, would require the media to respect the private interests of others, come what may. This syllogistic approach to the issue was simplistic and over-blown. In circumstances where (as has been seen) parts of the local press had done rather well at Strasbourg in previous years, it was arguably also cynical.

8.174　　The anxiety of the Government was amply demonstrated by the fact that the Lord Chancellor felt obliged to deal with the issue of privacy within minutes of introducing the Human Rights Bill in the House of Lords on 3 November 1997. Lord Irvine denied that the Government, in domesticating the Convention, was introducing a privacy statute. On the contrary, he was satisfied that the Government had resisted demands that it should. The best way forward was, in his view, 'strong and effective self regulation'. He stated:

> 'I say as strongly as I can to the press: "I understand your concerns, but let me assure you that press freedom will be in safe hands with our British judges and the judges of the European court". I add this, "You know that, regardless of incorporation, the

---

1　　See **3.191** et seq.

judges are very likely to develop a common law right of privacy themselves". What I say is that any law of privacy would be a better law after incorporation, because the judges will have to balance Art 10 and Art 8, giving Art 10 its due high value.'

8.175   He continued:

'More practically, I do not envisage the press going down to late Friday or Saturday privacy injunctions, disruptive of publishing timetables, if the press has solid grounds for maintaining that there is a public interest in publishing'.[1]

8.176   After alluding in this way to the interventionist role of the judiciary, it is perhaps odd that, less than a month later, the Lord Chancellor should in a conference speech have said he 'would not agree with any proposition that the courts as public authorities will be obliged to fashion a law on privacy because of the terms of the Bill. That is simply not so'.[2] In other words, the judges will develop a privacy law, but are not required to do so. What was the gap which it was anticipated on every side that they would fill?

8.177   The Government's White Paper had stated confidently that 'when the UK ratified the Convention the view was taken that the rights and freedoms which the Convention guarantees were already, in substance, fully protected in British law'.[3] At least so far as the domestic law of privacy was concerned, this was a considerable over-statement. So much so that it has become trite to point out that there is *no* law of privacy in this country,[4] even though, as Lord Hoffman has noted extra-judicially, 'the individual's right to dignity and respect is essential to a civilised community'.[5]

8.178   When the relevant community is no longer the village of medieval times but the global audience of the information era, it becomes exponentially more difficult to protect privacy. The traditionally piecemeal approach of the common law has to many come to appear inadequate.[6] Few could claim that it currently safeguards the citizen in the following respects identified by the then Consultative Assembly (now the Parliamentary Assembly) of the Council of Europe as forming part of any right to privacy: 'avoidance of being placed in a false light, non-revelation of irrelevant and embarrassing facts, unauthorised publication of private photographs, [and] protection from disclosure of information given or received by the individual confidentially'.[7]

8.179   The baleful inadequacies of the existing regime were revealed most starkly in the notorious case of *Kaye v Robertson*.[8] The actor, Gordon Kaye, was ill in

---

1   Hansard HL, vol 582, cols 1229–1230, 3 November 1997.
2   *The Impact of the Human Rights Bill on English Law* edited by BS Markesinis (Clarendon Press, Oxford, 1999), p 13.
3   *Rights Brought Home* (see fn 6 on p 7), para 1.11.
4   Although it has been argued that s 85 of the Copyright Designs and Patents Act 1988 was the first form of statutory protection for privacy in this country, albeit that it is framed as a moral right against the unauthorised use of commissioned photographs.
5   Delivering the Goodman Lecture on 22 May 1996 entitled 'Mind your own Business'.
6   A useful summary was provided by Balcombe LJ in *Derbyshire County Council v Times Newspapers Ltd* [1992] 3 All ER 65, and his comments were approved by Lord Keith in the House of Lords in the same case. As to the Derbyshire case generally, see **8.111**.
7   Van Dijk and van Hoof (see fn 6 pn p 45), p 489. Additional elements identified by the Nordic Conference of Jurists on the Right to Respect for Privacy in 1967 included the use of a person's name, identity or photograph without consent.
8   [1991] FSR 62. Consider also the press coverage of the tracing and exposure of Mary Bell, the convicted child killer, whose daughter was a Ward of Court (see *Re X (A Minor) (Wardship: Injunction)* [1984] 1 WLR 1422).

hospital and under sedation after brain surgery when a journalist and photographer from *The Sunday Sport*, posing as doctors, sought to interview him and take pictures. They were thrown out, but proceeded to publish what their newspaper described as a 'great old-fashioned scoop'. Much to the chagrin of the judges (including Bingham LJ (as he then was)) before whom the case came, Mr Kaye was left without any remedy in English law in circumstances where he would likely have succeeded in France or Germany. Arguments for an injunction based on libel, passing off, malicious falsehood and trespass[1] all failed, although the publisher was prevented by court order from suggesting that the actor had consented to its activities. What Mr Kaye had needed above all else was a right to sue for breach of his privacy but, as noted by Lord Justice Leggatt, such a cause of action 'has so long been disregarded here that it can be recognised now only by the legislature'.

8.180   The decision was subsequently criticised by Lord Lester,[2] who believed that Art 8 could have been adduced in a creative way, as could the common-law right of privacy, to which Lord Keith had alluded in *Spycatcher*.[3] Lord Bingham has also since doubted whether the decision in *Kaye* was right.[4] An odd feature of the case was that no-one in it referred to the decision in *Morris v Beardmore*,[5] where three members of the House of Lords had suggested that there was such a thing as a local right to privacy.[6]

8.181   *Kaye* is not the only outrageous example in this area. In *R v Brentwood Borough Council, ex parte Peck*,[7] the facts were that the Council had sold parts of its CCTV footage[8] to a production company, which had proceeded to broadcast some of the material on television. Certain frames showed the unsuccessful attempt of the applicant (who was identifiable) to cut his wrists. The court found that the Council had not acted irrationally, having as it did the right to release CCTV material to the media in hope of assisting the prevention of crime.[9]

---

1   Trespass, like nuisance, requires an interest in land which Mr Kaye, as a visitor to the hospital, did not have.

2   'English judges as law makers' [1993] PL 269 at 284–5.

3   For the Spycatcher case generally, see **8.98** et seq.

4   See his article 'Should there be a law to protect rights of personal privacy?' [1996] EHRLR at 456–457).

5   [1981] AC 446 at 461. Indeed, Sir Brian Neill has referred to Lord Denning's confident assertion in the House of Lords (Hansard HL, vol 229, col 638 in 1961), relying on the decision in *Prince Albert v Strange* (1848) 2 De G & Sm 652, that English judges would intervene to protect an infringement of privacy. See his chapter 'Privacy: A Challenge for the Next Century' in B Markesinis (ed) *Protecting Privacy* (Clarendon Press, 1999), p 2.

6   See also in this area *Michael Barrymore v News Group Newspapers Ltd* [1997] FSR 600 and *Stephens v Avery* [1998] 2 All ER 477, cases in which injunctions were granted to restrain the unapproved disclosure of information about private relationships.

7   [1998] EMLR 697.

8   It has been suggested that the average person may be filmed up to 300 times per day.

9   Consider also the notorious video cassette *Caught in the Act!*, comprising a compilation of CCTV material sold by security firms which the Home Office conceded it was powerless to stop. Only a copyright claim by Carlton Television led to a withdrawal of the cassette from sale. In *California First Amendment Coalition v Calderon* (1997) 956 F Supp 883, a federal district judge upheld what was said to be the public's First Amendment right to witness the execution of death-row prisoners.

8.182   Whether or not it is right that privacy has traditionally assumed such social significance that it has not needed to be protected,[1] senior members of the British judiciary plainly came to the view some years ago that the jurisprudential deficit that existed was no longer tolerable. In the case of *R v Khan*, for example,[2] Lord Nicholls mentioned 'the widespread concern at the apparent failure of the law to give individuals a reasonable degree of protection from unwarranted intrusions in many situations', before posing 'the important question whether the present, piecemeal protection of privacy has now developed to the extent that a more comprehensive principle can be seen to exist'.

8.183   It was against this background that, in the words of Sir Stephen Sedley, certain of the judges therefore picked up the ball and ran with it 'regardless of whether or not written rules gave [them] the right to do so'.[3]

8.184   This has been achieved incrementally and by the adoption and attenuation of existing causes of action such as trespass, nuisance, defamation, breach of copyright, breach of confidence (buttressed by data protection legislation)[4] and the Protection from Harassment Act 1987. These coincidentally track, to some extent, the limitations in Art 10(2) of the European Convention.[5]

8.185   Certain by-now celebrated comments in the case of *Hellewell v Chief Constable of South Yorkshire*[6] show this law-making technique in action. There, Laws J (as he then was) said that:

> 'If someone with a telephoto lens were to take from a distance and with no authority a picture of another engaged in some private act, his subsequent disclosure of the photograph would, in my judgment, as surely amount to a breach of confidence as if he had found or stolen a letter or diary in which the act was recounted and proceeded to publish it. In such a case, the law should protect what might reasonably be called right to privacy, although the name accorded to the action would be breach of confidence.'

8.186   This creative reliance upon an extended breach of confidence argument was seen in a later case where an interim injunction was granted to restrain the publishers of *The Sun* from further reproducing stills of a photo-shoot for an Oasis album-cover. The photographer had managed to evade elaborate security and Lloyd J found that 'the circumstances were such . . . that any reasonable man in the shoes of [the photographer] would have realised on reasonable grounds he was obtaining the information, that is to say the view of the scene, in confidence, at

---

1   See E Barendt's 'Privacy as a Constitutional Right of Value' in *Privacy and Loyalty* edited by P Birks (Clarendon Press, 1997) and D Feldman's chapter in the same volume 'Privacy-Related Rights and their Social Value'.
2   [1997] AC 558 at 582–583.
3   In his chapter 'Governments, Constitutions and Judges' in G Richardson and H Genn *Administrative Law and Government Action* (Clarendon Press, 1994).
4   As to which see also **7.51** et seq.
5   See **8.80** et seq.
6   [1995] 1 WLR 804. It has been suggested that a *Hellewell*-type argument would have been deployed in the case involving the photographs of Princess Diana exercising in a gymnasium, but the action was settled before trial.

least to the extent that he was obliged by that confidentiality not to photograph the scene'.[1]

8.187   It would therefore be wrong to characterise the existing state of the law as wholly deficient to protect privacy, for it is not. Of course, a danger has been in artificially straining existing common-law remedies to unintended ends and, at one point, Lord Irvine, when Opposition spokesman, felt moved to criticise what might 'sound to ordinary people like a judicial threat to legislation'.[2]

8.188   Nor does such flexible judicial law-making make it straightforward to predict the impact of the Act in this area, few cases involving press intrusion having reached the European Court, perhaps because they are in effect filtered out by the national courts of those numerous Member States which have had privacy statutes for some time, of which France is perhaps the most prominent example.

8.189   The different approaches here and abroad were pointed up in the case of John Sweeney. Sweeney was a BBC journalist, who had been refused permission to visit Brecqhou, the home in the Channel Islands of the prominent businessmen Sir David and Sir Frederick Barclay, but who landed nevertheless for the purposes of a television broadcast. The Broadcasting Standards Commission, which has, it should be noted, a (limited) statutory remit in privacy matters, concluded that this was an 'unwarranted infringement of privacy', although the regulator determined (and the High Court later agreed) that it had no jurisdiction to intervene in advance of transmission. The Barclays were, however, quite separately able to invoke French privacy laws as regards an article written by Sweeney for *The Observer*.

8.190   The breadth of French privacy law was again underscored in the case of Claude Gobler, former personal physician to the late President Mitterand, who admitted that for years he told lies about Mitterand's health, during which period Mitterand secured a second term in office, despite having told voters that he would be 'transparent' as regards his well-being. Gobler is reportedly petitioning the Strasbourg Court after Mitterand's family obtained an injunction against him for breach of privilege and medical confidentiality. He received a suspended prison sentence and was fined in the face of his lawyer's reliance on a public interest defence and the fact that privacy was being asserted on behalf of a dead man.[3] In the face of the best attempts of some British judges to fashion, prior to the introduction of the Act, a skein of privacy protection it is plain therefore that, compared to France at least, the jurisprudence in the UK has a long way to go before it can be said to amount to a privacy regime. What, however, of Strasbourg law? As appears below, its protection of privacy from press intrusion is nowhere near as robust as the media in the UK may have suggested.

---

1   *Creation Records Ltd v News Group Newspapers Ltd* [1997] EMLR 444. It is a moot point as to whether that case would be decided differently under the Act to the extent that the relevant photograph was already in the public domain, albeit formatted differently. Would court interference to prevent its further reproduction be proportionate and necessary?
2   Hansard HL, vol 572, col 1259, 5 June 1996.
3   See, for example, *The Independent*, 5 December 1999. The Duchess of York was awarded damages by a French newspaper which published photographs of her topless in the South of France. She had no remedy in the UK.

8.191   On the contrary, although the importance of personal autonomy generally was emphasised in *Niemietz*,[1] the European Court has, quite outwith any concerns about the inter-relationship of Art 8 and Art 10, placed limits upon the extent to which the private citizen can lawfully seek relief from media attention. For example, the case of *Winer v United Kingdom*[2] arose out of English defamation proceedings which had been settled, broadly on terms favourable to Mr Winer. He complained at Strasbourg about the absence of a remedy available to him for the publication of statements which, although true, infringed his privacy. The European Commission held that there was no obligation upon the British State to provide relief additional to the right to sue for defamation, *not least when to do so might infringe the European Convention right to freedom of expression*. The European Commission acknowledged that the then existing English tort of breach of confidence was too inchoate, but on balance determined that Mr Winer was adequately protected by local libel law. If *Winer* is any guide, it not apparent why certain media interests should have suggested that the domestication of the European Convention held such terrors for them. It has already been noted that the higher protection afforded political speech at Strasbourg has the effect that the more an individual puts his private life into the public domain (and particularly the world of politics), the more his claim to respect for his private life is reduced.[3] Many would not quibble with that. What is more surprising is the unsympathetic approach of the Strasbourg institutions to the privacy claims of those who are *not* politicians.

8.192   In the case of *Earl Spencer v United Kingdom*,[4] the European Commission held that applications by Earl Spencer and his then wife were inadmissible. The two had complained about the absence of a domestic privacy law following tabloid reports regarding Lady Spencer's medical treatment for alcoholism and an eating disorder. An unauthorised photograph had been taken from a public road of her walking in the grounds of a sanatorium. The Spencers sued one-time friends (who they believed had tipped off the media) for breach of confidence, and these claims were later compromised.

8.193   The Spencers argued at Strasbourg that the UK was under a positive obligation to guarantee their Art 8 rights. The absence of a local privacy law meant that they had no effective remedy under Art 13 and that Art 8 was violated. In response to this the European Commission held that the Spencers first should have proceeded with an action against the relevant parts of the local media for breach of confidence rather than go to Strasbourg direct and that, as such, they had not exhausted their domestic remedies. The European Commission was invited by the British Government to look at the status of domestic law since *Winer*. When it did, it reached the conclusion that the Spencers had failed to show that a breach of confidence action against the press would have been ineffective. It was for the national courts of the UK, through the common law, to 'develop existing rights by way of interpretation'. The European Commission agreed with the

---

1   See **7.20** et seq.
2   (1986) 48 DR 154. The European Court has on the whole avoided deciding whether Art 8 gives rise to a reputational right. In *Winer* the Commission looked at the state of the then existing English libel law in the context of Mr Winer's Art 8 application, but did not address this wider point. See also **8.148**.
3   See *Bruggemann and Scheuten v Germany* (1981) 3 EHRR 244.
4   (1998) 25 EHRR 105.

British Government that the law on breach of confidence here had developed since *Winer* where, unlike in the case of the Spencers, failure first to pursue a confidence claim locally had *not* been regarded as a procedural failure.

8.194   The Spencers therefore lost, but their advisors at least had the comfort of knowing that the European Commission believed that the absence of an actionable remedy in such circumstances could show a lack of respect for the applicants' private lives. The problem here is that, as the European Court has itself pointed out, the notion of 'respect' is not clear-cut and its ingredients will vary considerably from case to case. Traditionally, it is yet another area in which Contracting States enjoy a wide margin of appreciation in determining the steps to be taken to ensure compliance with the European Convention, giving due regard to national needs and resources.[1]

8.195   *Spencer* is on the other hand to be contrasted with *Neves v Portugal*,[2] in which a magazine publisher alleged a violation of his Art 10 rights where he was sentenced to 15 months in jail, fined and ordered to pay damages for the reproduction of intimate photographs of a businessman. The European Commission was clear that the punishment was not only proportionate but also necessary to protect the businessman's privacy. Set against that, in the case of *News Verlags GmbH and CokG v Austria*,[3] the European Court held that the publication of photographs of a suspected neo-Nazi letter-bomber was not a breach of the suspect's privacy on the basis that he was a long-standing extremist and was charged with offences going to the core of a democratic society. On the contrary, the injunction granted by a court in Vienna restraining the use of the photographs was an Art 10 violation because it was not necessary in a democratic society.

8.196   One case which conceivably would have been decided differently if the Act had been in force is *Bernstein v Sky Views Ltd*,[4] where a householder failed in an action for trespass where aerial photographs had been taken of his home without permission. Such a case is of some current relevance in circumstances where it has been reported that for £18 it will soon be possible to download from the Internet a photograph of anywhere in Britain.[5]

8.197   Aerial photography of one's home is more than merely trivial. However, is it serious enough to engage the European Convention when some years ago, Lord Bingham said he was clear that a domestic privacy regime 'should strike only at significant infringements, such as would cause substantial distress to an ordinary phlegmatic person'?[6]

8.198   The limited number of Strasbourg authorities in this area shows that, although the cases do not all point one way, the notion that the European Convention is ritually used to curb press invasions of privacy is wide of the mark. Consider the European Court decision in *Friedl* in this context.[7] In that case, the Strasbourg judges held (by 14:9) that the taking of photographs in a *public* street would not generally be an Art 8 violation, saying that:

---

1   *Neves v Portugal* Appl 20683/92.
2   See fn 1 above.
3   Appl 31457/96.
4   [1978] QB 479.
5   See *The Sunday Times*, 5 March 2000.
6   In a speech to the Association of Liberal Democrat Lawyers.
7   *Friedl v Austria* (1996) 21 EHRR 83.

'... the reason why the taking of photographs and the retention of the photographs were not regarded as [an] interference could be said to be mainly that, when the photographs were taken, the applicant was in a public place where anyone is in principle free to take photographs and where the taking of photographs can, in most circumstances, be considered a trivial act which must be tolerated by others, although some persons may indeed consider it unpleasant that someone else should take their photograph.'

THE GOVERNMENT'S DEAL WITH THE MEDIA

8.199   The experience of British newspapers at Strasbourg could scarcely be described as entirely unhappy, which no doubt prompted Lord Lester during the Parliamentary debates on the Human Rights Bill to criticise 'misguided public pressure from the press for a media immunity ... in relation to the protection of personal privacy'. In particular, he objected to an article in which Lord Wakeham, Chairman of the Press Complaints Commission, had suggested that the Human Rights Bill could, once enacted, become a 'villain's charter'.[1]

8.200   However, Lord Lester and Lord Wakeham at least agreed that the Press Complaints Commission should be given enhanced powers. Failing that, Lord Lester predicted that courts in the UK would go down the same road as in the USA, where free expression was accorded primacy, but where there were federal and State laws guaranteeing personal privacy.

8.201   In a significant contribution (again on the very first day of substantive discussion of the Human Rights Bill), the then Lord Chief Justice, Lord Bingham,[2] suggested that it was 'hard' to see how Art 8's guarantee could pose 'a threat to responsible organs of the press or the broadcasting media' (although his reference to the need for those organs to exercise responsibility will have escaped no-one's attention). Equally, he found it 'hard to see why this country – alone among European nations – should fail to reconcile [the European Convention's] competing principles in an acceptable manner'.[3]

8.202   A complicating factor that emerged early in this context (as in others) was uncertainty attaching to the reach of the Human Rights Bill. Granted that the BBC, funded by the licence-payer, would be very likely to be a public authority in the terms envisaged by the draftsman. What, however, about the independent television companies? Did the Human Rights Bill, as feared Lord Kingsland, create a conflict between 'publicly and privately provided television services'?[4] Lord Donaldson thought that there could be no difference between the BBC and the ITV companies and assumed that all were public authorities.[5]

8.203   Lord Williams, for the Government, thought that there was 'no difficulty' in this area. Channel 4 'might well' be a public authority, but private

---

1   Hansard HL, vol 582, col 1241, 3 November 1997.
2   At one time apparently a night lawyer for *The Daily Mirror*: see *Media Lawyer* (edited by T Welsh) Issue no 24 (November/December 1999) at p 19.
3   Hansard HL, vol 582, cols 1246–1247, 3 November 1997. Lord Bingham's involvement in the privacy debate has been substantial, indeed one of his most significant speeches on the subject was given only several days before his appointment as Lord Chief Justice was announced.
4   Hansard HL, vol 582, col 1238, 3 November 1997.
5   Hansard HL, vol 582, col 1293, 3 November 1997.

television stations might well not be. More specifically, he said that the Government's belief was that a newspaper would not be a public authority, in response to which Mr Edward Leigh MP complained some time later in the House of Commons that this would ensure that 'the Murdoch newspaper empire may be considered a private body while a small local parish church will be considered a public body because it conducts marriages'.[1]

8.204   Some further elaboration on the status of the BBC came from the Home Secretary, who suggested that 'the BBC is plainly performing a public function, and the House has long accepted that it should be the subject of much greater regulation than the press'. In fact, the Act leaves the BBC in an invidious position. The Government may be clear that it is a public authority as far as the Act is concerned, but the Strasbourg institutions were unable to resolve the issue when it came before them once before[2] and so far have reached no view as to whether the BBC can petition Strasbourg as an applicant.[3]

8.205   A significant proportion of the programmes now shown on British television are made by independent production companies. Suppose that one such company makes a programme which appears to involve an invasion of privacy. Is the European Convention engaged if the programme is sold to the BBC but not if it is sold to Granada? Some will say that that is indeed the result, as that is what Parliament intended. If so, it is likely to lead to significantly different editorial emphases across the broadcasting spectrum which is surely not desirable. It is to be hoped that judges would not stand idly by in that event, particularly if reminded of the positive obligations placed upon States to guarantee the European Convention rights of all their citizens.

8.206   How (this definitional issue regarding public authorities aside) did the Government envisage that the legislation would bear upon the supervision of the media in the UK? Perhaps not surprisingly, most of the focus in Parliament was on the position of Fleet Street. As to the press, Lord Williams said that 'the proper way forward [was] to have effective self-regulation by the [Press Complaints Commission]; that is to say, effective in terms of public support ... If there [was] effective self-regulation there [would] be no blemishes ...'.

8.207   Unintentionally or not, just after he had sought to quieten media concern, Lord Williams added: 'This law will introduce into our regime the necessity for those who intrude to understand that now legal sanctions may be *hurled* against them when formerly they were not'[4] (emphasis added).

8.208   All of this begged a fundamental question. If the Press Complaints Commission was the regulatory way forward, would it have public authority status or not? The Lord Chancellor had originally considered it would not, but changed his mind after seeing an Opinion of David Pannick QC that had been procured by the Press Complaints Commission and he confirmed this in a letter to Lord Wakeham, for whom the problem was methodology, not principle. The Human Rights Bill would, in his view, lead to the development of a common law of privacy

---

1   Hansard HC, vol 306, col 794, 16 February 1998.
2   *Hilton v United Kingdom* (1981) 3 EHRR 104.
3   *BBC v United Kingdom* (1996) 21 EHRR 97. See also **3.139** et seq as regards the ability generally of public authorities to be claimants under the Act and/or the European Convention.
4   Hansard HL, vol 582, cols 1310–1311, 3 November 1997.

when all were agreed that self-regulation was the way ahead. Only the rich would be able to enforce privacy rights in the local courts. Injunctions would lie against newspaper publishers and, even though the press would have a public interest defence, cases might take years to resolve and it would mean nothing more or less than 'an end to journalism'. Therefore, he wanted to take the Press Complaints Commission entirely out of the scope of the Human Rights Bill, even though, as Lord Lester reminded the House, that would also take out of the Bill a number of other media regulators including the Independent Television Commission, the Radio Authority, the Video Recordings Authority, the Broadcasting Standards Commission and even the Advertising Standards Authority.

8.209 The Lord Chancellor sought to persuade Lord Wakeham to turn matters to the advantage of the Press Complaints Commission. In debate, he quoted extensively from his letter to Lord Wakeham:

> '... the opportunity is that the Courts [will] look to the [Press Complaints Commission] as the pre-eminently appropriate public authority to deliver effective self-regulation, clearly balancing Article 8 and 10. The courts, therefore, would only themselves intervene if self-regulation did not adequately secure compliance with the Convention.'[1]

8.210 He then went on to remind Lord Wakeham of the underlying reality:

> '... the judges are ... poised regardless of incorporation of the Convention to develop the common law in their own independent judicial sphere. What I say positively is that it will be a better law if the judges develop it after incorporation ...
>
> Parliament, if invited to do so, might well pass a tougher statute outlawing invasion of privacy than the judges are likely to develop.'[2]

8.211 Far better, according to Lord Irvine, that 'the courts be able to adapt and develop the common law by relying on existing domestic principles in the laws of trespass, nuisance, copyright, confidence and the like, to fashion a common law right to privacy.'[3] The media's 'salvation' was in its own hands and could be achieved by establishing a 'beefed-up' Press Complaints Commission which could become 'the general arbitrator' in privacy cases, provided 'it did its job strongly and well'.[4]

8.212 Lord Lester remained adamant that the Government should not capitulate in the face of what he considered to be a misguided campaign by the media:

> '... it sticks in my throat when I read in newspapers that they are entitled to have the benefit of Art 10 ... but they must be somehow immunised against the effects of Art 8. There is no other democracy in the world where that is the case. It is not the case in the United States, the land of the First Amendment, where there is privacy protection and a protection of free speech. It is not the case in Australia, Canada, New Zealand, India or the rest of Europe. I know of no country which has in its legal system what has been advocated by some sections of the press ... I know of no case in Strasbourg which has ever threatened the freedom of the press.'[5]

---

1 Hansard HL, vol 583, col 784, 24 November 1997.
2 Ibid.
3 Hansard HL, vol 583, col 785, 24 November 1997.
4 Hansard HL, vol 583, cols 785–786, 24 November 1997.
5 Hansard HL, vol 585, cols 835–836, 5 February 1998.

8.213   The Government had time to consider how best to proceed in the face of such entrenched views by the time the Human Rights Bill first reached the House of Commons on 16 February 1998, when the Home Secretary, Mr Straw, immediately reiterated Government support for 'the freedom of the media' (an alarmingly broad concept, much broader than any generally-held notion of free expression, but which it is assumed he regarded as co-terminous) and its 'opposition to a statutory law of privacy'.[1] It soon became apparent, however, that Lord Lester's complaints of a week earlier in the upper House may have been borne of an awareness that discussions had been taking place between Government and representatives of the media, as Mr Straw immediately proceeded to announce that the Government proposed to table amendments to the Human Rights Bill in order 'to enhance press freedom in a wider way than would arise simply from the incorporation of the Convention into our domestic law'.[2] These amendments would in fact become s 12 of the Act, a provision which has no counterpart in the body of the European Convention itself and which is the only part of the legislation to address the question of a hierarchy of rights or what Lord Hoffman has called the conflict 'between good and good'.[3]

SECTION 12

8.214   Section 12 comes into play 'if a court is considering whether to grant any relief, which, if granted, might affect the exercise of the Convention right to freedom of expression'.[4] Not just that, but the Court must have 'particular regard' for Art 10,[5] a blanket stricture that is not easy to reconcile with the incremental approach adopted at Strasbourg.

8.215   Mr Straw said that he had tabled the amendments with the aim of enhancing press freedom. In fact, he intended that they apply also to 'broadcasters or anyone whose right to freedom of expression might be affected'[6] and it did not matter that a public authority was not involved in the relevant litigation. In other words, s 12 may be relevant in libel proceedings between two private individuals or between a company and a newspaper, further confirmation that the Act is intended to have more than merely vertical effect.[7]

8.216   Section 12(2) descends into specifics, stating that no relief should be awarded against a respondent who is not represented in court unless the applicant has taken all practicable steps to notify the respondent or there are compelling reasons not to do so.[8] Although this obligation to give notice arguably reflects what already happens in practice, Mr Straw thought that this 'would virtually rule out pre-publication injunctions being granted ex parte' – a long-standing concern of the media – and he envisaged that the occasions on which it would not be possible to give notice of an intention to go to court would be rare, indeed the only

---

1   Hansard HC, vol 306, col 776, 16 February 1998.
2   Hansard HC, vol 315, col 536, 2 July 1998.
3   'Human Rights and the House of Lords' [1999] 62 MLR 159 at 165.
4   See Appendix 1.
5   Section 12(4), see Appendix 1.
6   Hansard HC, vol 315, col 536, 2 July 1998.
7   Section 12(1), see Appendix 1.
8   See Appendix 1.

example the Home Secretary could think of was where national security issues were involved. If this is so, s 12(2) of the Act appears to consign applications for prior restraints *without notice* to legal history. Not that the legislation is aimed solely at without notice applications. Prior restraints generally are discouraged. Thus, s 12(3) establishes that no order is to be made by the court which would stop publication before trial, unless the judge is satisfied that the applicant is likely to establish at trial that publication should not be allowed.[1] The Home Secretary said that this provision was designed to ensure that the barrier that previously stood in the way of so-called Friday-night injunctions was made even higher in hope of protecting the media 'from what [amounted] to legal or legalised intimidation'.[2]

8.217 Here too, it is not apparent that this materially affects the legal position (ie before the Act) regarding defamation actions. It was already notoriously difficult to obtain an interim injunction to restrain a libel.[3] Section 12(3) would appear, however, effectively to import this degree of difficulty into other areas of law. In particular, the existing ability of applicants to obtain a judicial gag to restrain a breach of confidence is narrowed by s 12(3) very substantially. In such cases, applicants will now need to do more than establish on long-standing common-law principles that there is 'a serious question to be tried'.[4] The practical difficulty conceivably to be faced by judges is that interlocutory applications for restraints (however rare) will take longer to hear as applicants file (perhaps lengthy) evidence dealing with the merits (which would not previously have been necessary in most instances), specifically to show why they are 'likely' to prevail at trial.

8.218 The provisions of s 12 do not apply where the relevant relief or remedy is sought in the context of criminal proceedings.[5] This is potentially a significant exception, for it means that, insofar as s 12 extends media freedom,[6] that freedom cannot be invoked when challenging, for example, the reporting restrictions imposed in a high-profile criminal trial.

8.219 Justifying the exemption, the Home Secretary said that he was worried about judges in criminal cases being required to look at privacy codes,[7] but he neglected to mention that those judges will be obliged to have regard to the European Convention in any event.

8.220 Section 12(4) was the Government's attempt to reconcile the domestication of Art 8 with the media's perceived anxiety that a free-standing privacy law would develop. For that reason, it may be appropriate to reproduce it in full:

'(4) The court must have particular regard to the importance of the Convention right to freedom of expression and, where the proceedings relate to material which the

---

1   See Appendix 1.
2   Hansard HC, vol 315, col 537, 2 July 1998.
3   See *Bonnard v Perryman* [1891] 2 Ch 269.
4   See *American Cyanamid v Ethicon* [1975] AC 396.
5   Section 12(5), see Appendix 1.
6   Many commentators are not persuaded that s 12 has changed anything. Edward Garnier MP, a practitioner at the libel bar, thought it 'simply a gesture' to placate the press barons (Hansard HC, vol 315, col 553, 2 July 1998). More generally, he thought that 'the contest between freedom of expression and the right not to have one's privacy invaded had been overtaken by a little too much emotion and perhaps not enough reason' (Hansard HC, vol 314, col 426, 17 June 1998).
7   Hansard HC, vol 315, col 540, 2 July 1998.

respondent claims, or which appears to the court, to be journalistic, literary or artistic material (or to conduct connected with such material), to –
(a)   the extent to which –
    (i)   the material has, or is about to, become available to the public; or
    (ii) it is, or would be, in the public interest for the material to be published;
(b)   any relevant privacy code'.

8.221   On first review, this appears startling. Although the European Convention deliberately does not make Art 10 an absolute right, British judges are henceforth to have *particular* regard for it. This strong direction does not, however, displace Art 8 as regard – particular or otherwise – does not mean adherence.

8.222   Also startling is the deferment to the media in allowing it to determine whether material is 'journalistic, literary or artistic'. Absent rank bad faith on the part of the media, it is not apparent that a judge can go behind the media's claim that the material it holds (the subject of litigation, it should be remembered) falls within the protection afforded by s 12. The media can also decide for itself whether it is engaged in 'conduct' connected with journalistic material, which might mean conduct preparatory to a story of which not one word has yet been written. In short, it may be expected that the media, which had through the Press Complaints Commission negotiated with the Government the exception for 'journalistic, literary or artistic material' in the data protection legislation,[1] will seek to construe this phrase as broadly as possible.

8.223   Section 12(4) effectively extends the public interest defence to a breach of confidence claim to all other actions (including libel actions) involving 'journalistic' material, while also extending into other areas the 'public domain' defence at common law to a breach of confidence. Mr Straw said that the reference to material 'about to' become available to the public was to reflect the reality that stories may be published abroad or over the Internet, possibilities that in his view a court could not sensibly ignore.[2] This does of course hark back to the *Spycatcher* case[3] and it should not be difficult for media respondents to establish in many instances that a particular story is already in the public domain.

8.224   It is a moot point as to whether so-called 'pyjama' injunctions of the type obtained without notice on behalf of the Home Secretary to restrain the *Sunday Telegraph*'s story[4] about the Report of the Inquiry into the death of Stephen Lawrence days before it was due to be published will be seen again, s 12 having come into force. As *The Guardian* wrote at the time,[5] 'the ironies multiply', as it was the Home Secretary who sought that injunction and the Home Secretary who introduced the amendment that later became s 12.

8.225   Gerald Kaufman MP[6] sought an assurance in the wake of the Home Secretary's announcement that, if Art 8 could not trump Art 10, the reverse should also be the case, while Douglas Hogg MP[7] queried whether the amendments would pass muster at Strasbourg and might themselves be a derogation from the

1   Section 32 of the Data Protection Act 1998.
2   See Hansard HC, vol 315, col 539, 2 July 1998.
3   See **8.98** et seq.
4   See, for example, *The Daily Telegraph*, 23 February 1999 and **8.109**.
5   23 February 1999.
6   Hansard HC, vol 306, col 777, 16 February 1998.
7   Hansard HC, vol 306, col 778, 16 February 1998.

European Convention. The Home Secretary was clear that the amendments would be European Convention-proof, although it is interesting that he admitted that he had asked himself that same question.[1]

THE APPLICATION OF PRIVACY CODES

8.226   Section 12(4)(b) obliges local courts to have regard to any *relevant* privacy code. This means that a failure to adhere to such a code may be a factor to be taken into account when a judge is determining whether to grant an interim injunction. It is unclear what is added by the relevance qualification in this context. Is this meant to screen out reference by advocates to, for example, US privacy statutes or French laws which do, at least, closely follow the Strasbourg authorities? It is clear that it is not just the Press Complaints Commission's Code that is relevant in this context,[2] but also (suggested the Home Secretary)[3] that of the Broadcasting Standards Commission, the Independent Television Commission, the BBC's Producers' Guidelines and any written framework operated by a media company.

8.227   Media lawyers are familiar with these codes and an egregious breach of a code may, already be relevant to the assessment of damages in a libel action. The

---

1   Professor Ross Cranston MP, the distinguished academic lawyer (and now a Government Minister) made some interesting observations about the scope of Arts 8 and 10 towards the end of the Parliamentary debates on the Human Rights Bill. He said: 'Freedom of speech ... encapsulates our vision of democracy; it is essential to our democratic procedures. If we do not have freedom of speech, we cannot operate our democratic mechanisms. The protection of private life involves a range of concerns – our rights, for example, to individual autonomy, to reputation, to the protection of private reputation and to an individual name'. He described how the German courts distinguish 'between speech that informs, and speech that is mere gossip ... [and] also distinguish between speech motivated by greed, and speech that is in the public interest'. He went on: 'The German courts have considered the motives of the publisher, whether the speaker will benefit financially, the extent to which the information has been disseminated, the breadth of the restriction that the plaintiff wishes to impose on the defendant's speech rights and the methods used': Hansard HC, vol 315, cols 557–559, 2 July 1998.

2   The Commission's Code imports wholesale Art 8(1) of the European Convention. In its amended form (1 December 1999) it provides at para 3 as follows:
    '*Privacy*
    (i)   Everyone is entitled to respect for his or her private and family life, home, health and correspondence. A publication will be expected to justify intrusions into any individual's private life without consent.
    (ii)   The use of long-lens photography to take pictures of people in private places without their consent is unacceptable. Note – Private places are public or private property where there is a reasonable expectation of privacy.'
    There is then, unsurprisingly perhaps, a public interest carve-out as follows:
    '1. The public interest includes:
    (i)   Detecting or exposing crime or a serious misdemeanour
    (ii)   Protecting public health and safety
    (iii)   Preventing the public from being misled by some statement or action of an individual or organisation.
    2. In any case where the public interest is invoked, the Press Complaints Commission will require a full explanation by the editor demonstrating how the public interest was served.
    3. In cases involving children editors must demonstrate an exceptional public interest to over-ride the normal paramount interests of the child'.

3   Hansard HC, vol 315, col 538, 2 July 1998.

codes are, however, given an increased status by the Act (whether the media intended it or not) and it will be more important than ever before for newspapers and broadcasters to ensure that their staff comply with them, not least because the scheme of s 12 would appear to encourage a judge to grant an injunction to stop a story which is not code-compliant unless, that is, there is a public interest justification. Equally (and this is better news for the media) there may be judges who conclude that the ability of citizens to make a Press Complaints Commission complaint alleging infringement of privacy is enough to secure Art 8's guarantee of respect for private lives.

8.228   Section 12 does nothing to disturb the position that, for whatever reason, broadcasters remain subject to additional constraints, with a 'clear injunction' placed upon the BBC to ensure balanced coverage, whereas no such restriction is placed upon a newspaper unless prescribed by the Press Complaints Commission.[1]

8.229   The problem for claimants, numbers of whom are corporates, is that the Press Complaints Commission has no power to fine or seek a court order to secure a complainant's right to a private life.[2] Nor, indeed, can it require the publication of its adjudications (although it should be pointed out that compliance is habitual). As Sir David Calcutt noted in his report some years ago (and the Commission's Code has changed somewhat since Sir David's comments were made), the Commission was set up by the press industry and there is a perception that it is 'over-favourable' to it.[3] In view of its limited powers, the question arises whether this particular public authority (assuming, of course, it is one) is able to act in a way that is compatible with the Convention, at least as regards Arts 8 and 13 (but perhaps also Art 10), for if the Commission cannot punish by fine, can it secure respect for private lives?

8.230   The relevant industry codes are not themselves decisive in any event. Judges are not to be bound by them and this will most obviously be the case where judges conclude that the codes fall short of guaranteeing the domesticated Convention rights. Insofar, however, as the Act encourages a more intensive form of judicial review,[4] agencies such as the Commission may come under more rigorous judicial scrutiny if they appear not effectively to be securing Art 8's rights. What, for example, about a 'sting' operation of the type used by the tabloids which does not involve any breach of privacy (in terms of intrusion)? Will attempts be made, relying upon Art 8, to establish a French-style image right and a US-style right of publicity? Will the tabloid 'faking' of photographs, a technique examined by the House of Lords in *Charleston v News Group Newspapers*[5] be outlawed? These are all matters conceivably made more readily justiciable by the legislation.

1   Said the Home Secretary (Hansard HC, vol 314, col 411, 17 June 1998).
2   There is, therefore, nothing which would appear to justify the claim of the media commentator Roy Greenslade that the Commission will become a police officer more than a social worker (*The Guardian*, 7 June 1999) or of the Rt Hon Brian Mawhinney MP that it would become the 'Prior Censorship Commission' (Hansard HC, vol 306, col 794, 16 February 1998).
3   *Review of Press Self-Regulation* (1993) Cm 2135 at xi.
4   As to which see **6.289** et seq.
5   [1995] 2 AC 65.

8.231   The power of the statutory media regulators to fine will also be watched closely in the coming period. Will they any longer be able to mete out punishments of the kind imposed in December 1998 on Central Independent Television (a fine of £2m)?[1]

8.232   There are indications that the long-running idea of a single media regulator with over-arching responsibility for the convergent media has come to the surface again.[2] If established, a single regulator with a single privacy code might make for a more coherent approach to the development of a privacy standard. As the responsible Cabinet Minister, the Rt Hon Chris Smith MP, said, the traditional broadcasting approach of 'one to many' and the telecommunications approach of 'one to one' are fast disappearing in an age when news can be downloaded on a mobile telephone. A super-regulator would eliminate any tendency in the future to engage in forum-shopping among regulators (as the implications of the Act become more apparent) and might help to mitigate any perceived unfairness deriving from the fact that, for example, Channel 4 is (very probably) a public authority whereas Channel 5 (probably) is not.

8.233   Little so far suggests that s 12 specifically and the Act generally need hold great terrors for the media on privacy grounds, particularly if the early cases in which damages are awarded set a low tariff.[3] It is not even apparent how a privacy claim against a defendant which is not a public authority would be pleaded. The assertion without more that a newspaper had breached the claimant's privacy in violation of Art 8 of the European Convention would be liable to be struck out. It is conceivable that an appeal would lie from that decision at which it could be argued that the court had an obligation under s 3 of the Act to read a privacy right into the common law – but that gives rise to the difficulty that s 3 provides explicitly for an interpretative obligation in relation to statutes only. An alternative might be to frame a future privacy claim under an existing statute, such as the Data Protection Act 1998, before inviting the court to construe the 1998 Act in conformity with the European Convention. The problem there is that the factual matrix may not engage data protection law at all. In any event, the Data Protection Act 1998 has a wide carve-out for journalistic activity.[4]

8.234   The other alternative is, of course, for the court to be reminded of its own public authority obligations under s 6 and invited to provide the remedy. Last of all, a judicial review could be sought of the actions of, for example, the Press Complaints Commission. In circumstances where newspapers are in the coming years most unlikely to be designated public authorities and where the application of privacy rights in claims between private parties remains unclear, this may be the most popular route forward.

---

1   For programming code breaches in the programme, 'The Connection', made by Carlton UK Productions. See also **6.285** et seq.
2   *Wall Street Journal,* 2 December 1999.
3   As regards damages at Strasbourg and under the Act, see **2.66** et seq and **3.156** et seq.
4   Section 32 of the Data Protection Act 1998.

THE ACT'S IMPACT UPON THE CORPORATE RIGHT TO PRIVACY AND TO A REPUTATION

8.235   The case of *R v Broadcasting Standards Commission, ex parte BBC*[1] arose out of a BBC Watchdog programme based on film surreptitiously shot on Dixons' premises (although the secret filming was not in fact broadcast). Forbes J at first instance concluded that privacy, as referred to in the Broadcasting Act 1996[2] and when construed in conformity with Art 8 of the European Convention, was a right available to natural persons only and not to corporates.[3] He found this to be consonant not just with the Strasbourg authorities but also with US law.[4] His Lordship went further in finding that filming by subterfuge was not necessarily wrong unless it took place in circumstances of 'seclusion' – a feature absent in this instance because the filming was merely picking up what customers entering Dixons' premises could see for themselves.

8.236   Thankfully for the corporate interest, the decision of Forbes J was overturned by the Court of Appeal,[5] which held that the issue of privacy in the Broadcasting Act 1996 was not the same as that in Art 8. Lord Woolf pointed out that the notion of privacy as established in the European Convention was not the same as that used in the Broadcasting Act. He added:

> 'While the intrusions into the privacy of an individual which are possible are no doubt more extensive than the infringements of privacy which are possible in the case of a company, a company does have activities of a private nature which need protection from unwarranted intrusion. It would be a departure from proper standards if, for example, the BBC without any justification attempted to listen clandestinely to the activities of a board meeting. The same would be true of secret filming of the board meeting. The individual members of the board would no doubt have grounds for complaint, but so would the board and thus the company as a whole. The company has correspondence which it could justifiably regard as private and the broadcasting of the contents of that correspondence would be an intrusion on its privacy. It could not possibly be said that to hold such actions an intrusion of privacy conflicts with the ECHR.'

8.237   For the present, then, the corporate right to privacy, at least in the broadcasting context, has survived. The media will, however, undoubtedly wish to return to this subject, not least because Lord Mustill, whilst agreeing that the instant appeal should be allowed, did not believe that companies had a right to privacy. For him, privacy denoted:

> '... the personal "space" in which the individual is free to be itself [sic] and also the carapace, or shell, or umbrella, or whatever other metaphor is preferred, which protects that space from intrusion. An infringement of privacy is an affront to the

---

1   [1999] EMLR 858. The Court of Appeal judgment can be found at [2000] EMLR 587.
2   By virtue of s 107(1) of the Broadcasting Act 1996, the Broadcasting Standards Commission is required to draw up a code investigating matters such as 'unwarranted infringement of privacy'.
3   Even though s 111(1) of the Broadcasting Act 1996 refers to fairness complaints brought by an individual 'or by a body of persons, whether incorporated or not'.
4   A company's right to privacy is, however, recognised as part of Art 13 of the German Basic Law. Similarly in Canada: see s 8 of the Canadian Charter and the case of *Hunter v Southam* [1984] 2 SCR 145.
5   The general interest attaching to the issue of privacy was such that Liberty was permitted to make written submissions on the subject.

personality, which is damaged both by the violation and by the demonstration that the personal space is not inviolate ...'

He did 'not see how it [ie privacy] can apply to an impersonal corporate body, which has no sensitivities to wound, and no selfhood to protect ... A company can have secrets, can have things which should be kept confidential, but I see this as different from the essentially human and personal concept of privacy'. This issue is plainly very far from being closed.

8.238 What about the reputational rights of corporates? As has been seen, it is already probably the position that a body that is judicially reviewable in English law cannot maintain an action for defamation[1] and, unsurprisingly, the point has already been made that big business should not be able to bring libel actions[2] which in turn raises considerations under Arts 6 and 14. The argument against corporate libel claims can easily be put. Some multi-national corporations have an authority and influence of a kind historically the preserve of nation States. Their tactical (indeed strategic) use of libel actions to suppress criticism not only has a chilling effect upon freedom of speech but is disproportionate and in violation of any notion of equality of arms. Already there is a European Commission case which is authority for the proposition that a prohibition on group actions for libel is not a breach of Art 6,[3] so there is no certainty that the argument will fail.

THE ACT'S IMPACT UPON MEDIA LITIGATION GENERALLY

The scope of the evidence in judicial review applications affecting the media

8.239 In the past, evidence of the so-called 'chilling' effect of any restriction on freedom of expression risked falling outside the scope of a judicial review application. However, such material may now become highly relevant, all of which conceivably creates a difficulty for a court not readily able to carry out a fact-finding exercise.[4]

8.240 In the House of Lords case of *Simms and O'Brien*,[5] evidence was filed about the role of investigative journalists in helping to root out miscarriages of justice in 60 cases. There was also sworn testimony from Gareth Peirce, the criminal lawyer, who explained the importance of the media in overturning wrongful convictions. This may be a precursor of things to come.

---

1   *Derbyshire County Council v Times Newspapers Limited* [1993] AC 534. See **8.111** et seq.
2   Dave Morris and Helen Steel, the defendants in the notorious 314-day *McLibel* case brought by McDonalds, have petitioned the European Court on this point. See D Pannick's article 'Exposing the flaws in Britain's libel laws' *The Times*, 20 April 1999.
3   Appl 11862/85 (a UK case about gypsies).
4   I Leigh and L Lustgarten 'Human Rights Act 1998' [1999] CLJ 509 at p 525. This topic is more fully examined at **6.308**.
5   *R v Secretary of State for the Home Department, ex parte Simms and O'Brien* [1999] 3 All ER 400.

Active case management

8.241   Judges will need to take care that directions calling for the curbing of evidence, as for example, in the *Grobbelaar* case,[1] do not provoke a challenge based on Art 6.

Pre-action discovery in media cases

8.242   This is available in Part 31 of the CPR and it will be interesting to see the extent to which the wholesale coming into force of the Act has an impact upon the making of US-style pre-trial inquiries into the way in which press stories are compiled.

The Act's impact on reporting techniques

8.243   Related to this issue is the fact that, if journalists here want to avail themselves of the wider form of common-law privilege contemplated by the House of Lords in *Reynolds*[2] they (and, in overhead terms, the directors for whom they work) must ensure that their articles are researched and corroborated as never before. The great fact-checking departments of US newspapers may not yet have been reproduced on this side of the Atlantic, but if the media wants to enjoy a broad measure of *Reynolds*-type protection, they may have to be.

The Act and the Internet

8.244   In the wake of the settlement in the case of *Godfrey v Demon Internet*[3] and the decision of the US Supreme Court in the case of *Lunney v Prodigy*,[4] it is not clear to what extent the so-called Internet defence in section 1 of the Defamation Act 1996 will be improved by reliance on Art 10. Reports suggest that the liability of ISPs is to be tested at Strasbourg,[5] the argument being that they should only be liable if they know their transmissions are defamatory and untrue or are recklessly indifferent as to whether they are true or not. The likelihood must be that the issue will be ventilated in the High Court when the Act is fully in force long before the reported complaint gets to Strasbourg.

Article 10 and intellectual property

8.245   James Dyson, the inventor, is reportedly claiming an Art 10 violation as part of his objection to the renewal fees charged by the UK Patent Office.[6] He is apparently arguing that the renewal system militates in favour of large companies and that a patent is no different from the work of an author or artist.

8.246   Just as imaginatively, it has been argued that a ban on grey-market importation of, for example, a well-known brand of jeans may infringe Art 10, the

---

1   *Grobbelaar v News Group Newspapers Limited* (1999) *The Times*, 12 August. See generally Chapter 6.
2   See **8.115** et seq.
3   [1999] 4 All ER 342. See also *The Independent*, 4 April 2000.
4   *Lunney v Prodigy Services Co* 120 SC 1832.
5   *Outcast*, a gay magazine, is making the complaint after its website was apparently closed down by its service provider. See *The Times*, 18 April 2000.
6   *The Observer*, 11 July 1999.

rationale being that grey-market importers have a free expression right to tell potential purchasers that the grey-market product is as good as that sold by the manufacturer itself, only cheaper.[1] The notion that the right to freedom of expression could be used as a defence against a claim of trade mark infringement appears difficult, however, in light of Art 10(2)'s express approval of limitations placed on freedom of expression where the 'rights of others' are concerned. A more fruitful line of inquiry might instead be to object to the power to award 'additional' damages for copyright infringement under s 97(2) of the Copyright Designs and Patents Act 1988. Does this not have a disproportionate and chilling effect?

The Act and popular protest

8.247   In *Steel v United Kingdom*,[2] a breach of Arts 5 and 10 was established where the applicants were arrested after handing out leaflets outside a conference centre. The actions of the police were adjudged at Strasbourg to be disproportionate in circumstances where the protests were peaceful and there was no threat of disorder. This decision and the future development of the law of trespassory assembly in relation to Art 11 of the European Convention will be issues of importance to companies engaged in medical research or the study of genetically modified organisms. How will the Protection from Harassment Act 1997 be interpreted in this context? More generally, what impact does the Act have upon the limits of acceptable criticism of those in authority? In *Janowski v Poland*[3] a journalist had been convicted for remonstrating with a policeman. The European Commission found out this was not an Art 10 violation on the basis that public servants such as the policeman were entitled to carry out their duties with public confidence. They might, therefore, need to be protected from abusive attacks.[4] Such facts might seem of limited local application, but it has recently been reported that a website was shut down following a letter of complaint from the Lord Chancellor's Department where the website was being used to criticise named members of the judiciary.[5]

The scope of the 'reply to attack' privilege

8.248   The European Commission found that the publisher of *The Times* had not been subjected to an Art 10 breach when the High Court found that *The Times* had no qualified privilege when publishing an apology in a defamation action.[6] The press here will no doubt move to test this again.

---

1   See K Garnett QC 'A classic clash of competing rights' *The Times*, 11 January 2000.

2   (1999) 28 EHRR 663. See also, in this context, the decision of the European Commission in the case of *Hashman and Harrup v United Kingdom* Appl 25594/94: binding over hunt saboteurs to be of good behaviour where there had been no violence and no breach of the peace was too imprecise to be a sanction prescribed by law. It left the applicants unclear how they should behave in future. See too the case of *R v Redmond-Bate* (1999) *The Times*, 23 July and **8.249**.

3   (2000) 29 EHRR 705. This decision has been widely criticised. See, for example, A Lester 'Getting Off Lightly' *The Guardian*, 31 May 1999.

4   Prince Hans-Adam of Liechtenstein was recently found to have violated Art 10 by refusing to re-appoint a judge he sacked for disagreeing with him.

5   *The Independent on Sunday*, 7 November 1999.

6   *Times Newspapers Ltd v United Kingdom* (1997) Appl 31811/97, following *Watts v Times Newspapers Limited* [1996] 2 WLR 427.

CONCLUSION

8.249   In a recent case, Sir Stephen Sedley memorably set the scene in the period immediately before the introduction of the Act by saying that 'free speech includes not only the inoffensive but the irritating, the contentious, the eccentric, the heretical, the unwelcome and the provocative, provided it does not provoke violence. Freedom only to speak inoffensively is not worth having'.[1]

8.250   This is, in the end, a moral issue and where there is a clash between European Convention rights of (variously) privacy, reputation, free expression and to a fair trial it will be for the judges to endeavour to determine where society should draw the line, having, as has been seen, borne in mind the nature of the speech, the speaker and his audience, the terms of the speech and the interference with it.

---

1   *R v Redmond-Bate* (1999) *The Times*, 23 July. The Yorkshire police had for a time been arresting preachers adhering to the Faith Ministry (some of whom, it is reported, had been held in custody for up to 3 weeks): see *The Lawyer*, 6 September 1999. Alison Redmond-Bate had refused to stop preaching on the steps of Wakefield Cathedral and was convicted of obstruction. Sedley LJ threw out her conviction.

Chapter 9

THE PROTECTION OF BUSINESS ASSETS

INTRODUCTION

9.1   No right 'brought home' by the Act had more troubled origins than the right to property, the only clear economic guarantee to be found in the European Convention and one of only two rights to invoke the public interest as a justification for State interference.[1] The fear that such a safeguard would, by definition, favour vested private interests particularly and (less obviously perhaps) *laissez-faire* capitalism generally meant that even bare recognition of the principle proved politically contentious[2] and, as a consequence, it was omitted from the Treaty when it first opened for signature.

9.2   As has been seen,[3] the motivation of many of those advocating British incorporation of the European Convention throughout the 1970s and 1980s was the hope that it would lead to enhanced protection from governmental intervention in the property sphere. Such an aspiration gives rise to an obvious difficulty for, as pointed out by Holmes J, 'government could hardly go on if ... values incident to property could not be diminished without paying for every such change'.[4] Resolution of this conflict between the perceived sanctity of personal possessions and the pursuit of the public interest remains an enduring theme of modern democratic debate and the conflict, as seen in the drafting history of the European Convention itself, has often been referred to by the European Court in its determinations.

9.3   When the European Convention was being drafted, the then socialist Governments of the UK and Sweden provided the sternest resistance to its emergence. The creation of such a highly contentious guarantee would, it was feared, inhibit future social planning in a wholly unpredictable way.[5] Fifty years on, it is another Labour Government that, in the UK, has rendered the Protocol's protection more accessible through the medium of the Act.

9.4   Property interests were at least acknowledged, albeit in vague terms, when another multilateral instrument, the UNDR,[6] was adopted. Article 17 of the UNDR provides that 'everyone has the right to own property alone as well as in

---

1   Along with Arts 2(1) and (4) of the Fourth Protocol. See Appendix 2.
2   See **1.29** et seq.
3   See **1.39**.
4   *Pennsylvania Coal v Mahon* (1922) 260 US 293 (1922) as quoted by D Anderson QC in 'Compensation for Interference with Property' [1999] EHRLR 543 at 545.
5   In other Member States, the post-War settlement remains highly relevant in the context of Art 1 of the First Protocol (hereafter referred to as Art 1/1), with many European citizens asserting claims to land and other assets lost during the War or confiscated after it by Soviet Bloc countries. See, for example, *Panikian v Bulgaria* (1997) 24 EHRR CD 63, in which 35 years of continuing occupation was enough to engage Art 1/1, even though the applicant had acquired title from the Communist regime which had seized the land in question. See also *Elisabeta Vasilescu v Romania* (1999) 28 EHRR 241. Former King Constantine of Greece is seeking massive compensation in a complaint to the European Court about the confiscation of royal estates when he was deposed; see the *The Observer*, 15 November 1999.
6   See **1.15** et seq.

association with others' and that 'no-one shall be arbitrarily deprived of his property,' but no analogous provision made its way into the ICCPR or the ICESCR.[1]

9.5   By 1952, a compromise, conceiving of property interests as analogous much more to civil rights than economic entitlements, was reached in the European Convention context and a heavily qualified right to property (not, mark you, expressly termed as such)[2] was adopted in Art 1 of the European Convention's First Protocol. Its text is as follows:

> '*Protection of property*
>
> Every natural or legal person is entitled to the peaceful enjoyment of his possessions. No-one shall be deprived of his possessions except in the public interest and subject to the conditions provided for by law and by the general principles of international law.
>
> The preceding provision shall not, however, in any way impair the right of a state to enforce such laws as it deems necessary to control the use of property in accordance with the general interest or to secure the payment of taxes or other contributions or penalties.'

9.6   By extending its protection to 'every natural or legal person', Art 1/1, unlike other substantive features of the European Convention, explicitly includes within its reach commercial enterprises as well as, for example, majority shareholders[3] and non-corporate bodies such as the Greek Orthodox Church. The latter therefore had standing to complain to Strasbourg when some of its land was expropriated.[4] Companies have not been slow to allege violations of Art 1/1, but they have for the most part been no more successful than individuals for, although this is a guarantee which is much invoked, it is generally invoked in vain, as shall be seen below.

9.7   This is largely because Art 1/1 is predicated upon the basis that an even greater degree of latitude is permitted Contracting States than is conceded to them in Arts 8–11 of the European Convention[5]. In its terms, Art 1/1 permits the 'public' and 'general' interest to be invoked to override rights to property in contrast, for example, to the strict limitations placed upon any measures impinging upon the right to respect for private lives in Art 8, which must be 'necessary' to protect specified interests such as 'national security' and 'public safety'.[6]

9.8   What is more, the European Court has gone out of its way to ensure that the extensive qualifications in Art 1/1 are given a width which leaves governments with ample policy room for manoeuvre. Clements, Mole and Simmons go so far as

---

1   See **1.17**. The right to property has been recognised in EC law as a fundamental right: see *Hauer v Land Rheinland Pfalz* [1980] 3 CMLR 42, in which reference was made to Art 1/1.
2   FG Jacobs and RCA White in *The European Convention on Human Rights* (Clarendon Press, Oxford, 1996) call it 'a property right of sorts' at p 246 and also compare it in structure to Art 2, where the right to life is first enunciated as a general principle before the most extreme interference with that right is identified.
3   See *Yarrow v United Kingdom* (1983) 30 DR 155, where a shareholder action was in fact barred and *Kaplan v United Kingdom* (1982) 4 EHRR 64, where a majority shareholder action was allowed. See also **2.51** et seq.
4   See *Holy Monasteries v Greece* (1994) 20 EHRR 1.
5   As to the analysis of qualified rights generally, see **2.7** et seq and Chapter 5.
6   See Chapter 7.

to suggest that the second paragraph of Art 1/1 'almost amounts to a presumption that some form of control over the enjoyment of possessions is inevitable.'[1] Indeed, the margin of discretion left to national legislatures when implementing social and economic programmes in this area is so broad that there has yet to be a single case in which an initiative pursued by a European Convention State has been found not to be justifiable, at least in principle, *on public interest grounds* within Art 1/1. Thus, for example, the expropriation of land from Greek Orthodox monasteries, for the sole benefit of the Greek Exchequer, was found (in the face, it should be said, of what looked like some frustration on the part of the Strasbourg institutions) to be pursuant to a legitimate aim.[2]

9.9   Where property-related challenges have been successful, they have tended *also* to involve an infraction of the due process guarantee in Art 6(1)[3] for, as Harris, O'Boyle and Warbrick note,[4] the way in which Contracting States *procedurally* interfere with property rights may be relevant in determining whether in *substance* their actions conform to Art 1/1. Procedural infringements apart, however, it will be apparent from what follows that only the most blatant confiscations of property by public authorities have resulted in violations of the European Convention as, for example, when retrospective legislation was passed deliberately to deprive a company of an arbitration award in its favour against a government body.[5]

9.10   There is a further (domestic) reason why Art 1/1 promises more than it delivers for business and that is the evident disinclination of the Blair administration (and, indeed, the whole of the British political elite) any longer to pursue the kind of strategic social and economic legislation which once sparked disputes at Strasbourg involving the UK. Unlike in the past,[6] laws to (re-)nationalise the aircraft and shipbuilding industries or to force landlords to cede property to tenants at reduced prices are unlikely to find their way on to the statute book at Westminster in the foreseeable future and provoke challenges based on Art 1/1.

9.11   For all that, in the future Art 1/1 is likely to prove to be of assistance in many commercially relevant areas. A combination of Art 6(1)'s procedural guarantee and Art 1/1's property safeguards may, for example, necessitate radical changes to current methods of Inland Revenue investigation. Adjudication in the planning and construction fields may need to be modified. Even the substance of primary legislation will not be immune, this Government's proposals to create a ramblers' 'right to roam' having already been criticised as potentially infringing Art 1/1.

9.12   Although Art 1/1 may, in the era after public ownership, therefore have lost some of its resonance, it retains a core principle of value on which companies may still productively be able to rely.

---

1   L Clements, N Mole and A Simmons *European Human Rights: Taking a Case under the Convention* (Sweet & Maxwell, 1999), p 223.
2   *Holy Monasteries v Greece* (see fn 4 on p 298).
3   See Chapter 6.
4   See DJ Harris, M O'Boyle and C Warbrick *Law of the European Convention on Human Rights* (Butterworths, 1995), p 524.
5   *Stran Greek Refineries and Stratis Andreadis v Greece* (1994) 19 EHRR 293, see **9.17**.
6   See **9.43** et seq.

ASSETS COVERED BY ARTICLE 1 OF THE FIRST PROTOCOL

9.13   However contentious in political terms, the right to property has a long-standing pedigree in local law[1] and courts have not been slow to overrule the decisions of central and local government where there has been a perceived interference with that right.[2] In this context, one contribution made by the European Convention has arguably been to expand in Art 1/1 upon the range of interests denoted by the word *possessions*.[3] Although the Article is entitled (pursuant to the Eleventh Protocol)[4] 'Right to Property', it extends far beyond real estate. The French text variously defines possessions more broadly as *biens, propriété* and *usage de biens*, so it is unsurprising that *possessions* has been interpreted to extend beyond the purely corporeal to include, for example, a right to ownership or a right *in rem*.[5] Once again, as seen in relation (for example) to the operation of Art 6,[6] the Strasbourg institutions look for their own autonomous definition and the fact that an interest is not a *possession* in UK law does not mean that it is not a possession capable of protection under not just Art 1/1 but as a civil right under Art 6.

9.14   Interests that have found shelter within Art 1/1 include such disparate matters as:

– patents;[7]
– contractual entitlements;[8]
– fishing rights;[9]
– compulsory insurance schemes;[10]
– shares;[11] and
– judgment debts.[12]

9.15   In the words of Harris, O'Boyle and Warbrick, it is the 'acquired economic value of the individual interest' which is the key.[13]

9.16   Licences, which may after all be the single most valuable asset held by, for example, a broadcaster or an energy utility, can be possessions in European Convention terms. In the case of *Pudas v Sweden*,[14] the European Court suggested that the decisive factor was 'whether the licence can be considered to create for the licence-holder a reasonable and legitimate expectation as to the lasting nature

1   See, for example, *Attorney-General v de Keyser's Hotel* [1920] AC 508.
2   Professor Griffiths, from a perspective on the left, attributes this readiness to intervene to 'the idea that Parliament, in this field, was "interfering" with the common law'. See *The Politics of the Judiciary* 5th edn (Fontana, 1997), at pp 103–104).
3   It is regrettable that the text of Art 1/1 refers both to *possessions* and to *property*, even if both words are treated synonymously.
4   See **2.44** et seq.
5   *Gasus Dosier und Fördertechnik GmbH v The Netherlands* (1995) 20 EHRR 403.
6   See Chapter 6.
7   See *British American Tobacco Company v The Netherlands* (1955) 21 EHRR 409 and *Smith Kline and French Laboratories v The Netherlands* (1990) 66 DR 70.
8   See *Mellacher v Austria* (1997) 23 EHRR 364.
9   *Bauer v Sweden* (1989) 60 DR 128.
10   *Gaygusuz v Austria* (1997) 23 EHRR 364.
11   *Bramelid and Malmström v Sweden* Appl 8588/79 and Appl 8589/79, (1982) 29 DR 64.
12   *Stran Greek Refineries and Stratis Andreadis v Greece* (1994) 19 EHRR 293. Compensation too can be a possession: see *Garrett and Others v Portugal* Appl 29813/96.
13   See fn 4 on p 299.
14   (1988) 10 EHRR 380.

of the licence and as to the possibility to continue [sic] to draw benefits from the exercise of licensed activity'. The status of licences as protected possessions was confirmed and extended by the Strasbourg Court's judgment in the leading case on Art 1/1 of *Tre Traktörer Aktiebolag v Sweden.*[1] There it sufficed that revocation of a restaurant's drinks licence (which gave rise to no legal right in Sweden) had 'adverse effects on the goodwill and value of the restaurant',[2] affecting as it did one of the principal criteria for the running of the business. In other words, a licence is likely to be a possession within Art 1/1 where it creates a legitimate expectation about its durable nature and the ability to benefit from it.[3]

9.17 The evolutive thinking of the European Court as regards the meaning of possessions has been seen in two relatively recent cases. The applicants in *Stran Greek Refineries v Greece*[4] were faced with an unsubtle interference with the judicial process. They had claimed for costs they had incurred and the value of bonds they had deposited under a contract with the then Greek military junta to build an oil refinery, which the newly restored democratic administration terminated. Not only had the applicants made good their claims against the Greek Government in arbitration proceedings, but they had also successfully withstood two legal challenges, as a consequence of which the validity of the arbitration award and the amount due had been confirmed. At this point, retrospective legislation, without any provision for compensation, was passed to deprive the applicants of the fruits of their victories. In a unanimous decision, the European Court found a violation of Art 1/1. Specifically, it held that:

> '... the arbitration award ... conferred on the applicants a right to the sums awarded. Admittedly, that right was revocable, since the award could still be annulled, but the ordinary courts had by then already twice held – at first instance and in the Court of Appeal – that there was no ground for such annulment. Accordingly, in the [European] Court's view, that right constituted a possession.'[5]

9.18 In *Pressos Company Naviera SA v Belgium,*[6] the reasoning in *Stran Greek* was extended to cover claims that had *yet* to proceed to judgment. There a group of 26 applicants had initially sought compensation for damage to their ships. In respect of 23 of the applicants, negligence had been established and/or admitted on behalf of the State-run pilot service. Legislation with 30 years' retrospective effect was then introduced on ostensible public interest grounds to bar claims for damages for marine collisions. The European Court deemed all such claims 'possessions', adding that the effect of the change in the law was to deprive the applicants of their rights. The Strasbourg judges considered the Belgian Government's aims were legitimate but disproportionate for lack of compensation and refused to accept Belgium's objection that no claim had been recognised and determined by a final, dispositive judicial decision. In the view of the European Court, the applicants had claims in tort which came into existence as soon as damage occurred. Such claims were assets. Specifically, they were possessions within the meaning of the first sentence of Art 1/1 and they gave rise

---

1   (1991) 13 **EHRR** 309.
2   At para 53.
3   The implications of this for companies operating under local authority or regulatory licences is examined below at **9.86** et seq.
4   (1995) 19 **EHRR** 293.
5   Ibid.
6   (1996) 21 **EHRR** 301.

to a legitimate expectation on the part of the applicants. In other words, a possession in European Convention terms can be a contingent asset such as a claim for negligence.

9.19   The European Court has, however, sought to distinguish between mere aspirations (such as those of an heir during the lifetime of the testator),[1] falling outside the reach of Art 1/1 and economic interests which are sufficiently established to fall within it[2] and which may, as already noted, be broadly analogous to the civil rights or obligations falling within Art 6(1).[3] In the case of *Ian Edgar (Liverpool) Limited v United Kingdom*,[4] a complaint of an Art 1/1 breach was held to be inadmissible in circumstances where a British firearms distributor argued that the statutory ban on hand-guns introduced in this country in the wake of the Cullen Report into the Dunblane shooting was an interference with the peaceful enjoyment of its possessions and a deprivation. The reasoning at Strasbourg was that loss of future income of this sort fell outside the European Convention's scope. The applicant had no legitimate expectation that it would be able to continue dealing in a particular kind of weapon and it had in any event been statutorily compensated at market value.

9.20   In circumstances where the approach of the Strasbourg judges is resolutely fact-based, as a consequence of which it is generally necessary to eke out the salient principles by way of analogy, the interpretative task facing local courts in this area will be by no means an easy one, and one judge[5] has already found the judgment in the *Pressos Company Naviera* case 'difficult to reconcile' with the approach adopted in the more recent European Court ruling in the *National and Provincial Building Society* case.[6]

9.21   In the latter case, a dispute had arisen as a result of changes to the computation periods for tax on investment profits. Regulations were passed to provide for payments during a transitional period. They were found to be invalid for technical reasons following a successful domestic challenge by the Woolwich Building Society,[7] whose claim in restitution to recover tax paid pursuant to the relevant regulations later led to the repayment of £57m by the Inland Revenue.[8] Other building societies sought to emulate this 'independent and bold' achievement,[9] although their claims, whilst awaiting the ruling in the *Woolwich* case, were not far advanced. Recognising the danger, and in circumstances where the Inland Revenue admitted it had no defence, the Government passed retrospective legislation (not affecting the Woolwich Building Society) in three separate Finance Acts to close off any further challenge. In response, three building societies complained to Strasbourg.

---

1   *Marckx v Belgium* (1979) 2 EHRR 330. See also *Inze v Austria* (1988) 10 EHRR 394.
2   In *Matos e Silva v Portugal* (1996) 24 EHRR 573, the European Court found that rights had been exercised without protest over part of the old royal estate for almost 100 years. The income deriving from the estate was held to be a possession.
3   See **6.33** et seq. See also van Dijk and van Hoof (see fn 6 on p45), p 620.
4   Appl 37683/97, 25 January 2000. In the context of another ban, this time on certain beef products, see *Pinnacle Meats v United Kingdom* Appl 33298/96.
5   See Moses J in *Marks & Spencer Plc v Customs and Excise Commissioners (No 1)* (1999) 1 CMLR 1152.
6   *National and Provincial Building Society and Others v United Kingdom* (1998) 25 EHRR 127.
7   See *R v Inland Revenue Commissioners, ex parte Woolwich Building Society* [1990] 1 WLR 1400.
8   See *Woolwich Equitable Building Society v Inland Revenue Commissioners* [1993] AC 70.
9   *National and Provincial* (see fn 6 above) at para 89.

9.22   The European Court was 'especially mindful of the dangers inherent in the use of retrospective legislation which has the effect of influencing the judicial determination of a dispute to which the State is a party'. Furthermore, although the Strasbourg judges were anxious to express 'no concluded view' on the issue, they remarked that, absent a final judgment before a UK court, the applicants enjoyed 'at best a precarious basis' on which to assert that they had rights amounting to possessions. The retrospective intervention involved no element of double taxation and, in any event, the local law of restitution, at the time when the applicant building societies issued proceedings in the UK (and prior to the *Woolwich* ruling) was 'not in fact favourable to the outcome of [the applicants'] cases'. They had no final, enforceable judgment in their favour and the question of whether they had established that their claims constituted possessions was 'bound up with their complaints that they were unjustifiably deprived of those possessions'.[1] The building societies had hoped to secure a 'windfall profit', according to the Strasbourg judges, in exploiting a technical defect to avoid a tax payment. Although they were hoping to rely on the principle established in the Woolwich Building Society's test case, they had no legitimate expectation that Parliament here would not act to uphold its intention as expressed in the original fiscal regulations, an aim the European Court considered to be legitimate.[2]

9.23   Legitimate expectation in the context of Art 1/1 was also considered by the Court of Appeal in the recent case of *Heil v Rankin*[3] as a result of which certain levels of award in personal injury cases were reviewed upwards. The defendants and their insurers had argued that any changes operating retrospectively would not only be a deprivation of property but also a process breach under Art 6, but in a robust judgment the Court of Appeal said that any deprivation was in the public interest, on the basis that the aim was fair compensation for tort victims, that the European Convention did not inhibit the incremental development of the common law and that no legitimate expectation (as to the level of awards) prevented the retrospective effect of a court order. The case underlines the inventive potential of Art 1/1. It also underscores the difficulties that lie ahead for corporates seeking to rely on it.

9.24   For a *possession* to engage the right to property safeguarded in the European Convention, it needs to have some economic or pecuniary value which has been prejudicially affected as a consequence of the matter in dispute. The applicants in *Van Marle v The Netherlands*[4] had challenged a refusal to register them as accountants. Article 1/1 could, in the European Court's view, properly be invoked by the applicants on account of the effect that refusal of registration would have upon their business. The European Court found, despite the fact that Dutch law recognised no right of goodwill, that:

> '... the right relied upon by the applicants [might] be likened to the right of property embodied in Article 1 [of the First Protocol]; by dint of their own work, the applicants had built up a clientele; this had in many respects the nature of a private right and constituted an asset.'[5]

---

1   *National and Provincial* (see fn 6 on p 302) at para 168.
2   Ibid, at para 171.
3   [2000] 2 WLR 1173.
4   (1986) 8 EHRR 483.
5   Ibid, at para 41.

9.25 The applicants in *Van Marle* not only had a possession susceptible of European Convention protection, but that possession had been the subject of an unlawful interference. It is to the ingredients of interference that attention is now turned.

THE INTERFERENCES PROHIBITED BY ARTICLE 1 OF THE FIRST PROTOCOL

9.26 In the landmark case of *Sporrong and Lönnroth*,[1] the European Court construed Art 1/1 as comprising 'three distinct rules'. In the later case of *AGOSI*,[2] the *Sporrong* rules were described as follows:

> 'The first rule, set out in the first sentence of the first paragraph [of Art 1/1], is of a general nature and enunciates the principle of peaceful enjoyment of property; the second rule, contained in the second sentence of the first paragraph, covers deprivation of possessions and subjects it to certain conditions; the third rule, stated in the second paragraph, recognises that the Contracting States are entitled, amongst other things, to control the use of property in accordance with the general interest. However, the three rules are not "distinct" in the sense of being unconnected: the second and third rules are concerned with particular instances of interference with the right to peaceful enjoyment of property and should therefore be construed in the light of the general principle enunciated in the first rule.'[3]

9.27 The three *Sporrong* rules now need to be examined more closely.

9.28 The first rule is that Art 1/1 offers general protection against any interference with the peaceful enjoyment of possessions. Enjoyment in this context means more than having and holding. It imports a right to dispose of, destroy, sell, lease, lend or use private possessions generally, although there is as yet no suggestion that Art 1/1 (or indeed Art 8) confers a right to a home, unless the applicant is already in possession of it. Nor does it go so far as to mean a right to enjoyment in terms of environmental amenity. Similarly, although judicial determinations of private property rights may obviously engage Art 6(1), they generally do not engage Art 1/1.[4] A private tenant whose lease is forfeited by court order will, absent some form of horizontal application of the Act, therefore not be able to rely upon Art 1/1.[5]

9.29 For an interference with enjoyment to be established, it is necessary to show that the economic or market value of the asset in question has decreased.[6] The fact that, for example, aircraft noise renders enjoyment of a piece of land 'less pleasant' is not sufficient to engage Art 1/1,[7] although it may conceivably have implications under Art 8. On the other hand, the burning of property by the

---

1   *Sporrong and Lönnroth v Sweden* (1983) 5 EHRR 35 at para 61. See **9.119** for a detailed
      treatment of this case in the context of planning law.
2   *Allegemeine Gold-und Silberscheideanstalt v United Kingdom* (1987) 9 EHRR 1.
3   Ibid, at para 48.
4   See, for example, *Mairitsch v Austria* (1989) 11 EHRR 46.
5   See *Di Palma v United Kingdom* (1998) 10 EHRR 149 and **9.228**.
6   Therefore, minor infractions are probably not covered: see *Langborger v Sweden* (1990) 12
      EHRR 416, a case about a disputed 0.3% commission.
7   *Powell and Rayner v United Kingdom* (1990) 12 EHRR 355.

Turkish authorities in the course of a campaign against Kurdish groups obviously affected property values.[1]

9.30   Article 1/1 identifies two specific types of interference, to be construed in light of the first rule in *Sporrong*, which may conceivably engage the Convention:

– deprivation of possessions (the second rule); and
– control of the use of property (the third rule).

9.31   Whilst the European Court in *Sporrong* might have asserted that the three rules that underpin Art 1/1 are distinct, if not unconnected, it is not always clear from the Strasbourg jurisprudence against which parts of the Article (or against which of the three rules) particular conduct is to be tested. On occasions, indeed, a violation of Art 1/1 has been found without an infraction of any particular rule being identified. This is consistent with a tendency on the part of the European Court 'to assimilate all interferences with the peaceful enjoyment of possessions under the single principle of fair balance as set out in *Sporrong*,'[2] so any judicial imprecision at Strasbourg may not matter too much to the extent that the same benchmark is increasingly applied to all three *Sporrong* rules. Thus in *Papamichalopoulos v Greece*[3] the European Commission split 4:3 on the question whether a breach of the first rule (enjoyment) or the second rule (deprivation) had occurred. The European Court by contrast made a general finding that Art 1/1 had been violated.[4]

9.32   However broad-brush the judicial approach to Art 1/1 at Strasbourg, the fact remains that there will be instances where a claimant in future domestic litigation can identify an interference with his general enjoyment of possessions within the first *Sporrong* rule without there being a violation of the second or third rules in *Sporrong* in terms of an unjustifiable deprivation of property or unlawful control of the use of property. This was, as will been seen later, the approach adopted by the European Court in the *Sporrong* case itself.[5]

9.33   'Deprivation' (the second *Sporrong* rule) has been defined restrictively so that formal extinction of the rights associated with an asset must generally be shown, even though the European Court has on occasions been ready to 'look behind the appearances and investigate the realities of the situation complained of'.[6] A recent example of deprivation in the traditional sense was the enactment of a presumption that disputed land belonged to the Greek State, a measure which was found, without more, to amount to a deprivation in the *Holy Monasteries* case.[7]

9.34   The European Court, exceptionally, has been prepared to treat activities short of full legal expropriation as *de facto* deprivations in European Convention

---

1   *Selcuk and Asker v Turkey* (1998) 26 EHRR 477.
2   Harris, O'Boyle and Warbrick (fn 4 on p 299) at p 525.
3   See *Papamichalopoulos v Greece* (1995) 21 EHRR 439 and see **9.34**.
4   As discussed in Harris, O'Boyle and Warbrick (fn 4 on p 299), p 524.
5   See **9.119** et seq.
6   See *Sporrong* (fn 1 on p 304). In terms of looking at the reality of the situation, one may wonder what the Strasbourg institutions would make of the argument, apparently made for some years by the British Museum, that passing a law requiring the return by the Museum of the Elgin Marbles to Greece would be a confiscation within Art 1/1. See *The Economist*, 18 March 2000.
7   *Holy Monasteries v Greece* (see fn 4 on p 298).

terms. In *Papamichalopoulos v Greece*,[1] for example, a contested statutory provision passed by the Greek junta, whilst not effecting legal transfer of title, meant that the applicants were no longer in a position to sell or make any other use of their land. An Art 1/1 violation was established. In circumstances where the applicants' land had been commandeered by the military authorities without compensation, the Court found that:

> 'The loss of all ability to dispose of the land in issue, taken together with the failure of the attempts made so far to remedy the situation complained of, entailed sufficiently serious consequences for the [land of the] applicants de facto to have been expropriated in a manner incompatible with their right to the peaceful enjoyment of their possessions.'

9.35   Such cases are more usually treated as examples of control of use within the third *Sporrong* rule *even where there has been a wholesale seizure*,[2] so long as the 'taking' was purportedly effected in pursuit of the objectives contemplated in the second paragraph of Art 1/1 (ie acting in the general interest or to secure the payment of taxes or other contributions or penalties). To most eyes, a seizure of possessions makes for a deprivation and it is odd then that the Strasbourg institutions should often have euphemistically regarded seizures as examples of control of use. This was starkly shown in the case of *AGOSI*.[3] There the applicants had sold Krugerrands to buyers who defaulted on payment and who attempted to smuggle the coins into the UK. The bullion was seized by HM Customs and Excise and declared forfeit, even though the sellers had had the original transaction declared void by a German court. The European Court (disagreeing with the European Commission) found that this was a legitimate exercise in *control*, rather than *deprivation*. The fact that seizure was *intended* to enforce an import prohibition was crucial for classification purposes.

9.36   Another important forfeiture case is that some years ago involving Air Canada,[4] where HM Customs and Excise impounded an Air Canada jet on which a large consignment of cannabis had been found. The aircraft was not released until the airline paid £50,000, an administrative action the European Court (albeit on a split decision) considered a proportionate control of use in light of (a) the importance legitimately to be attached to combating trafficking in drugs and (b) several previous warnings to the airline about inadequate security. The Strasbourg institutions found that the British customs authorities had not sought to transfer ownership, but merely restricted the use of the aircraft. In terms of the facts of that case, this may be broadly supportable, but what about the decision in *AGOSI*, where the coins in question were not handed back or (more relevantly for the corporate sector) what about the revocation of a commercial licence, such as, for example, one for the extraction of gravel? Can this reasonably be described as control of use within Art 1/1 (rather than a deprivation) where it is done on environmental grounds?[5]

9.37   In light of these cases, it might be suggested that it does not matter under which head of Art 1/1 an interference is classified. Any such suggestion would,

---

1   (1993) 16 EHRR 440.
2   Such as of obscene materials, See, for example, *Handyside v United Kingdom* (1976) 1 EHRR 737 in which copies of the Little Red Schoolbook were seized and destroyed.
3   See fn 2 on p 304.
4   *Air Canada v United Kingdom* (1995) 20 EHRR 150.
5   See *Fredin v Sweden* (1991) 13 EHRR 784.

however, be misconceived and would be, in effect, to disregard the provisions of Art 1/1 itself which include additional requirements to be satisfied if a deprivation of possessions or a control of their use is to be justified. Even though the European Court's decisions have, as has been seen, tended to dilute these requirements, it is far from inconceivable that local judges will seek to bestow some substantive content upon them, thereby perhaps limiting the range of legitimate interference with property.[1]

MAKING USE OF THE GENERAL PRINCIPLES

9.38   The European Court has accorded a wide margin of appreciation to national governments in matters of property, whether the goals ostensibly pursued be in relation to town planning policy (as in the *Sporrong* case),[2] leasehold enfranchisement as an exercise in 'social justice' (as in the *James* case)[3] or even procedural tax law (as in the *National and Provincial* case).[4] Therefore, a challenge to the substance of the underlying policy aim enunciated by a national authority will rarely prove effective.

9.39   Article 1/1 is a heavily qualified right and, as with the other qualified rights in the European Convention (most obviously in terms of this book, Arts 8[5] and 10[6]), the Strasbourg institutions analyse complaints in a broadly similar way. Thus, as regards an alleged deprivation of property, they will review:

–   the existence of any public interest justification;
–   the proportionality of the steps taken in relation to the purported public interest justification; and
–   the legality of the steps taken.

9.40   Equally, it is important to note that, in addition to being heavily qualified, the second paragraph of Art 1/1 is permissibly worded. It asserts that the right to property shall not 'in any way impair' a State when *enforcing* laws (by inference abridging the property right) 'it deems necesssary'. Necessity in this particular context does not mean the existence of the 'pressing social need' called for when limiting free expression under Art 10.[7] Indeed, originally, the European Court declined to review the necessity criterion in the property context. At the outset, the Strasbourg judges suggested that Contracting States were the 'sole judges of the "necessity" of an interference' and that the European Court 'must restrict itself to supervising the lawfulness and the purpose of a restriction in question'.[8]

9.41   Subsequently, the European Court has proved ready to examine necessity,[9] even though national authorities continue to enjoy a wide discretion, as confirmed in the *Gasus* case.[10] In that case, the applicant company had supplied a

---

1   See *Padfield v MAFF* [1968] 2 WLR 924 for judicial readiness to imply limits to (even) an openly worded statutory power.
2   See fn 1 p 304 and **9.119** et seq.
3   *Taines v United Kingdom* (1986) 8 EHRR 123. See also **9.50** et seq.
4   See fn 6 on p 302.
5   See Chapter 7.
6   See Chapter 8.
7   See **5.29** et seq.
8   *Handyside v United Kingdom* (see fn 1 on p 306).
9   As in the *AGOSI* case (see fn 2 on p 306 and **9.35**).
10   *Gasus Dosier und Fördertechnik GmbH v The Netherlands* (1995) 20 EHRR 403.

cement mixer against payments by instalments. It retained title by way of security. The purchaser went bankrupt and the Dutch revenue authorities seized the mixer, as they were entitled to do under local law. The applicant argued that it was neither responsible for, nor could it have been aware of, the purchaser's tax default. Nonetheless, the European Court accorded the Netherlands power to 'pass whatever fiscal laws they considered desirable, provided always that measures in this field did not amount to arbitrary confiscation'. The fact that commercial creditors were aware of the element of risk involved in an instalment contract, and could provide for this by, for example, demanding payment in advance, did not render the Dutch Revenue's seizure and sale 'devoid of reasonable foundation'. The suppliers still had the right of judicial review and enjoyed a degree of priority over other creditors.[1]

9.42   While there may be some tactical benefit to be derived from showing that an infringement of *enjoyment* (in terms of the first rule in *Sporrong*) also meets the threshold required for an unnecessary *control of use* (in terms of the second rule in *Sporrong*) a much greater advantage is to be derived by bringing a claim based on *deprivation* (in terms of the third rule in *Sporrong*), in circumstances where the proportionality test is applied more strictly in cases of deprivation, where ownership can be lost, unlike in instances of control of use.[2] Not just that, 'a right to compensation is not inherent'[3] in control of use cases, a further reason for attempting to establish that a deprivation has taken place. The point is moot as to whether domestic judges will henceforth adopt the same approach as the European Court.

9.43   In *Lithgow v United Kingdom*[4] the applicants were owners of aircraft and shipping companies that were nationalised by virtue of the Aircraft and Shipbuilding Industries Act 1977, in keeping with a pledge made in the Labour Party's 1974 General Election manifesto. In order to value the companies, a 'price reference period' was selected, with compensation paid at a 'vesting date' 3 years after the price reference period. A decline in the relevant businesses combined with the effects of inflation over the intervening period led the British Government itself to admit that, by 1980, 'the terms of compensation imposed by the 1977 Act were grossly unfair to some of the [nationalised] companies.'[5]

9.44   The Strasbourg judges found that the policy goal pursued (ie nationalisation) had been debated extensively in Parliament and was one as regards which 'opinions within a democratic society may reasonably differ widely'[6] (although the applicants in fact had not contested the principle before the European Court). However disputatious, that did not make the goal, without more, a European Convention violation. As far as the means of implementing the goal were

---

1   In a powerful dissenting judgment, three judges considered that to 'seize goods which unquestionably belong to [a] third party is not indispensable to tax authorities' and was not proportionate.

2   In light of the European Court's reluctance to recognise seizure, forfeit and destruction as de facto forms of deprivation, this distinction has been described as 'untidy and unsatisfactory': see Anderson in *Compensation for interference with property* (1999) EHRLR 543 at 553.

3   *Baner v Sweden* Appl 1176/85, (1989) 60 DR 128.

4   *Lithgow v United Kingdom* (1986) 8 EHRR 329.

5   House of Commons Statement of the Secretary of State for Trade and Industry, 7 May 1980. See *Lithgow* (fn 5 above) at p 335.

6   Ibid, at p 373.

concerned, the European Court confined itself to examining whether a uniform basis for compensation was 'in principle unacceptable'. It noted, for example, that a common approach had administrative benefits. It saw that interest had been applied at base rate and concluded that, even in the absence of any provision to adjust for inflation, the mechanical steps for achieving nationalisation were such as 'the United Kingdom was reasonably entitled to take within its margin of appreciation'.[1]

9.45 Had hindsight no application in this context? As to that, even though the European Court was willing to consider the actual effects suffered by the applicants, the fact that the compensation paid had been shown over time to be inadequate still did not constitute a European Convention violation. The Strasbourg judges considered that the fact that the compensation scheme could have been justified, in principle, in 1977 was sufficient to ensure Convention-compatibility given the obvious need for forward planning inherent in legislation of the sort in dispute.

9.46 Whilst the compensation terms in the *Lithgow* case were deemed inherently 'material to the assessment whether a fair balance [had] been struck', the European Court regarded deprivation as special on the basis that 'under the legal systems of Contracting States the taking of property in the public interest without payment of compensation is justified only in exceptional circumstances'.

9.47 Businesses in the UK for many years have enjoyed protection from the confiscation of their property without compensation by the State, at least as regards the operation of secondary legislation.[2] In the context of tax law, this has meant that, if an 'objectionable rule was in secondary legislation rather than primary legislation then one could bring review proceedings upon the useful, if slender, fiction that Parliament would never authorise the Inland Revenue to act so unreasonably.'[3]

9.48 Confiscation without compensation is, it might be assumed, no longer part of any mainstream political agenda in advanced European societies and has not been so for some time. Although the concept tends to conjure up images connected with extra-parliamentary activity and revolutionary policies, it can in fact be put into practice in a variety of different ways. Thus, Greece was in default in introducing and passing legislation whereby it was presumed that disputed monastic property was in fact owned by the State without any provision for the payment of compensation whatsoever.[4] Less clear, however, is the extent to which the Act will improve a business's position where compensation is paid but is inadequate. In *Lithgow* the European Court said that:

> 'Compensation must normally be reasonably related to the value of the property taken, but Protocol 1, Article 1, does not guarantee full compensation in all cases.

---

1   Ibid, at p 381. However, Art 1/1 was violated in a case where compensation was not paid for 17 months and inflation was 70% per annum: *Akkus v Turkey* Appl 19263/92, 9 July 1997.

2   *AG v de Keyser's Royal Hotel Ltd* [1920] AC 508. The European Court, however, has agreed that compensation need not be paid where land is being unlawfully occupied in breach of planning permission: see *Ryder v United Kingdom* (1992) 11 EHRR 80.

3   See N Jordan's article 'The Impact of the Human Rights Act upon Compliance: The Taxation Viewpoint' in *The Human Rights Act and the Criminal Justice and Regulatory Process* (Hart Publishing, 1999), p 116.

4   *Holy Monasteries v Greece* (1994) 20 EHRR 1. When monastic lands had earlier been expropriated (in 1952), one-third of the market value of the land had been paid as compensation.

Legitimate objectives of public interest may justify reimbursement at less than the full market value; the nature of the property taken and the circumstances of the taking may be taken into account in holding the balance between public and private interests ... the Court will respect the national legislature's judgment in this respect unless manifestly without reasonable foundation.'

9.49   Therefore, provided there is a reasonable relationship between the amount paid and the market value of the property taken, compensation at less than the normal going rate or without, for example, allowing for inflation, may not give rise to a violation of the European Convention. What is more, the lack of proportionality in terms of the nexus between value and price must be profound before any system of compensation will fall outside the margin of appreciation.[1] Thus, the claim by the applicants in *Lithgow* that they should receive parity of compensation, based on market value, in common with those whose land was compulsorily purchased in the UK failed, not least because the practice internationally was adjudged to be decisive.

9.50   In the case of *James v United Kingdom*,[2] trustees of the estate of the second Duke of Westminster challenged the operation of the Leasehold Reform Act 1967, which had the effect of enabling tenants to purchase their homes in central London for sums substantially below their true market value. The landlords argued that there was no equivalent law in any other European Convention country and that the statute in question benefited individual tenants rather than the public at large. The public interest requirement in Art 1/1 would never be satisfied, it was argued, when simply transferring property from one private interest to another, because it would not benefit the community generally. Some of the beneficiaries, especially those who had just before acquired short-term leases, stood to receive a windfall enrichment[3] where they had, as yet, contributed little to the cost of building maintenance and where, following payment of the site value only, their interest had nonetheless been upgraded to full freehold status.

9.51   The Strasbourg judges were in little doubt about the deference they needed to pay Contracting States in this context. As they put it, 'the notion of "public interest" is *necessarily* extensive' (emphasis added). They continued:

'... the decision to erect laws expropriating property will commonly involve considerations of political, economic and social issues on which opinion within a democratic society may reasonably differ widely. The Court, finding that the margin of appreciation available to the legislature in implementing social and economic policies should be a wide one, will respect the legislature's judgment as to what is "in the public interest" unless that judgment be manifestly without reasonable foundation.'

9.52   In such circumstances, the European Court unanimously concluded that the remedying of perceived social injustices was a legitimate function of democratic legislatures.[4] The absence of a *direct* benefit to the community at large

1   See, for example, *Katikaridis v Greece* [1997] EHRLR 198.
2   See fn 3 on p 207.
3   The applicants adduced evidence suggesting that some of the beneficiaries, living in Belgravia, were not exactly destitute (with one buying the lease for £9,000 and reselling within a year for £116,000).
4   As such, rent control laws have been held to be a 'legitimate aim of social policy': see *Kilbourn v United Kingdom* (1986) 8 EHRR 81. See also *Spadea and Scalabrino v Italy* (1995) 21 EHRR 482, where the mass suspension of eviction orders to avert a homelessness crisis was held to be legitimate.

following a taking of property 'in pursuance of legitimate social, economic or other policies' did not render the legislature's judgment 'manifestly without reasonable foundation'.[1] Neither did the uniform or compulsory nature of the transfer scheme render the system 'irrational or inappropriate'. It was sufficient that 'uncertainty, litigation, expense and delay' could thus be avoided,[2] the European Court rejecting the trustees' argument that each enfranchisement agreement had to be tested against the European Convention.

9.53   The abandonment across Europe of public ownership as an instrument of State policy has served to reduce the contemporary relevance of the decisions in *Lithgow* and *James*, which involved clear and substantial interferences with property rights. The permissible area of discretion within which governments can lawfully operate remains, however, very substantial, because the concept of the general interest as referred to in Art 1/1 is inherently flexible and covers matters far removed from old-style nationalisation. Thus, in the case of *Mellacher v Austria*,[3] the European Court said that:

> '... the second paragraph [of Art 1/1] reserves to States the right to enact such laws as they deem necessary to control the use of property in accordance with the general interest. Such laws are especially common in the field of housing, which in our modern societies is a central concern of social and economic policies. In order to implement such policies, the legislature must have a wide margin of appreciation both with regard to the existence of a problem of public concern warranting measures of control and as to the choice of the detailed rules for the implementation of such measures.'

9.54   Such language serves to illustrate the uphill task traditionally faced by litigants seeking to persuade the European Court to abandon its deferential approach to the social and economic programmes of national administrations. On account of this approach, the conferring of positive obligations upon States to safeguard and facilitate European Convention rights has so far not bulked large as a principle invoked in Strasbourg cases engaging Art 1/1, even though it is by now an important feature of the jurisprudence affecting, for example, Art 8.[4] The only implied duty imposed on governments is to provide procedural safeguards and a regime for compensation. In fact, States can arguably impose greater duties upon their citizens in this area than is imposed upon States by the European Convention. As such, there was, for example, no violation when a private Swedish landowner was required on environmental grounds to plant trees.[5]

9.55   Whether or not the concept of the margin of appreciation is now imported into domestic adjudication or not,[6] the controversial history of Art 1/1 is such that a generous approach to State interference in property-related cases is very likely to be a feature of litigation under the Act. It is also likely that, as

---

1   At paras 45 and 46.
2   At para 50.
3   (1989) 12 EHRR 391.
4   See **5.17** et seq and **7.55** et seq. There is no suggestion, therefore, that the UK could be held liable by disaffected property-owners because of losses suffered through some systemic market collapse or, indeed, the effects of inflation: see *Gustafsson v Sweden* (1996) 22 EHRR 409. So too, failing to warn the public not to invest in pyramid investment schemes has been held not to engage Art 1/1: see *MN v Bulgaria* (1996) 88 DR 163.
5   *Denev v Sweden* (1989) 59 DR 127.
6   As to which, see **6.293**.

discussed below,[1] British judges may be anxious (like indeed their counterparts in Strasbourg) to limit the so-called horizontal application of the Act in the property sphere.

9.56   An Art 1/1 challenge is more likely to succeed where there is an absence of proportionality and the presence of aggravating features such as a failure to pay compensation. Both of these factors were in issue in one local case brought before the Act received Royal Assent, where the failure to pay compensation after salmon were destroyed by the authorities in accordance with regulations was adjudged illegal in circumstances where it was held that other measures could have been adopted.[2]

9.57   Delay may be another aggravating factor. It was conceded in *Sporrong* that the Swedish Government was entitled to earmark private property for compulsory purchase as part of its town-planning programme, but progress was so slow that the applicant landowners were left in a state of uncertainty for up to 23 years, which the European Court considered an 'individual and excessive burden'.[3] On the other hand, a factor militating against an Art 1/1 violation will be extensive public debate in advance of implementation.[4]

9.58   The first paragraph of Art 1/1 additionally allows for deprivations subject to 'conditions provided for by law and by the general principles of international law'. The approach to legal prescription in relation to the European Convention right to property is the same as that adopted in the other qualified rights in the European Convention. In other words, national laws curbing the relevant European Convention rights must be accessible, ascertainable and foreseeable.

9.59   The operation of this principle was illustrated in the case of *Hentrich v France*.[5] Liliane Hentrich bought a large plot of land in (ironically) Strasbourg. The local Commissioner of Revenue considered that the price agreed was manifestly below market value. In such circumstances, Art 668 of the French tax code permitted him to pre-empt the sale by payment of the purchase price plus a premium of 10%. France freely admitted that the power was exercised exceptionally as a deterrent against tax evasion. In the preceding year, there had been just 26 instances of pre-emption in the whole of the country. There was, nevertheless, no means of challenging the exercise of the power and the French revenue authorities had neither to give reasons for their decision to intervene, or to show fraudulent intent.

9.60   In a damning judgment, the European Court found that 'the pre-emption operated arbitrarily and selectively and was scarcely foreseeable'. Nor was it 'attended by the basic procedural safeguards' enshrined in Art 6(1). The power to intervene in these circumstances existed in no other Contracting State. There were other ways to curb tax evasion and the suggestion that the payment of a premium price could ever compensate for the loss of a home was questionable. Considered as a whole, Madame Hentrich had been required to bear 'an

---

1   See **9.223** et seq. In France, most planning restrictions do not apparently give rise to any entitlement to compensation. See J-B Auby 'The Influence of European Law on Planning' [1998] EPL 45 at 47.
2   *Booker Aquaculture Ltd v Secretary of State for Scotland* [2000] UKHRR 1.
3   *Sporrong* (see fn 1 on p 304) at para 69.
4   See *National and Provincial Building Society and Others v United Kingdom* (1997) 23 EHRR at 164.
5   (1994) 18 EHRR 440.

individual and excessive burden which could have been rendered legitimate only if she had had the possibility – which was refused her – of effectively challenging the measure taken against her'.

9.61   As far as the need in Art 1/1 for deprivations to accord with international law principles is concerned, it is conceivable that businesses domiciled outside the UK may be able to invoke the international law guarantee of 'prompt, adequate and effective compensation'[1] in respect of any property confiscated in the UK. The European Court, however, has robbed this stringent safeguard of much of its potential by allowing only those who are *not* nationals of the State in question to rely on it[2] and by classifying measures (as has been seen), as exercises in *control of use* which under international law would be likely to be deemed expropriations. A good example was the confiscation of property that took place in *Gasus*[3] where the cement mixer forfeited by the Dutch revenue authorities had in fact been sold by a German company under a retention of title clause and where the European Commission held that 'the deprivation of property which occurred [could not] be compared to ... measures of confiscation, nationalisation or expropriation in regard to which international law [provided] special protection to foreign citizens and companies'.[4]

9.62   Notwithstanding the fact that it appears to reflect the *travaux préparatoires*, this distinction in treatment sits oddly with the non-discrimination covenant to be found in Art 14[5] and the confirmation in Art 1 that the European Convention's protection extends to everyone within the jurisdiction of any Contracting State.[6] In the *Lithgow* case the European Court expressed itself satisfied that any differential treatment between State nationals and aliens had an 'objective and reasonable justification', but in an age of global companies and international capital markets this is beginning to appear threadbare and a good instance of an area in which some evolutive thinking by the Strasbourg judges is called for. [7]

THE RIGHT TO PROPERTY COMBINED WITH OTHER EUROPEAN CONVENTION GUARANTEES

9.63   The *Hentrich* decision shows the potential advantage to companies of coupling reliance upon Art 1/1 with covenants enshrined in other Articles of the European Convention where the 'threshold of justification is not nearly so lenient'.[8] This has not historically been lost upon practitioners, indeed the cases suggest that applicants' prospects at Strasbourg are generally improved by relying

---

1   See Harris, O'Boyle and Warbrick (see fn 4 on p 299) at 530–1.
2   See *James v United Kingdom* (see fn 3 on p 307) at para 61. Anderson describes the European Court's attempt to justify this distinction on the basis of an alien's increased vulnerability and lesser benefit from public interest measures as 'less than convincing' (see fn 3 on p 308) at p 549.
3   See fn 1 on p 308.
4   See European Commission Report A 306-B (1995).
5   See **5.44** et seq.
6   See Appendix 2.
7   See R Higgins 'The Taking of Property by the State – Recent Developments in International Law' in *Hague Rec*, vol 176 (1983–III) and Anderson (see fn 2 on p 308), p 549.
8   See J Coppel *The Human Rights Act 1998* (John Wiley & Sons Ltd, 1999), para 14.23.

on as many European Convention rights as possible. Of the other rights domesticated by the Act, two in particular should be borne in mind by businesses seeking redress for interferences with possessions.

9.64   Article 6(1) is very commonly combined with Art 1/1 in Strasbourg petitions. In *Sporrong*,[1] for example, Art 6(1) was found to have been violated by virtue of the absence of any tribunal in Sweden able to deal with the full range of matters in issue. The due process rights in Art 6(1), however, are no more absolute in the property context than in any other. Part of the background to the *Lithgow* case was that the British Government had established a dedicated system for the settlement of disputes arising out of the nationalisation of the shipbuilding industry before a specially formed arbitration tribunal. Restrictions placed upon the ability of shareholders to intervene did not violate Art 6 in circumstances where the European Court shared the European Commission's view:

> '. . . that this limitation on the right to direct access for every individual shareholder to the Arbitration Tribunal pursued a legitimate aim, namely the desire to avoid, in the context of a large-scale nationalisation measure, a multiplicity of claims and proceedings ... Neither [did] it appear, having regard to the ... Government's margin of appreciation, that there was not a reasonable relationship of proportionality between the means employed and this aim.'[2]

9.65   On this basis, *Lithgow* suggests that, when property matters are in issue, permissible limitations under guarantees other than in Art 1/1 may *also* be given an expansive reading, to the disadvantage of claimants.

9.66   The other weapon conceivably of general use in possessions cases is Art 14,[3] which guarantees enjoyment of European Convention rights without discrimination and in respect of which the deference accorded to Contracting States is more limited in scope. An imaginative corporate litigant will often be able to identify preferential treatment accorded businesses holding property in similar circumstances. Where such preferences are established, it is for Contracting States to establish objective and reasonable foundations for them.

9.67   Although State action is generally scrutinised closely under Art 14, violations as a result of discrimination have been rare in the property sphere. Indeed in *James*, the European Court applied the *same* margin of appreciation to Art 14 as it did to Art 1/1 in circumstances where the applicants had pointed to the fact that a small proportion of high-value tenancies had been granted exemption from the enfranchisement legislation. In this regard, the judges ruled that:

> 'The second head of complaint [Article 14] must be examined in the light of the [European] Court's finding under Article 1 of Protocol No 1 ... In view of the legitimate objectives being pursued in the public interest, and having regard to the respondent State's margin of appreciation, that policy of different treatment cannot be considered so unreasonable as imposing a disproportionate burden on the applicants.'

9.68   On the other hand, in the case of *Darby v Sweden*[4] the Swedish Government declined, with commendable candour, to argue that a legitimate aim

---

1   See fn 1 on p 304 and **9.119** et seq.
2   See fn 4 on p 308 at para 197.
3   See **2.12** and **5.44** et seq.
4   (1991) 13 EHRR 774.

underlay the discriminatory features of a church tax whereby only those who were permanently resident qualified for exemptions. The European Court found a violation of Art 14 in conjunction with Art 1/1. Generally, however, the fact that the taxation system may be deliberately redistributive and thereby differentiate between one income group and another will tend not to be a violation of Art 14, even where it positively discriminates (for example) in favour of women.[1] Differential treatment between resident and non-resident tax-payers will also not offend the European Convention if it can be justified rationally, although this has proved a fertile area for litigation in the context of EC law.[2]

9.69　Article 8 is relied upon increasingly at Strasbourg in combination with Art 1/1, often in environmental cases. This is considered separately below.[3]

FACTORS TO FOCUS UPON

9.70　It will be apparent from this brief survey of the Strasbourg jurisprudence that there will be substantial obstacles to be surmounted in proving to judges in the UK that private property interests should, on European Convention grounds, trump policies pursued by public authorities. However, many corporates will consider the burden worth taking up. Expense aside, there is no reason why they should not do so in circumstances where, so far as the State is concerned, it remains necessary to prove that the community interest did not fall excessively on the property owner and that the relevant public interest could not be secured without interfering with the citizen's possessions.

9.71　Against that background, it could be that the existence of the following factors may improve a company's chances of establishing an Art 1/1 violation:

- the infringement of a legitimate expectation;
- prolonged, unjustified delay affecting the enjoyment of possessions;
- the absence of adequate protection from the arbitrary operation of a policy affecting the enjoyment of possessions, leading to scarcely foreseeable results;
- the availability of alternative means for the State to achieve its objects and/or the absence of alternative means by which private parties may protect their interests;
- the disregarding of Art 6 requirements of procedural fairness, such as the giving of reasons and the referral of disputes to an independent tribunal, without objective justification;
- the absence of compensation, especially in cases involving deprivation;
- the adoption of an inflexible mechanism for the payment of compensation;
- the discriminatory treatment of companies in similar positions; and
- the absence of adequate public debate prior to decisions constituting interference with possessions.[4]

1　See *Lindsay v United Kingdom* Appl 11089/84, (1986) 49 DR 181 and also *McGregor v United Kingdom* [1998] EHRLR 354 and see generally **5.44** et seq.
2　See *Finezant v Schumacker* [1995] STC 306 and *ICI v Colmer* [1998] STC 874.
3　See **9.187** et seq.
4　See C Baker (ed) *Human Rights Act 1998: A Practitioner's Guide* (Sweet & Maxwell, 1998), p 404.

9.72   Having reviewed the general principles, their application by virtue of the Act to particular commercial sectors is considered.

THE SPECIAL POSITION OF UTILITIES[1]

9.73   Utilities regulators such as OFTEL are already well established as part of our administrative law system and will be public authorities as defined in s 6 of the Act.[2] What is more, independent bodies supervising industries on a self-regulatory basis could be amenable to European Convention challenges and the Press Complaints Commission has already been considered in that context.[3] The role of such non-statutory entities was looked at in the case of *R v ICSTIS, ex parte Firstcode*,[4] which arose out of an agreement reached between BT and providers of premium rate telephone services to create an Independent Committee on Standards in Telecommunications Services. This body was to issue a code of standards and discharge a dispute-resolution function. Although it was undoubtedly a creature of contract, rather than legislation, the Court of Appeal found that it exercised a quasi-public law jurisdiction – and there appears every likelihood that, therefore, it too will be a public authority in terms of the Act.

9.74   Not just the regulators but, as has been seen,[5] the utilities themselves will very likely be public authorities (as regards their public functions). This classification will need to keep pace with rapid changes in market dynamics. In time, today's monopoly providers may well find their advantageous position eroded by increased competition. Should that not affect their public authority designation? Conversely, can the argument be made that private companies become public authorities upon achieving market dominance?

Utilities as defendants under the Act

9.75   Article 1/1's guarantee of the enjoyment of possessions could conceivably be invoked against utility companies that refuse or restrict the supply of essential commodities, endangering the economic substratum and goodwill of dependent businesses, while cutting off domestic supply may raise implications under Art 8 (the right to respect for private life).[6]

Utilities as claimants under the Act

9.76   It may be anticipated that utility companies[7] will seek to invoke the European Convention (and, specifically, Art 6(1)) in connection with licence

---

1   See, generally, on this subject S Hamilton 'The Human Rights Act and the Regulation of Utilities' [1999] *Util Law Rev* 115.
2   See **3.86** et seq.
3   See **8.204** et seq.
4   The case is helpfully discussed by C Scott in 'The Juridification of Relations in the UK Utilities Sector' in Black, Muchinski and Walker (eds) *Commercial Regulation and Judicial Review* (Hart Publishing, 1998). Compare the case of *Mercury Communications Ltd v Director General of Communications* [1996] 1 All ER 575.
5   See **3.92** et seq.
6   See Chapter 7.
7   Subject to the all-important risk that utilities which are public authorities may conceivably not be able to invoke the European Convention on their own behalf: see **3.139** et seq.

modifications and revocations, which can have a material effect upon the value of businesses.[1] In particular, the increasing use of *individual* licence negotiations to set *general* regulatory standards and the alleged offering of preferential treatment in industries with broadly similar operating conditions potentially bear on various aspects of the European Convention.

9.77 This last issue has in fact already been tested in the domestic context. The *Scottish Power* case[2] arose out of Scottish Hydro's rejection of a licence modification relating to price control. A reference ensued to the then Monopolies and Mergers Commission, which found for Scottish Hydro on public interest grounds. The regulator subsequently declined, however, to extend the same concession to a Scottish Hydro competitor, Scottish Power. The Court of Appeal found that the regulator's attempts to justify such differential treatment were irrational. The homogenous market conditions affecting both operators were such that the (beneficial) consequences of the Monopolies and Mergers Commission report could not be limited to one operator only. Perhaps ironically, it is not apparent that this would necessarily give rise to an Art 14 violation in European Convention terms, in that the differentiation was not on the basis of a designated status, such as race or religion.

9.78 Utilities and other commercial licensees are susceptible to regulation in three broad phases:[3]

– *when a licence is granted*: generally following the satisfaction of statutory requirements and approval by a designated Secretary of State;
– *when a licence is modified*: usually by consent after negotiation with the relevant Secretary of State or regulator. Failing agreement, a competition reference will often lie and, as a last resort, recourse to the court may be available by way of judicial review; and
– *when a licence is renewed or revoked*: usually by the relevant Secretary of State or regulator.

9.79 The hope of a utility company to be granted a licence is likely to be classified as a mere 'expectation' that does not engage the European Convention, rather than a civil right or obligation in terms of Art 6(1)[4] or a right to property in terms of Art 1/1. The grant, refusal, modification or revocation of a licence may, however, be looked upon rather differently.[5] These are likely to be *civil obligations* in terms of Art 6(1), not least in circumstances where, in light of the substantial degree of discretion enjoyed by utilities regulators, they are unlikely to be able to rely upon the defence of statutory obligation in s 6(2) of the Act. Put another way, it will rarely be the case that regulators in the utilities sector are *required* by statute to make particular decisions affecting licences.

9.80 If the Act encourages what has been described as a 'seepage of law'[6] into the utilities sector, it may prove to be a mixed blessing. Recourse to litigation may undermine the culture of compromise and consultation inherent in the 'close

---

1   Some utilities licences can, for example, last 25 years or more.
2   *R v Director General of Electricity Supply, ex parte Scottish Power* CA (unreported) 3 February 1997, as discussed by Scott (see fn 4 on p 316).
3   See Hamilton (fn 1 on p 316).
4   See **6.33** et seq.
5   See, for example, *Benthem v The Netherlands* (1986) 8 EHRR 1.
6   See Scott (fn 4 on p 316), p 20.

and consensual nature of utility regulation'.[1] Therefore, the Act may act as a catalyst, testing procedural weaknesses in the current regime. To the extent, in particular, that they exercise both regulatory and executive functions in relation to licence negotiations (and, indeed, generally) it is at least arguable that utilities regulators are not 'independent' in the sense required by Art 6(1).

9.81   A non-interventionist approach, tending in its effect to give a specialist regulator the benefit of the procedural doubt, was demonstrated by the Strasbourg judges in a case arising out of a patent dispute involving British American Tobacco.[2] Its application to register a patent was turned down by the Appeals Division of the Dutch patent office. The Division's institutional structure was challenged by British American Tobacco, which pointed to the fact that its members were appointed by the executive and would be 'predisposed to accept the views of their colleagues in other branches'. British American Tobacco's claim was dismissed on the ground of the company's failure to exhaust remedies available in the Dutch courts. In a unanimous judgment, the European Court in any event recognised that 'in a domain as technical as that of granting patents there [might] be good reasons for opting for an adjudicatory body other than a court of the classic kind integrated within the standard judicial machinery in a country'.

9.82   Although this was a straightforward echo of the conclusion reached in *Bryan*,[3] it is by no means clear that the present regulatory regime in the utilities sector will be treated in the same way in the early cases brought under the Act.

9.83   Section 30 of the Utilities Act 2000[4] lays down licensing procedures in respect of which no appeal mechanism is established. Judicial review will lie from a modification to which a licensee objects, but a disaffected licensee is likely to say that this is inadequate to meet the requirements of Art 6(1) or indeed the procedural aspects of Art 1/1, while the regulator will no doubt contend that the scenario is in substance comparable to that in *Bryan*[5] and that no violation arises.

9.84   Such licence modifications are, more likely than not, controls of use within the *Sporrong* third rule[6] and energy regulators will need to show why such interference was justified, particularly where a modification causes loss to the relevant operator, not least in circumstances where the Bill makes no provision for compensation.

9.85   The Utilities Bill is in this respect a further example of the contemporary implications of the Act for commerce.

---

1   *Regulatory Relations in the UK Utilities Sector*, pp 20–27.
2   *British American Tobacco Company v The Netherlands* (1995) 21 EHRR 409.
3   *Bryan v United Kingdom* (1995) 21 EHRR 342 and see **6.71** et seq.
4   The Act received Royal Assent on 28 July 2000.
5   See fn 3 above.
6   See **9.26** et seq.

LICENCES AND LOCAL AUTHORITIES[1]

9.86   The Act will also have implications for local authority licensing, an activity which ranges from the supervision of public houses to music promotions. It will force councils to address the fairness of their application procedures, an area in which complaints have for a long time been made as regards what is perceived to be a cavalier approach on the part of many boroughs.[2]

9.87   As already noted,[3] in *Tre Traktorer*,[4] a licence to serve alcohol in a restaurant was adjudged by the European Court to be a possession. On this basis, therefore, it is likely that a liquor licence or a public entertainment licence in the UK will in be adjudged to be a possession protected by Art 1/1.

9.88   Article 1/1 serves to protect current entitlements. A licence holder who has a reasonable expectation of continuing to hold a licence has a European Convention possession but it appears which that Art 1/1 will protect those without an existing interest, such as a non-holder applying for a licence.

9.89   In seeking to show that there has been a breach of Art 1/1, a claimant will do well to persuade a court that a particular local authority is not pursuing a legitimate aim in invoking public order or health issues when dealing with a licence in a particular way. The claimant's best chance may be in arguing that a fair balance was not struck between the individual and general interest, or where the measures taken by the local authority were disproportionate as, for example, where a licence was revoked following a relatively minor breach of a licence condition.

9.90   The procedural guarantees in Art 6(1) are likely to be of greater assistance to companies seeking to challenge a licensing decision, not least because Art 6(1) can probably be invoked by those who do not already hold licences.[5]

9.91   Licensees and applicants for licences have a right of appeal to the Crown Court from decisions of licensing committees of justices in relation to liquor licences or to the Magistrates Courts (followed by the Crown Court) from decisions of local authorities. In all cases, there is a full rehearing. Decisions of justices or local authorities can also be challenged by judicial review. As there is a rehearing by a tribunal with 'full jurisdiction', the requirements of Art 6(1) are likely to be satisfied, even if there was a breach of the requirements of procedural fairness at the outset.[6] A third-party objector may, however, conceivably be able to make out a breach of Art 6(1) because a High Court judicial review is the only available remedy to a third party and this may be insufficient in terms of Art 6(1).

9.92   The possibility of appeal or re-hearing is, of course, of no obvious value to a company that requires a public entertainment licence urgently for the purposes of a one-off event such as a pop concert, not least where the company is a special

---

1   See generally on this subject the excellent conference paper by S Fitzgerald QC *Licensing, Local Authorities and the Human Rights Act* (24 May 1999).
2   See Discussion Paper of Business in Sport and Leisure on Local Authorities and Public Entertainment Licences.
3   See **9.16**.
4   *Tre Traktörer Aktiebolag v Sweden* (1989) 13 EHRR 309.
5   See *Benthem v The Netherlands* (see fn 6 on p 317).
6   See *Bryan v United Kingdom* (see fn 3 on p 318).

purpose vehicle established for precisely that event. In such circumstances, it will be argued that the decision of the local council is in effect determining the matter as a whole and that, as a consequence, the process safeguards inherent in Art 6(1) should apply at that point.[1]

THE ACT'S IMPACT ON TAXATION

9.93   The European Convention in Art 1/1 specifically protects the right of States to levy taxes – an obvious interference with possessions – and the Strasbourg institutions have indirectly copper-fastened this power by repeatedly holding that the assessment or imposition of taxes does not in general engage Art 6, on the basis that it is not a *contestation* of a civil right or obligation.[2] Even retrospective legislation, while looked at critically, is likely to be regarded as compatible with the Treaty.[3]

9.94   Notwithstanding the deference that the Strasbourg institutions have traditionally shown to tax gatherers, fiscal matters are likely, on account of the Act, to be subjected to close scrutiny as regards their European Convention implications. As will be seen, some current methods of revenue enforcement and prosecution in the UK sit uncomfortably with the European Convention safeguards in Arts 6 and 8. In general terms, the Strasbourg jurisprudence suggests that the corporate taxpayer stands a better chance of establishing a Treaty violation if it collaterally attacks process-related features of the taxation process rather than the substance of any given tax.

Challenging the substance

9.95   The Strasbourg institutions accept that a law passed to raise tax may 'adversely affect the guarantee secured [under Art 1/1] if it places an excessive burden on the person or the entity concerned or fundamentally interferes with his or its financial position'.[4] Therefore, national revenue authorities must act proportionately in establishing a fair balance between the individual and community interest. Although this would appear to be a helpful starting-point for a disgruntled tax-payer, findings of a European Convention violation are likely to remain extremely rare in light of the very broad discretion enjoyed in this area by Contracting States. This assumes, of course, that British judges follow the determinations of the European Court.

9.96   Harris, O'Boyle and Warbrick suggest that the power of States in fiscal matters is 'practically unlimited'[5] and, if that be so, it will be of some tactical importance for businesses seeking the benefit of the property guarantee in Art 1/1 not to have their cases characterised as tax disputes. In circumstances where the substance of a tax is unlikely to be incompatible with the European

---

1   See S Fitzgerald (see fn 1 on p 319), p 16 at para 43.
2   See **6.30** et seq.
3   See **9.17** and para **9.18**.
4   *Wasa Liv Ömsesidigit v Sweden* (1988) DR 58.
5   See fn 4 on p 299, at p 537.

Convention unless it is manifestly disproportionate[1] or wholly arbitrary, it will generally be much better to focus on possible violations of Art 6[2] and/or Art 14.[3]

9.97 There are numerous instances in the Strasbourg authorities of the leeway given to tax-gatherers. A complaint, for example, by Austrian companies about the operation of the PAYE system on the basis of the administrative burden it placed upon businesses there was unsuccessful,[4] as was a British challenge to the introduction of retrospective legislation to prevent the deliberate off-setting of commodity trading losses against tax.[5] A petition about the impact of certain national insurance contributions upon the self-employed also failed.[6]

9.98 The burden now placed upon the UK Government to preface Finance Bills with a s 19 statement of compatibility[7] may at least focus ministerial minds upon the need to strike a fair balance in tax matters, but arguments based on complaints as to the general level of, for example, corporation tax, would appear to be almost hopeless.

9.99 One area of possible challenge may arise out of the inflexible imposition of taxes irrespective of circumstances. For example, s 89 of the 1998 Finance Act imposes a 15% levy on the assumed growth of personal portfolio bonds whether or not they have in fact performed (this) well. In the past, the European Court has taken a dim view of such an approach. The *Katikaridis* case[8] arose out of a Greek law which presumed that traders benefited from the construction of major roads near their premises. In reliance upon this, the Greek administration refused to compensate the applicants when it expropriated their land for road-building purposes. In fact, the road constructed was a fly-over, from which the traders located underneath derived no benefit. This was found to be in violation of the fair balance principle to be struck under Art 1/1.

9.100 The issue of retrospective legislation in the fiscal context has already been examined as part of the general analysis of Art 1/1.[9] It was also canvassed in a recent domestic case involving *Marks & Spencer*,[10] in which it was common ground that the high street retail chain had overpaid VAT for years. Regrettably from its point of view, the Finance Act 1997 excluded the availability of refunds for amounts paid more than 3 (as opposed to the original 6) years before the making of a claim. Moses J found that this did not infringe Art 1/1 as it 'did not remove the possibility of a claim, [but] merely imposed a limitation period'. In any event, a detailed computation of Marks & Spencer's entitlement was outstanding. This meant that the company's claims did not constitute 'vested rights to restitution'.

---

1   See *Wasa Liv Ömsesidigit v Sweden* Appl 13013/87, (1988) 58 DR 163: a one-off wealth tax on savings and benefits was not a violation.
2   See Chapter 6.
3   See **5.44** et seq.
4   Appl 7427/76, (1976) 7 DR 148.
5   Appl 8531/79, (1981) 23 DR 203.
6   Appl 7995/77, (1978) 15 DR 198.
7   See **3.201** et seq.
8   *Katikaridis v Greece* [1997] EHRLR 198.
9   See **9.17**.
10   *Marks & Spencer v Commissioners of Customs & Excise (No 1)* (1999) 1 CMLR 1152. The case also involved a consideration of the EC law position.

More than that, he considered that Marks & Spencer enjoyed no legitimate expectation that a previous limitation period would ever be shortened.[1]

9.101   If the *Marks & Spencer* decision is a pointer to the future domestic treatment of European Convention points in tax cases, it would appear that the approach adopted will be one in which the tax-payer is unlikely to be given the benefit of the doubt, save perhaps where there are no transitional arrangements cushioning against abrupt, retrospective changes in revenue or excise law.[2]

Challenging the procedure

9.102   Penalties for failure to pay tax are likely only to breach Art 1/1 in so far as they are deemed disproportionate. However, the fact that decisions on enforcement are discretionary will oblige the Inland Revenue to ensure that its prosecutorial practices and its approach to mitigation is not discriminatory within Art 1/1 in conjunction with Art 14. The problem, as ever, remains the deference accorded Contracting States in the revenue area. In circumstances where the European Court confirmed in *Gasus* that it would 'respect the legislature's assessment unless it [was] devoid of reasonable foundation',[3] it is clear that the threshold to be crossed remains a very high one.

9.103   In the *National and Provincial* case,[4] the European Court agreed to overlook the fact that the British building societies were, at bottom, objecting to a tax liability (which on one view should not engage Art 6(1) at all)[5] by finding that the claim was 'closely linked' to a private-law restitutionary dispute. On this basis, it is at least arguable that any restitutionary-type claim to wrongly-paid tax engages Art 6(1). Similarly, a claim for damages by a company driven into liquidation following a failure to confer tax breaks on it was deemed to engage Art 6(1) in the case of *Editions Périscope v France.*[6]

9.104   In the early period after the Act comes fully into force, it may be anticipated that corporate taxpayers will argue that the whole of Art 6's guarantees (including Arts 6(2) and (3)) should be available to them when faced by an Inland Revenue prosecution.[7] The case of *AP, MP and TP v Switzerland*[8] arose out of a Swiss law imposing penalties for tax evasion that survived the death of the evasive taxpayer. Irrespective of any question as to their own personal involvement, the applicants therefore had inherited fines because of the conduct of their late husband and father. The European Court found that, in their severity, the penalties imposed went far beyond the recovery of outstanding debts and were penal in nature.

9.105   The status in European Convention terms of tax prosecutions has not yet been settled at a domestic level. Recent decisions by the Duty Tribunal have

---

1   The case went to appeal, where the European Convention points were not revisited (judgment of 14 December 1999).
2   See also *Nationwide Access Ltd v Commissioners of Customs and Excise* (unreported) 14 February 2000.
3   See fn 5 on p 300.
4   See fn 6 on p 302.
5   See **6.40**.
6   (1992) 14 EHRR 597.
7   Appl 1998/92, 18 January 1999.
8   (1998) 26 EHRR 541.

declined to treat the VAT penalty regime as a criminal matter,[1] but it is debatable whether this stance can be maintained. Also likely to be examined intensely are those instances where strict preconditions are attached to the exercise of rights of appeal[2] and where legal aid is not available to defend a tax or excise prosecution.

9.106 An interesting question is raised by the current practice of issuing notices under s 20 of the Taxes Management Act 1970, whereby the Inland Revenue can require the production of documents from (not only) the taxpayers it is investigating but also third parties. Issues of procedural fairness arise in circumstances where any of the recipients of such statutory notices are normally left with 30 days to object on the ground that compliance would prove 'onerous'. The service of such notices was challenged in a recent case on, amongst other matters, Convention grounds, but Lightman J appears to have had little difficulty in holding that Art 8's safeguards regarding confidentiality and privacy presented the Inland Revenue with no obvious difficulty. The notices in question were amply justified. They pursued a legitimate aim and were necessary in a democratic society to protect the taxation system.[3]

9.107 Nor is it clear that, in terms of notices served upon taxpayers, legal professional privilege can be maintained. The recent Court of Appeal decision in *Parry-Jones v Law Society*[4] made it clear that privileged documents would have to be disclosed in investigations involving a lawyer's own tax affairs. However, a Special Commissioner has subsequently suggested that this judgment is authority for the proposition that legal privilege can *never* be claimed to resist taxpayer notices.[5] Quite apart from issues affecting Art 8 of the European Convention,[6] any determination to break the privilege will doubtless encourage taxpayers to consider whether to take professional advice in the first instance and, where they do seek advice, for it to be given orally.[7]

9.108 The fact that Art 6 of the Convention may not be engaged in any given tax case does not render the taxpayer in every case devoid of all procedural protection. In *AGOSI*,[8] the European Court found certain minimum procedural requirements inherent in Art 1/1, even though Art 6 was found to be inapplicable. The interference with property rights in that case was such that the Strasbourg judges considered that the applicant should be afforded a 'reasonable opportunity to put its case'.[9]

---

1   See, for example, *Hodgson v Customs and Excise Commissioners* [1997] ELR 116. See also G MacFarlane, 'Duty Tribunal Cases' [1999] *The Tax Journal* 21 and M Conlon 'Human Rights and Taxation' (1999) 17 *VAT Intelligence* 1616.

2   See, for example, *Formix v Commissioners of Customs and Excise* (unreported) 13 November 1997 in relation to s 84(2) of the VAT Act 1994, which requires payment of all outstanding tax before an appeal can be brought.

3   *R v Inland Revenue Commissioners, ex parte Banque Internationale à Luxembourg SA* (unreported) 23 June 2000.

4   [1968] 1 All ER 177.

5   *An Applicant v An Inspector of Taxes* (1999) STI 888.

6   See Chapter 7.

7   F Ferguson 'Whose Privilege is it Anyway?' (1999) *Tax Journal* 511, 15–16. See also *Simon's Tax Directive* (1995) Issue 60, 3.151 ff.

8   *AGOSI v United Kingdom* (1987) 9 EHRR 1 at para 62 and see **9.35**.

9   Ibid, at para 88.

Challenging discrimination

9.109　　In the context of discrimination in taxation, the *National and Provincial* judgment confirms that not every difference in treatment will amount to a violation of Art 14. Indeed, the European Court was clear in that case that it must be established that 'other persons in an analogous or relevantly similar position enjoy preferential treatment, and that there is no reasonable and objective foundation for this distinction'. Where would this leave companies operating here but domiciled overseas who are treated less fairly than domestic companies?

9.110　　The fact that, despite considerable advance speculation to the contrary, no complaint on European Convention grounds was made to the Blair Government's so-called utilities windfall tax highlights the difficulty of establishing discrimination in this context. That tax was introduced in the Finance (No 2) Act 1997 as a one-off levy on the excess profits of privatised utilities. It was payable in two tranches, the second of which fell due on or before 1 December 1998, so it is by now of historical significance only. It says much, however, for the formidable deference shown by Strasbourg to national tax-gatherers that the windfall tax survived intact despite the fact that the tax was not borne by those who bought shares in the privatised utilities on flotation and later sold them – presumably at a profit – but was borne (in reality) by shareholders whose holdings had declined in value following the announcement of the imposition of the tax. Nor was the tax introduced to remedy any technical defect in legislation (a feature of the *National and Provincial* case),[1] but was aimed at companies which had already been taxed. Furthermore, it was unfair in its differentiation, not being levied on every company in any given industrial sector but only at particular companies within each sector. It may be on much the same basis that the imposition of levies upon current settlors for past profits of offshore taxes has been identified as a likely subject for an Art 1/1 complaint.[2]

9.111　　In the *Marks & Spencer* case,[3] the Commissioners justified the differential treatment of traders in different sectors on the basis that there was a discrete regulatory regime for each sector. Whilst the Court of Appeal expressed no concluded view on the matter,[4] Moses J had not at first instance considered this to be objectionable.[5] The Inland Revenue will no doubt be looking again at its selective prosecutorial techniques, notwithstanding this indication.

9.112　　Political exigencies may mean that personal taxpayers have more chance of establishing discrimination in the tax field than corporates. In spring 2000, for example, the British Government effected a friendly settlement at Strasbourg with two widowers deprived of benefit when their wives died when they would have received benefit if they had been women.[6]

1　　See fn 6 on p 302.

2　　See E Campbell 'Taxation and Human Rights' in *The Essential Human Rights Act 1998* (Wilberforce Chambers, 2000).

3　　See fn 10 on p 321.

4　　See the judgment of 14 December 1999 (unreported) at p 29.

5　　Ibid, at p 24.

6　　See *The Guardian*, 26 April 2000. The case was *Crossland v United Kingdom* Appl 36120/97. See also *MacGregor v United Kingdom* Appl 30548/96.

THE ACT AND PENSION SCHEMES[1]

9.113   Even though there is no European Convention right to a pension,[2] where pensions entitlements exist, they almost certainly satisfy Art 1/1's definition of 'possessions', most obviously where an earmarked, ascertainable share in a fund is created, but probably also where there is no identifiable individual share. The definition probably also extends to contributions made by an employer as part of a private pension plan.[3] In the case of *Gaygusuz v Austria*[4] the European Court concluded that, in relation to social security benefits at least, the European Convention's property right was engaged where 'entitlement [was] linked to the payment of contributions.' Non-contributory benefits appear for the present, however, not to be possessions engaging Art 1/1 and, as such, the European Convention cannot be relied upon as establishing a right to social security.

9.114   The large private pension funds will need to look closely at the Act's implications for their businesses. Are they public authorities too? In terms of their systemic importance, it would appear strange to treat them differently from the privatised utilities. However, it is difficult to see how their activities could be regarded as being as functionally public or as monopolistic as those of a railway company even in an era of private pension provision. Assuming, however, some indirect horizontal effect of the Act in this area as in others, questions are now likely to be raised as regards the human rights relevance of provisions (for example) for the maintenance of capital values and rules for the winding-up, transfer and assignment of funds.[5]

9.115   To the extent that pension rights can be brought within the European Convention's scope, any differentiation in entitlement based upon nationality and gender will be examinable under Art 14. No doubt few cases will prove as straightforward as *Gaygusuz*, however, where the Turkish contributor was excluded from benefit on the basis that it was reserved to Austrian nationals. Not surprisingly, a violation was found.

9.116   In the past, State pension entitlements have been viewed by the Strasbourg judges as analogous to rights granted by private employers.[6] Hence, such entitlements will probably be classed as 'civil rights' and covered by Art 6(1)'s procedural guarantees. This may require the Pensions Ombudsman, for example, to permit oral hearings and encourage trustees to give reasons for their decisions.

9.117   In two recent cases,[7] claimants sought to prevent their pension entitlements vesting in their trustees in bankruptcy. The Court of Appeal was not

---

1   The status of welfare benefits at Strasbourg is outside the scope of this book. In general terms, a claim for such a benefit will not engage the European Convention unless some process breach under Art 6 or Art 14 can be identified.
2   *X v Germany* Appl 2116/64, (1966) 23 CD 10.
3   *Stigson v Sweden* (1988) DR 57/131. See also *Szrabjer v United Kingdom* [1998] PLR 281 – SERPS payments were a pecuniary right within Art 1/1. There is little doubt that the Occupations Pensions Regulatory Authority will be designated a public authority in terms of s 6 of the Act. No doubt mindful of this, it has apparently altered its procedures.
4   (1997) 23 EHRR 364.
5   See, generally, on this L Hall and J Southern, *Human Rights and Pension Schemes*, Report of a seminar by William M Mercer Ltd (7 April 1999).
6   See *Lombardo v Italy* (1992) 21 EHRR 188.
7   *Dennisson v Krasner, Lesser v Lawrence* (joined cases) [2000] 3 All ER 234.

impressed, dismissing the claimants' argument that the susceptibility of their pension entitlements to claims by creditors could infringe their European Convention rights and doing so partly on the basis that Parliament had looked at the issue several times over a generation.

THE ACT'S IMPLICATIONS FOR PLANNING

9.118   The protection afforded by Art 1/1 to the 'peaceful enjoyment of possessions' has, as has been seen,[1] a broad application and equates with a right of property[2] – hence the Article's heading, added pursuant to the Eleventh Protocol on 1 November 1998.[3] The property right is frequently analysed as constituting a congeries of interests synonymous with ownership, including the right to dispose of and to use property as the owner wishes. In this context, it is not surprising that planning law engages the European Convention in many respects. It has already been noted[4] that the term 'possessions' has been given an autonomous meaning by the Strasbourg institutions and is not limited to physical ownership of goods[5] with the result that certain forms of intangible interest may fall within Art 1/1, such as the economic interest associated with a licence to exploit a gravel pit,[6] the grant of outline planning permission[7] and the goodwill in a business.[8] Article 1/1 is also highly relevant in circumstances where the imposition of planning controls by the State is, without more, inconsistent with an untrammelled right of property ownership and, in an age of heightened environmental awareness, such controls are likely to increase and be made the subject of multilateral agreement.

9.119   The *Sporrong*[9] case is the starting-point when considering the European Convention law on planning. In that case, the European Court sought to establish a balance between the protection of the corporate (or personal) and the community interest. The applicants[10] were the owners of two properties in the centre of Stockholm, an area earmarked for an urban redevelopment programme, part of which involved the construction of a viaduct leading to a major relief road. The applicants' land was first made the subject of compulsory purchase notices in 1956. The notices gave the city council 5 years to complete expropriation and have compensation determined by a tribunal. The notices were subsequently extended by the Swedish government for successive periods of (respectively) 23 years and 8 years. Prohibitions on construction by the applicants were also imposed at the outset and these lapsed after 25 years and 12 years

---

1   See **9.28**.
2   *Marckx v Belgium* (1979) 2 EHRR 350.
3   See **2.44**.
4   See **9.13** et seq.
5   See *Gasus Dosier und Fördertechnik GmbH v The Netherlands* (see fn 1 on p 308).
6   *Fredin v Sweden* (1991) 13 EHRR 784 (Commission report), at para 48.
7   *Pine Valley Developments Ltd v Ireland (No 1)* (1991) 14 EHRR 319.
8   *Fredin* (see fn 6 above) at para 51.
9   *Sporrong and Lönnroth v Sweden* (1983) 5 EHRR 35. The case apparently had a profound impact in Sweden in terms of raising consciousness about the European Convention. It became a weapon in attacking the Social Democrat establishment and in the process delayed the Treaty's local incorporation. See I Cameron in *European Civil Liberties and the European Convention on Human Rights* edited by CA Gearty (Martinus Nijhoff Publishers, 1997), p 230.
10   Cameron (see fn 9 above) says at p 230 that 'organised housing and business interests' lay behind them.

(respectively). The European Court held that the effect of these administrative measures was substantially to restrict the applicants' ability to use and dispose of their possessions. In the process, the measures had also interfered with the applicants' property rights.

9.120 In deciding whether this interference amounted to a European Convention violation, the Strasbourg judges held, as has been seen,[1] that Art 1/1 contained three distinct rules, incorporating the notions of interference with the right to the enjoyment of property (the first rule), deprivation of property (the second rule) and control of property (the third rule). Having found that the interference of the Swedish government was to be considered under the first rule, the European Court stated that its role was 'to determine whether a fair balance was struck between the demands of the general interest of the community and the requirements of the protection of the individual's fundamental rights'. It emphasised that the search for this balance was inherent in the whole of the European Convention and was also reflected in the structure of Art 1/1.

9.121 This approach as to whether or not a 'fair balance' was struck between the individual's right of property and the demands of the general interest has, since *Sporrong*, been conflated and it is now also used to determine whether a deprivation or control of property can be justified under the second and third rules identified at Strasbourg. In approaching any planning issue in the UK from now on, identification of a fair balance will be of great significance.

9.122 In *Sporrong*, it was held, albeit only by the narrowest of margins (10:9), that a fair balance had not been struck. It was considered legitimate for Sweden to implement a policy for town planning and the European Court accepted that a Contracting State should enjoy a wide margin of appreciation when so doing. The fact, however, that the applicants were left in a state of uncertainty as to their property rights for such a long period of time meant that they had borne what was described as an individual and excessive burden. It would only have been rendered legitimate if the applicants could have sought a reduction in the length of the prohibitions placed upon them or been able to claim compensation. Neither of these options had been open to them.

9.123 It will be apparent, therefore, that a fair balance may be achieved where effective procedural protection exists. To this extent, Art 1/1 has developed its own due process standard quite separate from Art 6(1).[2] Nevertheless, no Art 1/1 violation will be established where the applicant has failed to make use of such adequate procedures as are available.[3]

9.124 In much the same vein as *Sporrong*, violations were found by the European Court in two other planning cases, both emanating from Austria, in which the Strasbourg judges considered a number of deficiencies in the process whereby farming land was provisionally re-designated for building. They reviewed the length of the process (16 years), the absence of compensation and the applicants' inability in both instances to challenge the process because it was provisional in nature. The European Court found that these factors were not

---

1   See **9.26** et seq.
2   See Chapter 6. See also, by contrast, *Scollo v Italy* (1996) 22 EHRR 514, where it took nearly 12 years from the making of an eviction order for the occupiers to be removed and there was found to be no Art 1/1 violation.
3   See *Phocas v France* Appl 17869/91.

outweighed by the existence of any communal interest considerations[1] and were infractions of the right to peaceful enjoyment, ie the *Sporrong* first rule. Likewise, the introduction of an urban redevelopment plan in Montpellier which seriously affected the applicant owner of property in the case of *Phocas v France*[2] was also treated as an interference with peaceful enjoyment. However, no violation was found in circumstances where it was held that the applicant had failed to exhaust domestic procedures for the purchase of his property.

9.125   Another case where the European Court held that a fair balance was not struck was *Matos e Silva*.[3] There the applicant company's ability to use and deal with part of its land was greatly restricted by measures introduced by the Portuguese Government to create a nature reserve. The European Court determined that the applicants had, there too, borne an individual and excessive burden. For years they had cultivated the relevant area to extract salt and breed fish before the Portuguese Government had made a 'public interest declaration' that half of the company's land was needed for a public purpose, namely the creation of the nature reserve. Restrictions imposed on the use of the land made it impossible in practice to sell it. For 13 years, the company was left in a state of uncertainty as regards the future of its rights over the land – all this time without any compensation being paid. Although, as a matter of local law, the company's right to deal with its possessions had been left intact, its ability to do so in reality had been greatly reduced. Article 1/1 had been violated.

9.126   Nothing in the *Matos e Silva* decision is inconsistent with the often-repeated view of the Strasbourg judges that Contracting States are entitled to impose planning restrictions in the interests of the community as a whole. Those community interests may include the preservation of nature,[4] the maintenance of the green belt[5] and the protection of the environment.[6]

9.127   Further, as was emphasised in *Sporrong*, the European Court has tended to accord a wide margin of appreciation to States in matters concerning town and country planning policy, being reluctant to encroach into an area which can be highly complex[7] and with a high policy content and in respect of which the consensus of the Strasbourg institutions has traditionally been that governments are better equipped to find the requisite fair balance between private and public interests. This approach was emphasised in *Buckley*,[8] where the judges stated that:

> 'It is not for the Court to substitute its own view of what would be the best policy in the planning sphere or the most appropriate individual measure in planning cases. By reason of their direct and continuous contact with the vital forces of their countries, the national authorities are in principle better placed than an international court to evaluate local needs and conditions. In so far as the exercise of discretion involving a

---

1   See *Erkner and Hofauer v Austria* (1987) 9 EHRR 464 and *Poiss v Austria* (1988) 10 EHRR 231.
2   See fn 3 on p 327.
3   *Matos E Silva Lda v Portugal* (1996) 24 EHRR 573.
4   See *Fredin v Sweden* (see fn 6 on p 326).
5   See *Pine Valley v Ireland* (see fn 7 on p 326).
6   See *Matos e Silva, LDA v Portugal* (1996) above)
7   See *Allan Jacobsson v Sweden* (1989) 12 EHRR 56.
8   *Buckley v United Kingdom* (1997) 23 EHRR 101. See also in this context the European Commission decision on admissibility in *Mabrey v United Kingdom* (1996) 22 EHRR CD 123, where the maintenance of the green belt was considered to be a legitimate way of securing national economic well-being and, to that extent, within Art 8(2). See also the section on the environment at **9.178** et seq.

multitude of local factors is inherent in the choice and implementation of planning policies, the national authorities in principle enjoy a wide margin of appreciation.'[1]

9.128   There is no reason to believe that domestic courts will use the Act to take a more interventionist approach in the planning arena. In many instances, they will continue to defer to the judgment of the relevant planning authority, concluding (like the Strasbourg institutions) that the planning authority, as the specialist body vested with responsibility for choosing and implementing policy in this discretionary area (particularly where the exigencies may be intensely political), should be left to get on with matters. Any prediction as to the future propensity of local courts to reach their own views regarding the most appropriate planning decisions in any given situation depends, furthermore, upon the impact of the Act upon the scope and intensity of judicial review in this country, a substantial subject considered elsewhere in this book.[2]

9.129   British judges have shown in the past that they are prepared to scrutinise critically the exercise of administrative power which interferes with property rights.[3] It is also evident from *Sporrong* and from *Matos e Silva* that the European Court is also willing to find that a fair balance has not been struck between the private right to property on the one hand and the general interest on the other, when applicants are shown to have been subjected to long periods of interference with and uncertainty over their property rights as a result of bureaucratic inefficiency. In these (admittedly rare) cases, it is unsurprising that the European Court reached the conclusion that the relevant applicants had borne an individual and excessive burden.[4]

9.130   Complaints to Strasbourg about planning controls or restrictions are generally dealt with under the first[5] or third[6] rules enunciated in *Sporrong*, the European Court appearing to take the view that an applicant in planning cases will not generally have been deprived of property for the purposes of the second *Sporrong* rule even if the planning measures in question are extremely restrictive of the exercise of property rights, the rationale being that there remains an underlying proprietary interest which has not been taken away.[7] The exercise of a power of compulsory purchase, however, has been treated as a deprivation for the purposes of the second rule.[8]

9.131   Aside from wider issues of policy and discretion, the Strasbourg cases suggest that violations are less likely to be found where entrepreneurial

---

1   At p 129, para 75. The challenge in *Buckley* was in fact made under Art 8 of the Convention. However, the Strasbourg institutions have taken the view that there is an overlap between the necessity required to justify an interference with Art 1/1 and the right protected by Art 8. See *Howard v United Kingdom* (1987) 9 EHRR CD 91.
2   See **6.289** et seq.
3   See, for example, *Chesterfield Properties plc v Secretary of State* [1998] JPL 568 in which Laws J (as he then was) applied the 'anxious scrutiny' test to an interference with property rights in the form of a compulsory purchase order. See also *R v North Lincolnshire Council, ex parte Horticultural and Garden Products Sales Humberside Ltd* [1998] 3 PLR 1.
4   Excessive delay has also led to findings of a breach of Art 6(1) in planning cases. See, for example, *Erkner and Hofauer v Austria* (1987) 9 EHRR 464 and **9.124**.
5   See *Sporrong* at **9.119** et seq and *Matos e Silva* at **9.125**.
6   See, for example, *Fredin* and *Pine Valley* (see fns 6 and 7 on p 326 respectively).
7   See *Sporrong* at para 62.
8   See *Lithgow v United Kingdom* (1986) 8 EHRR 329 and *James v United Kingdom* (1986) 8 EHRR 123 and **9.43** et seq.

development companies have acquired land subsequently made subject to some form of planning restriction. The justification appears to be that developers are to be assumed to have accepted such a risk when purchasing the relevant land.[1] The fact that the applicant knew of a particular restriction on purchase[2] will also, not surprisingly, be considered material at Strasbourg. All these factors go to proportionality, as does the extent to which the restriction goes to prevent the use of the land.

9.132   Planning controls may, of course, also engage the liability of the State under Art 8, which guarantees respect for private and family life and the home.[3] In the past, applicants at Strasbourg have argued that particular planning measures have interfered with home and private life[4] and there is no reason why a company should not run the (albeit subsidiary) argument that a planning restriction violates Art 8, this on the footing that the *Niemietz* case established that an 'office' can in certain circumstances be a 'home'.[5] Ultimately, however, companies will continue to look primarily to Art 1/1 and Art 6 for the protection of their commercial interests in the planning sphere.

9.133   The Act may materially impact upon a number of specific features of local planning law as explained below.[6]

The development plan

9.134   In the UK it is the job of the local planning authority to prepare a development plan. This is a key feature of the planning process as there will be a presumption in favour of granting a proposal that accords with a development plan.[7]

9.135   It is conceivable that the adoption of a particular development plan may in Strasbourg terms amount to an interference with the right of enjoyment as articulated in the first *Sporrong* rule.[8] In *Katte Klitsche*, for example, a land-use plan, adopted by a local council, prevented the applicant from developing his land. On the facts of that case, the Strasbourg judges held that a fair balance had been struck between the individual and the general interest, but it is conceivable that a local planning authority could be found to be in violation of Art 1/1 by adopting a particularly restrictive development plan which ostensibly did not strike a fair balance.

9.136   The adoption of a particular planning policy in a development plan could constitute a civil right within Art 6(1)[9] and an objector to a development plan may arguably therefore be entitled to rely on the process safeguards set out in that Article where, for example, the local planning authority's reasoning in failing to adopt a particular recommendation leaves an objector uncertain as to whether

1   See *Fredin and Pine Valley* (see fns 6 and 7 on p 236 respectively).
2   See *Allan Jacobsson* (see fn 7 on p 328).
3   See Chapter 7.
4   See, for example, *Buckley v United Kingdom* (1997) 23 EHRR 101.
5   *Niemietz v Germany* (1992) 16 EHRR 709.
6   The following section draws heavily upon the excellent chapter by Iain Colville in *A Practitioner's Guide* (see fn 4 on p 315), p 278 et seq.
7   PPG1, at para 25.
8   *Katte Klitshe de la Grange v Italy* (1994) 19 EHRR 368.
9   See *Ortenberg v Austria* (1995) 19 EHRR 524.

to exercise a right of appeal to the High Court under s 287 of the Town and Country Planning Act 1990.

9.137   As Art 6(1) guarantees the right to a public hearing in the determination of civil rights and obligations, s 35B(4) of the Town and Country Planning Act, which provides that: 'No person shall have the right to be heard at an examination in public', raises an obvious fair trial issue. More than likely, however, a local court will follow the decision of the Strasbourg judges in *Bryan*[1] in holding that the availability of an appeal to the High Court under s 287 of the Town and Country Planning Act is sufficient to cure any earlier defect arising from the denial of a public hearing.

9.138   As such, the impact of Art 6 on planning appeals may be limited, given that in most cases the Town and Country Planning Act provides for a final appeal to the High Court on a point of law.

Paying for planning permission

9.139   Companies are particularly affected by the practice whereby a local planning authority frequently expects payment from those who are seeking planning permission for any substantial development.

9.140   It is hard to object to the notion that a developer, who may be seeking to construct a large site which necessitates improvements in area infrastructure, should make a financial contribution to a local authority. However, situations can arise when a developer is expected to make a payment towards infrastructure or another public scheme wholly unconnected with the developer's own proposal. Alternatively, there have been instances in which developers have sought to secure planning permission by making large payments to schemes which have (only) a tenuous connection with their own proposed development.[2]

9.141   So far local courts have been reluctant to impose any sort of control on planning 'benefit' schemes of this nature.[3] Such activities may, however, possibly amount to a violation of Art 1/1 to the extent that any curtailment of the right to property must not require a property owner to bear an individual and excessive burden. A company asked to make a payment towards a public scheme, which is wholly unconnected with its own hoped-for development, may be able to argue that its Art 1/1 guarantee has been the subject of interference. Specifically, it could be argued that the requirement that a company subsidise a public development scheme which is completely unrelated to its proposed development does not strike a fair balance.

Determination of a planning application

9.142   It is arguable that the balance that is presently struck in the British planning regime between the private right to property and the general interest is not in accordance with Art 1/1. Indeed, the Government's own Planning Policy Guidance states that local planning authorities are not concerned with protecting

---

1   *Bryan v United Kingdom* (1995) 21 EHRR 342. See also **6.71** et seq.
2   See, for example, *Tesco Stores Limited v Secretary of State of the Environment* [1995] 1 WLR 759.
3   See commentary by Michael Barnes QC in 'Planning and Compensation' in *The Essential Human Rights Act 1998* (Wilberforce Chambers, 2000) at pp 63–67.

the private interests of the individual.[1] The personal circumstances of the applicant for planning permission are, furthermore, only to be taken into account in exceptional circumstances[2] and personal circumstances will seldom outweigh more general planning considerations.[3]

9.143   That is clear, but local planning authorities, which are public authorities in terms of the Act, must now discharge their planning functions in conformity with the interpretative burden placed upon them in s 3 of the Act[4] and this will require to adhere to the guarantees in Art 1/1.

Rights of appeal from planning decisions

9.144   An applicant for planning permission can appeal to the Secretary of State against a refusal of planning permission.[5] There is then a further right of appeal to the High Court on the ground that the Secretary of State's decision was *ultra vires* or that any of the relevant statutory requirements have not been complied with.[6] Following *Bryan*,[7] the jurisdiction exercised by the High Court on appeal from the decision of the Secretary of State is likely to be considered sufficiently 'full' to comply with Art 6.

9.145   The right of appeal against a refusal or conditional grant of planning permission under s 78 of the Town and Country Planning Act is available only to the applicant for planning permission. It follows that a third party has no such right of appeal and has rather to rely on a challenge by way of judicial review to the decision of the local planning authority or a statutory right of appeal on a point of law as a person 'aggrieved'.[8] Even if an applicant pursues his right of appeal under s 78, a third party does not have a right to be heard at a public inquiry. Permission from the inspector is required.

9.146   The European Court decided in *Ortenberg*[9] that a third party is entitled to the protection of Art 6(1) when a grant of planning permission over neighbouring property adversely affects the value of the applicant's property and his enjoyment of it. In that case, the Austrian Government had contended that Art 6(1) did not apply because the right of a neighbour to object to planning permission in a matter involving the protection of the environment was a public-law right and, therefore, was not a *civil* right for the purposes of Art 6(1). The Strasbourg judges rejected the argument on the ground that the applicant was in substance complaining about an infringement of her pecuniary rights, because she alleged that the works envisaged on the neighbouring property would reduce the market value of her land and diminish her enjoyment of it. On the facts, there was found to be no breach because, although the applicant had no right of appeal, the subsequent detailed review by the local administrative court of her complaint was adjudged to be sufficient.

1   PPG1, para 39.
2   See *Great Portland Estates v City of Westminster Council* [1985] AC 661.
3   PPG1, para 38.
4   See **3.41** et seq.
5   Section 78 of the Town and Country Planning Act 1990.
6   Section 288 of the Town and Country Planning Act 1990.
7   See **6.71** et seq.
8   Section 288 of the Town and Country Planning Act 1990.
9   *Ortenberg v Austria* (1994) 19 EHRR 524.

9.147   The European Court has yet to consider whether the absence of a right of appeal against planning permission is a breach of Art 6(1). In *Bryan*,[1] a right of appeal against an enforcement notice to the Secretary of State was in itself held at Strasbourg to be insufficient, but because there was a further right of appeal to the High Court, on a point of law, the European Court concluded, as has been seen, that there had been no violation of Art 6(1).

9.148   A moot point in this context is whether the availability of judicial review or appeal under s 288 of the Town and Country Planning Act is sufficient to comply with Art 6(1). The Strasbourg judges in *Bryan* emphasised the:

> '... uncontested safeguards attending the procedure before the Inspector; the quasi-judicial character of the decision-making process; the duty incumbent on the Inspector to exercise independent judgment; the requirement that Inspectors must not be subject to any improper influence; [and] the stated mission of the Inspectorate to uphold the principle of openness, fairness, and impartiality.'

9.149   Further, when the European Court considered the fact that the High Court was not able to substitute its own findings of fact, it stated that such an approach could be expected in specialised areas of law such as the one at issue, 'particularly where the facts have already been established in the course of a quasi-judicial procedure governed by many of the safeguards required by Article 6(1)'.

9.150   It is certainly possible to argue, on the basis of the decision in *Bryan*, that there is insufficient Art 6(1) protection in the present system for a third party who is aggrieved by a grant of planning permission, because there is no right of appeal on the merits.[2] It also follows that a third party may be able to submit that there has been an infringement of Art 6(1) where an applicant for planning permission exercised his right of appeal to an inspector and the inspector refused the third-party permission to appear at the inquiry. The fact that the third party could apply for judicial review of the inspector's decision may be insufficient in European Convention terms when the third party had no opportunity to be heard before the inspector at the earlier appeal regarding the decision of the local planning authority.

Compensation and planning

9.151   There is no right to compensation in English law where the grant of planning permission on neighbouring land reduces the value of third-party interests and the effect of the grant of planning permission on third-party interests is not treated as a relevant consideration when planning applications are determined.

9.152   On the basis of the European Commission's decision in *S v France*,[3] one leading commentator has argued that a grant of planning permission for a development which does not create an actionable nuisance but which reduces the value of third-party land violates Art 1/1 unless compensation is paid.[4] In that case,

---

1   See **6.71** et seq.
2   See T Corner 'Planning, Environment and the European Convention on Human Rights' [1998] JPL 301 at p 307.
3   (1990) 65 DR 250
4   See Corner (see fn 2 above), p 309.

the applicant had complained of noise nuisance and visual detriment.[1] Her complaints were held to be inadmissible on the basis that the European Commission found that the compensation she had been paid was adequate. However, the Commission went on to state that the taking or affecting of property without payment would normally amount to a violation of Art 1/1 and it must be arguable that the value of property is 'affected' by a development on neighbouring land, even if the development does not constitute an actionable nuisance.

Enforcement action

9.153   A system of effective enforcement is essential to any planning control regime. A local planning authority in the UK may take enforcement action where there has been a breach of planning control. Such action can plainly have a drastic impact on corporate activity. Where such curtailment cannot be justified in the general interest, a company in the future may have the basis for an Art 1/1 complaint.

Planning contravention notices

9.154   Local planning authoritiess have powers under s 171C of the Town and Country Planning Act to seek information from owners and occupiers of land in order to establish whether there has been a breach of planning control. The section permits a local planning authority to serve a 'planning contravention notice' to seek information from owners and occupiers about activities and operations being carried out on their land. The Environment Agency has similar statutory powers.[2]

9.155   The recipient of the notice is required to complete it and failure to do so may result in prosecution. There are virtually no prohibitions on the use of information so obtained[3] and, as a result, it can readily be used not only to decide whether or not enforcement action should be taken, but also as a source of evidence in a subsequent prosecution, for example for failure to comply with an enforcement notice[4] or a breach of condition notice.[5]

9.156   This raises obvious European Convention implications. As has been seen,[6] Art 6(1) safeguards the right against self-incrimination as an aspect of a fair trial. The *Saunders* decision[7] confirmed as much. In the local planning context, local planning authorities are not *required* under statute to use the information obtained through coercive powers in subsequent prosecutions. If, on the other hand, local planning authorities exercise their information-gathering powers and seek to rely on the information so obtained against the provider in subsequent criminal proceedings, Art 6(1) will likely be engaged. Nothing in the *Saunders*

---

1   Visual detriment does not currently constitute a nuisance in English law.
2   Sections 23(1) and 71(3) of the Town and Country Planning Act 1990 and s 110 of the Environment Act 1995.
3   One example is, however, s 108(12) of the Environment Act 1995 – no answer given is admissible in subsequent criminal proceedings.
4   Section 179 of the Town and Country Planning Act 1990.
5   Section 187A of the Town and Country Planning Act 1990.
6   See **6.129** et seq.
7   See **6.132** et seq.

decision by analogy makes, however, the actual *gathering* of information by means of a planning contravention notice contrary to Art 6(1).[1]

9.157 The application of *Saunders* to domestic law in the property context was, as already seen, recently considered by the House of Lords in the case of *R v Hertfordshire County Council, ex parte Green Environmental Industries Ltd and Another*,[2] where requests for information had been served on Green Environmental Industries Ltd in accordance with powers under the Environmental Protection Act and where the Council refused to give any assurance that any information provided would not be used against the company in a subsequent prosecution. The House of Lords ruled that the gathering of information under coercive powers was not in breach of Art 6(1) because the information requests were in substance extra-judicial.

9.158 The limitations of the *Saunders* principle appear to be as narrow in this area as in others.

The burden of proof in enforcement appeals

9.159 The burden of proof in planning enforcement appeals may prove to be a fertile ground for challenge under the Act. A landowner has a right of appeal against the issue of an enforcement notice to the Secretary of State on a number of prescribed grounds.[3] It may, for example, be alleged that no breach of planning control has taken place, or that the activities engaged in do not amount to a breach.

9.160 The legislation does not state upon whom the probative burden rests, but it is conventionally accepted that the burden of proving the facts on which the appeal is based rests on the appellant landowner.[4] It will be apparent that it may be extremely difficult for a company to show that there has been no breach. It may be necessary to find fact witnesses in relation to matters that occurred some time in the past, especially if, for example, the defence relied on is that there has been no material change in use of the land over time. In these circumstances, Michael Barnes QC[5] argues that the law violates the right to use and develop property as protected by Art 1/1 and that it is not apparent that a 'fair balance' can be achieved if a property owner has the burden of establishing his own innocence.

9.161 The allocation of the burden of proof in enforcement proceedings may also obviously breach Art 6, provided (that is) that the right to use and develop land is shown to be a civil right. It is surely difficult, however, to contend that under Art 6(1) a company has a 'fair hearing' on appeal to the Secretary of State if it is required to prove its innocence. Some case can indeed be made out that the existing law is a breach of the presumption of innocence.[6]

9.162 The Secretary of State, as a public authority under the Act, will now have to address this issue when determining enforcement appeals. Judges will also be

---

1   For a further discussion of planning contravention notices and Art 6(1) see M Beloff QC and P Brown 'Planning Contravention Notices and the Right to Silence: The Impact of the Human Rights Act 1998' [1999] JPL December at 1069.
2   (2000) 2 WLR 373. See also **6.143**.
3   Section 174 of the Town and Country Planning Act 1990.
4   See *Nelsovil v Minister of Housing and Local Government* [1962] 1 WLR 404.
5   See fn 3 on p 331.
6   Ibid, at p 56.

bound to act in a way that is compatible with the European Convention under s 6(1) and it will be open to them to adopt an interpretation which does not place the burden of proof on the appellant.

Blight notices

9.163   Part IV, Chapter II of the Town and Country Planning Act 1990 establishes a compensatory scheme for those whose land is blighted by a project carried out in the general interest. The scheme operates in the following way: the owner of the proprietary interest serves a blight notice on the local planning authority and the authority then has to buy the land and pay compensation to the owner. Any diminution in value resulting from blight is ignored for the purposes of assessing the value of the affected land.

9.164   There is a tension between the existing statutory scheme and Art 1/1. A compensation scheme regarding blighted land seeks to strike a balance between the individual's right to property and the general interest in carrying out certain projects, such as (for example) motorway construction. The problem with the current system is that it restricts the categories of person who can serve a blight notice and receive compensation. Corporate bodies, in particular, are affected.

9.165   There are three categories of person who have a 'qualifying interest' in the service of a blight notice:

–   owner-occupiers of residential property;
–   owner-occupiers of agricultural property; and
–   owner-occupiers of other types of property if the annual value is less than (a current) £18,000.

9.166   The corporate sector generally falls into this last category. In many cases, a company will own property but will not be in occupation of it, having (for example) leased it. The company may suffer a loss if the property is blighted and it cannot be sold or can be sold only at a knock-down price. As matters currently stand, a business will not be compensated in such circumstances unless it is in occupation of the blighted premises.

9.167   Even if the company is an owner-occupier of the property, it may have a greater annual income than £18,000 (equivalent to a capital value of approximately £250,000). Here too, the company cannot serve a blight notice. In essence, it is only the interests of smaller businesses which are protected by the legislation and it may be difficult in European Convention terms to justify limitations that do not protect those who buy property as an investment or have property of more than modest commercial value.

Compulsory purchase[1]

9.168   The power of a local authority (which significantly for these purposes can include water and electricity companies acting under statutory powers) to acquire land compulsorily is plainly a serious invasion of a company's right to peaceful enjoyment of its property. This was acknowledged long before Art 1/1 came to be given direct effect through the Act. Lord Denning regarded it 'as a

---

1   See generally in this area the article by M Redman 'Compulsory Purchase, Compensation and Human Rights' [1999] JPL 315.

principle of our constitutional law that no citizen [was] to be deprived of his land by any public authority unless ... expressly authorised by Parliament and the public interest so demands'.[1] More recently, Laws J (as he then was) famously acknowledged that, however eccentric it sounded to some ears, Kwik Save's challenge to a compulsory purchase order made in respect of its store in Stockton-on-Tees raised a fundamental constitutional right.[2]

9.169   The relevant powers of compulsory acquisition[3] and the accompanying provisions for compensation[4] are scattered over a number of statutes. Compulsory purchase is a deprivation of property in terms of the second *Sporrong* rule. As such, the deprivation must in European Convention terms be in the public interest, subject to the conditions provided for by law and to the general principles of international law. As discussed above,[5] the European Court, when considering whether a deprivation is justified under Art 1/1, requires that a proper balance be struck between the individual's right to property and the community interest. So too, if the compulsory purchase is of a 'home' as understood in the European Convention context, Art 8 will be engaged.[6]

9.170   As has been seen, the fact that Art 8 may be relevant does not mean that a compulsory purchase order will not be upheld by a local judge if, for example, it was served on environmental grounds. In a recent decision Malcolm Spence QC (sitting as a Deputy High Court judge) held that 'provided the procedures are followed correctly and fairly and in accordance with the law, there is no infringement of Art 8 if the interference is held to be necessary for the preservation of the environment in the interests of the community'.[7]

9.171   Compensation provisions are, as has been seen,[8] a material factor in assessing whether a fair balance has been struck, and this is the case whether or not a disproportionate burden has been imposed on an individual. In *Lithgow v United Kingdom*,[9] the European Court stated that 'the taking of property in the public interest without payment of compensation is treated as justifiable only in exceptional circumstances'[10] and in light of that decision, it is highly improbable that a local authority in the UK could compulsorily acquire land without paying some compensation.[11]

9.172   If a British court follows the traditional approach of the Strasbourg institutions in according a broad measure of deference to public authorities, both as to what is in the public interest and as regards the payment of less than full

---

1   *Prest v Secretary of State for Wales* [1983] 266 EG 527.
2   *Chesterfield Property Plc v Secretary of State for the Environment and Stockton-on-Tees Borough Council* [1998] JPL 568.
3   See Part IX of the Town and Country Planning Act 1990.
4   See Land Compensation Act 1961, Compulsory Purchase Act 1965, Land Compensation Act 1973 and the Acquisition of Land Act 1981.
5   See **9.120** et seq.
6   See *Howard v United Kingdom* (1987) 9 EHRR CD 91.
7   *Miles v Secretary of State for the Environment* (unreported) 4 June 1999. No Art 1/1 infringement was also found. As regards the European Convention and the environment generally, see **9.179** et seq.
8   See **9.43** et seq.
9   (1986) 8 EHRR 329. See **9.43** et seq.
10   Ibid, at para 120.
11   One exception is the War Damages Act 1965 whereby no compensation is payable for expropriation in time of war (see also **1.37**).

compensation, a company's challenge to a local authority, relying on Art 1/1, is likely to be unfruitful.

Time-limits in planning cases

9.173   Certain of the statutory rights of appeal provided for in the Town and Country Planning Act share a common feature, which is that the appeal must be brought within 6 weeks of the order or act of which complaint is made. Is this problematic in terms of Art 6(1)? The objection could be made that the period is so short and inflexible as to amount to an infringement of the right of effective access to a court.[1] Set against that, the argument will forcefully be made that, without such a truncated period, local planning administration will become very difficult. Why, however, should the time-frame be different from the general requirement to be prompt when making an application for judicial review?

Costs

9.174   The rule that costs generally follow the event in litigation does not apply to planning inquiries. The successful appellant, in the majority of cases, has to bear the costs of the inquiry even where it has been established that the relevant local planning authority had no justification for commencing enforcement action or no good reason in the public interest to refuse planning permission.

9.175   It is an uncontroversial proposition that the taking of enforcement action and the refusal of planning permission may amount to an interference with the right of property[2] and there are grounds for arguing that a fair balance is not struck between the private and the general interest when the property owner has to bear the costs of an unjustified interference. The present system is very arguably a violation of Art 1/1, if not also Art 6(1).

9.176   At present, any costs application must be made at a planning inquiry before the final decision of the Secretary of State or appointed inspector is known. Before the final decision, an appellant is prevented from relying on all relevant facts in support of his application for costs. No doubt advocates will argue that this is a breach of the appellant's right to a fair hearing under Art 6(1).

Conclusion

9.177   While the Act gives direct effect to substantive rights which should help to challenge planning decisions, companies in reality face difficulties in persuading local courts that a particular planning measure does not pursue a legitimate social purpose or that the relevant planning authority has not struck a fair balance between the individual and the community interest. The exceptions will be where the facts are extreme and the planning authority is shown to have a wholly unjustifiable policy or is guilty of manifest delay and inefficiency in implementing a legitimate policy. For this reason, companies should regard procedural challenges under Art 6 as the most effective way of safeguarding their property rights in so far as those rights bear upon the planning regime in the UK.

---

1   As to which, see **6.75** et seq.
2   See Barnes (see fn 3 on p 331), pp 57–60.

THE ACT AND THE ENVIRONMENT[1]

9.178   No express right to environmental protection or to a clean environment is to be extracted from the European Convention,[2] an omission which critics point to as exemplifying the Treaty's limited post-War priorities. However, the criticism is overblown because, as will been seen, the Strasbourg institutions have begun to interpret the European Convention rights in a way that establishes some limited environmental safeguards.

9.179   That guarantees in this area have a crucial role to play in international human rights protection generally has been emphasised by Judge Weeramanty, Vice-President of the International Court of Justice:

> 'The protection of the environment is ... a vital part of contemporary human rights doctrine, for it is a *sine qua non* for numerous human rights such as the right to health and the right to life itself. It is scarcely necessary to elaborate on this, as damage to the environment can impair and undermine all the human rights spoken of in the Universal Declaration and other human rights instruments.'[3]

9.180   There is now a definite multilateral impetus to protect the environment[4] and EC environmental law is, for example, increasingly affecting the form of domestic planning law. Environmental impact assessments are now compulsory in many instances[5] while the Seveso Directive is aimed at preventing major industrial accidents and controlling construction in the vicinity of dangerous industrial sites.[6] Local planning law must comply with EC Directives safeguarding certain animal species[7] and the EU is generally entitled to take decisions concerning land use,[8] while the Treaty of Amsterdam has further emphasised the importance of environmental protection in EU policy-making.[9] Above all, the EU has emphasised that the precautionary principle (whereby preventative action is

---

1   See generally in this area J Thornton and S Tromans 'Human Rights and Environmental Wrongs' [1999] *Journal of Environmental Law* 35.
2   Unlike, for example, s 24 of the South African Final Constitution.
3   In a separate opinion in the *Case Concerning the Gabcikovo-Nagymaros Project between Hungary and Slovakia* on 25 September 1997, reproduced in N Grief's chapter 'Convention Rights and the Environment' in Betten *The Human Rights Act 1998: What it Means* (Martinus Nijhoff Publishers, 1999), p 142.
4   After a series of non-binding declarations (such as the Stockholm Declaration 1972 and the Rio Declaration 1992), the first binding international treaty – the UN/ECE Convention on Access to Information, Public Participation in Decision-making and Access to Justice in Environmental Matters ('the Aarhus Convention') – has now been signed by 35 countries and by the EU and is expected to enter into force in the next few years. It protects procedural rather than substantive rights, however. See also EU Directive 90/313/EEC on freedom of access to information on the environment.
5   Directive 85/337/EEC.
6   Seveso Directive of 24 June 1982.
7   Directive on Preservation of Wild Birds of 2 April 1979, Directive on the Preservation of the Natural Habitat of Endangered Species of 21 May 1992.
8   Article 130S of the EC Treaty.
9   It amends the Treaty of Rome by incorporating the principles of sustainable development and a high level of environmental protection into the stated objectives of the Treaty (Art 2). A new Art 6 states that environmental protection requirements are to be integrated into the definition and implementation of all Community sectoral policies and activities.

to be preferred to remedial measures) applies to environmental matters.[1] Such indeed is the range of EC law protection in this area that claimants may for the foreseeable future prefer to invoke provisions of the Community, as opposed to the Convention, legal order.

9.181   After a slow start, the Strasbourg judges have overcome an initial reluctance to carve out standards in this area[2] and now agree that, 'in today's society the protection of the environment is an increasingly important consideration'.[3] In analysing the Convention's implications for planning law,[4] it was noted that a Contracting State may legitimately promote the general or public interest by the introduction of controls to protect the environment. This aim may justify interference with the property rights of corporates, otherwise protected by Art 1/1, by the imposition of planning restrictions, provided only that a fair balance is struck between the interests of the community and the individual company.[5]

9.182   Restrictions may limit the way in which a company uses or develops land or the activities that it is permitted to carry out on land. A good example of this is the *Pine Valley* case,[6] which arose out of the first applicant's purchase of land with outline planning permission which was then sold to the second applicant. The Irish Supreme Court subsequently declared the outline planning permission to be void. Following a complaint to Strasbourg, the European Court found that this was an interference amounting to a control of use within the third rule in *Sporrong*.[7] The control was, however, legitimate as it was done in the general interest of protecting the environment. Although no compensation had been paid, a fair balance had been struck.

9.183   The *Pine Valley* decision suggests that Art 1/1 remains a poor starting point for a company objecting to a decision ostensibly taken on environmental grounds, on the basis that the European Court there said that it did not, 'in principle, guarantee a right to the peaceful enjoyment of possessions in a pleasant environment'. The European Convention is only likely to be violated where an identifiable individual or corporate interest has been affected in a tangible and damaging way without there being any offsetting public interest consideration.

9.184   A company whose activities are affected by environmental legislation and which requires a licence or authorisation to operate may be able to complain that its property rights have been infringed if its licence or authorisation is revoked or not renewed where it is able to show that the action taken was disproportionate or, for example, that no compensation was paid.[8] Article 1/1 could be relied upon when, for example, government measures, intended to

---

1   See Art 103R(2) of the Treaty of Rome, explicitly adopted in the First Recital to the
     Environmental Impact Assessment Directive (Directive 85/337/EEC as amended by 97/11/
     EC) and the First Recital to the Integrated Pollution Prevention and Control Directive
     (Directive 96/61/EC).
2   See, for example, *X v Germany* (1976) 15 DR 161.
3   *Fredin v Sweden* (1991) 13 EHRR 784.
4   See **9.118** et seq.
5   See, for example, *Fredin v Sweden* (1991) 13 EHRR 784 and *Matos E Silva Lda v Portugal* (1997)
     24 EHRR 573.
6   (1992) 14 EHRR 319.
7   See **9.26** et seq.
8   See **9.43** et seq.

safeguard public or animal health, cause disproportionate loss to a commercial enterprise.[1] Alternatively, a company might conceivably argue, relying on comments of the European Commission in the case of *Powell and Rayner*[2] that (for example) 'noise nuisance which is particularly severe in both intensity and frequency may seriously affect the value of a real property or even render it unsaleable or unusable and thus amount to a partial expropriation'.[3]

9.185   In fact, if it can in the new millennium be stated that a rudimentary form of environmental code is being carved out of the European Convention, it is being eked out not of the property guarantee in Art 1/1 but out of the safeguards for respecting private and family life to be found in Art 8, as is seen below.

Environmental protection and Article 8 – the potential liability of companies

9.186   Environmental litigation is likely to increase after the wholesale implementation of the Act. The most prominent targets will be the 'pure' public authorities,[4] such as central and local government, not merely on account of any polluting activities (for example) for which they are responsible, but also because they may have positive obligations to discharge in this area[5] in terms of the steps they should be taking to secure European Convention rights for all. Also under attack, however, will be hybrid public authorities, such as utility companies, insofar as certain of their functions are functions of a public nature for the purposes of section 6(3) of the Act. This will probably include public suppliers of water, sewerage and waste disposal services and energy and transport providers – all sectors with obvious environmental features. Such companies will understandably be at risk of claims based on the European Convention.

9.187   There are then the much greater number of private companies engaged in environmentally hazardous activities. They too will be monitored closely in the event that local courts seek, as part of their own obligations as public authorities in terms of s 6 of the Act, to uphold European Convention rights in proceedings between private parties. The extent to which action can be taken by one private party against another *directly* on the basis of European Convention rights remains a matter for debate,[6] but there is little doubt that, from now on, claimants will be able to bring actions based on existing torts against, say, the owners of a polluted site, whilst relying on a perceived European Convention breach to bolster their tortious claims. It will therefore be important for *all* companies in environmentally-sensitive industries to be aware of the implications for them of European Convention domestication.

---

1   The Scottish Courts have considered Art 1/1 in relation to an order for the destruction of salmon stocks in the interests of fish health without the payment of compensation. They decided that the measures taken were disproportionate: see *Booker Aquaculture Ltd v Secretary of State for Scotland* (1998) *The Times, Scots Law Report*, 24 September (see also **9.56**). The case has now been referred to the European Court of Justice. See also A O'Neill 'The Protection of Fundamental Rights in Scotland as a General Principle of Community Law' [2000] EHRLR 18.

2   *Powell and Rayner v United Kingdom* (1990) 12 EHRR 355.

3   See also *S v France* (1988) 65 DR 250.

4   See **3.86** et seq.

5   As regards positive obligations generally, see **5.17** et seq.

6   For an analysis of the so-called vertical and horizontal effect of the Act, see **3.74** et seq.

9.188   The European Convention contains, as already stated, no express provision for the protection of the environment but, in the case of *Powell and Rayner*,[1] the European Court determined that Art 8(1) guaranteed respect for a certain *quality* of private life. As will appear, that decision was the first in a series in which a developing environmental right was carved out of Art 8 rather than Art 1/1. Both Treaty guarantees do, to a degree, bear on environmental concerns. One protects (among other matters) the enjoyment of property (Art 1/1), while the other safeguards respect for the home (Art 8). One requires an interest in land (Art 1/1) while the other does not (Art 8). Given the overlap, it is strange that, in a considerable number of cases taken to Strasbourg, the two rights should not have been yoked together.[2]

9.189   In *Powell and Rayner*, the applicants were owners of property in (respectively) Surrey and Berkshire who mounted a challenge arising out of the noise levels from aircraft taking off and landing at Heathrow Airport, arguing that the Government's measures to reduce noise nuisance were inadequate. The Strasbourg judges accepted that Art 8 applied because: 'In each case ... the quality of the applicant's private life and the scope for enjoying the amenities of his home have been adversely affected by the noise generated by aircraft using Heathrow Airport'.

9.190   The European Court considered that it did not matter whether the complaints before them were approached on the basis of a positive duty on the State to take the requisite measures to safeguard the applicants' rights under Art 8(1) or in (the negative) terms of an interference to be justified under Art 8(2). The principle was in either event broadly the same, namely the identification of that fair balance which must exist between the interest of the individual and the community as a whole.

9.191   The operation of a large international facility like Heathrow was, the applicants agreed, of strategic importance to the UK and its continued development was a legitimate aim, even if the impact upon the environment could not entirely be removed. As a number of measures had in fact been introduced to abate noise and compensate residents affected by it, the European Court took the view that the policy imperative and the regulatory measures adopted did not give rise to a violation of Art 8(1), whether or not the State's obligations were approached in terms of negative or positive obligations. The margin of appreciation which was permitted in such a case had not been exceeded, neither had the fair balance struck been upset.[3]

9.192   In one sense the applicants' failure in *Powell and Rayner* was surprising because British householders in two earlier noise cases taken to Strasbourg and declared admissible there were able to settle with the Government on terms including the payment of compensation.[4] Those applications were, however,

---

1   *Powell and Rayner v United Kingdom* (1990) 12 EHRR 355. See also **9.184**.
2   See, for example, *Buckley v United Kingdom* (1997) 23 EHRR 101.
3   A case has been declared admissible by the European Court in which it is alleged that night flights into Heathrow amount to a violation of the local residents' rights under Art 8. See, for example, Press Association, 16 May 2000.
4   See *Arrondelle v United Kingdom* Appl 7889/77, (1982) 19 DR 186 (£7,000 paid). The European Commission had accepted there that the British Government was not responsible for the noise made by cars on the M23 but it was responsible for the motorway itself. See also *Baggs v United Kingdom* Appl 9310/81, (1985) 44 DR 13 (£24,000 paid).

arguably distinguishable from *Powell and Rayner* to the extent that the conditions in one instance were described as 'intolerable' and 'exceptional' and where there was evidence that the applicant's proximity to the noise made it virtually impossible to sell up and move.

9.193　　Although no violation was identified in *Powell and Rayner,* the case is a good illustration of the way in which claimants may be able to rely on Art 8 in environmental disputes. Its potentially broad application stems from the notion that Art 8 may place positive as well as negative obligations on public authorities as regards the protection of private and family life.[1] Article 8 additionally demands that a fair balance be struck between the (often competing) interests of the individual and the community. A violation will only be found if this balance has not been achieved. This was confirmed in *S v France*[2] in which *Powell and Rayner* was cited. Building a nuclear power station 300 metres from the applicant's home undoubtedly engaged Art 8, but no European Convention violation was found because the applicant had already been awarded FFr250,000 by the French authorities.

9.194　　In two subsequent cases the European Court did establish the existence of violations and, in the process, it has expanded the notion of respect for private and family life in the environmental context. In *Lopez Ostra,*[3] the Strasbourg judges determined, to begin with, that serious environmental pollution may affect individual well-being and prevent citizens from enjoying their homes because of the adverse implications for private and family life that pollution may present, not least in terms of the risk to health.

9.195　　The facts were that the applicant complained about a waste treatment plant that had been built by a private company 12 metres from her home in a municipality where there was already a heavy concentration of environmentally-insensitive industry. The plant had begun operations in the absence of a licence. Its fumes were soon affecting those living nearby, including the applicant's daughter, who became seriously ill. Although the Spanish authorities were not directly responsible for the toxic emissions, the European Court found unanimously that Spain was nevertheless in violation of Art 8, the local municipality having permitted the plant's construction on its land and subsidised its construction. The State had not struck a fair balance between the economic future of the town involved (even though, ironically, it had been hoped that the plant would reduce pollution in an industrial area) and the applicant's right to respect and effective enjoyment of her home and private and family life. Nor was it enough that the township had ordered the temporary shutdown of the plant and rehoused affected residents. The authorities were adjudged not to have taken sufficient measures to protect the applicant's Art 8 rights because they had

---

1　　Consider in the environmental context, for example, the extended burden arguably placed by the Act upon local councils to deal with the problem of abusive tenants. It has even been suggested that the failure of central Government to deal with the proliferation of leylandii trees could raise an Art 8 issue. See W Outhwaite and M Wheeler *The Civil Practitioner's Guide to the Human Rights Act 1998* (Old Bailey Press, 1999), p 76.

2　　See fn 3 on p 341.

3　　*Lopez Ostra v Spain* (1995) 20 EHRR 277.

allowed the pollution to continue and had even challenged two national court orders that the plant be closed temporarily.[1]

9.196 This case illustrates three points of particular interest to corporates. First, it demonstrates that an individual's quality of life may be infringed so as to breach Art 8 *even if his health is not endangered.* Invocation of the Convention therefore is not restricted to instances of extremely serious or life-threatening environmental pollution. Secondly, *Lopez Ostra* points up the residual liability of a State which fails adequately (or at all) to regulate the activities of private or commercial interests. Thirdly, it displays a willingness on the part of the Strasbourg institutions to award compensation for what is perceived to be environmental misconduct,[2] a willingness that the Act statutorily obliges local courts to take into account.[3]

9.197 In *Guerra*,[4] the protection afforded by Art 8 in environmental cases was extended further. There the European Court held that a State could be liable in European Convention terms for failing to provide necessary information to individuals which would enable them to assess the environmental risk to which they were being subjected. In *Guerra*, all 40 applicants lived within 1 kilometre of a chemical factory which was not State-owned, which had been classified by the Italian Government as a high-risk operation and where there had been a poisoning incident in 1976 as a result of which 150 people had been admitted to hospital. In 1988, a technical report had criticised standards at the site and the applicants complained that the local authorities had not taken sufficient practical action to reduce the risk of pollution and to prevent accidents. They also contended that inaction over several years before releasing the requisite information amounted not only to a breach of Art 8, but also to the right to life safeguarded in Art 2.[5] They further complained that the failure to inform the public about the hazards and the procedures to be followed in the event of an accident was a breach of their right to receive information as protected by Art 10.

9.198 The European Court (disagreeing with the European Commission) held that Art 10 did not apply because it did not place a positive duty on a State to provide information, but only prohibited a State from preventing a person from receiving information.[6] Article 2 was also inapplicable, although Judge Walsh and Judge Jambrek dissented from this, the latter making the point 'that the protection of health and physical integrity is as closely associated with the "right to life" as with ... respect for private and family life'.

9.199 Article 8 was adjudged, however, to be relevant. The close location of the applicants' homes to the factory meant that the toxic emissions bore directly on the applicants' right to respect for their private and family lives and the Strasbourg judges restated the view that there may be positive obligations inherent in the need to secure effective respect for such lives.

---

1   The applicant had also argued that there was a breach of Art 3 of the European Convention, which prohibits inhuman or degrading treatment, but the European Court rejected this allegation. See **9.215** et seq.
2   Approximately Ptas 25m were awarded.
3   See **3.160** et seq.
4   *Guerra v Italy* (1998) 26 EHRR 357.
5   See Appendix 2.
6   See **8.157** et seq.

9.200   In neither *Lopez Ostra* nor *Guerra* were public authorities the polluters. The issue in *Guerra* was whether the national authorities had taken the necessary steps to ensure effective protection of the applicants' rights. The applicants had waited in vain for essential information which would have assisted them in assessing the risks they were running and, as such, the national authorities had failed to fulfil their obligations under Art 8.[1]

9.201   The *Guerra* judgment will be a starting-point in future environmental cases in the UK. It is now persuasive authority for the proposition that not only are Contracting States under a duty to provide information to individuals about health risks and disaster procedures in the environmental context but that the duty may be engaged even if the hazardous operation belongs to a private company. A wholly practical consequence of the Act is that public authorities are now likely to demand that private companies engaged in high-risk activities carry out comprehensive risk assessments so that, at the very least, adequate information can be made publicly available to satisfy the positive duty placed upon emanations of the State. Utility companies designated public authorities under the Act as regards their public functions are very likely to have to make such information publicly available in any event.

9.202   The obligation on public authorities to provide information regarding risks to environmental health was later addressed by the Strasbourg judges in the case of *McGinley and Egan*.[2] The applicants there were British ex-servicemen who had been stationed on or near Christmas Island during atmospheric nuclear testing in the 1950s and who sought to establish whether they had been exposed to dangerous levels of radiation. Although no Art 8 violation was found (on a 5:4 split), the European Court stated that:

> 'Where a Government engages in hazardous activities, such as those in issue in the present case, which might have hidden consequences on the health of those involved in such activities, respect for private and family life under Article 8 requires that an effective and accessible procedure be established which enables such persons to seek all relevant and appropriate information.'

9.203   There was no breach on the facts because such a procedure was available, but the principle was clear. It is against this background that companies should anticipate that the Act will be a catalyst for tighter State controls over activities which pollute or endanger the environment. Firms that cause discharges or other forms of nuisance can expect that enforcement authorities, if only to forestall damages claims directed at them, will act with even greater haste than they may conceivably do at present. Companies engaging in hazardous activities such as incineration and open-cast extraction may additionally find that the necessary licenses or authorisations become harder to obtain once public authorities take on board the ramifications of Art 8.

9.204   The burden placed in environmental terms upon the corporate sector by virtue of the Act should not, however, be over-estimated. Although there would appear to be no reason why Art 8(1) may not in the future be invoked in most cases of nuisance, Art 8(2) allows for interference with the right to respect for home and family life in the interests of national security, public safety or the economic

---

1   Compensation of Lira 10m was awarded.
2   *McGinley and Egan v United Kingdom* (1998) 27 EHRR 1. See also **6.124** as regards the implications of the case for disclosure obligations in litigation.

well-being of the country. In particular, the European Court has granted a considerable margin of appreciation to States in the implementation of economic policies, as illustrated by the decision in *Powell and Rayner*.[1] Above all else, it requires to be emphasised that, to date, only two violations of Art 8 have been found by the European Court in the environmental context (namely *Lopez Ostra* and *Guerra*), both of which were highly unusual cases on their facts.

9.205 The dynamic development of European Convention jurisprudence in the environmental context has, furthermore, been slowed by the deference shown to States when the fair balance test has been applied and by the narrow victim test for standing which has limited the scope for complaint by pressure groups. These constraints may yet prove to be less significant in the UK, particularly if the traditional test for standing in applications for judicial review, which has in the past helped campaigning organisations to bring actions, informs the approach of British judges to the victim test stipulated in s 7 of the Act.[2] As in so many other respects, the early judgments may be decisive for the future development of the law in this area. Suffice for the present to say that recognition of public concern about environmental risk has clearly been evident in a number of recent domestic cases.[3]

Corporate claimants in environmental cases

9.206 This discussion has proceeded so far on the premise that it is the company which is the polluter. A company may, however, wish to argue that its own European Convention rights have been infringed by environmental damage. As has been seen already, the European Court has held that the notion of 'private life' in Art 8 may conceivably extend to certain business or professional activities.[4] Whether a manufacturing facility is also protected remains unclear, although there appears no reason in principle why such a facility should be excluded from protection.

Due process and environmental rights

9.207 The effectiveness of the procedural protection of underlying substantive European Convention rights (such as the right to property), that is guaranteed by Art 6, is discussed elsewhere.[5] It is clear that interference with other European Convention rights may engage Art 6 and amount to a *determination of civil rights and obligations*. A decision by a local authority or the Secretary of State

---

1   See **9.189** et seq. Arguments about the economic well-being of the country were also deployed against the applicants in a case about Canary Wharf (*Hunter v London Docklands Development Corporation* [1997] AC 655), which the applicants lost in the House of Lords on the basis that, as they had no proprietary interest in land, they could not proceed in nuisance. That decision now looks questionable in European Convention terms. See *Pemberton v Southwark London Borough Council* [2000] EG 135 and **9.229**.
2   See **3.123** et seq. Pressure groups may also be able to rely on provisions of the Aarhus Convention once ratified.
3   See, for example, *Enviroco Waste Holdings v Secretary of State for the Environment* [1996] Env LR 49 and *Secretary of State for the Environment v Redland Aggregates; R v Norwich City Council* [1998] Env LR 12. See also the article by P Shiner 'Environmental Protection Judicial Review and Human Rights' [1999] JR 43.
4   *Niemietz v Germany* (1992) 16 EHRR 97. See also **7.20** et seq.
5   See **9.64**.

authorising, for example, a factory or power station to carry on an activity which pollutes or endangers the environment may interfere with a company's right to property under Art 1/1 and its right to respect for its 'home' as safeguarded by Art 8. A company may seek to rely on Art 6 in order to buttress these rights. Alternatively, if a company is an entity carrying out the polluting activity for which authorisation or a licence has been given, it should be aware of the Art 6 implications of, for example, licence revocation. In *Fredin*, the owner of a gravel pit who had invested heavily in it was told not only that he had to stop excavations some months later but that financially he would need to secure the cost of making the site good. Neither demand was judicially reviewable and this was held by the European Court to constitute an Art 6 violation.[1]

9.208 There is no third-party right of appeal where a pollution control or waste management licence is granted in the UK.[2] As with the position in relation to planning decisions, the absence of an appeal on the merits may breach Art 6, despite the finding in *Bryan*[3] that the combination of an appeal to the Secretary of State or appointed inspector and subsequent review by the High Court was sufficient. There is no discretion to hear oral representations from a third party on an appeal to the Secretary of State in relation to pollution control and waste management licences – arguably another process breach.[4]

9.209 Nevertheless, third parties will encounter difficulties in relying on Art 6 in the context of environmental claims. In *Balmer-Schafroth*,[5] the applicants lived three miles from a nuclear power station and objected to the extension of its operating licence. They argued that they had been denied access to a tribunal for the purposes of objecting to the extension. The European Court held (dividing 12:8) that Art 6 was not applicable because the applicants had failed to show that the power station had 'exposed them personally to a danger that was not only serious but also specific and, above all, imminent'.[6]

9.210 If this approach is followed by domestic courts, it may prove difficult for individuals or companies to show that they are in sufficient danger to be able to bring a complaint under Art 6. Such a restrictive attitude will doubtless be criticised as under-estimating the importance of the preservation of the environment in community terms and as not being consistent with other developments in this area, such as the application of EC law's precautionary principle and the growing judicial recognition of the importance of the public perception of risk. Therefore, there is as yet no reliable indication that local judges will choose to restrict the application of Art 6 in the way that the majority of the European Court did in *Balmer-Schafroth*.

9.211 Whether, however, they express themselves as pungently as Judge Pettiti in his dissenting opinion is another matter. He said: 'The European Court's assessment of the tenuousness of the connection and of the absence of imminent danger is, in my opinion, unfounded. Does the local population first have to be eradicated before being entitled to a remedy?'

---

1   See fn 5 on p 306.
2   Compare the position in the planning context, see **9.146** et seq.
3   See **6.71** et seq.
4   See, generally, in this area P Shiner (see fn 3 on p 346), p 46.
5   *Balmer Schaforth v Switzerland* (1998) 25 EHRR 598.
6   Ibid, at para 40.

The right to life and the environment

9.212   Article 2 of the European Convention protects the right to life.[1] It prohibits a State from taking life intentionally. More than that, it requires that the State take effective steps to safeguard life.[2] It has been argued that 'life' must mean more than the opposite of death and that it implies a certain quality of life and not merely existence.[3] On this basis, Art 2 could, in theory, be relied on in support of an allegation that an environmental wrong has threatened life. The difficulty lies in establishing a causative link between the environmental damage and the threat to life.[4] Where such a nexus can be established, the conduct in question is likely in any event to be within the scope of one of the statutory offences that already exists in this country. As such, the giving of further effect to Art 2 through the Act may not make any material difference in practice. In any event, it may be a defence that relevant environmental standards have been adhered to. [5]

9.213   The majority of the Strasbourg judges in *Guerra*[6] did not consider the applicants' Art 2 argument, an Art 8 violation having been established. Two judges did, however, consider the issue in concurring opinions.[7] They both emphasised the need for applicants to show substantial grounds for believing that they faced a 'real risk of being subjected to circumstances which endanger their health and physical integrity and thereby put at serious risk their right to life'. Nevertheless, one of the two dissentents, Judge Jambrek, called for the Strasbourg jurisprudence on Art 2 to 'start evolving, to develop the respective implied rights, [and to] articulate situations of real and serious risk to life, or different aspects of the right to life'.

9.214   The European Court has made clear that a State is required to take positive action to protect the right enshrined in Art 2 (and, of course, in other Articles) and the scope of this right may expand in the future. It is possible, therefore, that State agencies in the UK could at some point be liable under Art 2 for failing to take action against a company engaging in environmentally dangerous activities. Would this extend, at the margins, to include the activities of biotechnology companies or to utility companies (whether public authorities or not) who terminate supply for non-payment? Firms engaged in water and sewage treatment, waste disposal and incineration or which operate power stations are certainly at risk if judicially classified as public authorities (in relation to their public functions), as appears likely. Beyond that, advocates may argue that the requirement of *intention* in Art 2 should be purposively read as covering recklessness and that inaction by public authorities as regards, for example, exhaust emissions or the operation of mobile telephone transmitters in the face of accumulated evidence will not be sufficient to enable them to avoid complaints based on Art 2.

---

1   See Appendix 2.
2   *McCann v United Kingdom* (1996) 21 EHRR 97.
3   N Grief (see fn 3 on p 339), p 143.
4   An example of a case where it was found that there was no causal link establishing a breach of Art 2 was in *LCB v United Kingdom* (1999) 27 EHRR 212. The European Court was not satisfied that the exposure of the applicant's father to radiation had caused her leukaemia.
5   See *LM and R v Switzerland* (1996) 22 EHRR CD 130.
6   See **9.197** et seq.
7   See opinions of Judge Walsh and Judge Jambrek and see **9.197** et seq.

Inhuman and degrading treatment and the environment

9.215   It was accepted by the European Court in *Lopez Ostra*[1] that environmental activity might conceivably violate Art 3 of the European Convention[2] if the conditions that an applicant lived in were so bad as to amount to degrading treatment. In extreme cases, a State could be liable under this part of the Treaty too, as could a utility classified as a public authority under the Act.

9.216   Grief suggests[3] that sewage discharges into the sea may, depending upon the facts, engage Arts 2 and 3. Whilst this possibility no doubt exists, a more likely use of the guarantees in these Articles in the commercial context is by claimants against, for example, rail companies, using Art 2 to bolster a private law claim for negligence following a track death and Art 3 in an action about (say) overcrowding.

9.217   It will be apparent from this very short explanation that even those parts of the European Convention furthest removed from corporate life, the first two substantive rights identified in the Treaty, may become necessary reading in boardrooms here.

Discrimination and the environment

9.218   Article 14,[4] which prohibits discrimination, can only be invoked in conjunction with one of the other European Convention rights. If an environmental complaint fell within one of the rights listed above, Art 14 could also conceivably be raised depending, that is, on the evidence showing a differentiation in treatment. In circumstances where parts of society are potentially exposed to greater environmental risks than others, the role of Art 14 is of some importance. There is a substantial literature in the USA about this issue (commonly referred to as 'environmental justice'), where the argument is made that racial and ethnic minorities and low-income groups are commonly exposed to greater environmental risks.[5]

9.219   Where public authorities in the UK fail to monitor the impact of environmentally-hazardous activities across all sections of the community, they should anticipate that Art 14 will be included in the claims made against them.

Conclusion

9.220   The need to protect the environment raises issues which cut across many of the European Convention rights domesticated by the Act. The impact on companies will come mainly from the increased armoury available to litigants seeking to challenge corporate activity which is alleged to harm or endanger the environment. Such litigants will now be able to argue that certain forms of activity infringe one or more of their human rights. On the other hand, putative claimants may encounter a strict application by local judges of the 'victim' requirement for standing in s 7 of the Act which may inhibit communal or group action – traditionally the basis for many planning and environmental protests in the UK.

---

1   See **9.194** et seq.
2   See Appendix 2.
3   See fn 3 on p 339 at p 146.
4   See **5.44** et seq.
5   See the helpful summary of the US position in Grief (see fn 3 on p 339), pp 158 et seq.

9.221   The fact that there is as yet no explicit European Convention right to a clean or healthy environment means that substantive protection of the environment has been made to fit into other rights which neither separately nor together constitute a comprehensive code. Despite the close connection between environmental issues and real estate, the procedural rights conferred by Art 6 and the limited information right in Art 8 may offer greater advantages for prospective claimants in the short term than the property right in Art 1/1.

THE ACT'S IMPLICATIONS FOR 'PURE' PROPERTY RIGHTS

9.222   The paramount importance of interests in and over land has recently been emphasised by Jean Howell:

> 'Even if a citizen has no rights to private property, he must have some sort of right, however loosely defined, to a place to live: there is no human activity which does not require, at the very least, access to land. Equally, property rights, whether in the form of freehold or leasehold ownership, or of an option to acquire property at a future date are a vital aspect of any commercial enterprise.'[1]

9.223   In such circumstances, it is perhaps no surprise that the European Commission should have held that a house in which the applicant has a legal interest but no legal permission to be in occupation was a 'home' within the scope of Art 8(1)[2] and this principle was confirmed by the European Court in *Buckley v United Kingdom*,[3] where a caravan, occupied (unlawfully) on the applicant's own land, was acknowledged also to be her 'home' in European Convention terms.[4]

9.224   Corporate landlords will find this unnervingly broad in reach. In an era in which organised squatters, eco-warriors and others jostle for media attention, what is a landlord to make of the observation of the European Commission in *G and E v Norway* that 'a minority group is, in principle, entitled to claim the right to respect for the particular lifestyle it may lead as being private life, family life or home'?[5]

9.225   Companies are plainly concerned to protect their proprietary rights in or over land. Furthermore, the rights of others, including lessees of company property, may influence the way in which companies conduct their affairs.

9.226   The instances cited above may be helpful therefore to the extent that they are illustrative of the way in which the Strasbourg institutions have tended to consider the way in which the provisions of the European Convention engage

---

1   In 'The Protection of Rights of Property in Land Under the Human Rights Act' in L Betten (ed) *The Human Rights Act 1998 – What It Means* (Martinus Nijhoff Publishers, 1998), p 168.

2   *Wiggins v United Kingdom* (1978) 13 DR 40. For a more restrictive view, see *S v United Kingdom* (1986) 47 DR 274. The position of tenancies held by same-sex couples was recently reviewed by the House of Lords in *Fitzpatrick v Sterling Housing Association* [2000] 1 FLR 271, where it was held by a majority of 3:2 that the male gay partner of a deceased tenant could succeed to the tenancy of the deceased.

3   (1996) 23 EHRR 101. See also *Gillow v United Kingdom* (1989) 11 EHRR 335 and *Mabey v United Kingdom* (1996) 22 EHRR CD 123.

4   See also *Turner v United Kingdom* (1997) 23 EHRR CD 181, another case about a caravan.

5   See generally the material in K Starmer's *European Human Rights Law* (Legal Action Group, 1999), pp 579 et seq.

private property rights. Even before the wholesale coming into force of the Act, it was apparent that the Treaty's use to protect a wide range of interests in land was becoming more common in local courts, such as in a case where the issue was whether Art 1/1 could be used to challenge the duty of a lay rector to pay for repairs to a church chancel.[1]

9.227   The vast majority of 'pure' property disputes involve private parties and rarely engage the responsibility of the State unless, for example, a private party is challenging legislation,[2] a planning measure or another form of State-imposed control.[3] The fact that the State has intervened to regulate private relations does not render it responsible, in European Convention terms, for the resulting consequences.[4] Therefore, the applicant in the *Di Palma* case[5] could not claim to have been deprived of her possessions by the State under Art 1/1 where the local court had ordered the forfeiture of a valuable long lease in accordance with the terms of the lease (the applicant having failed to pay the service charge). As far as the European Commission was concerned, the court order merely enforced a private law contract, freely entered into, between landlord and tenant.

9.228   What was more, the Commissioners found that forfeiture provisions were 'a common feature of tenancy agreements under the legal systems of all the member states of the Council of Europe'. The applicant's submissions in relation to Art 8 also failed on the basis that repossession was a legitimate interference within the exceptions provided in Art 8(2). Although only a Commission decision, *Di Palma* puts clear limits on the extent to which States are to be expected to regulate private property relations. It may also provide support for a broader argument as to waiver, in the sense that consent by contract may prevent any engagement of Art 1/1.[6]

9.229   In the same way, the fact that the Act is unlikely to have direct horizontal effect will mean that the protection offered by Art 1/1 in private property disputes will be limited. That is not to say, however, that legal authorities such as *Hunter v Canary Wharf*[7] will go unchallenged. In that case, the House of Lords held that occupiers of properties near Canary Wharf could not bring claims for nuisance, on the basis that they had no exclusive interest in the land affected by the nuisance of which complaint was made. This surely engages Art 8, whose protection is much broader.

---

1   See *Parochial Church Council of Aston Cantlow and Wilmcote v Wallbank and Another* (2000) *The Times*, 28 March – the duty arises under the Chancel Repairs Act 1932. The Court found that the fact that the cost of repairs could vary from parish to parish was not discriminatory. Articles 8 and 14 were also relied upon. See also *Jones and Lee v Miah* [1992] 2 EGLR 50, for a residential case in which the European Convention was referred to.
2   As in *Lithgow v United Kingdom* (1986) 8 EHRR 329 and *James v United Kingdom* (1986) 8 EHRR 123. See **9.42** et seq.
3   As in *Sporrong and Lönnroth v Sweden* (1983) 5 EHRR 35. See **9.119** et seq.
4   Thus, a charging order imposed in civil proceedings will not be an interference engaging Art 1/1: see *X v Belgium* Appl 7256/75 (1977) DR 8.
5   *Di Palma v United Kingdom* (1998) 10 EHRR 149 which followed the domestic decision in the same case: see *Di Palma v Victoria Square Property Co Limited* [1986] Ch 150. Note, too, that a repossession clause has been held at Strasbourg not to be a possession within Art 1/1: see *Antoniades v United Kingdom* (1990) 64 DR 232.
6   See also in this context *Holy Monasteries v Greece* (1994) 20 EHRR 1 at paras 76–78. As to the waiver of European Convention rights generally, see **6.170**.
7   [1997] 2 WLR 684. See also fn 1 on p 346.

Commercial landlords and property rights – as claimants

9.230   As a consequence of the Act, landlords may conceivably seek to argue that their property rights have been infringed if the Government introduces legislation which, for example, adversely affects their ability to extract rents. In *Ex parte Spath Holmes Ltd*, the Court of Appeal accepted that the right to receive a fair rent was a possession in terms of Art 1/1.[1] The applicant landlords had challenged an order of the Secretary of State which capped the rent payable in relation to regulated tenancies. It was held that the order was *ultra vires* the legislation under which it was introduced and it was struck down on that basis. Having considered that Art 1/1 applied in principle, the judges noted that balancing the respective interests of the tenants and landlords and determining whether the landlords or the taxpayer should subsidise any hardship arising was essentially a political issue. The evidence showed that the Government had consulted with landlords and had chosen not to accept their objections. The Court of Appeal concluded that, as such, the decision was not irrational.

9.231   As a consequence of the Act, local courts will henceforth also have to consider in appropriate cases of this sort whether or not a fair balance has been struck between the individual and the general interest in terms of Art 1/1.[2] This will be so, however reticent judges here are to be portrayed in the Act's early period as acting exorbitantly in policy areas.

9.232   Landlords may seek to argue that their right to property is infringed by the continued operation of assured tenancies or of tenancies which are still governed by the terms of the Rent Act 1977. The law governing assured shorthold tenancies gives landlords a statutory right to possession, a right which is extremely restricted in the case of old-style tenancies. This is arguably an interference with a right to possession of property under Art 1/1 which, in an age when little statutory protection is any longer given to tenants, arguably cannot be justified by a social policy pursued in the general interest. Conceivably Art 14, prohibiting discriminatory treatment, could also be invoked in this context.

Commercial landlords and property rights – as defendants

9.233   The fact that it is only public authorities which, by virtue of the Act,[3] are made directly liable for breaching European Convention rights does not mean that the Act is of no concern to private landlords. As has been seen, individuals can rely on European Convention rights in any legal proceedings.[4] This could include proceedings against a private landlord, even though in such proceedings claimants will almost certainly need to have available an existing, separate cause of action against the landlord and will not be relying solely on the breach of a European Convention right. Even so, in *Albany Homes Loans Limited v Massey*,[5] Lord Justice Schiemann, before the introduction of the Act, suggested that Art 8

---

1   *R v Secretary of State for Transport, Environment and the Regions, ex parte Spath Holmes Ltd* [2000] 1 All ER 884.
2   Howell (see fn 1 on p 350) at fn 58 on p 183 cites the Irish case of *Blake v Attorney General* [1982] IR 117, in which a statute restricting a landlord's right to possession was held to be unconstitutional.
3   Section 6 of the Act. See **3.73** et seq.
4   Section 7(1)(b) of the Act, see **3.124** et seq.
5   [1997] 2 All ER 609.

provided 'a clue to the solution to the problems' posed in a mortgage repossession case in terms of the need for the mortgagee to establish that possession was necessary for the protection of its rights – a statement that has alarmingly broad implications for private landlords.

9.234   A corporate landlord may, for example, face a challenge under Art 1/1 where it seeks to exercise powers under the Housing Act 1996 to take possession of a secure or assured tenancy on the ground that the tenant or a visitor has been guilty of anti-social behaviour.[1] It could be argued that that legislation imposes a disproportionate burden on the tenant when other legislation could be used just as effectively to combat anti-social behaviour.[2]

The position of housing associations

9.235   In addition to local authorities, housing associations may well be classified as public authorities for the purposes of the Act. Housing associations are often funded by a mixture of public and private sources. They may be public authorities under the Act when exercising some functions, and private bodies when exercising others.[3] Most housing associations are registered social landlords under s 2 of the Housing Act 1996. Not only do they receive public funds, but they are also subject to wide powers of policy direction and regulation. When carrying out regulated functions or publicly-funded functions, such housing associations will need to ensure that their activities conform to the European Convention rights given further effect by the Act.

9.236   A housing association therefore could find that it is faced with a number of challenges as a consequence of the domestication of the European Convention. In particular, it may foreseeably be argued that a particular housing association has failed to respect private and family life under Art 8 in the implementation of its housing allocation policy. Article 14 may also be engaged on account of the form of policy adopted.

Distress

9.237   The law of distress permits a landlord to enter on to the property of the tenant and seize goods to satisfy the payment of rent. This is done without court proceedings and whether or not the goods actually belong to the tenant. At common law, the landlord was merely permitted to retain the goods. Under the Distress for Rent Act 1689, however, a landlord has the power to sell the goods seized. It can be expected that tenants (including tenants of private landlords) will seek to resist the levying of distress by arguing that it is in breach of one or more safeguards in the European Convention and this issue has already been aired in the Scottish parliament.[4]

9.238   Distress may, for example, obviously be in breach of Art 1/1 by permitting a landlord to deprive a tenant (and even a third party) of his possessions. The question for consideration by local judges will be whether it is

---

1   Specifically, ss 144 and 148 of the Housing Act 1996.
2   Such as the Crime and Disorder Act 1998.
3   See s 6(5) of Act. See **3.73** et seq.
4   See *The Sunday Times*, 23 April 2000.

justified in the public interest. On the face of it, the law appears to place a disproportionate burden on tenants. The European Court has held, however, that Contracting States are entitled to control property and possessions to secure the payment of tax and that even a power to seize and sell a third party's assets to pay tax debts was in accordance with Art 1/1.[1] On this basis, it might be said that the doctrine of distress is not a violation of Art 1/1.

9.239   On the other hand, Art 1/1 also requires that a deprivation be *provided for by law*. It is not dispositive for these purposes that distress is sanctioned by domestic legislation. The European Convention requirement of lawfulness protects the individual against arbitrary conduct and demands compliance with the principle of legal certainty. The relevant law must therefore be sufficiently clear for citizens to know what their rights are. The Law Commission has criticised the rules on distress as not only arbitrary and artificial, but also uncertain due to the broad discretion placed in the hands of landlords and bailiffs.[2]

9.240   As distress involves entry into the tenant's home or premises, Art 8, guaranteeing respect for private and family life, is potentially in issue. In this context also, if a landlord's distraint is to be justified, it must be in accordance with law, pursue a legitimate aim and be proportionate.

9.241   Levying distress in order to protect the interests of creditors may well be necessary in a democratic society. As far as the requirement of proportionality is concerned, however, much may depend on the manner in which distress is levied, and specifically on factors such as whether the tenant was present, the extent of the search carried out and the number of people conducting the search. The Law Commission has commented in this regard that distress is usually carried out 'in a manner which may be intended to cause maximum inconvenience and unpleasantness'.[3] For so long as that continues to be so, landlords may be increasing the potential for challenges based on Art 8.[4] Certainly, it is difficult to see how distress carried out for non-payment of a television licence or a parking fine can be argued to be proportionate. There is, furthermore, no *obligation* to levy distress and a public authority engaged in distraining will not be able to rely on the defence (in s 6(2) of the Act) that it was statutorily compelled to act in the way that it did.[5]

9.242   Against this background, it is perhaps surprising that the due process requirements of Art 6 may not be of great assistance to tenants in challenging distress, despite the fact that distress is a remedy apparently without legal process. This is because the right to distrain presupposes that rent is owing and in many instances there will be no *contestation*[6] to engage Art 6. Where goods are wrongfully seized, however, there are a number of remedies available such as replevin, injunctions and damages which allow for determination of the tenant's rights by an independent and impartial tribunal. A third party also has access to the courts if distress is levied unlawfully.

---

1   See *Gasus Dosier und Fördertechnik GmbH v The Netherlands* (1995) 20 EHRR 403.
2   Law Com Report No 194: *Distress for Rent*.
3   Ibid at para 3.15.
4   For a case in which forcible entry to seize and sell goods was found not to be in breach of Art 8, see *K v Sweden* Appl 13800/88, (1991) 71 DR 94.
5   See **3.120** et seq.
6   See **6.30** et seq.

9.243   Odds are that a local court, as a public authority, may be constrained by its duty to act compatibly with the European Convention rights to develop the common law of distress in such a way that it cannot any longer be regarded as 'an automatic incident of tenure under a lease'[1] in the absence of express agreement between the parties. In short, the current domestic law in this area remains problematic in European Convention terms. But if that be so, how secure is the right of landlords to forfeit leases by peaceable re-entry?

Company mortgages

9.244   Mortgagees have the right to immediate possession of land. It is, however, an accepted practice that mortgagees only exercise this right where there has (first) been a default on the part of the mortgagor and by the bringing of possession proceedings. When a mortgagee institutes possession proceedings, the mortgagor is further protected by the terms of s 36 of the Administration of Justice Act 1970, by virtue of which a court can adjourn, stay or suspend the exercise of the right to possession and give the mortgagor further time in which to make payment.

9.245   The Court of Appeal has held in *Ropaigeleach v Barclays Bank*[2] that a mortgagee retains the right to exercise his right to possession by physical entry. If the mortgagee pursues this option, it bypasses s 36, which bites only upon a mortgagee who 'brings an action in which he claims possession'. Some protection for the mortgagor in this situation is provided by s 6 of the Criminal Law Act 1977, but it is only available if the mortgagor was physically present on the premises when entry to take possession was attempted. Further, there is no civil remedy; only criminal liability ensues.

9.246   It is strongly arguable that this self-help remedy, which may deprive mortgagors of both their property and their home, is in breach of Art 1/1 and Art 8. The remedy appears difficult to justify in the public interest when it may lead to families being locked out of their own homes without the benefit of due legal process. Article 8 arguments are, however, less likely to be persuasive in the European Convention context when a corporate mortgagor challenges possession by physical entry.

9.247   Such a form of self-help is, for all that, arguably disproportionate when an alternative procedure, by way of the institution of possession proceedings, is readily available.

Loss of interests in land caused by legislation

9.248   Minor interests in land must be protected by entry on the land register.[3] If minor interests are not registered in this way, they will not bind a subsequent transferee of the legal title, as a consequence of which the relevant interest will be lost with no compensation paid by the State.

---

1   Jonathan Kras 'Feudal Rights in the 21st Century' in *The Essential Human Rights Act 1998* (Wilberforce Chambers, 2000).
2   [1999] 4 All ER 235.
3   Except overriding interests which need not be entered on the register: see s 70(1) of the Land Registration Act 1925.

9.249   Land registration requirements may affect mortgagees. A mortgagee's legal charge on the land remains equitable until it is registered. A later mortgagee who registers the legal interest will take priority. As a result, the first mortgagee may lose its interest in the land.

9.250   One commentator has suggested that local law on the registration of minor interests may conceivably violate Art 1/1 in situations where it causes the loss of property.[1] Loss of a proprietary interest through a failure to register may, in theory, amount to a deprivation in terms of the second *Sporrong* rule. Very likely, however, local judges will be anxious to find that the existing statutory regime is justified as pursuing the general interest of legal certainty.[2]

9.251   It is also possible that a company that loses its interest in land as a result of the operation of the law of adverse possession could bring a similar challenge to the provisions of the Limitation Act 1980 which preclude the bringing of any action 12 years after it has accrued. Promotion of legal certainty in this context is certainly legitimate and a policy that, in effect, penalises those who fail to assert their property rights may be justified, but the fact that no compensation is payable raises the possibility of an argument under Art 1/1.[3]

The Act's impact upon countryside access

9.252   The Countryside and Rights of Way Bill was published by the Government on 3 March 2000 and since then ramblers' groups have hailed what is perceived to be a victory in prospectively gaining the so-called right to roam over 4m acres (one-ninth of the area of England and Wales) of mountain, moorland, heath, down and registered common land.

9.253   Companies that own land may obviously be affected if the Bill becomes law. The principal gripe of farmers is that they will apparently receive no compensation for any losses caused by the granting of access rights over their property, and the Country Landowners Association has already raised European Convention concerns in this context.[4]

9.254   Is the right to roam a violation of Art 1/1? It would appear to amount to a form of control of use in terms of the third rule in *Sporrong*.[5] Although the Government would be likely to succeed in establishing that the measures pursue a legitimate aim, namely access to the countryside in the general interest, there is conceivably an argument that a fair balance has not been struck between the communal and the individual interest. Landowners consider that the measures place a disproportionate burden on them, on the basis that they receive no compensation for an undoubted infringement of their property rights, in response to which it appears that the Government's position is that any losses or costs suffered will not be so material as to warrant the payment of compensation. Materiality may not, however, be persuasive in this context. It will be recalled that the European Court has held that the failure to pay compensation can only be

---

1   See J Howell 'Land and Human Rights' [1999] *The Conveyancer* 286 at p 304 and the Law Commission Report *Land Registration for the Twenty-First Century* [1998] Law Commission No 254.
2   J Howell ibid, at 305–306.
3   See C Harpum *Property Law – The Human Rights Dimension (Part 2)* [2000] 4 L & T Rev 29.
4   See, for example, *The Daily Telegraph*, 4 March 2000.
5   See **9.26** et seq.

justified in the most exceptional of circumstances.[1] Further, the payment of compensation in any event is an important element in striking a fair balance.[2]

9.255 The current debate in the UK about fox hunting is also of relevance in terms of the European Convention. Wholly coincidentally, the Strasbourg judges have recently determined an important case on hunting rights that has considerable domestic resonance. The case of *Chassagnon v France*[3] concerned the *Loi Verdeille* of 1964 whereby, simply put, small landowners were required to concede free access to hunters. The applicant landowners were affected by this. They also happened to object to hunting. The European Court found that:

> 'Compelling small landowners to transfer hunting rights over land so that others can make use of them in a way which is totally incompatible with their beliefs imposes a disproportionate burden which is not justified under the second paragraph of Article 1 of the First Protocol.'

9.256 If hunting was made a criminal offence in the UK, those with existing rights in the form of *profits à prendre* might seek to argue that criminalisation is tantamount to a confiscation of possessions. The availability and adequacy of compensation would conceivably be a decisive factor for a court which is required to decide whether the relevant measure is proportionate and strikes a fair balance.[4]

The Act and adjudication under the Housing Grants, Construction and Regeneration Act 1996[5]

9.257 The adjudication procedure established in the Housing Grants, Construction and Regeneration Act 1996 (the 1996 Act) is likely to face challenges under the fair trial provisions of Art 6(1) for a variety of reasons including the following.

(1) The requirement in s 108(2)(c) and (d) of the 1996 Act, whereby the adjudicator must come to a decision within 28 days of the referral of a dispute, could leave the respondent with insufficient time, particularly in a complex case, to prepare its defence.

(2) There is no requirement in the 1996 Act that the adjudicator be independent and impartial, even though his decision will often be dispositive. In many cases, the adjudicator may in fact have some connection with one of the parties.

(3) There is no requirement in the 1996 Act for a hearing, which is generally left to the discretion of the adjudicator. Most adjudications are decided on paper and Art 6(1) may become relevant if the parties are unable to comment on all the evidence.

(4) Adjudication is private, as is the decision of the adjudicator.

---

1   See *Lithgow v United Kingdom* (1986) 8 EHRR 329 and **9.43** et seq.
2   See *James v United Kingdom* (1986) 8 EHRR 123 and **9.50** et seq.
3   (2000) 29 EHRR 615. An Art 14 violation was also established.
4   The Inquiry into Hunting with Dogs chaired by Lord Burns looked specifically at the European Convention implications of any ban. Report dated 9 June 2000: see www.huntinginquiry.gov.uk. The Country Landowners' Association has reportedly claimed that a ban would engage Arts 8, 9, 10, 11 and 1/1: see *The Times*, 22 May 2000.
5   See generally R Button's article 'Changes ahead for adjudication' [1999] *Construction Law* May 11.

(5) The adjudicator may not be required to provide reasons.

9.258   By virtue of the 1996 Act, an adjudicator's decision binds the parties until it is taken to a higher tribunal, court or arbitrator. A local court will, in the event, be under a duty to act compatibly with European Convention rights by, for example, refusing to enforce an adjudicator's decision in circumstances where a fair hearing (or, indeed, any hearing) may not have taken place.

CONCLUSION

9.259   The open-textured nature of the European Convention's right to property appears on its face to offer corporate claimants considerable potential. In the event, the deference paid national authorities in this area has traditionally been such that, as in the case of other European Convention rights, the best prospect of establishing a violation in a property-type dispute may lie in the identification of an Art 6 process breach.

Chapter 10

THE ACT'S IMPACT UPON THE LEGAL SYSTEM

THE NUMBER OF CASES

10.1   It has been widely predicted that, when the Act comes fully into force, the courts will be deluged. Before the end of 1998, the suggestion was being made that 'human rights and pressure groups are already busily stacking up cases'.[1] On the other hand, it has been claimed that implementation late in 2000 was timed to ensure that it took place after the legal aid system was curtailed, with indications that the number of law firms offering legal aid may drop from 11,000 to 3,000. The charge is that this, together with the 'admirably obstructionist'[2] victim requirement in s 7 of the Act,[3] makes a litigation torrent unlikely. Whatever the position, it is noteworthy that the statutory ceiling on the number of High Court judges was raised on 25 November 1999 from 98 to 106,[4] in part because of the introduction of the Act. Meanwhile, 1,000 judges are to be given Internet access, again apparently on account of the Act.[5]

THE IMPACT UPON THE JUDGES

10.2   There are simply too many variables at play to predict with any degree of assurance what the volume and form of litigation under the Act is likely to be. What can be said with much greater certainty, however, is that judges will come under scrutiny as to their antecedents and beliefs more than ever before. Scotland, as noted, has already witnessed the remarkable spectacle of Dutch advocates successfully applying for three judges to be removed from a drugs case because the senior judge, Lord McCluskey, had recently expressed trenchant (and critical) views about the European Convention in a newspaper article.[6] In the

---

1   Frances Gibb writing in *The Times*, 26 October 1998. She expressed surprise that the Human Rights Bill had 'slipped through Parliament with the minimum of controversy'. This may, of course, be attributable more to the Government's overwhelming majority than to any lack of interest in the legislation. The press may have contributed to this in that very little of the Parliamentary debates was reported, according at least to the Home Secretary (see *The Daily Telegraph*, 21 October 1999).

2   See the article by L Clements 'The Human Rights Act: A New Equity or a New Opiate: Reinventing State Control' 1999 [26] 1 JLS 72.

3   See **3.123** et seq.

4   By virtue of the Maximum Number of Judges Order 1999, SI 1999/3138. See also Press Release, Lord Chancellor's Department, 10 November 1999. The Release quotes the Lord Chancellor as saying that there may be an estimated 1,000–2,000 *additional* applications for leave to move for judicial review in immigration cases after 2 October 2000. Even if only one in four cases led to a grant of leave, this would be an increase of 65% in the Administrative Court list. Similarly, appeals from magistrates' courts by way of the case stated procedure could increase by 70% in the first 2 years after implementation of the Act. Criminal cases going to the Court of Appeal could increase by one-third. Notwithstanding the influx of new judges, members of the Court of Appeal may still require to be diverted to the Queen's Bench Division to help out.

5   See *The Times*, 16 May 2000.

6   See **6.209**.

meantime, the head of the justice system, Lord of Appeal in Ordinary, Cabinet Minister and Speaker of the House of Lords, the Lord Chancellor, will not be immune from further analysis of his multi-functional role and calls for him to step down as a presiding judge in the Judicial Committee of the House of Lords have increased since the European Court's decision in the case of *McGonnell*.[1]

10.3   Nor will calls for judges to be appointed by some transparent and independent tribunal go away. Sir Nicholas Bratza, the UK's representative on the European Court, was interviewed for his position by a selection panel which included senior judges, civil servants and a lay representative and it is argued that this approach should be adopted for domestic appointments. Aspiring members of the US Supreme Court are grilled by the Senate Judiciary Committee and the received wisdom here is that any re-run in the UK of the kind of confirmation hearings affecting Judge Clarence Thomas and Judge Robert Bork would be unwelcome. Equally, a consensus is emerging that elevation to the Bench on the existing basis of secret soundings is no longer sustainable. The wholesale introduction of the Act (and specifically the requirements of Art 6(1)) mean that the issue can no longer be ducked.

THE IMPACT UPON JUDICIAL REASONING

10.4   The judges will no doubt heed the call of the Lord Chancellor now explicitly to have regard for the moral dimension attaching to particular legislation. Lord Browne-Wilkinson, the then most senior Law Lord, put it thus:

> 'As moral questions come before the courts in Convention cases the courts will be required to give moral answers to the moral questions. Moral attitudes which have previously been the actual, but unarticulated reasoning lying behind judicial decisions will become the very stuff of decisions on Convention points. The silent true reason for a decision will have to become the stated *ratio decidendi*.'[2]

10.5   Human rights considerations will dominate many cases and senior judges may find themselves in a position in which, on account of the domestication of the European Convention, they reverse their own, earlier decisions. In such circumstances, lawyers used to advising corporations in the context of a system based on binding precedent are plainly going to need to caveat their advice carefully.

10.6   There are, however, dangers in over-emphasising the moral dynamic and Dr Geoffrey Marshall has pointed out that a Lord Chancellor who, before he took up a Government appointment, once warned about judicial adventurism, has now exhorted the senior judiciary to 'subvert the clearly expressed intentions of the legislature by process of judicial massage or sleight of hands'.[3] There is no doubt that the senior judges recognise the risk and in a Privy Council case Lord Hoffman quoted with approval the comments of Kentridge AJ in the South African Constitutional Court when saying that: 'If the language used by the law-giver is

---

1   See for example, *The Guardian*, 9 February 2000 and **6.198** et seq.
2   *The Impact of the Human Rights Bill on English Law* edited by BS Markesinis (Clarendon Press, Oxford, 1999), p 22.
3   Letter to *The Times*, 31 October 1998.

ignored in favour of a general resort to "values" the result is not interpretation but divination'.[1]

THE IMPACT UPON THE LEGAL PROFESSION

10.7   The kind of cases initially brought under the Act will be a function in part of the specialist expertise of the lawyers involved. The European Convention was in its early days known in the main only to public international lawyers. In its second generation, as the Strasbourg Court began to make its presence felt, the Treaty came to be utilised by public lawyers in the UK. In the future, as the Act becomes suffused into British jurisprudence generally, the Act will become required reading for students and practitioners alike in every discipline. Legal training will accordingly need to adjust to the new dispensation. This is not merely a matter of a new constitutional law option. Private law, as has been seen, will be affected too. Can tort now be taught without reference to the *Osman*[2] decision at Strasbourg?

10.8   The Act not only requires transparency of judicial reasoning. It also calls for lateral thinking on the part of lawyers. Are they up to it? It will be ironic if they are not, because the Act is largely the inspiration of lawyers, both inside and outside the Blair administration. As James Young has noted: 'Not only was this a project of the political elite, it was the project of lawyers among that elite'.[3]

10.9   Lawyers are going to have to research new depositories of legal knowledge. They should, for example, be reviewing the decisions of the senior national courts of continental Europe. But how comparatively minded are British judges and lawyers? It has been suggested that Commonwealth judges are, perhaps ironically, more inclined to cite European cases than are British judges. Will this continue to be the case?

10.10   It is odd that, just a few years after English litigation procedure came fully to acknowledge the Strasbourg concept of the equality of arms, the Act should in a sense give an edge to those lawyers and clients with the financial capacity to fund the lateral thinking that the Act undoubtedly requires, for such thinking will undoubtedly be expensive. Claimants in a privacy case, for example, will want to cite national court decisions from the Continent – many of which have not gone to Strasbourg. This will take time, as there are no comprehensive European-wide law reports and many lawyers will not have access to any of the specialist series of human rights reports.[4]

10.11   Will the judges still tend to be drawn towards English-language judgments from the USA and South Africa rather than to decisions of the supreme courts in, for example, France and Germany, countries with very considerable

---

1   Quoted by Lord Hoffman in *Matadeen v Pointu* [1998] 1 AC 98 at 168.
2   See **6.54** et seq.
3   In 'The Politics of the Human Rights Act' 1999 [26] 1 JLS 27 at p 33, Young notes that the Rowntree Reform Trust Poll (quoted with approval in the House of Lords' debates on the Human Rights Bill) showed 76% of those asked in favour of a Bill of rights. They assumed, however, that this would be about social and economic rights, such as the right to free hospital treatment.
4   See Appendix 3 on finding helpful sources on the Internet.

experience not just of balancing competing interests but, perhaps more relevantly for UK purposes, of considering the extent to which constitutional or human rights covenants should bear upon disputes between and among private parties.

10.12   Whilst the objection to companies' invocation of the Act appears partial and discriminatory, the concerns broadly expressed about the risk of inappropriate cases brought under the Act is well made. Sir Stephen Sedley is reported as saying that, 'if all the legal profession does is use the Convention as the last port in a storm, much as *Wednesbury* irrationality is used in judicial review proceedings, then it will be rapidly devalued and sidelined'.[1]

10.13   Woe betide the first lawyers to bring a 'silly' Strasbourg claim or who routinely parade it as a 'makeweight ground of appeal'.[2] In the case of *R v North West Lancashire Health Authority, ex parte A and Others*[3] the court condemned, in a matter involving sex-change surgery, 'an unfocused recourse to Strasbourg jurisprudence, whether before or after the incorporation of the Convention into English law' as being 'positively unhelpful, cluttering up the court's consideration of adequate and more precise domestic principles and authorities'.[4] Will lawyers and their clients be let down gently or will poor points be punished in costs? If they are, there could be no more effective mechanism for blunting the impact of the legislation.

CONCLUSION

10.14   The aim of this book has been to demythologise this significant piece of legislation without expressing a view as to whether the statute is a desirable development or not. For some civil libertarians the Act will merely be a staging-post on the way to a full-blown domestic Bill of rights. That is of no immediate concern to the business community, the concerns of which are, perhaps, more prosaic and which will see the Act as a technical tool in some instances and as an institutional threat in others. Whether, on account of the statute's risks or rewards, it would not be remotely surprising if, in the early years after the Act's wholesale introduction, a considerable proportion of the landmark cases emanated from the commercial sector.

---

1   As quoted in the *JUSTICE* Bulletin, Autumn 1998.
2   Per Wall J in *In re F (Minors) (Care Proceedings: Termination of Contact)* [2000] 2 FCR 481.
3   *The Times*, 24 August 1999.
4   It has been reported that an evangelical Christian in Scotland is proposing to petition Strasbourg on the basis that the appearance of the digits 666 in her national insurance number gives rise to a breach of her Art 11 right to freedom of religion in circumstances where she has been told she cannot have a new number (see *The Sunday Times*, 5 December 1999). In the meantime, the UK Independence Party has pledged financially to support those resisting the abolition of imperial measures on the basis (perhaps ironically) that the actions of trading standards officers in enforcing the ban on the old system of weights and measures are an Art 10 violation (see the letter by Jeffrey Titford MEP to *The Daily Telegraph*, 11 November 1999). Meanwhile, a husband seeks to rely upon the European Convention for the right to bury his dead wife in his back garden (see *The Daily Mail*, 17 February 2000).

Appendix 1

HUMAN RIGHTS ACT 1998

(1998 C 42)

ARRANGEMENT OF SECTIONS

An Act to give further effect to rights and freedoms guaranteed under the European Convention on Human Rights; to make provision with respect to holders of certain judicial offices who become judges of the European Court of Human Rights; and for connected purposes.

[9th November 1998]

Introduction

1　The Convention Rights

(1)　In this Act, 'the Convention rights' means the rights and fundamental freedoms set out in—

(a)　Articles 2 to 12 and 14 of the Convention,
(b)　Articles 1 to 3 of the First Protocol, and
(c)　Articles 1 and 2 of the Sixth Protocol,

as read with Articles 16 to 18 of the Convention.

(2)　Those Articles are to have effect for the purposes of this Act subject to any designated derogation or reservation (as to which see sections 14 and 15).

(3)　The Articles are set out in Schedule 1.

(4)　The Secretary of State may by order make such amendments to this Act as he considers appropriate to reflect the effect, in relation to the United Kingdom, of a protocol.

(5)　In subsection (4) 'protocol' means a protocol to the Convention—

(a)　which the United Kingdom has ratified; or
(b)　which the United Kingdom has signed with a view to ratification.

(6)　No amendment may be made by an order under subsection (4) so as to come into force before the protocol concerned is in force in relation to the United Kingdom.

2　Interpretation of Convention rights

(1)　A court or tribunal determining a question which has arisen in connection with a Convention right must take into account any—

(a)　judgment, decision, declaration or advisory opinion of the European Court of Human Rights,
(b)　opinion of the Commission given in a report adopted under Article 31 of the Convention,

(c) decision of the Commission in connection with Article 26 or 27(2) of the Convention, or

(d) decision of the Committee of Ministers taken under Article 46 of the Convention,

whenever made or given, so far as, in the opinion of the court or tribunal, it is relevant to the proceedings in which that question has arisen.

(2) Evidence of any judgment, decision, declaration or opinion of which account may have to be taken under this section is to be given in proceedings before any court or tribunal in such manner as may be provided by rules.

(3) In this section 'rules' means rules of court or, in the case of proceedings before a tribunal, rules made for the purposes of this section—

(a) by the Lord Chancellor or the Secretary of State, in relation to proceedings outside Scotland;

(b) by the Secretary of State, in relation to proceedings in Scotland; or

(c) by a Northern Ireland department, in relation to proceedings before a Tribunal in Northern Ireland—

(i)   which deals with transferred matters; and

(ii) for which no rules made under paragraph (a) are in force.

Legislation

3 Interpretation of legislation

(1) So far as it is possible to do so, primary legislation and subordinate legislation must be read and given effect in a way which is compatible with the Convention rights.

(2) This section—

(a) applies to primary legislation and subordinate legislation whenever enacted;

(b) does not affect the validity, continuing operation or enforcement of any incompatible primary legislation; and

(c) does not affect the validity, continuing operation or enforcement of any incompatible subordinate legislation if (disregarding any possibility of revocation) primary legislation prevents removal of the incompatibility.

4 Declaration of incompatibility

(1) Subsection (2) applies in any proceedings in which a court determines whether a provision of primary legislation is compatible with a Convention right.

(2) If the court is satisfied that the provision is incompatible with a Convention right, it may make a declaration of that incompatibility.

(3) Subsection (4) applies in any proceedings in which a court determines whether a provision of subordinate legislation, made in the exercise of a power conferred by primary legislation, is compatible with a Convention right.

(4) If the court is satisfied—

(a) that the provision is incompatible with a Convention right, and

(b) that (disregarding any possibility of revocation) the primary legislation concerned prevents removal of the incompatibility,

it may make a declaration of that incompatibility.

(5) In this section 'court' means—

(a) the House of Lords;

(b) the Judicial Committee of the Privy Council;

(c) the Courts-Martial Appeal Court;

(d) in Scotland, the High Court of Justiciary sitting otherwise than as a trial court or the Court of Session;

(e) in England and Wales or Northern Ireland, the High Court or the Court of Appeal.

(6) A declaration under this section ('a declaration of incompatibility')—

(a) does not affect the validity, continuing operation or enforcement of the provision in respect of which it is given; and

(b) is not binding on the parties to the proceedings in which it is made.

5 Right of Crown to intervene

(1) Where a court is considering whether to make a declaration of incompatibility, the Crown is entitled to notice in accordance with rules of court.

(2) In any case to which subsection (1) applies—

(a) a Minister of the Crown (or a person nominated by him),

(b) a member of the Scottish Executive,

(c) a Northern Ireland Minister,

(d) a Northern Ireland department,

is entitled, on giving notice in accordance with rules of court, to be joined as a party to the proceedings.

(3) Notice under subsection (2) may be given at any time during the proceedings.

(4) A person who has been made a party to criminal proceedings (other than in Scotland) as the result of a notice under subsection (2) may, with leave, appeal to the House of Lords against any declaration of incompatibility made in the proceedings.

(5) In subsection (4)—

'criminal proceedings' includes all proceedings before the Courts-Martial Appeal Court; and

'leave' means leave granted by the court making the declaration of incompatibility or by the House of Lords.

Public authorities

6 Acts of public authorities

(1) It is unlawful for a public authority to act in a way which is incompatible with a Convention right.

(2) Subsection (1) does not apply to an act if—

(a) as the result of one or more provisions of primary legislation, the authority could not have acted differently; or

(b) in the case of one or more provisions of, or made under, primary legislation which cannot be read or given effect in a way which is compatible with the Convention rights, the authority was acting so as to give effect to or enforce those provisions.

(3) In this section, 'public authority' includes—

(a) a court or tribunal, and

(b) any person certain of whose functions are functions of a public nature,

but does not include either House of Parliament or a person exercising functions in connection with proceedings in Parliament.

(4) In subsection (3) 'Parliament' does not include the House of Lords in its judicial capacity.

(5) In relation to a particular act, a person is not a public authority by virtue only of subsection (3)(b) if the nature of the act is private.

(6) 'An act' includes a failure to act but does not include a failure to—

(a) introduce in, or lay before, Parliament a proposal for legislation; or
(b) make any primary legislation or remedial order.

7 Proceedings

(1) A person who claims that a public authority has acted (or proposes to act) in a way which is made unlawful by section 6(1) may—

(a) bring proceedings against the authority under this Act in the appropriate court or tribunal, or
(b) rely on the Convention right or rights concerned in any legal proceedings,

but only if he is (or would be) a victim of the unlawful act.

(2) In subsection (1)(a) 'appropriate court or tribunal' means such court or tribunal as may be determined in accordance with rules; and proceedings against an authority include a counterclaim or similar proceeding.

(3) If the proceedings are brought on an application for judicial review, the applicant is to be taken to have a sufficient interest in relation to the unlawful act only if he is, or would be, a victim of that act.

(4) If the proceedings are made by way of a petition for judicial review in Scotland, the applicant shall be taken to have title and interest to sue in relation to the unlawful act only if he is, or would be, a victim of that act.

(5) Proceedings under subsection (1)(a) must be brought before the end of—

(a) the period of one year beginning with the date on which the act complained of took place; or
(b) such longer period as the court or tribunal considers equitable having regard to all the circumstances,

but that is subject to any rule imposing a stricter time limit in relation to the procedure in question.

(6) In subsection (1)(b) 'legal proceedings' includes—

(a) proceedings brought by or at the instigation of a public authority; and
(b) an appeal against the decision of a court or tribunal.

(7) For the purposes of this section, a person is a victim of an unlawful act only if he would be a victim for the purposes of Article 34 of the Convention if proceedings were brought in the European Court of Human Rights in respect of that act.

(8) Nothing in this Act creates a criminal offence.

(9) In this section 'rules' means—

(a) in relation to proceedings before a court or tribunal outside Scotland, rules made by the Lord Chancellor or the Secretary of State for the purposes of this section or rules of court,
(b) in relation to proceedings before a court or tribunal in Scotland, rules made by the Secretary of State for those purposes,
(c) in relation to proceedings before a tribunal in Northern Ireland—

    (i) which deals with transferred matters; and

    (ii) for which no rules made under paragraph (a) are in force,

rules made by a Northern Ireland department for those purposes,

and includes provision made by order under section 1 of the Courts and Legal Services Act 1990.

(10)   In making rules regard must be had to section 9.

(11)   The Minister who has power to make rules in relation to a particular tribunal may, to the extent he considers it necessary to ensure that the tribunal can provide an appropriate remedy in relation to an act (or proposed act) of a public authority which is (or would be) unlawful as a result of section 6(1), by order add to—

    (a) the relief or remedies which the tribunal may grant; or

    (b) the grounds on which it may grant any of them.

(12)   An order made under subsection (13) may contain such incidental, supplemental, consequential or transitional provision as the Minister making it considers appropriate.

(13)   'The Minister' includes the Northern Ireland department concerned.

8 Judicial remedies

(1)   In relation to any act (or proposed act) of a public authority which the court finds is (or would be) unlawful, it may grant such relief or remedy, or make such order, within its powers as it considers just and appropriate.

(2)   But damages may be awarded only by a court which has power to award damages, or to order the payment of compensation, in civil proceedings.

(3)   No award of damages is to be made unless, taking account of all the circumstances of the case, including—

    (a) any other relief or remedy granted, or order made, in relation to the act in question (by that or any other court), and

    (b) the consequences of any decision (of that or any other court) in respect of that act,

the court is satisfied that the award is necessary to afford just satisfaction to the person in whose favour it is made.

(4)   In determining—

    (a) whether to award damages, or

    (b) the amount of an award,

the court must take into account the principles applied by the European Court of Human Rights in relation to the award of compensation under Article 41 of the Convention.

(5)   A public authority against which damages are awarded is to be treated—

    (a) in Scotland, for the purposes of section 3 of the Law Reform (Miscellaneous Provisions) (Scotland) Act 1940 as if the award were made in an action of damages in which the authority has been found liable in respect of loss or damage to the person to whom the award is made;

    (b) for the purposes of the Civil Liability (Contribution) Act 1978 as liable in respect of damage suffered by the person to whom the award is made.

(6)   In this section—

'court' includes a tribunal;

'damages' means damages for an unlawful act of a public authority; and 'unlawful' means unlawful under section 6(1).

9   Judicial acts

(1)   Proceedings under section 7(1)(a) in respect of a judicial act may be brought only—

(a) by exercising a right of appeal;
(b) on an application (in Scotland a petition) for judicial review; or
(c) in such other forum as may be prescribed by rules.

(2)   That does not affect any rule of law which prevents a court from being the subject of judicial review.

(3)   In proceedings under this Act in respect of a judicial act done in good faith, damages may not be awarded otherwise than to compensate a person to the extent required by Article 5(5) of the Convention.

(4)   An award of damages permitted by subsection (3) is to be made against the Crown; but no award may be made unless the appropriate person, if not a party to the proceedings, is joined.

(5)   In this section—

'appropriate person' means the Minister responsible for the court concerned, or a person or government department nominated by him;
'court' includes a tribunal;
'judge' includes a member of a tribunal, a justice of the peace and a clerk or other officer entitled to exercise the jurisdiction of a court;
'judicial act' means a judicial act of a court and includes an act done on the instructions, or on behalf, of a judge; and
'rules' has the same meaning as in section 7(11).

Remedial action

10   Power to take remedial action

(1)   This section applies if—

(a) a provision of legislation has been declared under section 4 to be incompatible with a Convention right and, if an appeal lies—
   (i) all persons who may appeal have stated in writing that they do not intend to do so;
   (ii) the time for bringing an appeal has expired and no appeal has been brought within that time; or
   (iii) an appeal brought within that time has been determined or abandoned; or
(b) it appears to a Minister of the Crown or Her Majesty in Council that, having regard to a finding of the European Court of Human Rights made after the coming into force of this section in proceedings against the United Kingdom, a provision of legislation is incompatible with an obligation of the United Kingdom arising from the Convention.

(2)   If a Minister of the Crown considers that there are compelling reasons for proceeding under this section, he may by order make such amendments to the legislation as he considers necessary to remove the incompatibility.

(3)   If, in the case of subordinate legislation, a Minister of the Crown considers—

(a) that it is necessary to amend the primary legislation under which the subordinate legislation in question was made, in order to enable the incompatibility to be removed, and

(b) that there are compelling reasons for proceeding under this section,

he may by order make such amendments to the primary legislation as he considers necessary.

(4)   This section also applies where the provision in question is in subordinate legislation and has been quashed, or declared invalid, by reason of incompatibility with a Convention right and the Minister proposes to proceed under paragraph 2(b) of Schedule 2.

(5)   If the legislation is an Order in Council, the power conferred by subsection (2) or (3) is exercisable by Her Majesty in Council.

(6)   In this section 'legislation' does not include a Measure of the Church Assembly or of the General Synod of the Church of England.

(7)   Schedule 2 makes further provision about remedial orders.

Other rights and proceedings

11   Safeguard for existing human rights

A person's reliance on a Convention right does not restrict—

   (a) any other right or freedom conferred on him by or under any law having effect in any part of the United Kingdom; or
   (b) his right to make any claim or bring any proceedings which he could make or bring apart from sections 7 to 9.

12   Freedom of expression

(1)   This section applies if a court is considering whether to grant any relief which, if granted, might affect the exercise of the Convention right to freedom of expression.

(2)   If the person against whom the application for relief is made ('the respondent') is neither present nor represented, no such relief is to be granted unless the court is satisfied—

   (a) that the applicant has taken all practicable steps to notify the respondent; or
   (b) that there are compelling reasons why the respondent should not be notified.

(3)   No such relief is to be granted so as to restrain publication before trial unless the court is satisfied that the applicant is likely to establish that publication should not be allowed.

(4)   The court must have particular regard to the importance of the Convention right to freedom of expression and, where the proceedings relate to material which the respondent claims, or which appears to the court, to be journalistic, literary or artistic material (or to conduct connected with such material), to—

   (a) the extent to which—
      (i) the material has, or is about to, become available to the public; or
      (ii) it is, or would be, in the public interest for the material to be published;
   (b) any relevant privacy code.

(5)   In this section—

'court' includes a tribunal; and
'relief' includes any remedy or order (other than in criminal proceedings).

13   Freedom of thought, conscience and religion

(1)   If a court's determination of any question arising under this Act might affect the exercise by a religious organisation (itself or its members collectively) of the Convention

right to freedom of thought, conscience and religion, it must have particular regard to the importance of that right.

(2)   In this section 'court' includes a tribunal.

Derogations and reservations

14   Derogations

(1)   In this Act, 'designated derogation' means—

(a)   the United Kingdom's derogation from Article 5(3) of the Convention; and
(b)   any derogation by the United Kingdom from an Article of the Convention, or of any protocol to the Convention, which is designated for the purposes of this Act in an order made by the Secretary of State.

(2)   The derogation referred to in subsection (1)(a) is set out in Part I of Schedule 3.

(3)   If a designated derogation is amended or replaced it ceases to be a designated derogation.

(4)   But subsection (3) does not prevent the Secretary of State from exercising his power under subsection (1)(b) to make a fresh designation order in respect of the Article concerned.

(5)   The Secretary of State must by order make such amendments to Schedule 3 as he considers appropriate to reflect—

(a)   any designation order; or
(b)   the effect of subsection (3).

(6)   A designation order may be made in anticipation of the making by the United Kingdom of a proposed derogation.

15   Reservations

(1)   In this Act, 'designated reservation' means—

(a)   the United Kingdom's reservation to Article 2 of the First Protocol to the Convention; and
(b)   any other reservation by the United Kingdom to an Article of the Convention, or of any protocol to the Convention, which is designated for the purposes of this Act in an order made by the Secretary of State.

(2)   The text of the reservation referred to in subsection (1)(a) is set out in Part II of Schedule 3.

(3)   If a designated reservation is withdrawn wholly or in part it ceases to be a designated reservation.

(4)   But subsection (3) does not prevent the Secretary of State from exercising his power under subsection (1)(b) to make a fresh designation order in respect of the Article concerned.

(5)   The Secretary of State must by order make such amendments to this Act as he considers appropriate to reflect—

(a)   any designation order; or

(b) the effect of subsection (3).

16   Period for which designated derogations have effect

(1)   If it has not already been withdrawn by the United Kingdom, a designated derogation ceases to have effect for the purposes of this Act—

    (a) in the case of the derogation referred to in section 14(1)(a), at the end of the period of five years beginning with the date on which section 1(2) came into force;

    (b) in the case of any other derogation, at the end of the period of five years beginning with the date on which the order designating it was made.

(2)   At any time before the period—

    (a) fixed by subsection (1)(a) or (b), or

    (b) extended by an order under this subsection,

comes to an end, the Secretary of State may by order extend it by a further period of five years.

(3)   An order under section 14(1)(b) ceases to have effect at the end of the period for consideration, unless a resolution has been passed by each House approving the order.

(4)   Subsection (3) does not affect—

    (a) anything done in reliance on the order; or

    (b) the power to make a fresh order under section 14(1)(b).

(5)   In subsection (3) 'period for consideration' means the period of forty days beginning with the day on which the order was made.

(6)   In calculating the period for consideration, no account is to be taken of any time during which—

    (a) Parliament is dissolved or prorogued; or

    (b) both Houses are adjourned for more than four days.

(7)   If a designated derogation is withdrawn by the United Kingdom, the Secretary of State must by order make such amendments to this Act as he considers are required to reflect that withdrawal.

17   Periodic review of designated reservations

(1)   The appropriate Minister must review the designated reservation referred to in section 15(1)(a)—

    (a) before the end of the period of five years beginning with the date on which section 1(2) came into force; and

    (b) if that designation is still in force, before the end of the period of five years beginning with the date on which the last report relating to it was laid under subsection (3).

(2)   The appropriate Minister must review each of the other designated reservations (if any)—

    (a) before the end of the period of five years beginning with the date on which the order designating the reservation first came into force; and

    (b) if the designation is still in force, before the end of the period of five years beginning with the date on which the last report relating to it was laid under subsection (3).

(3)   The Minister conducting a review under this section must prepare a report on the result of the review and lay a copy of it before each House of Parliament.

Judges of the European Court of Human Rights

18 Appointment to European Court of Human Rights

(1)   In this section 'judicial office' means the office of—

 (a) Lord Justice of Appeal, Justice of the High Court or Circuit judge, in England and Wales;
 (b) judge of the Court of Session or sheriff, in Scotland;
 (c) Lord Justice of Appeal, judge of the High Court or county court judge, in Northern Ireland.

(2)   The holder of a judicial office may become a judge of the European Court of Human Rights ('the Court') without being required to relinquish his office.

(3)   But he is not required to perform the duties of his judicial office while he is a judge of the Court.

(4)   In respect of any period during which he is a judge of the Court—

 (a) a Lord Justice of Appeal or Justice of the High Court is not to count as a judge of the relevant court for the purposes of section 2(1) or 4(1) of the Supreme Court Act 1981 (maximum number of judges) nor as a judge of the Supreme Court for the purposes of section 12(1) to (6) of that Act (salaries etc);
 (b) a judge of the Court of Session is not to count as a judge of that court for the purposes of section 1(1) of the Court of Session Act 1988 (maximum number of judges) or of section 9(1)(c) of the Administration of Justice Act 1973 ('the 1973 Act') (salaries etc);
 (c) a Lord Justice of Appeal or a judge of the High Court in Northern Ireland is not to count as a judge of the relevant court for the purposes of section 2(1) or 3(1) of the Judicature (Northern Ireland) Act 1978 (maximum number of judges) nor as a judge of the Supreme Court of Northern Ireland for the purposes of section 9(1)(d) of the 1973 Act (salaries etc);
 (d) a Circuit judge is not to count as such for the purposes of section 18 of the Courts Act 1971 (salaries etc);
 (e) a sheriff is not to count as such for the purposes of section 14 of the Sheriff Courts (Scotland) Act 1907 (salaries etc);
 (f) a county court judge of Northern Ireland is not to count as such for the purposes of section 106 of the County Courts Act (Northern Ireland) 1959 (salaries etc).

(5)   If a sheriff principal is appointed a judge of the Court, section 11(1) of the Sheriff Courts (Scotland) Act 1971 (temporary appointment of sheriff principal) applies, while he holds that appointment, as if his office is vacant.

(6)   Schedule 3 makes provision about judicial pensions in relation to the holder of a judicial office who serves as a judge of the Court.

(7)   The Lord Chancellor or the Secretary of State may by order make such transitional provision (including, in particular, provision for a temporary increase in the maximum number of judges) as he considers appropriate in relation to any holder of a judicial office who has completed his service as a judge of the Court.

Parliamentary procedure

19 Statements of compatibility

(1)   A Minister of the Crown in charge of a Bill in either House of Parliament must, before Second Reading of the Bill—

 (a) make a statement to the effect that in his view the provisions of the Bill are compatible with the Convention rights ('a statement of compatibility'); or

(b) make a statement to the effect that although he is unable to make a statement of compatibility the government nevertheless wishes the House to proceed with the Bill.

(2)   The statement must be in writing and be published in such manner as the Minister making it considers appropriate.

Supplemental

20   Orders etc under this Act

(1)   Any power of a Minister of the Crown to make an order under this Act is exercisable by statutory instrument.

(2)   The power of the Lord Chancellor or the Secretary of State to make rules (other than rules of court) under section 2(3) or 7(9) is exercisable by statutory instrument.

(3)   Any statutory instrument made under section 14, 15 or 16(7) must be laid before Parliament.

(4)   No order may be made by the Lord Chancellor or the Secretary of State under section 1(4), 7(13) or 16(2) unless a draft of the order has been laid before, and approved by, each House of Parliament.

(5)   Any statutory instrument made under section 18(7) or Schedule 4, or to which subsection (2) applies, shall be subject to annulment in pursuance of a resolution of either House of Parliament.

(6)   The power of a Northern Ireland department to make—

(a) rules under section 2(3)(c) or 7(9)(c), or
(b) an order under section 7(11),

is exercisable by statutory rule for the purposes of the Statutory Rules (Northern Ireland) Order 1979.

(7)   Any rules made under section 2(3)(c) or 7(9)(c) shall be subject to negative resolution; and section 41(6) of the Interpretation Act (Northern Ireland) 1954 (meaning of 'subject to negative resolution') shall apply as if the power to make the rules were conferred by an Act of the Northern Ireland Assembly.

(8)   No order may be made by a Northern Ireland department under section 7(11) unless a draft of the order has been laid before, and approved by, the Northern Ireland Assembly.

21   Interpretation, etc

(1)   In this Act—

'amend' includes repeal and apply (with or without modifications);
'the appropriate Minister' means the Minister of the Crown having charge of the appropriate authorised government department (within the meaning of the Crown Proceedings Act 1947);
'the Commission' means the European Commission of Human Rights;
'the Convention' means the Convention for the Protection of Human Rights and Fundamental Freedoms, agreed by the Council of Europe at Rome on 4th November 1950 as it has effect for the time being in relation to the United Kingdom;
'declaration of incompatibility' means a declaration under section 4;
'Minister of the Crown' has the same meaning as in the Ministers of the Crown Act 1975;
'Northern Ireland Minister' includes the First Minister and the deputy First Minister in Northern Ireland;
'primary legislation' means any—

(a) public general Act;
(b) local and personal Act;
(c) private Act;
(d) Measure of the Church Assembly;
(e) Measure of the General Synod of the Church of England;
(f) Order in Council—
    (i) made in exercise of Her Majesty's Royal Prerogative;
    (ii) made under section 38(1)(a) of the Northern Ireland Constitution Act 1973 or the corresponding provision of the Northern Ireland Act 1998; or
    (iii) amending an Act of a kind mentioned in paragraph (a), (b) or (c);

and includes an order or other instrument made under primary legislation (otherwise than by the National Assembly for Wales, a member of the Scottish Executive, a Northern Ireland Minister or a Northern Ireland department) to the extent to which it operates to bring one or more provisions of that legislation into force or amends any primary legislation;

'the First Protocol' means the protocol to the Convention agreed at Paris on 20th March 1952;

'the Sixth Protocol' means the protocol to the Convention agreed at Strasbourg on 28th April 1983;

'the Eleventh Protocol' means the protocol to the Convention (restructuring the control machinery established by the Convention) agreed at Strasbourg on 11th May 1994;

'remedial order' means an order under section 10;

'subordinate legislation' means any—

(a) Order in Council other than one—
    (i) made in exercise of Her Majesty's Royal Prerogative;
    (ii) made under section 38(1)(a) of the Northern Ireland Constitution Act 1973 or the corresponding provision of the Northern Ireland Act 1998; or
    (iii) amending an Act of a kind mentioned in the definition of primary legislation;
(b) Act of the Scottish Parliament;
(c) Act of the Parliament of Northern Ireland;
(d) Measure of the Assembly established under section 1 of the Northern Ireland Assembly Act 1973;
(e) Act of the Northern Ireland Assembly;
(f) order, rules, regulations, scheme, warrant, byelaw or other instrument made under primary legislation (except to the extent to which it operates to bring one or more provisions of that legislation into force or amends any primary legislation);
(g) order, rules, regulations, scheme, warrant, byelaw or other instrument made under legislation mentioned in paragraph (b), (c), (d) or (e) or made under an Order in Council applying only to Northern Ireland;
(h) order, rules, regulations, scheme, warrant, byelaw or other instrument made by a member of the Scotish Executive, a Northern Ireland Minister or a Northern Ireland department in exercise of prerogative or other executive functions of Her Majesty which are exercisable by such a person on behalf of Her Majesty;

'transferred matters' has the same meaning as in the Northern Ireland Act 1998; and 'tribunal' means any tribunal in which legal proceedings may be brought.

(2)   The references in paragraphs (b) and (c) of section 2(1) to Articles are to Articles of the Convention as they had effect immediately before the coming into force of the Eleventh Protocol.

(3)   The reference in paragraph (d) of section 2(1) to Article 46 includes a reference to Articles 32 and 54 of the Convention as they had effect immediately before the coming into force of the Eleventh Protocol.

(4)   The references in section 2(1) to a report or decision of the Commission or a decision of the Committee of Ministers include references to a report or decision made as provided by paragraphs 3, 4 and 6 of Article 5 of the Eleventh Protocol (transitional provisions).

(5)   Any liability under the Army Act 1955, the Air Force Act 1955 or the Naval Discipline Act 1957 to suffer death for an offence is replaced by a liability to imprisonment for life or any less punishment authorised by those Acts; and those Acts shall accordingly have effect with the necessary modifications.

22   Short title, commencement, application and extent

(1)   This Act may be cited as the Human Rights Act 1998.

(2)   Sections 18 and 20 and this section come into force on the passing of this Act.

(3)   The other provisions of this Act come into force on such day as the Secretary of State may by order appoint; and different days may be appointed for different purposes.

(4)   Paragraph (b) of subsection (1) of section 7 applies to proceedings brought by or at the instigation of a public authority whenever the act in question took place; but otherwise that subsection does not apply to an act taking place before the coming into force of that section.

(5)   This Act binds the Crown.

(6)   This Act extends to Northern Ireland.

(7)   Section 21(5), so far as it relates to any provision contained in the Army Act 1955, the Air Force Act 1955 or the Naval Discipline Act 1957, extends to any place to which that provision extends.

SCHEDULES

SCHEDULE 1

THE ARTICLES

PART I

THE CONVENTION

Rights and Freedoms

Article 2

Right to life

1.   Everyone's right to life shall be protected by law. No one shall be deprived of his life intentionally save in the execution of a sentence of a court following his conviction of a crime for which this penalty is provided by law.

2.   Deprivation of life shall not be regarded as inflicted in contravention of this Article when it results from the use of force which is no more than absolutely necessary:

   (a) in defence of any person from unlawful violence;
   (b) in order to effect a lawful arrest or to prevent the escape of a person lawfully detained;
   (c) in action lawfully taken for the purpose of quelling a riot or insurrection.

Article 3

Prohibition of torture

No one shall be subjected to torture or to inhuman or degrading treatment or punishment.

Article 4

Prohibition of slavery and forced labour

1. No one shall be held in slavery or servitude.

2. No one shall be required to perform forced or compulsory labour.

3. For the purpose of this Article the term 'forced or compulsory labour' shall not include:

   (a) any work required to be done in the ordinary course of detention imposed according to the provisions of Article 5 of this Convention or during conditional release from such detention;
   (b) any service of a military character or, in case of conscientious objectors in countries where they are recognised, service exacted instead of compulsory military service;
   (c) any service exacted in case of an emergency or calamity threatening the life or well-being of the community;
   (d) any work or service which forms part of normal civic obligations.

Article 5

Right to liberty and security

1. Everyone has the right to liberty and security of person. No one shall be deprived of his liberty save in the following cases and in accordance with a procedure prescribed by law:

   (a) the lawful detention of a person after conviction by a competent court;
   (b) the lawful arrest or detention of a person for non-compliance with the lawful order of a court or in order to secure the fulfilment of any obligation prescribed by law;
   (c) the lawful arrest or detention of a person effected for the purpose of bringing him before the competent legal authority on reasonable suspicion of having committed an offence or when it is reasonably considered necessary to prevent his committing an offence or fleeing after having done so;
   (d) the detention of a minor by lawful order for the purpose of educational supervision or his lawful detention for the purpose of bringing him before the competent legal authority;
   (e) the lawful detention of persons for the prevention of the spreading of infectious diseases, of persons of unsound mind, alcoholics or drug addicts or vagrants;
   (f) the lawful arrest or detention of a person to prevent his effecting an unauthorised entry into the country or of a person against whom action is being taken with a view to deportation or extradition.

2. Everyone who is arrested shall be informed promptly, in a language which he understands, of the reasons for his arrest and of any charge against him.

3. Everyone arrested or detained in accordance with the provisions of paragraph 1(c) of this Article shall be brought promptly before a judge or other officer authorised by law to exercise judicial power and shall be entitled to trial within a reasonable time or to release pending trial. Release may be conditioned by guarantees to appear for trial.

4. Everyone who is deprived of his liberty by arrest or detention shall be entitled to take proceedings by which the lawfulness of his detention shall be decided speedily by a court and his release ordered if the detention is not lawful.

5.   Everyone who has been the victim of arrest or detention in contravention of the provisions of this Article shall have an enforceable right to compensation.

Article 6

Right to a fair trial

1.   In the determination of his civil rights and obligations or of any criminal charge against him, everyone is entitled to a fair and public hearing within a reasonable time by an independent and impartial tribunal established by law. Judgment shall be pronounced publicly but the press and public may be excluded from all or part of the trial in the interest of morals, public order or national security in a democratic society, where the interests of juveniles or the protection of the private life of the parties so require, or to the extent strictly necessary in the opinion of the court in special circumstances where publicity would prejudice the interests of justice.

2.   Everyone charged with a criminal offence shall be presumed innocent until proved guilty according to law.

3.   Everyone charged with a criminal offence has the following minimum rights:

   (a)   to be informed promptly, in a language which he understands and in detail, of the nature and cause of the accusation against him;
   (b)   to have adequate time and facilities for the preparation of his defence;
   (c)   to defend himself in person or through legal assistance of his own choosing or, if he has not sufficient means to pay for legal assistance, to be given it free when the interests of justice so require;
   (d)   to examine or have examined witnesses against him and to obtain the attendance and examination of witnesses on his behalf under the same conditions as witnesses against him;
   (e)   to have the free assistance of an interpreter if he cannot understand or speak the language used in court.

Article 7

No punishment without law

1.   No one shall be held guilty of any criminal offence on account of any act or omission which did not constitute a criminal offence under national or international law at the time when it was committed. Nor shall a heavier penalty be imposed than the one that was applicable at the time the criminal offence was committed.

2.   This Article shall not prejudice the trial and punishment of any person for any act or omission which, at the time when it was committed, was criminal according to the general principles of law recognised by civilised nations.

Article 8

Right to respect for private and family life

1.   Everyone has the right to respect for his private and family life, his home and his correspondence.

2.   There shall be no interference by a public authority with the exercise of this right except such as is in accordance with the law and is necessary in a democratic society in the interests of national security, public safety or the economic well-being of the country, for the prevention of disorder or crime, for the protection of health or morals, or for the protection of the rights and freedoms of others.

Article 9

Freedom of thought, conscience and religion

1.   Everyone has the right to freedom of thought, conscience and religion; this right includes freedom to change his religion or belief and freedom, either alone or in community with others and in public or private, to manifest his religion or belief, in worship, teaching, practice and observance.

2.   Freedom to manifest one's religion or beliefs shall be subject only to such limitations as are prescribed by law and are necessary in a democratic society in the interests of public safety, for the protection of public order, health or morals, or for the protection of the rights and freedoms of others.

Article 10

Freedom of expression

1.   Everyone has the right to freedom of expression. This right shall include freedom to hold opinions and to receive and impart information and ideas without interference by public authority and regardless of frontiers. This Article shall not prevent States from requiring the licensing of broadcasting, television or cinema enterprises.

2.   The exercise of these freedoms, since it carries with it duties and responsibilities, may be subject to such formalities, conditions, restrictions or penalties as are prescribed by law and are necessary in a democratic society, in the interests of national security, territorial integrity or public safety, for the prevention of disorder or crime, for the protection of health or morals, for the protection of the reputation or rights of others, for preventing the disclosure of information received in confidence, or for maintaining the authority and impartiality of the judiciary.

Article 11

Freedom of assembly and association

1.   Everyone has the right to freedom of peaceful assembly and to freedom of association with others, including the right to form and to join trade unions for the protection of his interests.

2.   No restrictions shall be placed on the exercise of these rights other than such as are prescribed by law and are necessary in a democratic society in the interests of national security or public safety, for the prevention of disorder or crime, for the protection of health or morals or for the protection of the rights and freedoms of others. This Article shall not prevent the imposition of lawful restrictions on the exercise of these rights by members of the armed forces, of the police or of the administration of the State.

Article 12

Right to marry

Men and women of marriageable age have the right to marry and to found a family, according to the national laws governing the exercise of this right.

Article 14

Prohibition of discrimination

The enjoyment of the rights and freedoms set forth in this Convention shall be secured without discrimination on any ground such as sex, race, colour, language, religion, political or other opinion, national or social origin, association with a national minority, property, birth or other status.

Article 16

Restrictions on political activity of aliens

Nothing in Articles 10, 11 and 14 shall be regarded as preventing the High Contracting Parties from imposing restrictions on the political activity of aliens.

Article 17

Prohibition of abuse of rights

Nothing in this Convention may be interpreted as implying for any State, group or person any right to engage in any activity or perform any act aimed at the destruction of any of the rights and freedoms set forth herein or at their limitation to a greater extent than is provided for in the Convention.

Article 18

Limitation on use of restrictions on rights

The restrictions permitted under this Convention to the said rights and freedoms shall not be applied for any purpose other than those for which they have been prescribed.

PART II

THE FIRST PROTOCOL

Article 1

Protection of property

Every natural or legal person is entitled to the peaceful enjoyment of his possessions. No one shall be deprived of his possessions except in the public interest and subject to the conditions provided for by law and by the general principles of international law.

The preceding provisions shall not, however, in any way impair the right of a State to enforce such laws as it deems necessary to control the use of property in accordance with the general interest or to secure the payment of taxes or other contributions or penalties.

Article 2

Right to education

No person shall be denied the right to education. In the exercise of any functions which it assumes in relation to education and to teaching, the State shall respect the right of parents to ensure such education and teaching in conformity with their own religious and philosophical convictions.

Article 3

Right to free elections

The High Contracting Parties undertake to hold free elections at reasonable intervals by secret ballot, under conditions which will ensure the free expression of the opinion of the people in the choice of the legislature.

PART III

THE SIXTH PROTOCOL

Article 1

Abolition of the death penalty

The death penalty shall be abolished. No one shall be condemned to such penalty or executed.

Article 2

Death penalty in time of war

A State may make provisions in its law for the death penalty in respect of acts committed in time of war or of imminent threat of war; such penalty shall be applied only in the instances laid down in the law and in accordance with its provisions. The State shall communicate to the Secretary of the Council of Europe the relevant provisions of that law.

SCHEDULE 2

REMEDIAL ORDERS

Orders

1.—(1)   A remedial order may—

    (a) contain such incidental, supplemental, consequential or transitional provision as the person making it considers appropriate;

    (b) be made so as to have effect from a date earlier than that on which it is made;

    (c) make provision for the delegation of specific functions;

    (d) make different provision for different cases.

(2)   The power conferred by sub-paragraph (1)(a) includes—

    (a) power to amend primary legislation (including primary legislation other than that which contains the incompatible provision); and

    (b) power to amend or revoke subordinate legislation (including subordinate legislation other than that which contains the incompatible provision).

(3)   A remedial order may be made so as to have the same extent as the legislation which it affects.

(4)   No person is to be guilty of an offence solely as a result of the retrospective effect of a remedial order.

Procedure

2.   No remedial order may be made unless—

    (a) a draft of the order has been approved by a resolution of each House of Parliament made after the end of the period of 60 days beginning with the day on which the draft was laid; or

    (b) it is declared in the order that it appears to the person making it that, because of the urgency of the matter, it is necessary to make the order without a draft being so approved.

Orders laid in draft

3.—(1)   No draft may be laid under paragraph 2(a) unless—

(a) the person proposing to make the order has laid before Parliament a document
which contains a draft of the proposed order and the required information; and
(b) the period of 60 days, beginning with the day on which the document required by
this sub-paragraph was laid, has ended.

(2)   If representations have been made during that period, the draft laid under paragraph
2(a) must be accompanied by a statement containing—

(a) a summary of the representations; and
(b) if, as a result of the representations, the proposed order has been changed, details of
the changes.

Urgent cases

4.—(1)   If a remedial order ('the original order') is made without being approved in
draft, the person making it must lay it before Parliament, accompanied by the required
information, after it is made.

(2) If representations have been made during the period of 60 days beginning with the day
on which the original order was made, the person making it must (after the end of that
period) lay before Parliament a statement containing—

(a) a summary of the representations; and
(b) if, as a result of the representations, he considers it appropriate to make changes to
the original order, details of the changes.

(3)   If sub-paragraph (2)(b) applies, the person making the statement must—

(a) make a further remedial order replacing the original order; and
(b) lay the replacement order before Parliament.

(4)   If, at the end of the period of 120 days beginning with the day on which the original
order was made, a resolution has not been passed by each House approving the original or
replacement order, the order ceases to have effect (but without that affecting anything
previously done under either order or the power to make a fresh remedial order).

Definitions

5.   In this Schedule—

'representations' means representations about a remedial order (or proposed remedial
order) made to the person making (or proposing to make) it and includes any relevant
Parliamentary report or resolution; and
'required information' means—

(a) an explanation of the incompatibility which the order (or proposed order) seeks to
remove, including particulars of the relevant declaration, finding or order; and
(b) a statement of the reasons for proceeding under section 10 and for making an order
in those terms.

Calculating periods

6.   In calculating any period for the purposes of this Schedule, no account is to be taken of
any time during which—

(a) Parliament is dissolved or prorogued; or
(b) both Houses are adjourned for more than four days.

SCHEDULE 3

DEROGATION AND RESERVATION

PART I

DEROGATION

The 1988 notification

The United Kingdom Permanent Representative to the Council of Europe presents his compliments to the Secretary General of the Council, and has the honour to convey the following information in order to ensure compliance with the obligations of Her Majesty's Government in the United Kingdom under Article 15(3) of the Convention for the Protection of Human Rights and Fundamental Freedoms signed at Rome on 4 November 1950.

There have been in the United Kingdom in recent years campaigns of organised terrorism connected with the affairs of Northern Ireland which have manifested themselves in activities which have included repeated murder, attempted murder, maiming, intimidation and violent civil disturbance and in bombing and fire raising which have resulted in death, injury and widespread destruction of property. As a result, a public emergency within the meaning of Article 15(1) of the Convention exists in the United Kingdom.

The Government found it necessary in 1974 to introduce and since then, in cases concerning persons reasonably suspected of involvement in terrorism connected with the affairs of Northern Ireland, or of certain offences under the legislation, who have been detained for 48 hours, to exercise powers enabling further detention without charge, for periods of up to five days, on the authority of the Secretary of State. These powers are at present to be found in Section 12 of the Prevention of Terrorism (Temporary Provisions) Act 1984, Article 9 of the Prevention of Terrorism (Supplemental Temporary Provisions) Order 1984 and Article 10 of the Prevention of Terrorism (Supplemental Temporary Provisions) (Northern Ireland) Order 1984.

Section 12 of the Prevention of Terrorism (Temporary Provisions) Act 1984 provides for a person whom a constable has arrested on reasonable grounds of suspecting him to be guilty of an offence under Section 1, 9 or 10 of the Act, or to be or to have been involved in terrorism connected with the affairs of Northern Ireland, to be detained in right of the arrest for up to 48 hours and thereafter, where the Secretary of State extends the detention period, for up to a further five days. Section 12 substantially re-enacted Section 12 of the Prevention of Terrorism (Temporary Provisions) Act 1976 which, in turn, substantially re-enacted Section 7 of the Prevention of Terrorism (Temporary Provisions) Act 1974.

Article 10 of the Prevention of Terrorism (Supplemental Temporary Provisions) (Northern Ireland) Order 1984 (SI 1984/417) and Article 9 of the Prevention of Terrorism (Supplemental Temporary Provisions) Order 1984 (SI 1984/418) were both made under Sections 13 and 14 of and Schedule 3 to the 1984 Act and substantially re-enacted powers of detention in Orders made under the 1974 and 1976 Acts. A person who is being examined under Article 4 of either Order on his arrival in, or on seeking to leave, Northern Ireland or Great Britain for the purpose of determining whether he is or has been involved in terrorism connected with the affairs of Northern Ireland, or whether there are grounds for suspecting that he has committed an offence under Section 9 of the 1984 Act, may be detained under Article 4 or 10, as appropriate, pending the conclusion of his examination. The period of this examination may exceed 12 hours if an examining officer has reasonable grounds for suspecting him to be or to have been involved in acts of terrorism connected with the affairs of Northern Ireland.

Where such a person is detained under the said Article 9 or 10 he may be detained for up to 48 hours on the authority of an examining officer and thereafter, where the Secretary of State extends the detention period, for up to a further five days.

In its judgment of 29 November 1988 in the Case of *Brogan and Others*, the European Court of Human Rights held that there had been a violation of Article 5(3) in respect of each of the applicants, all of whom had been detained under Section 12 of the 1984 Act. The Court held that even the shortest of the four periods of detention concerned, namely four days and six hours, fell outside the constraints as to time permitted by the first part of Article 5(3). In addition, the Court held that there had been a violation of Article 5(3) in the case of each applicant.

Following this judgment, the Secretary of State for the Home Department informed Parliament on 6 December 1988 that, against the background of the terrorist campaign, and the over-riding need to bring terrorists to justice, the Government did not believe that the maximum period of detention should be reduced. He informed Parliament that the Government were examining the matter with a view to responding to the judgment. On 22 December 1988, the Secretary of State further informed Parliament that it remained the Government's wish, if it could be achieved, to find a judicial process under which extended detention might be reviewed and where appropriate authorised by a judge or other judicial officer. But a further period of reflection and consultation was necessary before the Government could bring forward a firm and final view.

Since the judgment of 29 November as well as previously, the Government have found it necessary to continue to exercise, in relation to terrorism connected with the affairs of Northern Ireland, the powers described above enabling further detention without charge for periods of up to 5 days, on the authority of the Secretary of State, to the extent strictly required by the exigencies of the situation to enable necessary enquiries and investigations properly to be completed in order to decide whether criminal proceedings should be instituted. To the extent that the exercise of these powers may be inconsistent with the obligations imposed by the Convention the Government has availed itself of the right of derogation conferred by Article 15(1) of the Convention and will continue to do so until further notice.

Dated 23 December 1988.

The 1989 notification

The United Kingdom Permanent Representative to the Council of Europe presents his compliments to the Secretary General of the Council, and has the honour to convey the following information.

In his communication to the Secretary General of 23 December 1988, reference was made to the introduction and exercise of certain powers under section 12 of the Prevention of Terrorism (Temporary Provisions) Act 1984, Article 9 of the Prevention of Terrorism (Supplemental Temporary Provisions) Order 1984 and Article 10 of the Prevention of Terrorism (Supplemental Temporary Provisions) (Northern Ireland) Order 1984.

These provisions have been replaced by section 14 of and paragraph 6 of Schedule 5 to the Prevention of Terrorism (Temporary Provisions) Act 1989, which make comparable provision. They came into force on 22 March 1989. A copy of these provisions is enclosed.

The United Kingdom Permanent Representative avails himself of this opportunity to renew to the Secretary General the assurance of his highest consideration.

23 March 1989.

PART II

RESERVATION

At the time of signing the present (First) Protocol, I declare that, in view of certain provisions of the Education Acts in the United Kingdom, the principle affirmed in the second sentence of Article 2 is accepted by the United Kingdom only so far as it is compatible with the provision of efficient instruction and training, and the avoidance of unreasonable public expenditure.

Dated 20 March 1952. Made by the United Kingdom Permanent Representative to the Council of Europe.

SCHEDULE 4

JUDICIAL PENSIONS

Duty to make orders about pensions

1.—(1)   The appropriate Minister must by order make provision with respect to pensions payable to or in respect of any holder of a judicial office who serves as an ECHR judge.

(2)   A pensions order must include such provision as the Minister making it considers is necessary to secure that—

   (a) an ECHR judge who was, immediately before his appointment as an ECHR judge, a member of a judicial pension scheme is entitled to remain as a member of that scheme;
   (b) the terms on which he remains a member of the scheme are those which would have been applicable had he not been appointed as an ECHR judge; and
   (c) entitlement to benefits payable in accordance with the scheme continues to be determined as if, while serving as an ECHR judge, his salary was that which would (but for section 18(4)) have been payable to him in respect of his continuing service as the holder of his judicial office.

Contributions

2.   A pensions order may, in particular, make provision—

   (a) for any contributions which are payable by a person who remains a member of a scheme as a result of the order, and which would otherwise be payable by deduction from his salary, to be made otherwise than by deduction from his salary as an ECHR judge; and
   (b) for such contributions to be collected in such manner as may be determined by the administrators of the scheme.

Amendments of other enactments

3.   A pensions order may amend any provision of, or made under, a pensions Act in such manner and to such extent as the Minister making the order considers necessary or expedient to ensure the proper administration of any scheme to which it relates.

Definitions

4.   In this Schedule—

'appropriate Minister' means—

   (a) in relation to any judicial office whose jurisdiction is exercisable exclusively in relation to Scotland, the Secretary of State; and
   (b) otherwise, the Lord Chancellor;

'ECHR judge' means the holder of a judicial office who is serving as a judge of the Court;

'judicial pension scheme' means a scheme established by and in accordance with a pensions Act;

'pensions Act' means—

    (a) the County Courts Act (Northern Ireland) 1959;

    (b) the Sheriffs' Pensions (Scotland) Act 1961;

    (c) the Judicial Pensions Act 1981; or

    (d) the Judicial Pensions and Retirement Act 1993; and

'pensions order' means an order made under paragraph 1.

Appendix 2

CONVENTION FOR THE PROTECTION OF HUMAN RIGHTS AND FUNDAMENTAL FREEDOMS

ROME, 4.XI.1950

'The text of the Convention had been amended according to the provisions of Protocol No. 3 (ETS No. 45), which entered into force on 21 September 1970, of Protocol No. 5 (ETS No. 55), which entered into force on 20 December 1971 and of Protocol No. 8 (ETS No. 118), which entered into force 1 January 1990, and comprised also the text of Protocol No. 2 (ETS No. 44) which, in accordance with Article 5, paragraph 3 thereof, had been an integral part of the Convention since its entry into force on 21 September 1970. All provisions which had been amended or added by these Protocols are replaced by Protocol No. 11 (ETS No. 155), as from the date of its entry into force on 1 November 1998. As from that date, Protocol No. 9 (ETS No. 140), which entered into force on 1 October 1994, is repealed and Protocol No. 10 (ETS No. 146), which has not entered into force, has lost its purpose.'

The governments signatory hereto, being members of the Council of Europe,

Considering the Universal Declaration of Human Rights proclaimed by the General Assembly of the United Nations on 10th December 1948;

Considering that this Declaration aims at securing the universal and effective recognition and observance of the Rights therein declared;

Considering that the aim of the Council of Europe is the achievement of greater unity between its members and that one of the methods by which that aim is to be pursued is the maintenance and further realisation of human rights and fundamental freedoms;

Reaffirming their profound belief in those fundamental freedoms which are the foundation of justice and peace in the world and are best maintained on the one hand by an effective political democracy and on the other by a common understanding and observance of the human rights upon which they depend;

Being resolved, as the governments of European countries which are like-minded and have a common heritage of political traditions, ideals, freedom and the rule of law, to take the first steps for the collective enforcement of certain of the rights stated in the Universal Declaration,

Have agreed as follows:

Article 1[1]

Obligation to respect human rights

The High Contracting Parties shall secure to everyone within their jurisdiction the rights and freedoms defined in Section I of this Convention.

SECTION I

RIGHTS AND FREEDOMS

Article 2[1]

Right to life

1. Everyone's right to life shall be protected by law. No one shall be deprived of his life intentionally save in the execution of a sentence of a court following his conviction of a crime for which this penalty is provided by law.

2. Deprivation of life shall not be regarded as inflicted in contravention of this Article when it results from the use of force which is no more than absolutely necessary:

    (a) in defence of any person from unlawful violence;
    (b) in order to effect a lawful arrest or to prevent the escape of a person lawfully detained;
    (c) in action lawfully taken for the purpose of quelling a riot or insurrection.

Article 3[1]

Prohibition of torture

No one shall be subjected to torture or to inhuman or degrading treatment or punishment.

Article 4[1]

Prohibition of slavery and forced labour

1. No one shall be held in slavery or servitude.

2. No one shall be required to perform forced or compulsory labour.

3. For the purpose of this Article the term 'forced or compulsory labour' shall not include:

    (a) any work required to be done in the ordinary course of detention imposed according to the provisions of Article 5 of this Convention or during conditional release from such detention;
    (b) any service of a military character or, in case of conscientious objectors, in countries where they are recognised, service exacted instead of compulsory military service;
    (c) any service exacted in case of an emergency or calamity threatening the life or well-being of the community;
    (d) any work or service which forms part of normal civic obligations.

Article 5[1]

Right to liberty and security

1. Everyone has the right to liberty and security of person. No one shall be deprived of his liberty save in the following cases and in accordance with a procedure prescribed by law:

    (a) the lawful detention of a person after conviction by a competent court;

(b) the lawful arrest or detention of a person for non-compliance with the lawful order of a court or in order to secure the fulfilment of any obligation prescribed by law;

(c) the lawful arrest or detention of a person effected for the purpose of bringing him before the competent legal authority on reasonable suspicion of having committed an offence or when it is reasonably considered necessary to prevent his committing an offence or fleeing after having done so;

(d) the detention of a minor by lawful order for the purpose of educational supervision or his lawful detention for the purpose of bringing him before the competent legal authority;

(e) the lawful detention of persons for the prevention of the spreading of infectious diseases, of persons of unsound mind, alcoholics or drug addicts or vagrants;

(f) the lawful arrest or detention of a person to prevent his effecting an unauthorised entry into the country or of a person against whom action is being taken with a view to deportation or extradition.

2. Everyone who is arrested shall be informed promptly, in a language which he understands, of the reasons for his arrest and of any charge against him.

3. Everyone arrested or detained in accordance with the provisions of paragraph 1(c) of this Article shall be brought promptly before a judge or other officer authorised by law to exercise judicial power and shall be entitled to trial within a reasonable time or to release pending trial. Release may be conditioned by guarantees to appear for trial.

4. Everyone who is deprived of his liberty by arrest or detention shall be entitled to take proceedings by which the lawfulness of his detention shall be decided speedily by a court and his release ordered if the detention is not lawful.

5. Everyone who has been the victim of arrest or detention in contravention of the provisions of this Article shall have an enforceable right to compensation.

Article 6[1]

Right to a fair trail

1. In the determination of his civil rights and obligations or of any, criminal charge against him, everyone is entitled to a fair and public hearing within a reasonable time by an independent and impartial tribunal established by law. Judgment shall be pronounced publicly but the press and public may be excluded from all or part of the trial in the interests of morals, public order or national security in a democratic society, where the interests of juveniles or the protection of the private life of the parties so require, or to the extent strictly necessary in the opinion of the court in special circumstances where publicity would prejudice the interests of justice.

2. Everyone charged with a criminal offence shall be presumed innocent until proved guilty according to law.

3. Everyone charged with a criminal offence has the following minimum rights:

(a) to be informed promptly, in a language which he understands and in detail, of the nature and cause of the accusation against him;

(b) to have adequate time and facilities for the preparation of his defence;

(c) to defend himself in person or through legal assistance of his own choosing or, if he has not sufficient means to pay for legal assistance, to be given it free when the interests of justice so require;

(d) to examine or have examined witnesses against him and to obtain the attendance and examination of witnesses on his behalf under the same conditions as witnesses against him;

(e) to have the free assistance of an interpreter if he cannot understand or speak the language used in court.

Article 7[1]

No punishment without law

1. No one shall be held guilty of any criminal offence on account of any act or omission which did not constitute a criminal offence under national or international law at the time when it was committed. Nor shall a heavier penalty be imposed than the one that was applicable at the time the criminal offence was committed.

2. This Article shall not prejudice the trial and punishment of any person for any act or omission which, at the time when it was committed, was criminal according to the general principles of law recognised by civilised nations.

Article 8[1]

Right to respect for private and family life

1. Everyone has the right to respect for his private and family life, his home and his correspondence.

2. There shall be no interference by a public authority with the exercise of this right except such as is in accordance with the law and is necessary in a democratic society in the interests of national security, public safety or the economic well-being of the country, for the prevention of disorder or crime, for the protection of health or morals, or for the protection of the rights and freedoms of others.

Article 9[1]

Freedom of thought, conscience and religion

1. Everyone has the right to freedom of thought, conscience and religion; this right includes freedom to change his religion or belief and freedom, either alone or in community with others and in public or private, to manifest his religion or belief, in worship, teaching, practice and observance.

2. Freedom to manifest one's religion or beliefs shall be subject only to such limitations as are prescribed by law and are necessary in a democratic society in the interests of public safety, for the protection of public order, health or morals, or for the protection of the rights and freedoms of others.

Article 10[1]

Freedom of expression

1. Everyone has the right to freedom of expression. This right shall include freedom to hold opinions and to receive and impart information and ideas without interference by public authority and regardless of frontiers. This Article shall not prevent States from requiring the licensing of broadcasting, television or cinema enterprises.

2. The exercise of these freedoms, since it carries with it duties and responsibilities, may be subject to such formalities, conditions, restrictions or penalties as are prescribed by law and are necessary in a democratic society, in the interests of national security, territorial

integrity or public safety, for the prevention of disorder or crime, for the protection of health or morals, for the protection of the reputation or rights of others, for preventing the disclosure of information received in confidence, or for maintaining the authority and impartiality of the judiciary.

Article 11[1]

Freedom of assembly and association

1. Everyone has the right to freedom of peaceful assembly and to freedom of association with others, including the right to form and to join trade unions for the protection of his interests.

2. No restrictions shall be placed on the exercise of these rights other than such as are prescribed by law and are necessary in a democratic society in the interests of national security or public safety, for the prevention of disorder or crime, for the protection of health or morals or for the protection of the rights and freedoms of others. This Article shall not prevent the imposition of lawful restrictions on the exercise of these rights by members of the armed forces, of the police or of the administration of the State.

Article 12[1]

Right to marry

Men and women of marriageable age have the right to marry and to found a family, according to the national laws governing the exercise of this right.

Article 13[1]

Right to an effective remedy

Everyone whose rights and freedoms as set forth in this Convention are violated shall have an effective remedy before a national authority notwithstanding that the violation has been committed by persons acting in an official capacity.

Article 14[1]

Prohibition of discrimination

The enjoyment of the rights and freedoms set forth in this Convention shall be secured without discrimination on any ground such as sex, race, colour, language, religion, political or other opinion, national or social origin, association with a national minority, property, birth or other status.

Article 15[1]

Derogation in time of emergency

1. In time of war or other public emergency threatening the life of the nation any High Contracting Party may take measures derogating from its obligations under this Convention to the extent strictly required by the exigencies of the situation, provided that such measures are not inconsistent with its other obligations under international law.

2. No derogation from Article 2, except in respect of deaths resulting from lawful acts of war, or from Articles 3, 4 (paragraph 1) and 7 shall be made under this provision.

3. Any High Contracting Party availing itself of this right of derogation shall keep the Secretary General of the Council of Europe fully informed of the measures which it has taken and the reasons therefor. It shall also inform the Secretary General of the Council of Europe when such measures have ceased to operate and the provisions of the Convention are again being fully executed.

Article 16[1]

Restrictions on political activity of aliens

Nothing in Articles 10, 11 and 14 shall be regarded as preventing the High Contracting Parties from imposing restrictions on the political activity of aliens.

Article 17[1]

Prohibition of abuse of rights

Nothing in this Convention may be interpreted as implying for any State, group or person any right to engage in any activity or perform any act aimed at the destruction of any of the rights and freedoms set forth herein or at their limitation to a greater extent than is provided for in the Convention.

Article 18[1]

Limitation on use of restrictions on rights

The restrictions permitted under this Convention to the said rights and freedoms shall not be applied for any purpose other than those for which they have been prescribed.

SECTION II

EUROPEAN COURT OF HUMAN RIGHTS[2]

Article 19

Establishment of the Court

To ensure the observance of the engagements undertaken by the High Contracting Parties in the Convention and the Protocols thereto, there shall be set up a European Court of Human Rights, hereinafter referred to as 'the Court'. It shall function on a permanent basis.

Article 20

Number of judges

The Court shall consist of a number of judges equal to that of the High Contracting Parties.

Article 21

Criteria for office

1. The judges shall be of high moral character and must either possess the qualifications required for appointment to high judicial office or be jurisconsults of recognised competence.

2. The judges shall sit on the Court in their individual capacity.

3. During their term of office the judges shall not engage in any activity which is incompatible with their independence, impartiality or with the demands of a full-time office; all questions arising from the application of this paragraph shall be decided by the Court.

Article 22

Election of judges

1. The judges shall be elected by the Parliamentary Assembly with respect to each High Contracting Party by a majority of votes cast from a list of three candidates nominated by the High Contracting Party.

2. The same procedure shall be followed to complete the Court in the event of the accession of new High Contracting Parties and in filling casual vacancies.

Article 23

Terms of office

1. The judges shall be elected for a period of six years. They may be re-elected. However, the terms of office of one-half of the judges elected at the first election shall expire at the end of three years.

2. The judges whose terms of office are to expire at the end of the initial period of three years shall be chosen by lot by the Secretary General of the Council of Europe immediately after their election.

3. In order to ensure that, as far as possible, the terms of office of one-half of the judges are renewed every three years, the Parliamentary Assembly may decide, before proceeding to any subsequent election, that the term or terms of office of one or more judges to be elected shall be for a period other than six years but not more than nine and not less than three years.

4. In cases where more than one term of office is involved and where the Parliamentary Assembly applies the preceding paragraph, the allocation of the terms of office shall be effected by a drawing of lots by the Secretary General of the Council of Europe immediately after the election.

5. A judge elected to replace a judge whose term of office has not expired shall hold office for the remainder of his predecessor's term.

6. The terms of office of judges shall expire when they reach the age of 70.

7. The judges shall hold office until replaced. They shall, however, continue to deal with such cases as they already have under consideration.

Article 24

Dismissal

No judge may be dismissed from his office unless the other judges decide by a majority of two-thirds that he has ceased to fulfil the required conditions.

Article 25

Registry and legal secretaries

The Court shall have a registry, the functions and organisation of which shall be laid down in the rules of the Court. The Court shall be assisted by legal secretaries.

Article 26

Plenary Court

The plenary Court shall

    (a) elect its President and one or two Vice-Presidents for a period of three years; they may be re-elected;
    (b) set up Chambers, constituted for a fixed period of time;
    (c) elect the Presidents of the Chambers of the Court; they may be re-elected;
    (d) adopt the rules of the Court, and
    (e) elect the Registrar and one or more Deputy Registrars.

Article 27

Committees, Chambers and Grand Chamber

1. To consider cases brought before it, the Court shall sit in committees of three judges, in Chambers of seven judges and in a Grand Chamber of seventeen judges. The Court's Chambers shall set up committees for a fixed period of time.

2. There shall sit as an *ex officio* member of the Chamber and the Grand Chamber the judge elected in respect of the State Party concerned or, if there is none or if he is unable to sit, a person of its choice who shall sit in the capacity of judge.

3. The Grand Chamber shall also include the President of the Court, the Vice-Presidents, the Presidents of the Chambers and other judges chosen in accordance with the rules of the Court. When a case is referred to the Grand Chamber under Article 43, no judge from the Chamber which rendered the judgment shall sit in the Grand Chamber, with the exception of the President of the Chamber and the judge who sat in respect of the State Party concerned.

Article 28

Declarations of inadmissibility by committees

A committee may, by a unanimous vote, declare inadmissible or strike out of its list of cases an application submitted under Article 34 where such a decision can be taken without further examination. The decision shall be final.

Article 29

Decisions by Chambers on admissibility and merits

1. If no decision is taken under Article 28, a Chamber shall decide on the admissibility and merits of individual applications submitted under Article 34.

2. A Chamber shall decide on the admissibility and merits of inter-State applications submitted under Article 33.

3. The decision on admissibility shall be taken separately unless the Court, in exceptional cases, decides otherwise.

Article 30

Relinquishment of jurisdiction to the Grand Chamber

Where a case pending before a Chamber raises a serious question affecting the interpretation of the Convention or the protocols thereto, or where the resolution of a question before the Chamber might have a result inconsistent with a judgment previously delivered by the Court, the Chamber may, at any time before it has rendered its judgment, relinquish jurisdiction in favour of the Grand Chamber, unless one of the parties to the case objects.

Article 31

Powers of the Grand Chamber

The Grand Chamber shall

    (a) determine applications submitted either under Article 33 or Article 34 when a Chamber has relinquished jurisdiction under Article 30 or when the case has been referred to it under Article 43; and

    (b) consider requests for advisory opinions submitted under Article 47.

Article 32

Jurisdiction of the Court

1. The jurisdiction of the Court shall extend to all matters concerning the interpretation and application of the Convention and the protocols thereto which are referred to it as provided in Articles 33, 34 and 47.

2. In the event of dispute as to whether the Court has jurisdiction, the Court shall decide.

Article 33

Inter-State cases

Any High Contracting Party may refer to the Court any alleged breach of the provisions of the Convention and the protocols thereto by another High Contracting Party.

Article 34

Individual applications

The Court may receive applications from any person, non-governmental organisation or group of individuals claiming to be the victim of a violation by one of the High Contracting Parties of the rights set forth in the Convention or the protocols thereto. The High Contracting Parties undertake not to hinder in any way the effective exercise of this right.

Article 35

Admissibility criteria

1. The Court may only deal with the matter after all domestic remedies have been exhausted, according to the generally recognised rules of international law, and within a period of six months from the date on which the final decision was taken.

2. The Court shall not deal with any application submitted under Article 34 that

   (a) is anonymous; or
   (b) is substantially the same as a matter that has already been examined by the Court or has already been submitted to another procedure of international investigation or settlement and contains no relevant new information.

3. The Court shall declare inadmissible any individual application submitted under Article 34 which it considers incompatible with the provisions of the Convention or the protocols thereto, manifestly ill-founded, or an abuse of the right of application.

4. The Court shall reject any application which it considers inadmissible under this Article. It may do so at any stage of the proceedings.

Article 36

Third party intervention

1. In all cases before a Chamber of the Grand Chamber, a High Contracting Party one of whose nationals is an applicant shall have the right to submit written comments and to take part in hearings.

2. The President of the Court may, in the interest of the proper administration of justice, invite any High Contracting Party which is not a party to the proceedings or any person concerned who is not the applicant to submit written comments or take part in hearings.

Article 37

Striking out applications

1. The Court may at any stage of the proceedings decide to strike an application out of its list of cases where the circumstances lead to the conclusion that

   (a) the applicant does not intend to pursue his application; or
   (b) the matter has been resolved; or
   (c) for any other reason established by the Court, it is no longer justified to continue the examination of the application.

However, the Court shall continue the examination of the application if respect for human rights as defined in the Convention and the protocols thereto so requires.

2. The Court may decide to restore an application to its list of cases if it considers that the circumstances justify such a course.

Article 38

Examination of the case and friendly settlement proceedings

1. If the Court declares the application admissible, it shall

    (a) pursue the examination of the case, together with the representatives of the parties, and if need be, undertake an investigation, for the effective conduct of which the States concerned shall furnish all necessary facilities;

    (b) place itself at the disposal of the parties concerned with a view to securing a friendly settlement of the matter on the basis of respect for human rights as defined in the Convention and the protocols thereto.

2. Proceedings conducted under paragraph 1(b) shall be confidential.

Article 39

Finding of a friendly settlement

If a friendly settlement is effected, the Court shall strike the case out of its list by means of a decision which shall be confined to a brief statement of the facts and of the solution reached.

Article 40

Public hearings and access to documents

1. Hearings shall be in public unless the Court in exceptional circumstances decides otherwise.

2. Documents deposited with the Registrar shall be accessible to the public unless the President of the Court decides otherwise.

Article 41

Just satisfaction

If the Court finds that there has been a violation of the Convention or the protocols thereto, and if the internal law of the High Contracting Party concerned allows only partial reparation to be made, the Court shall, if necessary, afford just satisfaction to the injured party.

Article 42

Judgments of Chambers

Judgments of Chambers shall become final in accordance with the provisions of Article 44, paragraph 2.

Article 43

Referral to the Grand Chamber

1. Within a period of three months from the date of the judgment of the Chamber, any party to the case may, in exceptional cases, request that the case be referred to the Grand Chamber.

2. A panel of five judges of the Grand Chamber shall accept the request if the case raises a serious question affecting the interpretation or application of the Convention or the protocols thereto, or a serious issue of general importance.

3. If the panel accepts the request, the Grand Chamber shall decide the case by means of a judgment.

Article 44

Final judgments

1. The judgment of the Grand Chamber shall be final.

2. The judgment of a Chamber shall become final

    (a) when the parties declare that they will not request that the case be referred to the Grand Chamber; or

    (b) three months after the date of the judgment, if reference of the case to the Grand Chamber has not been requested; or

    (c) when the panel of the Grand Chamber rejects the request to refer under Article 43.

3. The final judgment shall be published.

Article 45

Reasons for judgments and decisions

1. Reasons shall be given for judgments as well as for decisions declaring applications admissible or inadmissible.

2. If a judgment does not represent, in whole or in part, the unanimous opinion of the judges, any judge shall be entitled to deliver a separate opinion.

Article 46

Binding force and execution of judgments

1. The High Contracting Parties undertake to abide by the final judgment of the Court in any case to which they are parties.

2. The final judgment of the Court shall be transmitted to the Committee of Ministers, which shall supervise its execution.

Article 47

Advisory opinions

1. The Court may, at the request of the Committee of Ministers, give advisory opinions on legal questions concerning the interpretation of the Convention and the protocols thereto.

2. Such opinions shall not deal with any question relating to the content or scope of the rights or freedoms defined in Section I of the Convention and the protocols thereto, or with any other question which the Court or the Committee of Ministers might have to consider in consequence of any such proceedings as could be instituted in accordance with the Convention.

3. Decisions of the Committee of Ministers to request an advisory opinion of the Court shall require a majority vote of the representatives entitled to sit on the Committee.

Article 48

Advisory jurisdiction of the Court

The Court shall decide whether a request for an advisory opinion submitted by the Committee of Ministers is within its competence as defined in Article 47.

Article 49

Reasons for advisory opinions

1. Reasons shall be given for advisory opinions of the Court.

2. If the advisory opinion does not represent, in whole or in part, the unanimous opinion of the judges, any judge shall be entitled to deliver a separate opinion.

3. Advisory opinions of the Court shall be communicated to the Committee of Ministers.

Article 50

Expenditure on the Court

The expenditure on the Court shall be borne by the Council of Europe.

Article 51

Privileges and immunities of judges

The judges shall be entitled, during the exercise of their functions, to the privileges and immunities provided for in Article 40 of the Statute of the Council of Europe and in the agreements made thereunder.

SECTION III

MISCELLANEOUS PROVISIONS[1, 3]

Article 52[1]

Inquiries by the Secretary General

On receipt of a request from the Secretary General of the Council of Europe any High Contracting Party shall furnish an explanation of the manner in which its internal law ensures the effective implementation of any of the provisions of the Convention.

Article 53[1]

Safeguard for existing human rights

Nothing in this Convention shall be construed as limiting or derogating from any of the human rights and fundamental freedoms which may be ensured under the laws of any High Contracting Party or under any other agreement to which it is a Party.

Article 54[1]

Powers of the Committee of Ministers

Nothing in this Convention shall prejudice the powers conferred on the Committee of Ministers by the Statute of the Council of Europe.

Article 55[1]

Exclusion of other means of dispute settlement

The High Contracting Parties agree that, except by special agreement, they will not avail themselves of treaties, conventions or declarations in force between them for the purpose of submitting, by way of petition, a dispute arising out of the interpretation or application of this Convention to a means of settlement other than those provided for in this Convention.

Article 56[1]

Territorial application

1. [4] Any State may at the time of its ratification or at any time thereafter declare by notification addressed to the Secretary General of the Council of Europe that the present Convention shall, subject to paragraph 4 of this Article, extend to all or any of the territories for whose international relations it is responsible.

2. The Convention shall extend to the territory or territories named in the notification as from the thirtieth day after the receipt of this notification by the Secretary General of the Council of Europe.

3. The provisions of this Convention shall be applied in such territories with due regard, however, to local requirements.

4. [4] Any State which has made a declaration in accordance with paragraph 1 of this Article may at any time thereafter declare on behalf of one or more of the territories to which the declaration relates that it accepts the competence of the Court to receive applications from individuals, non-governmental organisations or groups of individuals as provided by Article 34 of the Convention.

Article 57[1]

Reservations

1. Any State may, when signing this Convention or when depositing its instrument of ratification, make a reservation in respect of any particular provision of the Convention to

the extent that any law then in force in its territory is not in conformity with the provision. Reservations of a general character shall not be permitted under this Article.

2. Any reservation made under this Article shall contain a brief statement of the law concerned.

Article 58[1]

Denunciation

1. A High Contracting Party may denounce the present Convention only after the expiry of five years from the date on which it became a party to it and after six months' notice contained in a notification addressed to the Secretary General of the Council of Europe, who shall inform the other High Contracting Parties.

2. Such a denunciation shall not have the effect of releasing the High Contracting Party concerned from its obligations under this Convention in respect of any act which, being capable of constituting a violation of such obligations, may have been performed by it before the date at which the denunciation became effective.

3. Any High Contracting Party which shall cease to be a member of the Council of Europe shall cease to be a Party to this Convention under the same conditions.

4. [4] The Convention may be denounced in accordance with the provisions of the preceding paragraphs in respect of any territory to which it has been declared to extend under the terms of Article 56.

Article 59[1]

Signature and ratification

1. This Convention shall be open to the signature of the members of the Council of Europe. It shall be ratified. Ratifications shall be deposited with the Secretary General of the Council of Europe.

2. The present Convention shall come into force after the deposit of ten instruments of ratification.

3. As regards any signatory ratifying subsequently, the Convention shall come into force at the date of the deposit of its instrument of ratification.

4. The Secretary General of the Council of Europe shall notify all the members of the Council of Europe of the entry into force of the Convention, the names of the High Contracting Parties who have ratified it, and the deposit of all instruments of ratification which may be effected subsequently.

Done at Rome this 4th day of November 1950, in English and French, both texts being equally authentic, in a single copy which shall remain deposited in the archives of the Council of Europe. The Secretary General shall transmit certified copies to each of the signatories.

Footnotes

1   Heading added according to the provisions of Protocol No. 11 (ETS No. 155).
2   New Section II according to the provisions of Protocol No. 11 (ETS No. 155).
3   The articles of this Section are renumbered according to the provisions of Protocol No. 11 (ETS No. 155).
4   Text amended according to the provisions of Protocol No. 11 (ETS No. 155).

Protocol to the Convention for the Protection of Human Rights and Fundamental Freedoms, as amended by Protocol No. 11

Paris, 20.III.1952

Headings of articles added and text amended according to the provisions of Protocol No. 11 (ETS No. 155) as of its entry into force on 1 November 1998.

The governments signatory hereto, being members of the Council of Europe,

Being resolved to take steps to ensure the collective enforcement of certain rights and freedoms other than those already included in Section I of the Convention for the Protection of Human Rights and Fundamental Freedoms signed at Rome on 4 November 1950 (hereinafter referred to as 'the Convention'),

Have agreed as follows:

Article 1

Protection of property

Every natural or legal person is entitled to the peaceful enjoyment of his possessions. No one shall be deprived of his possessions except in the public interest and subject to the conditions provided for by law and by the general principles of international law.

The preceding provisions shall not, however, in any way impair the right of a State to enforce such laws as it deems necessary to control the use of property in accordance with the general interest or to secure the payment of taxes or other contributions or penalties.

Article 2

Right to education

No person shall be denied the right to education. In the exercise of any functions which it assumes in relation to education and to teaching, the State shall respect the right of parents to ensure such education and teaching in conformity with their own religious and philosophical convictions.

Article 3

Right to free elections

The High Contracting Parties undertake to hold free elections at reasonable intervals by secret ballot, under conditions which will ensure the free expression of the opinion of the people in the choice of the legislature.

Article 4[1]

Territorial application

Any High Contracting Party may at the time of signature or ratification or at any time thereafter communicate to the Secretary General of the Council of Europe a declaration stating the extent to which it undertakes that the provisions of the present Protocol shall apply to such of the territories for the international relations of which it is responsible as are named therein.

Any High Contracting Party which has communicated a declaration in virtue of the preceding paragraph may from time to time communicate a further declaration modifying the terms of any former declaration or terminating the application of the provisions of this Protocol in respect of any territory.

A declaration made in accordance with this Article shall be deemed to have been made in accordance with paragraph 1 of Article 56 of the Convention.

Article 5

Relationship to the Convention

As between the High Contracting Parties the provisions of Articles 1, 2, 3 and 4 of this Protocol shall be regarded as additional Articles to the Convention and all the provisions of the Convention shall apply accordingly.

Article 6

Signature and ratification

This Protocol shall be open for signature by the members of the Council of Europe, who are the signatories of the Convention; it shall be ratified at the same time as or after the ratification of the Convention. It shall enter into force after the deposit of ten instruments of ratification. As regards any signatory ratifying subsequently, the Protocol shall enter into force at the date of the deposit of its instrument of ratification.

The instruments of ratification shall be deposited with the Secretary General of the Council of Europe, who will notify all members of the names of those who have ratified.

Done at Paris on the 20th day of March 1952, in English and *French*, both texts being equally authentic, in a single copy which shall remain deposited in the archives of the Council of Europe. The Secretary General shall transmit certified copies to each of the signatory governments.

Footnotes
1   Text amended according to the provisions of Protocol No. 11 (ETS No. 155).

Protocol No. 6 to the Convention for the Protection of Human Rights and Fundamental Freedoms concerning the abolition of the death penalty, as amended by Protocol No. 11

Strasbourg, 28.IV.1983

Headings of articles added and text amended according to the provisions of Protocol No. 11 (ETS No. 155) as from its entry into force on 1 November 1998.

The member States of the Council of Europe signatory to this Protocol to the Convention for the Protection of Human rights and Fundamental Freedoms, signed at Rome on 4 November 1950 (hereinafter referred to as 'the Convention'),

Considering that the evolution that has occurred in several States of the Council of Europe expresses a general tendency in favour of abolition of the death penalty;

Have agreed as follows:

Article 1

Abolition of the death penalty

The death penalty shall be abolished. No-one shall be condemned to such penalty or executed.

Article 2

Death penalty in time of war

A State may make provision in its law for the death penalty in respect of acts committed in time of war or of imminent threat of war, such penalty shall be applied only in the instances laid down in the law and in accordance with its provisions. The State shall communicate to the Secretary General of the Council of Europe the relevant provisions of that law.

Article 3

Prohibitions of derogations

No derogation from the provisions of this Protocol shall be made under Article 15 of the Convention.

Article 4[1]

Prohibition of reservations

No reservation may be made under Article 57 of the Convention in resepct of the provisions of this Protocol.

Article 5

Territorial application

1. Any State may at the time of signature or when depositing its instrument of ratification, acceptance or approval, specify the territory or territories to which this Protocol shall apply.

2. Any State may at any later date, by a declaration addressed to the Secretary General of the Council of Europe, extend the application of this Protocol to any other territory specified in the declaration. In respect of such territory the Protocol shall enter into force on the first day of the month following the date of receipt of such declaration by the Secretary General.

3. Any declaration made under the two preceding paragraphs may, in respect of any territory specified in such declaration, be withdrawn by a notification addressed to the Secretary General. The withdrawal shall become effective on the first day of the month following the date of receipt of such notification by the Secretary General.

Article 6

Relationship to the Convention

As between the States Parties the provisions of Articles 1 to 5 of this Protocol shall be regarded as additional articles to the Convention and all the provisions of the Convention shall apply accordingly.

Article 7

Signature and ratification

The Protocol shall be open for signature by the member States of the Council of Europe, signatories to the Convention. It shall be subject to ratification, acceptance or approval. A member State of the Council of Europe may not ratify, accept or approve this Protocol unless it has, simultaneously or previously, ratified the Convention. Instruments of ratification, acceptance or approval shall be deposited with the Secretary General of the Council of Europe.

Article 8

Entry in force

1. This Protocol shall enter into force on the first day of the month following the date on which five member States of the Council of Europe have expressed their consent to be bound by the Protocol in accordance with the provisions of Article 7.

2. In respect of any member State which subsequently expresses its consent to be bound by it, the Protocol shall enter into force on the first day of the month following the date of the deposit of the instrument of ratification, acceptance or approval.

Article 9

Depositary functions

The Secretary General of the Council of Europe shall notify the member States of the Council of:

(a)   any signature;
(b)   the deposit of any instrument of ratification, acceptance or approval;
(c)   any date of entry into force of this Protocol in accordance with Articles 5 and 8;
(d)   any other act, notification or communication relating to this Protocol.

In witness whereof the undersigned, being duly authorised thereto, have signed this Protocol.

Done at Strasbourg, this 28th day of April 1983, in English and in French, both texts being equally authentic, in a single copy which shall be deposited in the archives of the Council of Europe. The Secretary General of the Council of Europe shall transmit certified copies to each member State of the Council of Europe.

Footnotes
1   Text amended according to the provisions of Protocol No. 11 (ETS No. 155).

Appendix 3

USEFUL HUMAN RIGHTS WEBSITES

1.	Council of Europe	www.coe.fr/index.asp
2.	European Court of Human Rights	www.echr.coe.int
3.	European Commission of Human Rights	www.dhcommhr.coe.fr/
4.	Hudoc Human Rights Documentation	www.dhcour.co.fr/hudoc/
5.	Home Office Human Rights Unit	www.homeoffice.gov.uk/hract
6.	Lord Chancellor's Department	www.open.gov.uk
7.	Houses of Parliament	www.parliament.uk
8.	Court Service	www.courtservice.gov.uk/homemap.htm
9.	European Court of Justice	www.europa.eu.int/
10.	United Nations	www.un.org/rights/
11.	United Nations Commissioner for Human Rights	www.unhchr.ch/
12.	Northern Ireland Human Rights Commission	www.nihrc/org/

Appendix 4

BIBLIOGRAPHY

C Baker (ed) *Human Rights Act 1998: A Practitioner's Guide* (Sweet & Maxwell, 1998)

L Betten *The Human Rights Act 1998: What it Means* (Martinus Nijhoff, 1999)

P Birks (ed) *Privacy and Loyalty* (Clarendon Press, Oxford, 1997)

R Blackburn *Towards a Constitutional Bill of Rights for the United Kingdom* (Pinter, 1999)

P Chandran *A Guide to the Human Rights Act 1998* (Butterworths, 1999)

L Clements, N Mole and A Simmons *European Human Rights: Taking a Case under the Convention* (Sweet & Maxwell, 1999)

Constitutional Reform in the United Kingdom: Practice and Principles (Hart Publishing, 1998)

J Coppel *The Human Rights Act 1998* (John Wiley & Sons, 1999)

T Corner 'Planning, Environment and the European Convention on Human Rights' [1998] JPL 301

R Crawford Smith *Broadcasting Law and Fundamental Rights* (Clarendon Press, Oxford, 1997)

K Ewing 'The Human Rights Act and Parliamentary Democracy' [1999] 62 MLR 79

C Gearty (ed) *European Civil Liberties and the European Convention on Human Rights: A Comparative Study* (Martinus Nijhoff, 1997)

R Gordon QC and R Wilmot-Smith QC *Human Rights in the United Kingdom* (Oxford University Press, 1996)

D Gornien, D Harris and L Zwaak *Law and Practice of the European Convention on Human Rights and the European Social Charter* (Council of Europe, 1996)

S Grosz, J Beatson and P Duffy *Human Rights: The 1998 Act and the European Convention* (Sweet & Maxwell, 2000)

DJ Harris, M O'Boyle and C Warbrick *The European Convention on Human Rights* (Butterworths, 1995)

J Howell 'Land and Human Rights' [1999] *The Conveyancer* 286

M Hunt *Using Human Rights in English Courts* (Hart Publishing, 1997)

D Jackson *The United Kingdom Confronts the European Convention on Human Rights* (University Press of Florida 1997)

FG Jacobs and RCA White *The European Convention on Human Rights* (Clarendon Press, Oxford, 1996)

M Janis, R Kay and A Bradley *European Human Rights Law* (Clarendon Press, Oxford, 1995)

M Janis, R Kay and A Bradley *European Human Rights Law: Text and Materials* (Oxford University Press, 1996)

A Lester and D Pannick *Human Rights Law and Practice* (Butterworths, 1999)

Lord Lester of Herne Hill QC 'First Steps Towards a Constitutional Bill of Rights' [1997] EHRLR 124

I Loveland (ed) *Importing the First Amendment* (Hart Publishing, 1998)

BS Markesinis (ed) *Protecting Privacy* (Clarendon Press, Oxford, 1999)

BS Markesinis (ed) *The Impact of the Human Rights Bill on English Law* (Clarendon Press, Oxford, 1999)

G Marston 'The United Kingdom's Part in the Preparation of the European Convention on Human Rights 1950' (1993) 42 ICLQ 796

J Merrills *The Development of International Law by the European Court of Human Rights* (Manchester University Press, 1995)

H Mountfied 'Fundamental Human Rights Principles: Defining the Limits of Rights. The Concept of a Lawful Interference with Fundamental Rights' (UCL/*JUSTICE* Seminar notes, 5 October 1999)

A O'Neill *Judicial Review in Scotland: A Practitioner's Guide* (Butterworths, 1999)

W Outhwaite and M Wheeler *The Civil Practitioner's Guide to the Human Rights Act 1998* (Old Bailey Press, 1999)

K Reid *A Practitioner's Guide to the European Convention on Human Rights* (Sweet & Maxwell, 1998)

Rights Brought Home: The Human Rights Bill (Cm 3782)

AH Robertson and JG Merrills *Human Rights in Europe* 3rd edn (Manchester University Press, 1993)

P Shiner 'Environmental Protection, Judicial Review and Human Rights' [1999] JR 43

K Starmer *European Human Rights Law* (Legal Action Group, 1999)

M Supperstone, J Goudie and J Coppel *Local Authorities and the Human Rights Act 1998* (Butterworths, 1999)

The Essential Human Rights Act 1998 (Wilberforce Chambers, 2000)

The Human Rights Act and the Criminal Justice and Regulatory Process (Hart Publishing, 1999)

The Rt Hon Jack Straw MP and Paul Boateng MP 'Bringing Rights Home: Labour's plans to incorporate the European Convention on Human Rights into UK law', reproduced in [1997] EHRLR 71

The Rt Hon Lord Justice Sedley *Freedom, Law and Justice* (Sweet & Maxwell, 1999)

P van Dijk and GJH van Hoof *Theory and Practice of the European Convention on Human Rights* (Kluwer Law International, 1998)

J Wadham and H Mountfield *Human Rights Act 1998* (Blackstone Press, 1999)

INDEX

References are to paragraph numbers.

Trial process – *cont*
  oral hearing   6.167
  presence of defendant   6.167–6.169,
    6.175–6.177
    criminal case   6.167, 6.175
    waiver of right   6.169, 6.175–6.177
    without notice hearing   6.168
  press, etc, exclusion   6.178, 6.179,
    6.183, 8.155
  public hearing, *see* Public hearing
  reporting restrictions, *see* Expression,
    freedom of
  time for trial   6.184–6.187
    avoiding delay   6.185
    civil case   6.185, 6.186, 6.190
    criminal case   6.185, 6.188, 6.191–
      6.193
    'reasonable' time   6.186
    unreasonable, examples   6.189–
      6.193
Tribunal, *see* Court/tribunal

Unfair dismissal
  ceilings on awards   6.230
  delay   6.190
  qualifying period for claim   6.98
United Nations   1.14–1.17
  Covenants (ICCPR and ICESCR)
    1.15–1.17, 1.19
    privacy protection   7.7, 7.8
  Declaration, *see* Universal Declaration of
    Human Rights
  establishment of   1.14
  Human Rights Committee   1.19
  purpose   1.14
United States of America
  Amendments to Constitution   1.10,
    1.11, 6.4
  data protection issues   7.54
  Declaration of Independence   1.9,
    1.10
  'environmental justice'   9.218
  freedom of speech   8.8, 8.25, 8.27,
    8.48
  right to be left alone   7.10
Universal Declaration of Human
    Rights   1.15, 1.16, 1.21
  Covenants giving practical focus to
    1.17
  European Convention, relationship
    with   2.1, 2.12
  expression, freedom of   8.5
  fair hearing right   6.4

private life, protection of   7.6, 7.7
property rights   9.4
transformation into European
    Convention   1.28
'Unless' order   6.109
Utilities, privatised   3.89, 3.102–3.104,
    3.119
  effect of HRA on generally   9.80–
    9.82
  non-interventionist approach,
    case   9.81
  environmental liability   9.186
  licence issues   9.76–9.85
    'civil obligations'   9.79
    'expectation' of grant   9.79
    judicial review   9.83
    modification   9.77, 9.83, 9.84
    regulation phases   9.78
  property protection right   9.73–9.85
    claimant, as   9.76–9.85
    defendant, as   9.75
  public authority, whether are   3.89,
    3.102–3.104, 3.119, 9.74
  regulators of   9.73
  termination of supply for non-
    payment   9.214
  Utilities Bill   9.83–9.85
  utilities windfall tax   9.110
  victim, whether can be   3.140–3.142
VAT   9.100, 9.105, 9.111
Vertical effect   3.74, 3.75
Victim
  European Convention breach   2.49,
    3.135–3.138
  HRA breach   3.124, 3.129–3.142,
    3.152, 9.220
    claimant 'at risk'   3.139
    corporate public authority and
      narrow threshold   3.134
    invocation of tort action limited
      to   3.130
    judicial review requirement
      contrasted   3.131, 3.133,
      3.135, 3.136
    pre-election Consultation Paper,
      retreat from   3.131
    public interest groups, position of
      3.135, 3.138
    purpose of requirement   3.132
    Scotland   4.14
    State body/private utility   3.140–
      3.142
Vienna Convention   5.5
Waiver of rights   6.169–6.177
  public hearing right   6.172, 6.173